AF743351

THE GRID

	Definitory Hypotheses 1	ψ 2	Notation 3	Attention 4	Inquiry 5	Action 6	. . . n.
A β-elements	A1	A2				A6	
B α-elements	B1	B2	B3	B4	B5	B6	. . . Bn
C Dream Thoughts Dreams, Myths	C1	C2	C3	C4	C5	C6	. . . Cn
D Pre-conception	D1	D2	D3	D4	D5	D6	. . . Dn
E Conception	E1	E2	E3	E4	E5	E6	. . . En
F Concept	F1	F2	F3	F4	F5	F6	. . . Fn
G Scientific Deductive System		G2					
H Algebraic Calculus							

Other titles in the Maresfield Library by W. R. Bion

Attention & Interpretation
Elements of Psychoanalysis
Learning from Experience
Second Thoughts
Transformations

of related interest:
Grinberg, L. et al: Introduction to the work of Bion
Klein, M. et al: New Directions in Psychoanalysis

"And indeed there will be time
To wonder, 'Do I dare?' and, 'Do I dare?'
Time to turn back and descend the stair, . . .
Do I dare
Disturb the universe?
In a minute there is time
For decisions and revisions which a minute
*will reverse."**

*T.S. Eliot, "The Love Song of J. Alfred Prufrock," *The Waste Land and Other Poems*. 1930, New York: Harcourt Brace and Co.

CONTRIBUTORS

Frank Philips

Richard Alexander

Bernard Bail

Susanna Isaacs-Elmhirst

Betty Joseph

Albert Mason

Frederick Kurth

Herbert Rosenfeld

Frances Tustin

Richard J. Rosenthal

A.B. Bahia

Alfred Silver

Andre Green

Leon Grinberg

James Grotstein

Eliot Jaques

Melvin R. Lansky

Ignacio Matte Blanco

Donald Meltzer

Roger Money-Kyrle

Michael Paul

Hanna Segal

Hans A. Thorner

Robert H. Gosling

Martha Harris

Margaret J. Rioch

J.O. Wisdom

Robert J. Langs

Sidney Klein

Isabel Menzies Lyth

W. Clifford Scott

DO I DARE DISTURB THE UNIVERSE?

A MEMORIAL TO W.R. BION

edited by
James S. Grotstein

Routledge
Taylor & Francis Group
LONDON AND NEW YORK

First published 1981 by Caesura Press

Published 2019 by Routledge
2 Park Square, Milton Park, Abingdon, Oxon OX14 4RN
52 Vanderbilt Avenue, New York, NY 10017

First issued in hardback 2019

Routledge is an imprint of the Taylor & Francis Group, an informa business

Copyright © 1981 Taylor & Francis

All rights reserved. No part of this book may be reprinted or reproduced or utilised in any form or by any electronic, mechanical, or other means, now known or hereafter invented, including photocopying and recording, or in any information storage or retrieval system, without permission in writing from the publishers.

Notice:
Product or corporate names may be trademarks or registered trademarks, and are used only for identification and explanation without intent to infringe.

British Library Cataloguing in Publication Data
A C.I.P. for this book is available from the British Library

ISBN 13: 978-0-367-09947-3 (hbk)
ISBN 13: 978-0-946439-01-0 (pbk)

CONTENTS

ACKNOWLEDGEMENTS

I should like to acknowledge my gratitude to the late Dr. Bion and to Mrs. Bion for their cooperation in the preparation of this work. It began as a *Festschrift* to celebrate his eightieth birthday, but he died before it could be published. I am indebted, of course, to all the contributors because of their enthusiasm and their cooperation with my editorial requests. I should like to acknowledge my gratitude to Dr. Joseph Sandler, past editor of *The International Journal of Psycho-Analysis*, for his kind permission to re-publish the late Mr. Roger Money-Kyrle's article, "Cognitive Development," and the late Dr. A.B. Bahia's article, "New Theories: Their Influence and Effect on Psychoanalytic Technique." I am indebted as well to Mr. Thomas T.S. Hayley, the current editor of *The International Journal of Psycho-Analysis*, for his gracious permission to re-publish Dr. Sidney Klein's article, "Autistic Phenomena in Neurotic Patients," and Mrs. Isabel Menzies Lyth's paper, "Bion's Contribution to Thinking About Groups." I am also in the debt of Dr. Dinora Pines, Editor of *The Bulletin of the British Psycho-Analytic Society* for *her* permission to re-publish Mrs. Menzies Lyth's article.

Because of the long gestation period in the development of the *Festschrift*, I granted permission to some of the contributors to pre-publish their articles elsewhere. They are as follows: a) Dr. Robert Langs, who pre-published his "Some Communicative Properties of the Bipersonal Field" in *The International Journal of Psychoanalytic Psychotherapy*, Volume 7, 1978, and in *The Listening Process*, 1978, both books published in New York by Jason Aronson; b) Dr. Donald Meltzer, who pre-published his "A Note on Bion's Concept 'Reversal of Alpha Function,'" in *The Kleinian Development*, Part III: *The Clinical Significance of the Work of Bion*, Perthshire: Clunie Press, 1978; and c) Dr. Susanna Isaacs, who pre-published her "Bion and Babies" in the *Annals of Psychoanalysis*, Volume VIII, New York International Universities Press, 1980; d) and I, the editor of this volume, who pre-published a somewhat shorter version of "Who Is the Dreamer Who Dreams the Dream and Who Is the Dreamer Who Understands It?" in *Contemporary Psychoanalysis*, Volume 15, 1979, edited by Dr. Arthur Feiner, New York. I am grateful to the publishers of these pre-publications for offering "foster homes" for those articles until their publicational mother was able to welcome them home again.

My gratitude extends in full measure to my wife and children who have borne the brunt of my labor of love, and to my secretary, Ms. Cheryl Cole, for her laborious efforts.

". . . So much the rather thou Celestial light
Shine inward, and the mind through all her powers
Irradiate, there plant eyes, all mist from thence
Purge and disperse, that I may see and tell
*Of things invisible to mortal sight . . ."**

*Milton's *Paradise Lost*, Book III.

". . . omnem, quae nunc obducta tuenti
mortales hebetat visus tibi, et humida
circum caligat, nubem eripiam . . ."

Virgil, *Aenid, II*, 604

". . . The cloud, which intercepting the clear
light,
Hangs o'er thy eyes, and blunts they mortal
sight,
*I will remove . . ."**

*Joseph Addison, trans. *The Spectator*, No. 159, Sat., Sept. 1, 1711. Joseph Addison and Richard Steele.

Wilfred R. Bion
1897-1979

To Doctor Bion, In Memoriam:

We contributors affectionately dedicate these contributions to your memory as our means of giving thanks for your having disturbed our universes with your Language of Achievement. We recognize, moreover, that the influence of your work has already begun to disturb the universe of psychoanalysis and beyond. Our own efforts are offered in the hope that we too have acquired the courage to dare disturb.

—James Grotstein and the Contributors

Wilfred R. Bion:
The Man, The Psychoanalyst, The Mystic.
A Perspective on His Life and Work

Wilfred Ruprecht Bion's death on November 8, 1979 has thrust upon us the task of re-evaluating the impact he and his work have had on psychoanalysis in our generation. All those who have been in his presence, whether briefly or lengthily, swear-almost to a person-to the enormity of his vitality, to the power of his presence, to the humor of his dry wit, to the incisiveness of his thinking, and to the (sadly) anachronistic genteelness of his politeness and respect for people. His life story, such as I know of it, touches at many points onto the scroll of the Age of Heroes in which so many of our childhoods were so passionately spent vicariously. Bion may very well qualify as a modern equivalent of a classical hero, not only by virtue of his remote birth and his World War I exploits but also because of his being such a fearless champion of our Innocence (at least, for those of us who were his analysands) who grappled so handily with our dragons and enabled us to get through Blake's Forest of Experience onto the road to Higher Innocence. Yet from another perspective, one cannot read Bion's later works, particularly those which refer to the genius, the mystic, or the messiah, without applying that designation to him. What is a genius? To Bion it is one who is able to experience Truth ("O") without having to think about it (falsify it). To me it is someone who can see the mysterious in the commonplace, inquire into it, and transform the commonplace into the unusual. By both definitions Bion was a genius, or, as one of this caliber was designated in bygone times, a *wizard*.

There is enigma after enigma in Bion's life story, especially to an American such as myself. First of all, how did a man who was born in Victorian Imperial India in the city of Muttra, in the remote United Provinces, become a psychoanalyst? Yet he was not the only one. Once, while researching an article in an old issue of *The International Journal of Psycho-Analysis*, I chanced across the following obituary: "Claude Dangar Daly, Lt. Col., Retired." That an obituary of a retired British Indian Army officer should be printed in a psychoanalytic journal so piqued my curiosity that I read the whole obituary. Colonel Daly, while on frontier duty in Baluchistan, Northwest Frontier Provinces, recorded his dreams and sent them to Sandor Ferenczi. The latter prevailed upon him to consult Freud, whereupon this

British Army officer took a leave of absence, went to Vienna, was analyzed by Freud, trained by the Vienna Institute, and became a psychoanalyst. That this Indian Army officer became a psychoanalyst strikes me with wonder. The rest of the psychoanalytic world took no notice of this anachronistic crusader because his psychoanalytic contributions were few and did not gain attention. Yet the mystery remains—as in Hemingway's leopard on the snowline of Kilimanjaro—how did this Indian Army officer get from Khyber Pass to Vienna to become an analyst? The complacency and conformity of today's mores of psychoanalytic practice are challenged, I believe, by the incredulity of how anyone from that era and that remote area could ever find his way to becoming a psychoanalyst.

Major Wilfred Ruprecht Bion, D.S.O., who also made an odyssey similar to that of Colonel Daly, seems to have been more fortunate and did manage to acquire the attention of the psychoanalytic world and was more obviously that metaphoric leopard on the snowline of Kilimanjaro—wandering far off the course which his erstwhile onlookers might have conventionally plotted for him. His name is Hugenot, and his forebearers came to England after their persecution in France centuries ago. His father was a civil engineer of some prominence and was, for part of his life, Secretary to the Indian Congress. His services to the Crown were valued so highly that he was offered a knighthood but he refused it. Bion's mother allegedly came from a lower social class than his father, but her qualities of empathy and warmth were to make the profoundest impression on him. He was raised also by a maid and a governess, both Indian, who often spoke to him of tales from the *Mahabharata*, whose language he could not easily decipher but whose impact he was never to forget.

The mores of the class system of middle and upper class families in England and in the civil service of the empire were such that children, particularly the males, were sent off quite early to "public" school. Wilfred Bion was one of the many victims of this now questionable custom and was, accordingly, sent off on his own to England at the age of eight. To the best of my knowledge he was never again to return to India and was only planning to return there shortly before his death upon an invitation by a psychoanalytic group in Bombay.

In his "passage *from* India," where he was born on September 8, 1897, *this* army officer, football player, mathematician, painter, philosopher, classics scholar, physician, psychoanalyst, "dabbler" in Chinese, Greek, Latin and Hebrew, etc., etc., etc., came to England as a young boy and acquired one of the finest educations an aristocratic Edwardian England could offer. He was educated at Bishops Stortford College which he attended from 1906 to 1915. He later harnessed this education to the winds of his awesome imagination, after which he joined the Royal Tank Regiment on the Western Front and took part in the Battle of Cambrai, the first major engagement in which tanks were deployed against the Germans. Bion distinguished himself in this engagement and was summoned to London to be awarded the D.S.O.

by King George V. He fought in every subsequent major engagement on the Western Front until the armistice and was never able to forget the horror of those experiences or ever able to surmount the miracle of his survival.

He was demobilized late in 1918 and then went to Queens College, Oxford, in January of 1919 where he read Modern History. While there he fell under the influence of H.J. Paton, a tutor of philosophy, who introduced Bion to the works of Immanuel Kant, in particular, but also to other philosophers. This special input was to have profound influence on Bion's later work. While at Queens College, Bion distinguished himself in rugby and in swimming. He graduated in Modern History in 1921 but did not get a First, an honor which would have entitled him to a full-time academic career. Following graduation he returned to Bishops Stortford College to teach history and French. Oliver Lyth, in his Obituary of Bion, states that Bion reorganized the rugby football at the school and also was a coach for the swimming team. Lyth states, "There are odd recollections from 'old boys' of being got up at six in the morning by W.R. Bion to practise diving and swimming. During this time he also played rugby for the Harlequins." (Oliver Lyth, *Int. J. Psycho-Anal.*, 1980, 61, 269-274). It was during this time that Bion received a chronic injury to his left knee.

In 1923 or 1924 he left Bishops Stortford to study medicine at University College Hospital, London, and qualified in 1929. While becoming medically qualified, he became fascinated by the psychology of groups and by herd instincts, as espoused by Wilfred Trotter, the distinguished surgeon, who, as was so typical of many Englishmen of that and previous generations, had profound interests beyond his own profession. Trotter, like Paton before him, was also to have a powerful influence on Bion's later work. Bion achieved the Gold Medal for Clinical Surgery and qualified with the Conjoint Diploma in 1930. I believe it was after his qualification that he spent a short period of time as a medical officer in the R.A.F., following which he went to London (Circa, 1932), and began to practice psychiatry. According to Lyth, Bion had a post at the Institute for the Scientific Treatment of Delinquincy and was Medical Officer in the Department of Psychotherapy at the Maida Vale Hospital for Nervous Diseases, and, at the latter place, probably met John Rickman, with whom he was to have a personal analysis and then later a deep friendship. Bion was associated with the Tavistock Clinic from 1933 until 1948.

Upon entering psychoanalysis with John Rickman, Bion's training as an analyst in the British Institute for Psycho-Analysis began but was interrupted by the outbreak of World War II in September, 1939. During the war he was Officer-in-Charge of the Military Training Wing at Northfield Military Hospital for a brief six weeks, but, with the help of an outstanding group of colleagues, he was able to bring the effectiveness of group work into serious consideration. He wrote a paper about his work there entitled "Intra-Group Tensions in Therapy: Their Study as a Task of the Group," which appeared in *Lancet* in 1943. This was his maiden voyage into psychiatric literature and was also his first paper on groups. He had found a way of re-establishing group morale by achieving a common focus in a group approach which was later to be called the Tavistock method. He drew up a list of regulations which the members of the group were to undertake (according to Lyth): "1. Every man must do one hour's physical training daily, unless a medical certificate excuses him." Lyth points out how reminiscent this is of Bion, the swimming coach, at Bishops Stortford.

After the six weeks' stint at Northfield, Bion and Rickman went as Senior Psychiatric Officers to the War Office Selection Boards, where they innovated the selection of officers for the services. Their contributions were recognized, welcomed, and highly praised.

After the war, Bion returned to the Tavistock Clinic and was appointed Chairman of the Executive Committee. While there, he first published a series of papers which was to become collected into the monograph, *Experiences in Groups*, which was to thrust him into the position of fame beyond Britain's shores. He also resumed his psychoanalytic training which the war had interrupted. In the meanwhile, John Rickman, his first analyst, had introduced him to Melanie Klein and recommended that Bion continue analysis with her. Bion qualified as an analyst in 1947 and in 1950 offered "The Imaginary Twin" as his membership paper.

He began to play more and more important roles in the British Psycho-Analytic Society and became Director of the London Clinic of Psycho-Analysis from 1956 to 1962. He was Chairman of the Medical Section of the British Psychological Society in 1947 and gave as his address a paper entitled "Psychiatry at a Time of Crisis." He became President of the British Psycho-Analytic Society in 1962 and held the position until 1965. Upon Melanie Klein's death, he became Chairman of the Melanie Klein Trust.

Bion first married in 1940, but the marriage was fated to end tragically. His wife died shortly after the birth of their only child, Parthenope, in 1945. In 1951 he married Francesca, whom he met at the Tavistock Insititue of Human Relations and whose love and dedication were of paramount importance in his later life and career. Parthenope is now married to an Italian musician and conductor, and she has now qualified as a psychoanalyst. Bion had two children by Francesca: Julian, who is now a practicing physician, and Nichola, a linguist, who is working in publishing.*

While still living and practicing in Los Angeles, he could occasionally be observed walking around Beverly Hills at free moments, still bearing what resembled a military parade-ground gait. His accent was highly educated and, on occasion, a pronunciation such as "dis-ci-pli-nary" would betray a remnant of another, grander age—as did his infrequent special employments of such words as "macilent" and "definitory" reveal an education so infrequently attained nowadays—particularly in this country. Bion, an aristocrat from another time and another place on one level, is, paradoxically, a great

* I am grateful to Francesca Bion and Betty Joseph for some of these details.

commoner, albeit a most uncommon one. His political views remain unknown to me, but his humanity and democracy, his boundless belief in the "genius" within all of us, his detestation of class systems, his belief in the aristocracy of being human, his reverence for "common sense," his elimination of all cliches from his language, and his particular regard for individuality are at distant variance with what one might casually but inaccurately associate with *his* bearing and background but might accurately associate with the sacerdotal piety of psychoanalytic sanhedrinism around the world.

Bion frequently stated that nothing he has written was original. This statement has frequently been misinterpreted as false modesty. Likewise, his detestation for being idealized or regarded as unique may seem to borrow of the same illusion of modesty. Bion, the winner of the D.S.O., was not modest; he was gracious. I believe he meant to emphasize that knowledge generally, and psychoanalytic knowledge specifically, has been acquired as a legacy from countless forebears who labored in their Stygian darkness to formulate the truths which, like torches, are passed on from generation to generation down the corridors of time. We, the beneficiaries of this legacy, have the fecund input of countless generations sifting through our formative experiences. "Do we know to whom we should be grateful for the knowledge we have acquired?" Bion would often query. It is my impression tht Bion meant to emphasize that to one degree or another, we are all receptors of impingements of information from within and without. The numerous transformations in the propagation of knowledge render its origins progressively more obscure. At any given moment, therefore, a thought which we have just "created" might owe its origin to countless, diffuse, disparate antecedents generally beyond recall, as well as to "pure thoughts" themselves, his famous "O."

This idea of indefiniteness of the origin of ideas conjoins with another of Bion's conceptions: what I would call his disavowal of the cult of personality in psychoanalysis. Just as he is humble about the origins of his ideas, by the same token he eschews the assignment of a proper name of ownership to ideas—like Freudian or Kleinian—because it so saturates the space of psychoanalysis that it limits its creative growth. When once asked why he moved to Los Angeles from London, he humorously answered that "I was so loaded with honor, I nearly sank without a trace!"

The name Bion keeps cropping up more and more—and at varying places: the front page of the London "Times Literary Supplement," group therapy conferences, conferences on the treatment of psychoses, international psychoanalytic congresses, etc. I recently returned from the International Psychoanalytic Congress in Jerusalem where his name came up for ridicule by an internationally prominent psychoanalyst. The point of the ridicule was over Bion's advice to dismiss "memory" and "desire" from one's mind when one is conducting an analysis. That this was a more profoundly phenomenological, if not poetic, way of restating Freud's advice to listen with an open mind with free-floating attention seems to have escaped this prominent analyst. Bion was in this instance specifying the elements which obtrude our capacity for the requisite free-floating attention and cites Freud's letter to Lou-Andreas Salome as his inspiration for this notion.

His Work

Experiences In Groups

Bion's contributions are many and varied. I can only epitomize some of the thrusts of his work. He is best known to a sizable section of the mental health public for his unique way of looking at groups. By applying the rules of individual classical analysis (with a Kleinian emphasis) to the group as a single entity, he was able to discern that the individuals within it seemed to cluster into two different kinds of groups: (a) a work group whose members continued to focus cooperatively on the group's purpose or function; and (b) basic assumption groups who became resistant to pursuing the common purpose because of the obtrusion of a basic assumption common to each member of the resistant subgroup. The three different kinds of basic assumptions characterizing these groups are (1) fight or flight, (2) pairing, and (3) dependent. The procedures Bion applied to the study of these groups applied to groups of varying sizes and became known as the Tavistock method. Of particular significance is Bion's intuition into the creation of psychosis in the mob in relation to a group leader who is thought to be messianic, either in the positive or negative sense. His book, *Experience in Groups*, summarizes his findings on this subject.

Clinical Experience with Psychotics

His next period of work clustered around the clinical investigation of psychosis. In his works about this subject he was able to make penetrating and unique contributions to our understanding of the experience of being psychotic. His paper "The Imaginary Twin" (1950) already heralded the arrival of a very special new talent in psychoanalysis. It ingeniously dealt with a conception of the breast as the infant's first imaginary twin, and it also dealt with the link between the development of sight and the Oedipus complex, the link being that of curiosity, which was to adumbrate so many of Bion's later explorations. "Differentiation of the Psychotic from the Non-Psychotic Personalities" (1957) described a macroscopic splitting of the personality which long antedated Kernberg's "discovery" of personality splits in the borderline personality. His papers "Notes on the Theory of Schizophrenia" (1953), "Development of Schizophrenic Thought" (1956), "On Arrogance" (1957), "On Hallucinations" (1958), and "Attacks on

Linking" (1959), all examined the schizophrenic experience of nonthinking as due to the attacks on the linking of thoughts and objects. In these papers he was able to demonstrate and reconstruct the inchoation of psychotic experience from the mother's failure to contain the infant's fear of dying (as perceived by the infant who is to be psychotic). In so doing, he did for **Klein's psychology what Hartmann and Erikson were to do for Freud's - by** adding the adaptive principle to the understanding of mental reciprocity and mutuality. He was also to anticipate the emphasis of Winnicott and later of Kohut on the importance of empathy in the infant-mother bonding. It was here that the concept of the "container" and the "contained" first breathed life. In the progression of these papers Bion evolved a change in his attitude about projective identification and splitting in psychosis. Originally he believed that psychosis was due to violent splitting and projective identification of the patient's thoughts and of the mind which links the thoughts. Gradually, as he discovered the concept of the container and the contained and the attacks against links, he began to postulate that psychosis may be due to the infant's inability to split-off and to project adequately. In other words, it was deficient splitting and deficient projective identification—because of the lack of container to contain the split-off projections—which caused psychosis. His conceptions in this regard parallel that of Winnicott and Fairbairn, and antedate and anticipate the later work of Kohut.

Of even greater though less publicized importance, however, was his contribution on defective alpha function in psychosis. Alpha function, which roughly corresponds to Freud's primary process, is Bion's conception of a gating mechanism which receives the sensory data of emotional experience, processes it, "alpha-betizes" it, and transforms it into alpha elements for further mental "digestion" to be thought about or to become dream elements for postponement and storage. Classical analysis has generally assumed that psychosis presupposes an id and its instinctual irruptions which are driven by excessive primary process to overwhelm the ego. Bion's notion is seemingly the opposite: a defective and/or deficient alpha function which is less able to receive and therefore to dream about the sensory data of emotional experience. This defectiveness of alpha function predisposes to a vulnerability to psychosis by virtue of not being able to mitigate the impact of this data. Implicit in this newer conception is that Freud's "id instincts" are chaotic messages of a failing alpha function (primary process) which is no longer able to dream properly about reality, internal or external. But we shall hear more of alpha function later in this Introduction.

It was also during this period that he became interested in the alteration of the use of the sense organs in psychosis. He began to realize that the senses of the psychotic "do not talk to one another to make common sense," and, furthermore, that psychotics use their sense organs to project sensations into objects which then become hallucinations because of their propensity for abnormal projective identification (a concept he derived from Klein but developed further). The arrogance of schizophrenic thinking is in the smugness of believing one can "think" by evacuating thoughts *and* the organ which thinks the thoughts, the mind. He was also able to locate invariant internal objects in the psychotic's mind: (a) *the obstructive object*, which is the internalized transformation of the maternal image resulting from the psychotic infant's holocaustal attacks against, and dovetailing with, her. When internalized, this object becomes not only unwilling to contain projections, but it also attacks and obstructs the infant's attempts to be curious or attempts to contain or acquire knowledge; (b) *the bizarre object*, which is the result of a massive projection of the psychotic infant's feelings and perceptions, as well as the organ of perception and the organ of thinking, resulting in a mental denudation of the infant and a corresponding mutilation of the image into whom all this debris is violently projected.

His paper "On Arrogance" also extended Klein's formulations about the Oedipus complex, already an extension of Freud's, into a more global view of universal infantile catastrophe. In this pivotal paper Bion reminded us that the deeper tragedy of Oedipus—beyond incest and parricide —was the blinding of his eyes to Truth which thereby rendered him a mental cripple as a consequence of his arrogant epistemophilic curiosity to "know all"; the warnings by his mother and the already blinded Tiresias had been to no avail. By forfeiting his eyes and becoming a mental cripple, Oedipus became the paradigm for the lifelong mental invalid known as "every man." Bion was able to locate a triumvirate of symptoms in borderline and psychotic cases which consists of arrogance, curiosity and stupidity. They bespeak an infantile catastrophe which then transforms the arrogance of curiosity into the arrogance of stupidity, facilitated by the mind's being evacuated of thoughts via projective identification.

There is a decided change in focus toward the end of Bion's papers on psychosis. His paper, "A Theory of Thinking" (1962), constitutes a radical departure from his earlier clinical work. He was now to integrate his experiences with the analysis of psychotics and was ready to embark on the theme he had adhered to ever since: the nature of the mind. "A Theory of Thinking" was his first metapsychological paper. In stately cadence there follow *Learning from Experience* (1962), *Elements of Psychoanalysis* (1963), *Transformations* (1965), *Second Thoughts* (1967), *Attention and Interpretation* (1970), his *First* and *Second Brazilian Lectures* (1975, 1976), and his new psychoanalytic fictional trilogy, *A Memoir of the Future* (1977).

In describing Bion's metapsychology I find myself in the same situation as Rabbi Hillel when he was asked by a Roman general to recite the Hebrew scriptures while jumping up and down on one foot. He at least was clever enough to retort, "Do not do unto others what you would not have them do unto you!" I do not have so readily available an apothegm to offer in regard to Bion. Yet I should like to offer the following with the understanding that it is a painfully epitomized version of a rich treasury of thought.

In what follows, I am going to give my impressions of Bion's cosmic view of man and of his conceptions of metapsychology. I shall introduce these themes by first discussing Bion's use of language. Following this brief overview of his work, I shall then go into some greater detail about many of his important concepts.

Bion's Cosmic View of Man

To me, the essence of Bion's view of man from the perspective of psychoanalysis lies in the nature of preconception and its relationship to Truth, which I should now like to call "Truing," in order to designate its ongoing evolution. In Scripture Moses asked God how He was to be referred to with the populace, to which He replied, "Tell them that 'I am that I am!' " I really think a better translation from the Hebrew might have been " 'I am becoming; I am still becoming–God!' " The ever-becoming, always changing wavefront of becoming–in the form of preconceptions–is knocking on the door of our awareness when evoked by emotional experience. These preconceptions are, till then, the unborn children who must await the serendipity of Fate to be evoked–but, once evoked, become peremptory, that quality which Freud assigned to instinctual drives.

The unconscious psyche of Bion is older than man and is the mysterious source of creativity, imagination, evolution, and development. In my own contribution to this *Memorial* I have called this the Background Subject-Object of Primary Identification, the dream producer, etc. It is our Truing "O" which must, through us, constantly intersect with its counterpart, the "O" of the Other. The contact barrier of alpha function accommodates us to this potentially cataclysmic enterprise. Neurosis is a postponement of our rendezvous with the consequences of this fateful meeting, and psychosis is the abnegating disavowal and discrediting of it altogether.

Thus, Bion's cosmic view of the psyche is one in which we sit on the lap of our Godhead who is mysteriously connected to the Ultimate Godhead (Holy Ghost). "I"-ness consists, furthermore, in a prismatic refraction of the emanations of this Godhead and is known as the spiritual, scientific, and aesthetic vertices. Bion's man is more than man and almost a God–in other words, (s)he is transcendental like Nietzsche's "Uebermensch." Our sadnesses and our illnesses constitute both our recognition of our failure to live up to our Godliness *and* the agony of our stillborn preconceptions which hope to evoke us to return to our rendezvous with experiencing our unexperienced experiences–to becoming "O." Bion represents this as the transformation from Paradise Lost to Paradise Regained.

Bion's Special Use of Language

Bion was the bane of his publishers and the enigma of his audiences. His manner of speech and of writing presents startling clarities–often of delayed action–seemingly desultorily strewn about in complex recondite divigations and circumnavigations. In the next moment, he would make a giant leap without leaving his audience a roadmap or even faintest clue where he had gone. He always maintained—and erroneously so, I think—that he was merely speaking ordinary English. He never prepared his lectures; they were always spontaneous and innovative. Once, after being introduced to deliver the Franz Alexander Lecture, he began by saying, "I can hardly wait to hear what I have to say." The audience laughed, not knowing that Bion was serious.

Those who have been "supervised" and analyzed by him have also noted that peculiar admixture of confusion and clarity when in his presence. After many of my own analytic sessions with him, I would leave dazed and confused, believing that I had not understood much of what he had said—only to find that I was then remarkably clear with my own patients afterwards. During another moment in analysis, he gave me a series of interpretations which, unusually, caused me to say, "I think I follow you." His reply to that was an ironic, "Yes, I was afraid of that!" It was only then that I began to realize that Bion did not want to be followed or understood, let alone idealized. He wanted me and everyone who was in his presence to be responsive to his/her own emanations—and responses. I began more fully to "catch on" to his unusual manner of presentation after I had begun to comprehend the value of eschewing "memory and desire" with my own patients. The "selected fact" came one day when he chided me for trying to "understand" *him* rather than observe my own responses to his "second opinion" about my associations.

My next clue came from the Nobel Prize speeches from the medical laureates who spoke of the rationale for the CAT Scan (computerized axial tomography). Many different views of the object are taken from a variety of vertices around a perimeter which rotates in multiple planes if need be. In order to obtain a focus on a specific target object, say, in the interior of the body, everything around it (the obvious) must be obscured so that the hitherto obscured area can be illuminated all the more clearly. When this happens, the surfaces are blanked out—"by a beam of intense darkness," to quote Bion. The CAT Scan is a paradigm for Bion's method of thinking, speaking, and writing, I believe. His style helped him to tune into his own intuitive broadcasts, and he enjoined us to do the same. Actually, it can be said that Bion spoke the *Language of Achievement*.

An Overview of Bion's Metapsychology

Analytically, Bion is the product of the halcyon days of the British Psychoanalytic Institute when Klein still enjoyed a good reception by the classical members, especially by Ernest Jones and Edward Glover. Bion's first analyst, John Rickman, was classical but introduced him to Klein's theories and ultimately to analysis with Klein. Bion seems very much at home with Freud's writings and has tried more than any other Kleinian, in my estimation, to synthesize the key contributions of Freud and Klein.

Bion was intrigued by Klein's contributions about primitive mental states and began applying her theories and techniques to psychotic and borderline patients. It gradually became apparent to him that Kleinian theory, like Freudian theory, hypothesized a patient who dwelled in the third dimension and who had representations of objects who themselves were third dimensional who could, as a consequence of this fact, contain the projections of the projector. The patients *he* was seeing did *not* dwell in the third dimension but rather dwelt in a more limited one. The objects he was hearing about from his psychotic patients were not dimensionalized—full enough in depth—to be able to contain the patient's projections. The patient therefore must project within his/her own expanding space—like a patient in surgical shock where the capillaries dilate so extensively that the patient "extravasates within," analogized Bion. This observation led him to realize that the language of psychoanalysis, as well as language in general, was seemingly suitable for neuroses but not for psychoses. His reasoning was as follows: Freud, the intrepid pioneer and explorer of the mind, had made a brilliant discovery by locating the domain of the unconscious psyche. The conscious psyche, what today might be called the dominant hemisphere and its mental processes, are "sensible" insofar as it receives the data of experience from external stimuli (objects) by the sense organs which, as Freud pointed out, are noted in pleasure and unpleasure as their "codes" of differentiation originally. Freud further postulated, Bion reminds us, that the sense organ of consciousness was created to be "sensible" to internal stimuli as well as external stimuli.

The internal world of the psyche, however—what we might today refer to as being the non-dominant hemisphere—does *not* have a sense organ system analogous to that of the dominant hemisphere. Freud does say, however, that there is an organ of consciousness which is sensitive to psychical qualities, but it is not immediately analogous to the sense organs sensitive to the external world.

Thus, opined Bion, a newer way had to be found to address psychoanalytic attention to develop a keener reception to the "sense organ" of psychical qualities which respond to the "broadcast" of a "sender" who dwells in a domain quite unlike the three dimensional space of the external world. This *non*-sensual domain is even more complicated for the psychotic mind, and, whether psychotic or normal, seems to be characterized by a dimensionality which is not comparable with that on the outside, thus his subsequent, frequent references to "*the deep and formless infinite*" which he borrowed from Milton. Professor Matte Blanco refers to this as the domain of symmetricality, and I, as the domain of the zero dimension normally and the negative first dimension psychotically. Moreover, most of us have a neurotic personality *and* a psychotic personality, according to Bion, the consequences of which are that our psychical objects occur in a montage of delusional (hallucinatory) imagination (psychotic world), and neurological sensation (real world). We psychoanalysts need a way to screen out the quotidian noise of sensible life ("subject it to a beam of intense darkness") so as to be more responsive to the other message from the psychical world. This beam of intense darkness is the eschewal of memory and desire, the past and the future tenses of pleasure and unpleasure whose grammar and syntax underlie the sensible world of "understanding," comprehension, and "knowing."

Bion therefore sought to apply the Language of Achievement to the deciphering of the psychical world by suggesting *patience* on the analyst's part (after the suspension of memory and desire) until the scattered fragments of psychical elements began to cohere as *constantly conjoined elements*. One can liken this discipline to that of an exercise in meditation. When the analyst's patience is rewarded by his/her experience of a "selected fact" which gives him a clue as to the emerging coherence, (s)he has experienced the *security* emerging from a Transformation from "PS" → "D" (Paranoid-Schizoid Position → Depressive Position). In so doing his/her analytic container capacity has undergone *reverie* and, because of that, vulnerability, and has therefore experienced challenge, jeopardy, or threat–anxiety about the consequences. The analyst's reverie is a special deployment of alpha function which (a) prepares the analytic field for those "thoughts without a thinker" to emerge–both within the patient and within the analyst. Since they are unrehearsed free associations bilaterally, they are closer to representing *psychical objects* than if they had been "thought about sensibly." Thus the analyst's alpha function facilitates the activity of the patient's alpha function for his/her own transformations from "PS" → "D" so that his/her own inner, personal "O" can intersect with "O," Eternal Truth, in order to maintain the ineluctable pace of a continuing rendezvous with "O."

Bion believed that our receptivity to these psychical objects and their transformations could be thought to follow patterns which could be experienced from multiple vertices. **Principal** amongst these vertices are the scientific (ego), the religious (superego), and the aesthetic (id), but there are illimitable vertices depending upon the situation involved. Bion chose mathematics as a way of amplifying the scientific vertex. Mathematics had the advantage of being a language of signs and/or symbols which could conveniently represent objects in their absence and therefore facilitate a language useful for abstraction without the penumbra of associations typical of words. Furthermore, mathematics had undergone an epigenesis from third dimensional (Euclidian) space to analytic geometry (Descartes) and subsequently into algebraic calculus and was therefore even more suitable an instrument for a mind which dealt with dimensions far above the three of the sensible world. The application of mathematical rigor to the objects and the space of the psychical world had the effect of an ultimate refinement of their definition and purpose and was to give to psychoanalysis an unheralded system of logic as well as a basis for a newer and vaster cosmic view of the psyche. The construction, elaboration, and use of his grid was one of the outcomes of his employment of mathematical logic. This refinement can be analogized to the differentiating aspects of differential calculus, whereas the ultimate imagination or sensibly thoughtful use to which the results are put can be thought of as analogous to integral calculus. Later he employed Intuitionistic Mathematics from the Dutch School for even further refinement of his mathematical logic. Professor Matte Blanco's contribution in this *Memorial* will hopefully shed some light on some of Bion's uses of mathematical logic.

The second vertex of his cosmic view was Faith, not in the sense in which that word is used in the institutionalized religious sense, but in the transcendental sense, the Faith in Truth itself and its ultimate dependable oneness. Faith, to Bion, is the experience of at-one-ment which we are always trying to achieve—trying to become "O"—an experience which we all felt once upon a time and believe we are to feel once again—perhaps best expressed in Paul's First Epistle to the Corinthians—"Now through a glass darkly, then face to face." Each of our psychological words contains myriads of inherent preconceptions which anticipate experiences by realizations or rendezvous with them. These preconceptions live in a pretransformational state of commensalism within us until experience summons them. By "commensalism" I infer that Bion meant that countless preconceptions may exist peacefully within the psyche and be of no disturbance because they have not yet been summoned by their external counterparts to constitute a realization in experience. When this summons does take place, the preconceptions ("thoughts without a thinker") have now become serious conceptions to be considered by the already established state of the psyche (or group) after which either a symbiotic (mutually helpful transformation) takes place, or a parasitic one, in which one is dominated by the other to mutual disadvantage.

The third vertex is the aesthetic. Whereas Freud secularized and demonized the id into the mental representation of physiological irruptions, Bion seems to have regarded the primal unconscious as inherently imaginative, creative, and artistic. The artist is alpha function; the colors on its palate are the inherent preconceptions; and the canvas on which it is portrayed is the alpha screen, a contact barrier between consciousness and unconsciousness and can also be seen in the horizontal "C" level of Bion's grid in which imagery finds its way into phantasies, dreams, and myths. Bion was partial to the aesthetic vertex. He often used poetry and poetic imagery to emphasize its superiority to ordinary language in describing the psychical domain of "the deep and formless infinite." He even resorted to writing a three part novel, *A Memoir of the Future*, as another aesthetic exercise to illustrate his views of the mind in a language which could evoke and conjure rather than blatantly over-illuminate, as ordinary language does. Speaking of poetry, however, Bion had committed vast amounts of Roman, Greek, and English poets to memory. Rumor has it that he could quote Ovid, Vergil, Horace, and Milton almost indefinitely—and this is the man who espouses the abnegation of memory in order to converse in the Language of Achievement?

This Language of Achievement is the reformulation of imaginative recombination (second opinion as Bion often termed it) of what the analyst believes the patient to have expressed in his/her free associations. The analyst's interpretations are evocatively re-educative to the patient as second opinions rather than introjected per se. In underlining the fact of evocation in contrast to internalization, Bion is once again, like Lacan, realigning psychoanalytic theory to philosophical rationalism, as opposed to "tabula rasa" empiricism.

Bion's "Language of Achievement" is a way of talking about the new unsaturated word which can best express at that moment the approximation to Truth as it evolves with the analyst's patience. Language in general tends to become saturated and then begins to have a proliferation of meanings other than the one it was so designated by the thinker. He borrowed the term "Language of Achievement" from a letter Keats wrote to his brother in which the former also mentioned "negative capability":

"It struck me what quality went to form a man of achievement, especially in literature, and which Shakespeare possessed so enormously—I mean *Negative Capability*, that is, when a man is capable of being in uncertainties, mysteries, doubts, without any irritable reaching after fact and reason . . .

"The only means of strengthening one's intellect is to make up one's mind about nothing—to let the mind be a thoroughfare for all thoughts, not a select party."*

Bion's reverence for the mind is in contrast to our fear of it and to our fear of the "messiah thoughts" its relentless transmitter sends out. If he has reverence for the mind and the Truth it ultimately contacts, he also has reverence for his own ignorance and for all the glittering or half-glittering data-to-be which are lit up by each new mental sortie but which proliferate in the half-lights and penumbras of unknowability while we are exploring them. Ignorance, moreover, is that mental state best suited to conduct an inquiry into the psychoanalytic object. It corresponds to a "beam of intense darkness cast upon the patient's association" so that a little something may glimmer in the darkness. The glimmering or half-glittering data thus discovered are seductive sirens hinting at even richer treasure in the dark penumbra beyond. The mind can perish from disuse and from greed, I believe he believed.

He, more than anyone I know, had the courage to address himself to the dangerous instrument the mind represents—not so much because of its instinctual impulses, as Freud believed—but because of its capacity to have ideas. When we find Bion to be complex, then, may it not be that we have further to go to forget what we learned in order to dim the brilliance of *our* minds so that we may regain contact with the dangerous but dimly lit emanations from ideas which somehow Bion has been uniquely able to see more acutely? He *appears* complex and difficult to understand at times because his choice of words reveals his deliberate tendency to employ terms which are as devoid of saturation or of previous usage or of "understandability" as possible within the framework of coherence. He "paints" with words so as to

---

Letters of John Keats (two volumes), edited by Hyder Edward Rollins. Cambridge: Harvard University Press, 1958

evoke our own imagery or ideograms so that we can experience our imaginative response to his image(e)-inative evocations. He speaks the Language of Achievement, and he compels us to listen and to tune in to it so that we can re-discover the lost language of imagery which became pre-empted by the later language of "understanding." I for one once found him complex. I now find him to be quite sensible. I have been aided in this by his "advice" not to interpret him but rather to listen to my own responses to what he says. This simplistic logic has paid dividends.

Alpha Elements and Alpha Function

Bion's contribution to a theory of thinking constitutes a radical re-orientation of psychoanalytic theory into the direction of the mainstream of western epistemology. He lifted Freud's mechanistic biological reductionisms onto the higher plain of philosophical thought–particularly invoking the rationalistic pre-determinism of Plato and Kant and thereby augmented Freud's instinct theory with Plato's theory of inherent forms, pure thoughts, ("thoughts without a thinker") and Kant's a priori assumptions (things-in-themselves). Bion assumed that pure thoughts exist as inherent pre-conceptions and are older than the mind that thinks them. They are evoked from commensal passivity or innocuousness into active, disruptive epiphanies by the sense organ of consciousness as the latter is stimulated by events in the external and/or internal world. A mind is needed, Bion believed, to be able to think about these a priori thoughts ("thoughts without a thinker"). If Descartes stated, "I think, therefore I am!", Bion would state, "I am, therefore I have thoughts without a thinker which demand a mind to think about them!"

Thinking per se involves (a) the development or evolution of thoughts and (b) thinking about the thoughts by an apparatus of thinking known as the mind. The former occupies the vertical axis of Bion's now famous grid whereas the latter occupies the horizontal axis. The development of the organ of thinking, the mind, was necessitated in order to accommodate the former, the "thoughts without a thinker." Thus, thinking per se is a phenomenon forced upon the ego because of the pressure of "thoughts" which **have evolved** from sense impression transformations and from intuition. The evolution of thoughts proceeds along a genetic axis (the vertical axis of Bion's grid) as the thoughts emerge from sense impressions and are *transformed* by *alpha function* to produce *alpha elements* suitable for dreaming, experiencing, being thought about, and ultimately for mental action. His theory of transformations has always impressed me as a striking analogy to the Krebs Cycle of Intermediate Carbohydrate Metabolism–the biography of the change of a carbohydrate molecule on its way to ultimate utilization, maintaining its own invariant identity within its metamorphosis. Thoughts, like glucose, must emerge from a series of intermediate transformations so that the sensory and intuitive impacts of awarenesses can be slowed down to utilizable elements.

As I mentioned earlier, alpha function is a gating mechanism which receives the data of sensory and emotional experience, sensory in terms of the data of external experience, and emotional in terms of the data of internal experience. As such, it has a function of bimodal consciousness; e.g., external and internal worlds. It functions therefore as a frontier between two domains and tries to facilitate the communication between them. Alpha function represents in part, therefore, a porous repressive barrier between our consciousness and unconsciousness and/or internal and external worlds. Yet, as I stated above, Bion believes that the capacity to think, that is, to have an organ for thinking known as the mind, depends on the infant's acquiring his/her mother's alpha function to project into or onto. Thus, projection–reception forms an internal *thinking couple* within the infant. Bion also implies that alpha function is necessary for dreaming and that dreaming, in turn, is necessary in order to facilitate thinking and also to facilitate the capacity to sleep in order to guarantee a differential "membrane" between wakefulness and sleep. As such, alpha function also comprises a *dreaming couple*. All in all, one can see alpha function personified as an *experiencing couple*, which is then in series with the other two couples.

In *Attention and Interpretation* Bion implies yet another factor in alpha function, that of representing the Establishment in the Group proper or even in the internal group (intrapsychic group). The Establishment must prepare the way for the "messiah thought"—or the person bearing the "messiah thought"—to emerge. At the same time, the Establishment must prepare the members of the Group who have not been able to divine the "messiah thought" to be able to receive it without catastrophic change. In the probability of catastrophic change, the "messiah thought" must be challenged, falsified, or otherwise transformed. One can picture these transformations on Bion's grid as the relationship between definitory hypothesis as the emergence of the "messiah preconception" and its challenge by Column Two (psi). Dr. Frederick Kurth's contribution focuses on this relationship.

In psychoanalytic practice one can see many aspects of alpha function in the patient and in the analyst. In the former alpha function functions to generate feelings and thoughts as free associations which, in turn, are reflections of phantasies. These phantasies are manifestations of *imagination*, a key factor in alpha function. The analyst's capacity to divine the phantasy lies in his/her *intuition*. Intuition, in turn, is the capacity to divine the constant conjunctions and selected fact by which the phantasy or phantasies can be detected.

Transformations

As a result of alpha transformation, the transformed sense impressions seem able to become sensorily vivid in the course of their descent so as to register as dream thoughts (dreams by day or by night). I would think of this as their being given mythic license or dream status. The capacity to dream or to mythify sensory elements bespeaks an ability to organize random data into a narrative so as to gain procrastinational mastery and also to guarantee the division of sleep and wakefulness through being able to put some data "asleep" while being able to focus attention on other data. This is another way of stating the capacity to pay attention by putting other elements to sleep, and vice versa. Alpha elements create an alpha screen which permits this.

The transformed sense data then seem to link up with preconceptions, a mental reservoir of inherent (a priori) ideas waiting to be "realized" with their external and future counterparts—as already acquired ideas waiting to be re-mated with experiences, in either case resulting in the formation of a *conception*. Hunger could correspond to the "alpha-betized" sensory element which may then be dreamt about as a devouring breast, on one hand, or a fulfilling breast, on the other. A preconception which mates with frustration and seeks to evade frustration devolves into a "fugutive from thought," i.e., psychosis. A preconception which mates with frustration and in which the frustration can be tolerated or contained develops into the conception of "no breast" which then develops into the empty space in which the presence of the breast can be thought about. Thus the capacity for the development of the conception of "no breast" makes room for the capacity of thoughts to be thought about. *Learning from experience*, aided by the power of memory—and mother's capacity to dilute the frustrations through that *containment* known as *reverie*—fosters the development of thinking, that is, confidence that the painful reality can be modified. The modification of reality constitutes the horizontal axis of Bion's grid.

The Grid

Bion, the logician, reviewed all of Freud and all of Klein, separated out Freud's work of "Two Principles of Mental Functioning" and Klein's use of the paranoid-schizoid and depressive positions (and the employment of splitting and projective identification) to develop his now famous "grid" by which to locate the development, evolution, and transformation of all psychic elements and events. In so doing he has put something like a radioactive tracer on all feelings and thoughts which can be temporally and spatially located in the polar-coordinate system of a vertical genetic axis and a horizontal axis which represents the use to which the thought is to be put. Bion's conception of the grid represents one of the many applications of mathematical logic to psychoanalysis. The necessity for the application of mathematical logic to the study of psychical objects was something about which Bion felt very deeply. Toward his later years he more and more advised analysts to *abandon or to suspend memory and desire* as I have discussed earlier. To this he also appended the abandonment of *understanding*. Behind these injunctions, as I pointed out, were Bion's profound belief in the inadequacy of words, understanding, and sense data in general to apprehend the Truth of psychical objects in the internal world. Our relationship to the objects in external space is via the sense organs (of what we now call the dominant hemispheric organization which, in its sensory makeup, is neurophysiological). The sense organs were originally "discovered" by the infant from the vertices of pain, pleasure, and unpleasure. Thus, all data perceived by the sense organs is contaminated by the ancestry of the pleasure-unpleasure principle.

A word, thought, conception, concept, or formulation is a container (Establishment) which defines, refines, and confines the significance of non-verbal meaning within its boundaries. Life is always moving—"That which is is always becoming" (Plato), "The moving finger writ, and having writ, moves on . . .," etc. The Truths which words can only designate evolve and undergo evolutions because of the vitality of change itself. Understanding, like memory and desire, is like the need of an infant to grasp his/her beloved mother with his/her hands and/or other sensory organizations (eyes, etc.) in order to keep hold of her. In order to have object constancy, this infant must be able to allow mother to disappear (abandon memory, desire, and understanding) and allow her image *imaginatively* to appear in the presence of her absence.

Bion gradually awoke to the realization that language failed in its mission to approximate properly the study of psychic elements and was more suitable instead for non-animistic objects in the external world—as was western science itself. The internal world of the psyche has a language of its own. Psychoanalysis can explore it but has a more difficult time in translating it. Maybe art, poetry, music, religion, and mathematics can approximate it, Bion suggests. Why mathematics? Mathematics involves the use of signs or symbols which are devoid of meaning and therefore are free of memory and desire and, furthermore, can be used to designate objects on an ad hoc basis in a highly abstract, representational manner. The grid is one of the many applications of Bion's mathematical formulations. I shall discuss some of his other mathematical conjectures later in this section.

Bion's grid was at first devised by him as a diary of daily analytic experiences with patients. He later saw it as a convenient shorthand "computer" which could isolate the factors and elements of psychoanalytic objects and arrange them conveniently in cross-sectional space in such a manner so as to designate the invariants, constant conjunctions, and properties in general of psychical objects. In this being able to delineate psychical objects with greater mathematical specificity, conversations with colleagues as well as with oneself could be entertained. The grid can be thought of as a container (Establishment) which is comprised of a series of categories that Bion calls elements of psychoanalysis. They are functions of the personality which are formed by these factors and are phenomena which are observable through their primary and secondary qualities (in the Kantian sense) as having dimensions in the domain of sense, myth, and passion. The grid represents the abstract course of Learning through Experience as psychical objects undergo transformations from sense impressions to emotions and thoughts via a series of transformations from "O" (Truth) through "K" (Knowledge) to "O." As such, one can see a transformation from "PS" → "D." By this, Bion means that Truth may be too overwhelming for anyone except for the mystic to experience. It therefore must first be broken up through splitting and projective identification so as to be defended against until one is able to tolerate it, at which time a transformation into the depressive position takes place.

In a previous paragraph I have alluded to the vertical and horizontal axes of Bion's grid. Bion created this grid as a scaffolding device to be used to help the psychoanalyst organize his impressions about a *psychoanalytic object*, his term for the irreducible element of the patient's analytic experience. The evolution of the patient's sense impressions, their transformations via alpha function into utilizable or digestible mental objects, their modification by inherent preconceptions, their amplification by dream work or "myth work," and visualizations, etc., are all steps in the progression of development of the psychoanalytic element or object (the invariant in all these transformational processes) which ultimately ascends to the status of concept and conception. These "digestible" objects constitute what Bion refers to as a *definitory hypothesis*, an opening statement, so to speak, or a foreground element of attention which must then be challenged by the considerations of the second column on the horizontal axis (psi column), which represents an attempt to fault, to falsify, and to negate the definitory hypothesis. Column two therefore offers a background comparison and challenge to the newborn idea. Then the idea is further examined. An analyst may use this grid or any similar grid of his own choosing, Bion believed, in order to achieve a scientific standardization of his impressions about a patient, thereby putting his intuitions and his own capacity for emotional experience in a certain sector so as to achieve results which can be conveyed meaningfully to oneself and consequently to other analysts.

The Development of a Space for Thinking and Dreaming

It is as if the peremptory thought emerged, was transformed, and then was modified from a thing-in-itself (absolute) into an element of thought which could be dreamt, and therefore could be placed on a metaphoric table on the horizontal axis of the mind to be examined from many angles or *vertices* before corrective action is undertaken. This giant development requires space. Space develops as a legacy from the infant's being able to have a "thinking couple" inside him: (a) a self which generates thoughts, and (b) an internal mother who can modify or transform those thoughts, an "alpha mother," so to speak. The infant and his/her "broadcast" constitute the *contained*, and the receiving mother constitutes the *container*. Together, they comprise a *thinking couple* which, when internalized by the infant, becomes a model for thinking. The concept of the container is generally thought of today as a flexible rubber bag which expands with the impact of the infant's projections. What Bion really had in mind, I believe, was a container which, not only had a flexible coefficient of elasticity, but also was an instrument of interpretive transformation. One can use the analogy of the prism which refracts the monochromatic scream of the infant into the differentiated color spectrum of meanings which can then be arranged into hierarchies of importance for mental deliberation and for action. In so doing, mother's container function has not only absorbed the impact of the baby's screams, but has also translated the infant's organismic panic into signal anxiety with definitive realistic transformations into realistic danger, and of need-satisfaction. Omnipotence has been transformed into reality through mother's (and/or analyst's) interpretive function. Dr. Bernard Bail's contribution beautifully demonstrates this deployment of the container.

In order to achieve this the infant must be able to tolerate frustration enough to allow mother *her* space—and she is felt to reciprocate. This space becomes the hallowed space of thought. Bion's grid seems to be a sophisticated elaboration of the subject of Freud's theory of dream work as expressed in *The Interpretation of Dreams* (Freud, 1900). I believe Bion is saying that the original beta elements which impose upon the sense organs are internalized as *alpha elements* if permitted entry, the equivalent of *day residues* in the preconscious psychic system. These day-residue alpha elements are then seized upon by inherent preconceptions which are always searching to link up with realistic counterparts in order to surface and materialize. So far, this is straight-forward Freud, but there is one modification: Bion changed his focus from the importance of unconscious instinctual drives to inherent preconceptions (inborn knowledge). Freud states that the instincts, now imbued with their purloined day residues, are still barred from consciousness because of censorship and thus pull the now-instinctualized day residues into repression with them. Hence a repressive barrier is given to distracting day-residue material so as to guarantee peace of mind by day (during wakefulness) and by night (during sleep).

At the same time, the instinctual amalgam (instinct plus day residue—past *and* present) seems to *condense* or concentrate so as to achieve sufficient intensity so as to register on the day screen of perception, as visualization. Bion states that these visual images become the mind's way of storing mental accretions until they get linked up with mythic scenarios which take them onto varying forms of expression. Of all the interesting new ideas in this scheme, the one which impresses me most is Bion's conception of instincts. If I read Bion correctly, I believe he was suggesting that the ego's defense network is counterposed, not to instinctual drives, but rather to the awareness of their significance and ultimate meaning—of a preconceptive marriage with their realization. In short, defenses defend against the emergence of significance → meaning rather than to instincts per se.

It is my impression that Bion conceives of the content of the primary repressed—the unconscious proper—as inherent preconceptions which emerge as "thoughts without a thinker." Whereas Freud conceived of the primary repressed as instinctual drives intermixed with racial memory (such as the inheritance of the Oedipus complex, etc.), Bion seems to have a larger view of the unconscious, one in which it is the reservoir of all the possible inherent forms comprising potential awareness. His view connotes an inner cosmic vastness with a potential for virtually infinite realizations.

The Caesura and its Relationship to Significance and Meaning

It is most likely that Bion believed that the infant was born into an immediate awareness of something like the depressive position—that is, one of a unified and coherent psyche—which amounts to a sudden and frightening interface between the beta elements of reality which impinge upon the somatosensory awareness of external reality and, simultaneously, the intuitive arousal of preconceptions from the inner world of phylogenetic experience, which can include the awareness of all the ultimate **significances of any** or all events. Bion gradually came to believe that psychic birth occurred even before biological birth, and that inherent preconceptions could be stimulated by light flashes emanating from, for instance, stimulation on the developing optic pits at three months of fetal age. Every psychic moment, every mental event, every thought, every emotion, then, represents the immediate confluence of the external and the internal from the beginning of psychic life. The racial memory of preconceptions intercourses with the somatosensory impact of sensations to be molded into *significance*—and *meaning*. The amalgam rises to the surface by projective identification into the respective internal container for feelings which once used to be mother. For instance, the experience of hunger may mobilize the phylogenetic "memory" of being a prey and of being a predator in some metaphorical primeval rain forest. These inherent preconceptions may be programmed as phylogenetic "software" into the notion of the death instinct, which monitors death and danger, allows us to be anxiously aware of danger, and mobilizes the defenses against it. Programmed into the so-called life instinct would be the awareness of all the ramifications of need, desire, and pleasure, in which case the sexual nature of the Oedipus complex is an inherent preconception which is stimulated by the very act of need.

The interface of ultimate significance is first shielded by the passive stimulus barrier and mother's reverie, which is to allow for the postponement of these ultimate awarenesses which are to return in the mother container in the form of maturation, development, education, and, pathologically, the return of the repressed as symptoms. The first interface is primal repression and is effected by a splitting-off of a projection of these ultimate awarenesses in order to effect postponement. This period of splitting-off and projection in order to assure postponement is called the *paranoid-schizoid position.* The return of the split-off, the projected, and the repressed awareness is called the *depressive position*. In the sadness of ontogenetic maturity the truth of ultimate awareness can be given its fullest significance and meaning. The capacity to allow for this gradual re-entry of truthful significance in the shadow of sadness I have called the "dosage of sorrow" in my own contribution in this volume.

Publication

Freud's metapsychology was grounded in his neurological origins, and classical analysis to this date seems even yet to honor the neuronal discharge hypothesis as the central element of motivation. Melanie Klein did not seem to understand that her instinct theory was radically different from Freud's. It was not based on neuronal discharge but was, rather, based on the infant's need to contact a breast; it was a communicative theory, not a discharge theory. To Klein's *object relations communication theory* Bion added the *publication theory*. In Bion's terms this meant that the infant is communicating *and* also trying to get in contact with himself so as to be "known" or "self-conscious" in the literal sense of the term. This "publication" conjoins with communication (to objects) to seek correlation via feedback. Bion is constantly mindful that man is inherently a dependent creature who has only 180 degrees vision, not 360 degrees. A *second opinion* is therefore necessary for the human condition. This second opinion is implicit in all human bonding and is subsumed under "communication." Thus the senses of the individual, together (as "common sense") and individually, depend on the sense organs of the object with the second opinion, the object of *need*.

Publication without communication to objects leads to the grandiosity and isolation of psychosis. His theory of "publication" has foreshadowed the attempts of Kohut to establish a differentiation between the agenda of the narcissistic self and the object-relations self and thus anticipated the conception of "mirroring." Perhaps it would not be unreasonable to suggest that Bion has given psychoanalysis a *transcendental* perspective with hints of Carlyle, Emerson, and Nietzsche–in his conception of mind as always self-transcending.

Bion's Epistemological Sources

Bion's metapsychological ideas owe much of their uniqueness, I believe, to the fantastic sweep of his imagination, of his interests, of his education and of his background. One can often find Plato, Kant, Wordsworth, Keats, Shakespeare, Dante, Aristotle, and so many others walking through the paragraphs of his writings. His allusions are often exotic–the Andromeda spiral nebulae, the *Bhagavad Gita*, Intuitionistic Mathematics, Chinese hyeroglyphics, Jewish mysticism, archaeology, philosophy, the *Iliad*, the *Aeneid*, etc. (He studied history at Oxford and was much influenced by conversations with the philosopher A.J. Paton).

The allusions are not by chance. It is my impression that Bion had applied his rich educative background to the body of knowledge of psychoanalysis so as to put it in a continuity with the larger set of general knowledge–an epistemological synthesis, as it were. His concept of "C" elements and their linkages between sensations, dreams, and universal myths are but an example. Another example is his emphasis on inherent preconceptions, a notion which, as I alluded to earlier, is derived from Plato's Theory of Forms. Still others are his delineation of the "thing-in-itself" and "empty thoughts," ideas which have been propounded by Kant and "constant conjunctions" which he has borrowed from Hume. Bion's application of Plato and Kant has given psychoanalysis a rich new dimensionalization insofar as it specifies what Freud could only hint at when he referred to "id impulse." Bion changed Freud's conception of a neurophysiological mind into a vitalistic mind with infinite capacity for imagination–more than the sum of its instincts and their transformations, more than "id, ego and superego" can begin to convey. It is my impression that his "British pragmatism" is a fitting successor to Freud's all-too-Germanic scholastic romanticism.

Shifting Perspective and Vertices

Perhaps a word should be said about Bion the artist. He studied art for a year at the university of Poitiers and was much given to painting as a pasttime. I would not be surprised if his artist's eye were not responsible in some measure for his emphasis on shifting perspectives and vertices. When the subtlety of this emphasis is more deeply appreciated, we can see an enormously richer texture to the architecture of the inner world. I myself have been able to apply the concept of normal shifts in perspectives in the following way: When we speak of a good and a bad internal object, for instance, we are speaking from the viewpoint of an "I" assuming that distinction. On the other hand, the viewpoint from the "I" of the bad internal object is probably otherwise. *It* may feel itself to be good and that the so-called "good" internal object is "bad," for instance. All knowledge and feelings emerge from the initial judgements from different vertices, and therefore these differing vertices are implicit in the knowledge. In another contribution I have developed this thesis into the conception of the dual-track theorem. Abnormal shifts in perspective ("alternating pespectives") are more characteristic of psychotic minds, on the other hand.

Bion chose the term perspectives and then vertices rather than "points of view" in order to implement his conception that the senses themselves are prejudiced because they are dominated by memory and desire, which Bion **believes to be the deterrents** to speculative intuition. Thus, "points of view" conveys a sensory prejudice of the eyes and is not exact enough intuitively. The term vertex (and vertices) more ably conveys the mathematical rigor Bion had for so long a time tried to instill into psychoanalytic thinking.

Bion's Mathematics

Bion has made a significant contribution to psychoanalysis by postulating that contemporary psychoanalytic theory still corresponded to **Euclid**ian geometry insofar as it was limited to three dimensions of the senses. Geometry was liberated into its ultrasensual domain with Cartesian coordinates and the development of algebraic geometry. The psychoanalytic equivalent of this would be the development of intuition–that ultrasensual capacity to experience in domains beyond the reach of our tangible knowledge. The human being is still not caught up with being a sufficient "receiver" to the incredible "sender" he/she and other human beings are. Bion's views in this regard are connected to his conceptions of psychic space as being a continuing and varying relationship between the content and the container—both infrasensually and ultrasensually—so that relationships can exist in dimensions greater than three.

He delved into mathematical theorems at great length in order to seek unsaturated and more rigorous paradigms to apply to psychoanalytic experience. In this regard, he frequently mentioned Poincaire, whose formulations of set theory seemed to express a striking analogy to transformations from PS → D. From Poincaire, Bion then soared into the more rarified atmosphere of the Dutch School of Intuitionistic Mathematics which, as the name implies, deals with the mathematics of intuition—and the reverse. These mathematical expeditions were necessitated by Bion's dissatisfaction with his growing awareness that so much of psychoanalytic theory and knowledge had emerged from the "sensual band," that is, that they were products of the senses and were therefore subject to the prejudicial alteration of desire, which is but the future of the senses, as memory is the past. It was rigorous exactness and the unsaturated capacity for intuitive evolution that Bion was adventurously pursuing.

Religion, Mysticism, and Transcendentalism

Ultimately, Bion was to transcend the coldness of the mathematical paradigm and move on to the religious. He once commented to me, "Freud had unfortunately underestimated the place of religious passion in man's nature." Now using the religious vertex, Bion would replace "O" with "God" and would now suggest that great ideas (pure forms of thought, God) existed before there were men to conceive them. Mystics, thinkers, or messiahs, who have the capacity to achieve at-one-ment with God, are the receptors of this Truth which they must convert into a sensible language for dissemination to the non-thinkers of the establishment so that they can live, practice, and thrive in the penumbra of this Truth. The establishment container (religion or its counterpart) must be able to contain this Truth without catastrophic change. The container establishment must be both conservative in terms of the new Truth insofar as the latter must be preserved, but also must allow for the emergence of the change which the new Truth signifies, in which case, the Truth, or the Messiah who propagates it, is an evangelist—but of a new religion if the older establishment cannot adjust to it. Thus catastrophic change is the damage to the old Truth establishment which the new Truth causes to happen if the old Truth cannot adjust to it.

He then returned to his first major work, *Experience in Groups*, and looked at them once more but now from the religious vertex. You recall, that the work group was undermined by resistance groups which consisted of (a) a pairing group, (b) a dependent group, and (c) a fight-flight group. In an arcane reference in the original work Bion suggested that the genius (later to be called the mystic or the messiah) was, as a natural consequence, the offspring of the pairing basic assumption group. I take this to mean that the proper functioning of the work group (proper maturing, etc.) had become deficient and, by virtue of short-cutting of their scenario, they have defaulted on their agenda and therefore they have projected onto the next generation the additional burden of being their savior. From the religious vertex, Bion was to see a sequential succession to the basic assumption groups so that the pairing group produces the messianic leader upon whom they become dependent—as the dependency group. This dependency group now becomes a flight-flight group in regard to the leader-messiah, thanks to envy, and, upon the death of the messiah, must change again into a pairing group to prepare for a new messiah. (For a similar view of this complex notion, see Meltzer [1978].*)

Bion's Theory of Reality

His theory of "reality" is a striking answer to those who are critical of Klein for not recognizing reality. His emphasis in psychoanalytic technique is always, "Why does this come up *now*, or why are you telling me this at *this* time?" By so doing, he is emphasizing the "thing-in-itself," that irreducible element of reality (external or internal) which knocks on the door of the senses or upon one's intuition asking for recognition. This is prominently featured in the vertical and horizontal axes of his grid as the sensory impulse which is transformed from a beta element into an alpha element via alpha functioning, the successful functioning of which offers Truth as a necessary aliment for mental digestion and, further, allows for an alpha screen to be so deposited and formed that it can participate in the separation between sleep and wakefulness so that "digestion" and "action" can be separated. Robert Langs' contribution in this volume develops this idea further.

I beg indulgence for a momentary detour to develop Bion's theory of reality more fully. Claude Levi-Strauss, the structural anthropologist, has taught us that perhaps the deepest meaning of the Riddle of the Sphynx and the Oedipus complex is the notion of the theory of birth. He posits that there are two theories in primitive cultures about birth and also two structures in the primitive mind of the human being: the *autochthonous* and the *genital* theories. By autochthonous, he means born from oneself, self-generating, etc., whereas the genital theory predicates the necessity to have been conceived by parental intercourse. Parenthetically, I may add that in the ontogenesis of the child's phantasies about creation, the notions of female *and* male parthenogenesis are interposed (Christ from Mary, and Pallas Athena from Zeus) before the time of succession of the two-genital theory. In psychotic illness one frequently finds reference to the autochthonous theory in phantasies of birth and rebirth underlying seemingly more sophisticated birth phantasies, e.g., the Schreber case.

*Meltzer, Donald (1978). *The Kleinian Development: Part III: The Clinical Significance of the Work of Bion*. London: Perthshire, Clunie Press.

It was Freud who shoved the genital theory into the forefront of psychoanalytic theory, yet he was also the one who divided the mental apparatus into id, ego, and superego and *assigned autochthonous omnipotence* to the instinctual impulses of the id. Bion's theory, on the other hand, is quite unlike Freud's. It posits that all elements of the unconscious which rise to the surface; whether they be things-in-themselves, the "messiah thoughts," instinctual impulses, greed, envy, in fact, the whole panoply of the paranoid-schizoid position are always stimulated into awareness by some trigger element of reality which acts as a "genital" mate to have produced this awareness. The repressed does not return spontaneously by chance. This is an enormous revision of classical theory and places reality in a unique metapsychological framework.

Bion's theory of reality is especially cogent in the area of object relations. Classical Freudians generally assume that the infant's relationship to the breast is a *part-object* relationship, by which they mean that the breast function is all that the infant knows. Bion tells us, on the other hand, that the breast is a *linking* or *communicative* organ between infant and mother and is therefore not so much a *part-object* as it is a connecting organ—like a penis. In other words, object relationships, albeit primitive and barely differentiated, seem to exist from the very beginning. He has also clarified a point of enormous importance—once emphasized by Fairbairn—that the infant does not need the breast but rather needs the milk (experience) *from* the breast (*content* from the container, not the *container*). This notion augurs a very different kind of psychoanalytic conceptualization and technique for the treatment of neurotics *and* psychotics than does the classical. Bion's conception of the container and the contained is one example of this.

The Evolution of K → O

At this point, I should like to refer briefly to Bion's theory of thoughts and thinking, truth and falsehood, and memory and desire. In introducing this theme, let me distill one of Bion's contributions about thinking and lying via a parable: In the beginning there was Truth. In Its abject aloneness It was to ripple It s essence through that existential piece of resistance known as the human being and, in the eddy of that perturbance, be discovered by that human being anew from It s adventurous exploratory wave-front-echo. This eddy is called *experience*. The echo is the transformation of *Truth* as It is experienced by the beholder. The high point of Bion's conception is *experience*—that is, the origin of experience and the origin of our capacity to experience experience. The fate of experience is what Bion pleads our paying attention to.

Truth knows It s experience and requires no thinker to think It. The human being, who is the existential resistance I referred to, has been ordained to be persecuted, according to Bion, by an inexorable pressure of thoughts without a thinker which demand that the mind give them an audience for them to be thought about—especially upon the stimulation of the wave-front-echo of Truth which confronts the sense organs for attention–in other words, the experiencing of experience. Truth impinging from the outside upon the hapless human thus causes an inner perturbation which seems to rise to the occasion as if It hears the shibboleth of It s lost partner, the other Truth (like Plato's Androgyne), the one on the outside. Inner and outer Truth are fated to come together, and both are thoughts without a thinker because the Truth does not need to be thought.

I believe Bion is talking about the experience of the thing-itself which confronts us. This thing-in-itself is associated with Truth, God, eternal knowledge, and is located within us as well as on the outside. We also have emotions, feelings, and senses which color our perception of experience. Freud's notion of the primal unconscious was mainly that of instinctual drives–what Bion calls desire–but he dimly hinted at something else–primordial racial experience–what Bion refers to as inherent preconceptions (after Plato) or things-in-themselves (after Kant) in addition to desire. The mind had to be developed through countless evolutions in order to handle this noumenonological traffic, that is, the Truth, emerging as It hears Its shibboleth beckoning It from the outside. Once formed, the mind held on to its evolutional gain and learned that it had options. If it allowed the thoughts without a thinker this audience–if we could allow ourselves to experience it–then thinking per se did not have to take place. Instead, we self-transcend, which Bion calls an evolution in "O." In other words, the unconscious contains the inherent preconceptions, Plato's forms, Kant's things-in-themselves. Desires, that is, the instinctual urges or drives, are the adjectives of inner and outer experience and seek to modify them. They are not the primal nouns.

The options which are therefore available for the human being are as follows: (a) the experiencing of the experience (transformation in "O"); (b) the transformation of "O" into "K," in other words, facts about "O" in order to know enough about Truth so as to prepare for a future rendezvous with "O," yet necessitating a falsification of "O" by virtue of this detour through Knowledge because Knowledge cannot grasp Truth; and (c) the disavowal of Truth and transforming it into the lie which then absorbs the full use of thinking so as to maintain the Truth of the lie. The lie requires a thinker, as Bion cautions us. The Truth does not. All thinking begins as relative falsehood because it imperfects Truth and then, because of motivation (desire), can become the lie. Yet at the same time the thought-out lie is but the negation of the unthought and unthinkable Truth which is now a hostage in a miscreant container, the lie. In other words, thinking is inadvertent falsifying because it is motivated by desire, whereas repressing is lying by intent, and the content of the repressed is designated a lie which really contains the Truth. However, one can also see from this vertex that the ego itself is a falsifier in the very act of thinking because of the motivation or desire implicit in it. And here all this time we psychoanalysts–particularly those "liars" known as "ego psychologists"–have idealized the falsifying ego and demonized the id and superego. Furthermore, "understanding" may be one of the more sophisticated ways of avoiding the Truth while believing at the same time that one has arrived at it. Heisenberg's uncertainty principle states, in effect, that we alter or falsify Truth by our very observation–sensory apprehension–of it.

Bion has arrived at a conception of psychic functioning which assumes that true thinking is organized by alpha function and then publicated to the sense organ of consciousness. Secondary process, ironically, is the beginning of its falsification. Since secondary process is under the power of will, it is controlled by desire. The left brain "understanding" ego, attached as it is to volition, really contains instinctual drives all along in the form of volition or desire but has demonized the unconscious, the pure thinker, because of the dread of its meaning and significance. Defense mechanisms are volitional–instinctual–desire-inspired, and defend, not so much against instinctual drives, but against meaning and significance and also seek to modify them. The death instinct is not so much a drive per se as it is the defensive capacity to respond to the release of a preconception of a past Truth–apocalypse, chaos, etc.–which current experience has evoked into consciousness. It is the palimpsest of the agony of the species, and the defensive aspect of the death instinct rises to respond to its desperate primeval call.

From another vertex we can perhaps postulate that the transcendence which occurs through the experiencing of the experience–a transformation in "O"–constitutes self-knowing, whereas, once one has sent Truth into exile or barred its admittance, or banished it to an ignominious manger, it then becomes the lie to its namer and the Truth to its possessor, and thinking guards (seraphim) are posted to remind it that it is the lie and not the Truth–the defense mechanisms. It is otherwise known as human conflict, resistances, the defenses against the unconscious, human history, etc.

Psychoanalysis is that uncanny representative of Truth–"O"–which allows such an exploration of the mind that a second opinion can be offered about the lie to its liar with the ultimate hope that the lie dissolves so the Truth which it contains can then surface. Free associations, dreaming, etc., are random samples of pure inner Truth and pure thinking–thoughts without a thinker before falsification sets in. Psychoanalysis works like a hologram insofar as it produces a three-dimensional live image of a subject. A human being is revealed to be like all other human beings *and* to be an exquisitely unique individual at the same time. Being human occurs on these two tracks. We are always greater and lesser than we believe. The analyst's "discovery," to quote Bion, may be of "particular" but of no "general" importance. This in turn involves the capacity of the analyst to tolerate (respect) his own discoveries without having to believe they are of general significance or interest. In other words, according to Bion, the analyst must speak and listen to the Language of Achievement which is based upon negative capability, the capacity to bear or tolerate the frustration of doubt, of confusion, of ignorance, etc., until the relief caused by the appearance of the selected fact emerges. The evolution from the paranoid-schizoid position to the depressive position, according to Bion, is the transformational generative syntax of analytic transcendence, both for the patient and for the analyst. It is the transformation from patience to security.

Memory is the biography of past passions or desires and so tends to be falsified thereby—as does desire obfuscate the future. Although psychoanalysis relentlessly pursues memory and desires a cure, these passions, past and future, distort Truth by saturating or falsifying the empty moment when an evolution in "O" can occur—without preconceptions, without passions, without desire, without memory. Thus experience (thoughts without a thinker) can be experienced and allow self-transformation. Memory is best expressed in our self-transcendance. Our growth from what we have been to what we are into what we will be predicates the truest memory, which is the experiencing of the experience. Psychoanalytic technique must eschew memory and desire so as to allow the transcendence of experience. Understanding is a myth, a falsehood—on its way to becoming a lie—and subverts transcending experience. Psychoanalytic technique is like the polishing of shoes, how much polish one removes in the polishing is more important than how much one puts on. Memory—and knowledge—are meant to be forgotten—swallowed, so to speak so that they can allow a transformation of the container-self which needs to be silently altered by them. To hold onto experience or memory is to "mouth" it and thus preclude experience. Perhaps I can summarize all that I have stated above thus far by a quotation from *Ecclesiastes* (11:1):

> Cast thy bread upon the waters for thou shalt find it after many days.

That is but a summary of a synopsis of Bion's philosophical ideas about thinking.

Thus we can see that Bion believes that learning or evolving is really experiencing the experience. Our human capacity to tolerate the mating between the two lost halves of the Androgyne of Truth is self-transcendence —without memory—for the memory of the experience of the encounter becomes us. To hold on to the memory of it—to apprehend it—is to preclude the experience of it. Identification is the ultimate apprehension of the object and denial of the experience of it. Intuition is a higher form of mental process than is thinking. Thinking is merely the ad hoc use to which we put the harvest of intuition. True science is free association and dreaming—the products of alpha function, not thinking as we usually understand it, for free associations are without memory or desire. Science as we know it is handicapped because it requires the evidence of the senses.

And what is the product of this experiencing the experience so that the inner half of our androgyne meets its external counterpart—the realization of the experience? I believe Bion is suggesting that, when we do allow ourselves to experience the experience, we self-transcend by virtue of coming in contact with an aspect of ourselves which needs to be "known" to us. I am talking of the stirrings and yearnings of the archetypal preconceptions which, like Wordsworth's "unborn babies" or Michelangelo's "prisoners," strive and pray for the advent of the experiences which can release them from their immemorial marble—to be born. It is as if all our creations are but the rediscoveries which experiences release. Bion's transcendental view, then, is, I believe, that we walk in the shadow of our potential, transcendental, cosmic greatness, but are doomed only to get occasional glimpses of it through epiphanic surges as we mature.

I should now like to put Bion's concept of the thought without a thinker in juxtaposition to his concept of the container and the contained. If we consider the relationship between the mind and its thoughts as a paradigmatic expression of the container's relationship to its contained, then we can see, according to Bion, three distinctly separate relationships between the container and the contained: (a) *commensal*, by which is meant that the thought "O" and the thinker exists independant of each other, and furthermore, the thinker has not yet discovered the Truth or "messianic" idea from the thought "O." In this case, the container is as yet undisturbed by its thoughts because thought has not yet made an impression on the container; (b) *symbiotic*, by which is meant that the thought and the thinker (container have met and have transformed each other as a result. It might be called a "double Heisenberg" phenomenon in which the container modifies the contained and the contained modifies the container, that is, the thought modifies the mind and the mind modifies the thought. In this case, the thought is able to propagate, and the thinker is able to evolve; and (c) *parasitic*, in which case the thought and the thinker (container and contained) do meet but form an alliance in column two of Bion's grid, that is, the negating column, in which the meaning of the formulation emerging from the union of the thought and the thinker is known to be false (ego defense mechanisms in classical terms), but is erected against the "messiah idea" which, if experienced, would threaten either the container or the container would threaten the contained. In other words, a catastrophic situation is set up when a liberating "messiah idea" or thought is presented to the container and there is a movement from the tolerable commensal to the tenuous symbiotic to the near-catastrophic parasitic situation.*

Bion in Perspective

In reflecting the greater sweep of the epistemological traditions of Eastern and Western thought, the penumbra of Bion's metapsychology offers a larger and more dimensional template for psychoanalysis, one which can

*This is but a prefatory hint at *some* of the major points of Bion's work. I refer the reader to Grinberg, Sor and de Bianchedi [Leon Grinberg, Sor, Dario, and Elizabeth Tabak de Bianchedi (1975). *Introduction to the Work of Bion*. Translated from the Spanish by Alberto Hahn. Strath Tay, Perthshire: Clunie Press.] and to Donald Meltzer (1978). The clinical significance of the works of Bion.

contain yet surpass the current rigid neurological model of the classica psychoanalytic infrastructure. For the conception of a discharging id impulse to link up with man's inherent capacity for intuition and hunger for knowledge, the rigid doctrinaire dictates of left brain digital thinking must make allowances for its counterpart, the right brain's intuitive, global, spatial capacity to give significance and meaning to data. Freud, in my opinion, was a left-brain scientist whose intuitive capacity all but opened the door to the rich ore of the other brain but, like Moses, stopped short of the Promised Land because of his own saturation in "digital" science. Philosophy, epistemology, and "bilogic" (to use a term of Matte Blanco's) helps us even more fully to enfranchise the right brain's intuitive capacity. It is here that Bion's alpha function holds forth, as well as does his space-oriented "container" for feelings and thoughts. Bion's conceptions allow us to make more use of this holistic, intuitive capacity by freeing us from the concretizations and strictures of Freud's ultimately physiological orientation.

Was Bion a Kleinian?

When I was briefly in supervision with him before entering analysis, I asked him that very question. His answer was, "Heavens, no! I'm no more Kleinian than Melanie was. She always thought of herself as Freudian, but Anna (Freud) saw to it that she would be labeled 'Kleinian.'" Behind this anecdote about Klein's not being Kleinian lies, I believe, Bion's profound dislike for the confusion of personalities and theories. "Once Kleinian or once Freudian, it's no longer psychoanalysis," I believe he would state. He was analyzed both by John Rickman, a classical analyst, and by Melanie Klein. I believe he "digested" their legacy and became a *psycho-analyst*. When he suggests the abnegation of memory and desire, I believe him to mean one should desaturate ideas of dogma so that the analytic container can be opened for new possibilities rather than having to be saturated with Klein or Freud or Jung or the like. The psychoanalytic object must be discovered and rediscovered from different vertices. Yet it would never be safe to say that he is *not* Kleinian if that term be insisted upon. He had learned to play the instrument of phantasy with the notes of splitting, projective identification, manic defenses, and the like so that they emerge as a rare art form with beautiful arpeggios that would have made Klein proud.

Technically, therefore, Bion was more "Kleinian" than not. His extraordinary virtuosity produces such imaginative cadenzas of theory and practice that many of his commentators seem to miss the other side of Bion, the disciplinarian. His imagination is like a "clarinet run"; it can run off into exuberant and dithyrhambic directions but will return on key. That key is

In his: *The Kleinian Development*, Part III. Strath Tay, Perthshire: Clunie Press, for another view of Bion's work. I also refer the reader to Bion's work itself for a fuller development of his ideas. Any further delving into his thesis on my part would (a) transform me into his biographer, and (b) insult his work by presuming to be his translator.

Klein—and Freud! It was his belief that the proper basis of psychoanalysis is Klein's extension of Freud—and the phenomena of the paranoid-schizoid and depressive positions in addition to the theory of the Oedipus complex.

A thorough reading of Bion's works reveals that the irreducible building blocks for his metapsychology include Melanie Klein's conceptions of the *life and death instincts*—the phenomena of *greed and envy*—the theory of *splitting and projective identification*—the universality of the *paranoid-schizoid and depressive positions* (and their inter-relationship, and the *schizoid and manic defenses* apposite to them)—the theory of *internal objects*—her theory of the "*gap*" of separations between self and object, and the task the infant has in protecting the gap against destructive attacks from within—her belief in the inchoateness of *infantile omnipotence*—and her reformulation of the *Oedipus complex* to begin at an earlier time than Freud had indicated. Bion has borrowed from Freud's "Two Principles of Mental Functioning" and of the principle of *free association*. From these roots Bion has formulated the most advanced theory of thinking extant in psychoanalysis today, in my opinion.

Bion's Kleinian orientation has therefore been immense. With it he "Kleinianized" classical psychoanalytic theory and therefore firmly established the importance of her discoveries there. His elaboration of Klein's theories raised psychoanalysis to a structuralistic theory. In his postulation of the container and the contained, he seemed to be forever divining the structure which implicitly subtended or contained the mental contents he examined. Mental associations can be viewed as functions (in the mathematical sense) of the system or structures which they comprise. His conception of the inherent preconceptions is but one example. In this instance he is asserting that the inherent preconceptions act as "knowing" containers or predications for the contest they hypothesize to exist. Thus preconceptions can be looked at as the structural inferences which govern the analytic content of an hour. The concept of the grid fundamentally depends on this conception. In invoking the mathematical contributions of Poincaire, moreover, he was even more firmly entrenching himself in structuralism by virtue of the assumption made by Poincaire that the manifestation of a previously existing structure becomes apparent as the organism experiences change.

Yet it must be stated in fairness to Bion that he was far more than just "Kleinian." Bion's metapsychology transcends Klein's discoveries and carries Kleinian—as well as classical—analysis to far higher levels of attainment and conjecture. His insistence on the abandonment of memory and desire and the reliance instead on imagination and intuition have approached the fulfillment of Freud's dream to discover a separate logic for the internal world, a dream which Freud abandoned when he re-directed himself to the ego and away from the instincts. Bion has far transcended Klein in freeing psychoanalysis from the pleasures and displeasures inherent in instinctual life and has helped psychoanalysis to achieve, instead, access to its true heritage, pure thoughts and pure feelings—and the things-in-themselves to which they correspond.

Bion, Evidence of the Man   *Frank Philips*

EDITOR'S NOTE: *Mr. Philips has had the rare privilege of having been an analysand of Melanie Klein and of Wilfred Bion. His contribution is a reminiscence of Bion the colleague, Bion the analyst, and Bion the friend. It is a synopsis of tight compression which epitomizes a vast array of feelings and portraitures of intimate moments with a most extraordinarily interesting person.*

A Personal Reminiscence: Bion, Evidence of the Man

Frank Philips

My long association with Wilfred Bion, first in analysis with him, subsequently through long years of friendship, brings me to a realization of many matters. First, to describe them rather loosely, he understood psycho-analysis, found it to be in many respects inadequately used and set himself to do something about it. Thanks to his unusually penetrating insight and his need for truth and intolerance of alternatives to it, he brought to bear a cultured capacity for applying thought and common sense in rendering psycho-analysis not something more, but something *much more*. In achieving this, and in publishing the successive stages of his findings, he revealed to every psychoanalyst who really cares seriously for the matter the presence of an area of mind and personality that can be known and an immense area which can only be unknown for the time being, hence can only be conjectured to exist. For all this he will not be loved, human beings–many psycho-analysts of course included–being what they are. Fortunately a tiny minority will have found more truth about the matter of psycho-analysis through his work and genius.

My American colleagues who have also known in analysis, or in other circumstances, this noble character and extraordinarily creative psychoanalyst, will undoubtedly feel points at which their experiences with Wilfred Bion tally with mine. But an interesting aspect will be the shades of difference in our views, not the identity of them. There will be agreement, surely total, about the inherent quality of the man–the profound integrity, his humanity, and his awareness and respect for psycho-analysis. And thus for Freud, Melanie Klein, John Rickman, and many other people before and after Freud to whom all psycho-analysts must be grateful. In the same sense I think of his love and admiration of Shakespeare, Homer, Milton, the Bhagavad Gita within the Mahabharata, of Picasso, Michelangelo, Leonardo da Vinci, Monet, and of his delight in the poetry of Keats, Patrice de la Tour du Pin, Yeats, Gerard Manley Hopkins, Lautréamont, and a host of others. And not least I think of his love of music and of nature, of the wild-flowers of England and France, and of his watching, enthralled, during a fierce thunder-storm the flashes of lightning and hearing the cracking and pounding of the thunder.

I am also reminded of his experiences of life in the raw: those dreadful years in France in 1917 and later, his early experiences with patients, and his realization of the growing concern for our civilization tottering on its foundations, and not least the events–which one sensed at a distance–of his personal life which remained private and known only to himself. There was underlying everything his capacity for feeling and encountering love and hatred, both within and beyond himself, to a degree far exceeding the limits of most of us.

In the beginning of my own analytic adventure I could hardly have imagined that which was to emerge from a quiet impression which occurred in London in the early 1950's. Gradually, over the years, it matured and became a firm piece of reality. In the latter part of 1949 I had arrived from Brazil to go into analysis with Melanie Klein. During the five-days-a-week of the coming and leaving at Mrs. Klein's door-step, at 42 Clifton Hill, I noticed with some curiosity occasionally meeting a large, very solidly built man, with a broad face, a calm expression, and very dark brown eyes that looked at me directly. There was a very slight smile as though he was aware of the strangeness of what we both were doing in being there. Nothing beyond a usual greeting was said.

I was then in a very early stage of my analysis with Mrs. Klein. Wilfred must have been nearing the end of his analysis. Life in London went on as usual. However, in 1954 Mrs. Klein was feeling increasingly her advancing age—not long afterwards her health began to fail—and she suggested that I continue analysis with someone else. I had in the meantime met Wilfred in seminars and at the scientific meetings of the British Society and I had listened to what he had to say. Having an opinion sufficiently formed I had not the slightest hesitation in requesting him for a vacancy. I need not dwell on those years that followed, for all my colleagues in Los Angeles who knew him in analysis will recognize from their own experience something of what that meant. With the termination of my analysis, in 1961, there took place the International Association's Congress at Edinburgh. Wilfred gave his paper, A Theory of Thinking. A well-known American analyst who was also leaving the room in which we had been listening, said, "Well, *he* certainly knows his Plutarch."

My wife and I began to meet and know the Bions socially in the mid-60's. We lived on one side of Regents Park, they on the other. Time passed and life in London again went on as usual. Soon after the Bions went to Los Angeles my wife and I decided to accept an invitation I had received to return to Brazil to assist in the São Paulo Institute's training programme. After several years of my work here some of my colleagues agreed with me that it would be a good idea to invite Wilfred to visit Brazil and the Bions came for the first time in 1973. They spent a fortnight with my wife and myself during which Wilfred gave ten lectures to large audiences as well as supervision to a number of analysts and candidates. The effect was such that their visit was repeated in 1974, 1975 (spent at Brasília), and for the last time to São Paulo in April 1978. Wilfred had previously been to Buenos Aires where he was enthusiastically received. During the visits to Brazil he several times also visited the analysts in Rio de Janeiro.

As can easily be imagined the reactions of the people in Brazil were very varied. Many found it highly stimulating, some thought it intriguing, some considered it too difficult to take in, and various "old soldiers" simply declared it improbable. Since then the waves and the tides have swirled around in all the psycho-analytical circles in Brazil about what Wilfred had to say. But something important has happened and nothing will ever be the same again. The main thing this is what I am now going to mention. Up to 1973 the São Paulo Institute's training committee had provided a full course for teaching Freud and Melanie Klein. Following the 1973 visit arrangements were made to include Bion and this has been followed with all seriousness since then. Thus the whole course of training in São Paulo is devoted to the work of these three forces of psycho-analysis.

As in other years my wife and I were at our property in the Dordogne during July and August in 1973. This is in the south-west of France, some 100 miles from Bordeaux by road. The Bions spent some weeks with us there that summer. This inspired them to acquire a property of their own nearby; they on one side of a valley, we on the other. Wilfred loved the countryside, the planning of the architecture during the rebuilding of the house they had chosen, and pottering about in the garden, as well of course as doing a lot of writing. The farm villages in the region date from the 12th century. Wilfred had always loved England and France; although he spoke it but little he knew the French language very well. I never saw him happier than in those recent years when we met in this remote corner of the Périgord, formerly called part of the Aquitaine.

I now turn to a simple phantasy-construct of my own which I hope can be shared by others along with their own phantasies. We know that the influence of Wilfred's early childhood in India left in him a very deep impression. I think, in reflecting on it, that the analysis he had been able to have with Mrs. Klein, centering on the breast–that is in Kleinian terms–constituted a psychical center for the quality of universality which he possessed so thoroughly. I have reason to believe this through my own experience with Mrs. Klein. The matter can be carried further by all who care to undertake the reflection possible in reading Wilfred's books; he does not conceal reality. In itself this does not enable us to grasp the phenomenon of genius, but it is a way of looking at something in the man that has led to the title of this book.

Psycho-analysis as Wilfred found it, lived with it, suffered with it, and was faithful to it absolutely, left much to be desired. This awareness was, I believe, painful but it was not clarified immediately. It developed through a powerful need. This need was to make more truth available; it was transformed through psycho-analysis–the only thing we have–into a main objective with priority above all else. The consequence of his fertility of mind and tenacity of purpose led him to face the task with courage that became so habitual that it was part of him. The at-one-ment he stressed was an absolute objective.

When Wilfred and Francesca came to stay with us for the last time, in April 1978, he gave me a copy of his book "Seven Servants." He had written in it some dedicatory words. They are so expressive of him, so brief, so compassionate in his humour, that I can do no better than quote them in ending my contribution to this book.

> To Frank
> with every good wish for a long and absorbing servitude—from one slave to another
>
> Wilfred Bion

Can I say more, beyond wishing full satisfaction to those of my colleagues who feel they have known Wilfred Bion in a similar way?

CLINICAL CONTRIBUTIONS

On the Analyst's Sleep During the Psychoanalytic Session

by Richard Alexander

EDITOR'S NOTE: *It has long been known that there is more than merely an exchange of language which takes place in an analytic hour. The intrastructure of primitive "communication" seems to underly analytic dialogue and to traverse the ready-made conduit to achieve mysterious results if the analyst is not wary. The analyst's awareness of his/her response to a patient's "other language" can be critical to the outcome of the case, according to Doctor Alexander. This paper deals in depth with the nature of projective identification as it occurs transactionally in an analytic hour in order to preclude progression.*

On The Analyst's "Sleep" During the Psychoanalytic Session

Richard P. Alexander, M.D.

Commenting on the present state of psychoanalytic knowledge, Bion has been known to often state that inasmuch as we are engaged in a field which has been in existence for only some 100 years, that "we have just scratched the surface." The psychoanalytic contributions of Dr. Bion, however, have gone far, I feel, to lengthen and deepen this scratch and help us in finding our way. I have found this particularly to be the case in regards to the subject matter presented in this paper, where the application of a number of his theories and suggestions have shown themselves to be quite useful.

In a previous paper (1976), I drew attention to the relationship between the pathological withdrawal of the patient during the psychoanalytic session, leading to states of stupor and sleep—to those states of mind experienced by the analyst during the session, leading to *his* loss of interest or temporary lapse of consciousness. Relatively little appears in the literature on this latter situation, which will be the subject of this paper.

In his excellent monograph on the general subject of sleep and dreams, Scott (1976) makes mention of the analyst who sleeps during the session and expresses the importance of our further exploring this phenomenon. He suggests, however, that the analyst who becomes "bored and sleepy" may "become so guilty, that curiosity" about these feelings and experiences are "forgotten." Of course, Scott is in part here referring to the analyst's counter-transference feelings which no doubt contributes to the minimal literature on the subject. However, besides feelings of guilt, the experience itself is a very unpleasant one and for that reason is also perhaps prone to be "forgotten."

Dean (1957), for example, describes an experience with two patients in which his drowsiness became so acute and disturbing that he "desired more than all else that the hour end" so that he could take a nap, only to discover that at the conclusion of the hour, he again felt fresh and alert. Also, Schimel, (1976), describing a similar situation with a patient, writes that he felt "numbed and drugged" as if under the influence of a powerful narcotic. After dismissing the patient "it took many minutes," he states, to recover even when resorting to "breathing deep drafts of cold winter air." My experiences bear out that the distressful aspects they describe are quite typical.

Aside from the acute distress that may be experienced, is the *puzzling* nature of the situation with regard to not being able to understand what the "sleep" represents, or why the experience is happening. Calef (1971), in this regard, reports an instance during a session with a patient in which the analyst felt his own feelings to have "slipped away." He further described his mental state as being one in which he felt he had been "close to sleep but not asleep—though it could hardly be said that I was awake."

Experiences of this kind also have a disturbing effect on the analyst's capacity to achieve the desired state of free floating attention and the optimal balance between attention to the patient's feelings on the one hand and the analyst's feelings on the other hand. McLaughlin (1975) has pointed out that a kind of "alerting mechanism" which enables the analyst to recover from this sleepiness, propels the analyst to a state of "vigilance and readiness for action" resulting from superego—ego ideal pressures, which further has the effect not only of making our work less than pleasant but also detracts from our achieving this optimal balance. It is all these types of undesirable feelings and experiences that probably account for the relative absence of investigation into this subject, and points up the importance of furthering our interest in it.

In pursuing this problem, in the hope and effort to contribute further understanding, I would like to discuss it both from the standpoint of the patient, i.e., the type of patient that is capable of affecting the analyst's mind in this manner, as well as from the position of the analyst himself, i.e., counter transference feelings and experiences which may go beyond counter transference that have a disruptive effect on his (the analyst's) consciousness.

The Patient

With this in mind, I shall begin by presenting some clinical material from my most difficult and vexing case whom we shall call Mr. Y. This patient at times had the ability to render me helplessly sleepy from the moment he would begin speaking in the hour. This became a dreaded experience and I assure you had nothing to do with my general state of health and had as well no relationship to what is sometimes referred to as a depleted emotional state.

It was usually very difficult, even aside from the sleep effect, to glean significant meaning from the patient's talk. Since at first glance, however, his communication seemed coherent and always in plentiful supply, it was difficult to understand how the patient could be affecting me in this unpleasant fashion. In this regard, Bion (1967) has commented upon the point that "the fact that thinking and talking play such an important part in psychoanalysis is so obvious" as to escape the attention of the analyst. "It does not, however," he continues, "escape the attention of the patient who is concentrating his attack on linking and in particular the link between himself and the analyst."

However, even when on occasions I felt I was able to see a pattern forming which would make the formation of a link possible, an interpretation given for this purpose of promoting this result would seem to have no such effect. Worse yet, Mr. Y's response to my effort, rather than improving contact, would only again tend to render me sleepy, thereby producing a new and additional problem. A lack of progress also became apparent in relation to interpretations being addressed to the patient's tendency to frequently miss the Monday hour following the week-end break.

Although the content of such interpretation seemed correct and were even at times agreed with by the patient, there was little or no change in his behavior in this regard. This rather consistent missing of an hour during the week coincided with an idiosyncratic stylized and exhibitionistic manner of presenting himself at the start of each session as if he were saying "I've got it good, you've got it bad." Most puzzling of all was my tendency to become drowsy even when the patient was relating his dreams, as I would be left to wonder how it was that material coming from this unconscious realm would also have this effect on me.

My best clues, at this juncture, at understanding what was going on came as a result of my resolve to maintain attention after giving the initial interpretation in the hour. For example, soon after the onset of one such session, the patient started relating a story in his characteristic manner concerning a woman he was presently acquainted with and her young son, who now lived in Sweden. After his lengthy recitation of this story, I found it possible to interrupt to introduce an interpretation, stating that I thought he was also saying something about the remoteness of his relationships in general and that, in the session itself, the emotional distance that existed between us was felt to be something comparable to from here to Sweden; and also that the expanse that was symbolized by the distance between these two points, also expressed the degree to which he wished to remain remote from his unconscious, which contained the "young son" aspects of himself.

The patient responded with, "Yes, well–" and continued on with his story about the mother and son. Although his "yes" was said in a manner which indicated agreement, it became apparent then that his need to further elaborate on his story was felt by him to be of uppermost importance. His continuation at this point did not seem to be providing further pertinent information, and yet his style and skill in conversing resulted in my experiencing considerable doubt, as well as an unpleasant confusion with regard to my having been heard or responded to at all. It was now clearer to me that Mr. Y's return to his story provided him with a means by which he could stay a comfortable distance from me and the present by his living in the past; and at the same time have me be the one to experience this uncomfortable doubt and frustration in the present.

With this in mind, I pressed on, confronting the patient with his seemingly ignoring what I had said about himself and us. The patient responded as if to indicate some concern about the analyst stating, "Yes, I did hear what you said–I know I do that (ignore you) sometimes"–but then he again returned to his previous story as before. It was apparent that he was attempting to placate me and put me off by saying "sometimes I do it" meaning, not now, so as to be able to continue to maintain great distance from the present. This technique seemed to be serving two other purposes: one, to reassure me in a patronizing way that I had been heard and shouldn't feel rejected or insulted by his taking no heed of me, i.e., treating me as being almost non-existent, but at the same time reassuring me as if to say, "You're O.K." much as a disinterested mother might say to a small child who is tolerated but where no genuine interest is felt. At the same time, the patient, on returning to his story, seemed to be insulating himself with it and by his great quantity of words, preventing any true discovery of himself. The analyst in this situation may have as his alternatives, (1) accept the reassurances as a needy child might, or (2) become angry in lieu of accepting the patient's explanation. A direct expression of anger at this point, I felt, would only bring about a stronger and more clever denial by the patient, certainly producing no further movement.

The analyst in a dilemma such as this and thus prevented from establishing contact with his patient, might thus be encouraged to turn his interests away from the patient to other matters, or unwittingly to lose interest altogether and perhaps "sleep" to further avoid the frustrating nature of the situation. This latter attitude which had developed in the analyst in the past was something analogous to that of one who is presented with a seemingly insoluble problem where sleep and the hope for a better tomorrow seem to offer the only solutions. In this way, the patient, by living with his stories of the past, was avoiding contact in the present and slyly stimulating the analyst to wish for something better in the future.

In the present setting it began to dawn on me that, if my premise was correct, the patient must be trying to ward off extremely painful and frightening feelings related to feelings of inadequacy, smallness and unimportance which he was insidiously projecting into me through a constant barrage of splitting and projective-identification. His ability to manipulate the analysis through these means so interferred with my ability to function in my real identity as psychoanalyst that it had the effect, for all practical purposes, of rendering me very small and unimportant. At the same time, the patient's megalomanic insulation prevented him from being a patient.

His preference for maintaining this condition of absent analyst–absent patient finally became exposed when he responded to my further interpretation regarding his actions in analysis. For the first time the patient evidenced genuine emotion, angrily stating, "How dare you delve into my private life?" This response was quickly followed by an almost inaudible chuckle, suggesting that he felt his show of temper had revealed much too much of himself and as if to say that all would be forgiven and we could go back as before if I didn't do anything to provoke him again, much as a riled parent might react to a provocative child.

Mr. Y's resistance to and anger about having his "private life" exposed was related to his infantile feelings of loss and helplessness as well as infantile rage in response to these feelings. In this regard, Bion (1965) has pointed to the patient's resistance to self-discovery, or what he calls "being what one is," for fear of the revelation of very primitive impulses and/or psychotic anxieties and beliefs. The intricate nature of the patient's defense system and the method by which it could affect the analyst's mind, became more clear through understanding the function that the patient's dreams served.

In short, the patient made use of dreams to create and maintain the illusion of being in possession of or having entered into an idyllic state; while painful feelings were felt to be non-existent through their evacuation into the analyst and believing them to be safely contained therein.* This means of denial of mental pain through the employment of this massive split in the personality could be activated by the week-end break and/or any other intercurrent disappointment experiences in his outside life. Thus, the patient absenting himself from the subsequent hour was an expression of mental withdrawal now put into physical action. Through this means he could coherently feel well-off and believe the analyst was suffering the pain of loss and rejection, etc. It was the analyst's effort to interrupt the patient's pathological equilibrium by confrontation and interpretation which ultimately led to the angry comment with reference to his wanting his "private life" kept inviolate.

As the nature of the patient's intricate defensive maneuverings were increasingly revealed, Mr. Y began to make important changes, evidenced by a greater ability to maintain contact with the analyst, which coincided with the lessening of my loss of attention. He also gave information suggesting that his external relationships allowed for some genuine intimacy and sharing not present before.

During this period of improvement in the analysis, he also began more consistently to attend his appointments during the week. At one point during this phase of the analysis, it was necessary for the analyst to cancel a Monday session, resulting in the patient's again cancelling the next hour in his previously-characteristic manner. He initiated the third hour of this week with an apology, also in his usual manner, excusing the absence on the grounds that he had employed painters on Monday to redecorate his store and was required to remain with them on Tuesday until they had finished their work.

He then reported a dream in which he and his sister find themselves in a cold environment consisting of ice and snow, engaging in a sled race. In the dream, the course of the race is straight downhill and his sled comes in third place which Mr. Y seems willing to settle for. This dream indicated an important change had been made as it revealed for the first time significant content relative to the true structure of his personality and his "private" internal life.

Unlike previous dreams which expressed his belief that he possessed or experienced only the ideal situation or pure pleasure state, this dream showed his internal world as being full of cold and icy hostility. This self-

* The patient's employment of dreams in this manner is, I believe, a variation on the patient's use of dreams to serve solely an evacuatory function described by H. Segal at the U.C.L.A. Symposium on "The Work of Melanie Klein," April 16, 1977.

evelation was further borne out by his linking himself to his sister, a lesbian who lived alone and had never had a relationship with a member of the opposite sex, evidencing more clearly his hatred of two-ness. This was further demonstrated in his association to the "straight course" which Mr. Y felt was the quickest and thus "the safest approach," i.e., no danger of being thrown (rejected) by going around sharp curves (depending upon a complementary relationship where he was not in complete control). The content of this dream was also useful because the patient now was able to see and acknowledge the revengeful "tit-for-tat" nature of his behavior, i.e., "settling for third place (the third session in the week) triggered by my having to cancel the Monday hour. It was these feelings and the developing insight about them that he attempted to have covered over by the "painters" and his missing the subsequent hour. It had also been this defensive activity brought about by extensive splitting and excessive projective-identification* which had previously prevented progress in analysis and had so interfered with the analyst's capacity to think or remain attentive. The relevation of these anxieties of a real relationship resulted in the patient's becoming able to acknowledge his defensive smugness and his attempt to obtain cruel infantile satisfactions by showing off at the expense of developing a capacity for cooperative effort.

The Analyst

In discussing the conditions affecting the analyst's mental state, particularly those experiences affecting consciousness, for example: boredom, disinterest, sleepiness, etc., one immediately thinks of the significance of counter-transference. Racker (1968), in discussing the boredom or sleepiness of the analyst in these terms, describes it as a manifestation of "mutual withdrawal," wherein the analyst's withdrawal expresses his unconscious talionic response to the frustrating patient, brought on by the emptiness and futility of the patient's associations. Bion (1967), in commenting on the patient who attacks linking and "the capacity of both analyst and himself to talk or think" draws attention to a further determinant.

Although Mr. Y superficially evidenced no difficulty in talking, in fact his talk for a considerable time in analysis did little to facilitate communication, but rather impeded thinking. Segal (1977) also recently described a patient who attacked the linking capacity with "knifelike" efficiency which could be best detected by attention paid to the conscious derivative of the counter-transference feelings. Racker (1968) also emphasized the importance of making good use of these feelings so as to avoid "the danger of a vicious

* The concept of excessive projective identification originally put forward by Melanie Klein to emphasize frequency of the use of projective-identification has been expanded by Bion to include the excessive belief in omnipotence. See Bion, 1962, p. 308. It is the strength of belief in omnipotence which enables the patient to slip away into states of withdrawal, the peculiarity of which contributes to the analyst's inattention.

circle of reactions developing between them" which the patient unconsciously encourages to ward off "the intense dependence" that could develop if the analyst were to prove to be useful.

As mentioned earlier, patients may also be afraid to allow the analyst to be useful out of a fear of self-discovery–what Mr. Y referred to as his "private life." In endeavoring to get these patients *into* analysis, it is important to help them uncover their hatred of analysis and the determinants of this hatred, e.g., that analytic work leading to awareness of emotions contradicts their megalomania. Until this step is accomplished, the patient will continue to operate in a characteristic, compliant and/or contrived manner which makes for a false and/or "dead" analysis.

Mr. Y's dreams, as previously noted, served essentially as a self-reassuring function and were treated by him as if the events or feelings they depicted were real. Dreams of this kind function more like hallucinations, while real feelings of painful loss and rejection, which might normally appear in dreams, are split off and projected. The analyst's ability to use his mind effectively may be greatly compromised by the effect of these projections.

This type of unpleasant present that the patient is able to manipulate the analyst into serves also to stimulate in him (the analyst) the effects of memory and desire. Bion (1967-1970) has pointed out that it is focusing on memory–attention to the past, or desire–attention to the future, which serves to frustrate the analyst, demolishing his intuitive capacity as well as his link to the analysand. In stressing the importance of "eschewing memory and desire," Bion is taking Freud's (1972) lead expressed in the famous letter to Lou Andres Salome where he (Freud) writes of having to blind himself "artificially in order to focus all the light on one dark spot."

In applying Freud's concept further, Bion (1977) has drawn attention to the advantage that might accrue by not being unduly influenced by the content of the patient's speech so as to be better able to be alert to the phonation and to those "elements which lie outside the spectrum of thought." Attention directed in this manner goes a long way, he feels, to develop and maintain an optimum intuitive capacity in the analyst. The combination of attention directed to the patient's content *as well as* phonation has proved useful in dealing with the type of patient under discussion.

For example, Mr. G, another patient who at times rendered the analyst temporarily stuporous, was also frustrating because of a refractory response to progress. His underlying attitude, which inhibited personality growth, of "who needs it," i.e., depend on or value his object, had, as a result of interpretation, brought about some evidence of increased capacity for cooperation but had failed to produce significant change. In one hour during this period, Mr. G reported a dream wherein he is engaged in fellatio with his female companion.

This intercourse is abruptly interrupted by the sudden appearance of a dirty tramp, or hobo who terrifies the patient into breaking off the relationship. Associations failed initially to clarify the precise meaning of this terrifying object, although it seemed to represent an envious attack upon the sexual couple, i.e., mother-father, infant-breast, or mouth-nipple, as well as an attack upon the link bringing two objects together. In a subsequent hour, soon thereafter, the patient was able to acknowledge a new awareness of his "mind drifting" shortly after the onset of the session or during a verbal exchange, necessitating his request that I repeat the interpretation. This data clarified the dream symbolism with reference to the rivalrous *drifter* who functioned to destroy conscious mental functioning in general and interest and curiosity in particular. This impulse was motivated out of a wish to prevent accomplishment or progress and deny the significance of a complementary two-party relationship. The importance the patient placed on "drifting" as an expression of hostility against two-ness was helpful, also, in my becoming better able to understand the significance of his style of speaking.

This mode consisted of his verbalizing as if reciting from a sketchy outline and was thus devoid of feeling and deficient of meaning. In essence, his speech was designed to frustrate contact and encourage collusion in the direction of accepting the status quo. A model for this subtle but pathological verbal action of the patient would be that of remaining forever with the mother in an undifferentiated form.

A second mannerism of Mr. G, which had a similar effect and motive, was his tendency to speak so slowly and deliberately as to stimulate in me a painful sense of impatience followed by a tendency to lose concentration resulting in a tendency for *my* mind to drift. This ploy* of the patient, largely unconscious, had up to now escaped my attention, so attentive had I previously been to the content alone. Problems with regard to the *way* in which the patient relates which interfers with the analyst's capacity to think may also occur when the patient, as it were, suddenly and without notice *silently* disappears, i.e., becomes mentally non-existent or mindless.

This mindlessness does not occur with the magnitude seen in the schizophrenic patient who may feel non-existent to the degree of believing he is neither alive nor dead, but is sufficiently intense to cause the analyst to feel that he, indeed, is without a patient; a condition that leads to the analyst no longer having access to the "dark spot" on which to focus attention. The effect on the analyst of suddenly facing into the deep void produced by this type of patient withdrawal can be quite painful and is reminiscent of Milner's (1969) description of the "dark blankness" and the feeling of "having to climb out of treacle" experienced with her famous patient.

I had, for a time, an experience of this type with a young woman patient who had acknowledged a capability of "taking herself in and out of the analysis." These oscillations were manifestations of her efforts to cooperate on the one hand, but on the other hand to rid herself of mind when the analysis became "too hard." Later, she could describe her state of mind,

*The word *ploy* in this context refers to a complex series of omnipotent projective efforts contributing to character formation, manifested in part through his manner of speaking.

after I became able to point out her absence to her as being a condition in which thinking was suspended, or, in her words, "everything is just one big jumble," wherein she talks without thinking (empty words without meaning) and without awareness of the analyst as analyst.

In this patient, the analysis became too hard when she experienced a very primitive envious rage in response to discovering that she did not possess the analyst. This rage led to spoiling and devaluing attacks upon the analyst in phantasy; and because she anticipated terrible retaliation, she was unable to reveal these impulses. Feelings of worthlessness resulting from these attacks were also too painful for her to bear and were dealt with by further attempts to render the analysis and the analyst worthless, intensifying feelings of guilt.

These feelings, however, were quickly dispensed with by her engaging, in phantasy, in a ritual of self-punishment, thereby preventing any resolution of the problem. Instead, she attempted (unconsciously) to manipulate the analysis so as to cause the analyst to become isolated and left to engage in some form of desultory and unproductive activity. In this way she hoped to work off powerful feelings of envy and/or jealousy and deny the existence of aloneness.

Alternatively, she attempted to ward off these feelings by engaging in phantasies of carrying on a secret affair with the analyst. This belief, which originates and is maintained through phantasies of secret omnipotent anal penetration and projective identification* results in identity and geographic confusion and could clearly be noted by the patient in a recent Friday hour.

The patient started the session relating a dream in which she is crowded into a small area in the tail section of an airplane to see a "kiddie movie." Someone is trying to talk to her husband, which irritates the patient, who states: "Either talk or watch the movie—we can't do both."

As clearly as can be remembered the session proceeded as follows:

Analyst: I think you're trying to tell us something about the masturbatory impulses originating in your "tail section" which function to take you out of the real world—particularly as the weekend approaches.

Patient: Yes, it's either diarrhea or constipation—now it's constipation.

Analyst: Constipation when you feel you have control and possession of me as you prepare for the weekend break and diarrhea when you realize you don't have these powers and become frightened by your impulses—rage, envy and jealousy.

Patient: Oh, you're so smart (with obvious irritation in her voice). Did you see the movie "Annie Hall"? Its subtitle is "A Very Nervous Romance."

Analyst: You want to get me to talk about movies with you, like "kids" rather than do our analytic work together as adults—as you admit yourself, "we can't do both."

* See Meltzer, D. (1966), pp. 335-342 for further discussions of the workings of this mechanism of defense.

Patient: Yes (laughs). I try to trick you, but I'm glad you don't fall for my tricks. That *would* frighten me.

Analyst: It would make you feel you *really* had omnipotent powers.

Patient: Yes (nervous laugh).

In this brief exchange, the patient's attempt to "seduce" the analyst into colluding with the impulse to deny two-ness can be clearly noted. It is the patient's acting out of this denial and the phantasies described, which when undetected by the analyst, contribute to the analyst's loss of attention.

One method available to the patient, which for a time also escaped the analyst's attention but enhanced a silent "erotic transference," was the significance the patient placed upon the tone of *my* voice, to the *exclusion* of placing any value on the *meaning* of the spoken word. Since in this context, thinking is of no consequence to the patient, the intonation can be completely but stealthily used to reinforce the phantasy of an idealized situation, wherein she unconsciously believes she is being provided literal food or sexual stimulation.

Aside from the disconcerting effect that this action of the patient may have on the analyst's mind, its continuance also deprives the patient of the possibility of achieving further understanding. Since the patient thus becomes unable to learn from interpretations, frustration is intensified, while growth is nullified and dependence on the word as a thing-in-itself becomes dominant. The difficulty of dealing with this silent withdrawal, and phantasied efforts at seduction, may be contrasted with another young woman with similar psychodynamics, but who could maintain sufficient contact with herself during periods of withdrawal to be able to inform the analyst of her feelings and actions.

These withdrawal periods would similarly occur when the work of analysis was felt to be too painful, activating or reactivating feelings of inadequacy which were hated. The hatred of these emotions would, in turn, lead to the patient's mind "quitting," resulting in her feeling "walled off" from this painful reality through feeling "protected in a blanket of foam." In this manner, she could approach the nonexistent state of being, where she experienced "nothing." Had this patient not been able to verbalize some of this experience but had instead concealed it by "empty words" or complete silence, it is quite likely, I feel, that my optimum psychoanalytic mental state would have been interfered with, resulting in some aspects of drowsiness.

In speaking of the non-existent state, Bion (1970) has drawn attention to its origins as a place where time, feeling, or three-dimensional space, representing the place where the object was, is annihilated. The patient who suddenly lapses into stupor, described in my 1976 paper, appears to best approximate this state of non-existence. Bion feels that "non-existence" (when externalized) becomes an object "that is immensely hostile and filled with murderous envy towards the quality or function of existence wherever it is found."

It is frequently this murderous envy-producing silent withdrawal or empty wordiness that brings about the problems described in this paper. As one such patient comments, "I can achieve a feeling of well-being only by seeing someone else worse off." On the other hand, insofar as the state of feeling "nothingness" is incomplete, patients will frequently complain of bordom or insufficient achievement, which often contributes to their seeking analysis.

Mr. S.T., a young man of 26, illustrates a number of these points. Initially, he appeared to typify the All-American-Boy image, as evidenced by his frequent attractive smile, noted in the first interview. Later, it became clear that the smile manifested an attempt to cover up and control his hostile envy, and as a result of this effort, like a character in a Jules Feiffer cartoon, he had "become addicted to (appearing) nice."

Early in the analysis, the patient began to very suddenly become quickly silent—sometimes for several minutes from the onset of the session, or during the session following an interpretation. These silent periods at first had a devastating effect on my concentration, but as I became more familiar with the experience and became better able to sustain attention, I recalled Bion's (1977) recommendation with regard to considering the importance of achieving a condition of "'artificial silence' in order to hear very 'faint noises.'" By applying his suggestion, I discovered that it "worked" for me, too, as "I began (also) to hear sounds which formerly passed unnoticed."

For example, in one session, following an interpretation relative to his arrogant criticism aimed at tearing down the analysis, Mr. T became suddenly silent. As I listened carefully, I discerned something almost inaudible that, nevertheless, was detectable as a very definite *sigh*. When I pointed this out to the patient, he retorted, "—well, uh—that has—uh—I don't know how to put words to it, it doesn't compute, no point in having it around." I then recognized that during his "silence" the patient was operating outside the realm of thought and that the *sigh* was, in part, an expression of relief relative to his omnipotent belief of having evacuated something felt to be unwanted. It later developed that this "it" was at times felt by the patient to consist of considerable mass and weight, while at other times seemed to be fragmented and disbursed piece-meal. Most important at this juncture, however, was that what, at the outset of his silence appeared to be developing into a serious impasse, now through "sharpening my ears" gave promise of providing a fruitful result. At the same time, my consciousness, which was previously clouded, had changed to one of optimal anticipatory anxiety.

Summary and Conclusion

In this paper, the problem of the analyst becoming "sleepy" during a psychoanalytic session is studied from both the standpoint of the patient's actions, as well as how this action affects the analyst's mind. Various forms of patient withdrawal are felt to have specific significance in this regard and are delineated in some detail. A number of the concepts of W.R. Bion have been found to be particularly useful in pursuing this work.

References

Alexander, R.P. (1976). On patient's sleep during the psychoanalytic session, *Contemporary Psychoanal*. 12, 277-294.

Bion, W.R. (1962), A theory of thinking. *Int. J. Psycho-Anal.*, 43, 306-314.

—— (1965). *Transformations*. New York: Basic Books.

—— (1967). Commentary on the paper "Attacks on Linking." In *Second Thoughts*. London: Heinemann, 1967.

—— (1970). *Attention and Interpretation*, New York: Basic Books.

—— (1977). The Grid, In *Two Papers: The Grid and Caesura*, Rio de Janiero: Imago Editora Ltd.

Calef, V. (1971). Counter-transference and the emotional position of the analyst. Panel paper presented at a meeting of the So. Calif. Psychoanal. Soc. on Sept. 23, 1971. Also personal communication.

Dean, W.S. (1957). Drowsiness as a symptom of countertransference, *Psychoanal. Q*. 26; 246-247.

Freud, S. (1972). *Sigmund Freud and Lou Andreas-Salome Letters*. Edited by Ernst Pfeiffer. Translated by Wm. and Elaine Robson-Scott. London: Hogarth Press and the Institute for Psycho-Analysis.

McLaughlin, J.T. (1975). The Sleepy analyst; some observations of states of consciousness in the analyst at work, *J. Am. Psychoanal. Ass.* 23, 363-382.

Meltzer, D. (1966). The relationship of anal masturbation to projective identification. *Int. J. Psycho-Anal.*, 47, 335-342.

Milner, M. (1969). *The Hands of the Living God.* New York: Int. Univ. Press, 323-326.

Racker, H. (1968). *Transference and Countertransference.* New York: Int. Univ. Press.

Schimel, J.L. (1976). Discussion of paper by R.P. Alexander, *Contemporary Psychoanal.*, 12, 292-294.

Scott, W.C.M. (1975). Remembering Sleep and Dreams, *Int. Rev. Psycho-Anal.* 2.

Segal, H. (1977). On countertransference, paper presented at a meeting of the Los Angeles Psychoanal. Soc. & Inst. on Thurs. April 14, 1977. Also personal communication.

To Practice One's Art — *Bernard W. Bail*

EDITOR'S NOTE: *Doctor Bail has chosen the theme of the psychoanalysis of the dying patient as a vehicle to demonstrate the importance of Bion's newer view of the oedipus complex. In short, Bion emphasizes that the tragedy of Oedipus was less in the incest and parricide theme than it was in his enucleation of his eyes. Oedipus began with omnipotent and arrogant curiosity to want to know "all"; in ironic fact he could not stand to know "all" so he destroyed his capacity to know. It is likewise in the fable of the Tree of Knowledge in the Garden of Eden—we must not eat the fruit of that tree—for fear of knowing! It is the strictures against learning and knowing about the unconscious within the field of psychoanalysis which Doctor Bail chooses as his target.*

This contribution is a passionate plea, I believe, for us not to forsake our inquiries into the unconscious because of taboos, rituals, preconceptions, and the like. It is becoming all too fashionable for psychoanalysts to abandon psychoanalysis in favor of treatments which approach sentimentality because of awe and diffidence before what confronts them; e.g., psychoses, narcissistic patients, dying patients, etc. If the pursuit of Truth be fated to have a dark and troubled destiny, we the analysts must be the unshrinking companions of those who take that journey. Our very analytic technique is the ultimate reassurance that we are not shrinking from their experiencing their experience, and, in Doctor Bail's case, that we are helping them to realize by our analytic containment (which seems to continue during analysis) that the experience they are experiencing is merely that part of life known as dying, no more!

Dr. Bail's contribution, furthermore, beautifully and poignantly demonstrates what Bion really meant by the phenomenon of the "container" and the "contained." Bion's original description had to do with the infant's projection of his/her fear of dying into mother when, for instance, the advent of hunger mobilized the preconception of dying. Mother's capacity for reverie allows her to be a container for this projective identification by (a) being able to withstand the impact of her infant's agony, and (b) to "translate" the screams of the fear of dying (organismic panic) into its more realistic components, much like a prism refracts a beam of light into the components of the color spectrum, thereby transforming organismic panic into specific, signal anxiety or concern within the field of reality. Most people who refer to Bion's concept of containment imply the first meaning, that of mother's "elastic" capacity and also associate silence and/or passivity to this container function, but they ignore the translating or interpretive function that is crucial to the definition. This is specifically what Dr. Bail has not done—he has not ignored the obligation to translate (to analyse) the fear of dying in a patient who now has achieved, not just the preconception of dying, but the fullest realization that this is in fact her fate.

To Practice One's Art

Bernard W. Bail, M.D.

Le soleil ni la mort ne se peuvent regarder fixement.

La Rochefoucauld

While direct access to the truth is available, it would seem, to poets and mystics only, those less fortunate have finally been able, in this century, to take advantage of the most remarkable heuristic device of modern times: psychoanalysis. Yet Freud's discoveries rapidly became frozen into a rigid body of laws not to be transgressed at any cost. Thus, knowingly or not, Freud implicitly allowed those who followed him to reinstate the bliss of ignorance, and a series of "thou shalt not's" grew up around the original insights that should have opened up more pathways into the human psyche than has been the case. The extraordinary persistence to this day of such interdictions can be gauged with respect above all to the "narcissistic neuroses," deemed unamenable to analysis. We are still warned against analyzing schizophrenics, manic depressives and adolescents—despite the fact that these admittedly onerous tasks have been undertaken and a great deal learned in the process. What irony instead resides in the fact that, having given us the tools to understand this awful, forbidding conscience which terrorizes, constrains us to prayer, and virtually addicts us to superstition, Freud should somehow have given consent to successive generations of analysts to maintain this terrible force and keep it from perishing!

Thus enthroned in what has come to be the psychoanalytic Establishment, which has set forth guidelines for a good number of years for all aspirants, the respectability of certain taboos can hardly be accused with impunity. We are indeed reminded here of Cicero's views on the authority of those who teach: often an obstacle, he judged it, to those who want to learn. We must vigilantly guard our intrinsic freedom in this domain and, following Montaigne's example, begin among the liberal arts with that art which liberates us. Such man-made prohibitions on knowledge and exploration as I have been evoking thus far stem, I am convinced, from fear and ignorance. It is in this perspective, too, that the prohibition on the analysis of dying patients must inevitably be viewed. Indeed, the remarkable paucity of analytic literature on the subject cannot seriously be attributed to analytic patients' having a lower mortality rate than the general population.

Similarly, their analysts' failures to regard them as proper subjects for reflection must be discounted as a factor that would explain the absence of pertinent literature. The term "analyst" itself would seem a misnomer in a number of cases described by therapists who have made no attempt to adhere to the analytic model but have ignored it entirely or abandoned it early on in favor of psychotherapy. Those authors who address themselves to the issue of the dying patient frequently make use of the thinking of Kurt Eissler, whose 1955 book, *The Psychiatrist and the Dying Patient*, reflects in its title alone (the psychiatrist, not the analyst), a significant choice of therapeutic models.

In this paper I intend to discuss several aspects of the Eisslerian approach to the dying patient, an approach I find superficial in its failure to comprehend psychoanalytic insights and perhaps unwittingly treacherous to those patients it purports to accompany in their last months and weeks of life. I shall first state my major objections to Eissler's models. An examination of four contributors to the subject will follow, and in conclusion, I shall present a clinical case drawn from my own experience with a dying patient in analysis.

The Eisslerian "credo" has perhaps been nowhere stated more eloquently than by Florence Joseph in her article, "Transference and Counter-Transference in the Case of a Dying Patient," (1962): "I believe that what is essential is that the patient not be left to his loneliness and despair while he awaits death; that in the case especially of the patient who has undergone analysis, he be in close contact with his analyst; that the path they had trodden together in analysis for so many months and years in intimate communication, often on the deep unconscious level, should now enable the analyst to bring comfort to his patient in his final extremity." The notion of the analyst bringing comfort to the dying analytic patient is a noble one, perhaps, but it is unfortunately built on a shaky premise, namely that the unconscious is of little significance in the patient's final days on earth. We are in this way afforded just one of many examples of a certain intellectual confusion, for it is asserted time and time again that *the patient unconsciously knows he is dying*. If this is the case, then it is certain that on the deepest level no one can banish the loneliness and despair the dying patient must confront. The "comfort" it is within the analyst's power to bring to his patient differs, not only in degree, but in kind from the ultimately false reassurances the practitioner of the Eisslerian model hopes to purvey.

The denial of the patient's unconscious implied by this model has been shown to be reinforced by numerous attitudes, gestures and deeds on the part of the therapists who have provided the scant clinical material available to us on the subject. The knowledge the patient possesses of his imminent death is consistently avoided by these therapists who thereby repudiate everything that is courageous in man: the impulse to reveal the unconscious, to know the truth as far as one can know it, and to make as good use of it as one can. To deny the model of psychoanalysis at this particular time in the life of the analysand, the time when one ought to adhere more closely than ever to the analytic process, strikes me as a double betrayal: of the analysand on the one hand, and of intellectual honesty on the other.

Strictly speaking, the rationale implicit in much of the work on this subject is one which lends itself to destroying the analytic process *in general*, for we can *always* say (since we never know whether we shall be alive one hour from now): why not spare the patient loneliness and despair and make him more comfortable? What is left unspoken is that we wish to make *ourselves* more comfortable as well. In other words, where do we draw the line? Is a patient to be considered "dying" only when all clinical evidence available indicates that this death is imminent? If we do not know—and we do not—I think it is essential in the interests of exploration of our being to garner what knowledge we can about the extreme regions of human life, about dying, insofar as our store of knowledge of human affairs is still rather meagre.

While it is not my intent to belittle the contributions of Eissler and the other courageous men and women who have dared to look at what remains, after all, a forbidden aspect of existence, I must strenuously refute their general stance. The taboo against shedding light on the subject of dying, summed up in the dictum so often heard, "Do not interfere with the dying, let them die in peace," is tantamount, of course, to that original interdiction on eating of the fruit of the Tree of Knowledge. Curiosity is condemned, for we are to know neither of the beginning nor of the end of life. As to the former, we have gradually succeeded in pushing back the frontiers of our knowledge but the cloak and aroma of religion continue to mask primitive anxieties linked up with the obsidian fingers of the death instinct, taken seriously only by Melanie Klein and her followers.

Society has in the past assigned to the priest a role similar to that Eissler would appear to be recommending for the therapist of the dying patient, i.e., that of pipeline to the deity. We must reject this sort of pretense and be saddened at the loss of opportunity for exploration that it represents. Clinical experience has shown, moreover, that patients who are treated forthrightly do not wish rather to be fooled, but are genuinely grateful that an ordinary man, a psychoanalyst, is willing to go as far as man can, fearing neither the positive nor the negative transference. There is in such an experience the sense of adventuring to the very edges of our inner universe: those who do so should be respected as the astronauts of inner space in the same way as we respect those men we have propelled through the far reaches of outer space.

"The libido [of the dying patient]," Eissler (1955, p. 141) writes, "is then totally drawn into the process of binding the death instinct activated in the pathological process, leaving no surplus to maintain those functions which, under ordinary circumstances, are fed by libido . . . but the accretion of sublimated libido from without apparently eases the patient's struggle." With this citation I should like to present my second major objection to the Eisslerian model. To begin with, the confusion in the use of basic psychoanalytic concepts is striking: what can it possibly mean to suggest that sublimated libido may be provided "*from without*?" I would maintain, rather, that it is the interpretation of the conflicts of the patient (dying or not) as they relate to internal or external objects that results in a releasing of some libidinal forces with which to control the various manifestations of the death instinct. If this is what we believe is best for the living patient who we feel will continue to live till tomorrow and no longer—an act we make on faith—I cannot see how it is less true for the dying patient. Indeed anything short of this, such as avoidance of the truth as the analyst sees it, constitutes collusion on the analyst's part with the patient's destructiveness and can only hasten death.

It is my conviction that, contrary to an "accretion of sublimated libido from without," the patient's struggle is eased by truth. Truth through interpretation is love, is comfort for despair, is security against terror, is growth in the face of death, is friendliness in the face of loneliness; it is, in short, the summoning up of the most virtuous qualities developed by humanity in the course of its history.

With these general remarks in mind, let us now turn to several concrete examples of the avoidance of truth, the collusion between therapist and dying patient, which, it would seem, the Eisslerian model encourages at every point. In her article, Florence Joseph (1962) relies heavily on *The Psychiatrist and the Dying Patient* for confirmation of the approach she used with a young dying woman, Alice. Though her article affords us numerous instances of the type of collusion I decry, my point will be perhaps better taken if I restrict my discussion to four interrelated aspects of it.

The first aspect of collusion concerns the giving of gifts to the analysand. Joseph regards such comportment as not only justified, under the circumstances, but as desirable. She remarks that "spontaneous love without thought of obligation or return on the patient's part is a kind of antidote against death," (p. 27). Similarly, she notes that Eissler has written: "Then the gift will be experienced by the patient as a physician's giving him part of his own life, and the dreadful stigma of being selected for death will be converted into a dying together" (Eissler, 1955, p. 139). The beauty of such a sentiment is, I am convinced, entirely illusory. The notion of "a dying together" must be seen for what it really is: a well-intended device which unfortunately adheres to neither internal nor external reality but ends by duping the patient—and reassuring the therapist. But the patient is not really deceived: he knows at some level that the physician is not giving over part of his own life, nor would he, and that "dying together" is, of course, a phantasy which, like all such phantasies, is one of omnipotence, a denial of the helplessness he is subjected to in his moribund state.

Again, it must be stressed that the "antidote against death" which Joseph misguidedly seeks in proferring gifts to her patient can be found only in the replication of reality. For, as Freud's genius discovered, the death instinct we are to combat, even in its physical manifestations, may be neutralized by such infusions of truth (and thereby of libido into the mental economy) as interpretations can accomplish. Our task, in other words, is no different for the rapidly ebbing than for the slowly, imperceptibly dying patients that are the work of our everyday analytic practice.

Joseph's account of her treatment of Alice itself contains the very evidence one could make use of to support the contention that the patient knows very well he or she must die alone, that the therapist's "generosity" is ultimately of a rhetorical sort. Joseph ceased taking payment from Alice and brought her flowers on her weekly visit to her bedside. Her patient "laughingly scolded" her one day: "Freud would not approve of you at all." Indeed it may be asked: had the therapist the right to deny her patient her reparative gestures which went so far in recognizing what it cost the analyst to come and work with her and which, perhaps more importantly, represented a grand acknowledgement to her internal objects, those objects which, if not reinforced can only keep the patient depressed, quiet, anxious—even if possibly covered by manic denial? What then will be the toll upon the patient's state of mind—and upon her body? By refusing Alice's check, Joseph unwittingly deprives her of her feeling of potency, or richness, of capability, and tosses her into a state of weakness. She aids in this way the processes of deterioration, hastening death in her patient. The Eisslerian model, which effectively leaves little or no room for such reparative gestures, must subtly but surely speed up the dying process. While it might be argued that my position is cruel, it cannot seriously be denied that our existential situation is cruel and that there is nothing to be done about this state of affairs except to face up to it, and deal with it as best we can. The analytical model is *realistic*, whereas the Eisslerian one would appear to hinge on the religious, seeking, to bring comfort *in extremis*, ignoring the analytic tools that Freud passed on to us.

Nothing, moreover, is gained, in terms of expanding our knowledge about dying, by such collusion. No significant information comes out of Joseph's experience at least, although she appears to believe differently when she tells us that Alice's behavior could be interpreted as a regression to a pre-oedipal infant-mother relationship. That a state of regression might exist in a dying patient does not strike me as out-of-the ordinary. Have we really been enlightened as to the process of dying by this information? I hardly think so. What analytic patients are not in some state of regression? And isn't the same true of many post-analytic ones as well? Indeed it might be plausibly argued that in *all* of us such states exist. Any threatening situation that renders us helpless immediately lands us in states of phantasized omnipotence, which are pre-oedipal states most often arising in relation to the mother, vis-a-vis whom we suffer our helplessness most intensely, when we are ill-equipped to cope with it. Thus Joseph's description of this sort of regression in Alice scarcely adds to our knowledge of dying.* It is my conviction that the avoidance of truth with respect to the patient's unconscious has an inevitable repercussion upon the acquisition of truth in the domain of dying in general: to deny the unconscious results in intellectual stasis and prohibits accession to the truth. Indeed the question of the regression of the dying patient has not been adequately treated by Joseph or even Eissler, who perceives in it a possible longing for a past pleasure, the mother-child relationship. Merely to state that this is the last, the most intense, the grieved-for hope is insufficient. Perhaps we must look beyond the oedipal situation,

*It will be noted that throughout this article my preoccupation is not with death but dying. The distinction bears explaining: it is not the event—anatomical, after all—of death, about which we can say nothing, that is of interest to the analyst, but the process of dying which is, simply stated, the last period of living.

beyond the maternal-infant duo to glimpse a process of a completely different order: a *maturation process* which might be entirely desirable. Our minds must be open to this possibility and not be saturated with clichés so debased as to be meaningless to any reader or listener. I shall say more about this maturation process at length.

A third aspect of collusion in this area is related to the patient's dreams and the therapist's interpretation, or, as in Joseph's case, lack thereof. While admitting that Alice unconsciously knows she is dying, Joseph abstains from interpreting her patient's dreams of being the only passenger escaping from a sinking ship and from a burning, doomed airplane. Joseph explains her silence this way: "But never did she ask me to interpret her dreams, nor did she attempt to do so herself, although she was well-versed in dream interpretation and must have understood the symbolism." (p. 29.) Instead, the therapist's comment: "Oh, Alice, people do dream such horrible dreams under sedation" illustrates her attempt to deny the patient's unconscious knowledge, a denial with which Alice does not hesitate to collude. As we often see when a young analyst makes a wrong interpretation, the patient is quite ready to please himself or herself and the analyst by agreeing.

Finally, what is the outcome, *for the therapist*, of the Eisslerian approach to the dying patient? In Florence Joseph's case, it was, paradoxically, an enormous sense of *relief* after the patient's death. "It was scarcely a week after Alice died," she writes, "that I began to feel as if a burden had been lifted from my shoulders and shortly thereafter began to feel happy as I had not felt for months." (p. 33.) From this she infers that she might have resented the drain on her emotions and on her time and energy that dealing with Alice represented. I would suggest that such a drain *must* be the consequence of not hewing to an analytic model in the treatment of the dying patient. Briefly stated, the analytic model, by its refusal to encourage corollary demand on the analyst's energy, is as healthy for us as it is for the patient—which, if anything, again attests to Freud's genius.

What, then, is the temptation of the Eisslerian model? Might it not be the inability, on the part of many therapists, to recognize in themselves those very same primeval anxieties with respect to death that haunt their patients? The Eisslerian model alleviates such anxieties by joining therapist and patient alike in an alliance of omnipotence. Comforting the despairing, lonely patient, giving him gifts, refusing to give credence to his dreams, "dying together": these and similar notions reflect the extent to which primitive anxieties retain their hold over us. It cannot be recommended strongly enough that these anxieties be recognized at least intellectually by the therapist if he has not had an analysis of them.

Society, too, encourages adoption of attitudes favored by an Eisslerian-type model: it is impressed upon us, early on, that solitude is dangerous. Everyone ultimately lives alone just as everyone dies alone, yet the attractive though meretricious clamor of modern-day life serves constantly as a barrier to solitude. To be alone is to be lonely, or so we are led to believe. Groups, of which we seem never to be free from birth on, the family, school, profession; the propaganda of "sociability"; the cry of "learn to get along"–in all of this we can perceive the difficulty confronting the individual, the quasi-impossibility of attaining not the solitude of the hermit, but those stretches of aloneness that must be endured if one is to have any idea of his own world. So it is with dying: even in the extreme regions of life the individual is to be "spared" the confrontation with his lone self; a "dying together," in this perverse logic, must follow what amounts in most existences to a "living together" that has too often masked the truth.

It is unfortunate that the author of the communication under discussion chose not to give us a more complete description of the therapeutic services themselves. This is, regrettably, too often the case in the analytic literature available to us: an absence of precisely that clinical material without which our knowledge of this area must remain inadequate. Illuminating this last part of living might shed similar light on the first part, though this latter area is increasingly open to our scrutiny no doubt because of the optimism associated with the study of an organism that has exhausted its potentialities or has not fulfilled its promise, stirring up uncomfortable feelings in most people, analysts being apparently no exception to the rule.

To what extent these unacknowledged anxieties may be responsible for the lack of clarity one senses in an article such as "The Dying Patient," by Lawrence J. Roose (1969) is open to conjecture. The aetiology of the author's confusion apart, it behooves us to expose his mistaken ideas at once. Roose states his premise thus: "Assuming a minimal interference from counter-transference factors, the manipulation of the transference offered the patient a more promising way out of his dilemma through the facilitation of more primitive defense mechanisms in pursuit of the quest for the good mother through regression to the fantasy of reunion." The success of his approach to a dying patient he proclaims in these quasi-religious terms: "Death was miraculously transformed into ever-lasting life." The latter statement, it will readily be seen, closely parallels the earlier mentioned "dying together" phantasy in its evident emphasis on omnipotence. But it is chiefly with Roose's former statement that I must now take issue.

It seems to me that a certain ambiguity is apparent in Roose's text, for at the outset of his article, the author claims that "the psychoanalyst, with his special training and skill, is in a unique position to demonstrate that the use of psychoanalytic theory may extend beyond its strict application to those in psychoanalytic treatment." (p. 385) Does he really mean this? Apparently not, for Roose immediately qualifies his remark by adding that it is not "classical psychoanalytic procedures" which he has in mind. Rather he feels no psychoanalyst today can "rigidly restrict himself" to the latter. Roose concludes that he has envisaged such a liberty as "manipulation of the transference." It may be wondered what is meant by use of the term "psychoanalysis" in this article if the "manipulation of the transference" in which Roose indulges is to be taken seriously. How does such a manipulation manifest itself? Chiefly through the therapist's failure to respect the patient's unconscious–and indeed, at times conscious–knowledge of his imminent death. The patient, a doctor wavering consistently between acceptance of the truth and denial of it, was virtually begging Roose to help him come in contact with what was essential to him when he asked him, for example, whether to give up his professional phone. To have encouraged him to do so, to have in this way confirmed what he unconsciously knew, namely that he was no longer the doctor but the patient, the dependent one having to confront his essential reality rather than flee it as he had done with partial success for so long, would have constituted, in my view, the analyst's imperative task. Instead, by helping his patient to decide the issue in the negative, Roose further abetted his denial of the truth. The patient died as he lived, in a state of falsity.

The question of denial as raised in the article under consideration merits some clarification. It is not accurate that denial and consequent repression ultimately lead, as Roose appears to believe, to a phantasy of bliss, of reunion with the good mother. Why should the very real possibility of reunion with the Bad Breast—obviously represented in Roose's patient's case by the sister, the many unsatisfactory housemaids, and, before them, the mother herself—be so imprudently excluded? Indeed the good breast to this patient must remain, for the reader of Roose's article, a mystery, unless one conjectures that it was he himself he phantasied as the good breast, who needed no other person (internal object) and who later, by becoming a physician, could feel that many other people needed him. In any case, nothing assures us that a phantasy of a nature diametrically opposed to that Roose has suggested as the outcome of "successful" denial could not have resulted from such manipulation of the transference.

Finally, it is at best misleading to shore up one's arguments in favor of such departures from the analytic model by citing other authors with respect to reunion phantasies. They tell us nothing if more extensive clinical material has not been made available to us, as it has not in Roose's article. Freud's remarks on death, moreover, serve no purpose here: the issue is not death, but dying.

It is perhaps only in Janice Norton's account (1963) of her treatment of a dying patient that we may discern the *ideal* lineaments of the Eisslerian approach. Norton's is a story that combines the insight of the analyst with the care of a nurse, the practicality of an internist, the concern of a friend and the love of a mother. We could, without doing an injustice to her text, subsume it under the heading: "Analyst counter-transference reactions to a baby *in extremis*."

Norton's article raises once again the question of the extent to which strict adherence to the analytic method should be observed. The description afforded us of the dying patient she was working with must, however, give us pause: so much unfolds, in the treatment of this particular patient, that one would expect and hope for in the development of *any* analytic therapy, that the analytic model as such may indeed have been unnecessary. Mrs. B., Norton's patient, appears to be so open, so capable of verbalizing her mental states that we wonder whether such terminal conditions as hers lessened the resistances ordinarily met and struggled with or whether there exists an —as imperious as that existing in salmon homing up rivers whatever the perils or price—an urge in a human being when dying to fulfill his potential, to complete something (his life? his personality?) in a manner esthetically satisfying. As we experience with music, literature, painting, so do we perhaps seek to feel with respect to our lives: "that's the only way it could have ended," a feeling of esthetic rightness. Or does the need for such a maturation process waken in relatively few dying patients, much like the very few who come to us for psychoanalysis when all other ministrations have failed? They approach us still hungry, still searching, driven by elusive truth.

The wisest of men, Socrates, condemned to death by the cancerous hatred of truth in his society, was occupied with adapting Aesop's fables and the Prelude to "Apollo." Let him speak in his own words: "I did it in the attempt to discover the meaning of certain dreams, and to clear my conscience, in case this was the art I had been told to practice. It is like this, you see. In the course of my life I have often had the same dream, appearing in different forms at different times, but always saying the same thing: 'Socrates, practice and cultivate the arts.' "

A sentence of death failed to change Socrates' dream. The fundament of his personality remained secure, and he was at work in his last days interpreting his dream and, what is more, putting it into action in the present, where he seemed so capable of being, though not without a capacity for speculative thrusts into the future. We, on the other hand, cannot interpret the dream except to note the obtrusiveness of the day residue and the exquisite alliance of his dream life and his waking life. Indeed, it would appear to us that Socrates always practiced and cultivated his art. Would we, moreover, be guilty of too freely practicing our own art if we stated that the entire *Phaedo* could be taken as the free association to this dream? We would all be at liberty to select from the discourse whichever theme strikes us as being the iron core around which all the filings arrange themselves. For my part the following paragraph would best illustrate the latter:

> "Ordinary people do not seem to realize that those who really apply themselves in the right way to philosophy are directly and of their own accord preparing themselves for dying and death. If this is true, and they have actually been looking forward to death all their lives, it would be absurd to be troubled when the thing comes for which they have so long been preparing and looking forward to."

I quote from the *Phaedo* because it is here that Socrates confronts us with both the idea and the illustration of doing what he has always done, namely, be a philosopher. In his bones, in his soul, waking or sleeping, married, the father of children, questioner of men, expositor of truth, betrayer of deceit, citizen of the republic, soldier, victim, he was not like a philosopher but a philosopher.

Norton's patient was an exceptional woman whose courage in the face of death Norton describes as "extremely impressive." Little did it matter, then, that the analytic model was passed over. Mrs. B. functioned on a very high plane and would no doubt have succeeded in being analyzed regardless of the therapeutic model applied. Typical of this patient's basic personality structure was her liking for two psalms, both of which would appear to indicate a person with confidence in a kindly internal object called "the Lord." Norton's work may thereby have been greatly facilitated. So many of our patients unfortunately operate at lower levels of mental functioning, impelled by early infantile anxieties, bizarre part of objects, "beta elements," unlike this woman who appeared to have reached the calm waters of concern, care and trust, as expressed by Psalms 23 and 121.

It is clearly to patients such as Mrs. B., to relatively well-constituted human beings, that Eissler's comment, duly cited by Norton, may pertain: "It is conceivable that through the establishment of transference, through an approach which mobilizes the archaic trust in the world and reawakens the primordial feelings of being protected by a mother, the suffering of the dying can be reduced to a minimum even in the case of extreme physical pain." (Eissler, 1955, p. 119.)

In these specific instances only can some measure of success then be expected from the Eisslerian model. Far more frequently, it seems to me, the success, if such there is, of this model would have to be of an entirely illusory nature. For Eissler himself admits that his approach ideally requires of the therapist an impossible degree of psychological agility. "One of the greatest difficulties," he states, "seems to lie in the necessity for the psychiatrist to activate attitudes which seem contradictory." (p. 151) These attitudes are the following: (1) The therapist must give to the patient sublimated love in the form of affection, but "this affection must not be 'realistic,' as it would be when the physician loses a loved person of his own private orbit"; and, (2) the physician must be fully aware of the "dread involved in the certitude of death for this particular individual," yet he must not forget that such a death is an "organic event per se, deserving no other response but the one with which we bow to all other necessities of life." The therapist's failure to "balance" these contradictions can spell danger to the patient who will feel unloved, rejected or be drawn toward extreme acting out, says Eissler.

I could not disagree more. We should ask not only *how* such contradictory attitudes can possibly be maintained, but *why* they should be. It is not the therapist's role to regulate the intensity of an emotion, be it sorrow, pity or affection for the patient, but to put *all* such emotions, along with the patient's associations, to use in the furthering of the patient's self-knowledge. The goal of analytic therapy cannot be other than this. And why should the ego *voluntarily* tolerate such contradictions as Eissler deems necessary? He appropriates Hartmann's view of the ego as "organizing principle" to bolster his shaky arguments in this connection. Indeed, Eissler openly acknowledges the existence of irrationalities behind these contradictions, but fails to come to terms with the logical consequences of this admission by citing Hartmann with respect to the adequately differentiated ego's capacity to tolerate a certain degree of irrationality. What Eissler is in fact recommending for the therapist of the dying patient is none other than the high art of the *actor*. This pose must be unqualifiedly rejected.

The therapist's task is not to delicately balance contradictions, an unhealthy, impossible proposition, but rather to *undo* contradictions and expose behind them the irrationalities which Eissler unfortunately seeks to accommodate. It is finally this evasion of the truth which mars Eissler's book throughout and to which disturbingly little attention has until now been paid. In *The Psychiatirst and the Dying Patient* (1955), the most elaborate rationalizations, parameters, implausibilities are brought forward as their author contradicts himself time and again in the case histories. In addition to having lost valuable opportunities for exploring this little-known segment of life, the esteemed analyst, Kurt Eissler, in this book has set the example for generations of anlaysts to provide the same sterile reasons for *not* furthering our knowledge of dying.

A Dying Patient in Analysis

The patient had come to me recommended for psychoanalysis after several failures in psychotherapy. She was twenty-seven years old, small in stature, and dark hair covered her brow. She had a dirty look to her, and her dark bright eyes darted glances around the room. I was persuaded by the intelligent eyes, despite an obvious massive emotional illness, to undertake the analysis. Soon, as we all discover, sometimes to our chagrin, and sometimes as we expect, other symptoms came to be revealed. One was picking her nose uncontrollably until bleeding. In fact, this occupied a larger part of the analytic work than her phobia with paranoid reactions filling out the interstices of her personality. There were problems with her children, with her husband; terrors of unknown origin which would sweep her away; car accidents in which she narrowly missed death. There is no way to recount ten years of a psychoanalysis in this brief résumé, but one important fact became evident, and that was her tenacious wish for health, her determination to learn about herself no matter what the cost. It was this aspect of her personality that helped see her through the darkest miseries of her life when no relief seemed in sight, and when she would be stunned as other parts of her personality, unknown to her, landed her in predicaments which left her humiliated and hating herself. In time the dirtiness that was obtrusive, and on many occasions the smell of flatulence which soaked the room (for she lived almost exclusively in her bottom) also lessened and disappeared. She had been born and reared in New York of Jewish parents, and, as one so often hears, the father was kindly, reasonable, and loving in contrast to an argumentative, never-satisfied mother. She was the eldest of two children, her brother, Sy, being two years her junior. She did well in school but could not afford college, so her way was that of the business world. The family moved to California where she met and married her husband, who became a very successful businessman. The symptom which brought her to therapy was her fear of everyone, a fear so pervasive that she would spend her days peering through the curtains of her home, never showing herself. By this time she had two children, a girl and a boy, and there were problems with them already. She could be described as a borderline personality, or a severly obsessive-compulsive, with borderline features or a schizoid personality with depressive anxieties, depending on one's viewpoint; any one of these could front for the thing itself.

It was clear, after a piece of psychoanalysis, that Mrs. A. was infantile, was as ignorant about the realities of everyday life as she was about her children or her husband or about marriage, and, the key to it all, was exceedingly ignorant about herself. The task of psychoanalysis was no less than a construction of a personality for which she had substituted a life through omnipotence. By this I mean a life of infantile helplessness when confronted with the tasks which were simply behond her capacity. We negotiated two suicide attempts in the course of a ten-year analysis. Never were any parameters used, nor was there any hospitalization. Psychoanalysis in its usual form was adhered to, that is, interpretation of the material, of whatever nature, even to the very end of her life. It is germane, I think, though it cannot be part of this discussion,* that the patient's daughter committed suicide one year before Mrs. A. returned to me, thinking she was paying for the guilt over her daughter's death by psychosomatic symptoms.

A thorough examination of her physical symptoms revealed a carcinoma of the ovary. Surgery was performed, and chemotherapy as well as X-ray treatments were administered. In the course of events, she wanted to see and resume her analysis with me. I think it to be significant that the carcinoma struck this particular system, that is, the reproductive system, because I have rarely seen a patient with Mrs. A.'s intense hatred of sexual intercourse, by which I mean ultimately that of her parents. It is also noteworthy that so central a theme should have occupied her last days, but with quite a different feeling tone.

If I am correct in believing as I do, and as I suggested to Mrs. A in the second session, that she remembered with a part of herself—a fetal self—the sexual coupling of her parents and was terrified by the muffled noises, it is significant, then, that "sexual nightmares" (see below)—preoccupied her all her life until her death. I do not believe this to be a phantasy, that is, an event merely mental and/or imagined, but *a reminiscence of a real event*.

This complex of feelings was the central fact of her personality, and, though greatly attenuated by the psychoanalysis, so as to enable her to live a more than tolerable life, never was forgotten.

In the closing phase of the analysis, it was apparent to her, and she commented on it, that her marriage had become much happier, and she and

*A minute examination of analytical material might well help the physician in ascertaining those emotional assaults which cannot be contained mentally, thus breaching the mind, attacking the body and destroying it.

her husband were able to take vacations together, away from home for the first time. Her attitude to her mother had changed; by this time her father had died, and she was able to help her mother, in whatever way she could. She had become an outgoing woman, active in many areas, in civic and community affairs, in politics, and participated here at the local level in the party of her choice. She painted, played tennis. She had many friends, both male and female, and we both thought that the analysis had been sufficient and that terminating it was the right thing.

What follows is a transcript, reconstructed out of my notes, of several sessions with Mrs. A. a few years ago, during the last days of her life.

Transcript of Sessions with a Dying Patient in Analysis: First Session:*

MRS. A: Something is strange. I think I am dying. They keep saying I'm courageous, I'm brave, but it's not me. I'm not. I know it's not me. The doctors and nurses at the hospital would say that. But I'm a coward.

ANALYST: It seems to be important to have people confirm what one feels one is.

MRS. A: I sweat. The nurse wraps me in towels. It's awful. I remember what my mother used to say, that if you sweat, you'll catch cold, if your resistance is low, and die. And I seem to sweat a lot now. I get insulin. They test my urine. But I am afraid. I seem to be in a different world from everyone else. It's as if I've let go. There's a feeling of a plate glass between them and me. I'd like to hold on to that picture they have of me, but it's not me.

ANALYST: The fear is, if you let go—who are you and what are you? It is as if you were the infant who didn't know. In addition, what you always feared has come true—that mother was right. You have caught that kind of cold so there seems to be a very punitive mother and a very guilty you.

MRS. A: I used to read, watch TV. But I don't anymore. I lost all interest. I'd see a little boy fall or a man about to get hurt on TV and I'd feel it as if it were happening to me.

ANALYST: You feel as if you put yourself into them and could feel them, be them.

MRS. A: My mother was supposed to come Friday. She hasn't seen me in two months, but I was sweating so I called and told Sy I just couldn't see her. What shall I say—that I've got cancer?

My mother used to have pains. She used to tell me all about her pains. Now it's as though *I've* got them.

ANALYST: You feel as if you've put your pains into your mother, as if you were the infant with all those pains, trying to get rid of them. You felt responsible for your mother's pains and now they've been returned to you.

MRS. A: Jean and Kay [her friends] came over and cooked some soup. But I can't eat anything or drink anything. They also made some rice. It smelled so good that I wanted some, so I took a bit—but it hurt me.

*A paper reporting on this phenomena is in progress.

ANALYST: You felt the food was taken in and caused you pain—like mother's pain caused pain—and any food would be painful to take in. This would make physical pain worse.

MRS. A: Oh, I've forgotten what it was. A couple of months ago—my mind—I tried to hold on to my mind—I felt I couldn't. . . .

ANALYST: It's paradoxical to say, "to hold on to one's mind." What does that really mean: as if the mind were some material, substantial thing one could actually hold?

MRS. A: I mean my sense of reality.

ANALYST: Ah, then the mind—whatever it was—would be important, as important as infancy, and then there would be great difficulty, for you'd not have had much experience with your sense of reality then.

MRS. A: My eyes hurt, maybe it's the light—my left one more than the right. I don't know.

ANALYST: That's a way of saying your "I's" hurt, as if you were the infant just bringing these things into you—the things of external reality and internal—and they were painful.

MRS. A: I'm not brave. Instead I'm a coward—I do what I have to that's all. I've no choice.

ANALYST: Perhaps that's what courage is, after all; being a human being who does what she has to.

MRS. A: I feel I'm being pushed into a corner—with no chance of escape. At least if one's in jail there's always a chance of pardon. But I feel more and more pushed into a corner. Dr. A. came and removed fluid from my chest—1400cc. It felt as if my chest were being crushed.

ANALYST: That's strange, isn't it, when in reality there might be a feeling of more *room* in the chest.

MRS. A: I know, but yet somehow I feel it's the other way around. But today I don't have that feeling, of being crushed.

These last two weeks in hospital have been strange. I keep thinking and dreaming of life, death, babies, and I keep being afraid.

ANALYST: Perhaps that's what babies keep thinking of, in their way: of life or death, of how to survive, and being and feeling afraid, unlike all those stories of how much paradise infancy or childhood is! It fits in with your lack of interest in the things of the world, like playing Scrabble or watching TV or reading. There's all the work of coping with life or death. Others may fool themselves. But you've had enough analysis to feel how difficult it is to do that to yourself now.

MRS. A (nods): No, I don't fool myself. I can bear the pain of fluid drained out of my chest.

ANALYST: That's bearable—it's *finite*. But to bear the chronic mental pain of dying every day—to tolerate it—that too is part of the courage of everyday living for you even though, as you say, you have no choice. And to do it without screaming or yelling—like the nurses say other patients often do.

MRS. A: I used to talk to myself. As if I were the observer in my dream. And when I'd open my eyes the nurse would laugh or Tom [her husband] would laugh. I'd be saying—"Take care of the Baby."

ANALYST: It's as if you were both the adult and the baby at the same time. *Now* you can say it but *then* you might only have been able to cry. As a baby you would have been hoping mother would understand what you meant.

MRS. A: All I thought about or dreamt about was life—death—babies.

ANALYST: In the beginning that must be what one feels about. Perhaps in the end too; what to choose, except there is no choice now. . . .

Would you like to talk again with me?

MRS. A: Yes, I would, *unless something comes up*. [We both knew she meant death.]

Second Session:

MRS. A (in a very low voice): Well, the week hasn't been a bad one physically. I'm pleased with the progress I've made. They removed the subclavian I.V. But I feel like I'm in two worlds. I speak as if I were in a little room and no one hears me and the sounds are muffled and no one can answer me.

ANALYST: I would agree that you're in two worlds. One is the world of reality, that you're in right now as I talk to you; the other is the world of the womb in which you are remembering your parents' intercourse.

MRS. A: And I am full of fears. I had sexual *nightmares* during the week.

ANALYST: What do you recall of them?

MRS. A: They were all along the same line—In this one: Dr. Jones and his wife said I had to urinate before one. I woke up terrified.

ANALYST: Of whom or of what are you afraid?

MRS. A: I'm afraid of nausea. I had several attacks yesterday. They come on suddenly, there's no way to know when or why. They're "dry heaves" and they are so painful. I had several during the week as well.

ANALYST: Who is Dr. Jones?

MRS. A: I have no idea.

ANALYST: It would seem that one point is not so much the command to urinate, but I feel it has to do with a time of your life when you couldn't control your bladder, and you had terrible anxiety about your excretory habits. After all, nausea is or may be a prelude to vomiting—as if to get rid of something . . . obviously food, whatever else food might stand for.

MRS. A: I was able to urinate by myself yesterday. I'm very pleased with my progress—I could drink the tea—(she sips). I have to let it flow down so slowly or else I can pay for it for twenty minutes with pain.

ANALYST: It seems as if the dream contained a punishment. If you did *wet*—then the punishment would be nausea or ultimately—no food—if one follows out the train of thought.

MRS. A: I wish I could remember what you said and think about it.

ANALYST: What need is there of that? Unless you didn't understand what I said at the time. It would be like bringing up old digested food already used up—to redigest when all the food value was gone already.

MRS. A: No, I did understand what you said when you were saying it, but my mind slips. I can't read or concentrate and I can't hold onto things. . . . My mother came—finally. Chris told her on the way about the cancer—so that was a relief. Mom stared at me, then sat and held my hand—kissed it—kept kissing it.

ANALYST: Like a mother would a baby.

MRS. A: She didn't make any fuss, she didn't cry, she just sat there quietly the whole time.

ANALYST: You have just painted for me a picture of your mother we never saw in the whole of your analysis, quietly kissing away your pain. [Patient cried. Analyst waited, then continued.] When were you nauseous?

MRS. A: Well, I couldn't see Mom Friday last. I got too sick and had to cancel.

ANALYST: It was as if there was something you wished to get rid of and couldn't. Something you didn't want mother to know or to burden her with. Of course, I am not denying the tube in your nose or the illness itself, but I do want to call attention to these other reasons which I feel are so important in helping us understand the psychological contribution to your nausea.

MRS. A: And there is always this feeling of no control, of not knowing when I am going to get this way and feeling utterly helpless about that state. When I get up I want to push away the nurse. I want to do it by myself.

ANALYST: Well, we know from the past analysis how you feared helplessness and vulnerability—and yet what would a child do? An infant?

MRS. A: It must be awful . . . I watch Tom eat Chinese food, or I see someone eating on TV. I'm afraid of it and yet I want it so much.

ANALYST: This reminds you of the time you'd watch Sy at mother's breast—and lose control, as you once, more than once, told me, of how you ran up and began to hit Sy at that time. By the time you'd get through hitting Sy, not only would he be feared, but the milk—the first food you ever had—as well as its container would be feared; and yet at the same time wanted.

I think we can link the dream to the loss of control of your bad urine with which you attacked the mother and your feeling that the breast was taken away from you because of it, about which there was so much in the analysis. [She had had to be suddenly weaned at the age of three weeks when her mother developed an abcess.]

MRS. A: You're right. I did feel it like that. These dreams I had were nightmares. . . . I wish I could eat. If I don't make it I'll be sent back to the hospital.

ANALYST: Even this you feel would be a punishment–like the time you and Sy were sent to a home so as to gain weight. You felt it as a punishment even though you felt you went along to help and be with Sy. It's obvious it would be felt again today as a punishment.

MRS. A: If this is like infancy, I can't tell you how horrible it must have been to be perfectly still–full of fear physically, and mentally afraid to make a move for fear something terrible will happen–there is no way for me to be free enough to use anything.

ANALYST: I do feel this is as close as one can actually get to knowing something about these states of mind now forgotten. There are two things we ought to notice about your last remark: (1) it illustrates that mother had become a thing; you said "anything," and (2) she wasn't able to contain your pain, physical or mental. And you had to lie perfectly still because *you* couldn't contain your pain and indeed were terrified by any hint of it.

MRS. A: I look at myself in the mirror and Harry [her son], when he saw my hair fallen out was shocked. I was shocked, too, when I saw myself in the mirror, but I can't deny it–that's *me*–I can't run away from it.

ANALYST: I'm reminded of how you earlier tried to run away from your personality as we discovered before in your analysis. How you tried to run away from what you thought to be monstrous in it, which seems today to be something like a terrible punitive part if you don't do something–physically control yourself. . . . Or aren't you *really* talking about mental control: controlling your feelings which were ones of rage at the situation of helplessness when Sy came along, and at the parental sex that made you both.

But there is no running away from these monstrous feelings–or from your personality–instead, to be aware of it will help you cope not only with it but with your external world as well.

The fact of the matter is that today you *can* contain your personality such as it is and do take responsibility for it.

Third Session:

MRS. A: [she spoke at length of her physical state]: I just woke up at nine to get ready for you. [She was being a bit more sedated.] I'm getting Compazine every three hours so I don't have any nausea but I'm so sleepy. I tried to read but everything is so full of murder and bad things that I'm beginning to read *The Time Machine* which is trashy, but the other books upset me too much. I tried to think of what we talked about last week, but it was hard to recall.

My mother came Tuesday, with Sy. [This was related with a smile.]

ANALYST: Why are you smiling?

MRS. A: I don't know why . . . my mother worries me. She's going to be a problem. She comes and looks at me and says, "You don't look better.

Your throat is sore, why don't you gargle? What's to become of you?" Anyway, I was so bad that even though mother wasn't here for very long I asked Sy to take her home. I feel sorry for Sy because he wanted to stay. Tom's mother stayed and watched TV with him until quite late.

ANALYST: I wonder if you smiled just before in irony, was it a wry smile? Because this is not the kind of mother who helps, the one that was here the other day, but one who hinders. It's like the books, full of murders. But I was thinking: *The Time Machine* was your body, which you're reading, which you now feel is trashy.

MRS. A: I was so worried last week, I was so grateful that you'd talked to me. I felt you saved me. I could hear the nurses talking and I was afraid they'd both leave. I could only hear the murmur of the voices. It was holiday and I thought both would not be available—and it was frightening.

ANALYST: It was comparable to being the infant, feeling the mother would go away. Who then would look after you? Or it is even more primitive: the two breasts (the nurses). According to what we know, you did lose the breasts when you were three weeks old due to mother's infection. The anxiety could be that of dying.

MRS. A: I can understand that. It was terrible-terrible enough to feel these things today. I must make peace with my stomach, but how?

ANALYST: It is as though the stomach were the heart of you and you have to find out how to make peace with it—it's as if it got a bad meal, and were in pain, trying to reject the bad meal. If the meal were good, then there'd be no problem. This is in addition to the physical problem today, which I don't want to deny, the actual chemotherapy and its effect on the body, which is real enough.

MRS. A: I just got another injection on Tuesday—a chemotherapy injection. Tuesday was the day mother came, too; Tuesday, New Year's Eve.

ANALYST: All came together then, Life and Death.

MRS. A: I just got a picture in my mind of my mother: a long needle, standing up—with a huge eye.

ANALYST: You feel your mother comes and needles you instead of being a mother who can take away your hurts and pains, a mother who gives you bad milk, to put it in primitive terms. And I am felt to be a long needle, as well.

MRS. A: My mother has big eyes—you know, seeing everything.

ANALYST: Indeed you are also putting forward that these big eyes (I's) are capable of not only taking in a great deal but also of pushing out a great deal, pushing it into you. And it's very painful. And *my* big eyes, seeing everything, reflecting everything—also pain you greatly.

MRS. A: There's nothing I can do about my mother. She won't change.

ANALYST: I agree. But *you* have changed. There's a great difference between the way you were as an infant—so helpless, and yourself today with all your knowledge. And this may enable you to cope with your condition such as it is today.

Indeed it is as if Sy, your brother, neutralizes your mother. The problem is how to get more of Sy, figuratively speaking, and less of that mother—more good, less pain.

To sum it up, considering the totality of your feeling, I think there is a *positive* aspect as well in this discussion. Not only is this needle and eye a part of mother or myself or yourself—but it should be understood to be able to see everything wrong and to sew up the cares of the body and of the spirit. I want to remind you of the mother who, learning of her daughter's impending death—sat quietly, held and kissed her hand.

MRS. A: Well, I know our time is up now. Do I need to call? Will you come?

ANALYST: I'll come next week. There is no need to call.

Conclusion

Mrs. A died several days after her last session with me. She had been calm in the final days of her life, according to her husband. She had, on the day of her death, expressed interest in his work. As they conversed, her blood pressure suddenly fell, she felt weak, and asked her husband to get the doctor. Then she died.

The following material transcribed here in a somewhat compressed form from my notes, relates to the dream Mrs. A. earlier reported. This dream was highly condensed and offered myriad threads to be sorted out for interpretation. I ultimately came to view the latent content in these ways:

(1) The command to urinate could be taken literally in terms of an *evacuation* which would be essential in ridding her of her dying as well as her destructive parts.

(2) The patient's mother had prided herself on the fact that her daughter was toilet-trained, bowel and bladder, before the age of one. This clearly ties in the peculiar formation: "Dr. Jones and his wife ordered me to urinate *before one*." In reality, the patient had had to *control* her excretory functions before one year of age; in the dream she had to be able to *let go*. The reversal thus operated would create anxiety, for to urinate as commanded would doubtless arouse Mother's anger. The reversal affects, too, the major figures, Dr. Jones and his wife, who no doubt represent the analyst, that very analyst who had "saved" the patient's life precisely by allowing her to rid herself of her destructive parts in the analysis. The relief the patient had felt when she understood that the analyst could contain the bad things she projected into him is transformed in the dream into anxiety. The good analyst has become the persecutor, forcing her to risk angering her mother by urinating.

The peculiar formulation "before one" raises the question: can this "one" also be viewed as the equivalent of "one of us," since the command is given by the couple, Dr. Jones and his wife? Or does the "one" suggest copulating, sexual couple, i.e., "You must urinate before our couple (= one)"? The parental couple's intercourse having aroused such terrible feelings in the patient, her anxieties with respect to urinating in this dream can perhaps be better understood if we follow this train: to urinate is to destroy the parental intercourse; the damaged parental couple become persecuting objects taken into the patient's personality; she must get rid of these objects somehow. The very course of action she undertakes to save her life—getting rid of her destructive parts—is precisely that which threatens the parental intercourse. She must harm her good objects to disembarrass herself of her bad ones, hence the terrible anxiety she associates with this dream, which she refers to as "a sexual nightmare," one of many she claimed to have had around the same time.

(3) The association to the "dry heaves": these must be viewed as her valiant attempts *now* to get rid of her bad urine so as not to harm the parents. Yet the "dry heaves" also indicate her *incapacity to project* the dreaded substances (feelings) and persecutory objects out of herself. On perceiving the parental couple, who are capable of a sexual life, in the dream she responds with urinary soiling, but she also wants to evacuate this bad part of herself and *cannot*, just as the infant cannot stop his own phantasies. She knows she herself will be hurt by it if she can't somehow get rid of this bad urine: she will then have the damaged parents within her. It is not a person she fears but feelings. The "dry heaves" can easily be imagined to have a sexual meaning as well.

(4) A literal interpretation of "before one," taken again to mean "before one year old," might allow us to view the patient's terror in relation to this dream as the terror connected with the task before her: how to be "trained," how to control herself in a given, limited period of time—i.e., the time remaining in her life.

(5) Dying is felt to be a humiliation and a punishment. If the patient identifies with the parents, she fears she must suffer their fate, which is to be subjected to her burning attacks on them.

(6) The exhibitionism contained in this highly condensed manifest content of the dream can be linked specifically to the anxiety experienced by the patient in the early and middle phases of the analysis during which time she lived an extremely private, almost secretive life, including, naturally, its infantile components.

I was privileged, in the treatment of this patient, to reflect on the significance of the material she provided, exclusive of its use in the therapy. Though the content ultimately differed little from what one hears in other analyses, its intensity, to the analyst, is immeasurably greater. With a patient confronting imminent death, it is really only the analyst who must defend himself against that fact. Re-reading these transcripts today I am aware of the insufficiency of my interpretations on some issues, a fact which I attribute at least in part to the impact of the situation upon me. Yet the sessions do, I feel, give us an idea as to what a dying person is occupied with, as novelists and poets have tried to render imaginatively.

The study of dying is an attempt to give meaning to death as it is an attempt to give meaning to life. We are creatures who, consciously or not, insist upon such meaning. If history is, as it has been called, "an illustrious war against death," what more noble undertaking can there be than to investigate a personal history even if that one, under our tremulous glance, is already at an end? If the dying person seeks to know, who then may cavil at such a request by thinking "of what use is it?" As psychoanalysts we do not question what use a person makes of his death. The choice we have with the dying is the same as that we have with the living, prospective patient: we can refuse to participate in the analysis. In this we do not treat a body or a soul alone, but a whole life.

The dying patient gives us anew the gift of solitude. We as analysts can only give back to each analysand his life. His living and his dying must be centered in himself.

Psychoanalysis must be the fusing of two solitudes: the analysand must be able to be centered into himself so that he can be fused into the solitude and authenticity of the analyst, but only for the duration of the analysis. Afterwards, the solitudes must again be separate. Man in a group, paying heed to the group alone, is no better than an animal ceaselessly surveying its environment, unable to withdraw to contemplate his life.

As analysts we are privileged to come constantly into intimate contact with a segment, however short, of human life. We can reconstruct the beginning and childhood, and with luck we may be there at the very end of a patient's life. How, it may be asked, can we truly understand a life unless we can see it and be in it at the very end? Just as one age cannot be adequately understood unless we know and understand the previous one, a life cannot be understood unless we know it in its entirety. And here we are just beginning.

Submitted August 1977

References

Eissler, K. (1955). *The Psychiatrist and the Dying Patient*, New York: Int. Univ. Press.
Joseph, F. (1962). Transference and counter-transference in the case of a dying patient, *Psychoanalysis and the Psychoanalytic Review*, 49, 21-34.
Norton, J. (1963), Treatment of a dying patient, *Psychoanal. Study Child 18*, 541-560.
Roose, L.G. (1969), The dying patient, *Int. J. Psycho-Anal.*, 50-385-395.
Young, W.H. (1960), Death of a patient during psychotherapy, *Psychiatry*, 23, 103-108.

EDITOR'S NOTE: *Doctor Isaacs' contribution addresses itself to a fundamental contribution Bion made to Kleinian metapsychology which obviates the criticism which Winnicott and so many after him have made about Klein's ignoring of reality. The baby cannot "process" his experiences, as Doctor Isaacs reminds us that Bion has stated, unless (s)he identifies with a thinking mother-that is a mother who can think about him/her and his/her needs in a differentiating way so that corrective action ensues.*

Bion and Babies *

Susanna Isaacs Elmhirst

Bion has meant, and will mean, a lot to babies. This may come as a surprise, especially to those many, perhaps most, people working in the field of human psychology who believe that the activities of Bion's complex mind are so abstruse as to be incomprehensible and are thus irrelevant to the day-to-day reality of life, even to that of a working psycho-analyst, let alone to babies.

In these musings, offered in this *Memorial* to Bion, I want to consider the rôle of his work in furthering our understanding of the interaction between an infant and its environment in mental development. In that sense the title of this short essay may be misleading, for it does scant justice to the importance of those on whom babies depend. However, I hope to be able to demonstrate Bion's contribution to the solution of the nature versus nurture controversy as it applies to the growth of the mind from birth onwards.

My own first close contact with the man whose mental growth and productivity we are celebrating was as a candidate of the British Psycho-Analytic Society:

"Yes,
Dr. Bion can take you
in supervision for your second training case."

These longed-for words were momentarily a source of delighted relief and hope before I was struck with terror at the prospect of discussing my attempts at psycho-analysis with WRB himself. Bion, of the giant frame and master mind. How could I, a practical paediatrician turned child psychiatrist and psycho-analytic trainee, expect to apprehend and comprehend the mental manoeuvres of such a man. Should I waste his time with my bumbling efforts? Would I die of fright or be paralysed with nervousness so that I appeared stupid as well as ignorant? This was in England, in the mid-1950s, before Bion's sequence of books about the growth and functioning of the mind had been initiated with the publication of *Learning from Experience* in 1962. But he was already an impressive figure on the London, and world, psycho-analytic scene. He had also made a lasting impression on psychiatry with *Experience in Groups*, which had not then penetrated to paediatricians nor to me personally. However, Bion's serious but not censorious demeanour, his capacity to find something benign but perspicasious to say at scientific meetings and the way in which he drew respect and cooperation from all factions within the British Psycho-Analytical Society did not in any way justify my fears. But frightened I was. Luckily for me I was not too frightened to go to supervision with him and so began one of the great learning experiences of my life.

Isaacs-Elmhirst, S. ["Bion and Babies"]. This article was published in *The Annual of Psycho-analysis*, VIII (1980) 155-167. New York International Universities Press.

All that had ever come my way, personally and professionaly, had increased my conviction that how babies and children are cared for is of fundamental importance for their psychological, as well as their physical, growth throughout their lives. However, what drove, and drew, me into psychoanalysis was a search for answers to the problem of why could parents *not* provide the care they knew was needed and wanted to give. How could one four-month old baby literally die of pining when separated from its Mother in circumstances where others might merely mope, or even show no signs of perceiving the Mother's absence? How could one 10-month old baby develop an intractable autistic illness when the Father was ill for ten days and Mother agitatedly abstracted, though both were physically present? How could some parents force food into their babies despite their evident, conscious efforts to accept advice to the contrary? How could one understand or help a parent whose conscious plea for dry beds from a 7-year old was accompanied by a description of a better week, with 5 continent nights, as "he only did it for me twice last week"? What to make of a child, or her paediatrician's unconscious, when she stoutly maintained that "*My* doctor wants me to put a star on the chart when I *wet* the bed"?

In my first tentative efforts to explain to Bion what I observed and felt had been taking place in the psycho-analytic sessions I often fell back (in my view of it) on to memories stirred in me from my work with babies. To my surprise these notions were often enthusiastically greeted by WRB as "models," to be taken very seriously and the patients' responses studied for confirmation of their relevance and validity.

The effect could not have been more encouraging, then and in my continuing efforts to study feeling and imagination and give them due weight in each individual personality and its world. Bion was able to show how psychoanalysis was not separate from life, nor a substitute for it, but a method of microscopic distillation, making study possible if one could stand it. "Dr. Isaacs, if you were anywhere else but in a psycho-analytic session you would know what this patient is doing to you" is a characteristically compact communication, with its clear cut appreciation of one's perception and equally clear warnings against paralysing fear of, or exaggeration of the importance of, one's role as a psycho-analyst. It must have been during those years that Bion was working with, and thinking about, patients with thought disorders. So he was also involved with thinking about the development of a capacity to think.

It is evident to all those working in child psychiatry that a child's environment is of extreme importance in affecting its emotional development. Before this specialty came into being, family common knowledge and that of educationalists were in no doubt of the importance of nurture for the growth of personality. Since people's knowledge has been recorded in writing poets have spoken for the work of parents and babies in their descriptions of how adults are forever influenced by their childhood experiences. However, what has not been so apparent, except to those involved with the continuous care of babies from birth, is that what the child brings to the environment is variable and also vastly important in determining its personality growth. Indeed it seems to me that those who, like the Jesuits, claim to be able permanently to mould a person's development and ideology if given their care when young are making the assumption that they will be presented with a child in whom the fundamental steps toward human thought and concern have been taken in an earlier relationship, between the baby and its Mother.

To some extent, I think the stance of assuming the inevitability of satisfactory Mother-infant relations outside the uterus, as well as during pregnancy, was also taken by Freud. However Freud took the first essential, fundamental step in the scientific investigation of the child in us all, when he devised the technique of psycho-analysis. Abraham's application of this method to patients with manic-depressive illness opened the way to the study in adults of problems arising in the oral phase of babyhood. Melanie Klein, carrying on from Abraham, took the investigation to the very roots of character, and its disorders, in earliest infancy.

In choosing the names paranoid-schizoid and depressive position for two essential early infantile developmental states Melanie Klein had consciously in mind the relationship between infant experience and psychotic illness in adults. Winnicott perceptively accumulated and documented convincing evidence of how the basic healthy patterns of childhood personality growth can be distorted by family failure, and fostered by family achievement. But he called adult psychosis "a deficiency disease of infancy," deliberately implying that the environment was failing to provide necessary care as with the vitamin deficiencies. Winnicott misunderstood Melanie Klein's intense pre-occupation with her fascinating, but painful, discoveries about the fierceness of a baby's hatreds and the anguish of its struggle to resolve its conflict between the life and death instincts. He thought her constitutionally incapable of understanding the importance to an infant of the successes and faults of its environment. This misunderstanding reinforced a defensive stance, in himself and others, against awareness of the infants' contribution to the impact of the care being offered to them. In my view Bion's development of Melanie Klein's discovery of projective identification offers a resolution of the Klein-Winnicott misunderstanding. I think it also makes possible a reconciliation of the more rigid and vehement nature versus nurture protagonists.

Bion deduced and described how early infantile emotional states, pleasurable as well as painful, are experienced concretely and as such are not available for mental growth. These states cannot be thought about, imagined, dreamt of, remembered (as opposed to being repeated), until they have been transformed into abstract experiences. An infant cannot acquire this capacity for transforming its primitive experiences from beta to alpha elements, as Bion has called them, except by identification with an object capable of performing this fundamental function.

Such identification is achieved in healthy development via the use of projective identification as a normal mechanism. In this situation an infant evacuates it unmanageable, indigestible, conglomeration of good and bad experiences into the care-taking part object. This receptive part-object offers a realisation of the infant's inborn expectation, its preconception, that there is a somewhere in which the unmanageable can be made manageable, the unbearable bearable, the unthinkable thinkable. For the primary part-object, the breast in Kleinian terminology, does act, by a process which Bion calls alpha-function, upon the projected beta elements and render them into thinkable, storable, dreamable alpha-elements. These are projected into the baby and introjected by it. The result is an identification with a part-object capable of performing alpha function. Perhaps one should speak of a trace identitication, for the word identification can seem to describe so formal and final an activity. It can seem to imply that one contact with one manifestation of alpha function in an object and all is well. Certainly one sees such a misapprehension in young analysts who say "But I've made that interpretation," to which one can only reply that it is likely to need making and re-making on a million or more occasions, so it is with Mothers and babies. In my view the nature of a baby's need for repetitive experience, as though of a theme and variations, is worryingly and increasingly misunderstood by an influential section of paediatricians and child care personnel.

The receptive, part-object, alpha-function is usually provided for the baby by the Mother. It may be that this function *can* only be adequately performed for very young infants by the natural Mother, with 9 months experience of ante-natal involvement with her baby as a background. This is a view Meltzer has expressed at times. It may be that only women can tolerate and respond creatively to the impact of a healthy infant's normal projective identifications over a long period of time. It certainly appears to me that even if it should be a man who successfully performs for a baby the onerous task of receiving and responding to its projected experiences, at any time of the day or night that the need arises, the internal representation will nevertheless be of a good breast.

Be that as it may, Bion has given the name "reverie" to the capacity of the object to receive and respond creatively to the baby's projected, concretely experienced chaos and confusion. The word is lovely, with its thoughtful and gentle associations. But I sometimes wonder whether in choosing the word reverie Bion did justice to his own understanding of the emotional intensity of the relationship between Mother and baby, or analyst and analysand. For I do not think amongst the penumbra of ideas commonly associated with reverie is what Winnicott once called "the white heat" of a session. To me, and I think many others, reverie implies the availability of more time than is the lot of Mother and baby when a need for satisfaction arises.

A normal baby's capacity to tolerate frustration is very small. When a normal neonate experiences frustration it is in a terrible state of suffering, which feels endless to the infant. This sense of urgency that an infinite agony must be stopped right away is projected into the Mother. She must often, and normally can, react both appropriately and speedily. Reverie, or alpha-function, can occur almost instantaneously. But such responses, meeting the baby's pre-conceptions with appropriate realisations, must be repeated on innumerable occasions, and over a long period of time, if normal mental growth is to be built on a firm foundation. Yet if reverie means prolonged concentration with patches of musing, and of intense attention then it is indeed a very suitable word to describe the patient pre-occupation of a Mother with her infant or an analyst with his patient. For appropriate growth in sensitivity and depth in any relationship depends on the object learning from experience as well as the subject.

One thing that can go wrong in an infant's early life is that its Mother has not herself been able to develop an identification with a breast which can tolerate, and transform, the intolerable. Therefore, she cannot respond creatively, with reverie, to the baby's projections but has to rid herself, back into the baby, of un-nameable dread. Such a response interferes with growth of the infant's capacity to assess action and reaction, cause and effect, to put one and one together to make two, in other words it hinders the growth of a capacity to think.

A common way of attempting to conceal such a failure in herself is for the Mother to take a purely physical approach to an infant's distress. Young babies do need feeding so often that it is easy to see how such a view can be developed and clung to. Yet such an attitude can seriously jeopardize an infant's emotional and mental nutrition, especially when it extends to the material provision being seen as adequate from just any caretaker, baby-sitters, or house-keepers.

Bion's view is that if reverie is not associated in a Mother with love for the child and its Father that fact, like an incapacity for reverie, will be communicated to the infant, albeit in an unmanageable, indigestible way. He is speaking of the Mother's unconscious, as well as of her conscious mind. The implications are legion but this idea certainly throws some light on the reasons for the difficulties children have in one parent families, or those reared by adults with psychoses or perversions. In this short essay there is no room to explore such situations further. I want to move the focus of our attention to the variability of an infant's capacity to extract, and use for growth, what good the environment offers. But before doing so it seems relevant to mention that in a psycho-analyst counter-transference problems can be the equivalent of a Mother who cannot perform her function of reverie because she cannot love her baby or its Father. An analyst in such a plight may not be able to love his patient, or his patient's parents or former therapists.

I have been trying to show that Bion's idea of the breast as the prototype of the container, the recipient of the projected contents known by him as the contained, is not as static as the words sound or the symbol looks. I have been trying to indicate that throughout life people use each other, their environment, in this active way. They are in search of an active response. In infancy this interaction, with the breast as the container returning the altered contained projections to a baby who then becomes identified with the container, is utterly vital to mental growth and can only be achieved if the infant's containing objects are adequately capable of alpha-function.

Equally vital are the infant's reactions to the container's responses. Melanie Klein drew attention to the importance of envy as an innate characteristic which renders good experience bad. This, like other innate traits, is of variable intensity. Envy can be a crippling disability which, in both projective and introjective identifications, distorts good objects and potentially beneficial experiences.

No infant can survive at all without some identifications with good part-objects, so envious assaults result in a desperate sense of deprivation and frustration which increases the need for gratification and the difficulty of achieving any. Clearly any external deprivations compound the problem. Babies who have a serious innate problem with envy are in need of the most responsive and stable environment. We cannot yet identify these babies at birth or very early in life nor, if and when we do, is their environment easily enabled to provide the required sensitivity and continuity of care. Excessively envious projective identifications are even harder to tolerate, let alone respond to creatively, than are normal neo-natal communications. Even when such high standards of reverie are available introjective identification, as well as projective, are interfered with by envious assault in the infant.

Oliver Wendell Holmes, when asked to what he attributed his success in life, put it down to having discovered at an early age that he was not God. To some extent all infants and young children, healthy or not, are strongly influenced by the belief that their mental processes are magical and control the environment. Therefore any real, external, damage to hated objects is held by the infant to be its responsibility. Or it would be so held if the baby were not driven to desperate defenses against such an awful state of affairs, with the punishment and depression both threatening to overwhelm him or her. Among situations perceived by all infants as damaging to the object, and to the baby, is its disappearance externally. For babies "gone, not there" equals "bad, broken" and "broken" to some extent always equals "will break me." The absent object gives no evidence to the contrary and such evidence is essential. Furthermore the absence, the unavailability, of an essential object and the anxiety resulting from its disappearance both result in angry, greedy and envious responses and so leads to further attacks on whatever good internal representation of the object may have been achieved. I think the belief in personal omnipotence varies innately in individuals and is an important factor in determining an infant's response to the care it is offered. The relationship between omnipotence, narcissism, envy and the death instinct is the subject of a great deal of psycho-analytic study and discussion. Perhaps they are all names for the same inborn quality of disliking, or hating, what is, what exists, because it is not under the infant's, or adult's, control.

Whether or not this is so there does seem also to be an innate variation in the ego's capacity to tolerate the anxieties aroused by helplessness. This in turn clearly affects the extent to which a baby must resort to extreme attempts to defend itself from suffering.

Of particular importance in determining the growth of the human mind is the variable capacity of the individual to tolerate what Melanie Klein described as depressive anxiety. If symbol formation inevitably involves an experience of loss of the object as a material possession, which is Hanna Segal's thesis, then it appears that alpha-function must do so too. In my view capacities for alpha-function and symbol formation, if indeed they are not one and the same thing, will also turn out to be innately variable. I think a high tolerance of depressive anxiety is a fundamental factor in some babies capacity to develop more normally in disturbed and disturbing environments which would prove beyond the adaptive capabilities of infants less fortunately endowed.

Among many interesting facts about the type of environment in which a baby is most likely to be able to develop a capacity for thought are those emerging concerning sound and speech. Thinking is impossible without alpha-elements, so is truly symbolic speech. Not only is the sound of the human voice enormously important to babies, whose powers of discriminating one voice from another develop early and detectably. It can also be seen that even new-born babies respond rhythmically, with evident relief of anxiety, and often a manifest sense of pleasurable containment, to the language of an adult speaking to them. This remarkable phenomenon can be explained by the assumptions that introjection of alpha-function not only provides the infant with the tools for later pleasurable patternmaking but that from birth onwards there is an innate human capacity, probably also varying in strength genetically, to take pleasure in creative union of alpha-elements. Could this last capacity be none other than gratitude, as the basis of love? I think so.

Any of the innate or environmental barriers to normal identification with an object capable of alpha-function interfere with mental growth and with satisfaction and joy in growth. Beta-elements are not capable of constructive conjunctions with each other. The bizarre internal objects resulting from excessive envious projective identification are only capable of bizarre unions. These are inevitably unpleasurable and unhelpful, except to the perverse, omnipotent, sadistic aspects of the self. However, they are available for defensive evacuation. Alpha-elements and alpha function, may be rejected in favour of more primitive mental mechanisms for the very reason that they cannot be dealt with in this way.

Bion is fond of Keats' phrase "negative capability," using it to describe the breast's capacity for reverie, and the psycho-analyst's ability to promote mental growth without undue distortion. Both Keats and Bion have recorded for us, in their different ways, their belief that growth is attainable and beautiful but is never painlessly achieved. Both have told us that undue pain can increase the likelihood of distortions in natural growth. So it seems to me appropriate to end this tribute to Bion's work, and his courageously honest attitude to his work, with Keats' words:

> "Beauty is truth, truth beauty,"
> that is all
> Ye know on earth, and all ye need to
> know.

References

Bion, W.R. (1959). *Experience in Groups*. London: Tavistock.
Bion, W.R. (1962). *Learning from Experience*. London: Paul Heinnemann.

EDITOR'S NOTE: *Miss Joseph's paper is a beautifully sensitive example of a new trend in thinking by Kleinian authors. Thanks to Bion's questioning the* real *psychic birth of the infant (? fetus) in his book* The Caesura, *Kleinian therapists have become more sensitive and alert to very primitive states of mind which can be called "pre-paranoid-schizoid." Bick's and Meltzer's discovery of "adhesive identification" falls perhaps in this category. In brief, Miss Joseph is dealing with that type of patient who seems never really to have fully experienced being born and therefore never could really experience pain. They differ from the patients who employ schizoid or manic mechanisms and who therefore use splitting and projective identification to gain control of the object. The latter probably comprise that more common clinical entity subscribed under Mahler's* symbiotic states *of mind normally and pathologically, whereas Miss Joseph is perhaps dealing with Mahler's* autistic state. *In Bion's terms, one might call them fugitives from a Transformation in "O."*

Whatever it may be, Miss Joseph has poignantly removed the gossamer-veil off this type of patient and has allowed them to be "born" so as to experience the exquisiteness of real pain and therefore real pleasure.

Toward the Experiencing of Psychic Pain*

Betty Joseph

"People exist who are so intolerant of pain or frustration (or in whom pain or frustration is so intolerable) that they feel the pain but will not suffer it and so cannot be said to discover it . . . the patient who will not suffer pain fails to 'suffer' pleasure." This description of Bion's is central to my thinking in this paper. I want to describe a type of movement and a type of pain that I think is experienced at periods of transition between feeling pain and suffering it—a borderline situation. Some of our patients describe to us a certain type of pain which is, from their point of view, indefinable. The quality or nature of the pain is not comprehensible to them and they often feel that they cannot convey the experience to the analyst. It may appear to be almost physical, it may be connected with a sense of loss, but it is not what we would define as depression; it may contain feelings of anxiety, but it cannot just be seen as a sense of anxiety. It is, as our patients point out to us, "pain." It is this apparently indefinable phenomenon that I want to discuss here.

I am thus trying to describe a type of pain that emerges, I think, at moments when there is an important shift in the balance maintained by the personality—a shift and alteration of the state of mind, which can in some cases even be the precipitating factor that finally brings the patients into analysis. In others this shift is part of the analytic process, and if it can be resolved, can be a very positive step in terms of progress and integration. It is interesting to see how frequently it is felt to be almost physical, the patient locating it often in the lower part of the chest, and yet he or she knows clearly that he is not describing a physical condition, it is not hypochondriacal or psychosomatic, it is known to be mental. It is experienced as on the border between mental and physical. This type of psychic pain is, I believe, in many ways a borderline phenomenon, as I shall discuss again later.

Since the type of pain I am discussing is associated with a loss of a particular state of mind and psychological balance, I first want to consider the nature of this state. I have suggested that the pain is not just anxiety, not just depression. I shall indicate that it is linked with a greater awareness of the self and of the reality of other people, thus that it is linked with a sense of separateness; but it is not just these concepts that I am talking about—I want to explore the experience and the qualities involved. I think that it emerges in patients who, though in many ways living apparently satisfactory lives, have important areas of psychotic anxieties and whose defences have been operating comparatively successfully. They have to some extent achieved

*This paper is an expanded version of one given in October 1976 at a weekend Conference for English Speaking Members of European Societies organised by The British Psychoanalytical Society.

peace and freedom from conflict by the use of particular types of relationships with objects, which protect them from realistic emotional experiences. Basically I am describing an aspect of what Melanie Klein subsumes under the heading of projective identification. When this type of pathological tie breaks down, what they experience is new and unknown and is what they, and I here, are calling "pain." In the earlier stages of the analysis of such patients, anxiety and persecutory feelings are strong when these defences are felt to be threatened; as they are further analysed and progress is made, then I think the experiences changes from anxiety to "pain." This movement I shall refer to again later.

According to my experience, this kind of pain can arise however, not only during an analysis, as part of the analytic process, when we would expect it to be a gradual and slowly integrated process, but it can also arise outside analysis and indeed, as I have suggested, can be the thing that may finally bring a patient into treatment, when, for example, a particular type of relationship with an object alters and disturbs a previously held balance, then it is usually felt to be much more traumatic and violent.

The methods which such patients have been using to maintain their balance show considerable variety--but they have in common the employment of their important objects to contain parts of the self. This is sometimes achieved in a fairly total way, as with perverts who project themselves mentally or bodily into fetish objects like a rubber suit or a woman's body and thus keep free from anxiety and relating; it is sometimes achieved in a powerful but more limited way as when large parts of the self are projected into other people and not experienced as belonging to the self. Sometimes the process becomes more obvious to the analyst, as the patient having built up a whole delusional system involving specific areas of his life. For example, a patient will project parts of the self into the analyst in such a way that he perceives the analyst as being almost the same as himself in life or in personality, the patient's own difficulties usually being ascribed to the analyst with little or no insight and the analyst being seen as living a life which is very similar to his own, as, for example, isolated, friendless or liking the same kind of things. This may carry a conviction of a very close or intimate relationship with the analyst in the present or in the future. It means that there is no real relating, no differentiation.

In such patients, in the early period of the analysis, holidays and gaps can be non-experienced up to a point, because such patients retreat into their world and keep up a type of internal euphoric relationship with the analyst, which is quite different from an internal relationship based on the introjection of an object who has been experienced as physically real and valued, loved or hated. And we have to distinguish between the two. They do not "act out" or miss the analyst in the holidays because they seem able to maintain this euphoric idealised relationship, living in a kind of continual presence which does not permit of any distance. The slow breakdown of this type of internal relationship leads to very profound feelings of pain in gaps.

Because of the very concrete nature of this type of projective identification, the coming out of this state of mind is experienced equally concretely. One patient coming out of a partial delusional state of mind used the word "emerging," which was accompanied by great pain, another talked about being "pulled out." Some seem to see the experience in analysis as actually linked with operation scars. One such patient in a session felt an old operation scar pain being reactivated, others dream of scars huge and ugly. I am interested in the link between the experience of such patients as being cut out from, forced out or pulled out, and the whole idea of actual birth. This I shall discuss further later.

In order to look at the problem of this psychic pain in more detail, I want first to bring an example from one of the patients I spoke about earlier, where the breakdown of a rather specific type of relating helps to precipitate the individual into analysis. This example comes from a young woman who was in the latter part of her university career when she was considering analysis, and difficulties in her relationship with a rather older man finally helped to bring her into treatment. Her man friend, who came from a rather eminent scientific background, had at first been felt to be very interesting and desirable by my patient, but soon there was a shift and she found that she was taking him for granted as he became more and more devoted to her, fitting in with her wishes and demands, putting up with considerable criticism and even attacks as she found fault with him or his intelligence and so on.

At the same time, the relationship which had seemed to her very safe, as if they were very well matched and in love, became increasingly precarious, and she found she could hardly tolerate being away from him, could hardly let him go when they parted and could not tolerate the ending of endless telephone calls, etc. Then came a week when he, temporarily, gave up the relationship, and her pain became absolutely intense, and although they soon re-established it and she felt he was devoted to her, she needed constant reassurance of his devotion and continued to be in almost constant pain. She then slowly began to realize that the problem must be deeper because, despite his apparent devotion, she could never find peace.

I noticed that throughout this early period of analysis I hardly existed for her, but served as someone to come to to pour out her misery, and my role seemed to be an expectation that I should give her "understanding," which would put things right. She seemed to have little feeling about the analysis or myself as a person and was unaware consciously of any feelings about gaps or changes, but "understanding" did not help and she obtained very little relief at that time from being in analysis. I think what was happening was that this patient had some real difficulty about carrying a whole area of her feelings connected with being dependent, waiting and wanting and the anger, I think, associated with this. So long as this man friend was deeply dependent on her, almost clinging to her, she was all right, but the moment this shifted, however slightly, even the ending of a phone call, there was a panicky feeling which went into awful pain when he withdrew. I want to give an example from the very early part of the analysis.

A session would go something like this: the patient would come in, again describe the difficulties with her man friend; why did he leave her? Then she would describe the terrible feeling of misery and pain, why can't she trust him now, and so on. Then she came back with a very pressuring, strong, demanding question. Why did he change? I noticed that when I tried to help her to expand on what was going on, I would be met with a new barrage of questions. Why does it happen? What should she do now? And the questions in response to any interpretations became more imperious, more demanding and they seemed to dispense with anything I said and to go on nagging at me. Then I could show her that behind the problem with her friend was something associated with what she was doing with me. Whatever I said, she never gave herself time or the quietness to listen, absorb and digest but came back with a terribly urgent demand for more, quickly as it were, before the end of the session. Whatever I gave her did not seem adequate or did not come quickly enough, so it seemed to leave a terrible feeling of emptiness and hunger as if she could never get a sense of relief and so went on demanding more. But the way in which she would say, "Yes, but . . ." and come back to new questions was as if she was positively chewing at me or chewing into me, holding me concretely with her anxiety and demands. I think it is important to see how she experienced verbal understanding, which would pre-suppose a relationship between us, as of so little use and only a concrete thing like advice seemed to her likely to be of any help—which, of course, it actually was not.

Now the point that I am making here is not just that her behaviour in the transference was now mirroring her immediate relation with her man friend, invading, chewing and panicking, but I believe that the anxiety was that she could not manage a deep emotional relationship with anyone for rea- which were completely unknown then. There seemed to be a need for a relationship with her friend in which distance, difference, separations were wiped out as far as possible and he was kept clinging to her so that a whole desperate part was projected into him. When this structure started to collapse, first anxiety and then terrible pain emerged. I suspect that it was the breaking-down of a structured relationship which threatened to bring into the open various aspects of her relationships with the figures of her infancy. The one aspect that I began to know about was something of the controlling, invasive and chewing-up behaviour and the strange pressure that this brought to bear on me as a recipient, to try to ease her pain concretely with action as quickly as possible.

Now I want to move to the other side of the issue—that is, when the emergence of pain is part of the movement in analysis. The patient who has been living in a kind of delusional world begins tentatively to make contact with more realistic parts of his world and to the relationship with the analyst. These patients, as I have described earlier, tend to assume a kind of closeness, a very special relationship with the analyst, but at depth it seems to involve a phantasied projection of the self into the analyst's mind or body and the closeness is of this type, not one of relating and contact. Usually such patients do not realize this and believe they are most admiring and positive toward the analyst—which will turn out to be far from the truth.

It is the slow emergence from this state which brings extreme pain of an incomprehensible type, great distress which the patient often attempts to silence concretely with drugs or alcohol, believing there is no other way of dealing with it. The original reaction is often of a profound loss of a state of excitement or even of bliss, and therefore of impoverishment, and it is very important that the nature of the sense of impoverishment is eventually fully sorted out. But in long term such emergence gives to these patients a sense of greater emotional range and richness; or to paraphrase Bion's idea, the patient who now begins to have the possibility of suffering pain will also be able to suffer pleasure. I shall try to discuss this further by bringing a fragment of material from such a patient, B, a young woman writer who had one lively teenage son.

The background to the material is this. B had unconsciously been living in an unreal, quasi-delusional relationship with me, which appeared to extend into her other relationships—in which we were a very close idealised unit and very similar to each other. She had hardly been able to visualise me realistically. She had also apparently previously expected little of the analysis except some kind of remaining here; and however hard I worked and however much we achieved, she tended to lose contact day by day with what had been going on in the sessions. In the period that I am concerned with changes were taking place, particularly a new kind of realization of differences between us, which I would describe as her emerging from a blurred delusional world, and with this a greater appreciation and valuing of the day to day work, but also feelings of great pain.

B started by talking in a rather light, almost laughing way, being slightly humorous, which contrasted strikingly with the pain and difficulties she had been talking about in the previous session. Then she told a dream which she said had struck her with great horror. It was that she had had a second baby, though by no known father, as if no father was involved. It was as if the baby had been born all right but then a kind of hole had developed around the side of its cheek by the mouth, so that the mouth itself was like a great slit. There was the problem of how it would feed, because the milk would dribble out—it was vaguely incomprehensibly felt to be my patient's fault. She wrapped the baby up in a blanket and then saw that the slit was beginning to heal a bit, the baby looked somehow prettier. My patient's associations were to an aunt of hers who had recently had an operation but who had become disturbed immediately afterward and behaved in such a way as to open up, to tear open, some of the operation stitches, which the surgeon had then had to repair. This aunt had the same first name as my patient.

The dream seems particularly significant in this period when the patient was almost constantly in a state of intense pain, as if it contained some potential insight. First, I think that the baby is an aspect of herself now experienced as being born, emerging physically from a kind of idealised closed-in relationship with me—her delusional world concretely experienced. But the birth is not a natural one, but associated with being torn out—the operation scar. Now once she really starts to emerge all kinds of psychic troubles and possibilities begin to be opened up. One is the possibility of being responsible for herself and her mind and how it works, she feels in the dream vaguely responsible for the child's mouth, as her aunt is responsible for the damage to her operation scar, and the damage to the surgeon's work. Then she becomes incontinent, the milk will dribble out, which is exactly what had been happening between every session. It did not remain in and get digested.

This session had actually started with a kind of verbal incontinence, joking, a bit light, avoiding real issues. But very recently she had begun to get a grip on it, as if the mouth, in a very slight way, started to heal, to get a grip on the nipple, she was getting prettier! But if she really emerges, then a great deal has to be faced, such things as the fact that I have been there all the time working with her, that there has been a whole world of life going on and that her delusional world was a delusional world, and that babies have two parents, that our work needs her active work with me. She has not yet reached this stage of active responsibility for her mind, including its destructive and suicidal aspect that destroys progress in herself and undoes our work; this would involve "suffering pain." But she was moving in that direction. Suicidal feelings are very marked in patients emerging from these states of shut-in-ness because life itself is what they want to avoid since life, living, relating is exactly what stirs up so much pain and a whole gamut of feelings which have up to now been avoided. Destruction of the self and the mind that experiences is most attractive.

What I also want to stress here is the sense of confusion, not only the patient's own sense of confusion about what is happening, but also the apparent confusing and bringing together of many stages and anxieties: birth, oral anxieties—the dribbling mouth; apparently oedipal aspects—there was no father; fragments of potential concern and reparation—the baby is wrapped up, the mouth heals, there is a sense of vague self-reproach and so on. It seems that these patients who live so much in an unreal delusional world of projective identification have in their development ventured out to some extent—they are not actually psychotic—they have moved forward but never been able to hold on to and work through the basic steps of development, but have retreated immediately in the face of difficulties and anxieties back into their unreal world. As they emerge more fully in treatment, there is a breakthrough of a series of different stages and problems, as it were hinted at, touched on, but never really dealt with, which need to be teased out as the analytic work goes on.

This is, I suspect, associated with the unknown-ness of the nature of the pain, which is unable to be put under headings. The pain is not experienced as guilt in relation to impulses, concern about objects or the loss of an object; it has not this clarity. At this stage these patients have not achieved sufficient differentiation to reach and work through the depressive position. The nature of the pain is more unknown, more raw; it is more connected with the emerging into a live world. Retreat from it involves not so much the use of manic defences, but the slipping back into the use of more schizoid mechanisms to achieve peace, even though this involves destruction of progress or of the self, or an attempt to return to an undifferentiated state, as if inside the object. To put it another way, the experience of pain is not yet heartache—though felt often to be related to the heart—but it contains the beginnings of the capacity to feel heartache.

I think it is now understandable that these patients often seem to be the ones who have a puerperal breakdown when their own babies, particularly, I think, the first ones, are born. They tend to be comparatively comfortable and free from anxiety when pregnant, but the birth or the period immediately following delivery is frequently traumatic. My impression is that not only do they feel that the baby is being taken away from them, but they are so deeply identified with the baby, who is felt to be pulled or torn out of the mother's body, that the very early weeks can be most traumatic and precipitate a quite serious breakdown. The patient's own problem of being outside and born has never been adequately worked through.

I want now to return to a point that I indicated earlier, that is, the nature of the movement within an analysis toward the experiencing of this type of psychic pain. At first, when one is analysing the nature of the patient's projective identification into his objects, and there is some shift in the defences, the shifts are accompanied by anxiety and the quick re-use of the projective mechanisms to restore the old balance. It is only as these aspects are more integrated by the patient and there is a strengthening of the ego that a kind of willingness and active interest is felt in what is going on, externally and internally. It is then that, to my mind, psychic pain is experienced as such, and provided that the patient does not retreat from this, his capacity to suffer pain is increased. Bion describes the need for "the analytic experience to increase the patient's *capacity* for suffering even though the patient and analyst may hope to decrease pain itself" and he goes on to describe the relationship between pain and development, adding that this is "recognised in the commonly used phrase "growing pains," a point very relevant to my theme.

I want to illustrate this type of movement briefly. A patient, C, who had been very seriously withdrawn all his life and caught up in fetishistic phantasies, had begun to feel alive, with great pain and alarm, but also with a sense of increased emotional richness. For example, for the first time in his conscious life he had felt real attachment to his old mother. But there was also retreat. Shortly before the summer holidays he brought a dream, in which he was in a private hospital in his dressing-gown; something to do with a heart condition that he was worried about. Looking out of a window he was aware of a part outside, a kind of extension of the hospital, covering part of the street, where something was going on. A friend of his was going outside. His associations included a reference to his old night fears of his heart stopping and of dying. I suggested now a conflict between his remaining emotionally shut away inside and the notion of moving into contact with a world outside in which things were known to be going on, like leaving the analysis for the holidays with his eyes open, emotionally aware of it, and it might really be touching his heart positively. This suggestion rather moved him. He agreed, saying that it was odd that as he came into the session, he had looked at the date on his watch and noticed, most unusually for him, that the holidays would be here in a fortnight. Usually this only emotionally dawns on him a few hours ahead of a gap. By now, in the session, one could feel there was movement.

In the early part of his analysis when we had been able to analyse his profound projections into his objects there would be feelings of intense anxiety as in a dream recurring in his childhood, of dropping out of a globe into dark terrifying nothingness. Now we can distinguish this anxiety from a feeling of pain and worry about unknown feelings in relation to a world in which things are going on externally and internally. It is now the beginnings of pain where previously it was fragmentation, but he also knows that the pain contains something of richness and even, therefore, hope.

I am putting it this way because I feel that this type of pain has a quality of incomprehensibility to the patient and to the analyst. It seems to be a pain connected with people and life and if we can help our patients through this, then there is the possibility of a sense of responsibility for themselves and their relationships and their understanding and their impulses, and we get a real shift toward the depressive position with concern for people. But it is only part way toward the depressive position. If one assumes knowledge as to its content prematurely, I suspect that one helps a patient to harden up again. There is an additional technical point, that is, I think one cannot help patients to break out of the old methods of operating and emerge to the experiencing of this type of psychic reality and the beginnings of suffering psychic pain and get through it, except by following minute movements of emergence and retreat, experiencing and avoiding within the transference. "Knowledge" of these things is of no use to the patient. These two latter issues are essentially linked with Bion's own thinking: the one which he discusses frequently from various angles, that is, the importance of being able to stand not knowing—'negative capability.' The other concerns the value of distinguishing clearly, in our work, between "knowing about" and "becoming," between K and O.

I have tried to discuss a particular type of psychic pain that I believe belongs to the emergence from schizoid states of mind in wnich projective identification is strongly used. I have attempted to discuss it as a borderline phenomenon, on the border between mental and physical, between shut-inness and emergence, between anxieties felt in terms of fragmentation and persecution and the beginnings of suffering, integration and concern.

References

Bion, W.R. (1963). *Elements of Psycho-Analysis*. London: Heinemann.
—— (1965). *Transformations*. London: Heinemann.
Klein, M. (1946). Notes on some schizoid mechanisms, in *Developments in Psychoanalysis*. London: Hogarth Press; pp. 292-320.

Autistic Phenomena in Neurotic Patients

Sydney Klein

EDITOR'S NOTE: *Dr. Klein's contribution is a unique and timely addition to the psychoanalytic literature. The whole concept of neurosis is being fundamentally challenged recently by the new emphasis on borderline states which Bion was one of the first to suggest comprise a montage of psychotic and non-psychotic personalities existing independent of each other in the same individual. Dr. Klein makes the further refinement that this psychotic "twin" may be very much like, if not an actual remnant of, an autistically psychotic infant or child which has managed to survive virtually intact alongside an otherwise normal or neurotic personality in adulthood. Further, he makes the valuable distinction between primitive states and autistically abnormal states; therefore what persists is the residue of a psychotic catastrophe of infancy in the latter case.*

Autistic Phenomena in Neurotic Patients

Sydney Klein

In recent years there has been an increasing awareness amongst analysts that behind the neurotic aspects of the patient's personality there lies hidden a psychotic problem which needs to be dealt with to ensure real stability. This was particularly highlighted by Bion (1957) in his seminal paper on the differentiation of the psychotic from the non-psychotic part of the personality. However, I do not feel that this is still fully recognized. In the course of a periodic review of the progress of my analytic practice, and particularly of my patients' habitual modes of communication, I became aware that certain among them whom I thought of initially as being only mildly neurotic, some of whom were also analytic candidates, revealed during the course of treatment, phenomena familiar in the treatment of autistic children. These patients were highly intelligent, hard-working, successful and even prominent professionally and socially, usually pleasant and likeable, who came to analysis either ostensibly for professional reasons or because of a failure to maintain a satisfactory relationship with a husband or wife. It gradually became clear that in spite of the analysis apparently moving, the regular production of dreams, and reports of progress, there was a part of the patient's personality with which I was not in touch. I had the impression that no real fundamental changes were taking place. There is an obvious parallel with what Winnicott (1960) has called the false self, and which Rosenfeld (1978) has termed "psychotic islands" in the personality, but I do not think these terms quite do justice to what may be described as an almost impenetrable cystic encapsulation of part of the self which cuts the patient off both from the rest of his personality and the analyst. This encapsulation manifests itself by a thinness or flatness of feeling accompanied by a rather desperate and tenacious clinging to the analyst as the sole source of life, accompanied by an underlying pervasive feeling of mistrust, and a preoccupation with the analyst's tone of voice or facial expression irrespective of the content of the interpretation. There is a constant expectation of hostility and a tendency to become quickly persecuted at the slightest hint of the analyst's irritation or disapproval. Consciously the analyst is idealized as an extremely powerful and omniscient figure who also occurs in this guise in the patient's dream. As a concomitant, the patient denies his persecutory feelings in spite of the evidence subsequently given by dreams and other analytic material. For example, one patient offered to raise her fees as she felt so well, and I accepted her offer. The next night she dreamed of *a large white vampire bat and of a baby wriggling to escape from a tube being put into its foot for a blood transfusion*. It was obvious that although she had offered to raise the fees herself she experienced me as a vampire-like breast who was sucking her dry

Klein, S. ["Autistic Phenomena in Neurotic Patients"] This article first appeared in *The International Journal of Psycho-Analysis* 61, 395-402.

instead of filling her with life. Nevertheless her fear of me led to a firm denial of her persecutory feelings.

Another feature of the analysis is the tendency to bring up some topic which the patient seizes upon with obsessional rigidity but which is never worked through because of the inability to take in interpretations and deal with the problem. There is a striking similarity with the behaviour of autistic children who play with a ball or toy in a compulsive repetitive way and who scream and resist any attempt to interfere with or change the pattern of play.

Sooner or later, however, the patient's personality structure is made clearer by references in a projected form. For example, one patient said, "I can never get through to my mother. She seems to have an encapsulated relationship inside herself." Another described an autistic child she had seen in exactly the same terms. Yet another patient described herself as drifting away from me, even though she was interested in what I was saying, in exactly the way autistic babies are described as drifting away from their mothers. As soon as I was able to draw the patients' attention to these phenomena in themselves they began to dream about *being in walled towns or fortresses, stone buildings, etc.* In addition, crustaceous creatures began to appear in their dreams such as cockroaches, armadillos, lobsters, etc. (cf. Tustin, 1972). Previously these encysted parts of the self had been dealt with by projection into the body, producing various types of psychosomatic symptoms, or into other people.

I would like to describe one patient in some detail to illustrate my point. This female patient had politely but consistently denied all feelings about weekend or holiday separations even though the material pointed quite clearly to feelings of exclusion from the parental couple. Just prior to the second holiday break she suddenly developed acute abdominal pain and was rushed to hospital for removal of what turned out to be an inflamed ovarian cyst. Prior to the next analytic break she developed an acute swelling in her breast which was operated on and diagnosed as acute cystic inflammation. However, despite the operation she continued to complain of pain and swelling in both breasts. Subsequent sessions indicated that the swellings were equated with omnipotent appropriation by projective and introjective identification of her mother's genital and breast creativity. This was shown by a dream in which *she had two swellings on either side of her body* to which she associated sitting between two pregnant women at a dinner party. This was followed by phantasies of attacks on "the goose that laid the golden eggs." Moreover when she spoke of her feelings of insecurity and inability to maintain her confidence, which she equated with a structure of bricks collapsing, it became apparent that this was due to her attacking the cement which bound her together, namely my interpretations. Her own association of cement with semen showed her hostility to the creativity of both parents, who were not allowed to come together in her mind. Nevertheless, there was no overt expression of hostile feelings toward me which remained completely split off. Indeed there was little feeling of immediacy of emotional contact in the transference. Even when she agreed with what I said I did not feel we got any deeper. The model was of a baby with the nipple in its mouth but not taking in the milk.

However, after I had consistently drawn her attention to the lack of real emotional contact, in a Monday session a short time later she told me two dreams. In the first dream *she was driving up a hill in a red car*. Her association was that when she is without me at the weekend she stops going forward and feels like a child. She then told me the second dream in which *she was lying in a hospital bed in a room with her mother. There were cockroaches in the room and her mother was very angry with the nurse, while my patient was quite calm*. Her associations were that in her late teens she had had an operation for the removal of a dermoid cyst. Her mother came to visit her and was very angry with the nurse because she is very impatient and could not tolerate anything dirty in the room.

I interpreted that she was afraid that I was like her mother and could not tolerate anything dirty in her like a cockroach, but this was also because she was putting into me her own impatience and intolerance of anything which was not ideal. She agreed and said rather ruefully that she supposed she expects a land of milk and honey. She then added that she hates cockroaches. She remembered being with a girl friend and killing a big fat cockroach which her girl friend had been very frightened of. She laughed and said it was an act of friendship.

Now in the previous session there had been veiled and scattered but increasingly hostile references to this girl friend who had recently started analysis herself and had told my patient she was doing well. It seemed to me that under the guise of friendship she was denying her jealousy of her girl friend who in her phantasy was a new baby coming to me, and I interpreted that she turned me into a dirty cockroach and killed me off because of the hatred and jealousy that she experienced toward me at the weekend as a pregnant mother containing her baby sister and father's penis instead of being the ideal mother and breast who was there just for her. She said, "You have said this before but I don't see it. I must be blind. It is like looking at letters and not being able to put them together to make words out of them. It is the same with my husband. He gets furious with me and says that I don't take things in." There was a reflective pause and she said, "I must be a difficult nut to crack." There was another pause and she added, "but it's only like this when you talk about separation." I said that she kept herself in a shell in order to avoid the painful feelings I had just described.

To summarize, the dream of going up the hill in the car which then changed into a pedal car showed how the patient functioned by identification with me and my analytic potency. However, the fact that this defence failed at the weekend and she regressed to being the helpless child indicates that this identification was predominantly a contact one or what Bick has called "adhesive identifications." In the infantile position her anger with me as the mother containing father's penis and babies leads her to attack me and turn me into the black cockroach which then has to be killed off. The whole process has been previously encapsulated, i.e., in the dermoid cyst. which had then been dealt with by being cut out.

This patient had previously described how her mind drifted away in meetings because she felt afraid of her male colleagues and how she had always felt her father's words like bullets. In the next session she now returned to this theme and said that she was like a hedgehog, if she was feeling attacked either her quills shot out or she collapsed inside herself. When I interpreted that she was putting her own hostility into myself as father she said she did feel hostile. What was so painful was her feeling that he had no time for her. Every time she telephoned him he just said, "Hello," and passed her over to her mother. As a child and adolescent she always felt he was battering her with lectures and had no interest in her feelings or in common everyday events. She then recounted with intense feelings how she used to take her boyfriends home but how they had completely ignored her but sat adoring her father, who also ignored her. It was the most painful experience of her life, she said bitterly. "He robbed me of my femininity." When I tried to relate this to her feelings about myself and other patients she denied it. She was quite sure this wasn't so; I was kind, attentive, etc. However, she sounded quite hurt, and I then pointed out how she did feel hurt by me because when I interpreted her negative feelings she felt I ignored her positive, loving feelings. In fact a constant feature of the analysis at this time was that any interpretation of her negative feelings immediately made her feel extremely persecuted. During this period I had to proceed extremely cautiously but little by little she was able to voice feelings and produce dreams in which I was experienced successively as a hard-shelled beaked lobster, a cruel and treacherous Stalin who pretended to be genial but was really murderous, and then as more human but cold, hard and formal.

After this period she told me two dreams which shed some light on her difficulty in taking in understanding. In the first dream *her husband was talking on the telephone to a young girl who was staying with them and she cut the wire*. When I interpreted that not only was she cutting the links between her husband and the girl because of her jealousy of the relationship but was also jealous of the link between myself and my analytic babies, she said, "I don't understand." I then added that she didn't understand because she was also cutting the links between us as a result of the envy of the good link between us, and especially the link with the dependent part of herself. She then said, "I do understand that. It's like being in a boat and cutting the ropes pulling me ashore so that no one can help me. I am too proud. I take small things but not big ones." She then told me a second dream. *She was in the hairdresser's, and was kept waiting until the shop was empty. She then got so angry that she smashed two pairs of plates, each pair consisting of one large and one small*. Her association was that she had been to the hairdresser and changed her hairstyle but her husband had not noticed. The plates symbolized her capacity to receive and understand the analytic food for thought, which she smashed up when she could not bear the frustration experienced when she felt she was overlooked, especially if she felt I, like her husband, did not notice her attempts to change for the better. Her reaction to this interpretation was to say, "My father looked at me but did not see me and never listened either." After a pause she said that she now realized that her sexual phantasies toward her father and her wish for babies from him and other men, which we had previously seen, meant that she was prostituting herselt to get concrete proof that she was cared for. I told her that if she did not get all the food and care she wanted she destroyed what she did get, it was all or nothing.

At a later stage in the analysis, toward the end of the second year, what also emerged was her realization that she was using me as a processing plant in which I had to act as her eyes and her judgement, and function as someone refining and enriching her like a uranium factory, or giving her a blood transfusion. She revealed that the reason she projected her senses and her capacity to think into me was that if she stopped to think and make a decision as to what course of action to take she was afraid that she would become so paralysed by doubts about other possible courses of action that she would never move. Instead she got rid of her capacity to think and consequently behaved in a completely blind and confused way. This was described very vividly by her as pseudo-bravery, in which she acted very fast and destroyed what she called the monsters of doubt, which made her behave in what she called "constant hysterical action." It also became apparent that her paralysis by doubt was due to her fear that if she went ahead and committed herself to the analysis, this would result in her throwing herself completely into me, body and soul. This was partly due to her need to prove her commitment as a result of the projection of her expectations from others, particularly her father and myself. She admitted that she had always felt she needed her father's whole physical involvement because she had had so little of it as a child.

At the same time her fear of throwing herself inside me was due to the impulse to occupy and possess me as a mother full of imagined riches. This was felt as being carried out in such a violent way that she feared that she would get stuck inside me and would be unable to extricate herself. Even worse, she feared that in the process she would destroy my inside containing herself, expressed in phantasies of being buried alive in a mining shaft whose walls collapsed, a volcano erupting with tons of lava and a steam roller which could flatten everything.

However, as another holiday drew nearer at the end of the second year, it became clear that behind the possessiveness and jealousy of her more adult self, there was a desperate need to keep herself inside me because of the intense anxiety aroused in the infantile part of her by the approaching break. This time the impending separation brought into consciousness terrible feelings of my dying or abandoning her and of consequently dying or falling to pieces herself. She said she felt as if she were in a black space screaming for help. "I feel worse than an unborn baby, more like a mindless dog which can only be happy when its master returns." These primitive feelings of needing the analyst/mother in order to hold the infant together and prevent it from death and disintegration are basically what underlie the autistic defences I have previously described. The patient herself referred to her behaviour being like that of a child playing with a ball, which could not stop (just as I described the behaviour of the autistic child) because any suggestion of the idea of it not going on forever was like a small dose of death.

The interpretation of these intense anxieties brought a measure of relief to the patient but then led to phantasies that she could only get stronger by eating her way out of me and guilt at taking in life at my expense. As this was due to the feeling of being inside me again we could then see that apart from the primary infantile anxiety of separation she also got rid of the adult part of herself in order to make herself small enough to get inside me like Alice in Wonderland, this time because of a stubborn anger and spite at the separation. For the first time she was able to admit to murderous feelings about being left, both toward myself and toward the other babies felt to be taking her place inside, and in particular, anger at being made so much better that she could no longer regress to being the helpless infant.

This patient and others like her had a preoccupation with and a fascination for words. On one occasion when her husband had been away and not replied to a letter she had written him, she dreamed of *a letter being wrapped in wool*. The meaning of this dream was that no-words were experienced as cold and hostile. Similarly, in order to disguise her own hostile reactions she had to wrap up her own words to make them warm. This sensitivity to the analyst's tone of voice, which is partly due to the need to hang on to something for life and support, and partly due to the expectation of hostility, requires him to be alert to his own reactions. While there is no doubt that the visual deprivation caused by lying on the couch plays a part in the importance of the analyst's voice, it also has its roots in early infancy.

My patient's earlier difficulty in expressing her feelings seemed to be due partly to identifying me with a fragile mother who could not stand anxiety without breaking down, and partly due to identifying me with an omnipotent father who would crush any aggression or defiance or reject her love. It was this lack of a good stable container which I think led her to use her body as a container instead, with the consequent production of psychosomatic symptoms. In fact all my patients in this group experienced their mothers as anxious, insecure, controlling, overprotective and hypochondriacal, while their fathers were described as being either physically absent in their childhood or emotionally absent in the sense of being remote intellectuals heavily invested in academic or professional interests outside the family. However, the patient's material about being battered by words, and her excess of concrete thinking seemed to be related at a deeper part-object level to attacks by an object which contained by projection the split off hostility aroused by a frustrating nipple and the need to preserve it from this hostility, and the additional aggression toward this object for taking the infant's place. In this connexion I should like to mention that my patient had made various references to guilt and anxiety about incest. A dream in which *her body was split in half* was understood in terms of splitting off her sexual feelings from her oral ones. In the context of the session this led me to suppose that this incest taboo was originally based on the guilt and anxiety caused by primitive sexual feelings and desires directed toward the nipple which was felt at the same time to be in danger of being destroyed. In this connexion it is striking that for many years there seemed to be a taboo on the word nipple in the analytic literature. Although Freud used the word as early as 1905 in his paper on "A case of hysteria," even Melanie Klein hardly ever used it in spite of her voluminous writings on orality, and there have only been scattered references to it since, as Bradley (1973) described in his well-documented paper. A systematic differentiation of the nipple as a structure separate from, but part of the breast, the confusion of nipple and penis, etc., was first described by Meltzer (1963), i.e., nearly 60 years later.

Confirmatory material was furnished by another patient who described how his 4-week-old baby girl started to cry when he stopped talking to his wife when she was feeding the baby. As soon as he started to talk again the baby settled down. A few weeks later the reverse occurred. When he began to speak to his wife during feeding, the baby began to cry. In the context of the session it appeared that there is a change from an early experience of a good third object felt to be supporting the nipple to one in which it becomes hostile and intrusive. In other words, the absent third object, later called "father," is experienced as what might be called an aggressive masculine nipple. This was shown in a dream in which *the patient was being run down by a Jaguar car with a small rubber protrusion at the front* to which he associated a teat on a bottle.

Now, as Bion (1957) has pointed out, the fragmentation and projection of the sensory apparatus by the psychotic part of the personality leads to a penetration and encystment of the object which then swells up with rage. As a consequence words are not experienced as words but as hostile missiles, as my patient described. Seen in this light the acute cystic swellings of the patient I have described in detail can also be understood as being due to phantasies of projection of aggressive feelings and parts of herself into her internal objects, namely mother's nipple, breast and reproductive organs, which then swelled up and became persecutors. Bion also describes how in an earlier phase of development, i.e, pre-auditory, the infant has difficulty in using ideographs to form words. My patient's reference to not being able to put letters together to make words is relevant here and was due both to her attacking the links between objects and losing the capacity to restore them. In connexion with the projection of the sensory apparatus it is interesting that another patient who was much more disturbed, had a dream in which an old-fashioned gramophone horn was listening to him. In this case the capacity to hear had been projected so that the gramophone was then felt to be listening instead of playing. At a later stage he also dreamed of looking at a breast which had an eye in the centre looking at him, so that here the capacity to see had been projected.

To summarize, the autistic defence is primarily due to the avoidance of the pain caused by the intensity of the fear of death and disintegration caused by the absence of the containing nipple or breast. This surfaces as analysis progresses, not only at weekend and holiday separations but every time the patient makes a step forward and becomes more separate. In the patients I have described, these anxieties had previously been avoided either by projective identification with me and phantasies of being unborn and living inside me, by introjective identification with me as a hard-shelled object, and by adhesive identification leading to clinging to me as a placenta-like object which both feeds and detoxicates at the same time. The impact of these terrifying feelings on the analyst may be considerable, or they may have been previously modified by the reassurance gained by the fact that he usually retains professional contact with his own analyst or institute or indeed by using the institute itself as a container.

Technically, it is obvious that the patient's sensitivity to the tone of the analyst's voice must be matched by the analyst's equally sensitive but non-paranoid alertness to the underlying tone of voice and mood of the patient, In a previous paper on mania I described how the manic patient talked incessantly as a defence against feelings of inner emptiness. The type of patient I have described here does not, of course, have the same degree of disturbance, but it was noticeable that they were all extremely verbally fluent and two were informed by their parents that they could talk before they could walk. It seems that the premature development and hypertrophy of speech may be partly a defence against underlying feelings of emptiness and non-existence, and partly to overcome the infant's anxiety that his primitive feelings are not understood and contained. This precarious situation becomes confounded when the hypochondriacal mother uses the infant as a container for her own anxieties. In any event, speech was certainly used by these patients at certain periods either to maintain a link with the analyst or to avoid the link, rather than as a means of communication.

In other words, we have to recognize that although the patient appears to communicate at one level there is also a non-communication corresponding to the mute phase of the autistic child, and that what is not communicated are not only the aggressive but also the loving feelings which accompany the growth of the sense of separateness and the associated sense of responsibility for the self and objects. At the last Congress, Limentani (1977) also stressed the importance of learning to understand the moods and feelings of the silent patient and his difficulty in conveying his experience to students and colleagues. Is not this paralleled by the difficulty the pre-verbal infant has in conveying his sensations and feelings to his mother, especially the experience of being alone in a silent world?

It is my impression that recognition of the existence of the encapsulated part of the personality reduces the length of the analysis considerably, and moreover may prevent further breakdowns in later life. This was borne in on me when I treated several patients who had been analysed at earlier periods in their lives and who became very disturbed in the course of the process of ageing. There is one other important feature which repays observation in these patients, and indeed in all patients, namely the process of oscillation, which repeatedly occurs for example, between states of omnipotence and helplessness, activity and passivity, adulthood and infantility, psychosis and neurosis, primitiveness and sophistication of thought, and paranoid-schizoid depressive. Analysis of the oscillation leads hopefully to a more balanced state of mind and personality, in which the knife-edge of opposites is broadened to become a more solid basis of reflective thought.

Summary

I have described a group of patients who are seemingly successful in their professional and social lives, and who seek analysis ostensibly for professional reasons or for minor difficulties in their relationship. However, sooner or later they reveal phenomena which are strikingly similar to those observed in so-called autistic children. These autistic phenomena are characterized by an almost impenetrable encapsulation of part of the personality, mute and implacable resistance to change, and a lack of real emotional contact either with themselves or the analyst. Progress of the analysis reveals an underlying intense fear of pain, and of death, disintegration or breakdown. These anxieties occur as a reaction to real or feared separation, especially when commitment to analysis deepens. In the case I have described in detail the patient used various projective processes to deflect painful emotions either into other people, including the analyst, or into her own body. As a consequence the various objects or organs of the body swell up and became suffused with rage as a result of having to contain the unwanted feelings. This process leads in turn to intense persecutory fears and a heightened sensitivity to the analyst's tone of voice and facial expression. It would seem that the initial hypersensitivity of part of the personality is such as to lead it to anticipate danger to such an extent that it expels feelings even before they reach awareness. The sooner the analyst realizes the existence of this hidden part of the patient the less the danger of the analysis becoming an endless and meaningless intellectual dialogue and the greater the possibilities of the patient achieving a relatively stable equilibrium. Although the analyst has to live through a great deal of anxiety with the patient I feel that ultimately the results make it worthwhile.

References

Bion, W. R. (1957). Differentiation of the psychotic from the non-psychotic personalities. *Int. J. Psycho-Anal.* Vol. 38, pp. 266-275.

Bradley, N. (1973). Notes on theory making, on scotoma of the nipples, and on the bee as nipple. *Int. J. Psycho-Anal.* Vol. 54, pp. 301-314.

Freud, S. (1905). Fragment of an analysis of a case of hysteria. *S.E.* Vol. 7.

Limentani, A. (1977). Affects and the psychoanalytic situation. *Int. J. Psycho-Anal.* Vol. 58, pp. 171-182.

Meltzer, D. (1963). A contribution to the metapsychology of cyclothymic states. *Int. J. Psycho-Anal*. Vol. 44, pp. 83-96.

Rosenfeld, H. (1978). The relationship between psychosomatic symptoms and latent psychotic states. Unpublished Paper.

Tustin, F. (1972). *Autism and Childhood Psychosis*. London: Hogarth Press.

Winnicott, D. W. (1960). Ego distortion in terms of true and false self. In *The Maturational Processes and the Facilitating Environment*. London: Hogarth Press. 1965.

Using Bion's Grid as a Laboratory Instrument: A Demonstration

Frederick Kurth

EDITOR'S NOTE: *Dr. Kurth's contribution comprises a laboratory exercise in an analytic hour so as to demonstrate the use to which Bion's grid can be put. In particular, he tries to illuminate some of the uses and experiences of Column II of the grid, that second-from-the-left vertical column which is located next to Column I, which represents the just emerging "innocent" thought, feeling, or "knowingness" about the world; as a result, it functions as the negation to the new "messianic" ideas which originates thinking. Dr. Kurth's contribution helps us to see the intricacies and complications of the whole spectrum of Column II. He informs us that Dr. Bion had been greatly interested in this presentation, liked it, and was pleased that his grid had been put to such use. The grid, Bion said, was to be used so that one could "mull about in space" about clinical elements after the hour was over.*

Using Bion's Grid as a Laboratory Instrument: A Demonstration

Frederick Kurth

On the morning of May 12, 1889, Freud found his patient, Frau Emmy von N., in a surprising state. He writes,

> Contrary to my expectation, she had slept badly and only for a short time. I found her in a state of great anxiety, though, incidentally, without showing her usual physical signs of it. She would not say what the matter was, but only that she had had bad dreams, and kept seeing the same things. 'How dreadful it would be,' she said, 'if they were to come to life.'

Freud reports his experiences with this patient in *Studies on Hysteria*. In this monograph he describes also, for the first time, the phenomenon of transference, that dreadful coming to life from feelings of "estrangement," or "dread of becoming too much accustomed to the physician personally," or "frightened" at transferring distressful ideas to the figure of the physician.

Just a few pages before reporting his observations on transference, Freud noted a phenomenon which occurred while working with a hysterical symptom.

> While we are working at one of these symptoms we come across the interesting and not undesired phenomenon of "joining in the conversation."

He had observed this in his work with Fraulein Elizabeth von R.

> Further, her painful legs began to "join in the conversation" during our analyses. What I have in mind is the following remarkable fact. As a rule the patient was free from pain when we started work. If, then, by a question or by pressure upon her head I called up a memory, a sensation of pain would make its first appearance, and this was usually so sharp that the patient would give a start and put her hand to the painful spot.

I suggest, following Freud, that "joining in the conversation" is certainly not undesired: it textures the psychoanalytic experience. Furthermore, I suggest, the psychoanalytic conversation can be scientifically entered into so that one can know whether the verbal intercourse facilitates experience, making learning possible; or whether it's "just so much talk," interfering with experience and substituting a mnemonic exercise for learning and growth.

I shall attempt to demonstrate these hypotheses in several ways. I make a beginning by joining Freud in conversation with Frau Emmy von N. Nearly 40 years after recording his experiences with Frau Emmy, Freud characterized his presentation as "hardly going beyond the direct description of the observations." Nonetheless, so lively and so precisely does Freud record his work, that, in my judgment, it is possible scientifically to join him in an experience which took place nearly a century ago. I consider this fact heartening, for I shall present four psychoanalytic conversations of my own on the assumption that our fellow-workers will be able to join in these experiences sufficiently to allow for scientific intercourse. I shall then examine these conversations—Freud's and mine—using Bion's Grid.

The central theses of this paper are, first, interferences to the psychoanalytic conversation reflect interferences with experience and learning generally; second, the problem of learning, like the hysterias, has to do with experiencing sex. Problems with sex manifest themselves in the psychoanalytic relationship as problems with conversation. I propose to investigate interfering and facilitating elements of conversation.

Freud had his first conversation with Frau Emmy on May 1, 1889.

> She spoke in a low voice as though with difficulty and her speech was from time to time subject to spastic interruptions amounting to a stammer. . . . What she told me was perfectly coherent and revealed an unusual degree of education and intelligence. This made it seem all the more strange when every two or three minutes she suddenly broke off, contorted her face into an expression of horror and disgust, stretched out her hand towards me, spreading and crooking her fingers, and exclaimed, in a changed voice, charged with anxiety: "Keep still!—Don't say anything!—Don't touch me!"

Frau Emmy interfered—employing 19th century devices—with Freud's invitation for verbal intercourse. She ordered Freud to keep still, so that his words wouldn't touch her. She broke off the conversation.

This conversational pattern paralleled Frau Emmy's behavior in other relationships. After two courses of treatment with Freud, lasting seven and eight weeks respectively, she broke off with him permanently. Some years later Freud talked to another physician who had treated her and discovered,

> She had gone through the same performance with him—and with many other doctors—as she had with me. Her condition had become very bad; she had rewarded his hypnotic treatment of her by making a remarkable recovery, but had then suddenly quarrelled with him, left him, and once more set her illness going to its full extent.

A quarter of a century later Freud learned from one of Frau Emmy's children that "she had broken off relations with both her children."

There needs no ghost, come from the grave, to tell us in the 1970's, that Frau Emmy's relationship with Freud was congruent with her behavior elsewhere. What we want to draw attention to, nonetheless, is the fact that their conversation–the verbal intercourse–was the psychoanalytic "element" which precisely revealed her problems with sex. Furthermore, I propose to demonstrate that an interfering device intruded into a conversational experience–a hysterical device in the case of Frau Emmy–can be systematically detailed under psychoanalysis and its interfering function revealed as it comes into existence, to paraphrase Freud, while still on its native soil.

I shall now join Freud in conversation with Frau Emmy a year later, at the very end of her second stay with him. Frau Emmy had developed a new symptom.

> She kept on pressing her hands to her forehead and calling out in yearning and helpless tones the name "Emmy."
>
> This symptom had evolved at the time her chief complaint was of frequent states of confusion–"storms in her head" as she called them.

With several weeks of work Freud cleared up these difficulties by the use of hypnosis.

> Frau Emmy remained under my observation for some time longer, feeling perfectly well. At the very end of her stay something happened which I shall describe in detail, since it throws the strongest light on the patient's character and the manner in which her states came about.
>
> I called on her one day at lunch-time and surprised her in the act of throwing something wrapped up in paper into the garden, where it was caught by the children of the houseporter. In reply to my question, she admitted that it was her (dry) pudding, and that this went the same way every day. This led me to investigate what remained of the other courses and I found that there was more than half left on the plates. When I asked her why she ate so little she answered that she was not in the habit of eating more and that it would be bad for her if she did; she had the same constitution as her late father, who had also been a small eater. When I enquired what she drank she told me she could only tolerate thick fluids, such as milk, coffee or cocoa; if she ever drank water or minerals it ruined her digestion. This bore all the signs of a neurotic choice.

At this point Freud makes a momentous resolve, stochastically grasping with characteristic courage a fundamental of sexual experience.

> I therefore thought it advisable to recommend her to drink more and decided also to increase the amount of her food. It is true that she did not look at all noticeably thin but I nevertheless thought it worth while to aim at feeding her up a little.

Frau Emmy will have none of this, and a furious storm breaks out of her head and into her relationship with Freud. Emmy comes dreadfully to life.

> For the first time I failed to bring about hypnosis; and the furious look she cast at me convinced me that she was in open rebellion and that the situation was very grave. I gave up trying to hypnotize her, and announced that I would give her twenty-four hours to think things over. . . . At the end of this time I would ask her whether she was still of the opinion that her digestion could be ruined for a week by drinking a glass of mineral water and eating a modest meal; if she said yes, I would ask her to leave. This little scene was in very sharp contrast to our normal relations, which were most friendly.

Twenty-four hours later, Frau Emmy is docile and submissive. Under hypnosis Freud asks her, "Why can't you eat more?" And Emmy begins,

> I'm thinking how, when I was a child, it often happened that out of naughtiness I refused to eat my meat at dinner. My mother was very severe about this and under the threat of condign punishment. . . .

This is an astonishing conversation, for what one hears, albeit briefly and shadowed in hypnosis, is that a conversational experience enabled Frau Emmy and Freud to enter into the life of a dreadfully naughty child–Emmy –who refuses to be fed, touched or talked to, making possible a recognition that the punishment meted out for such naughtiness is condign. In short, they practiced psychoanalysis.

Freud's technical clumsiness–which many years later he thought might evoke pity–is inevitable at this early date and of no consequence. Bion writes,

> For my purpose it is convenient to regard psychoanalysis as belonging to the group of transformations.

Frau Emmy and Freud effected a transformation of a Case History into a conversational experience.

What I propose is that an invariant (Bion, 1965) under conversational experience is Sex, and the set of transformations when "making" conversation identifies this invariant. At this point I do not define Sex; nonetheless, I aim to investigate this invariant and to make its structure more explicit. The use of an undefined term, such as Sex, is common scientific practice. Freud writes,

> Zoology and botany did not start from correct and adequate definitions of an animal and a plant; to this very day biology has been unable to give any certain meaning to the concepts of life. Physics

itself, indeed, would never have made any advance if it had had to wait until its concepts of matter, force, gravitation, and so on, had reached the desirable degree of clarity and precision. The basic ideas or most general concepts in any of the disciplines of science are always left indeterminate at first and are only explained to begin with by reference to the realm of phenomena from which they were derived; it is only by means of a progressive analysis of the material of observation that they can be made clear and can find a significant and consistent meaning.

Bion writes,

> The name is an invention to make it possible to think and talk about something before it is known what that something is.

I suggest that what Freud called "joining in a conversation" is a transformation of mere talk into verbal intercourse.

I propose to present now four psychoanalytic conversations in which we have participated. Two consecutive sessions with a man in his second year of analysis will serve to demonstrate what I mean by interfering elements, as their existence becomes evident in the conversations. I shall discuss these elements at length and then demonstrate less bizarre interfering elements from two consecutive sessions with a woman in her third year of analysis. I shall then investigate these four conversations and those of Freud with Frau Emmy using Bion's Grid.

In presenting these conversations, quotes will bracket statements made by the patient; a dash will precede statements by the analyst.

The patient began the first conversation with a lengthy silence.
"I thought of something I can say. . . ."
—Which indicates you've thought of something you can't say.
"That's what I mean! Where does that come from?"
—From me. I said it.
"That's why I can't talk to you. You blow my mind. I can't stand it."
—I think you can't stand me. You can't stand me simply talking to you.
"I can't stand for you to be alive! There's this same obstacle, the Pain. It's in my head. It's always there. You just make it worse."
He again lay silent.
"Not that much to say."
—How much is that much?
"It's just the same thing. Have that deadening Pain in my head, and it's always sitting there. I just have to look at it."
—I would suggest 'that much' is enough to make you pay attention to the Pain sitting there, rather than to me, sitting here. You look at the Pain, which completely dominates your mind, so that you are unable to listen to me.

"If I take my eye off it, it'll just take over my mind. But while I'm doing that, I can't look at anything else. It just flips me out."
—I would draw your attention to the fact that you're busy looking, using your eyes, rather than talking and using words. Even if you look at something else—besides the Pain—it's still looking, not listening. Not listening, for example, to what I have to say.
"When I was driving here, I thought some people at a bus-stop were looking at me. They really got to me."
—Yes, which I think confirms the point I was suggesting: you think of me as looking at you and not as talking to you.
"They really got to me at the bus-stop. I was furious. The furious feeling just changed into the Pain, I guess. Everything I feel turns to Pain."
—I would suggest that 'looking' is experienced by you as being penetrated; it gets to you. And whether you are with total strangers who are as far away from you as the people at the bus-stop, or with me sitting here close to you, you feel you are being looked at and gotten into and become furious at what you experience as an attack.
"I just feel mad all the time. I feel everyone's looking at me and getting to me all the time. Whenever I'm talking to anyone, there's this warfare going on between our eyes. I spend most of my energy trying to cut down on this warfare of looking."

The obstacle or Pain, so concretely described by the patient, is an interfering element; it is always with the patient, and it interposes itself immediately with the beginning silence. The interposition becomes more violent as the conversation proceeds, although there is considerable fluctuation.

While heading for his office before the next session, the analyst ran to the elevator, barely catching it with the help of a lone passenger, the patient, who had not realized that he had been holding the elevator door for his analyst. They rode up in silence. The patient began the session itself with a lengthy silence.
"If I talk, it'll lead to a sticky situation. I just can't put up with it."
—I would suggest that you are talking about my meeting you on the elevator.
"When I saw you I thought: My God, it's him! The Pain became immediately worse. It's as though I need it for just such an emergency."
—The emergency, I would think, was to get rid of whatever feelings you were having as I tried to enter into the elevator.
"I wanted to say, 'Really crashing through that door, man.' I never could say that direct-out. The Pain was right there."
—Yes, and I would suggest that to enter into a conversation with me is felt by you as getting crashed into. Perhaps more accurately, any feelings you have from contact with me, either in the elevator or talking here with me, you experience as something crashing into you.

There was again a lengthy silence.
"When I'm here, I can't say anything. Yet I'm talking to you all the time in my head. I feel so stuck."
–I think you feel stuck with me. Perhaps we can now better understand your first statement today about talk leading to a sticky situation: talking to me leads to a sticky situation in that you then feel stuck with me.
"When I said last week I thought you were, well, you know, a dummy. . . . I just can't say it!"
–You just did. And I would suggest you are not saying 'Dummy' to me–the *word* 'Dummy'–but that you feel you are sticking into me something called Dummy.
"My whole body just went Blam! when I said it."
–And, when you said it again just a moment ago. You blam-ed me with Dummy, and now I am stuck with it. The difficulty of course, is that I'll blame you for sticking this bad Dummy into me. I'll blame you back, and the battle's on. Talking to me, then, really makes matters only worse for you.
"Can't stand it much longer. Feel getting madder and madder."
–Being stuck with me in your head and stuck with talking to me all the time in your head is maddening. I suggest you feel this unbearable situation is caused by my blam-ing you and crashing into you. You end up stuck with this maddening me who blames you and blams you, making you madder and madder.
"It's worse than the Pain."
–Yes, so you've decided apparently that the Pain stuck in your head is preferable.

The emergency or sticky situation the patient describes has two components: one, a feeling, triggered by the analyst entering the elevator; and two, what to do with a person-al feeling when actually present with that person.

I suggest a conversation entails talking directly to another person about whom one has feelings. This patient can't stand such a conversation, which he experiences as something crashing into him. An emotional contact which would provide opportunity for an analytic conversation gives rise instead to a grave emergency. The interposition of the Pain is an attempt to erect a barrier against being crashed into, whether in the elevator or talking from the couch. This raises the problem as to why he experiences a conversation as such a penetrating or being crashed-into phenomenon.

In point of fact, the patient is scarcely able to enter into a conversation –he can't talk. His wish to talk is blocked by the Pain and superseded by looking. He can only look or be looked at. The use of language as a facilitating structure in order to make contact with another person and one's feeling about that person, therefore, is not available.

What this patient calls Pain is a structure in his mind whose purpose is to protect him from being crashed into or invaded whenever he makes contact with another person, as in conversation. This patient experiences "entering into a conversation" as an emergency in which he will be entered into, and he attempts to deal with this threat by interposing the mental structure he calls Pain. He is unequipped to enter into a conversation with his partner through the interposition of a facilitating structure, such as language, and instead must resort to the use of an interfering element which stops the threat implicit in conversation. He must use and has constructed for such continuing emergencies a structure which interferes with conversation and protects him from doing it.

I don't suppose there's any question that this patient's Pain is a bizarre structure and as such would be classified, psychiatrically, as a psychotic element. For our psychoanalytic purposes, however, the importance of this structure is that it functions as an interfering element. I shall demonstrate with the next patient that elements structurally less bizarre can be equally interfering.

Bleuler, in discussing the fundamental symptoms of schizophrenia, writes,

> The most extraordinary formal element of schizophrenic thought process is that termed *blocking*. . . . It is of fundamental significance in the symptomatology and diagnosis of schizophrenia.

He describes psychic energy behaving like a viscous fluid in a system,

> but in 'blocking' the free-flowing fluid is suddenly stopped because somewhere a stop-cock was abruptly turned off.

I suggest this patient's construct—the Pain—and its interposing function psychoanalytically describe what Bleuler described psychiatrically. Blocking indicates the presence of a barrier erected against experience. Reality, both internal and external, is felt as too penetrating and too dangerous. Using Bleuler's analogy, the flow or process of experience is turned off.

The second set of conversations is from two consecutive sessions on a Thursday and Friday with a woman in her third year of analysis. The following background information is necessary for the reader to join in these two conversations.

This patient was recently divorced. She has two children: Charles, who is six years old and Phyllis, who is three. Charles has a tibial torsion and wears an orthopedic brace at night. The patient is chronically underweight; she finds eating a chore and rarely experiences hunger. She has had stages of alcoholism.

> The patient came in for Thursday's session and grazed the analyst's arm as she walked through the door. She threw her purse on the couch, hung up her jacket and, before lying down, looked intently at the analyst.
>
> "Didn't want to come in and just lie down."
>
> —You looked at me before you lay down.

"I wanted to see if you had brown eyes. Had a dream about a man with brown eyes. That's all I remember of it."

—You don't want to just lie down and talk, but to look into my eyes and to touch me, as you did when you came in.

"Amazed to hear you say that. Had thought about wanting to touch you yesterday. When I got home yesterday, my six year old embarrassed me. He knows I see you, and when I came in the house he said, 'If Dr. K's your husband, why don't you bring him home?' I was so embarrassed I blushed."

—You're amazed I say something any six year old knows: that you want to touch me.

"Feel like I'm getting a headache again. Had it this morning."

—I would suggest you prefer having a headache to having a husband. I can't touch your headache; I can't even talk to it.

"This morning, Phyllis asked me why I was taking aspirin. I told her I had a headache and she said, 'Can I feel it?' and put her hand on my head. She was so cute. I feel like I'm blushing. I really feel very uncomfortable."

—I think you feel uncomfortable that you don't really want to touch me but to simply swallow me like an aspirin—something you can bring home without any problem. I think you are also saying that you wouldn't even mind taking me home with you—I'd make a cute six year old, especially if I had brown eyes. What you don't want, however, is to lie down and talk with me because you ache; and you ache in ways that no three year old or six year old can understand or in any way help you with.

"I'm just so uncomfortable I don't see how I can stand it. I feel I'm going to have to run out of here. I just can't stay here. I don't know what's the matter with me. I've never had words affect me like this."

An important difference between this woman and the first patient, I suggest, is that she actively does what he experiences as being done to him. She enters the office and physically touches the analyst, looks penetratingly at him, seizes the couch by flinging her purse. The first patient, by contrast, feels crashed into at the elevator, looked at penetratingly from the bus-stop, and is dominated by the Pain.

An important similarity between the two patients is that for each the emphasis is on looking. She not only stresses looking at the analyst; she has a dream with nothing but eyes and a symptom—blushing—which co-features eyes. Furthermore, as she experiences feelings in the conversation, she develops a headache. This is not as psychically organized an interposing element as the Pain, but it is nonetheless interfering. Somatization, in this instance, interferes with the conversation. When the somatization was interpretively circumvented, she experienced a state of panic, similar to what the first patient described as an "emergency."

At the next session, a Friday, she came in quietly and put her purse down on the floor beside the couch; she kept her jacket on. She began with a long silence.

"I didn't think this morning that I didn't want to come."
–You're using very complicated syntax. I think what you're saying is that you wanted to come and see me.
"I can't say that. It's embarrassing. I was really thinking about taking little Charles to the doctor this afternoon."
–It's embarrassing for you to want to see me. That's something for six-year olds. You prefer something grown-up, such as a double negative. Or even a sick child to take to the doctor.
"I was up with him three times last night. The blanket had gotten tangled in his brace. I think his torsion is improved and that's a relief."
–I would suggest that you are bracing yourself at this moment with being grown-up, and being grown-up is a relief for you. It gets you up, so you're not feeling down. And not feeling little.
"I don't want to hear you. Feel very tense. When I was a child, I couldn't wait until I was grown-up. Hated being a child and spent all my time with grown-ups."
–I think those are grown-up statements, and you make them at this moment–and I'm not questioning their accuracy–to relieve your tenseness.
"Just want to get away from children! At breakfast Charles kept screaming for his cereal, 'I want it now!' "
–I suspect that you feel there is something I am screaming at you.
"Want to get out of here. Can't even stand you moving in your chair. Happened yesterday and frightened me. Feelings popped in, and I don't know what to do with them."
–I would suggest that you can't stand my moving in the chair today, my popping in, this Friday morning, and then popping out on the week-end.
"When I was driving here this morning, it was the first time I thought I would miss you on the week-end. And I can't stand that. It made me just furious at myself." She told a long dream. It is here condensed.
"I had a date with someone, but I had no clothes. A woman gave me hers, but they were spotted. I was trying to get the spots out. My date watched me very patiently. I kept working on a spot."
–I would suggest that you tell the dream at this spot to get away from our date.
"I don't know why that makes me feel so sad. I feel I can't stand it."
–I think you can't stand me, patiently talking to you.
"Why should just talking make me feel so bad?"
–Why should our just talking together make you feel so sad, or so furious, or so frightened?
"It does, and I can't stand it. I don't know what to say. I'm so aware of you, sitting there, and I can't stand it."
–I would suggest that at this moment you also feel so aware of yourself lying there but don't know what to say. You don't have the words, or at least the right ones to say what it is that's really going on.

"But you don't say words. I mean, the words you use aren't like dictionary words. You cut through words, and I feel I have nothing to hide behind."

–So that you're here on a date with me without clothes, the necessary words, and feel embarrassed and naked.

"If this hour doesn't end soon, I'm going to have to get up and leave. I feel I'm losing my mind."

The evidence is that, without this "mind" which she feels she's losing, she experiences a state of panic. I suggest that this mind may be thought of as a device which manufactures the kind of verbal syntax or speech which this patient thinks of as grown-up. If the functioning of this device is interfered with, then the patient experiences such feelings as embarrassment, tenseness, fright or panic. For her, childhood is that time needed for the construction of such a syntactic device, presumably through imitation of grown-ups; and adulthood is that time when one has available, for any contingency, this interposing structure. In its interposing function it corresponds to the first patient's mental device called Pain. It should be noted that the effectiveness of the interposition is not essentially related to the bizarreness of the structure.

The patient describes her son, Charles, screaming, "I want it now!" Her actual child, insisting on no delay, drives her from the house. The actual conversation which is immediate and happening is what she has to get away from and leave also. In the dream, however, matters are otherwise: there is no claimant *now*, only a "dream date." As is evident, a "dream date" is one which never happens. When the analytic conversation begins to "pop," she experiences the same need to get away immediately as she does with the child whose screaming threatens to wake her from her dream. She uses the dream as she uses grown-up talk: to get away from *now*.

In protecting herself by her devices against the penetration of *now*, she postpones experience. For her, experience doesn't happen, for she never has time for it. The child or conversation which she can't delay she also can't stand and must get away from. In short, the immediacy of experience is felt as an unbearable penetration. It is against such penetration that the syntactic device of grown-up talk or the telling of a dream is interposed. Her telling the dream, then, presents the problem to the analyst as to how to go about transforming an interfering element to a facilitating one.

It is manifestly clear from the dream that the patient isn't equipped for dates. She is unprepared for them: whether with childhood, for which she never had time, or now as a grown-up, for her analytic hour. She begins her date with the analyst by looking towards the future–that time later in the day when she will take her child to the doctor. She then looks to the past–the previous night when she had gotten up three times with him. When at last a conversation begins–experiencing feelings about a person one is talking with–she can't stand it. Such conversation makes her lose her mind, that is, her elaborate machinery for delaying a real date.

In analytically conversing with her, the effort to transform what is delayed and remembered to what is immediate and experienced is apparent. In working with the dream, however, a different kind of transformation is attempted. Note first that both Thursday and Friday dreams emphasize the visual: the man with brown eyes, the man looking at her as he waits, her looking at the spotted clothes, and so forth.

The problem is how to transform the visual experience of the dream into the verbal experience of a conversation. In linking clothes which are seen, to words which are heard, the analyst attempts to transform the visual world, that is, her dream world, into the invisible world of living language. Such language is not in the dictionary. She is not familar with it, as her statement on Thursday indicates, "I've never had words affect me like this."

It seems clear that this woman can't talk. Such speech as she has is spotty and serves her need to delay. Instead of conversational language, she has an elaborate panoply of delaying devices: difficult syntax, such as a double negative; grown-up activities as a mother of two small children; long dreams. At the beginning of the session, the analyst translates her syntax into conversational language by saying, "You wanted to come and see me." Her response is acute embarrassment. The embarrassment gives way to panic as her feelings about him intensify. She lacks the conversational equipment to make her feelings manageable—they scream at her. Language which facilitates a date is unavailable to her. She uses language to protect herself from experience.

I propose now to examine interfering elements in conversation with the aid of Bion's Grid. The Grid has proved itself a great help in my efforts to sort out these elements, and I shall demonstrate in considerable detail the usefulness of this scientific instrument. Familiarity with the Grid is necessary for the discussion which follows. I want to draw the reader's attention to Bion's *Learning from Experience, Elements of Psychoanalysis,* and *Transformations*. These books, in my judgment, comprise a body of work and represent a major development in the evolution of psychoanalysis as a scientific enterprise.

Bion defines elements as "functions of the personality." I find this useful in that an element which functions by interfering with the verbal intercourse is an interfering element. I shall assign such elements to Column 2 of the Grid.

All elements designated Column 2 have, for our purposes, a saturated factor as an invariant. Interfering elements or functions have other factors, but we shall not concern ourselves with these. I shall limit myself in this paper to factors in the functions of Ideation and make only brief reference to factors in the functions of Emotion.

An interfering element has a factor of saturation as an invariant, so that, like the noble gases, it is "satisfied." By contrast, a facilitating element has a factor of unsaturation as an invariant. A factor of unsaturation confers the quality of "unsatisfied" to such elements. Factors of unsaturation have a combining valency which makes their elements suitable for fresh combinations. Even as there are differences in combining valency among the unsaturated factors, so there are differences in the degree of saturation among saturated factors. In other words, I am going to group Column 2 elements according to differences in degree among the saturated factors. Freud's work with Frau Emmy von N. particularizes these concepts.

While working with Frau Emmy, Freud decides he is unsatisfied with her eating habits and her attitude toward nutrition generally. He aims "at feeding her up a little." Frau Emmy, however, will have none of Freud's feeding, so Freud concludes there is no point in continuing the relationship as his patient is "satisfield." She is satisfied not only with her self-devised diet, but also with her reasons for making the choices she does. Matters being thus closed, there is nothing for Freud to contribute. Emmy von N., *qua dietitian*, is an interfering element replete with saturated factors. Twenty-four hours later, "Emmy" opens up, bringing to life a life-long unsatisfying feeding relationship. We suggest that "Emmy" is a facilitating element with unsaturated factors. These make it possible for the psychoanalytic partners to have a conversation.

"Emmy" is an unsaturated element. It qualifies, therefore, for membership in the set of Transformations under Conversation. It is to be remembered that an element is a function of a personality. It is made up of factors, and these are infinitely varied—words, body-parts, emotions, things, etc. We'll give some examples from Freud in a moment. The use to which these factors are put is a function of a personality.

At the end of Frau Emmy's treatment Freud writes,

> I therefore made use of her hypnoses principally for the purpose of giving her maxims which were to remain constantly present in her mind and to protect her from relapsing into similar conditions when she had got home. At that time I was completely under the sway of Bernheim's book on suggestion and I anticipated more results from such didactic measures than I should today.

"Emmy," as an unsaturated conversational element contrasts with the saturation of "maxims" or "didactic measures" or suggestions." Frau Emmy's brother had given her a more primitive "satisfied" element:

> She told me further that in the course of her life she had had a large number of adventures with animals. The worst had been with a bat which had got caught in her wardrobe, so that she had rushed out of the room without any clothes on. To cure her of this fear her brother had given her a lovely brooch in the form of a bat; but she had never been able to wear it.

Brooches, didactic measures, suggestions, maxims are unsuitable for the set of Transformations under Conversation because they serve as saturated factors for interfering elements. As Freud indicates plainly in the instance of maxims, the aim is to provide the patient with saturated factors—when interfering with experience is the prescribed function—so that she might ward off whatever might attempt to enter her mind. The more effectively these interfering devices fill or saturate her mind the better.

I suggest that the bad dreams Frau Emmy dreaded coming to life indicates concern that saturated factors—dreams, hysterical symptoms, hypochondriasis—might become unsaturated, leaving her mind vulnerable to experience and in danger of functioning in the direction of change and development.

At this point I propose to classify some of the elements described by Freud using the Grid. These elements vary in sophistication, but all qualify for inclusion in Column 2—with the exception of the element Emmy—by having in common a factor of saturation.

I classify Frau Emmy's brooch as A2, a thing-in-itself. In so classifying it, I am not referring to the brooch as such but to its use as a saturated factor in the interfering function of Frau Emmy's personality. I classify as A2 the food Frau Emmy left untouched. More importantly, I classify as A2 the words of Freud that Frau Emmy insisted should not touch her. The dreams Frau Emmy dreaded coming to life belong in C2. I classify Freud's maxims as E2—conceptions designed to interfere with other conceptions; and his panoply of maxims as F2—a concept of didactic measures to interfere with learning from experience. Bernheim's book on suggestion as used by Freud we classify as F2. Frau Emmy's theories for not eating the food we classify as G2—a scientific deductive system with untouchable premises yielding infallible conclusions. Freud, with his unfailing straightness, gives a precise description of the "scientist" in G2:

> At that time I was completely under the sway of Bernheim's book on suggestion.

Freud noted that when he attempted to deal with Frau Emmy's G2—her scientific deductive system accounting for her not eating—"the explanation of mine made not the slightest impression on her." Actually, in the light of Freud's development, his being "completely under the sway of Bernheim" is F2. G2 indicates a structural rigidity significantly different from F2. Differentiating G2 from F2 is of considerable clinical importance.

An invariant in all elements of Column 2 is saturation. This invariant provides these elements with the property of being "satisfied." Note again the first interpretation reported in this paper with my first patient:

> The patient began the first conversation with a lengthy silence.
> "I thought of something I can say. . . .
> —Which indicates you've thought of something you can't say.

The interpretation attempts to draw the patient's attention to a Column 2 invariant: the patient waits until he is "satisfied" with what to say.

So far I have classified those functions which have a saturated factor as an invariant and interfere with a conversation in Column 2. I have classified also several interfering functions according to the appropriate Row on the Grid: Row A–b-elements; Row C–dreams; Row E–conception; Row F–concept; Row G–scientific deductive system. Classifying Column 2 functions according to their proper Row on the Grid makes possible a deeper understanding of the saturation valencies. Before pursuing this further, I shall put in the proper Row of the Grid some of the Column 2 elements that our two patients demonstrate. I shall describe an element in Row B and an element in Row D, two elements I did not demonstrate from Freud's work.

I classify our first patient's Pain as A2, a thing-in-itself. The second patient's pain–her headache–presents a more difficult problem, namely, where to classify hypochondriacal elements. In *A Midsummer Night's Dream*, Shakespeare describes the process of nomination, exemplified by poets, in this way:

> And as imagination bodies forth
> The forms of things unknown, the poet's pen
> Turns them to shapes, and gives to airy nothing
> A local habitation and a name.

I suggest that hypochondriasis is a kind of nomination, employing the vocabulary of body-parts and the syntax of body functions. Hypochondriasis gives to the airy nothing of the world of spirit–the non-sense inner world of human personality–a shape and local habitation. Hypochondriacal embodiment can serve as prelude to nomination, and in my experience the saturation of a hypochondriacal element is not as complete as an A2 element. Bion writes,

> Hypochondriacal symptoms may therefore be signs of an attempt to establish contact with psychic quality by substituting physical sensation for the missing sense data of psychical quality.

Hypochondriasis requires a name to indicate a variablity in saturation valency not possessed by A2 elements. I shall name hypochondriacal elements, A2 $\longleftrightarrow$ B2. A2 $\longleftrightarrow$ B2 names an element with a weaker saturation valency than A2.

At this point it may be helpful to look ahead. I am going to divide the elements of Column 2 into two sets. One set will contain the elements A2 $\longleftrightarrow$ B2 $\longleftrightarrow$ F2; the other set will contain the elements A2 $\cap$ G2. A2 $\longleftrightarrow$ B2 $\longleftrightarrow$ F2 will represent a set of Column 2 elements such that each member has a weaker saturation valency than members of the set A2 $\cap$ G2.

I classify our woman patient's headache as a hypochondriacal element, A2 $\longleftrightarrow$ B2. Her fussing three times during the night with her son's blanket tangled in his brace I classify B2. It is an α-element and makes "possible the formation and use of dream thoughts." (Bion, 1963) There is a link between the "missing" clothes supplied by the woman in the patient's dream and the blanket with which the patient supplied a proper covering for her child. The registration of this experience with her child indicates alpha function, since she subsequently made use of it in a dream. The evolution of alpha function is decisive for conversation, for alpha function signals functions in relationship. It provides the foundation for learning. It indicates a capability for intercourse and establishes the internalization of Sex. Alpha function, as nakedly as a jay-bird, announces the arrival of Sex.

The patient's "dream date" I put in C2. Her "mind" which elaborates grown-up syntax I put, tentatively, in E2, not G2. This patient has an interfering conception of verbal intercourse, yet it lacks the massiveness that is a necessary factor in a G2 scientific deductive system. Perhaps the F2 category describes her "mind" better, a concept of language which interferes with communication. The fact I want to emphasize is that interfering elements in the set A2 $\cap$ G2 have a saturation factor with a valency significantly greater than interfering elements in the set A2 $\longleftrightarrow$ B2 $\longleftrightarrow$ F2. In practice, whether an interfering element belongs in F2 or G2 can be most accurately determined, as already mentioned, through a continuing conversation. I classified Frau Emmy's "mind" exercised on the problem of not-eating as G2; under Case History, I concluded that it indicated a G2 scientific deductive system. The logician Charles Peirce gives an evolutionary description of G2 which I quote here to indicate the meaning I intend by the word "massive."

> It is terrible to see how a single unclear *idea*, a single *formula without meaning*, lurking in a young man's head, will sometimes act like an obstruction of inert matter in an artery, hindering the nutrition of the brain, and condemning its victim to pine away in the fullness of his intellectual vigour and in the midst of intellectual plenty. Many a man has cherished for years as his hobby some vague shadow of an idea, too meaningless to be positively false; he has, nevertheless, passionately loved it, has made it his companion by day and by night, and has given to it his strength and his life, leaving all other occupations for its sake, and in short has lived with it and for it, until it has become, as it were, flesh of his flesh and bone of his bone; and then he has waked up some bright morning to find it gone, clean vanished away like the beautiful Melusina of the fable,and the essence of his life gone with it. I have myself known such a man; and who can tell how many histories of circle-squarers, metaphysicians, astrologers, and what not, may not be told. . . .

I classify Rip van Winkle's sleep as G2.

I shall reclassify my patient's "mind" further on. On the basis of Peirce's description of circle-squarers and the like as paradigms of G2, her "mind" does not fit that category. For the moment I leave it in E2 or F2.

I want now to contrast the two subsets of Column 2, A2 $\cap$ G2 and A2 $\longleftrightarrow$ B2 $\longleftrightarrow$ F2, using some additional conversational material. I have indicated that the two sets reflect a difference in the saturation valency of the invariant under Column 2: the saturation factor in A2 $\cap$ G2 has a significantly higher valency. Accordingly, I classified my first patient's Pain as A2; it is a thing-in-itself that so saturates his "head" that the conversational partner has no room to enter. In fact, the aim of the partner is to "blam" something into the patient, leaving him stuck with it.

I shall present a conversation with this man which took place three years later. I shall show that the elements of the set A2 ∩ G2 are still demonstrable. However, the elements of Column 2, sub-set of Conversation, are also very much in evidence. For example, the patient's Pain no longer is only A2. It has acquired the properties of the hypochondriacal element; accordingly, I designate his Pain A2 ⟷ B2. The conversation is intended to demonstrate a set of transformations under Column 2, sub-set A2 ⟷ B2 ⟷ F2, as well as a set of transformations under A2 ∩ G2.

I cannot demonstrate the transformation of A2 to A2 ⟷ B2, which presumably had to precede the series of transformations within the new sub-set. A2 to A2 ⟷ B2 is decisively significant in dealing with the psychoses, and I am utterly in the dark as to its workings. It may be that the hypochondriacal element derives from elsewhere in the personality and does not indicate an evolution of A2. It seems to me a matter of first importance to elucidate the derivation of A2 ⟷ B2, or the dynamics of the transformation of A2 to A2 ⟷ Bs.

Before presenting the conversation, I want to say a word about the Rows of the Grid. These Rows indicate different ideational organization. As a working principle in my present work, however, I do not intend the Rows to signify a hierarchical structure. In my experience, *membership* in a sub-set is decisive, not *direction* within the set itself. For example, a dream—Row C—is neither higher or lower than Row B, alpha function. The set, A2 ⟷ B2 ⟷ F2 indicates those functions which are Transformations under Conversation. The set A2 ∩ G2 indicates those functions which are Transformations under Hallucinosis. The conversation that follows is intended to demonstrate that transformations under conversation may begin with the hypochondriacal element, A2 ⟷ B2; it also examples C2, D2, E2 and F2. I do not find that direction within the set itself is significant. However, membership in a set determines whether an element belongs under conversation or hallucinosis.

Here is the conversation; it is compressed:

"I got this gibberish in my head. Had it all morning."
—Gibberish something new?
"I think so. Noticed it the past few weeks. All this talking in my head. Makes no sense, really, but talking constantly.
—I don't understand.
"Questions pop in and then immediately the answers. Like something talking to me, but I can't stop it. It's in the way. A blockage, and I can't stop it."
—In the way of what?

"Of me! As I'm doing the chores about the place, the gibberish goes on. It's worse than a headache."
–But the gibberish, if I heard it right, let's you go on. Is that correct?
"Yea. It's not like the Pain. That just paralyzes me."
He lay silent a moment.
"The Pain feels different too lately, but I don't know how. The Pain is more . . . I don't know. It feels like a headache. Maybe it's more like a sorrow."
–Sorrow meaning an ache, a sadness?
"Yea, maybe something like that."
–So the headache is more an ache like a grief, rather than a pain.
"Hell, it's all fucked up!"
He again lay silent.
"I know that the gibberish is not the same thing as when I procrastinate."
–What's procrastinate?
"That's weird. I'll be thinking about all the things I should be getting done. Like the chores around the place. And while I'm thinking about them I think I *see* they're getting done. That's what I mean by procrastinate. It's like I'm in a dream. And that's different from the gibberish. Hell, I don't know what I'm talking about. All I know is that I'm preoccupied."
–You said the gibberish is questions popping in and then immediately the answers. What are the questions about?
"About everything, I guess."
–The chores?
"I guess. But it also gets in the way of doing the chores."
–When you procrastinate, for example, *see* the chores getting done rather than doing them–see the chores getting done as if in a dream, as you put it–does the gibberish go on as you're procrastinating?
"I guess they're kinda the same, but not exactly."
–If I understand you, I suggest the gibberish *talks* about the chores getting done, among other things it talks about, and the procrastination *sees* the chores getting done.
"Maybe that's right. The procrastinating's worse, though. It just takes over. It's like a god-damn ceremony, and you just gotta go through with it. Like the National Anthem before a football game. God-damn ceremony! You're just stuck with it. Nothing you can do about it. No way to be spontaneous!"
–Your dream, in which you dream the chores are getting done, becomes a ritual or a ceremony.
"Just feel trapped. Hell, it's all such a god-damn pain! The Pain goes on. The Pain is always there."
–The Pain you're talking about now is not the same experience as the headache which you associated with the sorrow. The Pain you're referring to now is that thing in your head.
"That's always there. But I had a strange thought the other day: I

> may be nuttier than a fruitcake, but without the Pain I wouldn't know it!"

I shall report the last part of this conversation in a moment. Three years earlier the patient had said,

> Have that deadening Pain in my head, and it's always sitting there.

I classified this element as A2. In this conversation, the patient said,

> The Pain feels different too lately, but I don't know how. The Pain is more . . . I don't know. It feels like a headache. Maybe it's more like a sorrow."

I classify the headache-sorrow as the hypochondriacal element, A2 ⟷ B2. If these designations are correct, then a transformation A2 to A2 ⟷ B2 may have occurred somewhere along the line, assuming an interrelationship. In my view, this indicates a change from Transformations under Hallucinosis to Transformations under Conversation. In my experience, the hypochondriacal element A2 ⟷ B2 had invariably evolved in those patients, however initially disturbed, in whom the analytic experience promoted development sufficiently for transformations under conversation. The difficulty is that whether one is dealing with A2 having latent A2 ⟷ B2 potential can be determined only retrospectively. The transformation of headache into ache or sorrow is extraordinarily vivid. I classify sorrow as Column 3; sorrow is an element in a more advanced set of transformations under conversation. In this session, this more developed conversational function is brief, as I shall soon show.

Except for such extreme states as Rip van Winkle's psychotic stupor or the end-times of the massive delusional state described by Peirce, conversation and hallucinosis comprise an admixture. I classified Frau Emmy as A2 ∩ G2; yet the conversational element *Emmy* emerged briefly, and a set of Transformations under Conversation became evident. My experience suggests that a quantitative factor under A2 ∩ G2 is decisive, but I do not know how to assess it. The patient certainly indicates that hallucinatory and conversational functions occur simultaneously.

The patient's conversation indicates four elements: Pain—headache—gibberish—procrastination—ceremony. I shall use the Grid to classify them. The four elements have a factor in common, namely saturation. Each element interferes with the patient, for example, gets in the way of his intent to do the chores. These interfering functions "pre-occupy" him, so that he has "no way to be spontaneous." Obviously saturation is an invariant in this set. The valency of this saturation factor is such, nonetheless, that we will classify the four elements as belonging to the sub-set of Transformations under Conversation. However, I shall take these same elements and classify them later as belonging to the sub-set of Transformations under Hallucinosis.

As a function of conversation, Pain–Headache is the hypochondriacal element, A2 ⟷ B2. Gibberish is B2. Its internal structure evidences the factor of reciprocity–questions and answers. Overall the conversation indicates unmistakably the function of reverie (Bion, 1962); reverie is the *sine qua non* of alpha function. Procrastination I classify C2, having the structure and function of a dream. Executive function is inhibited and visual factors predominate. The patient's ceremony is of particular interest. I shall classify ceremony as D2 ⟷ E2. This element may be thought of as representing a "marriage made in heaven." It is the mating of a pre-conception with a certitude. I shall refer to D2 ⟷ E2 as the element of ritual.

Before re-classifying these elements under Hallucinosis, I want to give the last part of the conversation.

> The session drew to a close. Suddenly the patient said: "So what! What the hell good is it! All right, so we know I do all that. So what! It doesn't get rid of it."
> –Oh but it does. You're *it*. And you want to get rid of what we know. We know we've been talking together. Not only that, at least from where I'm sitting, talking intimately and lively together.
> "So what!"

I classify the patient's So What as F2. It represents a concept of futility and is designed to interfere with any further conversational development. F2 represents the element of futility. F2 is designed to limit transformations under conversation to Column 2. F2 firmly shuts out such Column 3 rumblings for the patient as the element "sorrow."

This session demonstrates all elements of conversation in Column 2, including the element of hypochondriasis, the element of ritual and the element of futility. The Grid represents the sub-set of Column 2 Transformations under Conversation by:

A2 ⟷ B2 ⟷	D2 ⟷ E2 ⟶	F2.
(hypo-chon-driacal element)	(element of ritual)	(element of futility)

These same elements–Pain-Headache, gibberish, procrastination, ceremony, so what!–are also members of the sub-set of Transformations under Hallucinosis, A2 ∩ G2. A2 ∩ G2 does not represent development. The Pain which paralyzes the patient represents a beta element, not the hypochondriacal element. Under A2 ∩ G2, gibberish describes a violent and instantaneous back-and-forth "blam," as described by the patient in the first conversation. The patient speaks of the gibberish as a "blockage." Bleuler speaks of "blocking" in schizophrenia. Peirce describes an idea "lurking in a young man's head, will sometimes act like an obstruction of inert matter in an artery." The inert matter frequently consists of moral clumps produced by blam-ing, often directed against the self. The patient's explosive, "Hell, I don't know what I'm talking about!" is such a fragment of moral gibberish. Procrastination, in my judgment, is the decisive factor in the G2 element. G2, a scientific deductive system, is pure system. Its central focus is inaction. Scientific enterprise, which elaborates theories for their possible usefulness when making a future decision, is fundamentally contrary to G2 science. Freud "aimed" to do something, to feed his patient, to change through scientific effort his world. Freud acted in accordance with Bronowski's definition of science,

> Scientific knowledge is knowledge for action, not contemplation.

G2 science intends not action but ceremony. It is to be saluted, like a National Anthem, and humbly deferred to. Peirce describes the saturation which paralyzes all action of a G2 scientific deductive system:

> He has made it his companion by day and by night, and has given to it his strength and his life, leaving all other occupations for its sake, and in short has lived with it and for it, until it has become, as it were, flesh of his flesh and bone of his bone.

Early in this paper I noted "an important difference between this woman—my second patient—and the first patient: she actively does what he experiences as being done to him." Passivity in A2 ∩ G2 often indicates the high saturation valency; or "blam-ing," which interferes with action, is substituted for it.

Blam-ing is a central element in hallucinosis. I classify it A6. Transformations under Hallucinosis are largely carried out by and designed for blaming. I write this,

$$A6[A2 \cap G2] \rightarrow\cdot$$

By contrast, Transformations under Conversation, whether sub-set Column 2 or otherwise—which I have not discussed—have the element "conversing." I classify this element B6. Conversational transformations I write,

$$[A2 \longleftrightarrow B2 \longleftrightarrow F2] \longrightarrow B6.$$

It seems to me that the problem of psychoanalytic conversation, as instrumented by the Grid, can be usefully approached by an assessment of the factors that make up A6 and B6. I assume that elements of emotion have particular importance. I propose to investigate these elements in another paper in an effort to clarify further the interrelationship of A6 and B6.

I conclude that the element B6 is an invariant in conversational—or sexual—life. The element A6 is an invariant in hallucinosis.

References

Bion, W. (1962). *Learning from Experience*. (London: William Heinemann.)
—— (1963). *Elements of Psychoanalysis*. (London: William Heinemann.)
—— (1965). *Transformations*. (London: William Heinemann.)
Bleuler, E. (1911). *Dementia Praecox*. (New York: International Universities Press, 1940.)
Bronowski, J. (1965). *The Identity of Man*. (Garden City, New York: The Natural History Press.)
Freud, S. (1895). *Studies on Hysteria*. S.E., 2.
—— (1925). *An Autobiographical Study*. S.E., 20.
Peirce, C. (1955). *Philosophical Writings of Peirce*. (New York: Dover Publications, Inc.)

The Suffocating Super-Ego — *Albert Mason*

EDITOR'S NOTE: *In this contribution Doctor Mason has significantly pinpointed an internal object which is common to psychotics, asthmatics, and other psychosomatic patients. He believes the object causes claustrophobic anxiety and is characterized by omnipotence, omniscience, and omnipresence by virtue of the projective identification of omnipotence generally and of the qualities of the sense organs particularly into an object which is thus internalized in this awesome manner. In particular he believes that the fragmentation which leads to psychosis is the result of an anxiety which is a psychic equivalent to the panic experienced when respiratory function is threatened. In a separate contribution I wrote about the* magus *which I believed to be an internal object characterized by eerie, sphinx-like sorcerer qualities and composed of the projective identification of the epistemophilic instinct from the patient. I believe Doctor Mason is describing the same or similar object from another vantage point and is thereby casting a rich clinical light on a powerful internal enemy.*

The Suffocating Super-Ego: Psychotic Break and Claustrophobia

A.A. Mason

Introduction

This paper is an expression of gratitude to Dr. Wilfred R. Bion who supervised the first psychotic patient I treated by psychoanalysis eighteen years ago. His support and understanding helped me to complete a successful analysis of that case. This encouraged me to continue the psychoanalytic treatment of psychosis in ten further cases, eight of which continued analysis unto completion.

One of the findings of this experience is presented here with the hope that another generation of analysts might be encouraged to pursue the treatment and investigation of these disorders.

The Suffocating Super-Ego: Psychotic Break and Claustrophobia

This paper has arisen from my experience with two different clinical problems: First, the acute psychotic breakdown arising spontaneously or in the course of psychoanalysis. Second, the treatment of claustrophobia.

I found at times that these two apparently separate clinical problems unexpectedly turned out to be different facets of a similar problem. Patients who develop psychotic breaks suffered anxieties, symptoms, and defenses which had a marked similarity to those experienced by patients who had been treated for acute claustrophobic anxiety. Similarly, these claustrophobic patients frequently developed symptoms and anxieties of a psychotic nature. This, quite often, was especially noticeable when the claustrophobic anxiety diminished.

Detailed examination of the core dynamics of both these groups of patients has led me to believe that at times claustrophobia arises as the result of a defensive action against a psychotic breakdown, and a central issue is the type of super-ego structure present. It is to this particular super-ego quality that the substance of this paper is addressed.

The Super-Ego

The upright stance and the development of speech, along with the presence of the super-ego is one of the attributes of man that has raised him above the animal kingdom. This structure is responsible for his conscience, his morals, his ethics, his religion, and his esthetics. It is the source of all his spiritual aspirations and endeavors. However, the super-ego has also a side that becomes man's enemy, for as well as protecting and inspiring him, it punishes, tortures, reviles, and can destroy him. In fact, a great deal of our life is spent either in following the dictates of the super-ego or attempting with varied success to escape them. Freud (1923), who first described the super-ego, called it the heir to the Oedipus complex, its derivative, and its substitute. A child between the age of three and five, faced with the impossibility of his Oedipal wishes, because of his love for his parents and his fear of punishment, permanently incorporates and installs these parents inside his mind. This internal image of them has now become an internal object, which continues to live and act inside the child's mind, controlling, threatening, or punishing it whenever its Oedipal wishes attempt to make themselves known.

Melanie Klein (1933) continued Freud's investigation into the nature of the super-ego and her work expanded our understanding of it through her exploration of the early processes of introjection and projection. She developed Freud's idea that Oedipal super-ego was an installation of the image of the parents in the ego, and showed that this internal structure grew continuously by additional introjections from the outside world. Mrs. Klein also showed that the introjections which form the super-ego were not simply reflections of external reality, but contained also the child's projections into them. Thus the objects which formed the super-ego were a composite of external reality plus infantile projections.

Once this point was accepted, we came to realize that the infant's own contributions to the nature of its super-ego are as important and at times more important than those of the external world. Freud himself was puzzled by the exaggerated and distorted image the child had of his parents, and never satisfactorily explained it. Freud's view of the harshness of the super-ego was based on three ideas: 1) It was due to the individual's harsh aggressiveness turned against himself. 2) It was a continuation of the severity of the external authority. 3) It was based on the primal-horde father of prehistoric times. Mrs. Klein drew our attention to the early feelings of the child which are violent, uncontrolled and often too terrifying to contain. These feelings are then treated in the way that the child treats all frightening and intolerable internal states, and that is to project them into the outside world and into its objects.

The success of this manoeuvre is, however, limited; for at times the external terrors can themselves become so overwhelming that the child now re-introjects them in an attempt to control them. This process of projection and introjection and reprojection and reintrojection may be repeated over and over again in an attempt to deal with internal and external persecution. The formation of the super-ego is one result of this defensive process. The normal super-ego becomes the controlling agent of the dangerous id impulses-but the abnormal, or excessively destructive super-ego, i.e., that super-ego containing the infant's destructive projections, becomes itself felt as dangerous and as persecuting as the impulses it is supposed to control. Many disastrous consequences may follow in the presence of such a persecuting super-ego and the internal dynamics are reminiscent of the nationwide students' rebellion of the late 60s and early 70s. The students, under the belief that the establishment was oppressive and would not give them their due, or even listen to them, marched against their own colleges, smashing, looting, and destroying. The colleges and police attempted to suppress them, often using great force and violence. This produced even greater explosions of rage and frustration from the students and the situation grew increasingly violent and uncontrolled. One could say that psychosis had taken over.

When the super-ego is felt to be harsh and persecutory, it, too, may lead to a revolution of the ego and id impulses that are being crushed by it. A breakdown or breakup of the personality may follow where parts of the ego and the id are fragmented and projected with great violence. Sometimes the super-ego itself becomes the victim of the rebellion and is thrown out of office and projected into the outside world. When these fragmentations and projections occur clinically, they manifest themselves as psychotic breaks of a schizophrenic or manic type. This process has been described fully by Rosenfeld (1952). In attempting to avoid and in the treatment of this catastrophe, it is imperative to understand the nature of the formation of the persecutory super-ego, so that one can modify it, and the effects it produces.

The literature contains many papers that describe the severe, harsh, murderous and persecuting nature of the super-ego. In particular, those of Mrs. Klein (1926): She put forward that the super-ego existed much earlier than Freud described, and dated it at the beginning of the Oedipus complex and not as the heir to it. She also dated the Oedipus complex itself at the weaning stage of infancy.

This early super-ego is formed by the introjection of terrifying figures produced in fantasy by the child's sadistic impulses toward its object. In "The Psychoanalysis of Children," Klein (1932) suggested that introjection begins at birth and the incorporated object immediately assumes the function of a super-ego.

In 1952, she added to her concept of the super-ego as a persecutor by describing in great detail the formation of the envious super-ego.

In 1957, she had a change of view and stated that the super-ego develops with the two instincts, life and death, in a state of fusion and that the terrifying internal figures which result from intense destructiveness do not form part of the super-ego proper. They exist in a separate area, in the deep unconscious where they remain unintegrated and unmodified by normal processes of growth. These terrifying figures may in situations of stress infiltrate and overwhelm the ego. Mrs. Klein suggested that in the splitting-off of these frightening figures, defusion of the life and death instincts is in the ascendency and these extremely bad figures are not accepted by the ego. She also related these persecuting objects to dead and injured objects. (Meltzer [1969] elaborates on this aspect of the super-ego introjects later.)

Whether these early and terrifying figures are called primitive super-ego or are seen as totally apart from the super-ego, I fully agree with her idea that the presence of anything which strengthens them or allows them to in-infiltrate the rest of the mind is an important factor in psychotic breakdown.

My own observations suggest that there is something in the quality of these early internal figures that needs further elaboration. As Mrs. Klein wrote in her paper on the early development of the conscience, "The child's fear of his objects will always be proportionate to the degree of his own sadistic impulses. It is not, however, simply a question of converting a given amount of sadism into a corresponding amount of anxiety. The relation is one of *content* as well." The particular aspect of this content which I have observed cannot be described simply and I will attempt to explain it by describing several of its facets. One such facet has been studied extensively by Rosenfeld (1965), Meltzer (1973) and Bion (1959) and may be described as omnipotent, omniscient, and omnipresent. The common factor is the word "omni" meaning "all," thus: all-powerful, all-knowing, all-present. This super-ego quality creates a sensation in the mind of being watched by eyes from which nothing can escape. These eyes are cruel, penetrating, inhuman and untiring. They record without mercy, pity, or compassion. They follow relentlessly and judge remorselessly. No escape is possible for there is no place to shelter. Their memory is infinite and their threat is nameless. The punishment when it comes will be swift, poisonous and ruthless. An important effect of the omnipotent super-ego is the production of feelings of hopelessness which can result in either suicide or psychosis.

The hopelessness is engendered particularly by the feeling that the merciless, implacable quality of the internal watcher cannot be defied. Struggle against it is useless and resistance is futile. Added to this feeling of being constantly watched and threatened there is also the sense of being acutely listened to, smelled, and even having one's thoughts read, which gives some idea of the terror and hopelessness produced. These sensations create in the subject of their implacable scrutiny a feeling of being totally surrounded by irresistible forces which close in on them from all sides like the Iron of medieval tortures or the contracting room of Poe's "The Pit and the Pendulum." This particular form of persecution may not only cause a feeling of hopelessness in the subject, because of the belief engendered that no escape is possible, but the crushing and suffocating quality also produces panic and explosion, in a desperate attempt to escape, even at the cost of disintegration, The internal effect of the omniscient suffocating super-ego could be likened to an attack of acute claustrophobia of the mind.

Meltzer described the quality of paranoid anxiety that I am concerned with as terror, and believes it to be due to dead objects, particularly dead internal babies. Meltzer believes that the anxiety produced by these dead internal babies has an inescapable quality. He also described one outcome of the terror, which is a submission to the tyranny of a bad part of the self which promises to protect one against the terror. I fully agree with Meltzer about the importance of the inescapable quality of persecution of the super-ego but in addition to the consequences described by him believe that it is this very quality of the terror that produces anxiety of an explosive kind, which is extremely important in the formation of psychotic breaks. Moreover, I believe that when panic and psychotic breaks occur, it is because the persecution has become worse than inescapable, it has become suffocating and devouring. It therefore produces a violent reaction equivalent to that which occurs when respiratory obstruction or the fear of being eaten is experienced by any living organism, particularly as these two anxieties often occur simultaneously.

What are the roots of this implacable monster? The answer surely must originate in the equally implacable phantasies of the helpless infant, who is in reality so weak and so totally unable to defend himself, that his only weapon is his mind, aided by his organs of perception. So, all-powerful, originally, means the infant's all-powerful phantasies directed toward its primary object, the mother, or her breast. The child's controlling phantasies are strengthened by the use of a particular omnipotent mechanism described by Mrs. Klein (1958) as projective identification, where parts of the self are projected into the object, for many purposes, particularly to possess and control the object.

Mrs. Klein described the use of oral, urethral, and anal phantasies for this purpose. I believe that in addition to this, the organs of perception are of particular significance in this mechanism. The senses such as hearing, seeing, and smelling can all be used in phantasy to put parts of the self into the object as distinct from receiving perceptual stimuli from the object. This now imparts to the phantasy a controlling quality of great power. This process was first described by Bion (1958) in "On Hallucination." The capacities to see the object at a distance, to watch its every movement, to follow it around with one's eyes, all strongly support the feelings of omnipotent control. One even has the capacity to shut it out, i.e., annihilate it, by closing one's eyes, and bringing it back by opening one's eyes and letting in the light, just like God. The mere blink of an eye creates or destroys in phantasy one's objects. "Let there by Light!"

Hearing, too, can support phantasies of omniscience powerfully, not only because it supports sight, but also because it can function in the dark when sight is not possible. Hearing the parents speak, thus always knowing where they are and what they are about. Hearing them in bed and in intercourse all support phantasies of taking part in these activities, invading them and controlling them. The open door of the child's bedroom permits phantasies of control by hearing, as the night light gives it phantasies of control by seeing. Smell, too, allows the belief of taking part in the mother's activities, and the capacity to smell the breast is probably present from the beginning of life. Later on, smelling other bodily secretions can give the infant the belief that it is in contact with the intimate parts of the parents' bodies.

I see you, I hear you, I smell you, really means I touch you with my eyes, ears, and nose, and if I touch you I can hold, possess, and control you. In addition to these manoeuvres, there is also the phantasy of getting inside the mother with the senses; and seeing, hearing, and smelling take on the additional significance of knowing. To "know you," to "know about you," to "know all about you," contains always the phantasy of power and control over "the object." "Knowing," in this kind of phantasy means more than being acquainted with, it means in possession of. Knowing in Biblical terms means carnal knowledge, i.e., intercourse, and the knowing I am describing is very close to this in sense. It implies a penetration of the most intimate parts of the object, and therefore in phantasy controlling and possessing the object. "I see you," "I know you," "I know all about you," "I possess you": if one says and listens to these words, the sense and feel of their underlying phantasies become plain to us. "Knowledge" becomes power indeed in the child's mind.

I have already mentioned oral, anal, and urethral phantasies of affecting and controlling the object and would like to expand again on the quality of these phantasies. The child's cries are meant to affect the mother, but often in phantasy are meant to do much more than that. The piercing, the penetrating cry associated with the phantasy of control, and often the phantasy of projecting parts of the self into the object is believed and hoped by the helpless infant to possess and tie his mother to him. "I hear and I obey" is the phantasy counterpart that we and the object are meant to respond with. Sometimes the object does respond in just that fashion, following its own unconscious hope that when in the past it called imperiously or desperately, it had to be answered. The stark realistic fact that no one may be there, or even that if they are, they are not compelled to answer, is too frightening for the immature ego to tolerate. There is no single word that describes these invasive voyeuristic, listening and smelling phantasies, but when I describe invasive voyeuristic control, I am implying that senses other than sight may be used, sometimes separately and sometimes together, in the service of possessive invasion of the object.

The function of stools and urine in controlling the object is well-documented, but I would like to add a note about the phantasies that stools and urine are frequently felt to be the object or part-objects themselves. The thumb-sucking child, as Freud (1941) observed, has the hallucinatory wish-fulfillment that he possesses the breast or, as he wrote in his last words "*is* the breast." Mrs. Klein, expanded Freud's idea, and would have said that the child utilizing the phantasy of projective identification has projected its empty mouth into the breast and taken possession of the nipple, which it now holds in phantasy in its thumb, and can administer to itself. This nipple possessed and surrounded by the child's mouth, trapped and controlled, in fact virtually devoured, will later, when introjected into the ego, become a super-ego component which will be felt to surround, trap, devour and suffocate the child's personality in phantasy, producing the internal claustrophobia and acute psychotic breaks previously described.

Each of the three claustrophobic patients I have treated demonstrated marked oral fixation. One sucked his thumb from early babyhood to the age of 19, when he replaced it with cigarettes. Another could not be detached from her bottle and comforter until the age of 6 or 7. Even today, at the age of 57, she cannot venture out without candy, pills or breath mints in her bag, which still comfort and protect her.

The constipated stool may be similarly phantasied as the trapped nipple, felt to be now devoured and held and controlled, sometimes sadistically, in the rectum. Later, when it is introjected and installed as a super-ego component, it returns its former treatment to the infant's mind "with a vengeance." A patient had the following dream while suffering from an acute bout of constipation. "The King and Queen of England were held prisoner in the Tower of London in a dark airless dungeon. I would watch them through a small hole and think 'How have the mighty fallen.' One day, I went to see them and found they had been released—the dungeon was now filled with sun and air and was empty. I knew with a feeling of dread and panic that it could only be a question of time before they returned to become the head of the State and would throw me into an even deeper dungeon from which I could never escape."

These physical activities of sucking, crying, urinating, and defecating, and many others are thus added to the sensory activities, looking, hearing, etc., described previously, and together with phantasies of omnipotent and omniscient control help the child modify its feelings of extreme helplessness in relationship to its object.

The phantasies all give it the belief that the movements and life, inner and outer, of the mother are monitored, watched, and controlled, i.e., virtually devoured. In fact, the object is felt to be so trapped that not even a breath can be taken without the child's wishing it to be so. It is particularly this feeling, of not being able to breathe, which adds a quality of panic and desperation to the persecution that is conducive to fragmentation and breakdown.

It is certain that the infant's early perception of its primary object is not only a breast and nipple, but something that has the sound and movements of a living organism, particularly the sound and movements of respiration, as the child is held so closely to the mother's chest a great deal of the time.

When phantasies of controlling this primary object occur, they may become linked initially to phantasies of controlling the respiratory movements as well. I believe that this quality of breathing control, plus the quality of devouring the object, when re-introjected and installed as a super-ego component, adds to the already suffocating anxiety produced by the omniscient and voyeuristic components of the super-ego previously described. These four components—omniscience, voyeurism, devouring phantasies and breathing control—together make for a suffocating quality which is the cause of intense internal anxiety and which produces the tendency to rupture and explode.

Now, there are eyes, ears, and a nose inside of oneself, watching acutely over one's every movement and hearing one's every sound as well as a mouth holding one trapped and ready to swallow one. Added to all this is an omniscient quality which penetrates into one's deepest layers, knowing all about one's every activity, and holding one trapped and suffocated by this knowledge. This internal figure reminiscent of Orwell's Big Brother in the novel

1984 watches, and threatens continuously and also suffocates as it prevents any movement.

It is this feeling of having no freedom, no exit, no escape, that simulates the feeling of being unable to breathe, the mental equivalent of which, like all sensations of respiratory obstruction produces a violent panic, internal rupture and explosion—the psychotic break. Therefore, it is the roots of this feeling, i.e., the infant's intense, suffocating, omniscient, controlling and devouring phantasies and activities toward the object, and toward the analyst in the transference, which have to be minutely analyzed for relief to be obtained. I believe Bion hinted at this in *Elements of Psychoanalysis* (1963).

When the intrapsychic strain caused by the suffocating super-ego becomes intolerable, psychotic break due to fragmentation of the ego is probably the most extreme consequence that may follow. Other consequences or what may be called defenses against this strain that I have observed are as follows:

1. The use of drugs of all sorts, to blanket and dull the persecution of the super-ego. In fact, many drug addicts originally became addicted because they used their drugs as a self-administered treatment of the anxiety produced by the persecution of their super-ego. One could say that the addict who takes drugs to deal with the intolerable inner-tension caused by a suffocating super-ego is effecting the kind of therapy for himself that he often would get if he went for psychiatric treatment. Sometimes the drugs administered by psychiatrists are less harmful than those self-administered, but at times they are identical. Alcohol, heroin, the hypnotics and barbiturates are used frequently by patients for this purpose. It follows that taking these patients off drugs without adequate analysis of the persecutory anxiety will not only be futile, but will at times actually precipitate psychosis. It is even worse for some of these patients to be taken off drugs and confined to a hospital or prison, as this compounds the feeling of claustrophobia by adding a real external suffocation to the internal one. In such situations not only is psychosis a danger, but suicide may be attempted in a desperate endeavor to escape their terrifying feelings of suffocation.

2. The all-seeing, all-knowing super-ego may be projected into outer-space where it becomes the "God of Wrath" of the Old Testament. Presumably He can then be handled more easily by worship, placation, or merely because there is now more distance between Him and the self. I believe that the religious conversions experienced by many adolescents in particular are their attempts at solution of the suffocating tension suffered by them through their primitive super-ego. This religious conversion is sometimes an alternative to the drug solution, sometimes it accompanies the use of drugs, and sometimes it supersedes it.

One of my patients became extremely religious and orthodox during adolescence: in his words, "more orthodox than the priests." During his infancy, he was extremely controlling to his maternal object, both through direct demands and a chronic psychosomatic illness. Among his first words as a child were "get it" accompanied by an imperiously pointing finger. During adolescence he spent years "getting it" for God and being frightened and depressed if he felt that he had failed to please Him in any of His wishes. His psychosomatic illness was asthma, which trapped his mother at times in phantasy and fact, and then in turn, following projection and reintrojection, trapped him inside his own chest.

3. Fragmentation and projection of the super-ego into the patient's objects can also occur. This results in persecution of the "ideas of reference" type. The belief that one's mind is being read, that one is being controlled at a distance, that one is being hypnotized, all can be the result of the projection of the omniscient voyeuristic super-ego into one's objects and experiencing the "all knowing control" now being in them and being exerted toward oneself.

Two patients of mine occasionally projected their suffocating super-ego into their spouses. When this occurred, they both experienced intense feelings of suffocation when in contact with their wives. One could not bear any physical contact with his wife at all. Love-making was impossible and panic producing, and even sleeping in the same room was difficult to tolerate. His wife's breasts were experienced as "buffeting his face" and he had to break away dyspneic and panic stricken. He had been a thumb sucker until the age of 19–trapping and "suffocating" the nipple in his mouth constantly. His bouts of promiscuity with "unknown" women and even occasional homosexual episodes were totally in the service of escape from the feelings of suffocation that his wife's body produced. On analysis it could be demonstrated that she had become the receptacle into which his suffocating infantile mouth had been projected. This patient's anxieties seemed to date from as far back as feeding during infancy for according to his mother he would choke when he fed from her breast until her doctor adviced the use of a nipple shield through which her nipple protruded during feeding. When I recall how this patient would thrust his way into my office, sometimes bumping into me on the way: and how his voice bored into my head and his eyes penetrated me with a steely blue glance, I had little doubt that the nipple shield prevented him from asphyxiation because of his invasive thrusting into the breast. I often longed for the psychic equivalent of a nipple shield during sessions when he bore into my mind. From the patient's point of view the thrust was experienced the other way round, and he complained about my thrusting interpretations down his throat, and recalls how his mother "cornered" him in the morning with a bowl of corn flakes, and how suffocated he felt by her "pushing the food at him."

Another patient spent his weekends as a "cowboy"–roaming freely on the prairies, imagining he was free from any responsibilities, wife and children, all of whom made him feel asphyxiated. At times he became suffocated by the smog of the city and would drive furiously into the country to be able to breathe freely.

This patient had a long history of intensely possessive behavior toward his mother and many years of chronic constipation. When analyzed, his stools in phantasy were sometimes the breast and nipple of the maternal object, and sometimes the father's penis, swallowed or taken in per anum and trapped and held in his rectum. When he had periods of diarrhea, the trapped nipple and penis in phantasy were now expelled and experienced as either "smog" in the air or earthquakes on the ground threatening him. Both these phobias produced intense claustrophobic anxiety and attempts to run out of town and away from them.

On one occasion, I believe a psychotic break was narrowly averted by the analysis of his failure to pay his bill, which was unconsciously equated with trapping me in his "bank-rectum." He simultaneously developed great anxiety and persecution about the demands of his wife, children, and business, particularly in terms of financial demands, and felt annihilated and suffocated by them. He felt driven mad and talked about suicide as an escape from these impossible debts and demands.

It was finally the analysis of his withholding of money from me and the phantasies of what this was doing to me which enabled him to pay his bill, i.e., let go of me and a subsequent diminution of internal and external persecutory tension resulted.

A third patient who projected her super-ego into me during a session jumped out of my second floor window in a panic, as she felt too acutely suffocated to get out of the house by the slower route of stairs and door. She had been an extremely controlling child, mainly using illness to attach her mother to her. She also had a history of being four weeks in an incubator after birth, having been born prematurely. She had many memories and dreams, all describing an intense and controlling attitude toward breast, chest, and respiratory movements of her maternal object in me. Frequent dreams of persecution contained large animals breathing heavily which pursued her. Although there was a sexual element in the heavy breathing, it was also a return of a persecutor which now attacked her with its breathing. Internally she frequently experienced her own feelings to be too heavy and too violent to bear; this produced feelings of suffocation and panic. (Compare Dora [Freud, 1905] who also had asthma and was intensely controlling to her objects, maternal and paternal.)

4. Another common consequence of the suffocating super-ego is the production of the familiar symptom of claustrophobia.

Freud (1900) described a phobia as a projection and displacement onto an external object of inner conflicts which are causing a disturbance in the ego, so that the danger of developing anxiety now threatened not from the direction of an instinctual impulse but from the direction of a perception.

Melanie Klein (1946) related claustrophobic anxiety to the fear of being imprisoned inside the mother, following phantasies of invading and attacking the mother's body, using the mechanism of projective identification. Joan Riviere (1948) spoke of claustrophobia as due to a fear of retaliation following projective attacks on the object. Gehl (1964) linked claustrophobia to depression and en passant to paranoia and drug addiction, although he does not spell out the details. He does, however, confirm my own observations about the common occurrence of asthma and respiratory habits in conjunction with claustrophobia. My view that claustrophobia is both an internal state linked to persecutory super-ego phantasies of a suffocating nature and an external state brought about by the projection of this super-ego into an external claustrum encompasses and develops both Freud's and Klein's ideas. Klein seems to be describing a consequence following the projection of a split off part of the self into an object. She does not continue with the consequences of this primitive phantasy when the object is now introjected and forms part of the super-ego.

The claustrophobia I am describing, i.e., that due to the projection of the suffocating super-ego into an external claustrum, is a much more organized and detailed phantasy when analysed clinically. The claustrums commonly used are planes, elevators, crowds, cinemas, dentists, hairdryers, etc. All these things in external reality which of themselves can shut in and hold one confined can have the persecuting element of suffocation added to them by the projection into them of the super-ego qualities previously described. One claustrophobic patient once actually heard his father's voice in his head admonishing him, and after shaking his head "saw" his father's stern face in the outline of a mountain. This produced extreme feelings of being trapped and threatened by the mountainside and caused him to drive away in panic. Just as having one's God outside, it is no doubt more tolerable to have one's claustrophobia outside. There, one can attempt to flee from it, while if it is inside, it is inescapable.

5. In 1960, while conducting a research project for the Asthma Research Council of Great Britain on the psychotherapeutic treatment of asthma, I noted (1962) that three patients treated by me converted to claustrophobic anxieties after the remission of their asthmatic symptoms. The symptomatology changed from their chests to their minds, but the anxiety of being suffocated remained the same.

Since then, I have analysed four asthmatic patients and have noted that there were strong oral fixations in three of them. All had great difficulty in separation from their primary object, the breast. Later in their lives, the breast became equated with their inhalers which they also could not be separated from and which they carried constantly with them, trapped in their mouths or pockets. This "breast-inhaler" in its turn, after introjection, trapped them mentally as a super-ego component. It was then projected into their bronchi where it changed into asthmatic attacks which now suffocated them physically. Consequently, I believe that some asthmatics, particularly those characterized by broncho-spasm as distinct from swelling of the bronchial mucosa, fall somewhere in between the claustrophobias and the psychoses.

A conclusion of these findings would therefore be that the occurrence of certain types of asthma (consequence 5), the production of claustrophobia (consequence 4), like the worship of God (consequence 3), the production of paranoia (consequence 2), or the use of drugs (consequence 1), can all be defenses against psychosis. It also follows that extreme caution must be exercised in the analytic treatment of claustrophobia, as the return to the patient of those parts of the self projected out in defense may produce acute psychosis. The underlying anxiety must be elucidated, interpreted, and traced back to its origins, for the projected aspects of the personality to be accepted back safely. This is also true of all patients in whom psychotic breakdown is a danger.

I would also like to differentiate between the anxiety produced by the particular suffocating super-ego quality I have described, and the discomfort experienced whenever any form of concrete thinking is present in the patient.

Concrete thinking frequently arises as a result of the use of massive projective identification by the patient. When concretization is present, fusion with the object is also present in phantasy, and the mind does not think *about* the object, it thinks the object instead. Instead of the infant thinking *about* the breast, its thoughts *are* the breast. This omnipotent phantasy that the thoughts are the object produces a subjective feeling in the mind of a space occupying lesion. In contrast, thinking which is an abstract phenomenon does not produce the feeling of something literally present. The mind which literally thinks the breast becomes squeezed out of existence by the breast it has omnipotently produced. Subjectively this often produces a very uncomfortable feeling which is described variously as a pain in the head, a headache, a stuffed feeling, or other statements indicating the feeling of having two objects competing for one space. Sometimes a feeling of drowsiness is present, confusion is common, and associated symptoms of depersonalisation, unreality and deja vu phenomena are often present. In the most severe cases fragmentation and projection of this state of mind can occur. The patient typically cannot symbolise and literal thinking in which thoughts are felt to be identical with physical actions is present. Segal (1957) described this in her paper "A Note on Symbol Formation."

In contrast, the feeling accompanying the suffocating super-ego is invariably associated with a trapped sensation. The distress is similar to that produced by respiratory obstruction, accompanied by a wish to break out or break loose, panic frequently supervening. Concrete ideation is usually absent. The patient typically is anxious, distressed and agitated, cannot stay in one place and feels that he is jumping out of his skin.

Case History 1

This is a case history of a male, age 38, who is married with two children, a boy and a girl, who by profession is a pathologist and an experienced amateur astronomer. The patient's daytime life is spent staring down through lenses examining earthly bodies and his nighttime life is spent staring up through lenses observing heavenly bodies. In addition to these two "legitimate" voyeuristic activities, he is a movie buff with a decided predilection for pornography. There his voyeuristic activities are clearly concerned with the feelings of excitement he obtains as a result of the power and triumph he experiences watching forbidden and hidden secrets.

He is generally very concerned with sensual gratification of all kinds. He considers himself to be a fine cook, a wine taster, and avidly collects music records. His preoccupation with sensuality extends into his sexual activities which were compulsively promiscuous and casual. His partners were pursued with great initial excitement, and discarded rapidly after conquest. These women were all described at first in the same way as being bright, pretty, exciting, great in bed, and then after two or three sessions of sex they became a bore, a drag, demanding and dry. This dryness was also descriptive of their vaginas, which hurt and abraded his penis.

His penile skin problem was the last remnant of an infantile eczema once serious, but now confined to his penis and occasional flexures. His sexual activities focused a great deal on voyeurism, which was more exciting to him than the actual intercourse. His other complaints included severe allergies, mainly of an upper-respiratory nature which had been present much of his life, and for which he medicated himself continuously. He used a decongestant nasal spray once or twice almost every hour of his life. He also suffered from a serious lifelong hypochondriasis, at times of a delusional nature and at other times over-laying his real physical symptoms of skin rashes and allergic conditions. He had increasing anxieties regarding the loss of his potency in recent years; plus feelings of futility which at times progressed to hopelessness and deep depression.

He had a distinguished professional career with many honors and original achievements but was nevertheless totally dissatisfied with his life and accomplishments. His wife was not good enough for him, his children were not good enough for him and he himself was the worst of all in his own eyes. Nothing lived up to his expectations physically, mentally, professionally, or sexually.

His wife, who had been devoted and long suffering was beginning to come to the end of her patience with his demands, complaints, and sexual excursions which, in spite of his attempts to conceal, were discovered from time to time.

The dominant feature of his analysis was his preoccupation with his body, which was matched only by his preoccupation with his mind and the details of his analysis. He had spent fifteen years of his life being in analysis and has been my patient for the last five of these. The preoccupation with his body, his mind and his analysis went hand in hand with a dissatisfaction with all of them which was as profound as his fascination.

Unless he is interrupted the patient will spend the whole session discussing a particular complaint. If he experiences a pain in the neck he will describe in great detail: where it originates, the kind of pain it is, how frequently the attacks occur, how it affects his posture, the possible structures involved including bone, muscle, tendon, nerve, viscera, etc. In fact, he gives one a total differential diagnosis of neck pain. If I interrupt his minute preoccupation he complains that I am not listening. If I do not interrupt he complains that I am doing nothing for him.

The minute preoccupation and portentous predictions will suddenly vanish overnight, only to be replaced in a day or so with a similar complaint and preoccupation with ears, throat, rectum, duodenum, testicles, or whatever is the organ for the week. This obsessive scrutiny also occurs in relationship to his sexual, social or professional behavior. How did he behave at a dinner party last night? Did his joke fall flat? Did somebody smirk, did he stare too long at someone's wife or at her breasts? Was his behavior too obsequious or too aggressive or too seductive? When he talks about work reports they are always too long, too short, too clever, too obscure, or too something.

This immense time and energy devoted to the microscopic examination of himself was paralleled by an equally microscopic examination of his objects and me. He would comment after looking intently at me on my looks, my office, my voice, my interpretations, my general appearance, my humor and my state of mind. He would lie down and then comment on the couch being either too hot or too cold or too damp. He would comment that I had body odor today or perhaps my aftershave was too sweet. Sometimes he complained about my abdominal noises or told me to stop swallowing as it interfered with his thinking. At times he was convinced that he could even hear me blinking.

He paid particular attention to my breathing, its frequency and depth, etc., and on several occasions said that it prevented him from thinking, as the sound bored into his head. He would time my respirations and occasionally had to leave the office, as he claimed that he couldn't stand the sound or sight of them. My office was as closely scrutinized as I was and he would comment that it would smell of coffee or soup or bananas or other indescribable odors which were sometimes good and sometimes bad.

He boasted and suffered equally from hyperacute eyes, ears, nose, and skin. Sometimes his perceptions were accurate, usually they were exaggerated, at times they were frankly delusional. He projected into reality, constantly finding a little piece of something real and enlarging it monstrously by some projection, making a mountain out of a molehill.

As his real observations stretched into the delusional, his observations in the mental sphere did the same, for while he picked up small idiosyncrasies about me and other people, which were no doubt accurate, he stretched them in a way to support his omnipotent phantasies. He firmly believed he had a capacity to pick up extrasensory perceptions which then enabled him to know what people were thinking, and this belief shaded imperceptibly into supernatural ideas. The converse of this was also true, and at times he thought people could see what was in his mind or knew what he was thinking, and this shaded into the fear that they could affect or control him at a distance. He was also frightened of being controlled by me and others through the use of hypnotism.

Over the years it has become possible to reconstruct a picture of the patient as an infant, a child, and as an adult, who attempts, and at times succeeds, in exerting minute control over his objects. There also seems to be little doubt that his mother was over-anxious and spent a great deal of time ministering to his needs, both physical and mental. He learned with great skill the particular areas in which he could control her and his phantasies of omnipotent control were most effectively supported through the media of his illnesses. This technique was clearly much more successful than being good, bad, compliant, seductive or clever, all of which he had tried in turn.

The efficacy of illness in its power to chain one's loved objects securely to one is presumably through the attendant anxiety, guilt, and concern it stimulates in turn. Utilizing his skin, sinuses, middle ear, throat, and bowels he produced for himself a mother that had to become a nurse of great devotion and enslavement to him. His stools also played a large part in the obsessional controlling of his objects, and enemas were performed frequently, often being administered by both parents who would pay great attention to color, consistency, frequency, etc.

In the transference his behavior was likewise aimed at controlling and preoccupying me in his phantasy to the exclusion of everything else in my life. At times his obsessive scrutiny plus his invasive questioning had a curious way of assaulting my mind. He would make particularly evocative statements interspersed with subtle non-sequiturs, which gave me a sense of acute confusion. Sometimes he would evoke several conflicting ideas simultaneously producing a feeling of great uncertainty about what to say. These manoeuvres had the effect of causing me to feel oppressed, invaded, or suffocated, to wish to stop listening, or to terminate the session, or at times frankly to run away from contact with the patient.

The introjection of an object in which he had produced this effect no doubt played a large part in his own internal persecution of a claustrophobic nature. His phantasies of controlling me outside the session did work at times, as he could project into me anxieties bizarre enough and ominous enough to have just that effect. He knew only too well the signs and symptoms of every rare and malignant disease known to man, and would frequently leave me with the lingering doubt and anxiety that on this occasion I was going to miss the "big one," as he put it, and that while I was busy interpreting he was busy dying.

He also enlisted friends and colleagues who supported his anxiety about subtle symptoms and agreed that he could be affected by viral conditions, hypoglycemic conditions, hyper and hypothyroid conditions, various internal hernias, etc. As well as using his eminent physician friends, he frequently made hints of legal revenge which amplified his capacity to worry, control, and invade one's peace of mind.

In addition to his somatic versatility he attempted to control with his psychical productions, particularly by the use of dreams in sessions. According to the patient these were always strange, interesting, or fascinating, and indeed they always did succeed in being unusual either in content or form. If the patient had no physical symptom, he could always be counted on to bring a dream "unlike any we had ever heard before." I suspected that somewhere he had a storehouse of dreams for all seasons. They could be counted on to test or confirm the theories of Freud or Klein alike. They were doubtless present-day equivalents to the stools that he produced as a child, and it was difficult, even forewarned, to prevent oneself from being as engaged and occupied by his dreams today, as doubtless his parents had been in the past with his bowel functions.

Historically the patient had probably succeeded in producing in fact what he envisaged in phantasy—a mother tied to him in every conceivable way. Her capacity for a life free from him was not possible. On the few occasions when she escaped his control, her mind in phantasy and probably in fact, was invaded and preoccupied with him, so that he believed he was present in her life at all times. Even when she was with his father, he nonetheless presumed he was always there taking part in all their activities, sexual or otherwise.

In many dreams the patient appeared as a spider sitting in the center of a web and pulling into himself the helpless flies. These in phantasy were his mother and father, or myself in the transference, that he had trapped and hung as living food supplies, to be sucked dry at his leisure. On introjection, these omnipotently controlled parents formed a super-ego which gave him as little peace as he had given them. He felt observed all the time, with every action controlled and followed. He felt continuously scrutinized and measured against tremendous expectations. Is he doing too much, is it too little, is it good enough, and it never is! As he felt he had read their thoughts and minds, so his internal persecuting parents read his every thought. He had no place to hide, there was no leaf under which he could disappear. His sexual life too was exposed to them, and subject in his phantasies to their critical and disapproving gaze, which produced anxieties and failures in his performance. At times this super-ego became so constrictive and suffocating that he would become explosive in an attempt to escape its strictures. He feared having epileptic fits due to his clamped-down anger; in fact, he feared any contact with anger, believing that the only way to express it would be by explosive loss of control, as it had been so inhibited by his fear of his super-ego figures.

At times he felt so constrained by his skin he could barely contain himself on the couch. This skin had been preceeded by a constricting state of mind—a mental vise like skin which on analysis stood for his hyperacute constricting parents watching his every movement. He would tear at his skin, much as he had done as an eczematous infant getting some relief as he bled. (Free-flowing blood gives many wrist-slashing patients a feeling of escape from suffocating persecutors.) The geographical location of the persecuting super-ego would vary; at times it could be a voice in his head, at times it was a somatic state, a persecuting skin or back or throat or bowel. Situated in between the mental and the somatic persecutor was a hypochondriacal condition which was neither one nor the other, but could also make him feel constricted, suffocated, and explosive.

On two occasions he suffered breakdowns which clinically resembled acute mania. They were explosive attempts to liberate himself from what he felt were the intolerable confines of his work, wife, and children, who had become the repositories of his super-ego. He felt inextricably tied by them and felt they were draining him of all strength, energy, time and money, and would eventually literally kill him. "They are strangling and eating me alive" he would say. On one occasion he packed a bag, cashed all his money, and tried to disappear to the wide spaces of Canada. However, his escape produced feelings of confusion, depression, and guilt, and he had to return once again to what he felt was his bondage.

On a second occasion he again left his home, started using hallucinogenic drugs, went around with young girls, and spent nights with prostitutes. He had phantasies of blowing up the Pentagon or his university department, and he wrote books and papers furiously into the night, directed against established medicine and its corrupt practices.

On analysis it appeared that the patient had projected his crushing and suffocating super-ego into these various external persecutors and his break away from them and fight against them were his attempts to liberate himself from a persecution which he felt had become annihilating.

When one recalls the spider dreams wherein he was identified as the spider, sucking the life and juices out of his objects, one could see how an internal persecuting super-ego containing the spider part of himself would prove so terrifying. A dream that this patient had illustrates one aspect of this dynamic. He dreamed he was on a plane and seated next to him was the son of a friend of his. This boy was known to the patient as being a "smart-ass" and a "know-it-all," who was always in trouble with the police, school authorities, etc. The boy was asking my patient questions which were very obscure and esoteric, and was looking at him in a contemptuous and mocking way. My patient knew he could not answer these questions and would be humiliated and tortured if he couldn't. He was going to be strapped into his seat and the air would be let out of the plane. The thought of the confinement and suffocation made him frantic. He searched desperately for an encyclopedia to answer the boy's questions, but the boy's face leered at him mockingly and came closer and closer to his own. In desperation he felt the only thing he could do was to smash the window of the plane and jump out. His associations made it clear that the boy was a part of himself containing a particularly persecuting omniscience.

This omniscient aspect of himself was also seen as trapping, imprisoning, and suffocating, letting the air out and coming closer and closer to his face. The feeling of claustrophobia, wishing to smash the plane window and jump out, was an attempt to get away from this suffocating persecution. It was a feeling he frequently got in planes and cars and elevators and was clearly linked to a persecuting, mocking, imprisoning aspect of himself projected into these confining places and now experienced as crushing and annihilating him in their turn. The "smart-ass" boy was also linked to the patient's father who, since infancy, had made him feel trapped merely by his presence.

The patient also related this feeling to his state of mind prior to his two "break-outs" and which seemed to be the precipitating factor in the psychotic episodes described. Over the last three and one half years, particular attention has been paid in the analysis to his minutely controlling phenomena toward me in the transference. There has been a marked regression of somatic symptoms, and the persecuting hypochondriasis has diminished greatly. Finally, the patient's relationships to his objects, particularly his wife, have become markedly changed. His promiscuity has ceased and he now can feel comfortable at home instead of feeling suffocated. As his controlling and invasive phantasies toward me have been analysed, depressive and Oedipal material has occurred with greater frequency, doubtless as the consequences of his objects acquiring more of a life of their own.

Case History 2

The patient was a young man age 20. He was the middle-child in a family of three, with an elder sister age 24 and a younger brother age 13. His father was an architect and his mother a physician.

He had been hospitalized six months prior to beginning treatment with me for a mild psychotic episode, which was typically schizophrenic. He had hallucinations, paranoia, ideas of reference, depersonalization, and acute panic states. His breakdown was accompanied by feelings that there was a persistent voice in his head telling him he was dirty, worthless, and diseased, and that people in the street could read his mind and knew all about his obscene thoughts and his sexual preoccupations. At times he felt his clothes were suffocating him and wanted to tear them off. He felt suffocated in any crowded situation like a restaurant, cinema, elevator, etc. His mind also felt hot, crowded and filled with dreadful things that he longed to escape from by death or suicide. He feared, but also wanted to be locked away for life.

After 18 months of analysis, the patient brought me the following series of associations. He described a scene that he had witnessed on his way to his session which was liberally interspersed with phantasies and probably delusions. He stopped, he said, to watch a building crew at a nearby building site. There was a large group of men who were wearing red metal hats. These men were all colors—black, white, brown, and yellow—and were standing around smoking cigarettes, drinking coffee and beer, and eating sandwiches. They were also continually joking, playing cards, making visits to a little box to urinate and defecate, and seemed to be having a very good time except for an occasional fight that would break out among them. Each ten minutes or so the foreman would come around to inspect what they were doing and they would stop their joking, drinking, and eating, and do a little work to keep him quiet. They would put in a few screws and lay a piece of concrete still winking and nudging each other as they did so. The moment the foreman turned his back and left, they went back to their previous behavior. The foreman wore a silver hat and from time to time he would climb a ladder to a man seated on a platform at a table covered with plans, rulers, pencils, calculators, etc.

This man wore a gold hat and everybody called him "Sir." Gold hat issued orders to silver hat who ran down to the red hats trying to implement his orders and back again to gold hat reporting and getting fresh instructions. Silver hat was worried and harassed, running between the workers below and the boss above, and torn between the two, attempting to please and placate both. The work was getting done but slowly.

Suddenly the entire atmosphere at the building site changed and a hush descended over the whole place. Everyone looked up rather frightenedly to an extreme corner where there was a TV camera installed with a telephoto lens. This camera had everybody in its view as it could swivel 360° in all directions and it glowed eerily "like a fish's eye." The men immediately stopped their fooling around and stood frozen not knowing what to do. What was most frightening about the fish eye camera was its mechanical nature, its inhuman stare, and its unknown origin. No one seemed to know who was watching and recording, whose side he was on, what he was looking for, and what it would do. "You couldn't even breathe when it was on," my patient said, "without its knowing what you were doing." (The patient often describes his father in just those terms, i.e., when he gets home from work you can't breathe in the house without him jumping on you.)

The architect, according to my patient, thought it could be something the men's union had installed to check on him, but the men themselves thought it might be the "money-men" from New York who had Mafia connections and ruled even the unions.

As the patient was watching this scene he got the feeling that the men couldn't stand the tension produced by the TV camera any longer. He saw one of them reaching for a gun and thought he was going to shoot out the eye of the camera and also that one or two of these men were edging toward the wall in order to jump over it to escape, to break out. The patient became frightened at this point and ran away from the site to his session where he arrived 20 minutes late.

During his session he remembered that it was October 12, which was the second anniversary of the day he had been hospitalized. He therefore seemed to be reliving in phantasy as well as externally what had been an intrapsychic conflict two years ago that lead to his psychotic breakdown.

While the patient was psychologically unsophisticated, and had never heard of, let alone read, Freud, he seemed to be describing classically the levels of his mind. The red-hatted id impulses eating, excreting and fighting; the silver-hatted ego trying to bring some order to them; and torn between them and the gold-hatted architect super-ego. The super-ego was also linked directly to the father in reality, who was an architect by profession.

However, while the ego and the super-ego were responsible for control, discipline and order, they did not produce the anxiety, terror or hostility that the TV camera produced. The men did listen to the foreman and the architect, and curtailed their fooling around, but they were not intimidated by them and therefore did not respond with panic and hostility. The TV camera elicited quite a different response, because it was capable of seeing everywhere and producing a feeling that there was no escape from it. It was mechanical, which meant it had no human feelings to appeal to, therefore it was inplacable, and, in the patient's words, "you couldn't breathe without it knowing."

The TV camera can be likened to the primitive super-ego described by Mrs. Klein, which even the normal super-ego, gold-hatted architect, was afraid of. It was the trapped and suffocated feeling produced by this inhuman eye which caused hostility and breakouts to occur. ("One or two men edged toward the wall in order to breakout and one took out a gun which he was going to fire at the fish eye.") I believe this coincides with, and describes, when viewed intrapsychically, the beginning of the patient's psychotic break two years ago. I see this as a fragmentation and projection outward of parts of the id which was in violent rebellion against the feeling of entrapment produced by the primitive super-ego.

Historically, the patient had described how he spent many hours at night as a child creeping through the dark to his parents' bedroom. He would crawl along the corridor and listen outside the bedroom door for the parents' "quarreling." He always felt that they were quarreling about him and he would try to listen to hear exactly what they were saying. At times he would try to look through the keyhole and once tried to shine a torch through it to see if he could see what was going on. Sometimes he would creep outside the house and work his way along to a small balcony which was outside the window of the parents' bedroom. There he would spend hours listening and trying to get a glimpse through the curtain of what they were doing. He feared that his father was going to attack his mother and phantasied that he would rush in and save her. Some nights he even fell asleep on the balcony and would wake up in the early morning and hurry back to bed in case he was discovered. He was extremely terrified that one day his father would catch him and punish him severely.

We can see in the patient's childhood behavior the origins of this cruel, secret invasive television camera eye observing and recording everything, and which later introjected becomes his own internal observer debasing him. His eye and ears, like the fish eye, watched and recorded everything throughout the night. This cruel voyeurism was later projected into his father and then reintrojected into his own mind where it became installed as a primitive, cruel, all-seeing super-ego. When he phantasied that his parents were always quarreling over him or talking about him, he believed that he was always in their minds, i.e., he had invaded their minds and was between them even when they were supposed to be asleep and together. He also projected all sorts of cruel and sadistic phantasies into them and their intercourse which also became cruel and sadistic internal persecutors when reintrojected into his super-ego complex.

In the analysis, the patient's attitude toward me in the transference was similar in every way. He would bring dreams, material, or associations, not in order to obtain understanding through them about himself but to watch me and to learn about me by watching how I dealt with them. His material was like a series of Rorschach tests that he set me in order to observe what I did, how I did it, and thus to enable him to know how my mind worked, primarily to see what was wrong with it. This gave him feelings of triumph and superiority at my expense and produced a reversal of the patient-analyst relationship. He often had dreams where he would throw a stone into a pool to see what ripples it produced and watch how and where they went. Once he threw birdseed down to a flock of birds and laughed to see them fighting and squabbling over the seed. Once he arranged a window in a store and watched outside to see people's reactions to the various window dressings that he had arranged. These were all variations of his transference relationship to me. He would produce something and watch my response to it which, in my stupidity, I believed to be psychoanalysis and interpretations, while he secretly mocked and laughed at me as he did his "analysis" of me. I was scrutinized continuously, and could not so much as breathe without him knowing about it, controlling it, and, in his phantasies, arresting it at his will. His favorite television program was "Candid Camera," where a hidden TV camera watched people perform all sorts of things and a hidden audience would laugh at their expense.

Thus, the transference was also similar to his early behavior toward his parents. The frightening, suffocating, cruel TV camera super-ego was an introjection of his own cruel, voyeuristic eyes and attitudes toward objects projected into them and reintrojected where it formed a permanent and suffocating part of his mind. It was the suffocating, inescapable nature of this super-ego that was responsible for his later breakdown, which to him doubtless was experienced as a "break-out" from an intolerable prison.

If instead of breaking down the patient projected his super-ego into the outside world or his objects, he then suffered from paranoia or ideas of reference. Occasionally both catastrophies occurred simultaneously.

Case History 3

The following case illustrates a third component of the claustrophobic superego. The patient, an anaesthesiologist by profession, commenced treatment following a suicide attempt. He had been apprehended molesting sexually a female patient in the post-operative recovery period. He claimed to be assisting the patient's respiration while holding her breasts and compressing her rib cage.

During treatment he confessed to enjoying the feeling of complete power and control he experienced while anesthetizing patients, particularly after paralyzing their respiratory centers with drugs and washing out their CO_2 by forced respiratory movements. He would then continue the anesthetic which completely controlled respiration administered by a respiratory bag. He enjoyed the feeling of their life and breathing being totally in his hands. He employed controlled respiration even in minor surgical cases, when it was totally unnecessary, utilizing all sorts of rationalizations to justify this procedure.

He himself had suffered from acute claustrophobic anxieties in adolescence, and still suffered from life-long asthma and nasal congestion. He carried bronchial dilators in injection, pill and inhalation form with him constantly. Enclosed spaces would often precipitate asthmatic attacks for which he would use his inhaler or nasal decongestants to obtain relief. It was very doubtful whether he suffered from actual bronchospasm even though he wheezed on auscultation of his chest, for his lung and vital capacity studies were not typical of asthma.

He had many persecutory dreams about being chased by animals and men, and heavy breathing was often a feature of this persecution. On several occasions he strangled the attackers and cut off their air supply in order to escape.

In his analysis he frequently complained about my breathing. It persecuted him and he attempted to count or watch my respirations. This relieved him as he felt he gained control over them. At times he felt that he was being suffocated by my presence, my interpretations, or my "warmth." Once he said that my breath smelled so badly that it asphyxiated him and forced him to leave the session. This followed a session where he himself complained of passing flatus continuously. He had many bizarre phantasies concerning the gas he passed, believing it got inside people, and affected them in many ways, even at times sexually exciting them. His need to control breathing and his feelings that his own breathing was at times obstructed, both internally and externally, played a very important part in his analysis.

On several occasions when he became acutely anxious and thought he was going mad, he described his state of mind in terms identical to those he used when talking about his respiratory functions, i.e., crushed, trapped, held tightly, squashed out of existence, having no breathing space, etc. It was also clear from many dreams and associations that all authority figures and parental figures produced similar feelings of being hemmed in and suffocated, and their presence at times literally produced shortness of breath and asthma attacks which he would 'relieve' by the use of inhalers and bronchial dilators.

On reconstructing his infantile relationship to his mother, he emerged as an extremely controlling infant and child. He suffered from school phobia and would often stay home from school and spend his afternoons napping with his mother. She supported and probably encouraged his close attachment to her as she herself suffered from many phobias and feared being left alone. He recalls lying beside her in bed, originally with a bottle in his mouth, later to be replaced with his thumb, stroking the outside of her leg where it was cool.

In later life he frequently needed some cool outlet reminiscent of his mother's cool leg, like an open window or a draft, as he felt hot and suffocated without it. On the couch he would stroke the wall which he found cool and which gave him the feeling of being able to breathe more easily. His thumb-sucking persisted until he was 12 and was quickly replaced by cigarette, pipe-smoking, and chronic nibbling between meals. All these objects which were put into his mouth were linked on analysis to his mother's nipples in phantasy trapped and held suffocated. As an adult he was fascinated by women's breasts, cleavages, nipple outlines, and couldn't tear his eyes away from the rise and fall of their chests. This chest movement of women, on analysis, represented their separate life, mobility and freedom, and therefore had to be controlled in order to possess them and keep them tied as though they were a part of himself. The controlling of his objects was, on analysis, due to many different anxieties, the most prominent being to control his own inner feelings of persecution which arose in the absence of his objects. In this patient the absence of the good object in the outside world was never experienced as hunger, desire or longing, but instead as the presence of a dangerous and ravaging beast which has to be quieted or it would tear him to pieces, explode him to fragments, or drive him insane. His impulses of need or feelings of discomfort were always experienced as hoards of bees, ants or scorpions and his inner world was a collection of teeth, eyes and nails that gave him peace only when they possessed his object or usually part object. He would describe his feelings about women like the force which existed between magnets. It was either a violent surge toward them and smashing together when the poles were north-south, or an equally violent repulsion and springing apart.

This repulsion on analysis was identical to a claustrophobic panic reaction and followed the violent attraction which had led in his mind to his landing up inside his objects and becoming trapped and suffocated by them. The violent springing apart would now lead to another kind of panic, agoraphobic, based on being far away and feeling abandoned by the object. This, in its turn, produced a violent rush back to the object landing up inside once more and creating a claustrophobic-agoraphobic vicious cycle.

His mind, likewise, and internal objects identified with these impulses. At times his thoughts were jammed and smashed together like the poles in a magnet atrracting each other. At times his super-ego smashed and crushed the rest of his personality down under it, annihilating any resistance against it. At other times, as a reaction against the violent jamming together and the claustrophobia it produced, parts of his mind would fly apart and occasionally to pieces. He would then complain of feelings of dissociation, unreality, light-headedness, dizziness and confusion. Also, when his internal objects repelled each other or one sprang away from the other, he thought he was going mad, or becoming unglued, and suffered anxieties similar to those described by my other patients prior to psychotic breakdown.

Not only was it important for him to control the breathing of his objects as it represented their movement and life, but at times the gases which came from his objects were felt to be dangerous as they could control or poison him. Therefore control of his object's breathing was not only control of their separateness but also control of a persecutor. This necessity to control his objects' breathing would then be projected into his object and reintrojected into his super-ego where it controlled him and added another feature to the persecuting suffocation experienced internally. As well as the patient's omnipotent illusions about the gas coming from his anus, he had similar phantasies about the gas he produced from his mouth in the form of words or eructations. He had a long history of pride and pleasure at his eructing skills and could belch loudly and at will. His phantasies about this seemed to be related to the omnipotent nature of a gas, per se, i.e., it can penetrate secretly and quietly without its origins being detectable. Urine and faeces were less powerful as they could often be traced back to their origins by stains, etc., also they were more intangible and so much easier for the object to avoid.

Bringing up wind had the added triumphant pleasure of pleasing and delighting his mother as an appreciative gift following feeding. His "wind" had the kind of idealization and value that many patients attached to stools and urine when they could be equated with penises or food to excite or satisfy the object. All these omnipotent phantasies were also projected into his objects' gases and thus necessitated controlling them and their powerful phantasied effects.

A Note on Psychosomatics

My observations with asthmatic patients suggest that the bronchi and chest walls can be used as repositories for the suffocating super-ego in some patients. It is also probably that this phenomenon is only one of many somatic solutions to the unbearable persecution of the super-ego. My experience in the treatment of frequency of urine and stools also suggested that the spasm of the hollow viscus was linked to a persecutory super-ego, and the frequent evacuations brought relief of the mind as well as the body.

In the first case I described, the skin of the patient frequently stood for his constricting and suffocating phantasied parents, and his tearing holes in it enabled him to produce windows, which like the "cool wall" or "outer leg" of my third case, permitted him to breathe.

When Freud (1918) said of the Wolf Man "There is a wish to be back in a situation in which one was in the mother's genitals: and in this connection the man is identifying himself with his own penis . . ." he laid the ground work for the study of a vast group of somatic phantasies which is invaluable for the understanding and treatment of the psycho-somatic disorders. A man can identify not only with his own penis, but with his stools, urine, flatus, chest wall, breath, semen, in fact, all parts of his body and the body of his object. These processes are all achieved through the mechanism of projective and introjective identifications with whole or part objects. I have described this in case 3, when the patient, using projective identification, identified his thumb with the nipple and trapped it in his mouth, swallowed it in phantasy and imprisoned it in his rectum in the form of constipated stool. This in phantasy enabling him to take possession of the mother and her breast. In case 1, when the patient scratched himself until the blood ran, like the wrist-slashers who open their wrists to obtain relief, the patient is identified with his own blood which is escaping from his body which is identified with his object which is trapping him.

Many cigarette smokers get relief and satisfaction from the sight of smoke emerging as a cloud from their lips, and do not enjoy smoking in the dark. They are similar to the asthmatic patients whose air supply is trapped in the claustrum of their own bronchi and chest walls. These smokers are identified with the smoke, or air, being set free from the entrapping or suffocating object which in turn is identified with their chests or bronchi.

Any organ, or part of the body, can at times represent the object entrapping and suffocating the patient. The excretions and secretions, which liberate themselves from the patient's body, are equated with the escaping self, or part of the self freeing itself from intolerable suffocation. In this situation, projective identification is being used as a defense against suffocation produced by the presence of a constricting super-ego or the phantasy of being inside an object. Both these suffocating states of mind have themselves been produced earlier by phantasies of projective identification used in the service of control of the object.

It is as though, when the control has gone too far, the original omnipotent phantasies are put into reverse, to effect a rescue.

Summary

A particular quality of super-ego is described which can produce an anxiety of a suffocating nature. This anxiety is produced by certain kinds of super-ego components acting together or separately. Four of these components have been described.

(1) *Omniscience* (Omnipotence and Omnipresence)

(2) *Voyeurism* (Visual, Auditory and Olfactory elements)

(3) *Breathing Control* (Control of Respiratory and other movement. Control of dangerous gases)

(4) *Devouring* (Oral-trapped nipple, anal-trapped stool)

All these components are installed into the super-ego by the infant using the mechanism of projective identification which because of its omnipotent invasiveness imparts an invasive quality to the super-ego.

The consequences of the suffocating anxiety produced by the super-ego described are as follows.

(1) *Psychotic Break:* Fragmentation and projection out of ego and id. Sometimes fragmentation of super-ego.

(2) *Drug Use:* Self or psychiatrically administered. Relieves tension between super-ego and ego and id.

(3) *Projection Outward of Super-ego:*

(a) *Into the sky*—Religious conversions.

(b) *Into one's objects*—Paranoid relationship of suffocating nature—frequently leading to divorce or child runaway.

(c) *Into inanimate objects*—Elevators, crowds, planes, etc. Typical claustrophobia.

(d) *Into body organs (somatisation)*—Bronchi—Asthma; Bowel—Colitis; Bladder—Frequency; Blood-vessels—Hypertension, Raynauds disease.

Symptomatic treatment of (2) and (3) a, b, c, d may produce psychosis.

When a psychotic break threatens, the patient's monitoring suffocating phantasies toward the analyst in the transference have to be traced in great detail, and dissected carefully back to the underlying primitive anxieties producing these defences.

The transference present when this dynamic is in evidence is frequently of a nature I would like to call *voyeuristic*. Here the patient comes to the analysis in order to watch, observe and "know all about" the analyst rather than his own state of mind. Material is produced to see how the analyst deals with it, and to learn about the analyst's mind, and about psychoanalysis, in place of getting analysed. The patient's emphasis is on the examination of the analyst's secret shortcomings and not on his own. Excitement and feelings of power are produced by these observations, just as with the voyeur, and the patient's "cure" is to become a psychoanalyst, leaving the analyst as the patient.

References

Bion, W.R. (1958), On hallucination, *Int. J. Psycho-Analysis*, 39, 5; pp. 341-349.
— (1959), Attacks on linking, *Int. J. Psycho-Analysis*, Vol. 40, 5; pp. 308-315.
— (1963), *Elements of Psycho-Analysis*, London: Heinemann, pp. 19, 96.
Freud, S. (1893) Extracts from the Fliess Papers, Draft B Aetiology of neurosis, S.E., 1.; pp. 179-183 London: Hogarth, 1966.
— (1900), *Interpretation of Dreams, S.E., 4V.*, London: Hogarth, 1953.
— (1905), A Case of hysteria, *S.E., 7.*, London: Hogarth Press, 1953, pp. 1-122.
— (1918), An Infantile Neurosis, *S.E., 17*, London: Hogarth Press, 1955, pp. 1-122.
— (1923), *The Ego and the Id, S.E.*, 19, London: Hogarth Press, 1961, pp. 34-36, 38-39, 173.
— (1925), *Inhibitions, Symptoms, and Anxiety*, S.E., 20, London: Hogarth, 1959.
— (1941[1938]), Findings, ideas, problems. *S.E., 23*, London: Hogarth, 1964, pp. 299-300.
— (1947), Findings, ideas, problems, *S.E., 18*, 1964, London: Hogarth, 1964, pp. 299-300.
Gehl, R.H. (1964), Depression and claustrophobia, *Int. J. Psycho-Analysis*, 45, 2, pp. 312-323.
Klein, M. (1926), Psychological principles of infant analysis, *Int. J. Psycho-Analysis*, 7,
— (1932), *Psychoanalysis of Children*. London: Hogarth Press.
— (1933), Early development of conscience in the child, *Contributions to Psychoanalysis*. London: Hogarth Press, pp. 267-277.

—— (1946), Notes on some schizoid mechanisms, *Developments in Psycho-Analysis*. London: Hogarth Press, pp. 292-320, 1952.
—— (1952), On the theory of anxiety and guilt, *Development in Psycho-Analysis*. London: Hogarth Press, pp. 271-291.
—— (1955), On identification, *New Directions in Psycho-Analysis*. London: Tavistock, pp. 309-345.
—— (1957). *Envy and Gratitude*. N.Y.: Basic Books.
Mason, A.A. (1962), Asthma, *British Medical Journal*, Vol. 11, pp. 371-376.
Meltzer, D. (1969), Terror, persecution and dread, *Int. J. Psycho-Analysis*, pp. 49, 396-401.
—— (1973), *Sexual States of Mind*. Scotland: Clunie Press.
Riviere, J. (1948), Paranoid attitudes in everyday life and in analysis. Lecture to the British Psycho-analytic Institute, 1948.
Rosenfeld, H.A. (1952), Notes on the analysis of the super-ego conflict in an acute schizophrenic, *Psychotic States*. London: Hogarth Press, Chapt. 4, pp. 63-103.
—— (1965), *Psychotic States*, London: Hogarth Press, pp. 144-154.
Segal, H. (1957), Notes on symbol formation, *Int. J. Psycho-Anal.*, pp. 38, 391-397.

On the Psychopathology and Treatment of Psychotic Patients (Historical and Comparative Reflections)

Herbert Rosenfeld

EDITOR'S NOTE: *In that rarified atmosphere of the psychoanalytic treatment of the psychoses two names have emerged for unusual distinction for excellence, Wilfred Bion and Herbert Rosenfeld. I am hardly alone in according them the status of the two foremost authorities in the world on the subject. It is therefore a great privilege to be able to include Doctor Rosenfeld's contribution in this volume.*

His paper begins as a brief review of the development of Melanie Klein's formulations and their application to the psychoses, and then proceeds to compare some of his own theoretical formulations with those of Bion's. He demonstrates the confirmation of and congruity with Bion's theories which his own experience has revealed. This is especially true with the ideas of attacks on linking, attacks on the verbal and thinking apparatuses, the concept of the failure of maternal reverie, the importance of abnormal splitting and abnormal projective identification, and the importance of countertransference in the treatment of psychotics, amongst many. He also takes issue, however, not with Bion, but rather with those who follow Bion's injunction "to abandon memory and desire" in the treatment of patients generally. I believe Doctor Rosenfeld is here trying to make a distinction between suspension of memory preconceptions on one hand and patent amnesia on the other. Ironically, it has escaped most analytic critics of this injunction that Bion's "advice" is merely a poetically condensed way of implementing Freud's suggestion that the analyst should suspend judgment and allow his own free associations to appear.

On the Psychopathology and Treatment of Psychotic Patients (Historical and Comparative Reflections)

Dr. H. Rosenfeld, London

On this occasion I shall try to give some picture of the development of the psychoanalytic treatment of psychotic patients in England, but will concentrate mainly on Wilfred Bion's work and my own on this subject. Basically our work has much in common but we have frequently focussed on different aspects of the clinical problems we encountered. This is not surprising as the treatment and the research into the psychopathology of psychosis is a never ending source of making new connections and new discoveries. Both Bion and myself were profoundly influenced by our personal analyses with Melanie Klein and particularly by her views which she presented to the British Psycho-Analytical Society.

In December 1946, Melanie Klein discussed there in detail the development of the infant during the first three to four months of life, a phase which she named the paranoid-schizoid position and described for the first time the splitting mechanisms of the early ego, projective identification and the turning of the aggression against the self. She pointed out that there was a primary danger of the infantile self being destroyed by destructive impulses within. The external object, the mother in the feeding situation, and the libidinal impulses within the organism were acting as a defence against this destructive danger. However neither of these defences is generally successful in warding off the danger and under the pressure of this threat the ego tends to fall to pieces. She states: "The primary anxiety of being annihilated by a destructive force within with the ego's specific response of falling to bits or splitting itself may be extremely important in all schizophrenic processes." She also described in some detail the weakening and impoverishment of the ego resulting in excessive splitting and projective identification as a process where good and bad parts of the self were split off and projected into external objects. She stressed that the weakened ego became unable to assimilate internal objects who were then felt to dominate the ego. The weakened ego was also incapable of taking back in itself the parts projected into the external world. She again emphasised that these processes seemed to be at the root of some forms of schizophrenia.

When I began to treat a schizophrenic patient by psychoanalysis in 1943 I felt overwhelmed by counter-transference experiences which caused me considerable confusion and distress. During my analysis with Melanie Klein I gradually began to understand the force of my patient's splitting and projecting processes which I had been unable to observe and understand clearly. It is now generally known that the borderline psychotic patient stirs up early infantile "psychotic anxieties" in the therapist and only when these early experiences have become accessible and acceptable to the analyst as part of his experience in his own analysis will he be able to deal with his very disturbed patients with empathy and understanding. Bion emphasized the same point in *Second Thoughts* (page 162). He states that Melanie Klein believed that psychotic mechanisms could be found in all analysands and should be uncovered if the psychoanalysis was to be satisfactory. "There is no applicant for psychoanalysis who is without fear of the psychotic elements in himself and who does not believe he can achieve the satisfactory adjustment without having those elements psychoanalysed."

My analytic work with Mildred (1947) confirmed many of Melanie Klein's findings about splitting processes and projective identification. Eventually she responded well to the analysis and after that I was encouraged to accept some very severe schizophrenic patients for analysis in 1949, 1950 and 1953 and began to understand the very intense transference phenomena of these patients (see Rosenfeld 1952a, 1952b, 1964, and 1971). I observed that the schizophrenic patient was not only projecting good or bad parts of himself into objects but frequently intruded with his whole self into other objects which led to experiences of losing his self and to persecutory anxietites of being invaded by other objects. As the persecuting objects were frequently violently attacked by the patient and split up in many bits in order to get rid of them I realised that the appearance of hordes of persecutors which were often experienced as small animals or objects implied an unsuccessful attempt to destroy the persecuting objects. These objects became then still more persecutory and further extensive splitting and projection resulted. A hallucinated patient (1950) described that his mind seemed to be "all spread out in the world which was full of thousands of men," an experience which increased his feeling of perplexity and persecution. This process had similarities with Bion's description (1957) of the psychotic part of the personality where parts of the self become fragmented and projected into the outside world and are then perceived as bizarre objects.

In 1950 I described confusional states in chronic schizophrenias and faulty processes of reparation where split off parts of the self and objects were wrongly reconstructed which led to bizarre self and object formation. I also noticed that the states of confusion of parts of the self and object are particularly unbearable to the immature self and that abnormal splitting processes appear which cut the confused part of the self and object into pieces. These pieces are frequently described as bizarre or horrible by the patient. In 1950 I described a dream of a schizophrenic patient who observed a lobster creeping on top of another lobster and swallowing it up completely. Soon afterwards the patient saw a "horrid" object looking like bones and bits of the thorax running across the floor and he was terrified and tried to kill it. The patient felt that the dream pictured a terrible state of confusion where he felt that his sadistic self had swallowed up the breast (thorax) and proceeded to overpower and devour his good self. As the creature consisted only of bits of bones, it was clear that the confusion was quickly followed by fragmentation.

Clinically I concentrated in all my schizophrenic patients on understanding the intrusive process in the transference situation and found that when intrusion of the self became more intense the interpretive process became distorted and the patient experienced the analyst's interpretation as a concrete process, for example as criticism, advice or seduction. For example a positive transference interpretation was often misperceived as a declaration of love and contributed to the formation of a delusional transference. It appeared that excessive (omnipotent) projective identification was the cause of the development of concrete processes of thinking, which interfered with the use of language. H. Segal in her paper 'Some Aspects of the Analysis of a Schizophrenic' (1950) decribed these concrete thought processes of the schizophrenic patient in greater detail. She suggested that in psychotic patients there was an interference in the normal process of symbol formation and she suggested the term 'symbolic equation' for the tendency of the schizophrenic patient to confuse the real object with its symbolic representation.

Wilfred Bion contributed both to the theory and treatment of schizophrenia from 1953. In 1953 he gave a striking clinical picture of the intrusive transference in his description of the patient who felt he intruded into the analyst at the beginning of the session and had to be extricated at the end of it. He also found that the schizophrenic patient "uses words as things and as split off parts of himself which he pushed forcibly into the analyst." He demonstrated clinically how this severe splitting of the patient made it difficult for him to achieve the use of symbols and subsequently language. He also illustrated that the schizophrenic patient experiences verbal thought as catastrophic when he discovers the importance of it for recognising sanity. As verbal thought increases the schizophrenic patient's experience and understanding of psychic reality, which is exceedingly painful, he tends again and again to "turn destructively on his embryonic capacity for verbal thought as one of the elements which has led to his pain." Bion stressed the violent negative therapeutic reaction which occurs in the patient when he begins to use his verbal thought to realise the psychic reality, his hallucinations and delusions, inability to take food and to sleep. Intense hatred then appears against the analyst who is accused by the patient of driving him insane. The incapacity, or diminished capacity for verbal thought in addition to the attacks on verbal thinking are in my experience particularly important for the understanding of those schizophrenic patients who develop the schizophrenic process early on in life and who have severe speech disturbances. They are often regarded as mentally defective and only psychoanalytic investigation can reveal the schizophrenic process. Bion relates the negative therapeutic reaction to a defence against the severe mental pain which develops as the result of increasing insight and sanity which throws penetrating and often too glaring a light on the psychotic process. This negative therapeutic reaction is created by the normal sane part of the patient who cannot bear his insanity. This reaction reminds one of the resistance of patients who shrink from facing the working through of depressive anxieties and relapse to paranoid schizoid ways of thinking and feeling.

There are in fact quite a number of situations which create negative therapeutic reactions in psychotic patients. The faulty reparative process which follows the lessening of the splitting process in chronic schizophrenia can be regarded as a negative therapeutic reaction because instead of allowing the split up parts of the self and object to come together in a realistic way omnipotent destructive processes intervene to put the self and objects together in an absurd way. The most frequent negative therapeutic reactions occur when the saner more object related parts of the personality appear openly in the transference situation. This almost immediately mobilises violent opposition of the psychotic omnipotent structure of the patient's personality which feels threatened in its position of absolute power and domination of the patient. The omnipotent structures reassert their power by threatening the saner infantile dependent parts with death or try to destroy the positive link which has been formed with the analyst by making discrediting attacks on him to stir up distrust. These negative reactions or crises have been beautifully described by Hannah Green in her book "I Never Promised You a Rose Garden": the patient, Deborah, had been hospitalised for a delusional schizophrenic illness and was in psychotherapeutic treatment with Dr. Fried (Frieda Fromm-Reichmann). Gradually Deborah began to trust her doctor and told her for the first time in detail how her delusional system had developed. In her delusional world a figure, called the censor, claimed that he had the role of protector but he insisted that she kept her secrets to herself so that they would not be revealed to anybody in the real world. Deborah explained that gradually the censor became tyrannical. Other figures insisted that she was a captive and victim and that she could not escape from the delusional world which she called "Yr." After this important session Dr. Fried expressed her satisfaction with the progress and told her that there was much to understand and to study. She added, "you are not a victim now, you are a fighter with me for your good strong life." Soon after the session the patient became terrified and she felt that the censor and other figures of Yr made rumbling noises and seemed to be coming closer and she warned the nurse that she was afraid of an attack. She suddenly heard a gust of ridiculing laughter, but she did not lose consciousness. The censor's voice shouted in her inner ear. "Captive and victim: don't you know why we have done this. *We* planned your coming to the Hospital. *We* let you trust the doctor. You opened your secrets more and more. This is the final one. Now you have given enough of your secrets and you will see what she (Dr. Fried) will do, she and the world. And then the terrifying laugh occurred again. Later the full frightening punishment descended on her where she felt threatened with death by the internal figures, a crisis which was dealt with in the Hospital by putting her into a continuous bath under restraint. I often found that the negative therapeutic reaction in psychotic patients is introduced by mounting terror and it is difficult to find out from the patient details of this state, but sometimes a dream reveals details of the threatening situation. We shall discuss later the omnipotent psychotic organisation of the patient in greater detail.*

In 1957 Bion wrote a fundamental paper where he discussed in detail the differences between the psychotic and the non-psychotic aspects of the personality. In describing the psychotic part of the psychotic patient he stated that there were processes which appeared to be a withdrawal from reality but which were in fact caused by the dominance in the patient's mind and behaviour of an omnipotent phantasy that is intended to destroy reality and the awareness of it. He also emphasised that the delusion of the withdrawal from reality was caused by the powerful phantasy of projective identification which acts as if the perceptual apparatus of the patient could be split into minute fragments and projected into objects. This splitting process led to the formation of bizarre objects which consist of objects which contain, or encapsulate, minute particles of the patient's personality. Bion's description of the minute splitting of the ego confirms Melanie Klein's findings of the importance of processes of early ego fragmentation. However, Melanie Klein attributed the fragmentation to the power of the early destructive processes while Bion in this paper seems to suggest that the destructive process was intended for defensive purposes to destroy that part of the ego which is concerned with the perception of reality. I have observed attacks on the perceptive function of the ego, which often leads to an evacuation of the mental apparatus and consequently to a loss of the capacity for thought both in psychotic and certain borderline patients. The fragmentation of the ego and of the perceptive apparatus seems primarily related to a desperate defence against overwhelming destructive impulses and the persecutory anxieties related to them. It is the evacuation of the fragmented dangerous impulses and the persecutory anxieties relating to them combined with the perceptive mental apparatus which leaves the schizophrenic patient in a state of perplexity, helplessness and "nameless dread" (Bion).

As I mentioned before, bizarre objects in schizophrenia are created in many different ways, and I have the impression that most bizarre objects are in some way or other related to confusional anxieties. I am in total agreement with Bion that it is essential in the treatment of psychotic patients to differentiate between psychotic and nonpsychotic aspects of the personality. I also agree that omnipotence is the most characteristic quality of the psychotic part but I would stress that the omnipotence is bound up with the destructive narcissistic organisation which tries to destroy or interfere with the patient's relationship with real objects and therefore to reality. The

*In my paper, The Treatment of Psychotic States particularly Schizophrenia by Psychoanalysis in *Schizophrenia Today* (ed. by D. Kemali et al., the Pergamon Press 1976) I described a patient's dream where she was pursued by a murderer into the consulting room of a detective, after she had discovered two dead bodies who had recently been murdered. The murderer tried to kill her before she could reveal his existence. The patient saved herself by rushing into the detective's consulting room.

omnipotent destructive parts of the self try to lure the saner infantile aspects of the patient away from reality by promises of freedom from pain and anxiety and they often disguise themselves as benevolent and omnipotently ideal. Often the patient struggles against the powerful suggestive influence, but when the destructive force appears without disguise the patient generally feels paralysed by fear and begins to appease the threatening forces by submission. Often the persuasive force or influence strikes again when the patient is weakened by fear. Men may become identified with the aggressive force like a prisoner who changes his views under pressure of modern brain washing tactics so that he may actually make propaganda for the psychotic state and idealise it. For example a schizophrenic girl (1964) before a Christmas break lectured her analyst (Meltzer) on the value of masturbation and withdrawal from reality by stating that, "What makes insane people happy is good for them." Accompanying gestures showed that she referred to masturbation. She also insisted that "people who had been in concentration camps emerged as better people for having seen all the suffering," a statement which was gradually recognised as meaning that the patient's imprisonment in a cruel psychotic state combined with voyeurism gave her more love than the analyst who was going to desert her over the Christmas holiday. In this situation it was clear that the Christmas break stimulated the power of the patient's omnipotent narcissistic organisation, which had imprisoned her infantile self so that she talked like a Nazi prisoner who had become a Nazi through listening to all the Nazi propaganda. Fortunately it is mostly only in the acute phase of the psychotic illness that the sane part of the patient is completely overwhelmed and imprisoned in the psychotic part of the personality. Generally there are some remnants of the sane part which manage by verbal or non-verbal means to communicate with the analyst.

It is interesting that the significant work with psychotic patients does not usually occur in the area of the patient's conscious preoccupations, but is transmitted by non-verbal communication in the transference in very subtle ways. These are not easily identifiable but nevertheless can be perceived by a responsive and perceptive analyst. It seems that the psychotic patient uses a large variety of projective processes for communications with the analyst, and it is important to observe, as Bion pointed out, whether the patient has sufficient contact with reality so that the phantasies related to the projective identification are expressed sufficiently clearly so that the analyst actually becomes aware of the anxieties or feelings which the patient tries to force him to have (Bion: *Learning From Experience*, Chapter 12).

I shall now try to illustrate in some detail some of the difficulties of understanding and dealing with transference and counter-transference reactions in psychotic patients. A male schizophrenic patient who had recovered from an acute delusional episode several months previously came to analysis still suffering occasionally from delusional physical sensations of his body being influenced by certain people. The patient felt fairly positively in coming to his sessions and attended them quite regularly. However the analyst found that in most of the sessions he had to struggle against an intense sleepiness and it was difficult for him to observe the reasons for this sleepiness in the patient's material. One day the patient reported a dream where he was walking on a meadow with a boy and a girl. The patient was thinking of lying down on the meadow but then he noticed that the meadow was covered by thousands of bees and some other insects. Immediately after reporting the dream the patient complained that he felt too comfortable on the couch and that he feared he was being lulled into a false complacency which prevented him from feeling any anxiety. He then asked the analyst to allow him to sit up. The analyst confessed to me that he felt relieved by the request of the patient to sit up because he hoped that he might find it easier to control his overpowering sleepiness with the patient sitting opposite him. But his sleepiness, which made it very difficult for him to think, continued. The analyst did not interpret the dream in relation to the transference situation, which was understandable because at that time he had not been able to use his countertransference experience for the analytic work with this patient. In fact he felt that it interfered, or prevented him from functioning well. I felt that the dream and the patient's 'acting' of the dream in the session was important as it illustrated clearly that the patient had realised that he had some disturbing effect on the analyst and was afraid that the analyst was not able to help him to struggle against the disturbing force which he had projected into him. The bees would then represent projections, probably fragmented material which had covered the meadow, the analyst's couch and mind. There was no verbal evidence that the bees should be regarded as the fragmented bizarre object which Bion described, as the analyst's experience of sleepiness was apparently created by a non-verbal transmission from the patient. The struggle of the analyst against the sleepiness even increased after this session and he realised that he sometimes interpreted too quickly and too much in an attempt to keep awake. When the analyst permitted himself to respond more to the projections of the patient he became aware that the sleepiness projected into him had the effect of his listening to the patient in a way which seemed to persuade him to feel that everything was going well with the patient and there was nothing to worry about. This he could diagnose as the projection of the hypnotic power of the "psychotic forces" of the patient which were trying to intrude into and overpower his mind. Once, very fleetingly, some triumph was felt by the patient when he thought how powerless and impotent the analyst appeared to him in dealing with the powerful forces within the patient. Interpretation of an attempt of the patient to reverse the analyst-patient relationship was not rejected by the patient, but the disturbing overpowering sleepiness in the counter-transference reaction of the analyst still continued. The analyst then examined his own counter-transference experience in still greater detail. He began to realise that he felt while listening to the patient pulled away into a sleepy day-dreaming state which at first seemed to relate to the patient's material until he suddenly became aware that he was completely pulled away from the patient into his own day dreams. He then understood why he had to use such willpower to keep awake. Interestingly enough the patient almost simultaneously at this period of analysis explained to him that he had to use all his willpower to struggle with what he called the force because he needed the analyst's help to support the sane active part of his personality who wanted to get on with life and work. He indicated that if he gave into the seductive power of the force he would be in danger of falling into a trap from which he would not be able to pull himself out again. This time the analyst realised that his own counter-transference experiences were completely identical with the patient's reported experiences and his struggles. Up to that time the analyst had been generally in doubt about being able clearly to identify the struggles of the patient because he was never quite sure whether the patient's struggle was simply an attempt to forget and get rid of his psychosis and his delusions by splitting and projecting, or whether he was facing the "force" and struggling against what was clearly a psychotic force which was pulling him away from reality. It is interesting that when the analyst used his own counter-transference experience which had gradually convinced him that giving into the drowsy state of mind pulled *him* away from reality into his day dreams he was able to interpret the patient's struggle with much more sympathy, understanding and conviction and the patient responded to this by saying, "Now you really understand me." So it is clear that the non-verbal projections are an important tool of the psychotic patient to establish intimate communication with the analyst.

Bion has illustrated again and again, particularly in his description of psychotic patients, how much he used his counter-transference in understanding the patient's material. He also gave a detailed model of the early communication between the infant and mother which can assist the analyst to understand the purpose and meaning of the patient's projection which is particularly important in the understanding of non-verbal projections. In Chapter 12 of *Learning from Experience* Bion describes the importance of the mother's reverie which can discern the infant's state of mind even before the infant can be conscious of it. He regards the mother's reveries as the psychological source of supply of the infants needs for love and understanding. The capacity of the mother to have a state of mind which is open to receive the infant's projective identifications whether they are good or bad seems to change some of the confusions and unmanageable experiences of the infant into an understandable form, a process which Bion has called "alpha function." "In this way the infant's experience of frustration can gradually become more bearable and he can commit himself to a sense of reality. When the mother fails in this function a great burden is thrown on the infant's capacity to bear frustration." In his paper "Theory of Thinking" (on page 115) he says: "If the mother cannot tolerate the projections the infant is reduced to continued projections carried out with increasing force and frequency. The increased force seems to denude the projection of meaning and reintrojection is effected in similar force and frequency. He feels then an internal object is built up which starves its host of all understanding that is made available."

In the treatment of psychotic patients the patient tests again and again the analyst's capacity to bear his frustrating experience, his anxieties, confusion, his helplessness and hopelessness which he projects into him. The patient almost all the time fears that the analyst has become intolerant, will withdraw and even give up the treatment. He watches the analyst sometimes carefully for any signs of being distracted. He listens to his tone of voice to find out whether he is defensive or open to the patient's communications and he hopes that the analyst can understand and communicate to him in words what he (the patient) consciously or more frequently unconsciously tries to express. Any slight disturbance in the patient/analyst relationship can lead to serious misunderstandings; for example, when the analyst reacts too quickly before he has had any chance to experience fully what the patient is communicating to him, the patient feels rejected as he experiences the analyst's quick response as a refusal to accept his projection and he feels that his projects are thrown back at him.

I found that it is possible to observe in this very subtle relationship between patient and analyst how a sense of guilt can develop in the patient when he is not understood or when he experiences that the therapist is not in a receptive state of mind. I have noticed that some psychotic patients are extraordinarily sensitive and perceptive. They frequently do not want to communicate their perceptions to the analyst because they fear that this will be experienced by the analyst as intrusive and that they may hurt his narcissism which may put him on the defensive. It always takes a great deal of time to assist the patient in expressing himself freely so that he dares to allow himself to use his mind and to put into words what he has observed. It also needs usually a great deal of self observation on the analyst's part to accept his own reactions which are often only minimal mistakes and blockages, but which are often noticed by the patient. From the analyses of these patients I have the impression that they have been apparently unable to bear their awareness and perception of their mother's difficulties and anxieties in infancy and later on. So this problem seems to attack the infant's capacity to perceive, to lead to confusion and so the patients often present themselves as unobservant and stupid. This observation seems to confirm Bion's description of the internal object which prevents understanding and functioning. This internal object often appears to act as a superego which does not allow curiosity and observation of reality. In his paper on "Attacks on Linking" (No. 98 in *Second Thoughts*) he describes this early development of the superego. He emphasises here, that the link between infant and breast depends upon projective identification and the capacity of the objects to introject projective identification. Failure to introject makes the external object appear intrinsically hostile to curiosity and to the methods (namely projective identification) by which the infant seeks to satisfy it. I often found in severely traumatised patients,particularly if the mother was in addition unable to respond receptively to the communication by projection,that a superego is created which is almost identical to Bion's description.

Finally I want to discuss some aspects of Bion's work which have created controversy and I believe misunderstanding of his own intentions. In his book *Attention and Interpretation* (Chapter 4) Bion suggests that "uninhibited exercise of memories and desires is indistinguishable from, inseparable from and analogous to making preconception impossible by virtue of leaving no unsaturated element." He makes clear that the desire or the memory prevents an open mind if it occupies the "space" which should remain open. He also stresses that it is important that the analyst should avoid mental activity, memory and desire which is harmful to his mental fitness as some forms of physical activity are to physical fitness. Bion has frequently encouraged analysts not to close their minds by holding on to existing knowledge and so preventing the capacity to have an open mind to discover what remains unknown. I think Bion's advice if correctly used is of fundamental importance for analytic work particularly when one realises that something in an analysis does not work. If one first verifies in some detail what one has understood and known and what has seemed to be important and what has roused our interest but without apparent impact on the progress of the analysis we have to be completely open and without any prejudice and often it is this openness which leads to new understanding. It is very likely that it is the sensitivity of the patient to the analyst's state of mind which under such situations makes him feel more free to communicate.

However Bion's important advice not to misuse our memories has been taken by some analysts to mean that the more they can forget everything about their patient, the more inspiration and understanding of the patient will appear and they believe that any associations which may occur to him however disconnected it might seem to be is the interpretation and revelation which the patient requires. Bion himself has of course pointed out that some unexpected thought or phantasy which may appear in our mind may have some important meaning for our patient. However I want to remind you here of the experience of the analyst with the psychotic patient who made him sleepy and forced him into a state of inability to concentrate. It was only when he discovered that in his daydreaming his mind drifted completely away from the patient's material that he began to understand the important predicament of his patient and the patient's communication to him by projection. So the unexpected thought or phantasy which may appear in our mind has to be contained by us often for a long period in order to discover whether it may have any significance for our present work or is a distraction and interference which would seriously disturb the patient/analyst relationship if it was communicated to the patient as if it was an aspect of the patient's way of thinking and functioning.

In his description of clinical material in *Second Thoughts* Bion clearly demonstrated the importance of his memory in understanding the patients cut off or broken up thoughts, which he managed to link even when they appeared divided by intervals of many months.

So it is essential that we can rely on our capacity for memory but it seems to be important that we do not hold on obsessionally to our memories so that important bits of memories and understanding or even recognition of misunderstandings can freely appear in our mind when the situation warrants it.

Bion's description of the reverie of the mother implies that the mother remembers that she has a baby and remembers his needs and in addition is receptive to all his needs and communications or difficulties in communicating. There is a forgetting which is felt by the patient as being shut out or dropped from the analyst's mind and his thoughts which creates a deep hurt and a deep feeling of loneliness. So it is quite frightening to realise that there are quite a number of analysts who claim to be following Bion's work, who believe that the main virture of being an analyst is to forget. This misuse of Bion's advice is particularly dangerous in treating psychotic patients who need a particularly sensitive capacity of remembering and receptivity in the analyst to help them to find those memories, experiences and parts of themselves which they have evacuated, scattered and which seem often to the patient irretrievably lost.

Bion's advice of emptying our mind of desire particularly if it is so contrived that it affects our tone of voice and our way of communicating with patients can be harmful and also creates a strong feeling in the patient of being rejected by the analyst. It is,however,important to remember that our impatient desire to get on with the analysis and our expectancy of cooperation from the patient create great anxiety and feelings of persecution. It is important that our patients do not forget that we are human. I am sure Bion would agree with this.

References

Bion, Wilfred (1953). Notes on the theory of schizophrenia, in *Second Thoughts*, William Heinemann Medical Books, Ltd., London, pp. 23-35.

—— (1957). Differentiation of the psychotic from the non-psychotic personalities, in *Second Thoughts*, William Heinemann Medical Books, Ltd., London, pp. 43-64.

—— (1959). Attacks on linking, in *Second Thoughts*, William Heinemann Medical Books, Ltd., Lond, pp. 93-109.

—— (1962). The theory of thinking, in *Second Thoughts*, William Heinemann Medical Books, Ltd., London, pp. 110-119.

—— (1962). *Learning from Experience*. Chapter 11. William Heinneman Medical Books, Ltd., London.

—— (1967). Commentaries, in *Second Thoughts*, William Heinemann Medical Books, Ltd., London, pp. 120-166.

—— (1970). *Attention and Interpretation*. Tavistock Publications, London.

Klein, Melanie (1946). *Notes on Some Schizoid Mechanisms Developments in Psycho-Analysis*. Hogarth Press, London.

Rosenfeld, Herbert (1947). Analysis of a schizophrenic state in depersonalisation, in *Psychotic States*. London, Hogarth Press, 1965, pp. 13-33.

—— (1949). Remarks on the relation of male homosexuality to paranoia and paranoid anxiety and narcissism, in *Psychotic States*. London. Hogarth Press, 1965, pp. 34-51.

—— (1950). Notes on the psychopathology of confusional states in chronic schizophrenias, in *Psychotic States*. London. Hogarth Press, 1965, pp. 63-103.

—— (1952a). Notes on the psychoanalysis of the superego conflict in the acute schizophrenic patient, in *Psychotic States*. London. Hogarth Press, 1965, pp. 155-168.

—— (1952b). Transference phenomena and transference analysis in an acute catatonic schizophrenic patient, in *Psychotic States*. London. Hogarth Press, 1965, pp. 104-116.

—— (1964). Object relations of an acute schizophrenic patient in the transference situation, in *Recent Research on Schizophrenia* Ed. Philip Salamon, Psych. Research Reports of the American Psychiatric Association.
—— (1971). A clinical approach to the psychoanalytic theory of the life and death instinct: an investigation into the aggressive aspects of narcissism. *Int. J. Psycho-Anal.* Vol. 52, (Part 2), pp. 169-178.
Segal, H. (1950). Some aspects of the analysis of a schizophrenic. *Int. J. Psycho-Anal.* 31. pp. 268-278.

Psychological Birth and Psychological Catastrophe

Frances Tustin

EDITOR'S NOTE: *Mrs. Tustin has had a distinguished career as a child psychoanalyst and as an authority on autism. Her present paper is a distillation of some important observations and then conclusions which have been arrived at over the years of her clinical experience. First of all, she postulates that the infant continues a post-natal existence which, thanks to its mother's protective care, is very much like a continuation of the pre-natal situation. "Premature psychological birth" constitutes a catastrophe, Tustin suggests, which is then reinforced by the seeming domino principle of later disappointments, all under the aegis of the repetition compulsion. She makes the further point that, in the earliest aspects of post-natal life, projective identification is of less prominence than a "flowing over" from the infant to the mother. Additionally, the infant's primitive sense receptors have to deal with the dichotomies of hardness and softness, dialectics which occur in the feeding and in all later object-related situations, hardness being ultimately associated with male qualities and softness with female after first going through a protective or penetrating phase. She deals with the infantile phenomenon of "ecstasy" and "tantrums" as spill-overs of infantile states of emotions which must be handled by a suitable maternal container in order to postpone "precocious twoness" from developing.*

Mrs. Tustin seems to be stating that, side by side with the infant's differentiations, its state of primary undifferentiation must be optimally continued by the caretaking mother so that the model for containment can be introjected and optimal primal identification be exploited. This concept owes much to Bion's conception of maternal reverie but also goes a long way to dispel those attacks on Klein and her followers for not attending to external reality. Mrs. Tustin's contribution is a sensitive phenomenological testimonial to the "young infant's needs for parental support in bearing the ecstasy of 'oneness' and the tantrums of 'twoness,' if primal integrations are to take place."

Psychological Birth and Psychological Catastrophe

Frances Tustin

Introduction

Inspired by Dr. Bion's work this paper is based on psychoanalytic therapy with psychotic children and with the psychotic residues in neurotic children. It will suggest that the situation described by Dr. Bion as a *"psychological catastrophe"* is the result of a premature or mismanaged *"psychological birth"* and that this causes the cognitive inhibition and dysfunctioning which are outstanding features of psychotic states.

Psychological Catastrophe

From his work with adult patients, Bion has likened the situation which confronts a psychoanalyst, when working at depth with a psychotic patient, to that of an archaeologist who comes upon a ruined city, in the course of the excavation of which, due to the collapse and movement of rock strata, shards and other objects from earlier stages are found jumbled together with pottery and fabrications from later stages (Bion 1962). The appropriate nicety of this metaphor is well borne out by work with children. Clinical work at depth inevitably takes us back to the early stages of infancy. When working with psychotic states we find that, in infancy, developmental phases seem to have telescoped. Later stages seem to have been experienced precociously and out of phase, alongside current and earlier stages in a confused and disordered fashion.

Evidence of this comes from many writers. In their paper on Borderline Children, Rosenfeld and Sprince (1965) describe such children's precocious phallic development. When analysing these children they found "pseudo-phallic" elements inextricably intermingled with oral elements. This implies that the child's responses to the breast have been over-erotised. Meltzer and his co-workers confirm that this has been the case. (Meltzer, et al 1975). Winnicott has described the pseudo-maturity of patients who have developed what he terms a "false self" (Winnicott 1971). Helene Deutsch described the fragments of precocity found in "as if" patients (Deutsch 1942). Other workers have been impressed by the precocious development of certain ego functions such as musical or mathematical ability (albeit of a stereotyped kind), whilst other faculties remain in the psychological doldrums. Other writers have written of the "precocious ego development" (James 1960).

In this paper it will be suggested that the telescoping and jumbling of levelopmental phases, some of which develop precociously, is due to the rauma of a *premature* or *mismanaged* "psychological birth" (or perhaps nore accurately, to the cumulative trauma of such a catastrophe, since due o repetition-compulsion, the disastrous situation is repeated over and over ıgain in an attempt to come to terms with it).

Psychological Birth

., myself had begun to use the metaphor of psychological birth before neeting Anni Bergman at the Psychoanalytical Conference in London where he gave me the book written by Margaret Mahler, Fred Pine and herself alled "The Psychological Birth of the Human Infant" (1975). This is a nonumental work based on long experience with psychotic children and on neticulous observation of normal infants and children as part of a carefully planned research project. It is a classic in the field.

Applying Bion's work on "Thinking" to psychotherapy with psychotic children had led me to study certain aspects of the process of psychological birth which were not specifically dealt with by Mahler and her associates. Bion has added to our understanding of early infancy by drawing attention to the mother's capacity for empathic reflexion for which he uses the apt term of "reverie." Through his writings, we have come to realise that, in normal development, the newborn infant is sheltered in what might be termed the "womb" of the mother's mind just as much as, prior to his physical birth, he was sheltered within the womb of her body. This early womb-like state is also a result of the infant's lack of realisation that his body is separate from that of the mother.

Using a suggestion in a little known paper by Hermann (1929) that "flowing-over" is a precurser to *projection*, the present writer has suggested elsewhere (Autism and Childhood Psychosis, 1972), that "flowing-over-at-oneness" are processes by which the illusion of "primal unity" is maintained. It was suggested that these processes are earlier than *projection* and *identification* which imply some sense of bodily separateness between mother and infant.

There is another possibility which seems to contribute to the womb-like state of early infancy. It is tenable that, in spite of the caesura of birth, there is not an absolutely abrupt transition from the sensations associated with being inside the womb to being outside of it. Tactile sensations of being in the "watery medium" (Bion's term), appear to linger on and to be carried over into the child's earliest experience of the outside world. In using the term "oceanic feeling" for these early states, Rolland seems to have had something like this in mind (Rolland 1930, Freud 1930).

The poet Tagore wrote:

"On the seashore of endless worlds children play."

This line which was quoted by Winnicott in Playing and Reality (1971) is evocative for me of the unbounded timelessness of womb-like oceanic states. Work with psychotic states in childhood demonstrates that, if early oceanic illusions are prematurely interrupted, children *do not* play.

Dr. Derek Rick's research on the language development of autistic children demonstrated that such children had not the lalling and babbling sounds which seemed to be universal in the control groups of normal infants he studied, whether they were English or from foreign countries such as Egypt or Spain (Ricks 1975). It seemed that the autistic children had not "played" with the sounds which arise "naturally" from inbuilt predispositions. Instead they made sounds which were idiosyncratic to each individual autistic child and which they seemed to have concocted for themselves in the way that a normal infant will do later on when "play" with "natural" sounds is on the wane. This is in keeping with the artificiality of autistic children, and with the impression that they have missed an early "natural" stage of development. My thesis is that this is due to a premature or mismanaged "psychological birth" and the excruciatingly intense feelings associated with this.

Mismanaged or Premature Psychological Birth

This paper is dealing with elemental states which are normally deeply buried and not investigated. Individuals whose early infantile events were normal were relatively unconscious of them at the time they occurred and seem unlikely to have conscious memories of them later. A traumatic psychological birth is also covered over, and the individual only becomes affected by it if it disturbs his behaviour to such an extent that he has to seek psychiatric help. Other individuals with special talents may work over their psychological birth, whether traumatic or otherwise, through the medium of art, literature, music or religious rituals.

Psychological study of such states is difficult, for they were pre-verbal and pre-conceptual. Communication about them has to be by means of metaphor and analogy and these inevitably distort the original experience. The skill here is in finding the metaphor which is most apt. "Psychological Catastrophe" and "Psychological Birth" have seemed to me to be apt metaphors and "premature and mismanaged psychological birth" have seemed to me to be others. (Formulations about these levels seem best described as metaphors rather than concepts.)

In writing about such states we are making conscious, processes which are normally left unconscious and expressed through empathy and intuition. The mother of a newborn infant has a period of heightened awareness when through her "reveries" she can respond to elemental states in her child but, like the intense emotional experience of giving birth, these heightened states of responsiveness gradually fade to become dim and forgotten. However, communications about very early infancy seem likely to find an echo in the experience of earthy maternal women, in those men with marked feminine characteristics, or in men and women who follow one of the professions which develop deep maternal qualities. For others, communications about these states will not seem meaningful for they are deeply buried and should probably remain so.

However, in order to help ourselves and our patients, some of us are drawn into becoming aware of, and communicating about, these deep levels. Unfortunately this is an area of human experience about which vague, over-simplistic generalisations tend to be presented as precise facts. This is to be regretted, for these are states which need particularly cautious analysis and statement, plus an aptitude for evocative and apt description. It has seemed to me that in concentrating on physical birth and pre-birth, some workers in the field of psychosis are describing states which can often more feasibly be attributed to the womb-like state of early infancy. Such workers often seem to be concretising as bodily events, elementary psychological events which should be described as such. "Physical birth" may prove a helpful metaphor to patients for working over a difficult "psychological birth" but, in attempting to theorise about such states, we need to be more cautious and specific. Of course, if the physical birth has been a difficult one, then the psychological birth may be difficult, but this is not inevitable. It will depend upon the constitutional endowment of the infant, the events of early infancy and the quality of maternal sheltering he receives. Certainly, clinical material from deep levels seems to indicate that traversing the birth canal is not only a preparation for life itself, but is also a rehearsal for the "valley of the shadow of death." The parental attitudes during birth, the sort of sheltering he receives or, as the result of constitutional factors, he is able to use, will affect whether he will "fear no evil," i.e., whether he will develop "basic trust" and thus be able to bear the mistrust which is essential to survival.

Within the sane and healthy sheltering, but not entangling, of the post-natal womb, psychological integrations take place, just as bodily integrations took place within the physical womb of the mother's body. These are processes which are normally taken for granted, for they go on at relatively unconscious levels. They can only be studied if the post-natal womb seems to have been split open before these primal processes have become integrated. If this occurs, the processes are laid bare. In psychotic states this is the case and we become aware of processes and intense states of feeling which are not normally available to study.

Primary Integrations

Work with unintegrated and disintegrated states in children has led me to think that one of the earliest integrations which needs to take place is between "hard" and "soft" sensations. In the sensation-dominated state of early infancy the infant's primary distinctions are between "comfort" and "discomfort"—"pleasure" and "unpleasure." "Soft" sensations are pleasurable and comfortable. "Hard" sensations are unpleasurable and uncomfortable.

Gradually, "soft" sensations become associated with "taking-in"—with receptivity. "Hard" sensations become associated with "entering" and "thrusting." At some point, these become associated with the infant's bisexuality. "Hard" thrusting becomes "male," and "soft," "receptive" becomes "female." When, on the basis of a cooperative suckling experience, "hard," "entering" nipple and tongue are experienced as working together with "soft" receptive mouth and breast, then a "marriage" between "male" and "female" elements takes place. Out of this union of "hard" and "soft" sensations, a new way of functioning is born, that of firm, adaptable, resilience and toughness. This means that reality can begin to be processed, and sensation-dominated delusions will wither away. The world will begin to "make sense." And in this "making sense" of the outside world, the parents play a very important part. (The rudimentary psychological integrations which have just been described will, of course, be parallelled by neurophysiological integrations taking place in the child's brain and nervous system. These are not within my competence nor my province to describe, but I think they should be mentioned.)

In this account of basic integrations, the earliest situation is particularly difficult to describe because the sensation-dominated child is in a state of "oneness" with the mother. In this state, he is not likely to be aware of nipple, tongue, breast and mouth as separate entities. To describe as nearly as possible his probable state, we might say that "nipple-tongue" is "hardness" and "mouth-breast" is "softness." In a satisfactory suckling experience sensations of "softness" and "hardness" work together to produce a state of "well-being." "Well-being" is a psychological as well as a bodily experience. Thus, bodily sensations have been transformed into *psychological* experience through reciprocal and rhythmical activity between mother and infant. The stage is set for percept and concept formation. But this is a mysterious process and in this paper we can only hope to touch the fringes of it.

The foregoing is a bare outline of the processes of primary differentiation and integration as I have come to understand them. This understanding has mainly been obtained from a study of those children in whom the processes have been disturbed. Such children demonstrate for us the hazards which may have to be encountered before a salutory outcome is reached. Some of these will now be discussed.

Critical Situations for Primary Integrations

Clinical material from unintegrated and disintegrated children indicates that critical situations in primary integrations are those occasions when the infant becomes aware that "hard" and "soft" are both "me" sensations, and that both can emanate from the same source outside himself. It is at this stage that processes of projection are stimulated and get under way; processes of "flowing over-at-oneness" give way to *projection, imitation* and *identification*.

In Beyond the Pleasure Priniciple, Freud (1920) alerted us to the process of *projection* by which uncomfortable states are felt to be outside the body. "Comfort" is "me"–"Discomfort" is "not-me." "Softness" is "me," "hardness" is "not-me." This is well illustrated by a commonly reported feature of psychotic children, many of whom will only eat soft foods and reject hard lumps. With this dichotomy between the "soft me" and the "hard not-me," "twoness" comes into being. But, in this early phase of "twoness," the "soft me" is excessively vulnerable. This constitutes a critical situation. If the maternal sheltering is disturbed at this time, the infant feels exposed to "nameless dreads" (to use a telling phrase of Dr. Bion's).

The following extract of clinical material illustrates this situation as the child works over it in the protected situation of the psycho-analytic setting. The child seems to be trying to tell the psychiatrist about a time when his tender naked body felt unprotected from a hostile outside world. Just as we have to use metaphors for the description of these worldless states of awareness, so childen have to use picture language. This child's representation was moving and vivid.

Graham was twelve years old at the time when he worked over some of the elemental terrors to be demonstrated by the clinical presentation. He had been a "School Ditherer" (i.e., he was not an "out and out" school phobic). He found it difficult to go back to school on Mondays. He was seen once a week for psychoanalytic therapy by Dr. Etchegoyan who discussed the material with me in a weekly supervision time. (I am indebted to Dr. Etchegoyan for permission to use this material.)

October 22nd.	Graham had an accident to his dental plate and so did not come to his session.
October 29th.	Graham came and there was material about damage to his mouth which was related to infantile situations when he felt he lost the nipple of the breast which he had taken for granted as being part of his mouth, and then felt that his mouth was "broken"–"damaged."
November 5th.	Graham brought material about having precious things to protect but his special protection for these things gets "crashed." He then went on to describe an underwater situation with great vividness. He said he had seen this situation when on holiday in Devon (i.e., when he was apart from his therapist). He described a little baby crab whose mother was not there to protect it. Its shell had not

hardened as yet and it was pink and tender. It could easily have been attacked and eaten by the sea creatures which were around. In order to avoid this, it scuttled into an empty snail shell which was in the sea and there it was safe. Dr. Etchegoyan then talked to Graham about how he turned his hard back to protect his soft front. (This was an interpretaion we had discussed together previously.) Graham replied, "No, I protect my soft front with the hard buckle of my belt." He showed Dr. Etchegoyan a very large buckle that was on the leather belt which encircled his waist. He also said that he had hurt his left ear, twice, once yesterday and once today. Dr. Etchegoyan talked to him about his need to protect all the holes in his body because they were places where dangerous things could enter and where he could easily be hurt.

November 12th. Graham walked to the therapy room in a "somewhat disjointed fashion." He sat down and looked at the set of individual cupboards in which his own and the other children's toys are kept. (Each child has his own individual cupboard with his own key which will not open any other child's cupboard.) At first, as he looked, he touched his nails and put one nail inside the other as if extracting dirt. He then put his thumb in his mouth. Then, still looking at the cupboard, he fingered the buckle on his belt. He started to count the cupboards. Dr. Etchegoyan suggested that he was counting the cupboards to take his mind off his troubles, but she did not take up his fear of the other children as creatures who would attack his soft, pink, tender body which had so many open holes where he could be hurt and where dangerous things could enter, although she realised this later. (It seems to me that excessive vulnerability is one of the root causes of the massive use of obsessional mechanisms and that it is only by helping the patient with this vulnerability that obsessionality can be mitigated.) Graham, still looking at the cupboards, fingered the hard buckle on his belt. Then he joined and separated his hands by interlacing his fingers.

> Then, to Dr. Etchegoyan's consternation, he got up from his chair and rushed out of the room. He ran round the clinic building in a state of panic before returning to the shelter of his mother in the waiting room.

After this, there were several sessions when he refused to come to the clinic, but Dr. Etchegoyan kept in touch with Graham's mother by telephone. On one occasion, the mother told Dr. Etchegoyan with some embarrassment and bewilderment, that Graham had said that he was afraid that "monsters would come out of the little cupboards." Dr. Etchegoyan replied that she had realised that something like this had been worrying Graham and she hoped that he would come so that they could talk about it. The mother seemed very relieved that what she had reported had not sounded too peculiar and went on to report, with some amusement, that she had told Graham that he must know that monsters did not exist because he had never seen one. To which he had replied, "Why shouldn't there be monsters? Nobody has seen God but you say He exists!" After this discussion, Graham came to his next session.

Discussion of the Clinical Material

Dr. Etchegoyan, Graham's psychiatrist, is at the beginning of embarking on a study of the elemental depths encountered in child treatment. It was very instructive to her, as also to myself, to have such a striking illustration of their power to affect a child's functioning. (We often learn more when we have failed to understand a child's communications quickly enough, than when the therapeutic process flows smoothly and easily.)

This piece of material is a good illustration of the residues of unintegration which are encountered in the psychoanalytic treatment of neurotic children. It is also a good illustration of the importance of concentrating on psychic events rather than outside circumstances when dealing with "as if" levels of personality. Patients, at these levels, use outside events as a kind of psycho-drama. Their internal psychic life is negligible. Bettelheim's metaphor of an "empty fortress" is a very apt description of them (Bettelheim 1967).

It has been my experience that children often use underwater situations to express the early state of oceanic feeling. The little pink naked crab who has lost his mother is a telling picture of vulnerability. This excessive vulnerability makes Graham feel exposed to creatures who threaten him. This is the crux of his fear of school. The other children are not just children, they are "monsters"—all powerful things from the primitive depths which threaten him with death. Kind reassurance and rational reasoning offer no permanent relief. It is only by working over these elemental terrors through the infantile transference of the psychotherapeutic setting that the child can come to terms with them. Otherwise, he feels forever at risk. The psychotherapeutic setting seems to be a kind of incubator in which the psychological "prem" can achieve those basic integrations which he did not make in infancy. Without these, a sense of primal attachment and basic trust are not possible.

As the supervisor of this material, I learned something I had not previously known so clearly. I had become aware of such children's preoccupation with having an "extra bit" to their bodies. This always has to be a "hard" bit. The hard metal buckle was such an extra hard bit for Graham, and this made me aware of the ultra-protective nature of this hard extra bit. For me, this threw light on the commonly reported feature of some psychotic children who take hard things like metal trains to bed with them rather than soft "cuddly" toys as the normal child will do.

The underwater material shows another way of getting protection. The vulnerable Graham-crab enters the "hardness" of another creature. In this protective manoeuvre we see "intrusive identification (Meltzer's term) in action. This results in the "false-self" described by Winnicott; the "as if" condition described by Deutsch (1942). In later life, these patients live their lives through other people to an excessive and pathological degree. (They are the Strindbergs of this world.)

Encased in this "shell," such children are impenetrable to nurturing influences and their development is halted. Important basic integrations do not take place. It is one of the most difficult situations to deal with in psychotherapy. Removal of this protective manoeuvre brings the threat of a repetition of the "psychological catastrophe" from which the child has retreated.

This is the crux of the problem of non-integration or disintegration. Let me now summarize why this seems to be so. As was stated earlier, the child has experienced "twoness" too harshly, too early, too suddenly *for him*. In early infancy, comfortable "softness" is the prime consideration. To preserve this, the hard "not-me" is felt to be outside. But then this hard "not-me" is threatening. This seems to be the forerunner of the "stranger anxiety" described by Spitz (1963) for later stages of development. It seems possible that these "not-me" threats combine with the atavistic fear of predators from our animal ancestry to which ethologists have drawn our attention. Certainly, these "nameless dreads" often become focussed upon "creatures."

In his valuable paper on Imitation, Eugenic Gaddini (1969) tried to clear our minds about the psychoanalytic use of terms for early developmental situations and also to clarify for us the order in which early processes occur. Based on his own psychoanalytic work with adult patients and that of this wife Renata Gaddini with infants and children, he sees primitive rivalry as being even earlier than the primary envy described by both Klein (1957) and Jacobson (1964). This confirms my own experience. Children whose womb-like oceanic feeling is unduly disturbed seem to be faced by death-dealing "rivals" who could never exist in reality and whose threats are worse than death. Even "annihilation anxiety" seems too mild a term to describe the state of terror which either paralyses these children or causes them to behave in an impulsively irrational way, like dashing out of the consulting room or refusing to go to school. The threat is of a cataclysmic catastrophe which they feel they have already experienced, a repetition of which must be avoided at all costs (this needs detailed clinical material to make it meaningful to workers who have not experienced these elemental states).

This dichotomy between the hyper-vulnerable soft "me" calloused over by a hard impenetrable protection seems to be the basic situation in some forms of criminality. In his studies of murderousness, Dr. Hyatt Williams (1960) from psychoanalytic work with seven murderers in Wormwood Scrubs prison, has told us of the excessively tender feelings which such patients had beneath their callous exteriors. It would also seem to be a basic situation in some phobic patients.

So far, we have discussed states of unintegration, i.e., "hard" and "soft" sensations have not been integrated. But, in some psychopathologies we come upon disintegration, i.e., "hard" and "soft" sensations have been insecurely integrated, to break down under strain.

Critical situations would seem to arise when the attempt is made to integrate these basic states of sensation. When "hardness" penetrates "softness," excitement is produced. The prototype of this is when the hard nipple enters the soft mouth. If the excitement can be tolerated, it is pleasurable and the sublime state of "oneness" is maintained. But, the excitement can mount until a state of ecstasy is reached.

Ecstasy

Ecstasy can enhance the state of oneness experienced by mother and infant. Inbuilt predispositions seem to find exact coincidence in the outside world, and this seems to inaugurate and establish attachment to the mother. But, whether this attachment occurs will depend upon the maternal capacity to experience and bear such states of ecstasy within herself. If, for a variety of reasons, which may be part of a temporary passing phase, the mother's capacity to bear such extreme states is muted, then the infant is left to bear such states alone. In normal development, for much of the time, the mother will seem to "hold" (Winnicott) her infant together so that he does not disintegrate under the discharge of intense excitement. She also seems to contain (Bion) the discharges which are beyond the infant's capacity to bear and process. These are psychological as well as physiological. If the mother cannot hold her infant together in these intense states of excitement and cannot seem to bear the "overflow," and process it by empathy and understanding, the infant experiences a precocious sense of "twoness" which seems fraught with disaster. Instead of experiencing ecstasy as a peak of sublime oneness which helps him to feel "rooted" in a nurturant situation, the infant feels cut off from it. He feels adrift and alone. The insecurity of this precocious sense of "twoness" leads to pathological manoeuvres to reinstate the sense of oneness. In confusional psychotic children, these are adhesive and entangling in nature. They result in confusion with a maternal object from which it is well-nigh impossible to achieve normal separation in an appropriate and progressive way. The encapsulated children have the autistic delusion of being fused with the hard bit of the mother and of being protected by this encapsulation which is either total or of segments.

Precocious "Twoness"

Such children are aware of too much, too soon, too harshly, too suddenly for them. They experience an agony of consciousness which is beyond their capacity to tolerate or to pattern. Various protective autistic manoeuvres are used to deaden their awareness in order to avoid suffering. These result in their being out of touch with reality. Awareness of the outside world is inhibited or grossly distorted. Psychological integrations do not take place: behaviour becomes idiosyncratic. In extreme instances the child becomes psychotic.

The fact that the infant experiences "twoness" in a state which we loosely term "omnipotence," is also important. Omnipotence is a state in which the infant operates in terms of bodily sensations, rhythms and inbuilt pre-dispositions. Being newly born these have not been modified by reciprocal interplay with the outside world. In this state, the infant feels that his movements and urges make things occur, for example, that his crying results in "nipple-in-mouth" which seems to be the prototype for sensual completeness. However, precocious awareness of bodily separateness and "twoness" brings the knowledge that the nipple is not part of his mouth and that his movements do not always make for completeness and do not produce benign hallucinations. His unsatisfied crying mouth can then seem like a "black hole with a nasty prick" (as one child vividly described the situation of the breast which was absent from his mouth). This is a malign hallucination. Also, the frustration of the absent breast, of the uncompleted gestalt, is experienced as a tangible irritant, as a hard and painful friction—as roughness. Irritating friction produces rage and panic. When this reaches a crescendo of intensity it results in a *tantrum*—a *fit* of temper as we often term it.

Tantrum

On referral, autistic children often have a history of a passing phase of "*fits*" which do not seem to have been strictly epileptic in nature. Other children have a history of "tantrums" in infancy. I have found this to be a hopeful prognostic sign since it indicates that they have made some attempt to integrate the "hard" and "soft" facets of early experience. (Those psychotic children who have a history of having been an "exceptionally good baby" would seem to have remained in the state of making a dichotomy between the "soft me" and the "hard not-me." There would seem to have been little attempt to integrate these basic aspects of sensation, and thus, little friction and disturbance.)

The tantrum, like the ecstasy, needs nurturing which is capable of holding the child together through intense bodily-cum-psychological states. The mother also needs to seem to "contain" the bodily-cum-psychological discharges, expressed in such reactions as urination, defaecation and spitting, associated with the rage and panic of the tantrum. If these are not "contained" by the mother the delusion will be that they spread around in an uncontrolled and explosive fashion to bring about a catastrophe. (Meltzer's concept of the "nappy mummy" is relevant here.)

This "holding" and "containing" comes about through the processes of "flowing-over-at-oneness" described earlier. Unbearable bodily tension which is not understood, empathised and relieved by the mother quickly enough is experienced as a disturbing "overflow." It disturbs the illusion of "flowing-over-at-oneness." Unbearable bodily tension is uncomfortable. It feels turgid and hard. It is projected as "not-me." Thus, the sense of "oneness" is disturbed and "twoness" results, but in a way that is unduly painful and sudden and causes a precipitate coming together as a "self" which is not genuine—a "false self" as Winnicott has termed it.

Work with psychotic children has brought home to me the importance of this "overflow"—this "spill over" of psychological and physiological tension. The child experiences it as tangible body stuff which overflows out of his control. He cannot process it. He recoils from this dangerous stuff in the "not-me" outside world. Or, he may feel possessed by it and be unmanageably hyperactive. In early infancy, by her disciplined attitudes and behaviour the mother seems to control, channel and render harmless this overflow which is beyond the child's control. She acts as both analyser and synthesiser which if things go wrong, the psychoanalyst has to do in a more artificial way later on.

Over-Flow

There are many ways in which the mother can give the child the impression that she is giving way under the impact of the "over-flow." She may be absent in mind or in body. She may avert herself from noticing it and act as if it did not exist. She may be too permissive. She may be too strict or too teasing and thus provoke too much frustration and too much "over-flow." The worst situation seems to be one of gross inconsistency, of swaying between over-strictness and over-permissiveness in a way which is inappropriate to the particular child and the particular circumstances. The situation that becomes very clear in working with psychotic states is that bodily separateness from the mother has occurred too suddenly and too harshly *for that particular infant*. This has resulted in a precocious and false self which feels wounded or mutilated.

Pre-Animate States

Bion's term "container" seems very apt for the concretised functioning in terms of inanimate objects, which is under discussion. The early states of differentiation between "hardness" and "softness" take place before the important distinctions between "animate" and "inanimate" (to which Spitz has drawn our attention) are made or before they have become securely established. These early differentiations are the bedrock of human personality before the "humanness" of psychological functioning has emerged. They are physiological integrations with incipient psychological overtones which are extremely important in giving the personality its basic "set."

The psychotic child, who when taken to an educational psychologist for psychological testing, would only draw a ruined house and would do nothing else, was obviously communicating about a psychological catastrophe which he felt to be at the root of his being. This had seemed to happen to an inanimate "thing" and not to a person. This child had been suddenly weaned at four months of age and then separated from his mother. But, other children who manifest states of unintegration or disintegration have not necessarily had a geographical separation from the mother. Through no fault of their own, nor of their mother, the maternal sheltering has seemed to be shattered. As Bergman and Escalona have shown some children are hypersensitive and the "maternal shield" has not been adequate (Bergman and Escalona 1949). In another situation, a mother may find it difficult to "take to" and to empathise with her newborn child. In some cases, the mother was not emotionally "ready" for the birth of this baby. In other situations, the mother may find it difficult to empathise with the child who is very different from herself. A marked example of this is when a baby is born with a handicap such as deafness, blindness or spasticity. It requires a great effort of imagination to sense such a child's responses. In other situations, the mother may be depressed, or the father may be away from home, or the mother and father may be having a phase when they do not "get on" together.

These, and other situations which Dr. S. Tischler (1979) has described very feelingly, interconnect with each other to produce what seems to the child to be a "psychological catastrophe" at the root of his being. This has happened to a "body self"—a "felt-self"—of which the child has become aware prematurely. His self-representation is thus on a false basis and his body ego is defective. Such premature bodily separateness from the mother is experienced by the infant as the loss of a bodily part. This means that instead of normally-timed differentiation and integration, explosive disintegration or paralysed unintegration is the order of the day. In later life, such a child feels "cursed" rather than "blessed," for these situations are associated with states of omnipotence which result in feelings that are larger than life.

As D.H. Lawrence wrote:

> "It is a terrible thing to fall into the hands of the living God but a much more terrible thing to fall out of them."

This catastrophe has to be re-experienced and worked over if psychotherapy in later life is to reverse the pathological autistic processes.

Conclusion

The essence of the thesis developed in this paper is that the young infant needs parental support in bearing the ecstasy of "oneness" and the tantrum of "twoness," if necessary primal differentiations and integrations are to take place. The therapeutic setting acts as a kind of incubator in which the psychological "prem" can achieve those basic integrations he did not make in infancy. These extreme states are usually worked over within the privacy of parental sheltering. It seems somewhat indecent to lay them bare. Perhaps this is *one* of the reasons why psychosis seems so shocking and disturbing to normal individuals. Something is being made public which should be kept private.

Analysing such states seems rather like trying to put a dream or a nightmare under a microscope. It just cannot be done. It is a paradox that these crude states need extreme delicacy and subtlety in their delineation. To write about them often seems brash and clumsy, but not to do so seems a professional dereliction. It is hoped that the inevitable shortcomings of this paper will be offset by the fact that it has been written as an expression of gratitude to Dr. Bion who by his unique contribution to this most difficult area of study, has enabled many of us to rise phoenix-like from the ashes of psychological catastrophe to achieve psychological birth later in life than is normally possible.

References

Bergman, P. & Escalona, S. (1949). Unusual sensitivities in young children. *Psychoanalytic Study of the Study Child* 3/4, 333-352.

Bettelheim, B. (1967). *The Empty Fortress: Infantile Autism and the Birth of the Self*. New York: The Free Press; London: Collier/Macmillan.

Bion, W.R. (1962). A theory of thinking. *Int. J. Psycho-Anal.* 43, 306-314. ALSO IN: *Second Thoughts*. London: Heinemann, pp. 110-119.

Deutsch, H. (1942[1934]). Some forms of emotional disturbance and their relationship to schizophrenia. IN: *Neuroses and Character Types*. New York: IUP, 1965, pp. 262-281.

Freud, S. (1920). *Beyond the Pleasure Principle. S.E.* 18, 3-64. London: Hogarth Press, 1957.

—— (1930). *Civilization and its Discontents. S.E.* 21, 59-148. London: Hogarth Press, 1961.

Gaddini, E. (1969). On imitation. *Int. J. Psycho-Anal.* 50, 475-484.

Hermann, I. (1929). Das Ich und das Denken. *Imago*, 15.

Jacobson, E. (1964). *The Self and the Object World*. New York: IUP.

James, M. (1960). Premature ego development. *Int. J. Psycho-Anal.* 41, 288-294.

Klein, M. (1957). *Envy and Gratitude*. New York: Basic Books.

Mahler, M., Pine, F., and Bergman, A. (1975). *The Psychological Birth of the Human Infant*. New York: Basic Books.

Meltzer, D., Bremner, J., Hoxter, S., Weddel, D., and Wittenberg, I. (1975). *Explorations in Autism*. Perthshire: Clunie Press.

Ricks, D. (1975). Vocal communication in pre-verbal, normal, and autistic children. IN: *Language, Cognitive Defects, and Retardation*, N.O'Connor (ed.). London: Butterworths.
Rolland, R. (1930). *Prophets of the New India*. New York: Boni.
[Kut] Rosenfeld, S.K., and Sprince, M.D. (1965). Some thoughts on the technical handling of borderline children. *The Psychoanalytic Study of the Child* 20, 495-517.
Spitz, R. (1963). *Life and the Dialogue*. IN: *Counterpoint*, H.S. Gaskill (ed.). New York: IUP.
Tischler, S. (1979). Being with a psychotic child: a psychoanalytic approach to the problem of parents of psychotic children. *Int. J. Psycho-Anal*. 60, 29-38.
Tustin, F. (1972). *Autism and Childhood Psychosis*. London: Hogarth Press.
Williams, H. (1960). A psycho-analytic approach to the treatment of the murderer. *Int. J. Psycho-Anal*. 45, 532-539.
Winnicott, D.W. (1971). *Playing and Reality*. London: Tavistock.

Raskolnikov's Transgression and the Confusion Between Destructiveness and Creativity

Richard J. Rosenthal

EDITOR'S NOTE: Crime and Punishment *is a detective story and a great novel, but it may very well also have been one of the significant progenitors of psychoanalysis. No one reading this novel can remain unimpressed by the author's astuteness to the deeper dimensions of aberrant personality. Freud declared on his seventieth birthday that everything he had discovered was already present in Dostoevsky's work; Nietzsche proclaimed Dostoevsky the only psychologist from whom he learned anything.*

At the center of the novel is one of the most controversial figures in Western literature, and Dr. Rosenthal carefully utilizes the psychoanalytic "detective instruments" of Melanie Klein and Wilfred Bion to ascertain the states of mind of Raskolnikov. He makes use of Klein's delineation of primitive mechanisms and of Bion's conception of psychotic thinking, particularly the latter's notion of the domain of hallucinosis (-K), that cursorily improvised area of psychotic habitation where delusions of omnipotence reign supreme and from which the awarenesses of internal and external reality are barred admittance.

In so doing, Dr. Rosenthal is sensitively alert to the genius of Dostoevsky and to how the author is able to transform a horrifying tale of murder, from what might otherwise stand as a psychiatric case history, into elegant literature. On the one hand, we see ample evidence of autobiographical phantasies sifting their way through the sluices of the narrative into the mainstream of the story. But it is not to the author's personal conflicts that our attention is being directed. Dr. Rosenthal unravels the unconscious patterns found in the text itself, and then demonstrates how psychic mechanisms are rendered in literary terms—the use of projective identification, for example, and of physical space utilized in the representation of mental space.

What we are treated to in Dostoevsky's work are mental landscapes—*dream scapes from which there is no escape. It is for this reason, I think, that many people cannot read Dostoevsky; they find him too disturbing. Critical interpretations can serve to protect one from this disturbance, as can various religious and philosophical vertices. This may indeed be why so many readers came to view* Crime and Punishment *as a novel of self-discovery and progressive moral redemption. This is the point at which Dr. Rosenthal begins his re-interpretation and close textual analysis.*

This stimulating contribution was awarded the Jacques Brien Prize by the Los Angeles Psychoanalytic Institute for the best article submitted for the year 1980. I suggest it will not only cause us to look a little differently at the Raskolnikovs, Svidrigailovs, and Marmeladovs we see in our consulting rooms, but will send many of us back to re-read Dostoevsky's novel, and to do so with expanded understanding and appreciation.

Raskolnikov's Transgression and the Confusion Between Destructiveness and Creativity

Richard J. Rosenthal

Crime and Punishment is generally regarded as one of the world's greatest psychological novels. Most frequently, Raskolnikov is thought of as a man driven by his sense of guilt to get caught, to confess, and to be punished. I do not feel, however, that this is borne out by the text, at least not in the way it is usually understood. Nor do I go along with the oedipal interpretation of the novel that has been put forth by a series of psychoanalytically-minded writers. The first of these is assumed to be Freud (1928), although the only novel of Dostoevsky's that Freud specifically referred to was his last, *The Brothers Karamazov*. Joseph Frank (1975) has written a highly regarded article which reviews the factual errors found in "Dostoevsky and Parricide." It is Frank's contention (1976, pp. 25-28) that a number of the legends about Dostoevsky originated with or have been perpetuated by Freud's essay. In offering my reinterpretation of this great novel, I hope to not only address myself to formal elements within the narrative structure, but to suggest how the confusions found in reading *Crime and Punishment* reflect one of its central themes.

This novel seems to have provoked more intense reactions, more critical commentary, indeed more basic differences of interpretation, than anything else Dostoevsky wrote. The epilogue to the novel remains one of the most controversial areas of Dostoevsky criticism, specifically the question of Raskolnikov's moral regeneration. In fact, a good deal of these critical differences seem to stem from the critic's moral position vis-a-vis the novel.

Philip Rahv (1960) has suggested that we view *Crime and Punishment* as a detective story, but a special kind of detective story in which the murderer's identity is known from the beginning, and the problem for the reader is in discovering Raskolnikov's motive. Rahv sees the entire novel as converging toward the solution, and he takes his idea further by suggesting that the criminal is himself a detective intent on penetrating the mystery of his own motivation. "Never quite certain as to what it was exactly that induced him to commit murder, he must continually spy on himself in a desperate effort to penetrate his own psychology and attain the self knowledge he needs if he is to assume responsibility for his absurd and hideous act."

A number of other critics have also emphasized this dual progression: the quest for knowledge and the movement toward moral responsibility. Raskolnikov is often portrayed in the critical literature as an intellectual, a type of "thinking man." Richard Peace (1971) sums him up as "above all else, a man whose actions are based on cool and calculating reason." George Lukacs (1943) describes how Raskolnikov commits murder in order to "know himself," the crime being a test of his moral capacity. Edward Wasiolek (1959) also interprets the novel as a moral progression leading to spiritual redemption. "We find that Raskolnikov goes from pride to humility, hate to love, reason to faith, and from separation from his fellow man to communion with them." He sees the structure of the novel as built around two pivotal scenes, the murder and the confession. "The confession becomes the central point of the testing of Raskolnikov's rebirth."

This was close, apparently, to Dostoevsky's initial intention. In the *Notebooks for Crime and Punishment* (1931) he describes Raskolnikov: "N.B. His moral development begins from the crime itself, the possibility of such questions arises which would not have existed previously. In the last chapter, in prison, he says that without the crime he would not have reached the point of asking himself such questions and experiencing such desires, feelings, needs, strivings, and development."

None of this, however, found its way into the novel, as will soon become apparent. At every step of the way we see Raskolnikov deceiving himself in order to avoid responsibility. He is trying not to think, not to feel, not to confront reality. The novel is experienced in terms of this rhythm of avoidance and forced confrontation. When he goes off to Siberia, he is unchanged, unrepentent, and just as arrogant and angry as when he contemplated the murder. He appears to have learned nothing about himself or about his motivation for the crime. Why he has confessed is as big a mystery as the discovery of the motive for the crime itself.

I shall attempt to answer these questions, and in the process hopefully raise others, by approaching the novel from the psychoanalytic perspective so richly enhanced by the contributions of Melanie Klein and Wilfred Bion. This will enable us to understand the rage and destructiveness that Raskolnikov feels toward the nurturing mother, and the hatred of his own hatred which necessitates his rationalizations, his need to see mother and sister–indeed, all women to whom he is indebted–as robbing him and therefore deserving of his hostile attacks.

Splitting, the essential defensive operation which underlies all the others, gives Raskolnikov his name (raskol = to split). Excessive splitting is utilized along with idealization and devaluation, denial, omnipotence and primitive projection (projective identification) in order to avoid feelings of envy and greed, helplessness and dependency, and above all guilt, in relation to his mother.

Psychic murder, the attempt to annihilate painful and unacceptable aspects of the self, underlies the murder of the old pawnbroker and her sister. Raskolnikov believes that frustration and pain can be evaded by destructively attacking the part of the mental apparatus able to perceive them. Thoughts are treated as unwanted things, fit only for expulsion. Such pathological projective identification results in violent fragmentation and the disintegration of the personality; the evacuated particles are experienced as having an independent life threatening him from outside (Bion 1956, 1957, 1958a, 1962a, 1962b).

Crime and Punishment is more than a description of the shifting states of mind of such an individual. Without using first person narration Dostoevsky manages to place the reader partly within Raskolnikov's consciousness. The relationship between primitive projective mechanisms and narrative structure has been the subject of an earlier study (Rosenthal 1977). Critics may disagree about the meaning of Svidrigailov or Sonia, but they generally recognize that these two characters are meant to represent two aspects of Raskolnikov's personality. There is a sense in which *Crime and Punishment* resembles a dream, indeed a nightmare, in which all the characters are the dreamer, and all the action, the settings as well, are dramatizations of the various mental states of a single consciousness. By entering that world and becoming the dreamer, the reader shares in his experience, exciting and uncomfortable as it may be, and perhaps as confusing, too.

Before beginning a textual analysis of the novel, I would like to take one more look at the acquisition of knowledge in association with morality, but as seen from the vertex of the minus K (−K) link (Bion, 1962b, pp. 95-99). Knowledge can be used to misunderstand, in order to evade painful experience; the possession of knowledge may be used to assert one's superiority. The −K link raises morality above a scientific search for truth, but what is actually being asserted is "moral superiority without any morals." A superior object, which Bion calls a *"super" ego*, asserts its superiority by finding fault with everything. Relationships thus stripped of vitality and meaning become mutually spoiling and destructive. The link can be called *parasitic*, a term which perhaps better than any other summarizes the view of human relationships presented in Dostoevsky's novel.

The most important characteristic of this *"super" ego* is its hatred of anything it doesn't know, and its hatred of anything new, including any new development within its own personality, which it views as a rival to be destroyed. Infanticide is a theme which runs throughout this and most of Dostoevsky's other work. Hatred is directed also against the act of birth itself, viewed sometimes as a hostile ejection leading to disintegration or fragmentation, and at other times blamed for the feelings of smallness and helplessness and the persecutory awareness of how little one knows. *Crime and Punishment* is about precisely this kind of destructiveness; it is also a novel about creativity, including on some level, the writing of a novel.

I

"It would be interesting to know what it is men are most afraid of. Taking a new step, uttering a new word* is what they fear most . . . but I am talking

*Dostoevsky frequently used the same expression, "to utter a new word," in referring to his own creativity. For example, in a letter to his friend, the poet A.N. Maikov, May 15-27, 1869, he speaks of "the poet, as *creator and maker*" and writes, "only now you will have the power to utter the *new word, your new word!*" (Dostoevsky 1923, pp. 71, 77).

too much" (p. 2).* Raskolnikov, in the opening episode of the novel, expresses the awe with which men regard creativity. The spatial imagery associated with thinking something new, going where man has never gone before, provides one meaning of the word "transgression" in the title of the novel. The Russian word *prestuplenie*, unfortunately translated as "crime," more accurately means a stepping across, or more literally translated, a stepping over a barrier.

This initial scene utilizes the spatial imagery associated with *prestuplenie* on at least three different levels. While purusing his lofty thoughts about man's epistemophilic instinct, Raskolnikov is in the act of stepping across a different type of barrier. He is sneaking out of his garret, trying to avoid his landlady to whom he owes money and is ashamed of confronting. He must get past her open door, and across her threshold, in order to reach the supposed safety of the street. However, as he fearfully tries to get by her without being seen, he is not thinking of how to pay his debts. "The anxieties of his position had of late ceased to weigh upon him. He had given up attending to matters of practical importance; he had lost all desire to do so." His landlady represents a nuisance. "To be stopped on the stairs, to be forced to listen to her trivial, irrelevant gossip, to pestering demands for payment, threats and complaints, and to rack his brain for excuses, to prevaricate, to lie–no, rather than that he would creep down the stairs like a cat and slip out unseen" (pp. 1-2).

Raskolnikov's debt, his obligation to this woman, is experienced by him as a persecution. To the reader, she is an unknown presence on the other side of an open door; later, we will learn that she is easy to get along with, even generous, and his assumption that she would be demanding and threatening is part of the scene he plays out in his head. His responsibility to her is felt to be an enormous obstacle blocking his path. He tries to deal with it by avoidance, or by reducing it to insignificance. He has a momentary awareness that he is afraid of just such "trifles" as represented by the confrontation with his landlady. We are now in a position to state the second meaning of the threshold symbol. Raskolnikov's awareness of responsibility for, or obligation toward, another person is conceived of as a barrier. Many of his actions, including the murders, are an omnipotent attempt to step over his guilt. If this barrier does not exist, or if he can leap over it, then he believes he will be free.

The spatial movement of the opening episode is consistent with the birth imagery noted by a number of critics as appearing throughout *Crime and Punishment*. How appropriate that movement across the threshold separating the security of what is known, from the challenges of what is not, would be represented by, and representative of, the act of birth itself! Raskolnikov begins in the cramped and confining quarters of his little room

*Unless otherwise specified, references to *Crime and Punishment* are to the Constance Garnett translation. Pagination will be given parenthetically within the text.

where he had remained in bed, not caring about anything, rather lifeless. He struggles to get out, and has to overcome obstacles to do so. Once on the outside, life is teeming around him; there is brisk movement, and there are strong sensations. His mother, however, represented by the landlady who shelters and feeds him, is viewed not as the giver of life, but as the obstacle to being born. This is a tip-off, that whatever other crimes will be involved, robbery will be one of them. The mother has been transformed into an obstacle, her creative or nutritive capacities taken away from her.* Sure enough, Raskolnikov's musings about creativity, in his first spoken words to us, are both preceded and followed by associations to the robbery and murder of the old pawnbroker.

The idea of the murder makes Raskolnikov uncomfortable; so rather than considering it, evaluating it and perhaps rejecting the idea, he avoids it. He reduces it to a trifle. "It is not serious at all. It's simply a fantasy to amuse myself; a plaything! Yes, maybe it is a plaything" (p. 1). We will see over and over again that Raskolnikov deals with people by devaluing them, and with uncomfortable thoughts and feelings by getting rid of them, frequently by a forceful projection resulting in fragmentation into particles called "trifles."**

The importance of space in Dostoevsky's narrative structures had been noted by Bakhtin, who pointed out how Dostoevsky concentrates all the action in his novels at two points: (1) on the threshold (doorways, entrances, stairs, corridors) where crises and turning points occur; or (2) the square, open places where catastrophes and scandals take place (Bakhtin 1929). What has not been noted is the way in which Dostoevsky uses physical space to represent mental space, but in order to do this one would need some understanding of projective identification (Klein 1946; Rosenfeld 1969).

Raskolnikov's use of projection is dramatized for us by his efforts to get out of his building to the safety he imagines to be found on the street. The mechanism receives concrete representation as movement between inside and outside, or across the barrier between self and non-self. This placement of aspects of self where they don't belong, the resulting intrusion on others, is a transgression, all the more significant when there is some inkling that it is at someone else's expense. This is the third and most basic meaning

---

*This damaged and persecutory *threshold object* is a special example of the kind of *obstructive object* described by Bion (1958b). It will appear at the most crucial moments of the novel. Clinically, I have found phantasies about such objects most often associated with perverse behavior and psychosomatic illness. After writing this I learned that James Grotstein (1977) refers to a helpful *boundary object* which, along with the other internal objects, may be transformed into what he calls *impediment objects*.

**Ralph Matlaw (1957) has reviewed a closely related set of images, the bugs and insects that appear throughout Dostoevsky's writings, which likewise represent attempts to dehumanize or reduce various unacceptable attributes to insignificance. I am calling attention to the dynamics involved in such a process, the fragmentation and projection and the resulting feeling of emptiness, of being less able to defend oneself, of being easily overwhelmed. "Trifle" is probably the best translation of *pustjayaki*, which conveys insignificance, "nothing with nothing." The Russian word derives from *pustoy*, meaning "empty." This association is unfortunately lost in translation.

of the transgression symbolized by Raskolnikov's sneaking over his landlady's threshold.*

The open door, which will reappear at some of the most significant moments of the novel, represents Raskolnikov's failure to separate inside from outside, internal from external reality. Excessive use of projective mechanisms results in confusion both of self and others, and of fantasy and reality. Projective identification, in its emphasis on the obliteration of psychological separateness involved in projection, sheds further light upon the image of the parasite which likewise invades body boundaries, and cannot tolerate or survive separateness or separation from the host.

Raskolnikov's feeling of psychological depletion is accompanied by increased persecutory anxiety, a state of mind that is dramatized in this episode and repeatedly throughout the novel. Once he has, in effect, projected himself into the street, Raskolnikov has entered into "a complete blankness of mind; he walked along not observing what was about him and not caring to observe it" (p. 2). The crowds surrounding him are contrasted with the emptiness inside (his mind). His predominant sensation is smell, and he reacts with disgust to the stench around him. His heart is filled with accumulated bitterness and contempt, and he tries to avoid meeting anyone he knows. Suddenly a drunken man in a "wagon dragged by a heavy, dry horse" shouts, "Hey there, German hatter!" at the top of his voice and points at him. Raskolnikov reacts with terror and confusion. He is trying to be inconspicuous and his hat is too noticeable: a trivial detail that might spoil the whole plan. "Trifles, trifles are what matter! Why, it's just such trifles that always ruin everything" (p. 3). He had avoided his German landlady, reduced her to a trifle, only to be ridiculed for his German hat, another trifle.

The next scene contrasts with this one, as Raskolnikov visits the old pawnbroker, a "rehearsal" for his project. She opens the door a crack, and his first glimpse of her is nothing but her eyes, peering at him. He has brought something to pawn, his father's watch, which she dismisses as a trifle, not worth anything. He studies her and her surroundings, they complete their brief transaction, and he leaves. But a confrontation has taken place. He has looked her and his intended scheme in the face; and because of this, he realizes how loathsome and filthy his idea is. He feels the horror, the reality of it. At this moment psychic reality has been restored and he is at his healthiest. He recognizes his needs; he feels thirst, remembers not having eaten, experiences a desire to be with other people, and feels friendly to those around him. Chapter One had started with an avoidance followed by its consequence, and ended with a confrontation followed by its consequence. In seeing people and things as they are, Raskolnikov has become human, acknowledging his needs and feelings.

In this state of mind, he enters a tavern, where he makes the acquaint-

*See Roheim (1922) and Federn (1929) for some early psychoanalytic descriptions of threshold symbolism complementary to the way I have used it here. Freud (1900) refers to Silberer's description of threshold symbolism in dreams which concretely represent the transition from sleep to wakefulness.

ance of Marmeladov. The drunken ex-clerk's confession is a repetition of the first theme: indebtedness to a woman, efforts at avoidance, persecutory consequences. Marmeladov begins with an idealization of his wife, a view maintained throughout, which necessitates his frequent defense of her. "I am a pig, but she is a lady!" he proclaims. We learn of how she compares him to her first husband, and reproaches him for what he is not. Even when he worked hard, and put forth his very best effort, he could not please her. An idealized object is not a loving object; it is a demanding one! Marmeladov has no hope of living up to her expectations, and instead feels persecuted by her. His response is to steal money from her, in order to go on his drunken binge. His loud proclamations of guilt come far too easily, and don't lead to any constructive action. Such antics are a sham. He appears to have averted any feelings of responsibility for his behavior, and perhaps avoided his guilt as well.

Marmeladov has a need to idealize his wife, yet this doesn't stop him from presenting, if somewhat indirectly, his accusations against her. While some critics become involved in "blaming" either Marmeladov or his wife for their domestic catastrophe, others have attempted to tease out the difficulties, only to conclude that they deserve each other. Both husband and wife impose a straitjacket of expectations on the other; both idealize and blame. What we are witness to is a mutual projective identification in which both parties attack the other for their own shortcomings, a mutually spoiling couple, or what Bion might represent by the sign – (♀ ♂).

There is, however, another level to Marmeladov's suffering. At one moment in his rantings he becomes real; and if you listen to his speech, the feeling comes through. He has been avoiding going home, prolonging his drinking in order to avoid confronting his wife. It is not that she would pull his hair that matters; it would be better, he tells us, if she does. "That's not what I am afraid of . . . it's her eyes I am afraid of . . . yes, her eyes . . . the red on her cheeks, too, frightens me . . . and her breathing too . Have you noticed how people in that disease breathe . . . when they are excited?"*

Marmeladov cannot stand looking her in the face and seeing the suffering he has caused; far better is external punishment than this experience of responsibility. It is to avoid this recognition of guilt that he attacks both her and himself. One of the things that he seems to be avoiding is the awareness that his wife is dying, and that this renders him completely helpless. He is unable to tolerate the feelings of guilt at having harmed her, yet his efforts

*Snodgrass (1960) had commented about this paragraph: "This is a literary portrait of Dostoevsky's first wife, who had died of consumption in 1864 after a long illness involving much neglect and blame, and to whom he felt very guilty indeed." This would also be a reference to the author's mother, who died a similar death. With all the emphasis on the supposed murder of Dostoevsky's father, it seems to have escaped notice that it was either while his mother was pregnant with him, during the birth itself, or immediately after, that her consumption became sharply exacerbated. She was able to nurse Mikhail, born just one year before, but not him, nor any of her subsequent children. See Dave Magarshack (1961, p. 19) and Frank (1976, p. 23). We know that individuals born under such circumstances frequently retain the conviction that their growth and development, indeed their very existence, is at someone else's expense; that they are enormously destructive.

to run away from his guilt lead to further action which harms her even more, and eventually leads to both her destruction and his.

In the next chapter, Raskolnikov reads the letter from his mother, and in a communication that closely parallels Marmeladov's confession, there is offered another variation on the theme of indebtedness. Raskolnikov's mother draws attention to his failure to help her and his sister, and reviews all the hardships and humiliations with which they have had to put up. These sacrifices were made for him, and now sister Dounia is planning to marry Luzhin, an act of hopeless slavery akin to Sonia's prostitution. The letter leaves no doubt as to the sacrifice involved, and that it is being done out of love for Raskolnikov, and because of his "inability to provide anything more substantial."

We can now review the narrative sequence from landlady to pawnbroker to Marmeladov's wife to Raskolnikov's mother. Each woman is someone to whom a man is indebted; each is experienced as a persecutor, since it is on her account that the man persecutes himself. A progressive movement has been taking place: the landlady was unknown to us; the pawnbroker is briefly confronted; Marmeladov's wife is vividly described, although in the third person; Raskolnikov's mother represents herself through the letter. The effect on the reader, as it is for Raskolnikov, is of the woman coming closer and closer. The experience of being closed in upon is made even more striking by the progressive intrusiveness of the women.

Snodgrass presents an excellent delineation of the mother's method of guilt provocation: "She has learned the tender motherly art of introducing each item of accusation as if it were a matter of praise for her son or blame for herself. Thus she is able to insinuate as much blame as she likes without once relinquishing a convincing tone of saintly unselfishness and concern for others" (1950, p. 215). Since she keeps reminding Raskolnikov that all her thoughts and actions are motivated by love, the message presented is that love enslaves.* Raskolnikov feels overwhelmed by this latest version of his indebtedness to his mother, and, realizing that she will be coming to St. Petersburg and that he will have to face this obligation, feels stifled and has to run out in the street.

Wasiolek (1974), in discussing Snodgrass' article, takes issue with this view of Raskolnikov as "victim," and instead points out the protagonist's role in setting up such situations. Both critic's viewpoints are well substantiated. As with the Marmeladovs, it is not a question of who to blame, but of the mutually spoiling and destructive nature of the relationship. The mother's letter brings together a particular external and internal (psychic) reality until they coincide, thus heightening Raskolnikov's predicament. The two realities had been approaching each other in our narrative sequence, beginning with

---

*Snodgrass also reminds us how often characters in the novel give money or assistance to others, not out of any real concern for the person supposedly helped, but in order to make themselves feel more powerful at the other person's expense. The recipient feels not gratitude at being given something valuable, but that he has been taken advantage of and robbed.

their greatest disparity in the description of the landlady in the opening episode. After reading his mother's letter, Raskolnikov feels internally and externally persecuted. He is trapped, and expresses this when he recalls Marmeladov's question: "Do you understand, sir, do you understand what it means when you have absolutely nowhere to turn?" (p. 40).

How does Raskolnikov respond to his predicament? His guilt and helplessness turn to rage against his mother and sister, whom he feels are controlling him and persecuting him with their sacrificial love, but also against himself. Above all, he feels the need for action. "It was clear that he must not now suffer passively, worrying himself over unsolved questions, but that he must do something, do it at once, and do it quickly" (p. 40). This is a crucial idea in all of Dostoevsky's writings: the omnipotent solution. To do something, anything, gives one the illusion of power in place of helplessness. The action can be totally ineffectual and merely be a gesture to show one can do something. More often, it is destructive, and produces the opposite effect. It is at this moment that Raskolnikov's thoughts return to his murder scheme.

But first he reviews the alternatives open to him. He momentarily considers going to Razumihin, the one student with whom he had been on friendly terms. What follows is a comparison between the omnipotent and the legitimate way of doing things. Razumihin, whose name means "reason, good sense," demonstrates the kind of real strength that Raskolnikov lacks. Although in a similar financial bind, he has been doing translating, giving lessons, working at odd jobs. He can accept things as they are and make the best of them, and because of this, he has borne up under adversity. He is good-natured and liked by everyone. Raskolnikov, on the other hand, doesn't want the fruits of hard work, but "to get rich quickly." As he confesses to the maid, if he can't get rich all at once, he'd sooner starve. Furthermore he is arrogant and aloof and liked by no one. "He seemed to some of his comrades to look down upon them all as children, as though he were superior in development, knowledge and convictions, as though their beliefs and interests were beneath him" (p. 46). Suppose Razumihin helps him? Raskolnikov realizes that he would then be indebted to him, the last thing he can tolerate. He decides to put off seeing him until he does not need him—after the murder.

Raskolnikov sees a sixteen-year-old girl, drunk and disheveled, apparently having been seduced, and now about to be taken advantage of by a dandy he calls Svidrigailov, the name of the man who had tried to take advantage of his sister. Raskolnikov comes to her rescue, calls a policeman, offers money, then stops abruptly and is stung by revulsion. "Is it for me to help? Have I any right to help? Let them devour each other alive" (p. 45). It is striking that he doesn't say let him have her, or let him devour her, but let them devour each other, thus recognizing the persecution by the victim, perhaps augmented by projection of his own oral greed. He recalls his rage, not just at himself, but at his mother and sister.

His effort to aid the sixteen-year-old had consisted not just of calling in the policeman, or chasing away the dandy, or showing sympathetic support, but of giving her money. He then can ask himself whether it was his money to give, and concludes that his efforts to help her are at the further expense of his mother and sister. Helping another person is once again portrayed as detrimental to one of the parties—a robbery! Since he has no right to do good deeds, the only path left is to do bad ones.

The various elements in Raskolnikov's character are now brought together in his famous dream. Raskolnikov in the dream is seven years old, and is walking with his father toward the cemetery where his grandmother and baby brother are buried. As they pass a tavern, some kind of festivity is going on, with gaily dressed townspeople singing and drunk. There is a cart being pulled not by a great, strong cart horse, but by a thin, little sorrel beast, a peasant's nag. The cart's owner, Mikolka, tells all his drunken friends to get in the cart, then beats the nag to make her gallop. The drunken peasants laugh at the poor nag's feeble efforts, begging Mikolka to beat her harder. Mikolka goes into a rage, and he and the others beat the wretched nag to death. The little boy, terrified, rushes in to stop them, and puts his arm around the dead horse's head, kissing her eyes and lips. Raskolnikov wakes up in horror at the thought of murdering the old pawnbroker, but with a vivid image of beating her on the head with an axe, splitting her skull, the blood. His body feels as if it were he who had been beaten.

If the horse represents the old pawnbroker, it also stands for Raskolnikov. His mother and sister will be making part of their journey in a peasant's cart, and he, as head of the family since his father's death, is incapable of pulling his load. In the first chapter, a man had ridiculed him for his headwear from such a cart. Marmeladov had similarly been ridiculed in the tavern for his feeble efforts toward his family. The horse appears even more ridiculous when compared to its predecessor. Similarly, Marmeladov cannot compete with his wife's first husband; nor can Raskolnikov match up to how he feels he should be able to perform. This horse clearly cannot pull the cart by itself; it needs help. We see, however, how Raskolnikov views his own inadequacies. The horse, representing his weakness, is to be ridiculed, beaten, annihilated by the other aspects of his personality represented by Mikolka and the drunken villagers. Weakness and passivity are equated with uselessness and are despised. Raskolnikov will deal with this aspect of himself by projecting it into the old pawnbroker, and to a varying extent, into the other female characters in the novel.

So far, we have identified Mikolka with Raskolnikov, and the old horse with an unacceptable aspect of Raskolnikov and with the pawnbroker. Mikolka, in addition to representing superego qualities, personifies some of Raskolnikov's greed and selfishness. He insists on overloading the cart. He will take everybody, he says, and will force the nag to gallop. He keeps insisting that she is his property and that he can do with her as he pleases. "My property, mine!" he keeps repeating. At one point, however, Mikolka admits that her wretchedness, her suffering, is "breaking his heart," and that this is precisely why he feels like killing her. However, he immediately gets rid of his responsibility for her suffering by projecting his greed into the horse: "She is just eating her head off." Later on, during the beating, the efforts of the horse bring smiles even to the most sympathetic of observers. "To think of a wretched little beast like that trying to kick" (p. 51). These descriptions suggest a baby, both greedy and demanding, and incapable of taking care of itself or others, and therefore useless. There is additional evidence of this. After the horse is killed, the little boy holds her head and kisses it, just as at the end of the first half of the dream, he kissed the grave of his baby brother.

Most critics have ignored this first half of the dream. It is overshadowed by the horror and excitement, the dramatic imagery of the horse being beaten to death. Besides, the second half of the dream so closely approximates the murders. I believe the spatial movement of the dream helps clarify its meaning. The tavern is located on the way to the graveyard, and represents a manic defense (a psychic structure, or kind of barrier) against deeper, depressive anxieties. There is a feeling of having lost someone who is valued, two people, of whom he is being periodically reminded. But he tells himself in the dream that he had never seen his grandmother, and did not remember his brother at all, as if to emphasize that, not having seen them, he could not be responsible for what had happened to them. We have already noticed how Raskolnikov, and also Marmeladov, cannot stand seeing their victims, and how terrifying and guilt-producing are the eyes of the suffering. The horse in the dream is specifically beaten across the eyes, as if to blind it so that it will not be able to stare up at its attacker.

Raskolnikov attempts to get rid of unacceptable aspects of his personality by projecting them into the old pawnbroker and then murdering her. This is done in order to defend against guilt, and the fear that his destructive, greedy impulses have or will destroy the maternal imago that he loves and on which he depends. After the dream there is a flashback in which two minor characters, a student and an officer, voice Raskolnikov's own thoughts. The unknown student, this other student, is describing the pawnbroker as worthless, an object of contempt. Since her life is without value, to kill and rob her would be a humanitarian act, since so many others would benefit. "One death, and a hundred lives in exchange—it's simple arithmetic!" (p. 59). Here again we have the idea that for someone to benefit, someone else must be sacrificed, in this case, the old pawnbroker.

In addition, this other student emphasizes, it is the pawnbroker who greedily benefits at the expense of others. She is the blood-sucking louse, the parasite who wears out the lives of other people. (Again, a projection of the needy, greedy baby.) She is spiteful. The other day she bit her sister's finger out of spite. This step-sister, Lizaveta, is described here and throughout the novel as either like a baby or continuously pregnant. She was "kept in complete bondage like a small child" (p. 57). She is "like some little babe" (p. 55), and at the moment Raskolnikov kills her, "her mouth twitches pitiously, as one sees babies' mouths" (p. 71).

There is a peculiar ambiguity throughout the novel as to how many people Raskolnikov has killed. There is a repeated suggestion that Lizaveta was pregnant, so that there were three victims. Raskolnikov, however, usually refers only to his first victim, the old woman, as if there were just one murder. In the *Notebooks*, Dostoevsky is even more concerned with Lizaveta having been pregnant. At one point he writes, "They performed a Caesarian on her. She was six months pregnant. A boy, born dead" (p. 96). In a later notebook, he writes, "and she was murdered pregnant." This is followed by a note which is crossed out: "The old woman beat her when she was pregnant. I saw it myself. Pregnant, pregnant, sixth" (p. 165). In other notations, however, Lizaveta had already given birth and the child was known to Raskolnikov and loved by him.

In the dream, there is an additional image that I do not believe anyone has commented upon: standing next to the cart, a big fat woman in a red dress cracking nuts. This caricatured figure is further evidence for hostility against the pregnant mother. In the overheard conversation between the student and officer, there is a peculiar transition that offers additional support for this idea. The student, speaking of Lizaveta, says, "She is such a soft, gentle creature, ready to put up with anything." When the officer points out that he seems attracted to her, he replies "No, I'll tell you what. I could kill that damned old woman and make off with her money" (p. 58). I think what is being expressed are the hostile feelings toward the bountiful and life-giving mother, the wish to greedily attack and rob her, to scoop out her insides and empty her of her treasure.

Just prior to his murderous errand, Raskolnikov stretches out on his sofa and has a series of strange daydreams. One of them keeps recurring: an oasis in Egypt, the caravan is resting, the palms standing in a complete circle. All the party is at dinner, but he is drinking cool water from a stream: wonderful, blue, cold water. The sand glistens like gold. Several critics have interpreted this daydream as evidence of his beginning moral regeneration, but I think they have done so because of a lack of understanding of the vicissitudes of omnipotence. Admittedly the fantasy is deceptive: it is about water and the quenching of thirst. As George Gibian (1967) points out, water symbolizes creative, life-enhancing, positive forces in Dostoevsky's mythology. It seems ironic that Raskolnikov should be having creative thoughts at a time when he is about to commit such a destructive act. But this is typical of this particular state of mind. On the way to the pawnbroker's, he will be thinking about building fountains and extending the summer garden. Later in the novel, when Svidrigailov commits suicide, he will destroy himself surrounded by images of water, flowers, birth and creativity. Dostoevsky seemed to understand, at least intuitively, how mania and perversity can confuse good and evil, and masquerade destructiveness in the guise of its opposite.

Raskolnikov's oasis fantasy is a typical manic fantasy of omnipotent or oceanic reunion with a good mother, with oral gratification and sleep resulting. In the fantasy, he is not sitting down to dinner with the others, but has his own source of nourishment which is idealized. The basis of this is hinted at by the idea that things are not the way they appear; that sand is taken for gold. The fantasy is a way of denying dependency on an external mother. He can take care of his own needs; his circle is complete. Since he contains the source of all supplies, the external mother or her stand-in, the old pawnbroker, is worthless, or even a bad mother, and can be destroyed. Such fantasies also typically deny mortality and the passage of time.* His preoccupation with the fantasy keeps him in bed when he should be carrying out his plans. He is almost totally unprepared for what he is attempting, and is shocked when a clock strikes half-past seven and he realizes how late it is. His reaction is to deny the external reality by deciding that the clock is too fast. We recall that on his previous visit to the pawnbroker, he had given her his father's watch. Because the fantasy kept him in bed when he should have been on his way, he is still in the old woman's apartment when Lizaveta returns. The self-destructive aspects of the fantasy result in a second murder, the death of the good Lizaveta, and in his almost being captured.

Raskolnikov goes through the murders in almost a somnambulistic state. Having projected so much of himself into the old woman and Lizaveta has left him depleted and incapacitated. Throughout the novel, he faints, is physically weak, feverish, delirious, incapable of thinking. It is also obvious that he identifies with his victims and feels condemned, about to be killed, paralyzed, cut off from the living, dead.**

After having committed the second murder and robbed what he could, Raskolnikov is about to leave, when he experiences a shock of terror: the door of the apartment has been left unfastened and open. The most terrifying moment in the murder scene is contained in this image of the open door. During the murder, most readers identify not with the victims, but with Raskolnikov. At this moment of greatest vulnerability, he can be spied on or intruded upon. (Later, at another very private moment, when he is confessing the murder to Sonia, Svridrigailov will be eavesdropping through the door.) The open door, as I have previously noted, is closely related to the mechanism of projective identification and symbolically represents the breakdown of the separation of self and object representations, as well as the blurring or confusion of external reality and internal fantasy.

Having projected aspects of himself into the pawnbroker and then having murdered her, Raskolnikov then introjects and feels identified with the dead introject trapped inside him. The next part of the narrative is like a nightmare. Raskolnikov is trapped inside the apartment, an unknown somebody is coming up the stairs. "It seemed to him all at once that he was turned to stone, that it was like a dream in which one is being pursued, nearly caught and will be killed and is rooted to the spot and cannot even move one's arms." The unknown visitor stops outside the door. "They were

*Dostoevsky recognized the importance of such attempts to transgress the limits of time. In the *Notebooks* he wrote: "What is time? Time doesn't exist. Time is numbers; time is the relationship of existence to non-existence" (p. 195).

**Raskolnikov's identification with his victims, which is prominent throughout the novel, is also one of the ways he avoids conscious recognition of his guilt.

now standing opposite one another, as he had just before been standing with the old woman, when the door divided them and he was listening" (p. 73). Raskolnikov and his victim have changed places.

Now, standing on the other side of the closed door with two unknown gentlemen knocking and tugging to gain entrance, Raskolnikov feels at his most helpless. "While they were knocking and talking together, the idea several times occurred to him to end it all at once and shout to them through the door. Now and then he was tempted to swear at them, to jeer at them, while they could not open the door!" (p. 76). This would be the omnipotent solution, self-destructive in the extreme, but aimed at the momentary illusion of power as a defense against recognition of his helplessness. Throughout the rest of the novel, Raskolnikov will feel this destructive "power" at just those times when he is most helpless and out of touch.

The reader cannot help but recognize that it is not through any personal skills or abilities that Raskolnikov escapes from the pawnbroker's flat, but through something totally outside of his control, a continuation of the same accidents of fate that helped him in the carrying out of the crime. When he makes it back to his room, he flings himself on his bed and falls into not so much a sleep as a "blank forgetfulness" (p. 78). This is the end of Part One of the novel, and a good place to momentarily stop and summarize what has happened, and preview what is to come.

II

From the opening scene until the commission of the murder, I have focused on the progression of psychological events which culminate in Raskolnikov's attempt to annihilate the pawnbroker and what she represents. What Raskolnikov presents to himself as the creative act of a super-man, rationally operating on the basis of "simple arithmetic," I have attempted to describe in terms of the underlying non-rational factors which appear to be driving him. His "transgression," as I have pointed out, is not simply the murder of another human being, a stepping over the limits of law and order; rather it is a psychological transgression, related to three defensive maneuvers. As in the opening scene where Raskolnikov is attempting to avoid acknowledgement of his indebtedness and guilt in relation to another mother-surrogate, his landlady, he progressively seeks to "step over" this experience. On one level, he transgresses the boundary between self and other by his massive use of primitive projection mehcanisms. He deals with uncomfortable feelings by projecting them, and then feels persecuted when he sees the reminders of these feelings in the external world.

As Raskolnikov's indebtedness begins to stifle him, particularly with the arrival of this mother and sister, he is drawn to external action of a more and more omnipotent nature. The omnipotent act, as a means of denying helplessness, dependency, or guilt, becomes the second level of his attempt to find a solution. By this "new step," Raskolnikov attempts not to repair damage or find internal resolution, but to step over his guilt into a world of amorality. Instead of regarding the capacity for guilt and compassion as a mature and necessary human quality, it is experienced as a feminine or infantile weakness to be abolished or disowned. The mother-child relationship becomes the prototype of the mutually spoiling, poisonous couple, a view extended in the novel to relationships between men and women. Raskolnikov not only hates himself for caring, but he idealizes those whom he thinks are free of such concerns, those who are above such feelings and therefore in control: the omnipotent supermen.

In his need to deny his helplessness and dependency, any comparison between what has been given him and what little he is able to give in return becomes a painful humiliation. These feelings focus in particular on the gift of life itself. Not only can he never repay his mother, but he can never dupliate her feat. He idealizes creativity one moment and the next moment has reduced it from the long, slow process that it is, to a magically simple "new step" which will resolve all his difficulties. This serves the dual function of devaluing creativity, while establishing himself as the creator.

This third defensive strategy then involves not merely a random confusion between creativity and destructiveness, but a reversal of the two: essentially a manic defense in which guilt toward the mother is denied by seeing himself as containing the good mother; while the actual mother, or her surrogate, the pawnbroker, is bad and deserving of being destroyed. Thus the situation which Dostoevsky has portrayed at the pawnbroker's flat has occurred internally as well: Raskolnikov and his victim have changed places.

The pawnbroker contains a double projection. Not only is she the mother into whom Raskolnikov has projected his hostility, so that she becomes a caricatured bad mother; but by a similar mechanism, she comes to represent the bad baby, the parasitical louse, as well. As a result of his crime, Raskolnikov has also murdered Lizaveta, the generous, all-giving mother. In attempting to destroy his persecutor, he also murders the source of life and hope within himself, the internalized good object. The rest of this paper focuses on the consequences of such an act.

As Part Two begins, Raskolnikov is faced with a situation resembling the universal infantile fantasy of having greedily or sadistically attacked and destroyed the loved object. Hanna Segal (1952) describes this fantasy in which the loved object "is destroyed, torn into pieces and fragments; and not only is the external object so attacked but also the internal one, and then the whole internal world feels destroyed and shattered as well. Bits of the destroyed object may turn into persecutors, and there is a fear of internal persecution as well as a pining for the lost loved object and guilt for the attack."

In the absence of sufficient belief in the capacity to restore, the good object is felt to be irretrievably lost, and the situation hopeless. The ego resorts to a system of manic defenses under such conditions, in order to protect itself from total despair: denial of psychic reality, omnipotent control, and a regression to more primitive use of splitting and projective identification. A vicious cycle is set up in which regression leads to greater persecutory fears which lead to a greater use of omnipotent mechanisms. This could easily serve as a description of Raskolnikov after the murders. Dostoevsky, when he saw the novel emerging in this direction, initially planned to have Raskolnikov either think out or actually commit more crimes (1931, p. 56).

In discussing the rest of the novel, I will attempt to illustrate how Raskolnikov continues to use the defenses outlined earlier, in order to avoid confronting his guilt. I will portray him not as seeking to find punishment, but rather as using the external world—through omnipotent provocation, through acts of manic reparation, through acts of "confession" which contain neither contrition nor reparation, but are attempts to evacuate his feelings of helplessness and despair into others—to continue to avoid acknowledging any guilt, or responsibility toward his mother. In other words, I believe him to continue using the same defensive maneuvers after the murders as had caused him to commit the murders, and, as I will attempt to show, with not dissimilar consequences.

III

"Scraps and shreds of thoughts were simply swarming in his brain . . ." (p. 78). A moment later, Raskolnikov's preoccupation is with the external fragments, the things into which these thoughts have been transformed: rags of his clothing stained by his victims' blood, the trinkets taken from the old woman. He tries to hide these things, wanting no one, least of all himself, to see them. He attacks his perceptual apparatus, so that "his perceptions were failing, were going to pieces" (p. 81). He becomes obsessed with getting rid of the inanimate things into which have been projected bits of self and object (Bion 1956, 1957, 1958a, 1962a, 1962b).

These persecutory fragments are the latest version of the "trifles" that appeared throughout Part One and will continue to appear throughout the book. We now recognize them as the product of violent attacks on the mental apparatus and the inner world. Raskolnikov clutches hold of the scraps and trinkets, not knowing how to get rid of them. "For a long while, for some hours, he was haunted by the impulse to 'go off somewhere at once, this moment, and fling it all away, so that it may be out of sight and done with, at once, at once!' " (p. 82). He goes out, buries the objects under a stone, and feels momentary relief.

Thinking that by getting rid of these external reminders, he has gotten rid of the cause of his anxiety, he feels "an intense, almost unbearable joy" come over him. " 'It is all over! No clue!' and he laughed" (p. 97). His good feeling ceases when he approaches the boulevard where he had encountered the drunken girl, the dandy and the policeman. The memory is dealt with in characteristic fashion. He blames them for having existed and for reminding him now of the uncomfortable feelings he experienced in relation to them.

When, the next moment, he develops his first insight about the murders—that he did not do it for financial gain—his revulsion about what he had done and how he feels about himself is so intolerable that he feels he must do something to get rid of the feeling, must find someone else to contain it. "He had a terrible longing for some distraction, but he did not know what to do, what to attempt. A new overwhelming sensation was gaining more and more mastery over him every moment; this was an immeasurable, almost physical, repulsion for everything surrounding him, an obstinate, malignant feeling of hatred." "If anyone addressed him, he felt that he might have spat at him or bitten him . . ." (p. 98).

He goes to Razumihin for his distraction, but feels choked by his rage and tries to leave as quickly as possible. There is no question as to his being able to accept help from anybody. Before he manages to get away, however, there is a joke! Razumihin offers him a German text to translate, an article that "discusses the question, 'Is woman a human being?' And, of course, triumphantly proves that she is" (p. 100). Raskolnikov does not accept the article, and there is no discussion of it, although the idea has been introduced and could almost stand as a sub-title for the novel. Raskolnikov has murdered a woman and tries to convince himself that she was not a human being. He thinks of her as a worthless thing, a louse, an obstacle, a principle or abstraction. Sonia, as we will see, will either be devalued or regarded as an idealized abstraction. Women make excellent containers for evacuating unacceptable aspects of oneself.* To be female means to suffer, to be damaged, depressed, weak, passive—all that Raskolnikov is trying to avoid and finds so despicable in himself. The next time Raskolnikov will be at Razumihin's, he will say to him, "I am so sad, so sad . . . like a woman" (p. 169), one of the few times in the novel when he will acknowledge depressive feelings, although the entire novel is about his efforts to avoid them.

The next series of incidents confronts Raskolnikov with the loss of his good object. An elderly woman and her daughter take pity on him and thrust money into his hand. An offer of help, this time from a mother, has reminded him of his crime. He looks out at the bright, blue water of the Neva, and his gaze rests on the round dome of the cathedral, a particular sight that had always filled him with pleasure, the source of a marvelous and "mysterious emotion," only now it appears cold and blank and lifeless. He had murdered something within himself, the good maternal imago represented by the breast-shaped cupola. He stares at the coin the woman had given him and then throws it into the water. "It seemed to him, he had cut himself off from everyone and from everything at that moment" (p. 102).

On his return home, he lapses into a confusional state in which he reexperiences the helplessness and terror he felt at the pawnbroker's. In his delirium, he is trying to remember someone or something. He sees someone at his bedside "whom he seemed to know very well, though he could not

*In the *Notebooks* Dostoevsky wrote: "N.B. A woman is always only what we ourselves want to make of her" (p. 218).

remember who he [sic] was, and this fretted him, even made him cry" (p. 104). Of the murder he had no recollection, but "every minute he felt that he had forgotten something he ought to remember. He worried and tormented himself trying to remember, moaned, flew into a rage, or sank into awful, intolerable terror" (p. 105).

With sleep, good nursing, and the help of others, Raskolnikov's delirium clears; but after lying in his bed listening to them discuss the murder, after meeting his sister's fiance, Luzhin, and after learning that mother and sister will be arriving any minute, Raskolnikov again feels driven to action. His state of mind is characteristic: "Calm, self-confident, strong." "It was the first moment of a strange, sudden calm." "A sort of savage energy gleamed suddenly in his feverish eyes." "He did not know and did not think where he was going, he had one thought only: 'that all *this* must be ended today, once for all, immediately . . .* because he *would not go on living like that.*' How, with what to make an end? He had not an idea about it, he did not even want to think about it. He drove away thought; thought tortured him. All he knew, all he felt was that everything must be changed 'one way or another' he repeated with desperate and immovable self-confidence and determination" (p. 136). It will soon be obvious that, having "driven away thought," he is now mad. His feeling of power cloaks his helplessness; his need to do something, to get rid of the painful "this," sets up a vicious cycle rendering him increasingly helpless.

Raskolnikov gives away money, to a street musician, to prostitutes. His conversation is so peculiar a stranger fearfully crosses the street to get away from him. When joined by the police clerk, Zametov, Raskolnikov provokes him. First he teases him about his greediness and about his using his job to profit at others' expense. "You must have a jolly life, Mr. Zametov; entrance free to the most agreeable places. Who's been pouring champagne into you just now? . . . By way of a fee! You profit by everything!" (p. 141). Underneath the hostile teasing one senses a certain envy.

Raskolnikov then tells him he has been reading about the murder, reminds him of his fainting in the police station, and presents it in as suspicious a manner as possible. "Do you understand now?" he asks him and he laughs in the bewildered Zametov's face. This *omnipotent provocation* is a deliberate flirting with danger, in order to test his power and prove that he is in control.

Just as Raskolnikov felt like shouting at the two men trying to enter the pawnbroker's apartment, to swear at and mock them, he now experiences a similar impulse, "an intense desire again to put his tongue out." The gesture reveals, behind the facade of a powerful man, the child. When Zametov brings up another crime, Raskolnikov demeans the other criminals as children, simpletons. He describes how he would have committed the crime

*Three dots represent an ellipsis found in the original text, as employed by Dostoevsky. Three double-spaced dots indicates a deletion by the author of this article.

calmly, deliberately, self-confidently, without a trace of anxiety. Clearly, what is most important is to be in complete control. In Raskolnikov's bragging here, and particularly in contrast with the very different way he behaved during the actual murders and the way he continues to be overwhelmed by, and not in control of, his feelings, we begin to understand the importance attached to omnipotent control.

As we continue to follow Raskolnikov after his meeting with Zametov, he is still determined to "make an end of it all" (p. 150). After rejecting the idea of suicide, he is on his way to the police station to confess, when something happens to change his mind. He comes upon the dying Marmeladov, who has been run over by a coach and horses. Raskolnikov reacts "as earnestly as if it had been his father" (p. 155). Marmeladov represents the ineffectual, foolish father. But in this reversal of the dream, the horse kills father. Again, as in the dream and in the murder of the pawnbroker, the head is smashed. And, as the little boy did in the dream, Raskolnikov carefully holds the victim's head. They make their way to Katerina Ivanovna's where Raskolnikov takes charge, reassuring Mrs. Marmeladov, providing money, promising support. In the crisis, he assumes responsibility for the family as Marmeladov was unable to do, and as he was not able to do with his own mother and sister. He leaves feeling rejuvenated, and it is this which some critics have taken to be the beginning of his rebirth.

My impression is that it serves primarily as a kind of manic reparation. For the moment, Raskolnikov can forget about his helplessness and weakness and about his inability to help his family. In fact, after having just acquired a new family, he has forgotten entirely about his own. The murders also are momentarily erased, perhaps cancelled out by "arithmetic." There is a temporary feeling of power and control. " 'We will try our strength! he added defiantly, as though challenging some power of darkness . . . 'I believe my illness is all over. I knew it would be over when I went out . . . Strength, strength is what one wants, you can get nothing without it, and strength must be won by strength—that's what they don't know' " (p. 166). He appears to be challenging his enemies and experiencing a feeling of triumph over them. He sounds quite mad.

The subject of his challenge, the unseen enemy, are his persecutors. When he does not consciously recognize his uncomfortable feelings as guilt, he feels that someone is responsible for them. His efforts had been directed toward either getting rid of these uncomfortable feelings, "putting an end to it," or expressing rage toward those felt to be responsible. As a consequence of his actions at the Marmeladovs', he suddenly feels "pride and self-confidence grew continually stronger in him; he was becoming a different man every moment" (p. 166).

Normal reparation would be based on the recognition of psychic reality, the experiencing of the pain that this reality causes, and the taking of appropriate action to relieve it in phantasy and reality. The aim of manic reparation, on the other hand, is to repair the object in such a way that guilt and loss are never experienced. Manic reparation, as Hanna Segal (1964, pp. 82-83) explains, has three characteristics: (1) it is never done in relation to primary objects or internal objects, but always in relation to more remote objects; (2) the object in relation to which reparation is done must never be experienced as having been damaged by one's self; and (3) the object must be felt as inferior, dependent, and at depth, contemptible. There is no true love or esteem for the objects repaired; instead, they are being omnipotently controlled. It seems to me that Marmeladov's family, by being similar to, but not having the significance of Raskolnikov's own family, or the pawnbroker and Lizaveta , fits these characteristics.

Raskolnikov's boastings are more typical of manic triumph than of moral rejuvenation. Nor does he appear to be in touch with reality, since none of his statements is true. His illness is not over. He certainly had not believed it would be when he went out. This is an illusion of omniscience, in which he uses hindsight to convince himself that he is more in control than he is.* His feeling of strength is the biggest illusion. A little later when he will face his family in reality, the sight of his actual mother and sister will cause him to collapse in a faint.

If Raskolnikov had, in fact, helped the Marmeladovs out of a real feeling of compassion, the action might have left him feeling stronger. To be stronger, however, is not to feel powerful. If he had been stronger, he might have been able to acknowledge his weakness. To the degree that helping the Marmeladovs was done compassionately, he would also have been put in touch with depressive feelings—concern for their futures, grief, feelings about the dead Marmeladov, about his own family, about his own dead victims, guilt—certainly not triumph. As in other places in the novel where it occurs, the tone of triumph is an indication that what is being celebrated is a victory over reality, and usually a victory at someone else's expense.

Up to this point, I have stressed the manic aspects of his relationship with the Marmeladovs because I believe this feature of the relationship is most significant, and because it has been overlooked by other writers. Certainly there can be both manic and healthy aspects to behavior, and analysts are familiar with patients confusing the two, as, for example, when they make real progress, or accomplish something through hard work, but attribute it to their omnipotence, and then become manic. Raskolnikov's actions toward the Marmeladovs contain both manic and healthy aspects; and now, at the height of his mania, his feelings change. The manic defense is rarely complete; usually some depression is expressed. By the time Raskolnikov has reached Razumihin's house, he is no longer boasting of his triumph. He is subdued, reflective, depressed. He wants to tell Razumihin about his experi-

---

*There are many examples of this kind of self-deception, the most significant one being his later remark: "I am perhaps viler and more loathsome than the louse I killed, and I *felt beforehand* that I should tell myself so *after* killing her" (p. 239). Some critics have erroneously taken this as evidence that he knew before the murders that he would fail, and committed the murders in order to fail. His state of mind is a tip-off to the deception.

ence at the Marmeladovs', the impact of it on him, and he repeatedly admits to feeling weak. "I am so sad," he says, "so sad . . . like a woman."

There is another relationship which I think illustrates manic reparation: Raskolnikov's choice of love object prior to the murders. We first learn about Raskolnikov's fiancee from his friend, Razumihin. "The girl was not at all pretty, in fact I am told positively ugly . . . and such an invalid . . . and queer . . . it's quite inexplicable . . . she had no money either" (p. 189). Raskolnikov confirms the description and gives a hint as to the basis of the attraction. "She was such a sickly girl . . . quite an invalid. She was fond of giving alms to the poor, and was always dreaming of a nunnery . . . she was an ugly little thing. I really don't know what drew me to her then—I think it was because she was always ill. If she had been lame or hunchback I believe I should have liked her better still" (p. 201).

Raskolnikov's girlfriend was felt to be inferior, damaged both physically and mentally, and it appears that this was precisely what he liked about her. If she were more deformed he would have liked her all the more. Her damage was not something he had caused, therefore not something about which he need feel guilty. He could think of himself as her benefactor, rescuing her and restoring her; while at the same time, she could function for him as the representation of various ugly and unacceptable aspects of himself.

This relationship, which would have ended in marriage if the girl hadn't died, preceded Raskolnikov's scheme to murder the old pawnbroker. However, the two are very clearly related. In discussing his plan to marry the landlady's invalid daughter, Raskolnikov's mother says that the shock of hearing about it nearly killed her. " 'Do you think,' she adds, 'my tears, my supplications, my illness, my death perhaps from grief, our poverty would have stopped him then? *He would have stepped most calmly over all the obstacles*.' "* This links the "love affair" with the invalid girl with the murder of the old pawnbroker and Lizaveta. Both actions, one supposedly loving, the other destructive, are ways of avoiding guilt; yet both actions ultimately lead to the very thing they were designed to defend against: the death of Raskolnikov's mother.

The invalid girl is also linked to Sonia, whom some critics regard as her reincarnation. The discussion of this fiancee is almost immediately followed by Sonia's timid appearance at the door. Sonia is described as a child, overwhelmed with shyness, humiliated in the company of his family, and arousing in Raskolnikov feelings of pity and compassion, causing him to feel rejuvenated again. He and the reader are reminded of the previously-described scene at the Marmeladov's.

In the next episode of the novel, Raskolnikov and Razumihin visit the police inspector, Porfiry Petrovich, and the conversation turns to the article

*Here I differ slightly from the Garnett translation, which reads, "No, he would calmly have disregarded all obstacles." The verb used is *perestupit*, to step over, transgress. The noun would be *perestupanie*, meaning transgression, a variant of *prestuplenie*. See Mochulsky (1947, p. 305). Jessie Coulson (1953) translates the sentence: "No, he would have trampled coolly over every obstacle."

Raskolnikov had published on crime. In the article, he introduces his theory of the superman: that Man is divided into those few who are extraordinary and the majority of ordinary people, with the extraordinary having the right, even the obligation, to transcend the law in order to bring about some greater good. Ordinary men are limited by their sense of guilt, and Raskolnikov rather sarcastically describes how "they castigate themselves, for they are very conscientious: some perform this service for one another and others chastise themselves with their own hands . . . They will impose various public acts of penitence upon themselves with a beautiful and edifying effect" (p. 228). His tone is contemptuous, as if the awareness of conscience is a limitation, a weakness, a humiliation. One is reminded that when Raskolnikov did become aware of guilty feelings, he immediately experienced self-hatred and rage toward whomever was felt to be responsible for making him aware of the feeling, usually his victim.

One does not have to feel guilt about harming ordinary people since, according to the theory, they exist to be used. They "love to be controlled. To my thinking it is their duty to be controlled, that's because that's their vocation, and there is nothing humiliating in it for them" (p. 227). This is exactly the argument Svidrigailov will present, as we will see in a moment, although he will take it a step further by equating the ordinary people with women.

Now, who are the extraordinary people? They are "people with new ideas, people with the faintest capacity for saying something *new*" (p. 229). "Men who have the gift or talent to utter *a new word*" (p. 227). And how do these creative people go about their work? They destroy; their actions are destructive! Since we are describing envy of creativity, it is not surprising but that those who are destroyed are none other than the unconscious representatives of those thought to be most creative—a mother and her offspring, a pregnant woman.

On his arrival home, Raskolnikov continues the previous discussion with himself. "The real *Master* to whom all is permitted storms Toulon, makes a massacre in Paris, *forgets* an army in Egypt, *wastes* half a million men in the Moscow expedition" (p. 238), and gets away with it, even has altars set up to him. Why should he have to pay; why should he be made to feel guilty for one little crime? In continuing the comparison of himself with Napoleon, he is forced to recognize his limitations, guilt being the primary one that he cannot step over; and he experiences this as a humiliation.

He continues to vacillate between denying any guilt by devaluing his victim and thereby denying any significance to her murder,* and recognizing guilt, a limitation for which he immediately attacks himself and his victim as well. " 'The old woman is of no consequence!, he thought, hotly and incoherently . . . 'The old woman was only an illness . . . I was in a hurry to

*As Segal has pointed out: "An object of contempt is not an object worthy of guilt, and the contempt that is experienced in relation to such an object becomes a justification for further attacks on it" (1965, p. 71).

overstep . . . I didn't kill a human being, but a principle! I killed the principle, but I didn't overstep, I stopped on this side . . . I was only capable of killing'" (pp. 238-239). Here he is clearly telling us that it was not the act of murder that was the barrier—not Man's Law, but the feelings of guilt about harming another human being.

He then remembers that it was not just the old woman he had killed, but Lizaveta as well. "Poor Lizaveta! Why did she come in . . . It's strange though, why is it I scarcely ever think of her, as though I hadn't killed her? Lizaveta! Sonia! Poor gentle things, with gentle eyes . . . Dear women! Why don't they weep? Why don't they moan? They give up everything . . . their eyes are soft and gentle . . . Sonia, Sonia! Gentle Sonia!" (p. 240). Lizaveta, Sonia, who are gentle and good, but who inspire such guilt. Why don't they ever complain? They allow themselves to be drained, to be used. "They give up everything."

The passage reminds us of Marmeladov's confession, when after his pseudo-guilt, he describes the pain of looking into his wife's eyes and recognizing what he had done to her. Here Raskolnikov, as Marmeladov before him, is face to face with his guilt. Marmeladov's response had been to feel so uncomfortable that he would drink more, stay away longer, hurt his wife more, in order to avoid it. The student whose conversation Raskolnikov had overheard, and Mikolka in the dream, had expressed the same idea. It is as if each were saying: it broke my heart to look at her, to see what I had done to her, so I killed her.

Raskolnikov is troubled that these women accept things without complaining, without moaning. The women, by their passivity and acceptance, make him uncomfortable since they can't be seen as external persecutors with whom he can then get angry. Such anger would be righteous indignation, in effect, and experienced as liberating. Instead, the bad feelings attack him from inside; he can neither run from them, nor can he annihilate such feelings inside himself.

These feelings are felt to be attacking him, and when he loses consciousness, his ensuing nightmare represents his victimization by these internal persecutors and his feeling of having nowhere to escape. Raskolnikov sees himself in a kill-or-be-killed struggle which calls forth the need for greater action. In the dream, he is hitting the old woman on the head, and with every blow of his axe, she shakes with mirth at his impotent attempts to silence her, to annihilate her. As with the dream of the horse-beating, weakness is being ridiculed. This time, however, it is his supposed victim who is laughing at his weakness and who is seen as his tormentor. He realizes the door from the bedroom is open, and he hears laughter and whispering. He begins hitting her with all his might, and the laughter merely grows louder. He attempts to run away, but then realizes that all the doors to all the flats are open. The passage is full of people, people everywhere—on the landing, on the stairs—all silent, looking at him with expectation. He freezes on the spot, unable to move, and ends his paralysis only by screaming and waking up.

Dostoevsky presents this dream so that we first think its action is real. The open doors in the dream represent a breakdown of the ability to distinguish inner from outer reality. When Raskolnikov wakes up, he thinks he is still dreaming, and it takes him some time to realize he is awake. The first thing he sees upon opening his eyes is that the door to his room is open; Svidrigailov is standing in the doorway watching him. A fly is buzzing in the room, another carry-over from the dream. Raskolnikov twice asks himself if he is still dreaming. This device, the reversal of reality and the dream world, is used to introduce us, and Raskolnikov, to Svidrigailov. This demonic character is intended to represent Raskolnikov's omnipotence at its most successful, i.e., destructive. Significantly, he appears at the moment when Raskolnikov sees himself as most weak and helpless. Extraordinary measures, in the form of an omnipotent superman, are required in order to deny psychic reality.

Svidrigailov's first action in the novel is to step over the threshold into the room, and Dostoevsky significantly uses the same verb, *perestupit*, as a moment before he had had Raskolnikov use it in describing his failure. The threshold symbol again conveys the triple meaning previously discussed. Svidrigailov arouses Raskolnikov's curiosity by telling him that human beings, particularly women, love being insulted. Women enjoy being beaten; in fact, "One might say it's their only amusement" (p. 245). That Svidrigailov believes this and doesn't believe it is evidenced by his passion for young, innocent girls. His perversion is that he violates them, out of spite or envy. The pleasure of the perversion is that he knows they don't like to suffer. The attraction to innocence is to defile it.

Svidrigailov is intended to represent one aspect of Raskolnikov's personality, the idealization of destructiveness, taken to its furthermost extreme. His perversity is based on a reversal of good and evil, creativity and destructiveness, with a deliberate choice of the latter. Svidrigailov fascinates Raskolnikov, not because of a latent homosexual attraction, or because he acts out Raskolnikov's incestuous wishes for his sister, as several interpreters have suggested, but because he personifies the omnipotent superman who is in control of his feelings, steps over his limitations, and most important, is free of guilt. Svidrigailov tells Raskolnikov precisely what he wants most of all to hear: that he need not feel guilty about harming his mother and sister. He describes Dounia as a martyr. "She is simply thirsting to face some torture for someone, and if she can't get her torture, she'll throw herself out of the window" (p. 409). Women want to suffer; they love it; so rather than feel guilty, one should think of it as one's duty to take advantage of them.

A moment later, however, we get a very different picture of Svidrigailov in relation to Dounia. He is telling her that he loves her. "Let me kiss the hem of your dress, let me, let me . . . the very rustle of it is too much for me. Tell me 'Do that,' and I'll do it. I'll do everything. I will do the impossible. What you believe, I will believe. I'll do anything–anything!" (p. 425). He is telling her his feelings for her, but how pitiful he sounds. He idealizes her while negating himself. He is groveling, begging to be her slave, totally out of control. Again we are reminded that, in the world of this novel, to love means to be dominated both by one's passions and by the other person.

But then a change takes place in him, and "he came to himself." He is back in control, devoid of spontaneous emotion—and now Dounia is frightened, helpless. Even when she takes out a loaded gun and points it at him—in fact, particularly then—he is in control. Svidrigailov is asserting his bravery, erasing his previous humiliation. He is in control of his emotions and above it all, while looking death in the face. His domination and control appear complete. When she drops the gun, he feels that he has been saved from his dark isolation, but the next moment the look in her eyes tells him otherwise. "'Then you don't love me?' he asked softly. Dounia shook her head. 'And . . . and you can't? Never?' he whispered in despair. 'Never!'" (p. 428). His fate is sealed with this recognition of psychic and external reality. All thoughts of taking advantage of her sexually, of dominating or using her, are discarded. The confrontation has dramatically illustrated the difference between controlling another person as a part object, and having a real relationship based on recognition of separation and independence. It is this recognition that makes Svidrigailov seem more heroic, indeed healthier, than Raskolnikov; although, curiously enough, it is the same point upon which the former character is "doomed" and the latter "saved."

The next chapter contains the preparations for and details of Svidrigailov's suicide. He first visits Sonia in order to arrange for her future, as well as that of her little sisters and brother. He then visits his fifteen-year-old fiancee, to explain his absence and to provide for her also. His generosity, the good deeds he performs, have caused critics to point out his apparent indifference to morality, that he doesn't distinguish between good and evil and is equally capable of both. We are reminded of Raskolnikov, thinking about fountains and gardens and beautifying the city, while on his way to commit murder. Svidrigailov's actions, however, do benefit others, and as he is the first to recognize, will serve to keep the children of both families out of the clutches of someone like himself.

He thinks of Dounia. "Who knows?—perhaps she would have made a new man of me somehow . . " (p. 435). She would have been his salvation. A relationship with a woman is thought of as the way of connecting to life. The impossibility of this can only increase his envy, and so his thoughts focus on his hatred of birth, children and creativity. "How I dislike the sound of trees . . . I never have liked water" (p. 435). He dozes off, and in his sleep continues to be annoyed with little things, with multiplicity and various images of fecundity which persecute him. A mouse runs over his body. He thinks of flowers, lots of flowers in abundance. He listens to the pouring rain, and in a marvelous perversion of a birth symbol, thinks of how the river will overflow its banks and the cellar rats will swim out. He imagines killing himself under a great bush, drenched with rain, with millions of drops dripping on his head. There are flies in his veal. The revolt of the passions, represented by trifles.

He dreams of a young girl of fourteen dressed all in white, lying in a white silk coffin surrounded by a profusion of flowers. He remembers the girl, who had taken her own life after he had seduced her. We feel it now as he feels it: as the end of his innocence and hope, the annihilation of his capacity to feel. He then has a second dream, this one of a neglected child, a five-year-old girl who turns into a shameless harlot, her face the laughing face of *his* depravity.

The pair of dreams is similar in a number of ways to Raskolnikov's first two dreams. We recall that Svidrigailov had first appeared as Raskolnikov was waking from his second dream, as if in response to Raskolnikov's recognition of his own helplessness. Now Svidrigailov recognizes his own helplessness. In his last action before the suicide, he cannot even catch a fly.

The actual suicide takes place outside a big house, the great gates of which are closed, as if to reconfirm that the mother's body is unavailable and the separation from the good object permanent.* At the entrance to the house is a little man, a Jew wearing a soldier's coat and an Achilles helmet. The image of this weak, ineffectual man masquerading as a soldier is the image of omnipotence, a little boy pretending to be powerful. By being referred to as Achilles, he is identified with the unvanquishable hero, the all-powerful superman who cannot be touched by others, cannot be defeated, except through his one fatal flaw. Svidrigailov had stepped over the barriers. His flaw? By acknowledging the futility of omnipotent control, he has recognized his emptiness and isolation. He realizes that his destructive forces have destroyed the object that he loves and on which he depends, not only as an external object, but internally as well. His aggression has destroyed his own capacity to give and receive love. The ensuing fragmentation and paranoid reorganization of his world does not stop him from recognizing what he has done. It is for this reason, I think, that Svidrigailov touches us. He is sympathetic and quite different from the incarnation of evil Dostoevsky had initially intended.

A central idea running throughout the novel, and embodied in the respective fates of Svidrigailov and Raskolnikov, is that whether one ultimately gains salvation or perishes is dependent upon a relationship with a woman. Woman is felt to be absolutely essential in order to survive; one is dependent on her since she provides something one is unable to provide for oneself. The vulnerability involved in acknowledging this is surmounted by denying the woman's independence or separation from oneself; she is devalued, treated like a part object, controlled. There is no gratitude for what one receives from her, and it is absolutely necessary to avoid any feeling of guilt about how one treats her. In addition to Svidrigailov and Raskolnikov, variations on this theme are provided by Marmeladov, Luzhin, and Razumihin.

Luzhin clearly is the most negative and unsympathetic character in the

---

*This location is carefully chosen by Svidrigailov, after considering a number of other possibilities. At one point he notices the importance he's attaching to such a choice: "I've become more particular, like an animal that picks out a special place . . . for such an occasion" (p. 435). The last words he hears then, the little Jew repeating "You can't do it here, it's not the place" (p. 440) contain a particular irony. Svidrigailov has a *sense of place*, in contrast with the intrusive Raskolnikov; it is ultimately this sense of his own psychological place which determines his suicide.

novel, and Razumihin the healthiest. Luzhin tells us that "Dounia was simply essential to him; to do without her was unthinkable," and gloats over his plan to reverse the tilt in their relationship so that it is *he* who is on the pedestal, worshipped and admired by her, and regarded as *her* saviour. Her helpless position excites him, since it enables him to reverse roles with her, to turn the tables on this woman who has so much more than he does. "Here was a girl of pride, character, virtue, of education and breeding superior to his own (he felt that), and this creature would be slavishly grateful all her life for his heroic condescension, and would humble herself in the dust before him, and he would have absolute, unbounded power over her" (p. 267). In all relationships between man and woman, one either dominates or is a slave.

The role of slave belongs to Razumihin, who has fallen in love with Dounia on first sight, and during their first meeting babbles: "I am talking nonsense, I am not worthy of you . . . I am utterly unworthy of you!" (p. 175) ". . . you are a fount of goodness, purity, sense . . . and perfection . . . I want to kiss your hands here at once on my knees . . " (p. 176) and at this point he falls on his knees on the pavement and tries to kiss her hands while Dounia and her mother protest and wonder about his sanity. Attempts are made to attribute his behavior and speech to his being drunk.

Razumihin idealizes Dounia. From the first time he lays eyes on her, he has her on a pedestal labelled "Goodness, purity, sense, and perfection," and he falls on his knees to worship and serve her. Naturally, he feels unworthy in relation to such perfection. There are various reasons for idealization, including protection of the idealized object from being damaged or harmed, which would stir up feelings of loss, sadness, and guilt. A woman on a pedestal is kept at a safe distance. We learn that however ridiculous Razumihin may have been behaving, however out of control, he felt more comfortable with his idealization. Should Dounia have "been dressed like a queen, he felt that he would not be afraid of her, but perhaps just because she was poorly dressed and that he noticed all the misery of her surroundings, his heart was filled with dread and he began to be afraid of every word he uttered, every gesture he made" (p. 188).

Unlike Raskolnikov, however, Razumihin doesn't blame the woman for the feelings she stimulates in him, nor does he attempt to control such feelings by controlling her. There is no attempt to manipulate Dounia or to reverse their relationship; in summary, none of the omnipotent controlling and projective mechanisms we have come to associate with Raskolnikov. Razumihin accepts responsibility, not only for himself, but for helping Dounia, her brother, and their mother. He is the only one of the five men who is capable of making reparation.

In the three meetings that Raskolnikov has with Sonia, he makes extensive use of projection, and there is a recapitulation of much that I have already described. Initially he is cool, tries to break down all her defenses, and attempts to show her the realities of her situation at their worst, the futility of all her efforts. He torments her with just what he has been tormented by: his failure to provide for his family. "You must look things straight in the face at last," (p. 286) he tells her—precisely what he cannot do.

He does not relate to her as an individual, but as a kind of psychic toilet into which he can evacuate. This is frequently the function of the prostitute. He tries to make her feel helpless, useless, guilty, humiliated about revealing herself. By manipulating these feelings in her, he can remain uninvolved and in control. But then he realizes that all his cruel reproaches, his predictions of a terrible future, his suggestion that she kill herself—all these things she has thought of before, perhaps many times; she doesn't even notice his cruelty. Sonia appears uncorrupted by her experiences; she remains pure amidst all the dirt. He is intrigued by her ability to tolerate his attacks.

Raskolnikov finds out her solution: God! "She is a religious maniac." He forces her to read to him the story of Lazarus from the New Testament. His motive is perverse, destructive. She used to read to Lizaveta, and now she is revealing her "secret treasure" to him. "Raskolnikov saw in part why Sonia could not bring herself to read to him, and the more he saw this, the more roughly and irritably he insisted on her doing so. He understood only too well how painful it was for her to betray and unveil all that was her *own*" (p. 283). After all, he had come to reveal his painful secret to her. That he succeeded in relieving himself at her expense and in reversing their roles leaves him feeling momentarily triumphant, but also confused as to their separate identities. "We are the same," (p. 288) he tells her.

Raskolnikov relates to Sonia's suffering and submission with contempt and hatred one moment, while idealizing it the next. Neither response is personally directed to Sonia. In the middle of his cruel abuse of her, he suddenly bends down to the ground and kisses her foot. But don't take it personally, he tells her; "I did not bow down to you, I bowed down to all the suffering of humanity" (p. 279). A little later he explains that she had been chosen to hear what he had to say before he met her, indeed before the murders, when her father had first spoken of her.

After confusing and frightening her, he leaves in the same spirit of manic triumph as when he left the Marmeladov house. "Break what must be broken, once for all. . . . Freedom and power, and above all, power! Over all trembling creation and all the ant-heap! . . . That's the goal, remember that! That's my farewell message" (p. 287). We notice that, particularly in this state of mind, his parting metaphor is a destructive one. Raskolnikov never talks about reparation, the need for fixing or mending things, putting things aright.

The second time Raskolnikov visits Sonia, he has come to tell her who killed Lizaveta. Raskolnikov's responses to Sonia alternate, depending upon whether her response to him increases or decreases his anxiety and guilt. When she shows him that she can tolerate his attacks without being harmed, and that she can accept him, his discomfort is made more tolerable and he can show insight into his difficulties. But first he realizes that she is waiting, expecting something from him which he feels inadequate to deliver, he feels uncomfortable, and characteristically blames her. "Suddenly a strange, surprising sensation of a sort of bitter hatred for Sonia passed through his heart" (p. 351). He raises his head and looks intently in her eyes and to his surprise, sees neither victim nor persecutor. "There was love in them; his hatred vanished like a phantom." Like a good mother, she is able to contain his hateful feelings, and modify them through love.

He recognized his mistake; he had taken his helplessness and the urge to get rid of the feeling immediately, to project it violently, for hatred. "It was not the real feeling; he had taken the one feeling for the other. It only meant that *that* minute had come." "*That* minute" means that it is time to confess; but with ambiguity intended, it also refers to what was for him a similar experience. "His sensations that moment were terribly like the moment when he had stood over the old woman with the axe in his hand and felt that 'he must not lose another moment.' "

Significantly, he had come to tell her about Lizaveta. Lizaveta and Sonia are similar, and asking Sonia's forgiveness in some way cancels out the murders. It is important also that Raskolnikov does not actually tell Sonia, but that it is communicated, as are a series of other important feelings and states of mind–projections we would call them–through the eyes, by looking into the other person's face and experiencing what they are communicating. "You can't guess?" he asks. "Take a good look." Then, "he looked at her and all at once seemed to see in her face the face of Lizaveta." She looks, as Lizaveta did, like a frightened child. "Her terror infected him. The same fear showed itself on his face" (p. 353). When she realizes what he has done, she does not say anything. Again she intently stares into his face. He cannot stand her look and begs her to stop torturing him.

This was not at all the way he had imagined it would happen. But then she throws herself on her knees before him. "There is no one–no one in the whole world now so unhappy as you!" His heart softens and tears come to his eyes. "Then you won't leave me, Sonia?" (p. 354). Up to this point, she has accepted everything, not made him feel guilty, even made him feel that she needed him. Just as he had always tried to rid himself of any weakness, any uncomfortable feeling, he had assumed that she, his family, everyone, would want nothing to do with him, once they knew. She had accepted him.

But now she mentions his giving himself up. He recoils, becomes hostile. Furthermore, she expects an explanation. She tries to make the murders understandable, and he realizes that he himself does not understand, that he does not have an explanation to give her. When she makes a comment that again indicates her acceptance of him, his anxiety decreases, and he is able to reflect and momentarily have some insight. "I came to you for one thing–not to leave me. . . . Because I couldn't bear my burden and have come to throw it on another: you suffer too, and I shall feel better!" He has been seeking relief without reparation, absolution without repentence. Her response, to point out that he is suffering too, again makes his feelings more tolerable. "We are so different," he acknowledges at last. "We are not alike" (p. 356).

Still trying to find an explanation, he tells her about his Napoleon theory. Sonia is repelled at his failure to see what he has done. "I've only killed a louse, Sonia, a useless, loathsome, harmful creature" (p. 358). She does not accept this, and points out that he is responsible for killing a human being. This he does not want to hear—and he responds to the painful reality of her intervention as if it were an attack. His response is to attack himself, in the manner we first noticed with Marmeladov. Everything Raskolnikov says here is correct; but it is, in a sense, irrelevant. First of all, he avoids saying anything about the crucial point she has brought up: that he has taken a human life. Second, his verbal attack on himself is a caricature of conscience. It does not put him in touch with any responsibility for what he has done, or lead to any positive action, any desire to change. I'm worse than that, he tells her; "I am vain, envious, malicious, base, vindictive and . . . well, perhaps with a tendency toward insanity." He could have stayed in the University, could have worked like Razumihin does, "But I turned sulky, and wouldn't. (Yes, sulkiness, that's the right word for it!) I sat in my room like a spider" (p. 359).

Since this is not an acceptance of guilt or responsibility, we are not surprised when it abruptly changes direction into an attack on others. He believes other people are stupid, that they won't change, and that "it's not worth wasting effort over it . . . And I know, Sonia, that whoever is strong in mind and spirit will have power over them. Anyone who is greatly daring is right in their eyes. *He who despises most things* will be a law-giver among them and he who dares most of all will be most in the right!" (p. 359. Italics mine). What clearer expression could we possibly receive of the *"super" ego* which asserts its superiority by finding fault with everything!

When Sonia interrupts him and slows down his ravings, he calms down and, I think, momentarily returns to the deeper stimulus for the crime. He insists that it was not related to guilt for his mother and sister, but "to murder for my own sake, for myself. . . . It wasn't to help my mother that I did the murder—that's nonsense. . . . I did the murder for myself, for myself alone." If we were not wondering about his protesting too much, his next denial is even more suggestive. "Whether I became a benefactor to others, or spent my life like a spider catching men in my web and sucking the life out of men [sic], I couldn't have cared at that moment" (p. 360). Again, the symbol of his oral greed and guilt: the spider and the louse, who live off others and suck them dry.*

He decides, at the end of their meeting, that he has been in too great a hurry to condemn himself, that he should make a fight for it. He also feels differently about Sonia. Whereas he had felt that he could use her to get rid of his suffering, now he feels that he has only added one more burden and

*The spider, which recurs in Raskolnikov's thoughts about himself and is also used to represent Svidrigailov, is probably the most well known symbol of the oral destructive danger of being loved. The spider is associated with the threat of maternal engulfment based upon projection of the child's oral-aggressive impulses. See Abraham (1922), Sterba (1950), and Little (1966). In the paragraph just quoted Raskolnikov avoids acknowledging that women, particularly representatives of the mother, are the target of his aggression.

that now he has to worry about feeling guilty about her. "He felt once more that he would perhaps come to hate Sonia, now that he had made her more miserable. Why had he gone to her to beg for her tears? What need had he to poison her life?" (p. 365).

Raskolnikov's confession to Sonia has not only reminded him of his feelings at the time of the murders, but has repeated the very dynamics which led to his committing them. Having gone to Sonia out of desperate need, he now experiences their relationship as ruined. His feelings are a mixture of guilt and anger; he doesn't know whom to blame. He had felt weak and inadequate before a woman whom he perceived as expecting more from him than he could give. Characteristically, he responded to this with rage. Almost simultaneously, he suspects that it was he who was demanding, who was asking too much of her. Since his use of projective mechanisms results in confusion of self and other, he doesn't know which of them went too far.

Raskolnikov's efforts to escape from any clear understanding of his position require other people whom he can use as recipients of his projections, and blame for his difficulties. Identification with these projected aspects of himself results in feelings of suffocation and claustrophobia. It is significant that Svidrigailov and Porfiry Petrovich, the only two people who understand something of his psychological make-up, repeatedly tell him that what he needs is fresh air.

His need for adversaries, other people with whom he can be angry, is plainly stated: "No, better the struggle again! Better Porfiry again . . . or Svidrigailov. . . . Better some challenge again . . . some attack" (p. 380). Thinking of his mother and sister, and now of Sonia, reduces him to panic; therefore, he needs someone like Porfiry or Svidrigailov to rail against. They are external persecutors, and his counterattack is directed externally. He feels right, vindicated, and strong.

When, after a conversation with Razumihin, he believes that Porfiry suspects him and has set up a plan to get him, he feels "renewed; again the struggle, so a means of escape has come." Note the words with which he describes the shift from internal torment to externalized struggle. "Yes, a means of *escape* had come! It had been too *stifling*, too *cramping*, the burden had been too agonizing. . . . From the moment of the scene with Nikolay at Porfiry's he had been *suffocating, penned in* without hope of escape" (p. 384. Italics mine). Porfiry tells him: "If you ran away, you'd come back of yourself. *You can't get on without us*" (p. 397). It is because of this, and particularly because he cannot risk losing or harming Sonia, that he confesses.

Just prior to his going to confess, he is visited by his sister. When Dounia talks to him about expiating his crime by facing his suffering, Raskolnikov explodes. " 'Crime? What crime?' he cried in sudden fury. 'That I killed a vile noxious insect, an old pawnbroker woman, of use to no one! . . . Killing her was atonement for forty sins. She was sucking the life out of poor people. . . . Only now I see clearly the imbecility of my cowardice, now that I have decided to face this superfluous disgrace. It's simply because I am contemptible'" (p. 466). According to Raskolnikov, he is contemptible because he is weak and cowardly. The crime is stupid and clumsy because it failed. "I am further than ever from seeing that what I did is a crime," he rails (p. 447).

After Dounia leaves, he thinks to himself, "'But why are they so fond of me if I don't deserve it? Oh, if only I were alone and no one loved me and I too had never loved anyone! *Nothing of all this would have happened*'" (p. 448). By now, we can appreciate the truth of this for Raskolnikov, and know what burden of guilt is subsumed under the name of love. We also notice that he is still blaming others, the pawnbroker for being so greedy, his family for loving him; and he still is speaking of the need to break things rather than repair them.

When Raskolnikov goes to the police station, his cowardice gets the better of him and he leaves without confessing. The avoidance is momentary, however, for the sight that waits outside is more than he can stand. "There, not far from the entrance, stood Sonia, pale and horror-stricken. She looked wildly at him. He stood still before her. There was a look of poignant agony, of despair, in her face" (p. 457). The moment climaxes the novel by juxtaposing with Marmeladov's fearful look at his wife's eyes, and Svidrigailov's complaint about Dounia's look killing him. It also repeats the spatial movement of the opening scene, the woman waiting at the threshold, obstructing his path. Raskolnikov cannot stand to look into Sonia's face, and thereby experience what he is doing to her; he lacks the courage. "His lips worked in an ugly, meaningless smile. He stood still a minute, grinned and went back to the police office" (p. 457).

IV

The Epilogue, as Wasiolek (1959) points out, is a "source of perpetual embarrassment to the apologists for Dostoevsky." Artistically weak though it may be, it remains psychologically consistent with the preceding sections of the novel. One can appreciate the wisdom of not ending with the confession, for the obligation to confess under the circumstances just described provides Raskolnikov with the opportunity to feel angry again. In addition, now that he has stopped running physically, the narcissistic aspects of his personality become more discernible (Rosenfeld, 1964).

Raskolnikov's mother has become seriously ill. Her thoughts are continuously about her son, and she becomes deranged in her efforts to reassure herself that he will return. She knows nothing of his trial or his imprisonment, and is given no explanation for his disappearance. Raskolnikov, we are told, worries about her a great deal; but even though he predicts that her progressive depression will soon end fatally, neither he nor any of the others consider telling her even the partial truth. The knowledge of what happened is withheld from her, and what she doesn't know kills her.

Just as Raskolnikov dealt with unacceptable aspects of his personality by attempting to get rid of or annihilating them, so he believes his family would treat him the same way, and would want to get rid of him if he is guilty, or weak, or even wrong. In his anticipation of his mother's rejection of him, he deserts her first. She is made to feel that her son has abandoned her, and she goes mad and perishes because of it. There is almost a feeling of revenge here, a turning of the tables. That it seems so unnecessary adds to its cruelty. Could her fate have been any worse if she had been told the truth? This has usually escaped notice, even by those readers who recognize the killing of the pawnbroker as a symbolic or displaced murder of the mother.

There is an additional reason for this seemingly senseless death. Raskolnikov needs to destroy the original source of love and gratification in order to eliminate the source of envy. This idea is substantiated by the way in which things are brought about. Raskolnikov's mother expects him to return in nine months and she goes through elaborate preparations for his arrival, gets his room ready, etc. She dies of disappointment; her wish is denied. His birth, or rebirth, does not take place, at least not to her. His subsequent rebirth is contrasted with her sterility, her frustrated hopes and expectations.

Raskolnikov's resurrection resembles the murders in several respects. Both events are immediately preceded by phantasies of oceanic reunion, so that fusion with an idealized internal mother makes the external mother no longer necessary. It is as if Raskolnikov is saying that he does not need her; he can do it better himself. This would be the ultimate robbery. First a hostile substitute for the mother was killed off, and then the real mother herself.

In the second half of the Epilogue, Raskolnikov no longer is struggling with feelings of guilt; nor does he show a capacity for concern about others. As he himself declares, "My conscience is at rest" (p. 467). Raskolnikov is isolated from all the other men. He can be comfortable in his isolation precisely because all his needs are fulfilled by Sonia, whom he controls and treats as a part of himself. Despite Raskolnikov's crime and status as a prisoner, she considers herself beneath him in every respect. She is always available, expects nothing of him, is satisfied to be his slave. The other prisoners refer to her as the "good little mother," an additional clue as to what Raskolnikov has accomplished by his domination and control of her. She is willing to give all ("Lizaveta, Sonia. . . . They give up everything"), and she demands absolutely nothing in return. If he looks at her, or notices her existence, she is grateful. Meanwhile, he treats her with contempt, and does not acknowledge any awareness of need for her. In fact, she is experienced as needing him. A perfect narcissistic relationship, in which both dependency and need are either denied or projected into her.

The dream of the microbes is difficult to interpret as evidence of moral redemption. Shaw (1973) points out that Razumihin had earlier asked Raskolnikov, "Caught the plague or something?" a folkish expression loosely translated as "Are you crazy?" Unlike Raskolnikov's previous dreams, the dream of the microbes is not a dream at all; it is a fable or myth.* It recapitulates the argument presented in his article and in his discussion with Porfiry Petrovich, and is perhaps the most explicit statement of what I referred to in my introduction when I discussed Bion's concept of −K. Raskolnikov's microbes "were endowed with intelligence and will. Men attacked by them became at once mad and furious. But never had men considered themselves so intellectual and so completely in possession of the truth as these sufferers, never had they considered their decisions, their scientific conclusions, their moral convictions so infallible. . . . Each thought that he alone had the truth" (p. 469).

These microbes are the latest version of the persecutory, minutely splintered particles that had resulted from forceful primitive projections and had attacked both Raskolnikov and Svidrigailov at their most desperate moments. Holquist (1974), in his discussion of the dream, points out that the infecting particles, translated in most English editions as microbes, would more accurately be trichinae, for the Russian *trixiny*. Not only is this a well-known parasite, but it is usually associated with pigs or swine, which reestablishes the theme of oral greed and exploitation, the emotional factors of −K. We are not surprised when we hear how this knowledge is used, that "all men and all things were involved in destruction."

The rest of Dostoevsky's myth describes the relationship between the individual possessing this knowledge and his group. Bion has written about three such stories, the myths of Eden, Oedipus, and Babel, each of which deals with man's quest for knowledge and his subsequent punishment by an angry god (Bion 1963). I would like to compare Dostoevsky's myth with the one I think it most resembles:

> "All were excited and did not understand one another . . . The most ordinary trades were abandoned, because everyone proposed his own ideas, his own improvements, and they could not agree . . . Men met in groups, agreed on something, swore to keep together, but at once began on something quite different from what they had proposed. They accused one another, fought and killed each other."

> ". . . immediately the builders became embroiled in misunderstandings. If a mason told a hod-carrier 'Give me mortar!' the carrier would hand him a brick instead, with which the mason would angrily kill the hod-carrier. Many were the murders done in the Tower; and on the ground also, because of this confusion; until at last work slowed to a standstill."

While each of the three traditional myths deals with the quest for a specific kind of knowledge, I am suggesting that the Babel myth, quoted on

*If we consider that the capacity to "dream" preserves the personality from psychosis (Bion, 1962b, p. 16), then Razumihin's question would be answered in the affirmative, and Raskolnikov is perhaps furthest from the truth in this fable about the attainment of self-knowledge. Appropriately, he has this experience while in the hospital.

the right (Graves, 1963 p. 126), deals with artistic creativity. Under the supervision of the architect Nimrod, men attempt to build a tower reaching where man has never been before, crossing the threshold of heaven itself into the domain of the gods.* Their punishment for this transgression is the fragmentation of language. If we consider that the punishment fits the crime, what greater punishment for a poet or artist than to be deprived of the opportunity to communicate through language, to be reduced to babbling?

Whereas each of the three traditional myths may begin with the premise that the quest for knowledge is sinful, Dostoevsky has presented us with the consequences of knowledge sought in the service of envy and greed. It is no wonder that the notion of intrusiveness is so persistent, and the knowledge always felt to be acquired at someone else's expense. The dream of the microbes is a restatement of Raskolnikov's theory of creativity, which is also a theory of the superman. Not surprisingly, this dream of world destruction has a loophole, the chosen few who are saved from the plague, exceptional men "destined to found a new race and a new life, to renew and purify the earth." These super-supermen are invisible; in a statement that I think foreshadows the ending of the Epilogue we are told that "no one had seen these men, no one had heard their words and their voices."

After the dream, Sonia is not there, and Raskolnikov for the first time since his confession is worried about her. He learns that she is ill with a cold. Has she been infected by the microbes of his dream? He is forced to recognize his need for her, particularly when there is reason (the microbes) to fear that harm had come to her as a result of his treatment of her. This is made even more explicit by the way in which he learns of her illness. Her letter to him parallels the previous letter from his mother; in each case a woman had suffered on his account, and not told him about it until later.

When Raskolnikov looks out of the window of his hospital room, and sees Sonia standing by the entrance, waiting for him, the sight of her "stabbed him to the heart." The novel had both begun and ended with such a spatial and emotional configuration; in the opening episode in relation to the landlady, and at the novel's close when Sonia waits outside the police station. In each case, the woman is a threshold object, and being reminded of how he has treated her is more than he can bear. In the first instance he was driven to murder; in the second, to confess. Now once again Raskolnikov feels he must do something!

What follows is his resurrection and sudden awareness of love. It is ushered in by his second mystical daydream. The imagery is quite similar to the one preceding the murders. The desert caravan, with its resting camels, is now a tribe of nomads, like Abraham and his flocks. There is sunshine and

*In her article on "The Oresteia" (1963), Klein discussed *hubris*, which she felt was regarded as sinful primarily because of greed and exploitation of the mother. "Greed links with the concept of *moira* (which) represents the portion allotted to each man by the gods. When *moira* is overstepped, punishment by the gods follows. The fear of such punishment goes back to the fact that greed and envy are first of all experienced toward the mother who is felt to be injured by these emotions and who by projection turns in the child's mind into a greedy and resentful figure. She is therefore feared as a source of punishment, the prototype of God."

singing, and again a sense of timelessness. The nomads, those wanderers who owe allegiance to no one but themselves, give Raskolnikov a feeling of freedom. It is this sense of freedom which Raskolnikov has been seeking throughout the novel: freedom from responsibility for others, freedom from dependency, freedom from guilt.

The fantasy is followed by a sudden feeling of joy, the kind of letting go typically described as part of the mystical experience. Characteristically, also, Raskolnikov's love for Sonia is unspoken, communicated visually by looking into one another's eyes. It is an immediate, total, all-or-nothing experience. It takes Raskolnikov further away from moral redemption in that he does not deal with his crime, the murders, nor with his previous treatment of people; he forgets about them. When he begins to think about his previous torment of Sonia, he immediately stops himself. "But these recollections scarcely troubled him now; he knew with what infinite love he would now repay all her sufferings" (p. 471). His future deeds will cancel out his previous misdeeds. In the end, he was right; it is all arithmetic! "Everything, even his crime, his sentence and imprisonment, seemed to him now in the first rush of feeling an external, strange fact with which he had no concern" (pp. 471-472).

This sudden lack of concern echoes the opening scene in the novel when Raskolnikov experienced similar feelings (or a lack of them) in regard to his landlady and his indebtedness to her. By repeating the birth imagery, we are also brought back to the opening scene, perhaps having gone full circle. Sonia and Raskolnikov have another seven years in Siberia; but as to the regeneration of Raskolnikov's character, Dostoevsky tells us that would be another story.

References

Abraham, K. (1922). The spider as a dream symbol. *Selected Papers on Psychoanalysis*. New York: Basic Books, 1953.

Bakhtin, M. (1929). *Problems of Dostoevsky's Poetics* (tr. R.W. Rotsel). Ann Arbor: Ardis, 1973.

Bion, W. R. (1956). Development of schizophrenic thought. *International Journal of Psycho-Analysis* vol. 37, 344-346. In *Second Thoughts*. London: Heinemann, 1967.

— (1957). Differentiation of the psychotic from the non-psychotic personalities. *International Journal of Psycho-Analysis* 38, 266-275. In *Second Thoughts*, 1967.

— (1958 a). On hallucination. *International Journal of Psycho-Analysis* 39, 341-349. In *Second Thoughts*, 1967.

— (1958 b). On arrogance. *International Journal of Psycho-Analysis* 39, 144-146. In *Second Thoughts*, 1967.

— (1962 a.) A theory of thinking, *International Journal of Psycho-Analysis* 43, 306-310. In *Second Thoughts*, 1967.

— (1962 b). *Learning from Experience*. London: Heinemann.

— (1963). *Elements of Psychoanalysis*. London: Heinemann.

Coulson, J. (1953). Tr. *Crime and Punishment* by F. M. Dostoevsky (Norton Critical Edition, ed. G. Gibian). New York: Norton, 1975.

Dostoevsky, F. M. (1866). *Crime and Punishment* (tr. C. Garnett). New York: Bantam, 1959.

— (1923). *Letters and Reminiscences* (tr. S. Koteliansky and J. M. Murry). Freeport, New York: Books for Libraries Press, 1971.

— (1931). *The Notebooks for Crime and Punishment*. I. Glivenko, Moscow & Leningrad; rpt. ed. & tr. E. Wasiolek . London: Univ. of Chicago Press, 1967.

Federn, P. (1929). An everyday compulsion. *International Journal of Psycho-Analysis* 10, 130-138.

Frank, J. (1975). Freud's case-history of Dostoevsky. *T.L.S.* July 18. Rpt. in *Dostoevsky the Seeds of Revolt 1821-1849* Princeton: Princeton Univ. Press, 1976.

Freud, S. (1900). *Interpretation of Dreams. Standard Edition*. 5, p. 504.
—— (1928). Dostoevsky and parricide. *Standard Edition*. 21, 177-194.
Gibian, G. (1955). Traditional symbolism in *Crime and Punishment. PMLA* 70, 979-996.
Graves, R. and Patai, R. (1963). *Hebrew Myths: The Book of Genesis*. New York: McGraw-Hill.
Grotstein, J. S. (1977). The psychoanalytic concept of schizophrenia: II. Reconciliation. *International Journal of Psycho-Analysis* 58, 427-452.
Holquist, J. M. (1974). Disease as dialectic in *Crime and Punishment*. In R. L. Jackson (ed.), *Twentieth Century Interpretations of Crime and Punishment*. Englewood Cliffs, New Jersey: Prentice-Hall.
Klein, M. (1943). Some theoretical conclusions regarding the emotional life of the infant. In *Developments in Psychoanalysis*. London: Hogarth Press, 1952.
—— (1945). Notes on some schizoid mechanisms. In *Developments in Psychoanalysis*. London: Hogarth Press, 1952.
—— (1963). Some reflections on 'The Oresteia.' In *Envy and Gratitude and Other Works 1946-1963.* Delacorte Press/Seymour Lawrence, 1975.
Little, R. B. (1966). Oral aggression in spider legends. *American Imago* 23, 170-176.
Lukacs, G. (1943). Dostoevsky. In R. Wellek (ed.), *Dostoevsky A Collection of Critical Essays*. Englewood Cliffs, N.J.: Prentice-Hall, 1962.
Magarshack, D. (1961). *Dostoevsky*. New York: Harcourt, Brace.
Matlaw, R. (1957). Recurrent Imagery in Dostoevsky. *Harvard Slavic Studies*. 201-225. Cambridge: Harvard Univ. Press.
Mochulsky, K. (1947). *Dostoevsky His Life and Work* (tr. M. Minihan). Princeton: Princeton Univ. Press, 1967.
Peace, R. (1971). *Dostoevsky, an Examination of the Major Novels*. Cambridge: Cambridge Univ. Press.
Rahv, P. (1960). Dostoevsky in *Crime and Punishment. Partisan Review* 27, 393-425.
Roheim, G. (1922). The significance of stepping over. *International Journal of Psycho-Analysis* 3, 320-326.
Rosenfeld, H. (1964). On the psychopathology of narcissism: a clinical approach. *International Journal of Psycho-Analysis* 45, 332-337.
—— (1969). Contribution to the psychopathology of psychotic states; the importance of projective identification in the ego structure and the object relations of the psychotic patient. In P. Doucet and C. Laurin (ed.), *Problems in Psychosis*. Amsterdam: Excerpta Medica.
Rosenthal, R. J. (1977). Dostoevsky's use of projection; psychic mechanism as narrative structure in *The Double*. (Presented to the International Dostoevsky Society, August 1977, Rungstedgaard, Denmark.) In press.
Segal, H. (1952). A psycho-analytical approach to aesthetics. *International Journal of Psycho-Analysis* 33, 195-207.
Segal, H. (1964). *Introduction to the Work of Melanie Klein*. London: Heinemann.
Shaw, J. T. (1973). Raskolnikov's dreams. *Slavic and East European Journal* 17, 131-145.
Snodgrass, W. D. (1960). Crime for punishment: the tenor of part one. *Hudson Review* 13, 202-253.
Sterba, R. (1950). On spiders, hanging and oral sadism. *American Imago* 7, 21-28.
Wasiolek, E. (1959). On the structure of *Crime and Punishment. PMLA* 74, 131-136.
—— (1974). Raskolnikov's motives: love and murder. *American Imago* 31, 252-269.

THEORETICAL CONTRIBUTIONS

New Theories: Their Influence and Effect on Psychoanalytic Technique

A.B. Bahia

EDITOR'S NOTE: *This paper is reprinted here, having first appeared in the* International Journal of Psycho-Analysis *in 1977 (Vol. 58, pp. 345-363). I am indebted to the Estate of Doctor Bahia, Doctor Rosa Beatriz Pontes de Miranda, and Doctor Joseph Sandler, the latter as Editor of the* International Journal of Psycho-Analysis, *for their permission to republish the work. My editorial decision to requisition it for the* Memorial *was due to the unusually clear light it threw on the significance of Klein's and, particularly, Bion's emendations of the classical oedipal theory on one hand and the classical theory of memory and repression on the other. Doctor Bahia succinctly and cogently integrates Klein's and Bion's work into a newer theory of psychoanalytic technique. In particular, he has focused on the "myth" of classical analytic technique which suggests that the recovery of memory bespeaks the suppression of repression. Instead, he invokes Bion to suggest that memory itself is saturated with desire and is always "screen memory," and therefore is as devious from truth as it is revelatory. Memory is the past tense of desire and therefore designates a motive to change the future as one has changed the memory of the past, all to evade the unexpectedness inherent in the space of* now.

I believe this to be a seminal paper for psychoanalytic theory and technique. Its very theme accounts for the "Via Dolorosa" which has characterized the history of psychoanalytic development, whether in the historic conflict between psychoanalysis and all the institutions of the lay world, or the conflict between "Kleinians" and "Freudians" for the patent rights on the Holy Grail. Truth must remain free, open, and changing and must not be hampered by memory or desire or the intolerance of change.

New Theories: Their Influence and Effect on Psychoanalytic Technique

A.B. Bahia, Rio de Janeiro

> Controversy is the growing-point from which development springs, but it must be a genuine confrontation and not an impotent beating of the air by opponents whose differences of view never meet (Bion, 1970, p. 55).

I

Introduction

In his introductory note to Freud's first six works on psychoanalytical technique, James Strachey (1958) points out the relative scarcity of texts on this theme by the creator of psychoanalysis. He goes on to remark that Freud never ceased to maintain that mastery of psychoanalytical technique could only be achieved through clinical experience, never from books. Strachey adds: "clinical experience with patients, no doubt, but, above all, clinical experience from the analyst's own analysis."

The cornerstone of technique is, thus, experience from the analyst's own analysis which, according to Freud (1937*a*, p. 249), should be periodically resumed "at intervals of five years or so." Based on his own experience of undergoing or re-undergoing analysis without idealization, the analyst realizes the problems of the development of psychoanalytical technique better than anyone. Such development has to be limited to "exercises with ideas," following trends of thought which have stemmed from Freud's first discoveries.

However, exercises can be as exhausting and challenging as any other activity. Freud (1914) pointed out that the theory of psychoanalysis can be defined as:

> an attempt to account for two striking and unexpected facts of observation which emerge whenever an attempt is made to trace the symptoms of a neurotic back to their sources in his past life: the facts of transference and resistance. Any line of investigation which recognizes these two facts and takes them as the starting-point of its work has a right to call itself psychoanalysis, even though it arrives at results other than my own (p. 16).

Although this remains valid in its general terms, its recognition in specific clinical practice is very difficult. What may appear to be resistance may be, in fact, a veiled manifestation of a positive transference relationship and,

Bahia, A.B. ["New Theories: Their Influence and Effect on Psychoanalytic Technique"] This article first appeared in *The International Journal of Psycho-Analysis* 58, 345-364, 1977.

conversely, an ostensibly positive but hostile transference may become a barrier to the progress of an analytical process. But Freud's synthesis remains true: psychoanalytical theory still is an "effort to make transference and resistance understandable." Only, in order to grasp these concepts clearly, understanding their meaning in connexion with the development of psychoanalytical technique, one must provide wider and at the same time more precise terms of reference which will enable new interpretations of meanings to show up within the total historical pattern of psychoanalysis.

It should be recognized that in Freud, as in later authors, there are "seminal moments" the study of which helps in understanding new tendencies which they inspired. Identifying such "moments" is difficult and, given the extraordinary richness of Freudian clinical experience and critical elaboration, perhaps even useless. Moreover, to the risks of one's own limitations are added the restrictions of time and space imposed on such endeavours.

Recognizing and accepting these difficulties, the present work sets out to study the appearance and development of new trends within psychoanalytical technique. This study follows three main lines of reference: the first is Freud's synthesis—"the effort to make transference and resistance understandable," adding that the two facts referred to (transference and resistance) are a result of repression and are based, as Freud stressed throughout his whole work, on the processes of "remembering" and "forgetting": psychological mechanisms inherent in the phenomenon of *repression*. The second line is the renewal of some of the concepts concerning primitive anxieties, introduced by a reappraisal of the Oedipus conflict, as postulated by Melanie Klein after her experience in analysing children. The third line is the clinical concept of the *loss of contact with reality*, as described by Freud (1924*b*) in cases of *neurosis* and *psychosis*. I shall relate to each of these, "indicators": (1) saturation of the mind by memory and desire; (2) intolerance of frustration and incapacity for thought; (3) simultaneity of the pleasure principle and the reality principle.

II

1. The Significance of "Remembering" and "Forgetting" According to Freud

In an essay on the nature of preconscious mental processes, Kris (1950) remarks that "Freud's ideas were constantly developing, his writings represent a sequence of reformulations, and one might therefore well take the view that the systematic cohesion of psychoanalytic propositions is only, or at least best, accessible through their history."

The facts concerning the intimate connexion of "remembering" and "forgetting" with the processes that rule repression, however, seem to contradict Kris's statement. In fact, analysing Freud's writings with reference to the laws which seem to regulate the relationship between repressive processes and "remembering" and "forgetting" phenomena, one does not find that "continual reformulation." On the contrary, one seems to be faced with an impressive unity of point of view along the years.

From the "Studies on Hysteria" (Breuer & Freud, 1893-5) to the "Constructions in Analysis" (Freud, 1937*b*) one can derive the same technical postulate: that in the course of psychic processes amnesia indicates repression, and the appearance of a recollection, on the other hand, always means a suppression of repression. But as soon as we state this apparently so reliable principle, we can see a disturbing exception. The facts are neither so clear nor so well established. Adopting the critical approach recommended by Kris and considering all occasions on which Freud handled the phenomena of "remembering" and "forgetting," we find that there are memories which, far from indicating suppression of repressive mechanisms, rather imply a direct manifestation of their action. Those recollections that contradict and confuse the links painstakingly established by Freud between "forgetting" and repression, on the one hand, and "remembering" and suppression on the other, are—needless to say—the so-called "screen memories."

As is well known, in his study of this type of memory, Freud distinguished a peculiarity in the temporal relationship between the covering recollection and its hidden real contents, namely between retrogressive or retrospective, and progressive or advanced memories. But (as Freud himself remarked) it is not the temporal relationship between the "screen memory" and the "covered experience" that is important. The fundamental fact is that in "the so-called earliest childhood memories we possess not the genuine memory-trace but a later revision of it" (Freud 1901, pp. 47-48). In other words, Freud's clinical findings and his concept of "screen memories" contradict the identity previously established in his writings, between the appearance of a recollection and the suppressing of the repressive process. His own explanations are not very encouraging:

> Out of a number of childhood memories of significant experiences, all of them of similar distinctness and clarity, there will be some scenes which, when they are tested (for instance, by the recollections of adults), turn out to have been falsified. Not that they are complete inventions; they are false in the sense that they have shifted an event to a place where it did not occur—or that they have merged two people into one, or substituted one for the other, or the scenes as a whole give signs of being combinations of two separate experiences (Freud, 1899, pp. 321-322).

From these remarks one can see that Freud is comparing the processes of screen-memory construction and dream construction. "Screen memories" are not "genuine" recollections, but dream distortions created by the memory process, mutilated or metaphorical allusions to the "genuine," "complete" recollections.

But what in fact is a "genuine," "complete" recollection? How can it be defined, by which elements can it be recognized? Certainly, no help is to be had from the idea that "screen memories," nearer to dream structure than to memory structure, might *possibly* represent an exceptional memory process. In fact, if they occur in a "certain number of childhood recollections," what guarantee can we have that they are not present in the whole memory process? Granted that they occur only in some of the cases, how to proceed, in a particular case, in order to identify a recollection as a memory of a real fact, as a "genuine" memory, and not only a distortion disguising a fantasy? And, more, how to reconcile the meaning of the displacement of a "screen memory" with the accepted identity between a memory "in general" and the suppressing of repression, when this displacement is nothing but an effect of repression? In order to give an answer to these embarrassing questions, one must reformulate the meaning hitherto given to "remembering" and "forgetting" within the analytical process. This reformulation, moreover, can and must be done bearing Freud's works in mind.

Kris's warning concerning the "constant developing" of Freud's ideas, reminds us that this reformulation should not mean unconditional reacceptance of the total suppression of gaps of memory as a condition for cure. The Freud who in his "History of an Infantile Neurosis" (1918) tells us how he obtained new analytic material from his patient by fixing a date for the termination of the treatment, must certainly be superseded. Nowadays, we would call that famous "infantile material" a mental construction by the so-called Wolf Man, designed to get from Freud the satisfaction, in a degraded form, of instinctive, primeval needs, not sufficiently clarified by analysis.

But a clue can be found from the "other" Freud, the one who found—with such sagacity and scientific rigour—the concept of "screen memories." In one of his writings on this subject Freud (1899) expressed his suspicion that all conscious infantile recollections show us "our earliest years not as they were but as they appeared at the later periods when the memories were aroused." Freud concludes, baldly: "in these periods of arousal, the child-memories did not, as people are accustomed to say, *emerge*: they were *formed* at that time. And a number of motives, with no concern for historical accuracy, had a part in forming them, as well as in the selection of the memories themselves" (p. 322).

2. "Saturation" of the Mind by Memory and Desire

It is difficult to understand how Freud could have established two concepts about the memory process—one linking the suppressing of repression and the arousing of memories, and the other marking "screen memories" as the work of repression—without ever putting the two together for a comparative study. Everything points to the conclusion that if Freud had compared the two concepts, he would have called the memory process, in its entirety, a huge "screen memory," a "fantastic construction," in which "remembering" and "forgetting" are not antagonistic but complementary instruments, both with the same function, i.e., transforming external reality in accordance with instinctual needs.

In this sense, one can say that we all, whether successful or unsuccessful in our personal lives, in sickness or in health, actively creating or actively hallucinating, are, to some extent, genuine "*fabricators of memories*" (Bahia, 1956).

This "falsifying," "screening" character of the memory process is taken to its logical conclusion by Bion in his concept of "saturation" of the mind by memory and desire. This concept, as will be seen, underlies one of the most fertile trends of psychoanalytical technique in our day.

Apparently, what Bion claims is not very different from what Freud meant when he wrote about "free-floating attention." Thus Bion (1970) remarks: "a fallacious but helpful description . . . is that the practising analyst must wait for the analytic session to 'evolve.' He must wait not for the analysand to talk or to be silent or to gesture or for any other occurrence that is an actual event, but for an evolution to take place" (p. 28).

Bion goes further. Considering memory as "a container" for the "evacuations" or projective identifications, he proposes, as an active routine during analytical work, the avoidance of memories and desires of any kind. This, including the wish to "cure" the patient. He thinks it "a serious defect to allow oneself to desire the end of a session, or week, or term," since "such desires erode the analyst's power to analyse and lead to progressive deterioration of his intuition" (Bion, 1970), pp. 26-54).

Similarly, Bion stresses that "forgetting" is not enough, one must try positively to stop memories and desires. In this context he quotes a letter of Freud's (to Lou Andreas-Salomé) in which he suggests a method of reaching a mental state to compensate for the obscurity of certain objects of investigation: "I had to blind myself artificially to focus all the light on one dark spot." Bion proposes a constant watchfulness in keeping memories and wishes away, noting that this does not mean any lack of desire to get in touch with psychic reality. On the contrary, this would be the best—and possibly the only—way to reach an effective contact with that reality.

In his own words, "the more the analyst becomes expert in excluding memory, desire and understanding from his mental activity, the more he is likely at least in the early stages, to experience painful emotions that are usually excluded or screened by the conventional apparatus of 'memory' of the session, analytical theories often disguised desires or denials of ignorance."

What would the mental state be that is most likely to replace the mental saturation resulting from "attachment" to memories, wishes and previous "understandings"? According to Bion, the word that would approximately convey what he means is "faith." Faith in the existence of "an ultimate reality—the unknown, unknowable, 'formless infinite,' " out of which only a small portion can be known during an analytical session. Such faith, characteristic of scientific endeavour, "must be distinguished from the religious meaning with which it is invested in conversational usage."

In other words, only when disrobed of all artifice, lacking any sense of "anticipation," not *saturated* by memories, desires or previous "understandings," only then can an analytical session take place and "evolve" in an atmosphere of scientific truth.

As an illustration, take the following passage from a session with a recently married patient, three months under analysis. During the session, the patient's mental "saturation" by memories from previous sessions hinders the stimulus of new perceptions and the "evolving" of the present situation. Feelings of fear toward "the unknown" are also present. It should be stressed incidentally that this and all other instances of clinical material included in this paper should not convey any impression of the material being at all exceptional. These instances should be seen as mere illustrations which may recall something in the reader's own experience.

> P.: I remember last session, when you interpreted something concerning my wife . . . [pause]. By the way, it was connected with last Wednesday's session, I remember it well . . . How was it again? [pause of approximately 4 minutes].
>
> A.: I doubt whether you really can recall the last session, or last Wednesday's. What you are doing is trying to be sure that nothing is happening now. Or is going to happen. But those sessions you mention are over, and you know they can be of no use now.
>
> P.: Yes, I know, yes . . . but why am I afraid then?
>
> A.: I didn't say you were afraid. I only said . . .
>
> P.: [interrupting] But I am. At least, I feel I am afraid of you.
>
> A.: Perhaps this fear, as well as the "memories" about last week's sessions, are something created by you in order to get the illusion of being a helpless child, protected by a strong authority—myself, in this case—against anything new which might arise in your mind now.
>
> P.: But that is absurd! How could I feel at the same time protected and afraid of you?
>
> A.: Because you transform me into this authority I mentioned, though you know that I am not a protective or frightening figure.
>
> P.: Well, I remember that such was and perhaps still is my relationship with my father. . . . But I have already learnt a lot here, one thing being that you are not going to "father" me . . . [pause]. I appreciate this . . . [laughs]. Funny; I'm not afraid any more. Now I even feel encouraged to tell you that I had sexual contact with my wife on Saturday and that it was not satisfactory . . . I don't know why, but I felt I had to produce that coitus.
>
> A.: You talk about "producing" that coitus, not simply having it. As if you were an automaton or a machine for producing

coitus, on the assumption that you are obliged to do it. Exactly as you feel obliged to produce recollections here, or to force yourself to talk. You cannot be here simply, without feeling compelled to do something.

P.: By the way, you know my father inherited a flat from my deceased brother. Well, he offered me that flat for a very low rent . . . 700 or 800 cruzeiros a month, I don't remember which . . . I was going to accept, taking the way of least resistance, as I did before. . . . But then I thought it better to put some money aside, as I'm doing now, in order to buy my own flat . . . Fortunately my wife is of the same opinion . . .

A.: Now you seem to recognize that it is better for you to have an independent mind and life. With no fear of me and without that need to turn me into a protective authority.

III

1. Melanie Klein's Reappraisal of the Oedipus Complex

This short paper is obviously no place for a detailed description of Melanie Klein's discoveries in children's psychoanalysis which brought about a reappraisal of the Oedipus complex. Some reference to her findings is indispensable, however, as it will enable us to assess more precisely the directions or trends of the new developments in psychoanalytical technique.

Of two main findings, the first regards the period in which the Oedipus conflict arises as much earlier than was thought in the classical Freudian view. For Melanie Klein, the triangular situation starts with the period of weaning, perhaps even before. The second finding, which later helped to establish the concepts of the paranoid-schizoid position and the depressive position is that "the different phases (especially in the initial stages) merge more freely in one another than was hitherto supposed" (Klein, 1928, p. 214).

These two findings of Melanie Klein's have markedly overshadowed another finding, present in her whole work and extremely important, especially for the development of technique. We mean the connexion, which she always made a point of stressing, between *frustration*—at any level of the libido's organization (oral, anal or genital) and with any kind of object (part or whole)—and the awakening of the *epistemophilic* impulse.

So she states (Klein, 1928): "Oedipus tendencies are released in consequence of the frustration which the child experiences at weaning" (p. 202). Melanie Klein also stresses the fact that "the ego is still little developed when it is assailed by the onset of the Oedipus tendencies and the incipient sexual curiosity associated with them." And more: "one of the most bitter grievances which we come upon in the unconscious is that these many overwhelming questions, which are apparently only partly conscious and even when conscious cannot yet be expressed in words, remain unanswered." Moreover, during this phase "the child cannot understand words and speech" (Klein, 1928, p. 204), and the evolution of the psychic processes depends primarily on the relationship between mother and child: "the visible mother thus provides continuous proofs of what the 'internal' mother is like, whether she is loving or angry, helpful or revengeful" (Klein, 1940, p. 313).

According to Klein (1928), "the early feeling of *not-knowing* has manifold connections," the frustration being more intense as the child "knows nothing definite about sexual processes" (p. 204). Emphasizing the importance for the individual's total mental development of the early connexion between the epistemophilic instinct and sadism, Klein explains: "this instinct, activated by the rise of Oedipus tendencies, at first mainly concerns itself with the Mother's body, which is assumed to be the scene of all sexual processes and developments. The child is still dominated by the anal-sadistic libido-position which impels him to wish to 'appropriate' the contents of the body" (p. 204). Later (Klein, 1946), clarifying her views, she states that the assault on the breast develops into assaults against the mother's body—even before she is apprehended as a whole person—and that the assaults follow two main lines: one is the predominantly oral impulse to bite, to suck, to grab and to rob the good contents of the mother's body; the other is the anal, urethral impulse to expel dangerous substances into the mother's body.

These would be, in synthesis, the forms through which "the epistemophilic instinct and the desire to take possession come quite early to be most intimately connected with one another and at the same time with the sense of guilt aroused by the incipient Oedipus conflict" (Klein, 1928, p. 204). The later elaboration of the concepts of the depressive and paranoid-schizoid positions does not make the connexion between the early arousal of the Oedipus conflict and the epistemophilic instinct any weaker; on the contrary, it becomes more fertile, as might be expected. From being sadistic, egoistical and voracious, the early sexual curiosity in the paranoid-schizoid position changes into an altruistic impulse to "discover" ways and means to repair and preserve the inner body of the mother, its own mind and the external world, characteristic of the depressive position and origin of all later sublimations (Klein, 1955). It is this impulse to "see" and to "know," together with its inevitable frustration in permanent movement within the psyche, which concerns one of the main trends in the development of psychoanalytical technique today.

2. Intolerance of Frustration and Incapacity for Thinking

Since Bion's (1957) work on "Arrogance," this attitude—or the feeling of omnipotence related to it—has been interpreted as a basic incapacity to tolerate frustration. Bion's work sets out to study the appearance, in a certain type of patient, of references to curiosity, arrogance and stupidity which are "so dispersed and separated from each other that their relatedness may escape detection" (p. 86).

In order to clarify the connexion between these references, the analyst, according to Bion, should take them as "evidence that he is dealing with a psychological disaster." Bion sees the Oedipus myth "from a point of view which makes the sexual crime a peripheral element of a story in which the central crime is the arrogance of Oedipus in vowing to lay bare the truth at no matter what cost." As a result, the emphasis of the myth is put on the following elements: "the sphinx, who asks a riddle and destroys herself when it is answered; the blind Tiresias, who possesses knowledge and deplores the resolve of the king to search for it, the oracle that provokes the search which the prophet deplores, and again the king who, his search concluded, suffers blindness and exile" (p. 86).

Clearly, this reappraisal of the Oedipus conflict in other terms does not imply depreciating or underrating the tortured and universal character of the sexual "crime and punishment," mirrored in the classical Oedipus interpretation. We are offered another light on the parable. Seen from this angle and expressed in terms of the analytical experience between two persons–one analysing, the other analysed–both are subject to identical, though different manifestations of curiosity, stupidity and arrogance, which circle around the "crime" of wanting to know the truth at all costs. Most awkward of all: "the analytic procedure itself is precisely a manifestation of the curiosity which is felt to be an intrinsic component of the disaster (Bion, 1957, p. 87). Thus the very act of analysing the patient makes the analyst an instrument in hastening regression and turning the analysis into a piece of "acting out." One alternative, according to Bion, is to accept the regression and the "acting out" as inevitable and give a detailed interpretation of what happens in the session.

The three phenomena, any one of which may be absent at any one time, which make up or indicate the psychological "disaster" mentioned above, are equally important and mutually dependent, but only two of them, curiosity and arrogance, will be dwelt on here. In fact, the clinical experience of any analyst shows that under that oedipal arrogance–"I want the truth whatever it costs"–there always lies ill-concealed omnipotence refusing to admit its incapacity to tolerate the frustration of "not knowing." Whether the incapacity to tolerate "not knowing" appears in the analyst, or in the analysand, or in *both at the same time, the difficulty of tolerating "not knowing"* is a sign of the painful process of developing the capacity for not anticipating knowledge, for refusing impossible comprehensions, in the acquiring, in fact, of reality perception, which can be achieved only through *experience*.

These considerations are developed further in Bion's (1961) "Theory of Thinking" where, in contrast to most theories on the subject, he states that "thinking is a development forced on the psyche by the pressure of thoughts and not the other way round" (p. 111). His model for illustrating the theory is that of an infant whose expectation of a breast is linked to a realization of a no-breast available for satisfaction, experienced as an "absent" breast *inside*.

In his description, Bion (1961) stresses:

> the next step depends on the infant's capacity for frustration: in particular it depends on whether the decision is to evade frustration or to modify it. If the capacity for tolerating frustration is sufficient, the "no-breast" inside becomes a thought and an apparatus for thinking it develops, [which] initiates the state described by Freud in his "Two Principles of Mental Functioning," is which dominance by the reality principle is synchronous with the development of an ability to think (p. 112).

If, however, the capacity for tolerating frustration is inadequate, the bad internal "no-breast" confronts the psyche with the need to decide between evasion of frustration or its modification. The decisive factor in the choice of evasion is always the incapacity to tolerate frustration.

The consequence of this incapacity is an overdevelopment of the apparatus for projective identification, i.e., an "apparatus suited only to mental 'evacuation.' " Bion's proposed model for this development is "a psyche that operates on the principle that evacuation of a bad breast is synonymous with obtaining sustenance from a good breast" (p. 112).

An example may clarify these assertions. An obsessive patient, under analysis for several years, showed a series of reasoning rituals, providing her with the illusion of omnipotent control over persons and situations, notwithstanding the frustrating everyday reality. These frustrations, however, were not really "suffered" because an omnipotent fantasy would immediately renew the illusion of control. Among these reasoning rituals one stood out: the exercise of doubt before any decision, under the pretext that "one should not do anything precipitately."

At a certain period in her analysis—many aspects of her obsessional armour already well worked out—the patient brought to the session a number of worries about her daughter, a 16-year-old adolescent, based on some "real facts." The daughter, said the patient, had just finished high-school and did not intend to go on with her studies, which was a source of disappointment to the mother, whose university activities made it impossible for her to accept the "daughter's transgressions." Giving up her studies was only a minor transgression, for, as the patient saw it, the daughter had other, more serious failures: bad companions, marijuana smoking a strange fauna of hippie friends, one of whom seemed to have sexual relations with her daughter. All this oppressed the patient enormously, and she got more and more overwhelmed with doubts as to how to approach the daughter. She knew that she must talk to the girl; she was sure, in her own words, that she had to exchange ideas with her daughter, but she did not know how to do it.

From all this, it was possible to interpret the patient's wish to make a husband out of the analyst, in order to turn him into the picture of the "ideal father" the patient thought she had not been able to provide for the daughter. And, at another psychic level, the wish to transform the analyst into her own mother, who would take care that the patient would not poison or spoil the benefits of the treatment through the "marijuana" of her own doubts. And in spite of her "understanding," the real dimension of her relationship with her daughter remained untouched, and facts kept repeating themselves: the young girl's late hours, marijuana smoking, hippie friends and possibly her sexual promiscuity with them, the patient realizing her urgent need to talk to the girl, but not knowing how: she might hurt the girl's feelings, or say "something violent," she knew "her own temper," and so forth.

Here is a fragment from a session, during which the patient's obstinate resistance to giving up the omnipotent illusion of controlling everything was acutely present as well as her believing her thoughts to be able to control reality. At the time, the patient could not accept the frustration of not being able to know by *anticipation*:

P.: Well, Doctor . . . I feel very anxious about my daughter . . . I really don't know how I should talk to her and I worry about time passing . . .

A.: Perhaps you are more worried about time passing and your unwillingness to expose yourself . . .

P.: [interrupting] To expose myself to what?

A.: You know what, but you refuse to admit it: to expose yourself to talking to your daughter, as a mother, in a simple way, not prophesizing any misfortunes or troubles . . .

P.: I don't think so, Doctor . . . I still don't see enough . . . I haven't thought about the problem enough . . . I have to understand it better . . .

A.: In the name of better understanding, you postpone any action, which postponement you then proceed to bewail.

P.: [discouraged] Yes, that's right . . . a vicious circle . . .

A.: This circle can be broken, if only you would accept the fact that you cannot know beforehand how the talk with your daughter will go.

P.: But why all this fear, Doctor?

A.: Is it really fear? It seems to me to be more a need to keep intact a theory about yourself, which you already know to be false.

P.: What d'you mean?

A.: You know very well that you cannot anticipate anything concerning this talk with your daughter. Only through getting in touch with her will you learn something and be able to really help her.

P.: [after a prolonged pause] Yes, but I think it is not only with my daughter . . . it is a more general thing; I don't like to risk trying anything, without knowing exactly how it will turn out.

A.: As here in our session . . . Neither you nor I will ever be able to know, in advance, how a session will go.

It was precisely this perception of her own refusal to contact her daughter, as well as the analyst, refusals based on her fear "of learning through experience," not learning through foretelling, that led that patient to a constant evasion of frustration and to an intensified obsession about understanding "the truth" better. The truth at all costs, like Oedipus. This caused the patient's mind to be inundated with premonitions, doubts and cautious postponements.

Incapacity to tolerate frustration results thus in an incapacity for thought, which becomes more and more obvious as the processes of projective identification appear more intensely and frequently. This situation arises during psychoanalysis in the guise of an excessive belief in omnipotence, of knowing everything, anticipating everything, foreseeing everything.

IV

1. Contact and Loss of Contact with Reality

The discovery that saturation of the mind by memory and desire, on the one hand, and the incapacity to accept frustration, on the other, are responsible for the appearance of a feeling of omnipotence and omniscience, leads to the problem of *contact with reality*. This contact is a primary function of the ego, so to test its natural functioning becomes an important touchstone in psychoanalytical technique. There is no doubt about the practical value of this constant testing in analysis. Two different lines of approach, however, have been followed. Although both of them are deeply rooted in Freud's work, they differ in their conceptual basis and in their technical application in clinical practice. One of them (Hartmann, Paula Heimann, Winnicott) focuses on concepts established by Freud in his "Analysis Terminable and Interminable" (1937*a*). The other (Bion) derives from Freud's views on the "apprenticeship" of contact (Freud, 1911) and "loss of contact" with reality in neuroses and psychoses (Freud, 1924*b*).

Hartmann, according to whom the word ego—even between analysts—is often used ambiguously, bases his ideas on Freud's reformulation of the structure of the mental apparatus, as stated for instance in the sentence "each ego is endowed from the first with individual dispositions and trends, though it is true that we cannot specify their nature or what determines them" (Freud, 1937*a*, p. 240). Hartmann (1950) then proceeds to show that the "ego, in analysis, is not synonymous with 'personality' or with 'individual'; it does not coincide with the 'subject' as opposed to the 'object' of experience and it is by no means only the 'awareness' or the 'feeling' of one's own self." In this context Hartmann stresses that the ego is a "substructure of personality and is defined by its functions," among which the most notable are "the organization and control of motility and perception"; the function of being a protective barrier against excessive external and internal *stimuli*; and that of postponing action by means of thought.

This multiplicity of functions, according to Hartmann, is responsible for what he calls "the many contrasts of the ego," for since its origin the ego has been opposed to the instincts, but, at the same time, one of its main functions is to help gratify the instincts; it is the seat of insight but also of rationalization; the ego "promotes objective knowledge of reality," but at the same time, by means of identification and social adaptation, is the bearer of environmental prejudices. In other words, precisely because of the variety of the ego's functions, one can infer that the mind is one and indivisible even when in conflict. It is thus inappropriate to attempt to link certain functions of the psyche (like the objective knowledge of reality) to certain systems (for example, the ego), and other functions (social adaptability to the prejudices of the group, for instance) to other systems (the superego). As Freud foresaw (1937*a*) in one of his last papers, in the light of recent findings, "the topographical distinction between what is ego and what is id loses much of its value for our investigation" (p. 241). In the end, everything becomes ego.

Basing her work on Freud (1937*a*), Paula Heimann (1960) goes further than Hartmann in her ideas on the working of the ego, particularly concentrating on the ego's contact with reality in the processes of sublimation. While she recognizes that sublimation has a paramount role in the artist's make-up, Heimann nevertheless adopts the view that one should not treat these problems as different from the ordinary man's, since sublimation "is a continuous process rather than an occasional happening." Thus she notes that "many quite ordinary associations have in fact a sublimatory quality," especially "the patient's interest in the analytical process." According to her "the early stages of analysis are usually mostly devoted to instinctual and emotional problems, whereas in later stages problems related to the use of ego capacities tend to predominate" (Heimann, 1959).

From this angle, Heimann (1959) was able to lay down certain concepts, extremely valuable in theory and in practice: (1) the analyst must keep in close contact with the patient's conscious and unconscious ego at the time; (2) the analyst should not act as "a superego figure but as a supplementary ego for his patient"; (3) especially during the sublimatory activities of the patient—which she finds to be very frequent—the analyst should be "a bystander, a non-interfering presence," since in sublimatory activity, in the exercise and performance of his innate and singular endowments, the individual is once more alone.

This last concept fits in well with the so-called "paradoxical fact" described by Winnicott (1958), that the individual's capacity to be alone depends on the child's experience of having been alone in the presence of an object toward which he feels neither indifferent nor inhibited. This experience cannot be explained in terms of object relations, since it should be basically an experience of the self.

2. Simultaneity of the Pleasure Principle and the Reality Principle

As stated above, there is another line of thought which is different in origin and conceptual basis, and is thus applied differently in clinical technique. In order to be able to comprehend this line clearly one should go back to Freud's first ideas on "learning to contact reality" during the primary development of the individual, and on "loss of contact with reality" such as he described in neurosis and psychosis.

In order to establish a fundamental difference between neurosis and psychosis, Freud (1924*a*) stated that *"neurosis is the result of conflict between the ego and its id, whereas psychosis is the analogous outcome of a similar disturbance in the relations between the ego and the external world"* (p. 149). Only a few months later, however (reminding us of Kris's remark about Freud's "constant developing" of thought), Freud (1924*b*) revised his ideas, recognizing that this pattern would only apply to the first phase of the process, and that after this "every neurosis disturbs the patient's relationship to reality in some way." Moreover, he admitted that neurosis offers "a means of withdrawing from reality," signifying in its more severe forms "a flight from real life." The initial difference is expressed thus in the final outcome: "in neurosis a piece of reality is avoided by a sort of flight, whereas in psychosis it is remodelled." Or, in other words, "neurosis does not disavow the reality, it only ignores it; psychosis disavows it and tries to replace it" (p. 185). He concludes:

> There is, therefore, a further analogy between a neurosis and a psychosis, in that in both of them the task which is undertaken in the second step is partly unsuccessful. For the repressed instinct is unable to procure a full substitute (in neurosis); and the representation of reality cannot be remoulded into satisfying forms . . . (p. 186).

There is thus no doubt that Freud was aware that neither in neurosis nor in psychosis can the individual succeed in "withdrawing" completely from reality. Both neurotic and psychotic patients "withdraw" momentarily from reality, in order to return later to it, each in his own way, once the desired modification has been reached or at least the "one which was possible."

Solidly supported by considerable experience with psychotics, Bion developed these findings sketched by Freud and obtained very important, detailed descriptions of the functioning of the schizophrenic personality, in which four main factors seem to be active: (1) an unsolved conflict between life and death instincts; (2) predominance of destructive impulses; (3) hatred toward inner and outer reality; (4) a tenuous but tenacious object relationship.

> This peculiar endowment makes it certain that the schizophrenic patient's progression through the paranoid-schizoid and depressive positions is markedly different from that of the non-psychotic personality. This difference hinges on the fact that this combination of characteristics leads to a massive resort to projective identification . . . [and] its deployment by the schizophrenic against all that *apparatus of awareness that Freud described as being called into activity by the demands of the reality prinicíple* (Bion, 1955*a*, p. 38).

Assuming, on the other hand, that when Freud wrote about the ego's allegiance to reality he was "speaking of the development he described as taking place with the institution of the reality principle," Bion (1955*b*) suggests two modifications to Freud's description: (1) that the ego is never wholly withdrawn from reality (as remarked, this had already been observed by Freud); and (2) that the withdrawal from reality "is an illusion, not a fact, and arises from the deployment of projective identification against the mental apparatus listed by Freud." What happens is that the contact with reality is not wholly missing, but is "masked by the dominance, in the patient's mind and behaviour, of an omnipotent fantasy that is intended to destroy either reality or the awareness of it" (p. 46).

These two modifications proposed by Bion have an important effect on clinical practice, for "in the severe neurotic there is a psychotic personality concealed by neurosis, as the neurotic personality is screened by psychosis in the psychotic" (Bion, 1955*b*, p. 63).

Strangely enough, similar ideas have been developed, by Bion, from Freud's writings on "Loss of Reality in Neurosis and Psychosis" (Freud, 1924*b*) on the one hand, and from the "Two Principles of Mental Functioning" (Freud, 1922) on the other. Both sets of ideas complement each other, having equally important effects on theory and practice.

As well as the two studies on the ego's contact with reality, in neurosis and psychosis, we also find in "Two Principles of Mental Functioning" another very fertile concept, later developed by Bion with surprising effect on psychoanalytical practice. In fact, when describing the "two principles," taking primary unconscious processes as his starting point, whose tendency, "easy to recognize, is the pleasure-unpleasure principle, or more shortly the pleasure-principle" (Freud, 1911), Freud described how, trying to get satisfaction through hallucinatory means, is abandoned "because of the non-occurrence of the expected satisfaction." He then introduced the idea of "succession" in the systematizing of a new principle, the "prinicple of reality," which would cause series of adaptations to appear gradually, slowly developing the ego's functions (attention, notation, judgement of reality, control of motor discharges through thinking), all of them enabling the individual to contact his own instinctive needs and the external world.

It would seem that Freud admitted a period of full instinctual satisfaction before a later squaring up to reality. However, Freud himself recognizes—in a footnote to the same work (Freud, 1911)—that such a schematic description can be seriously criticized, since "an organization which was a slave to the pleasure principle and neglected the reality of the external world could not maintain itself alive for the shortest time" (p. 220). The concept of the sexual instincts, behaving in a auto-erotic way, insulated from frustrating situations (which are what create the institution of the reality principle) can only be a fiction. Freud himself admitted this, noting that he used the concept as a didactic tool only.

The pleasure principle and the reality principle are therefore permanent and parallel realities. It is exactly this fact (which, until very recently was not considered sufficiently) that Bion has been stressing since his very first studies on the disorders of thought and thinking. Going further, Bion (1962), "believing it may be possible to give some idea of the world that is revealed by the attempt to understand our understanding," proposes a "theory of functions" which cannot be reviewed here in all its details, but in general is so valuable for understanding important changes introduced in psychoanalytical technique that it must be outlined.

For example, implicit in Freud's (1911) study on the "Two Principles" is that the distinction between the "external world" and the "principle of pleasure/pain is irrelevant to the theme of comprehension," since both can be dealt with by the theory of the alpha-function. Expressed more clearly in Bion's (1962) own words, "an emotional experience occurring in sleep does not differ from the emotional experience occurring during waking life in that the perceptions of the emotional experience have in both instances to be worked upon by alpha-function before they can be used for dream thoughts." Insofar as the alpha-function is successful, "alpha-elements are produced and these elements are suitable to storage and the requirements of dream thoughts" (Bion, 1962). But "if alpha-function is disturbed, and therefore inoperative, the sense impressions of which the patient is aware and the emotions which he is experiencing remain unchanged" (Bion, 1962). These sensorial impressions and unchanged emotions were called beta-elements by Bion (1962): they "are not amenable to use in dream thoughts but are suited for use in projective identification."

What naturally follows is that "failure of alpha-function means the patient cannot dream and therefore cannot sleep," which implies that the capacity for dreaming preserves the personality from what is virtually a psychotic state.

In other words, much nearer to the terms used by Freud (1900), if the patient is unable to work on his emotions through the "residues" of each day's sensory impressions, transforming them into dream thoughts in the same way as a normal person does, it is because both phenomena (sensory impressions arising from reality and the *transformation* of emotions into alpha-elements) occur *simultaneously*.

Thus, Bion (1962) asserts, Freud's statement which suggests that the reality principle follows the pleasure principle "needs modification to make both principles co-exist." As a consequence, a procedure of very great significance for psychoanalytical technique becomes vital: the patient's theories about himself or about others must be confronted at every analytical step with reality. For in dreams, just as in wakefulness, the nub of an understanding of thought and its malfunctions "is the link between intolerance of frustration and development of thought."

A brief example will show more explicitly the connexions between the pleasure principle and the reality principle, on the one hand, and the patient's difficulty in experiencing the simultaneity of both and achieving *contact*, on the other. The patient is a young married woman, intelligent and sensitive. Under analysis for two and a half years, she came assiduously to the sessions, but kept up her reserved, detached attitude the whole time. Among her defences against *contact*, two were very conspicuous: the tendency to "explain" everything and everyone, and a certain compulsive drive to adopt an attitude of indifference, refinement and "distance" toward other people's and her own need for contact. She was very cautious about showing any amorous or even friendly feelings toward the analyst and, in a general way, toward anybody around her. During the session from which a fragment is quoted below, these personality traits were already markedly diminished. But fear of contact was still very pronounced.

P.: When I was on my way I was thinking how much I wanted to come . . . I don't know why . . . [pause].

A.: Why do you have to know why? Why not simply see that you wanted to come here and accept it calmly, waiting for what will happen?

P.: Yes, I don't know . . . [pause]. My sister-in-law decided to travel alone to Europe . . . She is separated from my brother but that isn't the reason, no . . . She says that since her unmarried days, she has wanted to do this—to travel alone, to stay in some country until the money is all spent and then return . . . I could never do that . . . I think that as long as I haven't finished everything I have to do here, reached the end of my studies and got my degree, I can't think of travelling.

A.: I believe that, to a certain extent, you too want to stay alone, all by yourself, with no interference from myself. But you consider the association with me, here—and in a certain way also your marriage—as a kind of prison, which you know really to be inside you. You want to get rid of a mental, emotional state that disturbs you, but you do not really know what it is.

P.: Yes, that's true, I do not really know . . .[long pause]. I'm recalling Christmas dinner at my parents-in-law's . . . Everything was all right, but I didn't really fit in with everyone . . . So I decided to go into another room and I sat there on the sofa, all by myself.

A.: You did travel, as your sister-in-law did . . . alone, until the money was spent; the money is your capacity to isolate yourself from the others, *as you are doing here, now.*

P.: Yes . . . but I forced everybody to notice me, they all came to ask me what the matter was, why I was sitting there so alone and silent . . . the story you've already been into . . . exactly the same.

A.: Do you mean what I said about the pleasure you get out of hiding yourself in order to make the others *find* you?

P.: [anxiously] Yes, that's right . . . exhibitionism, isn't it?

A.: I didn't say so. You want to make a critic out of me since this seems to be the only way for you to feel I go along with you.

P.: What I know is that they are a bunch of fools . . . that is what I thought then.

A.: Perhaps you feel you might be the fool, when you realize your mistake in believing that you make yourself noticed by forcing people to "find" you in your isolation.

P.: But at least I do make myself noticed, don't I?

A.: No, and you know you don't. I believe you have a suspicion that your "success" in making yourself noticed was in fact just a show of social politeness by your in-laws. And you feel foolish because you are afraid you might not attract a real interest in yourself, since . . .

P.: [interrupting] Why? . . .

A.: Because you are the first one to consider your own person as unimportant; you do not care very much for yourself. That can be clearly seen from the way you acted: going into the other room means—there, as well as here, in our session—"getting out" of yourself into something artificial, into the pose of drawing attention to yourself. And I think you have noticed that this does not bring you any nearer to yourself. At best, it is a method for "fools" only, for you and for me, who continue to be fools, both of us, that is, without any real contact. It seems that you are getting tired of this method of "going out" of the room in order to be "found." All the consideration and care you wanted for yourself are delegated to others: your parents-in-law, your husband and I remain the only people able to feel consideration for you. You yourself, not.

P.: How strange! This is exactly how I feel!

It is unnecessary to go deeply into the fragment given above to see the patient trying hard to evade the unease and guilt arising from her own lack of interest in herself and from the lack of contact between herself and people around. In fact she feels guilty because she senses the small esteem she has of herself.

Here is another example, in which one can see how reality and omnipotence delusions are handled by a patient with great troubles concerning contact, in the face of veiled but strong menace of imminent mourning (mourning for the self and mourning for the object). The patient, who had begun analysis two-and-a-half years before, is a refined, well-educated person, who has a "double image" about herself, of which she is only half conscious. This double image, frequently apparent during the sessions, shows on the one side a positive, well married, professionally successful person—a university teacher; on the other side she behaves, to herself and to the analyst, as a "rejected child," in the middle of a chaotic family, without harmony or affection. Every time the analyst tries to show this to be a covering-up of guilt feelings for having undone the family "inside" her, the patient always answers with "facts": her father was a rake who always had mistresses, her mother didn't care and took no part, her brothers were self-centered.

This is a session, during the week-end, crucial for this patient's development in analysis.

P.: Father called me yesterday and showed me some lymphatic glands which had appeared on his neck . . . he asked me to feel them . . . I wonder why . . . [silence for some minutes].

A.: You seem worried about it.

P.: Why, yes, I don't know, he always enjoyed excellent health, he is still a very handsome, strong old man, though he is 70 . . . I don't know . . . Then he said he must talk to me . . . About his business, his firm . . . Everything is O.K., but he said I should be informed . . .

A.: I think you have realized that your father is seriously concerned about his health . . . those lymphatic glands . . . and he wants you to know his intentions, in case something more serious should happen.

P.: [clearly and intensely annoyed, for the first time since she started analysis] Oh no! It is not that at all . . . I know father: he's always been like that . . . He wants to throw his problems on me . . . whenever he got himself a new mistress he always had to tell me everything . . . Besides, my brothers are there, in the firm. I don't understand anything about business . . . I'm a professional in the liberal arts . . .

A.: I think you are afraid to face the fact that your father needs you as a daughter, not as a business expert.

P.: No, not at all. You want to "force" worries on to me too . . . It's not that at all [long peroration on the father's personality, his selfishness]. He is very selfish, he sees only his own troubles . . .

A.: Could it also be that you are being selfish yourself, in refusing to notice that something serious might be happening to him?

P.: No; I don't think so, no. You don't know him. And it's no use keeping on about it.

A.: You think I'm "forcing" my own worries on to you, is that it? Well, if you feel like this, let's leave it. I might be wrong, perhaps not. Why be upset?

P.: [after some minutes of silence] I'm thinking that next Sunday is Father's Day. Yesterday I went out with my two children to buy a television set for my husband; as a gift from the kids to their father . . . It was a real trial, I can tell you—was, no! is . . . First, I went to a shop intending to get a "Philco" . . . I filled in all those papers to buy on the installment plan . . . They told me to take the set and then, once I got it home, it wouldn't work properly . . . I went back to the shop to complain, but they hadn't got another set of the same type, and they wanted to "force" another make on to me . . . I got very angry. I had already paid for that special type, and after all it is sheer *dishonesty* . . .

A.: You want to say that you want to have a certain kind of analysis, during which you think only what you want to think; your father's illness and caring for him do not come into this special "set." And if I do not sell you this type of "apparatus-for-negation-of-reality," I'm being dishonest. But perhaps you might be the one to feel dishonest, for you are not using the qualities you possess to help your father.

Three days later, in the first session of the following week, the patient arrived at the consulting room weeping, let herself drop on the sofa and stuttered: "You were right—the histological test showed that my father has a lympho-sarcoma . . . The doctors said, he has three to four years to live . . ."

Without needing to go into details, it should be observed how tenacious the resistance is shown by the patient to both perception of external reality—the "threat" of her father's illness—and, at the same time, to perception of her own internal psychic reality, represented by her feeling of guilt at refusing any *contact* with either perception.

All this can be clearly seen in her associations with the TV set. It is significant that only after the analyst honestly admitted he might be wrong in his insistence on pointing to the patient's worries and guilt feelings, did these associations arise. From this moment on, the gap between the patient's "hesitation" in accepting her external and internal realities and the analyst's "haste" in bringing her as soon as possible into contact with it disappeared.

V. Consequences

It is well-known fact that whenever there are important new departures in psychoanalysis, resistance to them appears to a degree proportionate to the importance or validity of the departure, and to the "convenience" of accepting or discarding the new elements. Doubts are expressed whether the new discoveries are genuine developments, or manifest or covert "resistances" to fundamental psychoanalytical findings and postulates.

This situation, which greets the appearance of any new departure in any field of science, seems to be more evident in psychoanalytical theory and technique, which thus run the risk of perpetually oscillating between immobility and petrification on one side, and light-headed acceptance of "revolutionary" new fashions, on the other.

But, as Jones (1948) remarked: "If psychoanalysis is to remain a branch of science, it is evident, that, now that Freud's ability to continue his magnificent impetus has been extinguished, advance beyond the limits he reached is inevitable."

Nowadays, precisely as in the days of Melanie Klein's discoveries, the facts repeat themselves. So Jones's words remain valid and might even be regarded as a norm for thought and action for every psychoanalyst, for going beyond Freud's limits *is* inevitable. Thus one should not be surprised at the enthusiastic responses or strong rejections awakened by the "new tendencies" in the theory and practice of psychoanalysis. The "cautious" contributions to ego psychology made by Hartmann, Winnicott or Paula Heimann, or the "revolutionary" innovations by Bion represent the same thing, i.e., advancing "beyond the limits reached by Freud." Enthusiastic acceptance and strong suspicion can be clearly observed, for instance, in the opinions expressed by participants in a discussion of one of Bion's works (1967), where "grateful praise" is given by John Lindon, honest objections based on personal experience are raised by Marjorie Brierley and Herbert Herskovitz, and gross subjective misinterpretations of the author's thought are offered by A. Gonzales, Jules Eisenbud and Thomas French.

Nonetheless, considering the present situation, there is really no cause for such "commotion," as Jones has called it, since there is nowadays much more accumulated experience, and the sources of the new developments are more clearly visible.

Looking back on the development of the ideas handled in the present paper, one can see now that three main aspects have contributed to the new evolutions within psychoanalytical technique: (1) "saturation" of the mind by memory and desire (preconceptions, distortions, anticipations); (2) inability to cope with frustration and incapacity for thinking; (3) the simultaneity of the pleasure principle and the reality principle. These aspects may stem respectively from three original sources: (1) the significance of "remembering" and "forgetting" according to Freud; (2) the revaluation of the oedipal conflict by Melanie Klein; and (3) Freud's studies on "Loss of Contact with Reality in Neurosis and Psychosis" (1924*b*) and on "Two Principles of Mental Functioning" (1911).

Obviously, this choice of "points of reference," together with the effort to link them to their sources in Freud's and Melanie Klein's original thought, brings consequences which seem to us of very great value for the theory and practice of psychoanalysis.

1. The first consequence is to confront the analyst and the analysand even more unequivocally with the necessity to be truthful. In fact, once the mind is free from the distortions, falsifications and subterfuges through which memory tries to "explain" the past and desire tries to "anticipate" the future; once the psyche is confronted with the impossibility of evading frustration through omnipotence; once the constant *simultaneity* of the principles of pleasure and reality is perceived—the personality is inevitably driven by facts into accepting truth and, step by step, into taking possession of itself.

To reach this goal, always painfully and slowly, is not a privilege given only to Bion's work, much less to the *points of reference* discriminated in the present paper.

Freud had already remarked that the relationship between analyst and patient is based on a "love of truth" and "on a recognition of reality" (Freud 1937*a*), free from all illusions or self-deceptions—an opinion certainly shared unanimously by all psychoanalysts. However, by identifying precise and richly significant "indicators," such as Bion has supplied, it may be easier to observe and interpret all the different forms of truth evasion and even to consider and interpret the phenomenon of lying, not so much as a form of "acting out," but as a psychic distortion, differing in each individual, but inherent in the human situation.

In Bion's (1970) words, "the reality of the problem becomes apparent when the psychoanalyst must ask himself: can a liar be psychoanalysed? (p. 97). But is there anyone who is not a liar to some degree in the psychoanalytcal situation? Memory and desire, saturating the mind, the evasion of frustration, show how difficult and universal it is to achieve an acceptance of a reality free from all illusion and error, as Freud wanted. Therefore, as Bion (1970) remarked, although "by definition and by tradition of all scientific discipline the psychoanalytic movement is committed to the truth as the central aim," in practice things are not so simple. "The patient, especially if intelligent and sophisticated, offers every inducement to bring the analyst to interpretations that leave this defence intact and, ultimately, to acceptance of the lie as a working principle of superior efficacy" (p. 99). If, however, "the emotional upheaval against which the lie is mobilized is identical with catastrophic changes, it becomes easier to understand why investigation uncovers an ambiguous position which is capable of arousing strong feelings. These feelings relate to an outraged moral system; their strength derives from risk of change in the psche" (Bion 1970, p. 99).

"The risk of change in the psyche"—this is the phrase which seems to make a synthesis out of the ultimate fear of the personality of its own progress. This hostility toward the naturing process grows more intense at the moment when maturity seems to demand the subordination of the pleasure principle and the emergence of the reality principle.

The other advantage in choosing our "points of reference" is the greater concentration required of the patient on his own mental and emotional processes, *here and now*. Needless to say, the concept of "here and now"is not new: it is intrinsic to the original development of the idea of transference, as postulated by Freud many times and subtly enriched by Melanie Klein's contributions, based on children's analysis. Strictly speaking, the concept was originated by Brentano, perhaps the first to give it a dynamic value in the relationship between man and his world.

The immediate and more remote consequences of disrobing the mind of memory and desire, and of recognizing how impossible it is to avoid frustration, are that, unaided by constructions of the memory designed to "explain" the past, and by *omnipotent anticipations* "forecasting" the future, the personality is forced to face the unforeseen situation of the *here and now* in a peculiarly stark way. And at this difficult moment–or at this sequence of difficult moments–when "self theories" begin to fail, together with "autobiographical legends" about "how I am," based on "how the past happened" (or how my family was, especially my parents); at this moment, analysis really starts.

All this is summed up in one basic obligation–being truthful, *here and now*. Once accepted, this permits a reappraisal of the whole analytical situation.

2. *Truthfulness, here and now*–binding the analysand and the analyst–demands that the analyst constantly keeps in view the patient's compulsion to repeat his outmoded patterns of behaviour in transference. It is noteworthy that Freud postulated compulsion to *repetition* to account for mental reactions to external danger (recurrent anxiety dreams in war-neuroses), and for "the method of working employed by the mental apparatus in one of its earliest *normal* activities–children's play" (Freud, 1920) but most of all thinking of psychoanalytical patients' insistence on old ways of acting and thinking. As is well known, he turned this "repetition compulsion" into one of the mainstays of psychoanalytical technique. From it he derived the highly-developed speculative and clinically-based concept of the "death instinct."

Psychoanalytical practice over many years has only confirmed Freud's speculations about the "repetition compulsion." Nevertheless, the time seems to have come to put on a firm basis the conviction that these findings do not account for the whole analytical situation, but only for a very important part of it. The idea of replacing "infantile neurosis" by "transference neurosis" may be an indispensable tool for the development of an analytical process, but has grown monstrously, preventing the impartial observation of the "new facts," that is the non-repeated, which occur in any analytical situation. This is so to the extent that original and fertile ideas have finally perished, become sterilized, defeated by the all-embracing range of this concept of the "compulsion to repeat." This has happened, for instance, to Winnicott's (1951) observations about transitional objects and transitional phenomena.

In fact, these two terms, which were introduced by Winnicott to define an intermediate area of experience between thumb-sucking and toys, between oral erotism and a true object relationship, or between primary creative activity and the projection of what has already been introjected, represent a very valuable contribution to the understanding of the emotional development of the child. In the same way, he stresses that the task of accepting reality is never finished, and no human being is entirely free from pressure to relate internal and external realities, but that an abatement of this pressure is given by an intermediate area of experience, not subjected to challenge. One must watch for the phenomena in this area carefully, he goes on, especially such as appear in adult creativity (art, science, religion). All lose their substance and their life when one tries to demonstrate—as Winnicott did—basing oneself on clinical material, that such transitional phenomena (normal and pathological) are mere "repetitions" of phenomena from the patient's earliest childhood.

Using the idea of "repetition compulsion" like this, as an all-embracing net, bars any possibility of ever observing new facts under a new frame of reference, as for instance the analytical situation *here and now*. This excessive subordination to the idea that the present repeats the past, that the present is the past itself, represents one of the most extreme forms of saturation of the mind by the tricks of memory and by the dominion of pre-established knowledge. Both analyst and analysand can be a prey to this subordination, and together find disappointment in the experience of a "negative therapeutic reaction."

Clinical facts and theoretical concepts seem, more and more, to show that what an analysand reveals even during one single analytical session, cannot necessarily be entirely explained as "compulsion to repetition," as a manifestation of the "death instinct."

Though he will show many "mental habits," based on the omnipotent belief that it is possible and even desirable to evade frustration through distortion, subterfuges and, in the most serious cases, through open, fully conscious lies, he will also show vital traits, derived from Eros and non-repetitive, arising out of the *new, unique situation*, never experienced before by the patient in his life.

Obvious as all this may appear, it is often enough ignored in clinical practice. Or it is misinterpreted as "positive transference." But it is not so. These truly new phenomena have little to do with transference, and show a new relationship between the patient and his own self, or with the real person of the analyst, *here and now*, without reference to a previous object, internal or externalized. As Paula Heimann (1950, p. 114) rightly remarked: "not everything a patient feels about his analyst is due to transference." Even a theorist in general psychology like Francis Irwin, not in any way especially linked to psychoanalysis, has very acutely observed that "the clinician may be overlooking the motives that are now effective in behaviour because of his interest in uncovering the long history that has made the person what he is" (Irwin, 1951, p. 234). Moreover, it should be stressed that the "exact moment and place" of the analytical session is not the only venue for a patient to achieve insight. No matter what may happen during an analytical session, the mental capacity of the patient and the totality of his life transcend the limits of any given analytical moment.

Psychoanalytical thought has become dangerously bounded by the concept of "repetition" and of "permanency of previous patterns of behaviour": much in the analytical field does not support this impression of petrification and immutability. Bion believes that the idea of the immutability of a patient, even for short periods, is based on a gross, primitive view of the continuity of the individual. For him, believing that no change can occur within a period of 24 hours is based on a grossly macroscopic vision of the human being, for "the mental phenomena with which we are confronted cannot possibly have remained unaltered even if no analysis had been done." He recalls that, "the mental phenomena should reveal invariance and it should be possible to observe the invariants embedded in these phenomena, but an invariant is a characteristic *not of permanence but of transformation*' (Bion, 1970, p. 52; my italics). He stresses that "characteristic of the mental domain is that it cannot be contained within the framework of psycho-analytic theory" (*ibid.*). With understandable surprise, he puts the question (Bion, 1970):

> Is this a sign of defective theory, or a sign that psychoanalysts do not understand that psychoanalysis cannot be contained permanently within the definitions they use? It would be a valid observation to say that psychoanalysis cannot contain the mental domain because it is not a container but a "probe" (p. 72).
>
> [He proceeds:] the formulation that I have tried to further by using the symbols ♀ and ♂ minimizes the difficulty by leaving ♀ and ♂ as unknowns whose value is to be determined (p. 73).

3. I hope to have made clear, through the different sections of the present paper, that the same "occurrences" that slow down or make the progress of the patient's analysis difficult, may also happen to the analyst, though on a different scale and in a different way. *Saturation of the mind by memories and desire, intolerance of the frustration of not knowing, difficulty in contacting reality*, or even *loss of contact with reality*–due (among other reasons) to the lack of perception of the simultaneity of the pleasure principle with the reality principle–are phenomena that can also appear in the analyst. For him we might say that *it is the saturation of the mind* by memories and preconceptions, and the arrogance of knowing, which lead to his *loss of contact* with the patient's internal and external reality.

One thing should be made quite clear: accepting these extremely important facts does not in the least imply an acceptance of the use of the so-called countertransference as an indispensable working-tool for the analyst. On the contrary, nothing is further away from our point of view than the very questionable opinion expressed by Winnicott (1947): "the patient can only appreciate in the analyst what he himself is capable of feeling" and that, for the sake of objectivity, the analyst must "be able to hate the patient objectively." Much nearer clinical reality, in this context, are the views held by Paula Heimann (1960), for whom it is precisely the analyst's behaviour "as a supplementary ego (not as a superego) which makes repetition change into modification."

Anyway, be it as described by Winnicott, or in a more flexible way, according to Heimann (1950), Gitelson (1952) and others, it seems to me that countertransference is nothing but a momentary "negative success" for the patient, in that, through projective identification, he achieves the *pushing* of some aspects of his self on to the mind of the analyst, who then becomes motivated by "unexpected" feelings of love or hatred. Heimann (1950), in slightly different words, recognized this fact when she stated that countertransference shown by the analyst is not only part and parcel of the analytical relationship, but a creation of the patient, part of the patient's personality. In other words, motivated by "successful" projective identifications of the patient, the analyst's capacity to correctly observe and interpret given clinical material is reduced by an undesirable block in his mind. Of course, this is bound to happen sometimes during analysis, to a greater or lesser degree. But to make out of this "accident" a working-tool, by definition, seems to me totally inadmissible. If the phenomenon appears very often in his practice, this is a sure indication that the analyst has to go back to psychoanalysis.

It is my contention that the wisdom gained by, first, freeing the mind from memory and desire, in accepting the inevitability of frustration and the simultaneity of the reality principle with the pleasure principle, and, secondly, understanding *compulsion to repetition* as *part* only of the analytical situation, not its entirety, is more far-reaching. The "reductionist" interpretations or constructions as used by Freud in his "Constructions in Analysis" (1937*b*) seem to lack a scientific basis. The dubious therapeutic value of such "constructions" is based on a magical belief in the "liberating" role of memory. This belief is a residue, as we have seen, of the pre-historical stage of psychoanalysis, when the method was still imprisoned in mechanistic concepts of "trauma" and "catharsis."

Certainly, it is not easy for the analyst to adopt this set of often risky technical procedures in practice. For this reason, Bion recommended them only to the analyst whose own analysis had brought him far enough to recognize the paranoid-schizoid and depressive positions. Unless he has gone through such a deep-probing process, the analyst may tend to feel himself immersed in a kind of catatonic stupor, especially during the first stages of an analysis, which may be very difficult to tolerate. If, however, he is able to endure this difficult period, eventually he will be rewarded with an *insight*, whose existence and depth he could never have suspected. *The analyst, however, must be very careful not to overrate his capacity for insight*. For, as Freud (1937*a*, p. 229) himself observed, "we must not take the clarity of our own insight as a measure of the conviction which we produce in the patient."

Summary

This paper aims at studying ideas which have contributed to the development of psychoanalytical technique, from Freud to our present time, with special attention to Bion's findings.

Three aspects of trends which seem to be basic to psychoanalytical technique at the moment are emphasized: (1) the "saturation" of the mind by memory and desire (preconceptions, distortions, anticipations); (2) inability to cope with frustration and incapacity for thinking; and (3) the simultaneity of the pleasure principle with the reality principle.

These aspects stem from three original sources: (1) the significance of "remembering" and of "forgetting" according to Freud; (2) the reappraisal of the oedipal conflict by Melanie Klein; and (3) Freud's studies on "Loss of Reality in Neurosis and Psychosis" (1924*b*) and on "The Two Principles of Mental Functioning" (Freud, 1911).

This conceptual revision leads to consequences of extraordinary practical importance:

1. Once the mind is released from the distortions, falsifications and subterfuges by which the memory tries to "explain" the past and the desire seeks to "anticipate" the future; once the psyche faces the impossibility of evading frustration through omnipotence; and as the simultaneity of the pleasure principle and the reality principle is understood, both analyst and analysand can concentrate with special application on the "here and now" situation, and face more unequivocally the need to be truthful.

2. To be truthful "here and now" implies the recognition that not all events in the analytical situation are necessarily repetitive, although they include repetitions. If the theory of "compulsion to repetition" is looked at critically, quite the opposite can be verified; that is to say, the analytical process evolves constantly toward the new, thus discarding schematic reductionism to childhood.

3. From observation of facts, countertransference can be said to be the result of successful projective identifications by the patient, which implies that it is questionable as a working-tool.

A version of this paper was presented to the 4th Brazilian Congress of Psychoanalysis in 1973 and was published in Portuguese in 1973, in *Revista Brasileira de Psicanálise*, Vol. 7, pp. 5-50.

Dr. Bahia died in 1974. This is the last paper he wrote, and it is according to the wishes and due to the efforts of Dr. Bahia's friends and colleagues in Rio de Janeiro that its English translation is now published posthumously.

References

Bahia, A. B. (1956). Repression, memory and amnesia. Rio de Janeiro: Servico de Documentacão do MEC.
Bion, W. R. (1955*a*). Development of schizophrenic thought. In Bion (1967*a*).
—— (1955*b*). Differentiation of the psychotic from the non-psychotic personalities. In Bion (1967*a*).
—— (1957). On arrogance. In Bion (1967*a*).
—— (1961). A theory of thinking. In Bion (1967*a*).
—— (1962). *Learning from Experience*. London: Heinemann.
—— (1967*a*). *Second Thoughts*. London: Heinemann.
—— (1967*b*). Notes on memory and desire. *Psychoanal. Forum* 2, 272-280.
—— (1970). *Attention and Interpretation*. London: Tavistock Publ.
Breuer, J. & Freud, S. (1893-5). Studies on hysteria. *S.E.* 2.
Freud, S. (1899). Screen memories. *S.E.* 3.
—— (1901). Childhood memories and screen memories. *S.E.* 6.

—— (1911). Formulations on the two principles of mental functioning. *S.E.* 12.
—— (1914). On the history of the psychoanalytic movement. *S.E.* 14.
—— (1918). From the history of an infantile neurosis. *S.E.* 17.
—— (1920). Beyond the pleasure principle. *S.E.* 18.
—— (1924*a*). Neurosis and psychosis. *S.E.* 19.
—— (1924*b*). The loss of reality in neurosis and psychosis. *S.E.* 19.
—— (1937*a*). Analysis terminable and interminable. *S.E.* 23.
—— (1937*b*). Constructions in analysis. *S.E.* 23.
Gitelson, M. (1952). The emotional position of the analyst in the psychoanalytic situation. *Int. J. Psycho-Anal.* 33, 1-10.
Hartmann, H. (1950). Comments on the psychoanalytic theory of the ego. In *Essays on Ego Psychology*. New York: Int. Univ. Press, 1964.
Heimann, P. (1950). On countertransference. *Int. J. Psycho-Anal.* 31, 81-84.
—— (1959). Bemerkungen zur Sublimierung. *Psyche* 13, 397-414.
—— (1960). Countertransference. *Br. J. med. Psychol.* 33, 9-15.
Irwin, F. (1951). Motivation. In H. Helson (ed.), *Theoretical Foundations of Psychology*. New York: Van Nostrand.
Jones, E. (1948). Introduction to Melanie Klein (1948).
Klein, M. (1928). Early stages of the Oedipus complex. In Klein (1948).
—— (1940). Mourning and its relation to manic-depressive states. In Klein (1948).
—— (1946). Notes on some schizoid mechanisms. In J. Riviere (ed.), *Developments in Psycho-Analysis*. London: Hogarth Press, 1952.
—— (1948). *Contributions to Psycho-Analysis*. London: Hogarth Press.
—— (1955). On identification. In M. Klein, P. Heimann & R.E. Money-Kyrle (eds.), *New Directions in Psychoanalysis*. New York: Basic Books.
Kris, E. (1950). On preconscious mental processes. *Psychoanal. Q.* 19, 540-560.
Strachey, J. (1958). Editor's Introduction to S. Freud's 'Papers on Technique.' *S.E.* 12.
Winnicott, D. W. (1947). Hate in the countertransference. In *Collected Papers*. New York: Basic Books, 1958.
—— (1951). Transitional objects, transitional phenomena. In *Playing and Reality*. London: Tavistock Publ., 1971.
—— (1958). The capacity to be alone. In *The Maturational Processes and the Facilitating Environment*. London: Hogarth Press, 1965.

Psycho-Semiotic Structures:
An Interdisciplinary Study of the
Relationship Between Psychoanalysis and the
Semiotic of C.S. Peirce

Alfred S. Silver

EDITOR'S NOTE: *Dr. Silver has been a long-time student of the American linguist-philosopher, Charles Sanders Peirce whose discovery of the semiotic is only now beginning to have a significant effect on modern psycholinguistics. Peirce's work is complex and difficult to understand. Dr. Silver has diligently surveyed and summarized the main threads of Peirce's work and has attempted to integrate his seminal theories with those of Bion. First of all, Peirce elevated Saussure's linguistic dyad of sign → object to a triad in which an interpretant (subject "I") is the important third agency which interprets the object via its sign (de-sign-ate). From his theory of thirdness, Dr. Silver develops Peirce's conception of symbol formation and pragmatism (pragmaticism) and ultimately explores the rationalistic preconceptions of Plato's theory of forms and Kants synthetic a priori concepts—all in an attempt to explore the inner being of subjective "I," the interpretant, inferer, and intuitor of those objects which it is already predisposed to know (by their sign) as is inherent in subjective "I"-ness. It is at this point that Bion's inherent preconceptions link up with Peirce so as to emphasize the importance of subjective, imaginative conjecture in the absence of memory and desire—to discover or rediscover the object by availing oneself of the "manic," that is, the epiphanic irruption of the "thing-in-itself," the sign—to find its counterpart in the outer world.*

A Psychosemiotic Model: An Interdisciplinary Search for a Common Structural Basis for Psychoanalysis, Symbol-Formation, and the Semiotic of Charles S. Peirce

Alfred S. Silver

Introduction

The elaboration of symbols may be the most universal but also the most enigmatic of accomplishments of man's cultural development. Small, curiously shaped artifacts have been uncovered at sites in Syria dating from Neolithic times, probably tenth millenium down to the third millenium, B.C. These tokens which represented partcular animals, plants, and articles of economic importance to the nomadic tribesmen of the region remained essentially unchanged until the third millenium when in the region of Ebla they appeared inside clay bullae in which they had been sealed after having had their form and design impressed on the exterior of the soft clay container. This development led rapidly to the realization that the actual tokens were no longer needed. The bullae were flattened into tablets, and the figurative impressions evolved into "word" markers. These in turn were abstracted into alphabetical (digital) symbols. These developments were associated with the explosive emergence of an urban civilization. If these events are taken as a possible beginning of a history of which the present crises of civilization are a continuation, then it may be agreed that clarification of the nature of symbol formation is of great importance.

The purpose of this communication is to explore: (1) the nature of the psychic activity called symbol formation; (2) the structure of symbols and signs formed by personalities capable of learning from experience; and (3) those structures formed by personalities incapable of proper symbol formation and hence subject to impaired dreaming, thinking and learning from experience. This exploration will focus on the ambiguous triadic relationship between (a) an object to be symbolized, (b) a second (symbolic) object invented or discovered to stand in symbolic relationship to the first, and (c) the symbol-former who stands in the triad as a third. In this complex role of "third" the symbol-former affects and actually is affected by the relationship of sign to object. The theory of this triadic relationship is necessarily both a cognitive theory and a theory of affect; I believe it demonstrates the inseparability from the egocentric subject. The investigation will attempt to elucidate some vital aspects of the connection between symbols and more primitive signs to which the unique triadic structure is common. I will attempt to demonstrate that these more primitive signs are ultimately linked to the body as "feelings" completing the link between soma and psyche.

Investigations into the nature of symbols, symbolism, and symbol formation have often arisen out of the need to understand these phenomena as an important aspect of "the arts." Symbolism here is often taken to be a special means of expression and communication (Arnheim, 1954; Langer, 1957)—a non-conceptual "language" with great powers of persuasion. This mode of thinking about symbols extends into the art of politics and propaganda, ethnological observations of myths, rituals, taboos, and into religious beliefs and practices generally (Levi-Strauss, 1968). The study of symbols leads to the realization that verbal and mathematical language is made up of *abstract symbols*, evidently a different kind of symbol, full of meaning but only abstractly linked to human feelings. At times they are only linked to those feelings of wonder and curiosity which motivate their use in the search for knowledge. Thus, symbols can be conceived as being instruments of expressing our feelings to one another as well as being the instruments of meaning and understanding. In addition, I hope to show that symbol formation is the means of creating the significant objects with which we populate the world that we inhabit. I shall try to develop some of the evidence from which we may conclude that the concept of "sublimation" must fall under this aspect of symbol formation.

Freud's early experiments with hypnotic techniques were transformed into a genuine cultural revolution. He realized that memories, phantasies, dreams, and hysterical symptoms were all symbolic events or symbolic products of psychic work whose origin and meaning might sometimes be ascertained by what amounts to symbol interpretation (Freud, 1896). The birth of pyschoanalysis may have occurred in that caesura when Freud realized that several of his young Viennese "hysterics" had misled him, and themselves, by phantasies of sexual contact with their fathers. They misunderstood these phantasies to be memories of actual events which for too long had been successfully urged upon Freud as historical fact. In this historical moment a creative hypothesis occurred to Freud regarding a symbolic phantasy which previously had the impact and consequences of a factual experience. The error of his earlier assumption about "historical evidence" led Freud to the exciting discovery that a new science was needed. Freud realized that confusion among the phenomena of predisposition, perception, conception, phantasy, and memory is an expected and potentially understandable feature of mental action requiring a unifying theory by means of which these confusions could be understood. I am suggesting that theories of symbol formation need to be better integrated with psychoanalysis in order to further this aim.

Freud's resistance to the fullest implications of his own discovery is well known. We cannot deny that this probably represented a cultural resistance to a revolutionary paradigm. In truth his genius carried him well beyond any reasonable expectation of success in pushing his discoveries forward. We must not overlook the continuation of this resistance into the present day. It is exemplified by the scorn and rejection which met Bion's (1970) plea for abandonment of memory and desire in the listening posture especially to be adopted in analytic sessions. This advice is, after all, only a reminder that psychoanalysts, in their relation to their patients, should not adopt the posture of those hysterical Viennese ladies in both their relation to their fathers and in their relations to Freud. Rather, the openness to discovery which Freud struggled to achieve in uncovering the vicissitudes of phantasy and symbol formation should be adopted. An inevitable consequence of the present communication, I believe, will be to clarify the relationship of *transference* phenomena to symbol formation and its structurally degenerate or primitive forms.

There continues to be an urgent need to develop as far as possible the meaning of Freud's discovery concerning the ambiguity of fact and phantasy. Even at the present time symbols are generally regarded in psychoanalysis primarily as a feature of "primary process" along with condensation and displacement. Further elaboration of the important part played by symbol formation in psychoanalytic theory is dependent upon the synthesis of psychoanalytic knowledge with the perspectives of modern philosophical and logical knowledge of symbol formation contained in the Doctrine of Signs. It is equally true that modern theories of signs are in need of further elaboration. This can only come with the unification of logical theories of signs and psychoanalytic understanding of unconscious symbolism.

Before proceeding further in the development of this needed synthesis, I shall briefly describe the concepts I believe to be implied in the term "symbol," a term used in conflicting and overlapping senses by authors in various fields and even within the same field. What I believe to be denoted by the term "symbol" is conveyed by the following ideas. *Everything in the world that we understand is known by some sign or symbol of its existence.* The primal object-world of preverbal existence is known to us through its transformations in the symbols of dreaming, thinking, and playing (including the aesthetic transformations in myths and the arts). Unconscious phantasy, which we interpret from the analysand's verbal (and other) behavior, is taken as symbolic or, ultimately, at least significant of the primal world. Jones (1916) postulated that unconscious symbolism refers to objects which consist of parts of the self, blood relatives, matters of life, birth, and death. Additional clinical work in subsequent years especially by Melanie Klein and her colleagues, has tended to establish the primal object-world as consisting of phantasies of the outside and inside of the mother's body, containing the father's penis and the unborn babies. These phantasies are confused with aspects of the self. Through psychoanalytic technique we discover that the infant exists in the primal object-world in a state of undifferentiated "transcendental at-one-ness" or "con-fusion" with that world.

Progressive expansion and clarification of the infant's understanding from that confused primal state depends on expanding symbol formation, whereby one thought gives rise to another thought, one object gives rise to another object, and the state of transcendental fusion is relinquished. The infant forms symbols of primal objects. His life and journey outside the primal tie with the womb, breast, and biological family require his adventurous exploration of vastly larger worlds filled with objects which are of great importance. Despite their symbolic connection to primal objects and their great value as objects-in-themselves they are the actual source of what one is dependent upon for the continuation of life beyond the primal world.

To the extent that there is interference or aberration in the infant's ability or will to turn away from his transcendental primal world toward other objects which become "knowable" as symbols of the primal objects, the phenomenon of symbol formation is interrupted or deformed. This does not mean merely a restriction or deformity of dreams and imagination; it means impoverishment of that individual's whole world, including the physical and cultural world as well as emotional attachment to that world through impoverished and alienated unconscious connections. What I mean by symbol formation requires the integration of two general symbol-forming functions: First, the establishment of a *preconception* (Bion, 1963) regarding the object to be symbolized, "an unconscious function," is necessary so that the symbol is properly connected as a sign of what is already *known* (in the sense of *present as experienced* in the primal object-world). Second, *realization* (Bion, 1963) of the emerging symbolic object requires perceptual and conceptual judgment by the symbol-former. This establishes the symbol as an object of interest and value in its own right with meaning of its own for the symbol-former. The integration of these two functions of the symbol-former, inner directed and outer directed, is highly vulnerable to any condition, external or internal, which affects his state of mind to alter his intentions and the relationship between preconception and realization.

The psychoanalytic understanding of symbolism has benefited very little from philosophical theories of symbol formation which developed contemporaneously with and subsequent to the work of Freud. There are several reasons for this failure. First, philosophers pride themselves on scrupulously avoiding the psychologisms and mentalisms which psychoanalysts must confront and need to understand. Therefore, philosophical theories, in the area of epistemology as well as in linguistics and in the phenomenology of symbols in general (semiotics), were meticulously developed to avoid contamination by subjectivism. When philosophers are forced to inquire as to the ostensible subject whose theories, experiences, and knowledge are under consideration, they tend to resort to the presupposition of a generalized epistemic subject. This subject is rational, logical, and scientific; in short, it is an idealized philosopher-subject whose intentions and values are in logical accord with and predictable from direct observation of his actions.

A second difficulty impeding the advancement of psychoanalytic theory through deeper understanding of the symbolic process was the occurrence of the revolution in linguistics initiated by Ferdinand de Saussure (1915) which began almost simultaneously with Freud's work. The linguistics revolution was based on a tentative theory of signs and symbols which

Saussure called *semiology*. However, the thrust of Saussure's semiology emphasized the symbolic character of language and the evolution of cultural systems based on, and containing, language as their infrastructure. Structural studies in literature (Barthes, 1967), mythology, and anthropology (Levi-Strauss, 1963) owe a great debt to the Saussurian linguistics which led to an academic revolution of considerable significance. The semiology, that deep structure of the symbolic function whereby *things* might be transformed into dreams and symbolic objects, was never fully developed. In my opinion, the Saussurian model also failed to properly take into full account the part played in symbol formation by the *individual* (subject). It therefore became concordant with scientific and philosophical (positivistic and behavioristic) trends of the day (which have more recently become subject to serious challenge). For this reason the semiology as well as the linguistic, literary, mythological, anthropological, and other cultural disciplines, while all pointing to the Freudian unconscious, abandoned the symbolizing infant at the very threshold of the most fascinating questions.

Despite the weaknesses in the Saussurian model, psychoanalysts such as Rosen (1969) and Edelson (1975) have attempted to clarify the problems of symbolic function in their clinical analytic work by using this model. Lacan (1968) has developed a semiologic model which is fundamentally based on Saussure but has carried the model to greater depths thereby raising interesting and extremely important issues. Some of these are taken up here indirectly as a consequence of the confluence of some of Lacan's concepts with those concepts arising out of the semiotic model of Peirce.

Melanie Klein's (1930) pioneering analytic work with psychotic children portended a breakthrough in relating the vicissitudes of symbol formation to phases of psychic development. Her clinical work emphasized the interpretation of symbolic phantasy appearing in play and enabled her to discern the details concerning the child's developmental struggles with the primal object-world as revealed in unconscious symbolism. In her work the interpretation of the patient's verbal associations, "play-acting," and the symbolism, condensations, and displacements all came together as indicative transformations of primitive physicalistic action in the primal object-world.

Hanna Segal's paper, "Notes on Symbol Formation," (1957) constituted a milestone in that it clearly distinguished aspects of abnormal symbol formation and related these to psychoanalytic theory, especially in terms of the Kleinian developmental positions (i.e., paranoid-schizoid and depressive positions). Moreover, Segal introduced certain essential features of a logical theory of signs derived from the work of Charles Morris (1938), the most essential of which was *the triadic relation of the subject (symbol-former): (1) to the object to be symbolized, and (b) to the symbol*. Morris has been a major interpreter of these principles which were developed by Peirce (Buchler, 1955).

The last impediment to the development of a logical theory of signs—the removal of which could aid psychoanalytic theory—resides in certain problems surrounding the most psychologically promising philosophical theory of signs: that developed by the American philosopher, Charles Sanders Peirce. His work began earlier, but was generally considered contemporaneous with that of Saussure as well as of Freud. Unfortunately there is little evidence that Peirce's work was known or much regarded by Freud or Saussure, for Peirce worked in relative isolation and obscurity in New England after a relatively early exile, perhaps in part self-imposed, from the Cambridge establishment. He was poorly and, at best, intermittently published during his lifetime. Despite the difficulty in general dissemination or acceptance of his ideas, Peirce now is described by many observers as the most original philosopher of his time. His major contribution was the creation of the philosophical system known as *pragmatism*. His theory of symbol formation is an outgrowth of the pragmatic view. However, Peirce remained in obscurity as did most of his life's work including his theory of signs, while his younger colleague, William James, expounded and developed his own version of the pragmatic doctrine, incidentally becoming a pioneer psychologist in the process. While Freud did meet James briefly on his trip to America, there is no evidence of any great interest on his part in the work of James or of Peirce

A brief reading of Peirce's work reveals great difficulties in the understanding of his ideas. His writing is dense, provocatively opaque and aggressively defiant of easy understanding. The style is archaic; difficult ideas are expressed with utmost accuracy, but often in a manner which challenges the courage of the most curious and sympathetic student. Peirce calls his theory of signs the *semiotic*, a word last used by John Locke. Peirce's semiotic corresponds with the *semiology* used by Saussure a short time later, deriving from the Greek root for seed, *semen*, but carrying the connotation of signal-bearer (semaphore).

Peirce's philosophical lineage runs from Plato through Duns Scotus and the scholastics to Kant. It is said that Peirce, during his teens, memorized both editions of Kant's "Critique of Pure Reason" (Moore, 1964). Peirce's strong affinity for the rationalism of Kant (whose transcendental dialectic, and synthetic a priori concepts were, I believe, essential presuppositions of Peirce's semiotic conception of symbol formation) endangered his reputation as a philosopher. This and his outspoken contempt for Bertrand Russell probably would have condemned Peirce's philosophy and his theory of signs to obscurity even had his disposition been more congenial and had his academic status been correspondingly more acceptable to his contemporaries in Boston. It is only in the 1970's that there has been a strong enough shift away from the deterministic and positivistic position of the philosophy of science to permit a widening of interest in Peirce.

It is my intention to demonstrate the usefulness of Peirce's theory of signs for the understanding of signs and symbols (and symptoms) in psychoanalytic theory. My purpose is not merely to show the application of this theory for understanding symbols in dreams and phantasies, but to demonstrate that the structure and dynamics of symbol formation provide a basis for a theory of thinking and for an understanding of the schemata whereby the mental operations of knowing, judging, and of creativity are to be understood. Under the broadest possible definition I would include all intelligent actions by man in his efforts to adapt to his environment by accommodation or to change his environment by assimilation of it. In this sense there is an asymptotic transition from symbols (as unconscious phantasy, dreams, language, myths and social rituals) to construction and use of interplanetary space vehicles as instrumental *signs* and *symbols* of man's purpose.

Pragmatism As the Basis of the Semiotic (and of Psychoanalysis)

Peirce's pragmatic philosophy and his Doctrine of Signs came to the very brink of psychology where he was forced to stop. It is for this reason that his ideas offer a means for unification of the logical with the psychological through psychoanalysis. In making this link it is necessary to become reacquainted with the features of pragmatism which afford the necessary connections. Although pragmatism as a philosophical system was taken over by William James and others, and while many features of the system subsequently were disavowed by Peirce in his retreat to the use of the term "Pragmaticism," the features of pragmatism described here do accord generally with Peirce's conception and offer the possibility of further psychological development. They are reviewed here to demonstrate the basis for Peirce's phenomenology and semiotic which offer hope for a unification with psychoanalysis.

Pragmatism may be characterized as a system of thought which attempts to assess the relationship of human values to the instruments we have devised for the conduct of life (Kaplan, 1961). "Pragmatism" comes from a root which means act or deed. Just as Socrates brought philosophy down to the marketplace from the clouds, pragmatism brings philosophy down from the academy to the laboratory, the studio, and to the consulting room. However, pragmatism does not replace practical considerations for sound theorizing. On the contrary, pragmatism views sound theorizing as the chief instrument which rational man has devised. This instrument of hypothesis-formation was presented by Peirce in the form of a model or theory of signs.

The pragmatic philosophy pre-eminently attempts to formulate the meaning and purpose of the relationship between human values and the facts of our technological world which confront us so ominously. Pragmatism is both a humanistic and scientific philosophy. Most scientific philosophies derive from the natural sciences, especially physics and mathematics; but biology, psychology, the social sciences, and the humanities have been most influential for, and influenced by, pragmatism. Indeed, both William James and John Dewey made important contributions to psychology as their pragmatic philosophies extended quite naturally into the area of the subjective.

It is a principle of pragmatism that every experience occurs in a concrete, biological and cultural matrix, and that the conceptions that grow out of experience are conditioned by that matrix. The problem of understanding the meaning of experience is relative, not to the opinion or perspective of the philosopher, but it is concretely rooted in the context in which the particular experience occurs. *It is from the vertex of the experiencer that the meaning of the experience must be understood*. It is not too strong, I believe, to say that this should be a first principle for psychoanalytic interpretation as well, a fact which has been re-emphasized by Bion (1965).

Peirce held that the existence of a belief is demonstrated by actions based on the belief. He held that the Cartesian who argues powerfully on behalf of his belief that all thinking begins with *doubt* rather than with *belief* is belied by the obvious strong belief from which his argument begins! A meaning is to be analyzed as an indefinite set of hypothetical propositions, with the antecedent of each stating a human purpose, interest, value, aim or intention, and the consequent indicating the outcome of appropriate action. In this way we go from concrete human experience based on purpose and value, to instruments of action which include the gamut of rules, representations, language, concepts, mathematics, and technology or art, all of which have significance in determining the outcome of the experience. These instruments can be identified as signs and symbols as well as objects or facts. The mind can be considered to contain the schemata for the use of symbols in order to give meaning to things, events, experiences, and actions. In this context the extension of mind, aided by its instrument of space exploration, reaches indefinitely past our solar system. In its symbolism, mind extends its phantasy world into the deepest celestial black hole and, through it, into the expanding universe beyond, about which we have the least, even indirect, experience. This statement is meant not only to reflect the infinite sweep of the symbolizing mind through its access to the world of phantasy-objects, but it is also meant to emphasize the importance of action in the material world of forms as the ultimate test and function of mind as suggested by Peirce's criticisms of the Cartesians and by my emphasis on technology and art as actual extensions of mind. In other words Plato, the artist-philosopher, was right in insisting on the philosophic search for form the *eidos*; and Peirce was right in his pragmatic insistence on the return to the world of action and objects—but always through the schema of correct theorizing (the semiotic) which points toward a true form. The extension of symbolization to include material forms of technology as instrumental signs and symbols is also meant to place the psychoanalytic concept of sublimation in its proper context under the rubric of symbol formation. The things of the objective world about which we understand anything can only have become known by signs or signals which we have somehow experienced: hence "understood things" are already experienced at least sufficiently to provide a sign constituting a preconception. This is the paradox of pragmatism (and of symbol formation). *All knowledge and meaning evolves through signs of objects which must already be known in some sense: reason does not begin with doubt, but rather begins with pre-existent belief.*

Pragmatism rests on behavioral psychology in the sense that mind, consciousness, and meaning are not to be construed as explanatory categories of cause and effect. Rather, they are instruments of action. Since this action consists of a social or interpersonal or, more broadly, an intersubjective relationship, mind cannot be contained under the skin or in the brain. Stimulus response behaviorism is to be seen as a victim of the reductionist fallacy of "nothing but." The recurring human yearning for causal (teleological) relationship takes the form of this tendency to analyze and deduce from general to particular in order to impose a sense of security and determinacy. This replaces exploration by scientific method with the deceptive reassurance of scholastic deductive systems which always return to the absolute as the omnipotent creator.

Pragmatism takes a predictive and experimental view of truth. Accordingly, truth is that which we are able to know about things by doing something with them. Mere looking is to be considered a significant action, yet the principal of contextualism requires that knowledge and truth increase in relation to the richness provided by the multiplication of signs, each of which may be thought of as providing an additional context or dimension to meaning. The signs whereby we know the object and progressively change it into a subject of knowledge, a fact, a concept, a rule, or a law (or establishing it as a "lie").

Classical epistemology set itself the task of justifying the movement of knowledge and thought from the self to the world—a problem for a solipsist who can never be satisfied that he exists in a real world. We are in the world to begin with, says the pragmatist, and thought is directed to the question of how we can move from one part of it to another and change it or be changed by it. The answer to this question lies partly in logic. In the most general sense, logic is semiotic. Logic for a pragmatist is what men do, a method to be pursued in order to move from a belief through doubt regarding that belief until a belief is reached which (for the time being) satisfies all remaining doubt in the community of those properly eligible to doubt. A system of such beliefs is called a science, and this method of reaching it, called logic, can also be called scientific method as it always occurs in a particular concrete, biocultural context. Pragmatism agrees that logic is concerned not necessarily with how men often, unfortunately, do think but how they quasi-necessarily must think—not on the basis of some absolute analytic formula but on the basis of the course of logical norms derived from their grounding in what happens when we think in one way or another. Peirce's theory of thinking is based on "what must be the character of all signs used by a 'scientific intelligence'; that is to say, by an intelligence capable of learning by experience—the modes of thought of a god, who should possess an intuitive omniscience superseding reason are put out of the question." (CP2.229)* In other words, Peirce insists that genuine thinking emerges from

*References made to CP refer to *The Collected Papers of C.S. Peirce:* Vol. 1-6, C. Hartshorne & R. Weiss (eds.), 1931-1935; Vol. 2-8, A.W. Burks (ed.), 1958. Cambridge: Harvard University Press. Numerals before the point refer to volume, and numerals after the point refer to paragraph.

experience; that the necessary pre-existent knowing must be a preconception derived from particular experience, not a direct gift of unmediated "god-like intuition."

For millenia philosophers have striven to avoid mentalism and psychologism in their theorizing since this opens the door to the most fanciful of beliefs and conceptions. However logic, as first defined by Peirce as a semiotic, is broader than the formal logic of Aristotle and the scholastics, broader than the formal symbolic logic of Boole, of Frege (and of Peirce), and broader than the formal systems of mathematics; for these only provide elegant deductive and analytic reconstructions of knowledge already acquired. Their schemata function elegantly in making transformations either of truths or of Alice in Wonderland fantasies with equal facility, thus demonstrating their adroit agility in ignoring the need to reconcile intrusions of psychologism into human experience. The pragmatic logic is concrete and particular, not merely formal and abstract. It is psychology connected by symbolism to the world. But it is still restricted to the sort of psychology which Peirce described as possessed by a scientific intelligence capable of learning from experience. Pragmatic logic is the use made by a psychology which is consistent with and true to the world to which it is linked by signs and symbols; it is also consistent with and true to itself, in some sense subsumed under the notion of presupposition, while at the same time being forced to accept its imminent fallibility.

When it is put to him as a riddle, the pragmatist logician will assert that even if you call it's tail a leg, a lamb has but four legs, though he may grant you that in some sense its tail may be conjectured to be a leg. The pragmatic logician hypothesizes, predicts and judges. He makes synthetic propositions leading from particular facts about the world to symbolizations and conceptualizations meant to properly represent and expand upon the facts. He understands that the particular fact he starts with is to be taken as a *belief*, to which is attributed *purpose* and *value*, to be called into question by judgment and doubt; and the symbols and concepts predicated are also understood to be beliefs subject to being further called into question in turn by being made to serve as preconceptions for higher realizations. He stands by the pragmatic maxim of Peirce (CP.597) that the beliefs derived from inquiry should not block the road of further inquiry. Such beliefs which do block the road ultimately act as foreign bodies, experienced as alien, dead and yet malevolently haunting, a preconception degenerated into a prejudice or delusion, carried heedlessly beyond the point at which inquiry requires them to be subjected to further doubt. *I hope to show that psychoanalytic objects are prone to become just such alien and foreign impediments which require proper symbolization in order to be elevated from the status of personified "things" (characterized as "part-objects" and especially "bizarre objects" [Bion, 1967]) to that of meaningful thought.*

To say that facts and concepts are beliefs is to point out that they also involve human values, since purpose and intention are imbedded in belief (Kaplan, 1961); it is purpose which determines value. It is only when the value implicit in what are taken as facts is not felt to be problematic that facts are considered already significant, that is, already evaluated and called "Objective." Correspondingly, what are taken as values are facts, events, and things whose objective aspect is already taken for granted, leaving to our attention the problematic aspect of intention and purpose. Thus, the problematic logic restores to "respectability" the "subjective" problems of freedom, justice, political and personal responsibility, as well as the problems of proper form and aesthetics: all these matters are rescued from this abandonment as "non-sense" by positivistic philosophy of science which demands strict objectivity for matters which deserve serious consideration.

The pragmatic logician believes that man enters into a transaction with the operative world of thingness by signifying, symbolizing, and conceptualizing an aspect of it; he does this by engaging his subjective intentions, purposes, and judgment of values in the transaction. In the world of science and technology a discovered scientific fact may appear to be entirely objective, but this semblance of truth appears only because the value aspect of the fact has already been considered a resolved question. It may be that the scientific fact is valued as a tool or instrument for the discovery of further facts, or the value may be held to be in its practical usefulness. When the value aspect of scientific facts is finally called into question (such as is presently happening in regard to the facts of power technology), all the values previously thought to be resolved within the entire scientific enterprise may be called back into question in a catastrophic challenge to paradigms long considered beyond doubt (Kuhn, 1962).

Since man is not self-contained, he is required to predicate questions about the world of things in which he must live and in which he is contained. This must take place via transactions. Through transactions, the world of things is given significance and symbolism by one's particular subjective world of purpose, beliefs, and in light of one's value system. This transaction is immanently fallible since it depends on the consistency and complementarity between the objective and subjective worlds. This consistency is closely connected to "reality testing."

The structural relationship between subjective values (and presupposed facts) and objective facts (and presupposed values) mediated by symbol formation attempts to resolve the conventional dualities between not only values and facts but also between emotion and reason and indeed between subjectivity and objectivity. This is not to assert that values and facts which are acceptable for one system can be imposed without conflict on another system in which they may function destructively. An example of this is the conflict between values for political groups as opposed to family groups described by Machievelli in his classic study of power.

Theory of Signs—Confusion of Terms

It is my belief that the theory of signs may be extended not only to what Peirce called the signs of how men quasi-necessarily must think, which he took to mean how men "should think," but will include in an extended psycho-semiotic schema the signs of how men (fortunately or unfortunately) do think. If I am justified in this claim for a semiotic model capable of assimilating the semiotic to psychology, and psychology to the semiotic, then I must address both disciplines—but in what language? In this regard I shall follow the usage of Peirce as far as possible in designating the semiotic elements and showing the position of the psychological element.

The term *sign* is used generically for the vehicle of representation for which Peirce also uses the somewhat awkward *representamen* (in an attempt to elude the familiar ambiguities in the terminology of signs and symbols). The term *symbol* is intended to be restricted to those signs (or representamina) whose meaning is conveyed abstractly by codes which are generally thought of as derived by the dictates of social convention, chiefly, but not entirely, linguistic. The formation of symbols so defined constitutes the sine qua non of language, conceptual consciousness, and human culture. This definition of *symbol* is somewhat in conflict with psychoanalytic and much ordinary language usage in which the word *symbol* and *symbolism* carry strong connotations of the emotional expression associated with concrete symbolic objects.

It is important to retain the ability to use the terms *symbol, symbolic*, and *symbolism* for signs which refer to absent objects, especially objects which are absent by virture of repression or disavowal—for the fact is that there is usually no felicitous grammatical alternative even though this sort of symbol seems very different from abstract linguistic or mathematical terms. The ambiguity which complicates the term "symbol" is revealed in the example of an actual crucifix in contrast to the linguistic term. Both symbols are derived by cultural convention and designate an absent object—but one also constituting a "symbolic object" with a value and meaning of its own in the present.

In contrast to his use of *symbol* for the abstract aspect of representation, Peirce used *icon* for a representation by likeness, analogy, and physical similarity; he used *index* for a representation by contiguity such as in pointing and signaling or in the "fit" of sign to object as of key to lock. After surveying the various usages employed by authors in the psychological, philosophical, linguistic, literary, aesthetic, and anthropological disciplines, one is soon convinced that insistence upon a particular usage solves nothing. Further, it is of much less importance than a clear understanding of the issues involved and an awareness of probable terminological discrepancies. For example, Peirce makes clear that in practice symbols are seldom if ever pure in their abstractness, carrying iconic and indexical connotations including their emotional expression as well (CP2.231). For the soldier home from the war, the sight of the Statue of Liberty and the feel of the motherland beneath his feet carry the symbolic force of abstract conceptualization. But the iconic and indexical significance of the experience add the powerful dimensions of imagery, immediacy, concrete particularity, and actuality to the symbol meaning. All acting together can be said to consist of a multi-dimensional symbolic experience. The full expressive power of the iconic and indexical significations together can best be expressed under the rubic of *symbolism.*

An alternative manner of expressing the complexity of symbolization is that of Cassirer (1957) who refers to symbolic *pregnance* and three hierarchic aspects of symbol formation—the expressive, representative, and conceptual. In either case social transmission of concepts and rules is furnished by the symbolic component which is conceptual, while the natural feeling sense is expressed and represented by the iconic and indexical content of the *pregnance* derived from the analogical relationship of sign to the physical object. A conceptual symbol such as Anglo-Saxon expletive may be more meaningful by virtue of the iconicity and indexicality (with which it is pregnant) than by means of the concept it conveys.

Peirce's Phenomenology

The theory of signs or semiotic proposed by Peirce is a direct outgrowth and manifestation not only of his pragmatic philosophy but of his phenomenology (Buchler, 1955). The principal feature of Pierce's phenomenology is his differentiation of *qualities, actualities*, and *meanings* into ultimate categories. Pure qualities can be understood as a field of potential meaning, e.g., pure color, which is presumed to inhere in things as a "category of firstness," "just being itself" until experienced and revealed by an iconic sign of likeness which stands in analogical relationship to its object. A particular field of properties enabling a sign to represent certain objects was referred to by Peirce as the *ground* or *idea* of the sign. A quality which is a mere "potential existent" in the "category of firstness" must be actualized by the "outward clash" of subject with object. This brute actuality of existence occurs in the "category of secondness" which could be described as a *meaningless, immediate* object-relation which is revealed by an indexical sign of the immediate experience but which, being caught up "inside" the experience, lacks perspective, context, understanding, or dimensionality. But from another vertex, such interactions appear dyadic and one-dimensional.

It is in the ultimate phenomenological "category of thirdness" that the meaning of an object-relation is given for the subject experiencing the relation. Both firstness and secondness are vividly experienced but are only *inferred* existents, insofar as they are understood or known. According to Peirce (CP5.264), even to be aware of a color or a pinprick requires at least a minimal judgment that the color or pinprick was perceived. *The irreducibility of perceptual judgments is a key Peircean concept which establishes the link of thirdness and the existence of a semiotic structure as an invariant in all forms of knowing from the merest percept to the most sophisticated argument or concept* (Buchler, 1955). Nevertheless, qualities and brute actualities are vividly experienced, often more so when the neutralizing and inhibiting effects of understanding (through fuller symbolization and conceptualization) are minimal in the experience. This is an obvious connection between the theory of signs and the Freudian theory of the neutralizing function of the ego and the unreliability of "consciousness" in theories of thinking, knowing, and understanding.

The Semiotic Triad

Peirce's semiotic triad of Object, Sign, and Interpretant is a model of logical thought structure which is not concerned with psychological aberrations. The model describes an equilateral triangle with Sign (S), Object (O), and Interpretant (I), each at its respective vertex. *A sign is something which stands for or at least points out or signals something to someone.* The triad may be said to reveal a sign of an object to an interpretant. Both object and sign may be external objects but may also be mental images. The Interpretant is always mental and can be thought of as "the proper significate effect" or "signified thought." The elements of the triad are not to be considered as existing in any series of *dyadic* relationships. "The interpretant stands in a genuine triadic relationship to its object such that its sign is determined to have the same relationship to its object as that in which the interpretant stands to the same object" (CP2.227). Peirce's concept of thirdness contains the notion of context or perspective. The third is the agency of understanding, standing in the position of metalanguage. Thirdness is required for an interpretant to give meaning and significance to a reaction between objects (an object-relation). The interpretant as third is not only the observer of the sign-object-relationship, but it is also in an active relationship with both and cannot stand aloof from them, being part of a triad. The consequence of this is the ambiguous circumstance where the brute reactions betwen things or the abstract relations between thoughts will be molded in conformity to the form in which the subject's thoughts are already molded. "Not only will meaning always, more or less, in the long run mold reactions to itself, but it is only in doing so that its own being consists" (Buchler, 1955). Not only is thirdness that which imparts meaning to reactions by its interpretant function in relating object to sign, but by virtue of its subsequent transformations, the interpretant imparts the meaning which it has acquired to future triads of meaning. In Peirce's words, "It is that which is what it is by virtue of imparting a quality to reactions in the future" (Buchler, 1955), that is to say, in subsequent triads. The interpretant thought of the present serves as the preconception for semiotic objects in further evolutions of signification. Thirdness establishes dimensionality in an object-relation which thereupon enters the world of representable space-time intervals in which indefinite proliferation of dimensionality can develop, predicate, and determine the evolution of meanings.

Peirce demonstrated by means of existential graphs that dyadic relations can only move along a straight line meaninglessly and never can branch out to provide fully dimensional matrices of ongoing but undetermined development. The triadic form provides an indefinite number of complex relationships, the development of any one of which reveals purpose, direction, context, and the ascribing of meaning. Meaning is always a prediction or predication of the future and is therefore the development of [mental] action.

The First Two Branches of the Semiotic

The semiotic has three branches corresponding to (S), (O) and (I) of the triad. However, the division between these three branches is never clearly defined due to the interdependence and interpenetration of one with the other. The first branch rises from the vertex of the Sign. It was called *speculative grammar* by Peirce and *syntax* by Charles Morris (1938). It may be thought of as "what must be true of signs in order that they may embody any meaning" (CP2.297). This syntactical aspect of signs was evolved by Peirce as a complex classification involving the possibility of a total of sixty-six classes of signs (CP8.344). These classes ranged from a sign as the mere appearance of a possible quality to a symbol as a fully abstract general law. Between these extremes are signs ranging widely in degrees of concrete particularity in their own character as sign or in their relation to object or to the interpretant. Of special importance among these complex classifications is the character of signs mentioned earlier which accounts for the difficulty in terminology based on the way that the sign represents its object: as *icon* (likeness), *index* (direct existential connection without regard to likeness), and as *symbol* (denoting object by rule, law, or convention or what Peirce calls a "habit"). The participation of icons and indices in sign formation is a part of the natural and physical qualities of signs. They are necessary for meaning to retain a connection to individuality and the senses. Theyare necessary for expression and communication, an essential for human relationships and interaction with the environment. But the conceptualizations which are uniquely essential to human interactions and cultural continuity rest directly on the symbol. "Symbols grow. They come into being by development out of other signs, particularly from icons, or from mixed signs partaking of the nature of icons and symbols. We think only in signs" (CP2.300).

The second branch of Peirce's semiotic trichotomy is what he called *logic proper*, and he defined it as the formal science of the *truth* of representations. Logic here is taken to be the semantic dimension of the semiotic, and the vertex of analysis is the denoted object of the sign. The analysis of the illative character of the semiotic need not detain us here since this leads in the direction of Peirce's pioneering studies in the field of semantics and also in formal symbolic logic. However, it should be noted in this regard that Peirce (CP6.552-8) developed the notion of a retroductive (abductive) inference as distinct from deductive and inductive inference. By this designation, Peirce intended to identify the manner in which a hypothesis is formulated from experience as a form of logical inference. This radical innovation by Peirce related to his belief that hypotheses are formed. That is, questions are asked and inquiries are made by means of an inference which proceeds from particulars of experience to general rules or laws. This is in contrast to deductive and inductive inference by means of which the testing of a hypothesis proceeds from generals to particulars as analytic propositions. The notion of hypothesis formation as a logical (retroductive) inference has been rejected by Reichenbach (1951), Popper (1959), and others who in fact deny that the formation of hypotheses is any business of science at all. Nevertheless, I believe that the notion of hypothesis formation illuminates the structural character, not only of hypotheses, but of beliefs, judgments, and scientific inquiry, all of which have in common aspects of symbol formation based on the semiotic. These notions are of great importance since they are the basis not only of creative thinking in general but the discipline of interpretation as well (including psychoanalysis and modern hermeneutics).

The Third Branch of the Semiotic

The third branch of the semiotic is that whose vertex is the interpretant. Other than the interpreters of Peirce, there has been a tendency, particularly in studies emanating from Saussurean linguistics, to treat symbolism and sign theory as the dyadic relation of sign or symbol to object. The formulation employs the term *signifier/signified* which tends to gloss the structural relationships and blurs the perspective of the symbol forever. This procedure results in a de-emphasis or outright exclusion of subjective element. Far from being regretted, this is a consequence devoutly hoped for by strict empiricism which welcomes any means of heightening the objectivity of a scientific method.

For Pierce, too, the problem of the interpretant was vexatious, for his scientific background and his pragmatism seemed to demand a return to the world of objective experience for meaning to be determined. Peirce, however, could never fully forsake his youthful fascination with Kantian rationalism. For him the whole universe is perfused with signs whose meanings are in part supplied by a subjective actant who determines what the relation of sign to object (the significant truth) shall be for him. The third branch of the semiotic was called pure or speculative rhetoric by Peirce and, sometimes, "methodeutic"—"a method for discovering method" in human inquiry generally. Even psychoanalysis suffers from the temptation to evade the ambiguity of the subjective by interpreting the analysand's experience as historical fact (as Freud did at first with his hysterical Viennese ladies). It is in this context, the need to interpret from the subjective vertex, that Bion's injunction to abandon memory and desire can be understood. It is Bion's "methodeutic," a method for standing aside from the subjective vertex in order to interpret the "methods" of the analyst and as revealed in his "memories and desires" directed toward the analyst "confused with a primal object and eventually, it is hoped, as a separate symbolic object."

It is clear that Peirce considered the third branch of the semiotic to be of extreme interest and importance. It is the science of how signs exercise their power to appeal to a mind, and especially how one sign gives birth to another, and one thought brings forth another. He called this third branch of the semiotic, "the highest and most living branch of semiotic" (CP3.364). However, he recognized that "the practical want of a good treatment of this subject is acute" (CP2.105). He recognized that the time was not yet right for a full and systematic exposition of the "methodeutic" functions of the semiotic subject. He was able to offer only a beginning for any further attempt to develop a science of the subjective which would link the doctrine of signs to psychoanalytic understanding of the "self" and its links to the object-world through symbol formation.

Peirce was able to offer a theory of emotional, energetic, and logical interpretants (thoughts emerging in the subject as a product of symbol formation). "These first logical interpretants stimulate us to various voluntary performances in the Inner World. We imagine ourselves in various situations and to be animated by various motives. We proceed to trace out the alternative lines of conduct which the conjectures would leave open to us. We are, moreover, led by the same inward activity, to remark different ways in which our conjectures could be slightly modified. *The logical interpretant must, therefore, be in a relatively future tense*" (CP5.481, italics mine). It will be noted from this description that the emotional and energetic interpretants may continue to participate in symbol formation in the conceptual realm by evoking iconic and indexical dimensions in the symbols and concepts. It will also be noted that Peirce's logical interpretant consists of imaginative as well as logical conjectures, that is, images which are rather representational fantasies.

In embarking on the third branch of the semiotic Peirce had projected himself into the realm of the inner world and of psychology. It was on the wings of the rich psychological content of his speculative rhetoric that Peirce's pragmatism carried his younger colleagues and successors into the field of psychology itself. These relationships were not well understood. Peirce thought his interpretants were to be studied as aspects of signs (the first branch). His highest logical interpretant contained or was contained in an *interpreter*, a duality he could not resolve and which continues to be argued in various contexts today.

From Semiotic to Psychology

Peirce was painfully aware of his inability to carry through the analysis of the third branch of the semiotic. In retrospect it appears that his analytic genius put him in touch with the evidence needed to guide him somewhat further into psychological theory, but his concerns that irrationality might affect his philosophical theorizing restrained his explorations in this area. In his essay on the "Law of Mind" (CP6.102-111) there appears his protest against the occult and the transcendental which he obviously felt to exert an uncanny attraction for him despite his orthodox scientific training." ". . . I was born and raised in the neighborhood of Concord–I mean in Cambridge–at the time when Emerson, Hedge, and their friends were disseminating the ideas that they had caught from Schelling . . . or from God knows what minds stricken with the monstrous mysticism of the East. But the atmosphere of Cambridge had many an antiseptic against Concord transcendentalism . . . . Nevertheless, it is probable that . . . some benignant form of the disease was implanted in my soul, unawares, and that now, after long incubation it comes to the surface, modified by mathematical conceptions and by training in physical investigations." In the same essay he protested against the obvious need, in a theory about the dialogue of ideas, for some mental agency that could connect an idea with a past and therefore theoretically absent idea. "...To say, therefore, that they are similar can only mean that an occult power from the depths of the soul forces us to connect them in one's thoughts . . . ."

Thus in 1892 Peirce disavowed further investigation of a *psychological* concept in favor of taking up an involuted, labored, and unproductive *logical* argument for a theory of "Synechism" which he described as a universal continuity of associations. He suggested but then dismissed the notion that the past idea might be present in the next thought, *vicariously*. For in 1892, five years before a definitive paper on "The Theory of Signs" he was unable to formulate a hypothesis with which to answer his own question, ". . . how the past idea can be related to its vicarious representation." Nor does it appear that he ever attempted fully to develop the idea of symbol formation as a kind of vicarious representation. Neither did he pursue fully the notion of the prior thought as a preconception. Although the mysterious "interpreter" of his highest logical interpretant offered a way out, he could not find a way to reach "I" as Will or the occult force of innate predisposition despite his explicit contempt for the notion of a cartesian *tabula rasa*. Neither could he orient himself in terms of the Kantian I-in-itself.

Preconceptions of the Symbol-Former

Since Freud's revolutionary explorations into those dark and occult regions of the mind, we are empowered to marshal certain arguments of Peirce and place them in context with psychoanalytic theory to provide a psychosemiotic theory of thinking. It appears that Peirce's study of the semiotic begins at a relatively well advanced level of symbol-formation and one which, as a consequence of Peirce's philosophical and logical approach to the problem, deals with semiotic object and sign mainly as external phenomena. Despite the reassuring quality of everyday rationality surrounding his examples, he quickly unveiled the paradox that *a sign or symbol must already "know" something about its object in order that the sign could have any means whereby it could know what to point out or represent.* "The sign can only represent the object and tell about it. It cannot furnish acquaintance with or recognition of the object; for that is what is meant in this volume by the object of a sign; namely that with which it (the sign) presupposes an acquaintance in order to convey some further information concerning it." (CP2.304). "It is impossible for a sign to convey any information about an object to a person if that sign has absolutely no relation or reference to anything about that object with which that person has the slightest familiarity or acquaintance." (CP2.243). An example of this odd but vitally important fact is the following: to an aborigine, in his first exposure to civilization, a street sign not only fails to convey the idea of a street of a certain name, but fails even to convey the idea that it is a sign of another object. The simple truth of overriding importance is that all signs and symbols must arise and be *in-formed* first by some presupposition in the mind of the symbol-forming subject before further structuring (based on the phenomena of perception, conception, etc.) can evolve a significant or symbolic object with its own character and importance.

The quotation from Peirce from which comes the title of the volume, *A Perfusion of Signs*, (Sebeok, 1978) begins in this way, "It seems a strange thing when one comes to ponder over it, that a sign should leave its interpreter to supply a part of its meaning." In this statement Peirce acknowledged his awareness that meaning is furnished to the semiotic by the subjective vertex of "I" in some important context. In this statement he also shifted the name of the subjective operator from interpretant, to interpreter, thereby acknowledging that the subjective vertex is not merely a passive receiver of symbols and concepts; it also plays the active role of symbol-former. If we now add Peirce's description that "the sign is that which is determined to have the same relationship to its object as that in which the interpretant stands to the same object" (CP2.305) and ask who it is that makes these determinations, we should require the same conclusion: that the subjective vertex of the triad has an active creative role as well as being a significant effect. Peirce's awareness of the active and creative role of the symbol-former is illustrated by this statement: "The reaction of sign to object is molded to conform to the meaning imputed to their relationship by the interpreter of the semiotic." (CP5.265). The meaning by which it molds reactions is said to be the only thing of which its (the interpreter's) being consists.

The ideas of Peirce concerning the complex functions of the subjective vertex of the semiotic, although unstructured within any coherent concept gradually become clear. His notions require, among other things, an a priori and "occult knowing" in order to provide at least a preconception and predisposition so that further significance may evolve. Awareness of this necessity was acknolwedged but strongly resisted by Peirce as told in the autobiographical fragment previously quoted. If we take his historical narrative not only as factual but also as a symbolic transformation of a phantasy at the deepest level of a primal object world already molded and "informed" by inherent preconceptions, then we should, if our theory has any merit, be able to locate in Peirce's narrative evidence of the existence of that primal object world.

I believe that this deep and occult level can be discerned even from such fragments as are given. A construction of the phantasy reveals Peirce's feeling that in close proximity to his birth there emerged a strong belief in transcendentalism (translatable in psychoanalytic jargon into a belief in infantile omnipotence). Despite this he tried hard to eradicate this omnipotence within himself by the antidotes available to him in the struggle to achieve the kind of thinking which develops through genuine symbol formation and scientific conceptualization. Nevertheless, he goes on, I believe, a benign germ of that early omnipotent "thinking" persists. He feels forced to consider this as evidence of "an occult demonic power in the depths of my soul" which has the ability to connect inherent preconceptions to "things" in order that they eventually may be experienced as significant objects: in this phantasy there appears a method which, although imbued with traces of the germ of omnipotence (germinal ?), explains how an object may be experienced in order that a sign may further signify it. Peirce gives us cause to consider, with him, the possible existence, not only of unconscious preconceptions, but of an unconscious subjective entity capable of connecting a thought with a prior thought—the concept (which he had already learned in his youth from Kant) of the un-manifest self of pure apperception, the "I-in-itself." This idea is, of course, old and allied in traditional wisdom to the idea of the soul.

There is a profound awareness of an ineffable force within most "self-aware" creative people. Pascal phrased it in the aphroism that "The heart has its reasons—which reason knows not of." For reasons which were uniquely his own as well as partaking of reasons deeply typical of human development, as we shall see, Peirce "averted his gaze" from these transcendental and occult notions in his conscious judgments. But he was unable to evade the necessity of a theory connecting pre-existent and particular notions to more and more general (and logical) symbols and interpretants. A manifestation of this conflict was his development of the retroductive inference theory, as alluded to earlier. This theory was a bold attempt to explain hypothesis-formation in terms of the scientific method as an illative and inferential phenomenon. In this way he attempted to translate the connection of signs to objects and to preconceptions into an entirely rational phenomenon. How far he succeeded is still disputed, but his view appears to be at least as valuable heuristically as that put forward by the school which states that the formation of hypotheses has nothing to do with scientific method at all.

The search for the symbol-former appears to be very much like the search for man's "glassy essence," that of which he is most ignorant. This mystical creative force becomes manifest in the uncertain tension of the relationship between the semiotic sign and its object. From one side there is a creative force which invokes some knowledge of the otherwise occult primal object in the form of presupposition or preconception. From the other side, a percept is formed based on iconic and indexical properties of analogical *likeness and fit* of some "thing" observed and compared to the primal object. It is on the anvil of symbol formation where likeness and fit can never be absolute, where the links of meaning accumulate, and where dreaming and thinking are creatively interwoven and artfully forged together in the form which the symbol-former had imagined in the first place.

To understand the relationship between the symbol-forming subject and his world, perfused through and through with signs and symbols, requires that the connection between the proposed sign and its object be in some sense analogous to a pre-existing connection between the symbol-former and the object. In the "Critique of Pure Reason" Kant (Korner, 1955) stated, "We cannot represent to ourselves as connected in the manifold anything which we have not, ourselves previously connected."

The logical necessity for some kind of pre-existing connection gives rise to a question about the paradox of infinite regression and has been the source of the most grievous doubts and uncertainties concerning theories of thinking and of creativity, not to mention metaphysical theories. The resistance of Peirce to the concept of a symbol-forming subject which would serve as an "occult and demonic power of the soul" connecting past thoughts to present and future thoughts is understandable. Even more interesting is the difficulty experienced by Freud who, having dared to conceptualize the dark recess of innate and instinctual presupposition and predisposition, also demonized and alienated this seemingly chaotic and autochthonous creative force by relegating it to the realm of "id" (it-ness rather than I-ness).

To reclaim the primal presuppositions and predispositions as quintessential elements of the "glassy essence" of the symbol-forming subject requires that we acknowledge the compound and multiplex character of a subjective entity capable of willing and judging, growing and creating. There is, of course, nothing new in this mystery, but it is necessary to explore it in order to see the lengths to which deterministic and radically empiricist science has gone to deny and oversimplify this truth.

First, let us examine a straightforward model for a pre-existent subjective world such as I am supposing to exist as a creative generator for a symbolic world of meaning. Examples abound in the creatures around us whose intelligence more predominantly consists of this preformed aspect. Avoidance of such examples can only be attributed to the hubris of ancient constraints against reducing man's exalted spiritual status—apt testimony to the fragility of man's faith in his own creativity.

There is a common European songbird which migrates nocturnally, employing celestial navigation whereby it can orient itself correctly even if blown a thousand miles off course (Tinbergen, 1951). Here one can no longer avoid the acknowledgements of an innate internal object-world associated with innate predisposition to action. Adaptive survival depends on its existence in relation to external reality within a symbolic relationship as we have defined it. Accompanying the innate schema (amounting to a map, a sextant, and a chronometer) are agitations and body orientations which are signs constituting preliminary external evidence of a dialogue betwen internal and external object-worlds. The enactment of this dialogue in the course of migration reveals an astonishing capacity in these small creatures for "reality testing" which is made possible by highly developed semiotic function. An innate semiotic schema capable of being realized by symbolic connection is essential to the natural order of things, whether as an I.R.M. (Innate Releasing Mechanism or schema) realized by an external releasor object (Tinbergen, 1951), or by the preconceptions and actions characterized by Freud as the instincts and their vicissitudes in man. The semiotic requires that the object be already known in some dimension in order that the signs, symbols, and significant objects may evolve. The cultural evolution in man through his gift of verbal symbolism in no way mitigates against more primitive ties to physical and somatic objects and analogic signs. In fact, as I have pointed out above, there is a logical necessity for the existence of this connection. The very nature of the semiotic structure provides for the intimate connection between these more primitive physical analogical signs with which man's verbal symbols are pregnant.

The innate "knowing" to which I allude is not claimed to be discovered in the semiotic of Peirce but rather is implied there and in his (and Kant's) philosophy. Peirce's phenomenology implies that pre-supposed "knowing" is to be found in the experiences of firstness and secondness where they exist prior to conceptualization as raw material for dreaming. These experiences exist concretely and pre-representationally in a strange world vacillating from the null to the one-dimensional states of mind which exist outside representational space-time dimensionality. These are peculiar states of mind which I hope presently to define.

It is necessary to acknowledge skepticism when dealing with preformism and innatism. But this issue could apparently be side-stepped by recourse to the old assumption of a *tabula rasa* and the additional assumption that early "introjective processes" are the earliest source of preconceptions. The prevalent scientific tradition views subjectivism and innatism as the most outrageous aspect of psychologism and mentalism. Piaget (1970) calls for "a differentiation between the *individual subject* who does not enter at all, and the *epistemic subject*, that cognitive nucleus which is common to all subjects at the same level," who is grudgingly accepted to the extent his operations free him from his spontaneous egocentricity. Most of all, Piaget objects to Chomsky's (1968) innate linguistic schema, hoping for the validation in the near future of a "structuralist hypothesis" by which "we would have an explanation of linguistic structures that disposes with too heavy-handed an innatism." (Piaget, 1970). This gentle sounding and rather feeble appeal by Piaget against the innatism implicit in Chomsky's deep linguistic structures is only a final protest against Kantian rationalism including all forms of priorism, preformism, and innatism which he fought against brilliantly and implacably all his life; for his science was based on deterministic, positivistic, and behavioristic criteria which enriched our understanding of directly observable and measurable phenomena, but rejected hypotheses which suggested the existence of an egocentric intelligence which antedated and might make a mockery of his "objective" observations.

Nevertheless there still remains that principle of symbol formation which states that a sign cannot create or discover the object which it represents; rather, it is fitted by the symbol-former to point to and represent the object which that symbol-former already "knows" as a presupposition. The primacy of the preconception is implicit in Kant's *Critique of Pure Reason* (Korner, 1955) in which his synthetic prior categories constitute an early portent of the semiotic of Peirce. The Kantian categories of the understanding were to be applied through schemata whereby these pre-existent concepts could be applied to things given in perception. The schemata were described as procedural rules of the imagination in procuring an image for a concept. The concept was tied to understanding, and its empirical instances are tied to perception. The schema (like the semiotic) has, so to speak, a foot in either domain. The whole far-flung Kantian system might be viewed as an effort to show that an innate conceptual structure is required to determine whether that which is given in perception is objective. In this Kant is saying that it is not only the external world which structures the internal world by the agency of synthetic ego function; but the internal world by means of innate structural schemata which actively structures that which is given by the sensory apparatus, imposing conceptual criteria of objectivity on the external world.

The Multiplex Symbol-Former

I do not mean simply to equate Kant's synthetic a priori concepts with Freud's id. I intend to show an essentially ambiguous relationship between innate preconceptions and the "things" to which these preconceptions are fused, forming the primal object-world. The manner in which this primitive world is formed is occult, transcendental, and omnipotent. It can be discovered and understood by means of psychoanalytic technique; but from the subjective vertex it is a state of con-fusion and is "known" only as meaningless "felt" experience (representing Peirce's categories of firstness and secondness). These have no discrete separateness, no inside or outside, no gap, no caesura. Despite the occult character of this kind of experience it is this which provides the "fore-knowing" which Peirce's phenomenology established as necessary in order that a sign could know what to point to in order to represent an object to its interpretant: this is the first task of the symbol-forming subject. Having accomplished this task, the signification and symbolization of the subject can proceed; and for this work the gap or caesura between sign and object must be the first boundary. It enables the subject to have an experience which can be understood because the gap prevents the object from falling inside or engulfing the sign (symbolic object). Should this state of separateness be sustained, a state of thirdness is established. Should the boundary collapse, con-fusion and loss of dimensionality will again prevail. Should the boundary and symbolic relationship be sustained, the potential for growth is immense. In this growing world inner and outer are necessary and predominantly complementary. In man's biological and cultural life the relationship between object and sign is both analogically and digitally coded. That link of meaning and significance between sign and object, as operated by the symbol-former at the vertex of the third branch of the semiotic, embodies the essential property of indeterminacy and ambiguity. It is the uncertainty in this link to the future which ennobles man or demeans him through the freedom which is entailed in this uncertainty. Man's freedom of will is embodied in this link, as in his struggle for self-determination.

The meaning link of the semiotic can be said to have a disambiguating function in that it is the agency whereby the symbol-former impresses his experience and prior understanding onto the chaos of the thing-in-itself. It is demonstrated by the notion that language is less ambiguous than the unconceptualized "things" which the symbols and concepts of language are invented to indicate, make sense of, and transmit as history. At the same time, this link is a re-ambiguating agency in that it enables the symbol-former to employ the creativity implicit in Will to evolve a brave new world, but always with deference to the images of the past. A successful hypothesis may simplify past problems but often opens the future to unanticipated complications. How the functions of the symbol-former are apportioned and carried out have long fascinated and troubled man. Kant (Korner, 1955) approached the problem in this way: "In introspection I am at times aware of myself and perceive myself after the fashion of an object. My empirical self (as object) must therefore be distinguished from *myself in itself* which is unknowable. This 'self of pure apperception,' the *I think* which must be capable of accompanying all my presentations, is not located in time. Of the self of pure apperception I am conscious not of how I appear to myself, or of how I am in myself, but only that I am. The introspected or empirical self is knowable and known. The self of pure apperception (the self-in-itself) is thinkable but cannot possibly be known."

Kant's self of pure apperception was regarded by Schopenhauer (1956) as the self of pure will, an irrational force. This concept was enhanced by the ideas of Vico (1968) and the German anti-enlightenment philosophers epiphanized in Neitzsche which formed a powerful current leading to the concept of *the id* and *the potent self* of the instinctual, purposive, innate predispositions and presuppositions. In the semiotic this self is non-objective and invisible, for its leading principle is its deeply unconscious existence; it is manifested only as that premonition of the primal object which enables it to be signified and symbolized by the selves of perceptual and conceptual judgment. This mystic self was known in Indian philosophy as Atman, the unmanifest and undifferentiated self in oneness with Brahman: the ultimate reality transcending differentiation and equivalent to Kant's thing-in-itself. In Exodus, the unmanifest appears as the ultimate theological self: "And Moses said unto God: 'Behold when I come into the children of Israel, and shall say unto them: the God of your fathers hath sent Me unto you, and they shall say to Me: What is His name? What shall I say unto them?' And God said unto Moses: "I AM that I AM,' and he said: 'Thus shalt thou say unto the children of Israel: 'I AM hath sent me unto you.' " The ancient belief is expressed in the existence of an unmanifest subjective entity who always hovers behind the scene. This entity represents the nameless creator who becomes manifest only in the signs and symbols with which he perfuses his universe. In the Christian theology, the pope is such a symbol, serving as the Vicar of Christ. To the extent God-like infallibility is claimed for the Vicar, the concreteness of symbols is called into question and the vicarious, that is to say symbolic character of the pope as representation rather than actual substitute is subject to challenge.

The Ambiguity of Subject-Object

The early Eighteenth Century counter-enlightenment scholar, Giambattista Vico (1968), was perhaps the first Modern to attempt a systematic analysis of the essential ambiguity existing in the penetration of man's subjectivity into the void of thingness. He saw man as the mythopoeic creature, the possessor of poetic wisdom which casts his relation to the world in the indirect form of metaphor, symbol, and myth. This informing structure corresponds to the "shape of his mind" and determines his perceptions. However, Vico saw this as a complementary relationship. The world of symbols, language, and institutions are created and impressed upon man as ritual, habit, and customs to which he must accommodate himself because these forms impress a conventional meaning on his life. Man becomes more and more dependent on the increasing complexities of these forms because they contain his existence. According to Vico, the nature of man is his history, a complementary process of self-creation. Within the domain of history and the humanistic and social disciplines I would include psychoanalysis and what I am calling the psycho-semiotic.

The transition between the natural and cultural sciences lies at the point where signs, based on natural likeness and actual analogical fitness, evolve into the culturally determined and encoded meanings of abstract symbols and concepts. In these areas Vico pointed out (Berlin, 1979) that we have a special relation to the objects of our investigation. We are, like our subject matter, human; we claim an understanding as participants in an active process - as mere observers cannot. If we wish to understand anything human, we must do more than exercise our simple perceptions. We must also exercise imagination and intuition in the service of somehow entering into the lives and outlook of other human beings and their productions. These intuitions include a sense of fitness of what looks or sounds right. This reflects on the iconicity and aesthetic expressiveness of the "new" method as well as on its conceptual appreciation.

Berlin claims that Vico's special mode of understanding marks the discovery of a central difference between the humanities and natural science. This belief corresponds to a discipline of humanities which is separated from the natural sciences by its method of interpreting the "text" of human cultural productions. This method is known as hermeneutics (Steele, 1979). While this division is a significant one, it is possible that Berlin is assuming a conception of the natural sciences which is too superficial. Recent researches in the philosophy of science by Kuhn (1962) reveal that even ordinary experimental interpretations in physical science are laden with preconceptions, concepts, and categories that may undergo radical change in the course of scientific development. If natural science is in the act of rethinking how it may use radically different means of interpreting natural phenomena, if even their observations are "theory laden," then the objectivity of all science in some sense must remain open to further inquriy (in the event that entrenched preconceptions collapse). In relation to objective science being laden with categories and preconceptions, it is worth recalling Kant's Transcendental Deduction (Kant, 1949, 1958). He held that knowledge of an object involves perceiving it and judging how it falls under a pure concept of the understanding (an a priori concept or category).

Kant held that perceptual judgments alone produce only "it appears to me" propositions. The objective unity of pure apperception is that which unifies (a) the manifold given in perception with (b) the "I think" through an a priori concept of the object. *Objectivity can never be given by mere empirical experience alone. Objectivity and "reality-testing" are forever dependent on the meaning-link between one (empirically sensed) object and another (preconceived) object*. This is determined by the exploratory dialogue between them and is the essence of symbolization. As Kuhn has pointed out, and as the Oppenheimer affair bears out, there is a recurrent collapse of basic preconceptions or paradigms of human science (and of the human state of affairs in all domains). This bears damning testimony to the vulnerability of man's symbolic and conceptual world (collectively as well as individually) to break down as the result of the accumulation of the detritus of badly assimilated and eventually alienating concepts. These concepts undergo a catastrophic disintegration in the face of new, powerful, discordant and penetrating predisposition, and consequent discordant "truths" appearing as the result of further inquiry.

Attempts to make clear and definite the character of the semiotic triad and of the dynamics of symbol formation inevitably run aground on the shoals of functional and structural ambiguities. It becomes evident that the various perspectives must be *tried* in order to provide the context which may eventually enable the explorative journey or odyssey, as it were, of symbol formation to manifest some meaningful and productive direction. Ironically, it is precisely the need for a perspective or context in what Peirce called thirdness that is both essential and inherently ambiguous in symbol formation. The symbol-forming subject is embarking upon a difficult exploratory voyage of discovery in which he must leave the primal world of safety and security behind. To relinquish this paradise, he must acknowledge his present and future unfittedness for that nursery-world. He must recognize that his future requires his launching a voyage of discovery for a new world, a world only recognizable at first by means of similarities and likenesses to the old paradise which he is now relinquishing.

To succeed in this highly complex enterprise, the symbol-former must be capable of performing the multiplex duties of captain, navigator, and crew. He must carry on an empirical and experimental relationship with the landmarks discovered in this alien sea. This relationship is based on dim memories of old landmarks which are rapidly fading from his world of experience. They derive from once remembered dreams which are now only felt in his bones. He is guided by his passions and parental initiation rituals. Dependent on these doubtful guides, he relies on his wit and on sharpness of eye. If misfortunate disasters befall the expedition, and in the event of catastrophe, it is no wonder that navigator, captain, and crew may fly apart. In the wake of disaster the purpose of the exploration may be abandoned and forgotten in favor of wild and terrifying phantasies that pursue to no avail a once forgotten paradise.

The use of metaphor to develop the theme of a symbol formation should not be derided nor devalued since metaphors, myths, and parables themselves are each a form of symbolization and demonstrate the difficulties in clarifying this complex theme.

Commensalism

A metaphor of considerable interest in understanding the difficulties in the path of symbol formation is based on a notion derived by Bion from its biological usage. This is the concept of *commensalism*. Bion's use of the commensal relationship to express a state of mind was not highly developed (Meltzer, 1978). My use of the term is an attempt to highlight certain aspects of Peirce's category of thirdness which I believe can be further clarified through the concept of commensalism. The term comes from ancient roots meaning "mess mates" or "to eat from the same table" (O.E.D.). To understand this metaphor one must visualize a continuum of object-relations in which the generic term "symbiosis" may designate the dependency of one organism upon another. At one extreme on this continuum appears the mutual parasitism constituted by a predator-prey relationship. This is a hopeless dyadic relationship in which there is invasion or engulfment of one organism by another in a one-dimensional link (Peirce's secondness) without awareness of any external context so that predator becomes prey and prey becomes predator endlessly. Hopelessness is assured by the absence of any awareness of an external source of nurture or replenishment. At the other extreme on this continuum is the commensal relationship involving a separateness and dependency. The commensal relationship is fundamentally triadic, invoking the Peircian category of thirdness. The third in a commensal triad may be thought of as the representative of the world "outside." This link brings awareness of boundaries, negation, separateness, and dependency. But it establishes a bond to resources as well as limitation and establishes meaning, understanding, and perspective. Thirdness is a category which establishes hope for not only a third, but a multi-dimensional world.

The Oedipus complex, if eventually worked through successfully, has an outcome manifested by healthy symbol formation and is an example of commensalism in which *the dependency relationship of the triad supersedes any dyadic relationship within it*. As tragically represented in the Oedipus myth, the murder of Laius and absence of the paternal vertex of the triad leads to a mutually parasitic dyadic experience which has no development, growth or heritage in either time or space. The relationship of Oedipus to Jocasta was one of secondness, regressing from first to null-dimension. It did not exist in true dimensionality and had no legitimate past or future.

Dialog-Analog

Between semiotic object and sign lies the link which is a void of separateness and bond of significant connection between two worlds. In order that true symbol formation and conceptualization develop, a dialog must evolve between these worlds. This dialog will enable the transcendental world of occult and primitive objects revealed by their primitive innate predispositions and preconceptions to impress its intentions and purposes upon the world of representational and dialectical understanding. This dialog is the heart of cultural evolution for it transforms a world of physical events whose signs are analogical into a humanistic world which can and must still cherish the objects of its physical needs but expands through symbolic and conceptual signs a representational spatio-temporal world of culture and creativity.

A model for the struggle toward the enlightenment—which comes with the achievement of culturally coded and therefore culturally communicable and transmissible symbols—is provided by the struggle for enlightenment to be found in the dialogues of Socrates and Plato. In discussing Plato's view of the struggle of emerging thoughts in the Socratic and Platonic dialogues, Friedlander (1958) states, "Allusion is made to the orphic symbol of the mud in which the mind's eye is buried . . . . The imagination is caught in images of hollowness and caves. The caves holding the inmates in chains . . . are a symbol for the world of the senses perceived by the eye . . . . Liberation is from darkness to light . . . . The dialectical journey begins with the liberation . . . . Connected with it is the turning around . . . involving the whole body and soul. The upward movement that follows is common to the paths of love, death, and knowledge. Everywhere, toil and labor accompany this striving." But the path upward is revealed to be painful, and liberation must be compelled upon the slaves. This is clear from the "Parable of the Cave." Referring to the liberator, "If they could lay hands on, and destroy him who attempts to break their chains and to lead them upward, they would kill him." In this striving on the path of understanding, according to Friedlander," . . . the Platonic dialogues mirror these two modes of knowledge in the two movements which lead to the *eidos*: mania and dialectic." The two modes of knowledge to which Fridlander refers are, from the inside (mania and intuition) and from the outside (dialectic and analysis).

It may be illuminating for psychoanalysts to contemplate the opinion of philosophers in the tradition of Plato: that knowledge is guided from within by intuition in the actions subsumed under the term mania. Even more illuminating may be the opinion of that great intuitionist philosopher, Henri Bergson (1913): that, "Intuition is the sympathy by means of which we project ourselves into an object in order to achieve identification with that element in which it is unique and which is inexpressable." Here we have as one side of the dialogue a movement of the mind which I have referred to as preconception and predisposition. This does not involve true symbol formation which would create nameable or describable representations. Rather, the preconceptions are reflected or mirrored back to the subject from the semiotic object mediated only by minimal natural iconic analogic signs that form extremely narrow triads. These splinter-like triads produce, in Peirce's terms, only a degenerate thirdness—hence only a one-dimensional relationship consisting of a dyad in effect, giving an experience of "secondness." It is my belief that this quasi-mirroring process (in which realizations, symbolization, and conceptions have been thwarted and short-circuited) constitutes the phenomena which have given rise to the term projective identification. It is most interesting that Bergson's statement (derived from introspection) anticipates the definition of the phenomenon of projective identification which Melanie Klein (1946) put forward some thirty-five years later from purely clinical observations. Bergson's hypothesis was published originally in 1911, the year in which Freud (1911) published the Schreber case and observed that in paranoids "symptom-formation" could be attributed to the mechanism of projection.

In the psycho-semiotic view, "symptom-formation" may be translated as concrete proto-symbol formation, i.e., one-dimensional identification: a pseudo-conceptualization due to an experience of extremely narrow perspective. This in turn is associated with a primitive semiotic whose sign is so poorly evolved that it is indistinguishable from its primal object which contains primitive preconceptions; it may even be a likeness of some bizarre fragment of a primal object (mirrored back as a bizarre identification) rather than having evolved through bonafide triadic symbol formation. In other words, Bergson's "intuition," Freud's "symptom-formation," and Klein's "projective identification" have essentially the same psycho-semiotic structure: a narrowed triad that functions cyclopically and which is experienced phenomenally in "secondness" (in one-dimension) as a concretistic brute actuality—an ineffable signal, an immediate symptom, or a confused identification.

It is important to make clear the vital phenomenological distinction between the "mirroring" which occurs in the narrowed triads of mania, intuition, and pseudo—or proto—symbol formation from the "reflections" characteristic of conceptual thinking. The mirroring refers to the effect produced prototypically in paranoid identification when hostile predispositions are felt to emanate from even inanimate objects, but scientific interpretation leads to a realization that these hostile signs emanate or are projected out to the object and mirrored back without further significant development. They are falsely identified as belonging to the accused and blamed object which is the recipient of the projection. On the other hand, true reflective thinking occurs as a critique of the understanding and is the manifestation of pure reason. It occurs when the empirical self and the empirical object of scrutiny are observed and their relationship judged by the (un-manifest) self of pure apperception (the I-in-itself) which acts as "third" in this triadic object-relation. The basic distinction consists in the fate of the preconception.

In symbol formation, the preconception may be said to be projected into the object as a means of drawing attention to the object so that the perceptual and conceptual apparatus will be enabled to locate, symbolize, and conceptualize a multi-dimensional and representational object which is differentiated and recognized by the subject as separate and objective, or integrated by the subject as "thought." Proper identification is subject to "reflection" by the subject aided by the perspective provided by his triadic relationship to object and sign. In the case of the various forms of pseudo-symbol formation, the preconception is concretely merged with the object without permitting a separate symbolic object to emerge and evolve. The subject's preconceptions tend to return directly and concretely back to the subject without differentiation or symbolic elaboration by perspective and thirdness. This is an object relation which is predominantly experienced one-dimensionally. It is potentially fraught with hallucinosis and repetition.

If one reviews the rather astounding complexity of the third branch of the semiotic, that of the symbol-former whose labors may be represented by his aspects called, after Kant, the "I KNOW," "I WILL," "I SEE," "I THINK," and the great unmanifest creator "I AM"; it will be recalled that all these aspects of subjectivism are required to vitalize and "subjectify" the thingness presumed to lie outside and separate from the subject so that "things" may be "identified" and "objectified."

Understanding of an object-relation develops as the signs of the experience multiply and evolve. This can be represented by the increasing space-time interval in the link joining sign to object. Fullness of understanding comes with the proliferation and integration of multiple signs forged together in the relation between object and sign. Complementary signs and symbols accumulate from every conceivable perspective. The object-relation is understood through the common symbolic code by the entire community of thinkers and considered to be "the truth" as a matter of "common sense." These signs may include historical context as well, and since every conceptualization points from past to future, not only space but time is involved in the full symbolic integration accompanied by the analogical signs of sensibility and individuality.

The World of Concrete Phantasy

To comprehend progressively how the meaning link between object and sign fills and expands to create a symbol pregnant with meaning is no simple matter. *Meaning begins with analogical and individualistic signs which establish the roots of identification*. To understand how these proto-symbols then are elaborated to become filled with the codes of a cultural heritage, it is necessary that we re-examine the dialogue between "mania" and "dialectic."

It is insufficient to remain confined to a triadic model in which the mania of innate predispositions influence and predispose an object. In this way it may serve as the preconception for a "vicarious" experience with the actuality of an "external world" (whose "reality" and "truth" are settled dialectically). *The unlimited potential of this creative symbolic link is made possible by the ability of the symbol-former to absorb and integrate the accretions of both natural and cultural signs and to use these conceptualizations as preconceptions to construct the objects of the ensuing triad in the evolving dialogue of triadic thought*. In the next ensuing thought this increasingly complex preconception enters the symbolic schema. The complex linking of one triad with another occurs in this way and reveals the dialogue opening out to the world of dimensionality. It is the product of the labor of the symbol-former. He effects the transformation by a continual metamorphosis of interpretant into ensuing preconception, creating a spiral of triads "unfolding" as the dialogue proceeds in some "direction" in space-time. This same phenomenon has been described, I believe, as the "hermeneutic spiral" (Steele, 1979).

In distinction to the unfolding of sophisticated spirals of thirdness, an experience may be signified only by some inexpressible feeling. The sign of such an experience may only be manifest in some physical action, perhaps only inside a primitive autonomic or kinesthetic system. However, I would take as an irreducible principle that a subjective experience must be manifested by some sign of *embodiment*, otherwise the experience could not be said to be actual. This is true even if the embodiment is only known by the signs of its denial in the form of some symptom such as depersonalization or alexithymia. This principle is of great importance in that it establishes the phenomenological necessity that an experience, to have any actuality or even potential quality, must be *contained* or *embodied*. To say that a thought is simply "projected" is to propose an object-relation involving only one object hence entirely hidden in the null-dimension. Let me hasten to add that "projection," as referred to by Freud (1911) and by many others (Green, 1980), as a general and normal imaginative phenomenon, is a symbolic experience which is readily understood to be occurring in representational space-time, often poetic or metaphoric, but in its phenomenal category of thirdness. It is very different from the so-called "projection" of paranoia—a concept as outmoded as that of the "unembodied wish" of pre-object-relations theory.

Emerging into view in recent years from behind an increasingly wide panorama of "symptom formation" is a form of "thinking" which does not lend proper understanding to experience. It is not helpful to confuse it with or compare it to "primary process." In these states of mind the link of symbolization is attacked and disrupted; the symbol-former is unable to maintain a triadic, commensal relationship with sign and object. A meaning-structure (semiotic) like any other object in the world can only be determined to exist by virtue of a sign or signs which point to it or at least signal its existence. Nevertheless psychoanalytic theory postulates the existence of a state of mind which transcends the need for signs. Such a belief amounts to a transcendentalism which denies separateness, embracing de-differentiation and mysticism. This state of mind disregards the scientific fact, and the mathematical proof of it by Gödel in 1931, which states that the truth of a proposition can only be validated from a vertex outside its own system. Matte Blanco (1975) demonstrated a logical basis for presuming the existence of such a transcendental state of mind by means of symbolic logic. He found the basis for a "merely potential logos" existing as "the symmetrical unconscious." He pointed out that such a structure must exist in the null-dimension. The latter can be conceived as a state of collapse by implosion or of disintegration by explosive expansion. In either case it becomes structureless, totally boundaryless, and theoretically undiscoverable, lacking any sign of existence. Peirce's exposition of the semiotic described the triad as an equilateral triangle, strongly implying symmetricality. But he also recognized "degenerate" states of thirdness, introducing the idea of asymmetry. Yet he was unable to formalize his "methodeutic" to the point where semiotic triads could be seen to require sufficient asymmetry for thoughts to follow some more or less definite direction in their evolution to finally "come to the point."

Matte Blanco (1975) reproached the Kleinian school for defining a paranoid-schizoid developmental position associated with internal and external objects which, they claimed, existed in an unconscious phantasy-world dominated by omnipotence of thought in a boundaryless world devoid of past and future, without dimensionality—a world occupied by confused and undifferentiated objects. In short, it is Matte Blanco's symmetrical unconscious world in which the idea of internal and external objects could not occur. The criticism has merit since Kleinians appear to have put themselves in the same position occupied by Kant when he inferred from the concept of *phenomenon* that its negation, *non-phenomenon* (noumenon, thing-in-itself), must also exist. But Kant soon found himself predicating a considerable philosophical system on a non-phenomenon whose existence he could only hypothesize. The semiotic triadic structure permits a more affirmative demonstration of the problem.

One must postulate a world model based on the Peircean triad. The triangular line forming the triadic model constitutes the boundary of the representational world of space-time intervals and full dimensionality. Outside the triadic boundary line it is postulated that the symmetrical phantasy-world exists. No signs or representations could be known in that world since it is based on transcendental belief which denies even the minimal separation which must exist for symbolization or even the barest signification which requires a linking relationship between object and sign. The phantasy-world outside the boundary must be hypothesized to consist, in Bion's (1963) terms, of undifferentiated beta elements.

However, based on clinical phenomena such as paranoid identifications and on Peirce's concept of "perceptual judgment," it is possible to suggest that there is a boundary domain consisting of extremely asymmetrical, narrow, and at times fragmentary triads. The primal objects in these scarcely differentiated structures must exist at or outside the boundary in concrete (unconscious) phantasy, but are linked *across the boundary line* to signs located within the representational space-time world. The most rudimentary signs are physicalistic, scarcely differentiated from the primal objects they represent. The boundary domain triads are so narrow that they are experienced as one-dimensional, linear dyads, lacking in perspective and in various ways deficient in the criteria for true symbol formation. At the same time these boundary phenomena furnish the evidence which allows us to bridge the caesural gap between the concrete phantasy-world and the spatio–temporal world of achievement. The boundary domain can be seen as a developmental continuum as well as a gap.

Emerging into full space-time dimensionality from the one-dimensionality of the boundary line are the transitional oneiric and ludic phenomena characterized by iconic and indexical signs, but they are also characterized by the emergence of symbolism. Symbol formation is marked by the inhibitory constraints imposed on phantasy by the demands of truthful space-time representation and structural rules of proper conceptualization. The penalty to be paid for multi-dimensionality and perspective is the increasing "scientific" doubt which accompanies one's experience—which in the absence of these constraints associated with symbol formation would have the full reign of unchecked delusional certainty. Outside the boundary line no definite horizon of the boundary domain can be clearly demarcated. However, as signs become more concretely physical and rudimentary, the narrow triads are subjected to increasing fragmentation, splintering, and disintegration. Movement in this direction may be felt "concretely" as a sinking into the dark domain of the null-dimension characterized appropriately by Bion (1962) in view of the associated attack on communication and expression as "nameless dread."

The use of the term "boundary line" is not meant to refer to the recently popularized clinical borderline syndrome; however the relationship between what is described here and that syndrome may well be called into question. The signs characteristic of this concrete boundary world are not symbols, properly speaking. They do not represent absent or lost objects since in this world separateness, absence, loss, past, future, and outside do not truly exist. Here the physicalistic manipulospatial actions are premonitory to dreaming and thinking. Visual and auditory signs may not yet be integrated to build up or round out representational dimensionality, as pointed out by Paul and Carson (1980). The concrete world of phantasy could be said to be that into which meaning and understanding are to be perfused by symbol formation as the work of relinquishing the primal object-world is undertaken. Exploration across the boundary into the spatio-temporal world progressively evolves through dreaming, playing, and thinking the experiences which otherwise are merely felt concretely as "things" to be manipulated "ego-centrically" and one-dimensionally. It is evident that the boundary structures are open to the resources of the primal object-world which must continue to function as a psychic well-spring, from which the elements and purposes of dreaming, thinking, and personality development may emerge in the triadic spatio-temporal domain. This exploration is not unimpeded by the truths of the material and natural world which impose hardships and frustrations on experience. It is in this context that Bion saw the paranoid-schizoid position and its physicalistic phenomena as developmental and basically constructive in function (Bion, 1965).

But just as dreaming, playing, and thinking capitalize on concrete phantasy, so may the reverse, regressive situation develop and prevail. For in the interest of disavowing and escaping from dependency on the symbolic object world of representational but separate reality, and in order to regain the transcendental paradise of the primal world, the subject may capitalize on already acquired conceptual and symbolic experience and the mimicry so natural in the boundary line world of analogical iconic signs. Here, verbal symbols may be employed concretely as substitutes or symbolic equations (Segal, 1957) for primal objects. An autistically devised pseudo-code of analogical significance may be surreptitiously substituted for or imposed upon the culturally dictated code of abstract symbols. Such a system may involve material objects used as a surreptitious means of clinging to primal (autistic) objects in concrete phantasy while being passed off as "transitional objects" as delineated by Tustin (1980).

In schizophrenia and certain perverse personality disorders, analysis may reveal that a highly bizarre and distorted concrete phantasy world has evolved into the simulacrum of a spatiotemporal world of sophisticated conceptualizations. Such highly evolved frauds are perpetrated to deny dependency on genuine symbolization and valuable symbolic objects in the material and cultural worlds and often employ intimidation and violence in the attempt to carry off the deception by coercing objects in the symbolic world to become dependent upon the psychotic personality. When human beings cannot be perverted to collude with the phantasy of dependency upon the psychotic subject, such subjects may turn to inhuman, perhaps chemical, objects with which this perversion of dependency can be played out. The problematic and essentially ambiguous possibilities which reside in that link of meaning between symbol and object can be illuminated more clearly by use of clinical material which provides a graphic model of the theoretical possibilities available in symbol formation.

A Clinical Case Example

The patient is a thirty year old female whose personality is characterized by extreme gentleness and profound disavowal of aggressive feelings. She has a history of recurring suicidal depressions associated with relationships marked by extreme polarization of intense idealization and subsequent crushing disappointment. At first, her sessions with me tended to correspond to this pattern, being characterized by unbounded enthusiasm followed, often within the same session, by very abrupt withdrawal and loss of contact which she was able later to describe as sinking helplessly into dark confusion followed by the sly emergence of a cold-blooded, suicidal and secretive attitude. But in many sessions it was clear that I, in the transference, had abruptly become the terrifying murderer with whom further contact was impossible. Only gradually would this surreptitious and hostile opposition subside. Occasionally, an extra session was necessary to provide opportunity for the patient to regain sufficient containment and confidence to avoid an impending catastrophe.

Lately, however, the situation improved, and the patient made more active efforts not to slip into the terrifying phantasies which so concretely removed her from contact with me. In a mid-week session, she was able to relate an experience that had recently occurred on two different occasions. In both she had suddenly been confronted by actions which she interpreted as sexual provocations which aroused a sense of betrayal and horror accompanied by an even more terrifying feeling of her mind "going faster and faster" until there was a sudden explosive feeling followed by an overpowering heaviness, then total confusion and even disorientation, all of which gradually subsided within a few hours. On both occasions her companions noticed nothing beyond her apparent detachment. In the same session in which these episodes were related to me she recalled with great satisfaction a lecture in her physics class concerning a remarkable space-time diagram which she tried to describe to me and then brought with her to the next session.

In the ensuing session, she was able to make a significant connection between her own recent dissociative experiences and the space-time diagram (Figure 1). This space-time diagram which she presented me is essentially in keeping with modern relativity theory (Weidner, 1980). The boundary of the

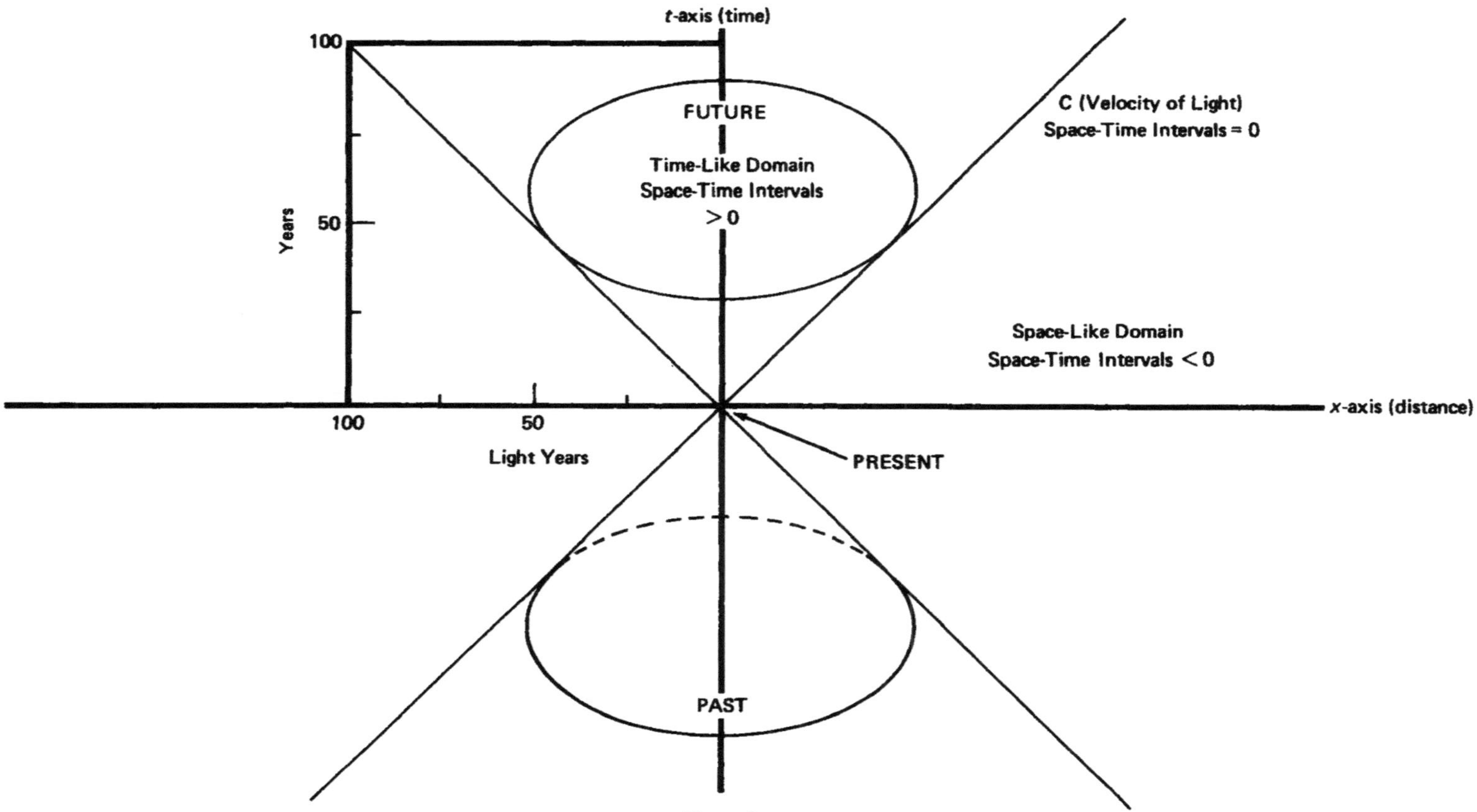
t-axis (time)
100
50
Years
FUTURE
Time-Like Domain
Space-Time Intervals
> 0
C (Velocity of Light)
Space-Time Intervals = 0
Space-Like Domain
Space-Time Intervals < 0
x-axis (distance)
100
50
Light Years
PRESENT
PAST

Figure 1

space-time cone shown in Figure 1 is a consequence of the limitation imposed on space-time dimensionality by the velocity of light, "C," Einstein's constant. The slope of the boundary of the cones determined by "C," the velocity of light, establishes the "time-like" domain of past and future for an observer in the present, located at the vertex linking experiences in the past to those in the future. The velocity of light may be interpreted as the maximum velocity which a signal (an elementary sign) can attain to point out an event or object to an observer in the present time. If this were not so, then experiences of objects and events would be unbounded and unlimited by time and space. However, this post-Galilean space-time diagram clearly differentiates the "time-like" domain of dimensionality within which an observer in the present can "make contact" with events and objects without transcending the velocity of light. This he does by means of a system of signs which are capable of making the necessary connections. Outside the boundary of the cone of the "time-like" domain and beyond the reach of signals, signs, and symbol formation lies the "space-like" domain. It is beyond experiencable events and objects for an observer in the present time vertex. This domain appears to correspond to the world of concrete phantasy and transcendence in contrast to the temporo-spatial world of representational thinking.

From the clinical material cited, it is clear that my patient associated her recent personal catastrophic experiences with accelerations of thoughts and subsequent crashing through the boundary and out of contact. These associations emerged from her presentation for analysis of the space-time diagram.

Figure 2 is a construction based on the space-time diagram of Figure 1. In this diagram the boundary of the cone of representational dimensionality is taken to correspond to the boundary of the psycho-semiotic triad. The observer in the present is taken to represent the symbol-former, (I), at the subjective vertex. An event or object, (O), on or outside the boundary line is subject to the crushing velocity which prevents signs or signals from reaching the symbol-former, (I). It is only when the boundary object, (O), is represented by a second object, (S), which exists well inside the boundary of the space-time domain where signal velocity is much reduced, that meaningful contact through symbol formation can be established. The notation, (K) designating this domain follows the transformational notation used by Bion (1967) for the domain of knowledge in contrast to (-K) which he used to designate the negation of K, a domain which is not simply equivalent to the domain of concrete phantasy, as I shall try to demonstrate presently. In further development of the idea of the boundary phenomenon, Figure 2 also contains an object, S′, scarcely inside the boundary and creating a narrow triad with (O) and (I). There is also an object, S″, which appears outside the boundary to make a (perverse) triad in the domain of (-K) which is falsely claimed to be a symbolic object such as (S) located in the representational space-time cone.

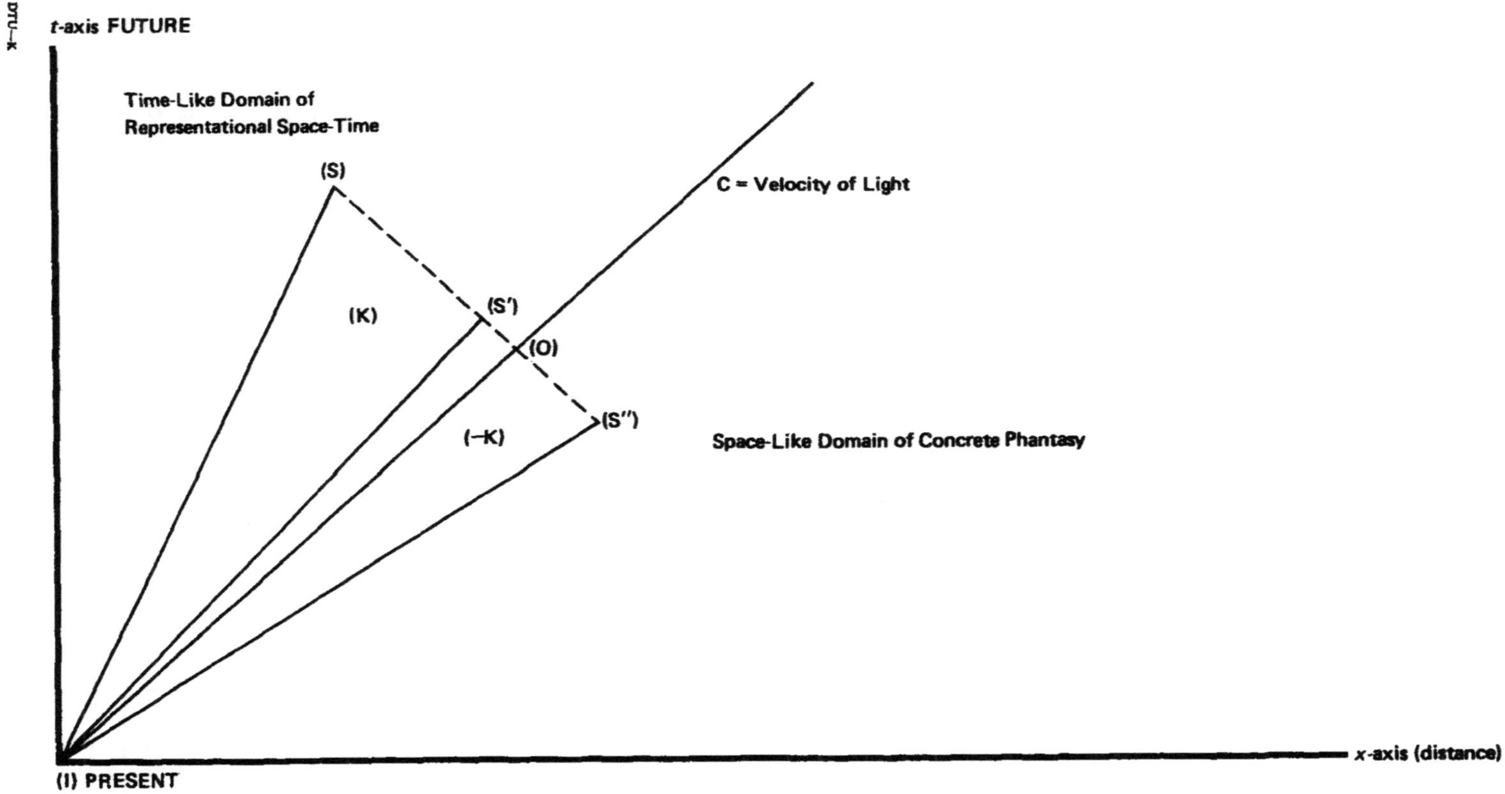
t-axis FUTURE
Time-Like Domain of
Representational Space-Time
(S)
C = Velocity of Light
(K)
(S')
(O)
(S'')
(−K)
Space-Like Domain of Concrete Phantasy
x-axis (distance)
(I) PRESENT

Figure 2

My patient's enthusiasm regarding her discovery of the space-time diagram derived from her realization that her terrifying experiences had a significant basis and could be interpreted and "understood": that as her thoughts began to accelerate, culminating in an explosive sense of confusion and "crushing weight" followed by a period of "absence," she must have been, according to her own account, "going too fast to control my own thoughts and feelings, so I must then have struck the boundary and crashed through!" For this patient the concrete domain was dominated by hostile, cruel, and terrifying thoughts felt by her to be alien objects which had been totally disowned and of which she consequently has no conscious experience except as their passive victim. The incompatibility resulting from this disavowal was revealed by her likening the difficulty when it was interpreted to the problem of "the matter-antimatter split." The appearance of very exciting, aggressively seductive thoughts associated inevitably by her with the threat of abandonment or betrayal resulted in a marked acceleration and explosive evacuation through the space-time boundary of these feared and hated iconic symbols and identifications. There was a dawning realization that earlier she had caused these "hostile objects" to accelerate through the boundary and slip out of contact, only to realize later the consequences: that once out of contact with dimensional reality and through the boundary these "hostile objects" had taken over and caused her to become identified slyly as a different personality ("part of an antimatter world") in which she became a cold-blooded, would-be murderer of the identity and person which existed in her "ordinary" space-time world. The "explosions" of more recent events indicated the development of active, even aggressive, resistance to easy slippage into the "(-K)" state of mind in which perverse concrete phantasy attempted to pass itself off glibly and superficially as genuine creative thinking while smugly and sadistically rationalizing and plotting murderous (self) destruction.

Putting aside the question of (-K) structures for the moment, let us reexamine the constructive evolution of symbolic objects from (S') to (S) as revealed in Figure 2. This evolution corresponds to the energy shift and decrease of velocity characteristic of the shift from the peremptory urgings of the primitive drives to the development of the so-called neutralization barrier resulting from the synthetic and inhibitory function of the ego. However, it will be noted that when these functions are depicted as evolving from narrow boundary triads to those of fuller symbol formation, no sharp dichotomy is observed to describe a movement from a primary to a secondary process.

The boundary structures, (S'), of Figure 2 are of particular interest. The narrow triads might be called proto-symbolic since structurally and developmentally they differ from symbols primarily in that their sign is analogical, physicalistic, and poorly differentiated from the object, although the sign lies inside the boundary enclosing the space-time world while its object remains outside this representational world. Whatever the particular vicissitudes accounting for their appearance, these boundary triads are structurally incapable of true conceptualization which requires fuller symbol formation. The boundary structures (S') are laden with preconceptions and lack sufficient thirdness to permit mature reflection and self-criticism. Self-criticism becomes possible when sufficient openness of the triad permits the subject to submit his thinking and creative theories to the deductive or inductive analysis in which concepts are traced back to their referent (denotatum). The two functions, hypothesis formation and formal deductive analysis, constitute the operation of a "hypothetico-deductive system." No such "insights" occur in the "narrow-minded" boundary structures. Such a system can only exist when the semiotic object has already been abstracted from its roots in concrete phantasy by participation in the hermeneutic spiral. In the domain of boundary structures true conceptualization and critical analysis do not legitimately occur. The phenomena that do occur can be understood by describing the particular forms these boundary triads may take. As pointed out earlier (Buchler, 1955), Peirce, in a discussion of the irreducible nature of the triad, pointed out that the simplest perception must be in fact mediated by a semiotic structure *if* that perception is *known* beyond the instant of its occurrence. He argued that although a simple percept may be experienced as if it were immediate (not mediated) it must involve a perceptual judgment which establishes a triadic structure involving the subject who links and judges the experience. In such a primitive triad judgment by the weak "third" does not necessarily empower him to "criticize" the experience. I believe the structure of percepts and perceptual judgments constitutes a boundary triad experienced dyadically and, although lacking perspective, is precisely the kind of experience which can be integrated with other signs to establish a growing base for true symbol formation and conceptualization when conditions are auspicious. In this case the judgment involved in the perception enables the subject to learn from experience.

Intuition is a second form of boundary structure which is undoubtedly universal in human experience, but widely devalued, discounted or discredited along with its proponents, by hard-nosed empiricists. Peirce (Buchler, 1955) counted intuition among those notions to which man is denied access simply because of his incapacity to experience or understand anything without the mediation of signs. His argument is made against the common belief that man may be capable of direct, unmediated, and unstructured knowing. But intuition as defined and structured by Bergson, as pointed out earlier, with its history traceable at least to Plato, corresponds to the notion of primitive preconceptions and predispositions. These arrive in the boundary structure from the domain of unconscious phantasy. That these belong to the boundary domain is attested to by the familiar fact of creative conceptualizations in many fields that began with the unexpected impact of inchoate "feeling" experiences which can be understood as simple signs of a motivating preconception in unconscious phantasy. These feelings in intuitive structures constitute a physicalistic sign which appears in the dimensional world inside the boundary but so close to the boundary line as to be hardly differentiated from its object which, though remaining in the concrete domain, is linked to its sign across the boundary line. Although the term, intuition, generally is reserved to describe a vague but valuable experience, indicative of a "creative gift," only a relatively small modification of usage separates it from the ineffable feelings which are associated with states of mind such as may occur in paranoia of phobia. In these states, crushing or splitting attacks may produce disintegration of sophisticated multi-dimensional conceptual structures. The disintegrated triads may include narrow boundary structures manifesting, among other things, the iconic signs which are experienced as intuitive knowledge, usually about terrifying but indescribable events. This use of the term, intuition, is meant to emphasize the common structural base shared by a variety of epiphenomena.

Another example, familiar to psychiatric residents as the Von Domarus Principle is the peculiar reasoning employed by schizophrenic personalities. As an attempt to unravel the mystery, a theory of "logic of predicates" states that the schizophrenic personality reasons by means of an invalid syllogism in which major and minor premises are connected by identical predicates. Thus, if I am Mary and the mother of God is Mary, then I must be the mother of God. This solution to schizophrenic thinking is paid scant attention since it rarely fits and never enlightens. First, schizophrenics, like the rest of us, are usually generating hypotheses, not making deductions (syllogisms). His hypotheses may sound like "profound" deductions when he speaks out of the delusional certainty that characterizes the narrow boundary triads which are, in effect, one-dimensional, lacking the perspective of thirdness. His hypotheses and the interpretations of his therapist may be experienced as concrete and possibly dangerous objects since, for him, the most abstract symbol or concept exists only in the brute reality of a one-dimensional world. When he is exhibiting this state of mind, symbols are "things" used to pursue his desires and manipulate his world. A patient named Michael angrily told me never to refer to him as Saint Michael—because saying "Saint" is the same as saying "say ain't." Therefore, if I called him Saint Michael I was really (but secretly) saying he ain't Saint Michael! In the narrowed boundary triads, symbols and concepts are simply substitutes for primal objects concretely equated with them in order to act out the physicalistic maneuvers and manipulations of the concrete phantasy world. We all theorize by a "logic of predicates", but the theorizing of the schizophrenic is a pretense used to draw us into his own concrete phantasies because of his refusal to leave them behind. The chain of predications in creative thinking unfolds into an open-ended spiral of evolving concepts which bear a symbolic value connecting them to previous objects (including primal ones) but also provide increasing value as part of the multi-dimensional world of achievement.

Despite the need to see the one-dimensional boundary triads behind percepts, intuition, the "logic of predicates," and the symbolic equation (Segal, 1957), it is necessary to appreciate that personality development requires a continuous creative flow of phantasy across the space-time boundary. It is when the personality does not give up clinging to primal objects in the boundary structures that thinking loses or does not acquire the advantages of commensal relationship with the symbolic and conceptual world. The mode of thinking which occurs in the boundary structures is common to all of us at times; it is sought as a refuge from ambiguity. The term projective identification introduced by Melanie Klein (1946) has become a source of contention partly because it has become a short-hand definition for the indefinitely wide gamut of boundary line triads characterized by concrete one-dimensionality, and the manipulo-spatial maneuvers that lead to confusions in which a wide variety of mis-identifications, misconceptions, and pseudo-symbol formation result often with disastrous effect on understanding. Among the peculiar phenomena typical of the one-dimensional boundary line experience is the delusional certainty associated with its absence of perspective. This results from the lack of separation of (S') from (O).

The collapse of the meaning-link between sign and object immediately attacks the meaning of the relationship between (I) and (O) as well since the lack of perspective threatens a further collapse into the null-dimension, there being no means of understanding the experience when the experiencer is inside the experience or fused with it without any means of observing or representing it. The unbearable threat of nullity may lead to repair of the structure, but it may lead also to the triad (Figure 2) designated by (S"). This is a model of a psychotic structure.

When the narrow triad (S') is on the boundary line of the space-time cone and constructive identification, compatible with space-time experience and growth is occurring, concrete phantasy can be considered as achievement-oriented phantasy which provides the raw elements for emerging dreams and conceptualizations. But there are many great hazards in the path of such peaceful fulfillment of one's phantasies and dreams, and frequent opportunity for repeated *dis-illusionment*. This inevitably produces a considerable period of postponement in the one-dimensional boundary line which Melanie Klein described as the paranoid-schizoid position. Beneath the ongoing dreaming, symbol formation and conceptualization there must also be an ongoing production of concrete phantasy by means of which the unknowable noumena are transmuted progressively into dimensional objects and their representations and abstractions, to be given value and eventually adjudged as to their truth. Otherwise, creativity and discovery could not continue.

Another significant contribution of Bion (1959) involves the tragic circumstance which turns postponement of symbol formation into total disavowal, hatred of the truth, and a turning away from space-time experience to the realm of what Bion calls (-K). This contribution of Bion to the Kleinian concept of projective identification is his notion that the paranoid-schizoid position and projective identification may not only represent a developmental phase but may instead be directed arrogantly against the development of commensal dependency. The narrow triad of (S") in figure two reveals the semiotic sign to be lodged outside true space-time intervals, in the space-like realm of concrete phantasy. This will be seen to be a perverse relationship since each semiotic cycle demolishes and disintegrates more of the primal object world hurling the fragments away from the boundary line of space-time reality and deeper into the (-K) realm thereby progressively stripping their connection with common sense truth of space-time dimensionality. The perverse dynamics as revealed by this model lead to the regressive attack on the meaning link and the equally regressive denudation of the representational world of imagination. Instead, the internal world of concrete phantasy is filled with destructive lies and becomes more and more committed to delusion. As pointed out earlier, this psychotic subject must rely on seduction, covert intimidation, or overt hostility since he is in truth totally dependent for survival on a world which he disavows or which he claims is dependent on him.

Conclusion

The attempt to construct a psycho-semiotic schema produces a structure which is characterized by certain features which together could be considered the phenomenal basis of symbol formation. The structure of the psycho-semiotic is that of a hypothesis. The hypothetical consists of an antecedent portion which is a particular experience; a *consequent* portion which consists of a *meaning* which is more general and not entirely contained in the antecedent; and a connecting *sign* which creates and synthesizes meaning and significance but is nevertheless a sign or symbol of the denoted antecedent as well as the vehicle for the creation of the connoted consequent. The creative work involved in forming the psycho-semiotic is a product of synthetic mental function (symbol formation) involving the expenditure of mental energy. It also might be called "creative thinking." This must be distinguished from analytic or deductive thinking which is computational, formal, must obey the rules of logical necessity (excluded middle, identity, contradiction), and rearranges rather than creates meaning from experience. The analytic function tests hypotheses, but only formally, by deducing whether a connoted consequent refers back to the antecedent term which it claims as its denoted referent. This formal test does not investigate the phenomenal basis of the meaning given to the actual experience of particular objects. This can only be accomplished by the "mental experimentation" which Peirce (Buchler, 1955) called "abstractive observation" by which is implied symbol formation by means of the semiotic, the formation of hypotheses.

The confusion that still surrounds the differentiation of synthetic from analytic thinking continues to lead to stifling misconceptions and misunderstandings such as those of Meissner (1980) who wishes to deny the connection between projective identification, symbolic equation, and the "Von Domarus Principle" because they are not related by logical necessity. In his yearning for formal validity, he overlooks that these phenomena may be related, not deductively or by logical necessity, but related because they are all derived from the same phenomenal flaw in symbol formation. Primitive identification, symptom-formation of paranoia, symbolic equation, and the logic of predicates, all are derived concretely by analogical (iconic) signs, (S'), from the antecedent object at the boundary line rather than through the understanding properly created in the perspectives of representational space-time by true symbol formation.

The analysis of psycho-semiotic structure may provide a basis for renewed investigation of so-called "reality-testing." Peirce's pragmatic logic establishes a basis for testing which demands more than formal deductive validations. The pragmatic logic demands a structure by means of which the actuality of experience through concrete phantasy is truly and properly linked by symbol formation to conceptualization or identification. This should properly be called "truth testing" rather than "reality-testing" since the soundness of the symbolic structure is a matter of consistency with cultural convention on an internal basis of con-sensual or common-sense consistency (Bion, 1963). This is related to truth in the pragmatic sense by which is meant a belief consistent with the beliefs of the community of so-called scientific thinkers; those qualified to doubt. This criterion allows for the emergence of creative departures from the previously accepted hypothetical consequents (interpretants). This concept of truth contrasts greatly with the pragmatic concept of the real. In a pragmatic sense, that which is brute, actual, and directly experienced, is the most real. In this sense a delusion is most highly qualified to be defined as "real" for its realness is not challenged by other possible consequents given in the understanding provided by other perspectives in the representational space-time of true symbol formation.

Another aspect of the psycho-semiotic is its structural analysis of the essential indeterminacy and ambiguity of meaningful experience. The foundation of ambiguity is the contribution of both innate preconception issuing from the "inside" and the empirical contribution entering the structure of meaning from the "outside" through the sensory apparatus. Both contributions are required for the creation of a meaningful and truth-bearing world. From this basic situation arise many other ambiguities. One of these is the ambiguous relationship which develops between the "instinctual drives" (id) and those motivations of ritual and taboo (superego). By means of the transformational cycles of the psycho-semiotic it is possible to visualize how each symbolization cycle integrates the product of preconception and predisposition with the products of perception by means of judgment, into conceptualization. Thus, the inside and the outside are brought together in representational space-time where the combined product of symbol formation is employed as successively more sophisticated preconceptions for succeeding cycles in the evolving hermeneutic spiral. In the event that the subject refuses to subject preconceptions to the modifications of symbol formation, persistent narrow boundary triads in effect "mirror back" distorted preconceptions which are passed off as symbols, but which would be better designated as some variety of projective identification. This difficult and progressively more complex integration is made possible by the ambiguous character of the symbol-forming subject who must not only be, in part, an empirical self experiencing an object, but also must be the I-in-itself creating, regulating, and observing the relationship which is the meaning link and foundation of "truth" in symbol formation and reason. Like Emily Dickinson's metaphor of an exasperated Diogenes, the ambiguous symbol-forming "I" must exclaim,

"I'm out with lanterns,
Looking for myself."

The resistance to truth is manifested by the attempt to destroy ambiguity by destructive attacks on the link of meaning between symbol and object. With the destruction of this link, the triad narrows down, and representational space-time is lost. In intact triads, the "thingness" of the object world is more and more symbolized, and the resultant representations more and more enter the internal space-time world as aspects of self known as "thoughts." This progressive integration creates more and more ambiguity and uncertainty as to whether a symbol is to be regarded as an object, a thought, or as an aspect of self; however, the presence of ambiguity and doubt always leaves room for further inquiry and understanding. This integration of the self and object world must be contrasted with the confusion of self and object which occurs when truth is attacked and the "thingness" of objects is confused with concretistic preconceptions resulting in the pseudo-conceptions of chimerical conglomerations of perceptions with primitive affections and predispositions. This attack on truth is aptly described by Emerson's *Sphinx* as seen by that wise old inquisitor as she demanded the truth, exposing the lie of projective identification to Oedipus, the flawed symbol-former, who had delusionally created her from his own preconceptions.

"The old Sphinx bit her thick lip—
Said, 'Who taught thee me to name?'
I am thy spirit, yoke-fellow,
Of thine eye I am eye beam.

"Thou art the unanswered question;
Could'st see thy proper eye,
Always it asketh, asketh;
And each answer is a lie."

References

Arnheim, R. (1954). *Art and Visual Perception, a Psychology of the Creative Eye*. Berkeley: University of California Press.

Barthes, R. (1967). *Elements of Semiology*, trans. A. Lavers & C. Smith. London: Cape.

Bergson, H. (1913). *An Introduction to Metaphysics*, trans. T.E. Hude. London: Allen Lane.

Berlin, I. (1979). *Against the Current: Essays in the History of Ideas*. New York: Viking Press.

Bion, W. (1959). Attacks on linking. IN: *Second Thoughts*. New York: Jason Aronson, 1967, pp. 93-109.

—— (1962). *Learning From Experience*. New York: Basic Books.

—— (1963). *Elements of Psycho-Analysis*. New York: Basic Books.

—— (1965). *Transformations*. New York: Basic Books.

—— (1967). *Second Thoughts*. (London: William Heinemann.

—— (1970). *Attention and Interpretation*. London: Tavistock Publications.

Buchler, J. (1955). *Philosophical Writings of Peirce*. New York: Dover.

Cassirer, E. (1957). *The Philosophy of Symbolic Forms*, Vol. III. New Haven: Yale University Press.

Chomsky, N. (1968). *Language and Mind*. New York: Harcourt Brace Jovanovich, Inc.

Edelson, M. (1975). *Language and Interpretation in Psychoanalysis*. New Haven: Yale University Press.

Freud, S. (1896). Further remarks on the neuro-psychoses of defence. Footnote, p. 168. *S.E.*, 3. London: Hogarth Press, 1962.

—— (1911). Psychoanalytic notes on an autobiographical account of a case of paranoia (dementia paranoides). *S.E.* 12 1-64. London: Hogarth Press, 1958.

Friedlander, P. (1958). *Plato, Vol. I, An Introduction*, trans. Hans. Meyerhoff. Princeton: Bollinger.

Green, A. (1980). Negation and contradiction. This volume.

Jones, E. (1916). The theory of symbolism. IN: *Papers on Psychoanalysis*. London: Bailliere, Tindall & Cox, 1920, pp. 87-144.

Kant, E. (1949). *The Philosophy of Kant*, ed. Carl J. Friedrich. New York: Modern Library.

—— (1958). *Critique of Pure Reason*. trans. J.M.D.Meikeljohn. New York: Modern Library.

Kaplan, A. (1961). *The New World of Philosophy*. New York: Random House.

Klein, M. (1930). On the importance of symbol formation in the development of the ego. IN: *Contributions to Psycho-Analysis, 1921-1945*. London: Hogarth Press, 1948, pp. 236-250.

—— (1946). Notes on some schizoid mechanisms. IN: *Developments in Psycho-Analysis*, ed. Joan Riviere. London: Hogarth Press, 1952, pp. 282-320.

Korner, S. (1955). *Kant*. Baltimore: Penguin.

Kuhn, T. (1962). *The Structure of Scientific Revolutions*. Chicago: University of Chicago Press.

Lacan, J. (1968).Lacan and the discourse of the other. IN: *The Language of the Self*, trans. A. Wilden. Baltimore: Johns Hopkins Press, pp. 160-273.

Langer, S. (1957). *Problems of Art*. New York: Scribners.

Levi-Strauss, C. (1968). *Structural Anthropology*. London: Allen Lane.

Matte Blanco, I. (1975). *The Unconscious as Infinite Sets*. London: Duckworth.

Meissner, W. (1980). A note on projective identification. *J. Am. Psa. Assn.* 28, 43-67.

Meltzer, D. (1978). *The Kleinian Development*. Perthshire: Clunie Press.

Moore, E. & Robin, R. (1964). *Studies in the Philosophy of Charles Sanders Peirce*. Amherst: The University of Massachusetts Press.

Morris, C. (1938). *Foundations of the Theory of Signs*. Chicago: University of Chicago Press.

Paul, M. & Carson, I. (1980). A contribution to the study of dimension. *Int. Rev. Psycho-Anal.* 7, 101-112.

Piaget, J. (1970). *Structuralism*. New York: Harper & Row.

Popper, K.R. (1959). *The Logic of Scientific Discovery*. London: Duckworth.

Reichenbach, H. (1951). *The Rise of Scientific Philosophy*. Berkeley: University of California Press.

Rosen, J. (1969). Sign phenomena and their relationship to unconscious meaning. *Int. J. Psycho-Anal.* 50, 197-207.

Saussure, F., De. (1915). *Course in General Linguistics*. New York: Philosophical Library, 1959.

Schopenhauer, A. (1956). *Selections*. De Witt H. Parker (ed.). New York: Scribner.

Sebeok, T.A. (1978) (ed.) *A Perfusion of Signs*. Bloomington: University of Indiana Press.

Segal, H. (1957). Notes on symbol formation. *Int. J. Psycho-Anal.* 38, 391-397.

Steele, R. (1979). Psychoanalysis and hermeneutics. *Int. Rev. Psycho-Anal.* 6, 389-411.

Tinbergen, N. (1951). *The Study of Instinct*. Oxford: Clarendon Press.

Tustin, F. (1980). Autistic objects. *Int. Rev. Psycho-Anal.* 7, 27-30.

Vico, G. (1968). *The New Science*, trans. T.C. Berginand & M.H. Fisch. Ithaca: Cornell University Press.

Weidner, R. & Sell, R. (1980). *Elementary Modern Physics*, Third Edition. Boston: Allyn & Bacon, Inc.

EDITOR'S NOTE: *Doctor Green has been inspired for quite some time by the work of Bion and Winnicott. The present paper is an attempt to delineate the derivatives of two categories of infantile relationships to objects, one having the capacity to say "no," and therefore is interpersonally directed, and the other not able to say "no," and therefore is directed toward inanimate objects (things). Dr. Green's fascinating elucidation of "things" and "no" emphasizes Bion's conception of the pathological splitting which takes place in schizoid personalities in which the awareness of need of a human object is split-off from the object and assigned to an inanimate object instead* (Learning from Experience). *Further, he attempts to define the internal psychic play space for "no," that is the space for negation, which is, Dr. Green quickly assures us, but a "yes" to a contrary wish—since "no" does not exist in the unconscious. What the author seems to be saying throughout the article is that "no" and "yes" are but complementarities which occur as constant conjunctions; one does not clinically appear without the other. The final portion of Green's article seems reminiscent of Bion's* Transformations.

Dr. Green's essay must be understood in the light of the contributions of the French School of linguistic structuralism which includes the works of Saussure, Barthes, Jacobson, Levy-Strauss, Lacan, and many others. This school has particularly assigned great importance to the phenomenon of binary opposition in language formation. This binary opposition of constantly conjoined elements comprises the essence of ambiguity. I believe it is the structure of latent ambiguity in the analytic patient's mind—its transformation as ambiguities to the analyst—then followed by the analyst's momentary resolution of the ambiguity via interpretation to the patient—that constitute the Ariadne's Thread through Dr. Green's contribution.

This contribution is an essay on the nature of the interphase of ambiguity between two complementary, not merely dialectical, systems of logic, primary and secondary process. It is most fittingly read after Dr. Alfred Silver's insofar as the latter helps pave the way for an understanding of the former.

Negation and Contradiction

Andre Green

> He had spoken the very truth and transformed it into the veriest falsehood.
>
> It is a curious subject of observation and inquiry, whether hatred and love be not the same thing at bottom. Each, in its utmost development, supposes a high degree of intimacy and heart-knowledge; each one renders one individual dependent for the food of his affections and spiritual life upon another; each leaves the passionate lover, or the no less passionate hater, forlorn and desolate by the withdrawal of his object. Philosophically considered, therefore, the two passions seem essentially the same, except that one happens to be seen in a celestial radiance, and the other in a dusky and lurid glow.
>
> Hawthorne, *The Scarlet Letter*

THINGS AND "NO"

At the December 1974 meeting of the American Psychoanalytic Association S. Abrams and P. Neubauer presented a paper entitled "Object-orientedness: the person or the thing." Using all the resources of psychoanalytic ego-psychology in the comparison of two children, faithfully and regularly observed in minute detail, their paper studied two types of object-orientedness: toward people and toward things. The discussion contrasted the child whose object relationship bound him mainly to persons, and the child whose object-relationship was bound to things. As I listened I was struck, apparently more than were the authors of the communication, by one fact. At a given age, each child possessed a vocabulary of five words. At least on first catching the ear, so to speak, there was no notable difference as far as four of these words were concerned. They designated persons who normally were around the children: Mommy, Daddy, little sister or brother, the maid, etc. But they differed significantly on one point: the child whose object relationships created a bond between him and things said "This" while the child whose object relationships were oriented toward persons said "No." I was struck by this connection between the predominant interpersonal (or intersubjective) relationship and the use of negation.

Spitz (1957) recognises—as have many before him—that the concept of negation and the constant use of the semantic "no" for communication are specifically human patterns. Yet his study of the prototypes of "no" in the area of motor activity—the infant's rotating and nodding movements of the head—reminded me irresistibly of the difficulties I had in communicating with the Greeks during my vacation: the Greek "No," which is phonetically similar to the French "non," means "yes," while the voiceless gesture which expresses the negative in Greek is a vertical, down-up movement resembling the up-down movement that accompanies the French "oui." It took me a while to get used to it for I wondered if I was not altogether confusing the messages of these undoubtedly friendly people.

To return to the work of Abrams and Neubauer, it seemed to me that it could be deduced from their study that thing orientedness (object "objectivation") was essentially realistic and merely brought about a duplication of presence, just as the "da" in the cotton reel game only calls attention to the fact that the reel really is there. Person orientedness, on the other hand, accompanied as it is by the use of negation, made me think of the relations that could be established between negation and the absence that the child playing with the reel expresses by "o-o-o." The reel is not there: *I affirm that I deny*. At this point I could embark on paths of speculation. However, I will abstain from doing so and reflect first on these connections between affirmative and negation in clinical theory.*

Positivistic Clinical Theory

Clinical theory is positivistic. It translates into metapsychological jargon the results of an observation bearing on the visible, the observable, that which testifies to the responsive mind. Yet psychoanalysis takes as its object the unobservable and the repressed. True, though theoretical language has remained positive in character I intend to suggest (somewhat arbitrarily) a different formulation of a certain number of clinical clichés based on patients whom I shall imprudently designate by their usual labels, in spite of our natural distrust of such generalisation.

The Hysteric Condenses

But it is because the hysteric, in his repression, strives to create every sort of gap between language and body, that he over-condenses.

The Obsessive Displaces

But it is because the obsessive cannot resist the temptation to bring into contact essentially alien elements that he goes on endlessly displacing.

The Phobic Avoids

But it is because the phobic eroticizes danger that he makes it appear where there is none and projects it onto objects or situations. Space is safe at last when he has become panphobic. Nothing can then arouse his fear unexpectedly since everything has become frightening.

*See my remarks on the cotton reel game in Green (1967) and Green (1970).

The Melancholic is Mourning an Object

But it is because the melancholic has finally been freed from the object of his passionate hatred that he imprisons its ghost by offering up his ego to restore its life.

The Paranoid Projects and Regards His Projection as a Reality

But it is really because the world and other people are entirely indifferent to him and because he can believe in nothing that he over-rationalizes external reality and develops a passionate relationship with it.

The Schizophrenic Splits and Disintegrates

But it is really because he is passionately attached, in mutual parasitism, to the mother's oneness, that he becomes dissociated.

These are nosological references which describe psychical reality from a distance. Let us put them aside and enter, instead, the analytic situation.

A Clinical Illustration

The patient, whom I shall call Ninon, I considered to be a deeply disturbed hysteric, and she had suffered an ulcerated colitis in the course of her treatment. After ten years of analysis with her I found myself, not for the first time, in a distressing situation. I shall say nothing of this patient's material. I shall say only that I was upset by her responses to my interventions. Three of these, in particular, seemed noteworthy to me. [She would say "Don't know" every time the associations became sufficiently explicit for her to draw the interpretation that she should have found for herself, and that I was expecting her to find for herself.] "I know!" she would say in an annoyed tone, replying to my interventions, and meaning: "You haven't told me anything new. I knew that already; it's obvious;" the implication being: "It's worthless." Finally, in other instances, she used to say peremptorily "No!" and accompany this with a veritable body discharge, as if she were lashing out on the couch, which reminded me of what Freud and Bion have said about the evacuation of unpleasant stimuli through motor activity.

One day, however, she related the "tomato-rice episode." Due to her mother's ambivalence and complicity, this patient did not attend school until she was eight or nine years of age. She had rationalised her phobia of leaving her mother by her fear of not knowing at school. She would, moreover, be stricken mute in front of strangers (especially the doctor whom her mother patronised assiduously) and suffered from anorexia.

One day her mother had made her a dish of tomato-rice. She made up her mind not to eat it. Furious, her mother began chasing her all over the apartment and trapped her in a corner. She tried to force her daughter to eat. The spoon was pushed against the barrier of her tightly clenched teeth and managed to force her mouth open. But, predictably, the rebellious child spit the mouthful out. The enraged mother, determined to win at all costs, then said to her, "If that's the way you want it then you'll go to school!" She dragged her there despite screams and tears.

My patient's reaction to the manifest content was to speak of it as a traumatic experience. Of course, it was one, except that what is missing from this is the secret desire of my patient who, without knowing it, wanted nothing more than to go to school. In fact, it was her mother's ambivalence that prevented her from doing so. The proof is that she came out first in class on the first test, but when she told her mother about it, the mother seemed upset that in the future her daughter might not be happy with anything less than the highest mark. I must admit that, at the time, the tomato-rice story fascinated me to such an extent that I risked falling for the manifest content. It was only later, on a specific occasion, that I understood that her "no" reproduced her refusal of the tomato-rice and that it was to be taken as a "yes." To be more precise, I would say—as I told her later on—that as she was so completely committed to expressing her *negative affirmation*, the apparent expulsion really carried with it, in the opening necessary for the utterance of this "no," a "yes" which slipped surreptitiously into her. This was her way of introjecting—the word has now been said—the interpretation. After this intervention, she had the feeling that her analysis had more progress in a few weeks than it had in ten years.

We shouldn't speak too quickly of *defence mechanisms*. Besides, a defence mechanism is, in essence, negative. No matter how strongly one asserts something, it is always a denial of something: That somewhere there is an attack being perpetrated in which one may oneself be both attacker and attacked. Instead, let us go right to the heart of the matter: to the consideration of Freud's article, "Negation," which I find both his most remarkable and his least satisfactory.

Negation

Negation characterizes a relationship, not an object (Lyotard, 1971). Negation does not have a specific place within language; language as a whole is sustained by negation. "The negative consists in this: that the terms of the system have no existence other than their value and that this value is conferred upon them entirely by the regulated intervals that they maintain among themselves." (p. 120). My patient, in the tomato-rice episode, was defending her discontinuity with her mother. For what she feared above all—probably because she desired it—was this mastery her mother had over her which made a closed universe of their relationship. It is easy, then, to conclude, with the logicians, that "*there is no negative without affirmation*."

Lyotard designates three modes of "no":

1) The grammarian's and the logician's negation (negative propositions).

2) The discontinuity discussed by structuralists and linguists when describing language, its spacing, intervals and invariance.

3) The logician's and the analyst's lack.

When, in the paper I read at the London Congress (1975) I emphasized the complementary anxieties of *separation* and *intrusion*, I was really talking about optimal spacing: about *useful distance* (Bouvet) and *efficient difference*. But what Freud says takes us even further. Marsal, in Lalande's *Vocabulaire de la Philosophie* (1968) observes, in the footnote to the article on the work "Negative," that "negative" admits of two opposites: "*affirmative*" and "*positive*," which are not synonymous. At times, to negate falls into the category of "assertions." (Think of what Freud [1925] says: "'It's *not* my mother,' so it *is* his mother.") At other times, to assert and to negate are two members of the category of "judgement." This indeed compels Freud to bring in the function of judgement. Nonetheless, he reverses the order in which the two kinds of judgement usually appear: he puts first the judgement of attribution (good-bad) and then the judgement of reality (existence-non-existence), a philosophical feat from which I do not believe we have yet drawn all the consequences.

This article leads us to a system of binary oppositions at every level: good/bad, existence/non-existence. But also suggested are the antithetical pairs Cs/Ucs and self/object. My patient says "no" to herself and to me simultaneously. *And through this denial she says "yes" to both of us*. This present emphasis on counter-transference (I need hardly point out that I did not enthusiastically welcome her peremptory "no's" to my interpretations) does not stem from some analytic game of hide-and-seek in which transference and counter-transference chase each other around and around. *Counter-* (in the sense of "close to")* transference evokes transference and transference counter-transference. And does not transference already refer to a place outside that which is taking place? What is going on is the product of what has been *transferred*, displaced, from a place which is only indicated to us by the hypothesis that it is not here alone that the process is going on but that it has already transpired and that, what is more, it will continue to go on elsewhere. *Transference seizes upon that drifting object in the analytic setting which is fed by counter-transference*.†

But there exists another conception of the negative, as the logicians

*Translator's Note: In French, "contre" can mean both "contrary to" and "close to" (Example: "tout contre moi = "close to me.")

†Counter-transference is here utilised in the broadest sense: in the reaction of the analyst to the transferenceof the analysand for the holding and maintenance of the analytic setting.

have seen: the pure concept that has no opposite. Here—to remain within the Freudian framework—no duality is called into play. The Eros-Death instinct opposition is shattered in the aporia of *primary absolute narcissism*, the zero degree of excitation. The commentary this would require is too lengthy to be dealt with now, so let us remain with Freud's 1925 article. In other words, let us stay within the bounds of the dual relationship (the relationship of the 2) and leave aside that zero which the human mind has so much trouble in understanding—especially when we listen to our patients, who always *cathect* something—even the aspiration toward Nothingness.

External reality is first denied, rejected and declared alien. It can be regained when the establishment of the reality principle, that is, of the secondary thought processes, recreates an equilibrium between the system of internal relationships and that of external ones. The discovery of the object is really a re-discovery. If we come to a dead-end because of the paradoxes implied by a proposition of this sort, it is truly because we do not wish to be disturbed by the most troublesome questions. We analysts understand one another. We understand one another so well that we no longer understand anything.

Freud's brilliant manoeuvre was in not hesitating to slide the discussion of language (which has its own logic) into that of the one he calls "*the language of the oldest—the oral—instinctual impulses*." Do instinctual impulses, then, have their own language? Or is this merely a metaphor? No, it is a necessity. It is impossible to deal with instinctual impulses except through language since, in contrast to orgasmotherapy or primal scream therapy, psychoanalysis is restricted to verbal communication. It can conceive of instinct only through language. Nevertheless, the types of discontinuity are here diametrically opposed to language.

The "language" of instinctual impulses implies a mental space (an economy of the space containing instinctual tension-discharge processes) quite different from the mental space involved in language (which economy is the result of tension-discharge processes of thought).

The essential point with respect to the introjection-expulsion opposition—and this will be the main argument of my paper—is that expulsion (or rejection; I am not talking about projection) does not do away with the contradiction. Rather, it duplicates it. Without wishing to provoke, let me call your attention to *Mao Tse-Tung's* remarkable essay, "On Contradiction" (1937). Mao quotes Lenin: "The two basic (or two possible? or two historically observable?) conceptions of development (evolution) are: development as decrease and increase, as repetition, *and* development as a unity of opposites (the division of a unity into mutually exclusive opposites and their reciprocal relation)." Mao then adds, "The fundamental cause of the development of a thing is not external but internal: it lies in the contradictoriness within the thing." (p. 313).

In other words, *the original act of expulsion*, which Freud conjectured as attending the birth of a pleasure ego, opens up within the subject a pleasure-unpleasure relation which will have to be resolved by repression. In short, there is a vertical splitting inside-outside, immediately followed by a duplication of the contradiction, within the inside element, between desirable (to the conscious) and undesirable (to the conscious, but desirable to the unconscious). Mao says: "One divides into two." He talks in the tradition not only of Hegel but also of Heraclitus.

However the solipsistic position, which consists in expelling external reality, is an amputation. External reality will very soon *be missed. The object of what is missing is in external reality.* That is why the internal contradiction must be reunited with this external reality from which it has cut itself off. One way we know of dealing with this amputation is autoeroticism—the perfect symbol of the turning inwards on the subject's own self which implies *splitting of the ego* (analogous to that which occurs in mourning) wherein the body replaces the outside world. The body amputates one of its members in order to set it up as a *quasi-object, an analogue of the object, a double of the object.* Then follows a series of couplings: the breast is replaced by the thumb, the reel follows upon the thumb. Language—substituted for the reel—is reduced to its simplest expression, o-o-o-da, two expressions which are not at all synonymous. The logic of binary opposites still retains its prerogatives but the opposites have been infiltrated by dissymetry. The relations between mouth and breast, between child and mother are characterized by an inbalance—the *difference in potential* which will have to change into a potential difference.

Lyotard is right to emphasize the fact that the introject-expel impulse cannot be simplified into a mere relation of nourishment. Eating and spitting out are mere acts of thought and cognition. If we choose to ignore this concept it is like summoning thought into action, like a deus ex machina, at a point of genetic development. It should be said, though, that in order for the child to have access to *the play of thought (au jeu de la pensee)*, the mother, as in the case of Freud's daughter, must go away. In other words, someone other than the child must be the object of her desire, of which the child will never be more than a symbol. This is an invitation to a shifting of psychic spaces. The absence of the mother has to be linked with her potential reunion with the father.

This system of opposites that Freud traces here through the example of negation continued to obsess him. It makes an appearance in quite unrelated situations. It is in language: re-read *Jokes and their Relation to the Unconcious* (Freud, 1905)—it is all there. And even more specifically, it is in the article that linguists have disputed and so misunderstood, "The Antithetical Meaning of Primal Words."

Counter-Interpretation and Counter-Construction

Let us go back to the session, with Freud. In "Constructions in Analysis" (1937) Freud is still very much involved with his work on negation, which was by then twelve years old. He tells us that the work of analysis "is carried on in two separate localities, that it involves two people, to each of whom a distinct task is assigned." For once he is not satisfied with assessing the patient's response in terms of resistance; he analyses it instead. This is worth remembering. In the case of the patient's accepting the construction, says Freud, his "yes" is by no means *unambiguous*." (italics mine). And a little further on he states, "A 'no' from a person in analysis is quite as *ambiguous* as a 'yes'." (italics mine). What, then, should we trust? The formula (already mentioned in the article on negation): " 'I didn't ever think' (or,'I shouldn't ever *have thought*')'that' (or, '*of that*')." This is a remarkable formula which allows for the coexistence of past and present (I didn't ever–I shouldn't ever have), of the indicative and the conditional (if you hadn't told me) of intransitive and transitive (that, or of that) wherein thought is at once its own object and the thought of something, namely of an object. *This is a formula which admirably condenses negation and affirmation*.

I propose to talk of *counter-interpretation* and *counter-construction* as the analysand's immediate reaction to the analyst's message. "Counter," here, means "*juxta*," independent of its positive or negative connotations. But Freud goes further. He adds that what will allow us to go beyond the ambiguity is the train of associations. In other words, the immediate effect of the interpretation or construction in the explicit counter-interpretation or counter-construction will be evaluated by the sequence of associations–that is, the production of the complementary element of the couple born from the interpretation or the construction alone. For truth, as Freud concludes, can be arrived at only through its distortions.

This leads us to a consideration of the function of resistance. Far from being the obstacle to ours, it is its lever. Without resistance there can be no transference. There cannot be any obligation to make *the detour* which is the surest sign of the *return* of the repressed. Respect for resistance is, therefore, not merely an ethical rule of non-intrusion. It is a concern for the preservation of the force of detour, thanks to which the conductive work on the diverted elements will enable us to fully appreciate what has returned, and which had to be diverted by the ego. This conception was already present in the *Project for a Scientific Psychology*, with the notion of side cathexis. This can equally well be applied to the idea of defense, which is often interpreted in a tactical perspective, whereas it is really a matter of *strategy of opposites* in analysis. Is it necessary to insist that the analyst himself is tricked and double-crossed by this strategy when he wants to get directly to the point? He becomes a Cassandra. He tells the truth but is not believed.

Contradiction and Circularity

In short, it is six of one and half-a-dozen of the other. One can perceive the feeling of *malaise* which periodically throws us back into contradiction and periodically demands that we free ourselves from this paralysis in which "yes" and "no" reflect one another as if each were mirror of the other. Paradox is a game of the mind, and no human relationship is tolerable if the ambiguity ceases to be more than just a limited condition. I would like to remind you of a quote from Freud on the Oedipus complex that will bring us back to familiar ground. In *The Ego and the Id* (1923) Freud, for the first time, described the total Oedipus complex, that is, the positive and negative complex whose elements you know. But, in this text, Freud made some passing remarks which appear, to me, to be important. He points out that the simple—that is, the positive—Oedipus complex is described as such for *practical reasons*. This means that he is alluding, with this common term, to a concept found in the *Project*: that of practical thought, the kind that must solve a problem, decide a matter. He illustrates the two-fold structure of the Oedipus complex by bisexuality—that is, by the fact that every individual, whatever his sex—his sexual identity—combines within him the sexuality of *both* of his progenitors, his parents. In other words, the expulsion of the Other's sex returns in Oedipal bisexuality through a dual identification. He goes on to say something more important, namely that, as far as the earliest object-choices and identifications are concerned, it is difficult to have "*a clear view of the facts*" (italics mine). In my opinion, he means that, with respect to the earliest relationships, *object-choices and identifications would not have to be separate and distinct*: they could thus contain within them a basic contradiction. Finally, Freud makes a remark of major importance when he says that "it is still more difficult to describe *the facts in connection with the earliest object-choices and identifications intelligibly*" (italics mine).

Here we are at the heart of the contradiction. On the one hand, we have these sets of facts and relationships which do not correspond to our standards of *intelligibility* (that is, to those of secondary thought processes) and, on the other hand, we have before us the theoretical task of describing them *intelligibly*. Therein lies the major paradox of Freud's work which speaks of *primary logic in the terms of secondary logic*. This is also the paradox of psychoanalytic practice: *hearing with one's primary ear, speaking with secondary language*. That is why it is sometimes preferable to remain silent rather than artificially inject secondary forms of communication (even if their content aims at primary communication) where primary logic is at work.

This, in my view, explains the shifting of the psychoanalytic referent we find in certain theoretical contributions: the Oedipus and castration complexes are replaced by the primal scene, which is their *primordial double*, the one in which object-choices and identifications are not mutually exclusive but at once contradictory and complementary. However, we have not escaped from the contradiction.

Once again I would like to quote Mao Tse-Tung. Mao writes that "qualitatively different contradictions can only be resolved by qualitatively different methods" (p. 321). If it is necessary to have a thorough knowledge of all the contradictions of a given situation, nothing could be more mistaken than to treat them all in the same way. "There are many contradictions in the process of development of a complex thing and one of them is necessarily the principal contradiction whose existence and development determine or influence the existence and development of other contradictions." (p. 331).

Thus, in the dual Oedipus complex, the means of breaking out of the circularity lies in the feature which makes of the psychically bisexual child a unisexual being. After elucidating the principal contradiction/secondary contradiction split, Mao rediscovers the principal and secondary aspects of the principal contradiction within the latter. Citing Lenin, Mao says, "*Dialectics* is the teaching which shows how *opposites* can be and how they happen to be (how they become) *identical*–under what conditions they are identical, transforming themselves into one another, why the human mind should take these opposites not as dead, rigid, but as living, conditional, mobile, transforming themselves into one another." (p. 337).

"No" Does Not Exist in the Unconcious

It would take a certain naiveté to think that, in dealing with these questions, I could have forgotten that "no" does not exist for the unconcious. "No's" separating force would seem to have no place in this discussion. As I reflected on this problem I became aware of the reason behind the epistemological scandal surrounding the death instinct. How can it be called an instinct? I do not intend to discuss the validity of the concept of the death instinct now. But I will say that Freud, who maintained that all drives are active, that is, affirmative and positive, needed to attribute to this disjunctive tendency, which is the negation of the tendency to form larger and larger wholes, the status of an instinct, i.e., an active force. Thus one escapes even less from contradiction inasmuch as this separating capacity *ensures spacing* and establishes discontinuity. That is, it protects against the dissolving powers of continuity in the fusion with the object and guarantees the existence of individualising separation.

But let us leave aside the death instinct and return to the unconcious and to dreams, the "royal road" that leads to it. Chapter VI, not VII, is the richest chapter in the book. I would like to quote a passage from it that is worthy of attention. "The way in which dreams treat the category of *contraries* and *contradictories* is highly remarkable. It is simply disregarded. "No" seems not to exist as far as dreams are concerned. They show a particular preference for combining contraries into a unity or for representing them as one and the same thing. Dreams feel themselves at liberty, moreover, to represent any element by its wishful contrary: so there is no way of deciding at a first glance whether any element that admits of a contrary is present in the dream thoughts as a positive or a negative." (p. 318).

I shall give a clinical illustration of this, taken from Ninon's analysis. After I had given an interpretation that was a little too much of a summary, she made a gesture indicating sharp disapproval and destructive rejection of me which, however, she elaborated better than was her custom. I understood that a tremendous movement of transference, of rapprochement, had taken place. At the next session I conveyed to her my feeling that her refusal was linked to a very great closeness against which she was mobilizing all her resources of negation, for fear, I told her, of an acting-out in relation to me. It was as though the words of my interpretation were capable of inducing not only thoughts and desires but also acts that had to be cleared away. She answered, "Since you're talking about acting out, I'm going to tell you the dream I had. I dreamt I was an analyst, sitting in an armchair like you are [in my interpretation I had mentioned this desire of hers] and I had Serge Gainsbourg* as a patient. On the couch he told me that he wanted to sleep with me [We had also touched on her avoidance of transference by her affair with a man]. I hesitated, then I gave in and in the dream he turned out to be impotent. I wondered: why Serge Gainsbourg?" Then she remembered having recently seen him on TV and thought that this wild man, this indomitable rebel who claimed he wanted to be bound to nothing and nobody, had nevertheless wound up falling for Jane Birkin, whom my patient found pretty and who had also been on the TV show. He had even given her a child [her desire, brought up in the previous session]. The TV show interviewer had asked the singer—and this is a sign of the times—if he ever dreamed. The answer was, "Never. I take barbiturates." [an illusion which refers back to my patient's own use of tranquilizers]. She then immediately grasped the meaning of this dream as representing *someone who never dreams*. She called it an *anti-dream*.

Before coming back to Freud, I would like to open a parenthesis. Listen to this passage from *Milinda Panha* (1964), a collection of Indian texts dating from approximately the second century B.C. to the second century A.D.

"Reverend Nágasena, in regard to him who has a dream as a portent—does his mind, going along of its own accord, seek that portent, or does that portent come into the focus of his mind, or does anyone come and tell him of it?

'It is not, sire, that his mind, going along of its own accord, seeks for that portent, nor does anyone else come and tell him of it, but that very portent comes into the focus of his mind. As, sire, a mirror does not go anywhere to seek for a reflection, nor does anyone else, bringing a reflection, put it on the mirror, but from wherever the reflection comes, it appears in the mirror.' " (Vol. I, Part IV, Division 8, p. 128).

Contradictions in Dreams

In this same Chapter VI, in the section concerning the means of representation, Freud considers logical relations. On the one hand he states that dreams

*Well-known French singer.

have no means at their disposal of representing the logical relations between the dream thoughts. But when even they seem to be present, Freud thinks this is "*part of the material of the dream-thoughts and is not a representation of intellectual work performed during the dream itself.*" "A contradiction in a dream," says Freud, "can only correspond in an exceedingly indirect manner to a contradiction *between* the dream-thoughts" (Freud's italics). This "*between*" clearly indicates that, for Freud, thought is the link between the terms. He goes on to concern himself with trying to find out how dreams can express this link. Very simply, dreams do away with the "*between*" by means of condensation: "They reproduce *logical connection* by *simultaneity in time*." (His example is Raphael's painting of the School of Athens.) This observation is extraordinary for it shows that the non-existence of "no" is the same as the non-existence of time. *Simultaneity takes the place of successive action in time*. All the same, the causal relation of successive action is not entirely excluded. It comes back into the picture through displacement: the transformation of one image in the dream into another or the transformation of the dream which gives way to another dream.

"*The alternative 'either-or' cannot be expressed in dreams in any way whatever*."

This is the crux of the matter. I quote again: "One and only one of these logical relations is very highly favoured by the mechanism of dream-formation: namely the relation of similarity, consonance, or approximation—the relation of 'just as.'" (pp. 319-320). This is analogical thought at work. "Similarity, consonance, the possession of common attributes—all these are represented in dreams by unifaction, which may either be present already in the material of the dream-thoughts or may be freshly constructed. The first of these possibilities may be described as 'identification' and the second as 'composition.' Identification is employed where *persons* are concerned: composition where *things* are the material of the unification. Nevertheless composition may also be applied to persons. Localities are often treated like persons." (p. 320).

All of modern psychoanalysis gets enmeshed in the type of contradiction Freud is referring to: persons-things. It is less an opposition between animate and inanimate than between persons and objects—though I know the difference between thing and object. This juxtaposition refers back to the relation between the whole object (person) and part-object (the whole and the part), Identification and composition inter-refer as methods of unification. The series that starts with incorporation and ends with identification will oblige us to return to that mode of composition or alienation represented by possession (in the medieval sense), through the image, the ghost, the double. Here the double comes back with double meaning.

Freud quotes from the Bible—Joseph interpreting Pharaoh's dream: "This dream, O King, although seen under two forms, signifies one and the same event . . ." Finally, everything can be summed up in one sentence: contradictions are treated like analogies. So, when Freud ends the chapter by asserting that dream-work "does not think, calculate or judge in any way at all: it restricts itself to giving things a new form," we understand that this exclusion of the function of judgement from the ability to transform is based on the work of analogical thought. This kind of thought neglects differences or, rather, puts to work another kind of difference which takes liberties with the differences of secondary logic. But to what extent does it do so? What is at issue here is interpretation.

This is a dual question: the interpretation that is the dream itself,
i.e., the dreamer's interpretation,
and:
the interpretation of the dream, i.e., the
analyst's interpretation.

Analytic Work and Introjection

The dream-work and the interpreter's work complement each other. What strikes me as unusual in Freud's work on dreams is his way of speaking about dreams "from the inside," like a stowaway. Furthermore, what is astonishing is the way he puts all the resources of his secondary thought processes at the service of the primary thought processes, of the dream. That is, there is a constant to-and-fro in which secondary logic moves into the background to allow primary logic to speak and be heard. For us, Freud, with secondary logic, explains the laws of that universe we visit every night without having fathomed its logic before him. At any rate, the path to dreams, like the path to the unconcious, is the object of the mediation of the ego—of the dreamer who relates the dream afterwards, during his session.

As we are all aware, analysis is only possible in the union of the analysand's free associations and the analyst's evenly-suspended attention, the aim of which is to encourage the analyst's free associations while *judgement* remains benevolently neutral. *Fluctuat nec mergitur.** But it is not a matter of floating to the point of falling asleep—which, it should be said in passing, does not happen only to analysts. As Bertram Lewin (1950) observed, the patient in analysis is torn between his desire to dream and his desire to sleep. Silence can ensure this function. But silence never disappears. In the analytic couple, one of the two partners is always silent. Thus, the function of silence, while someone is speaking, can always be delegated to the Other. But silence can sometimes speak louder than words, and behind the noise of the words speech can be silent.

We shall try to describe how analytic work is accomplished, with this attenuated but not entirely eradicated presence of contradiction, since, despite our efforts to make contact with the primary processes, the secondary ones are only half-asleep. This is the moment to recall that analytic dis-

*"She is tossed by the waves but does not sink": motto of the city of Paris, to which Freud often referred.

course is a contradiction in terms. Saying everything that comes into one's mind is, as we know, an impossible task. What is more, we are the first to become bored with the productions of certain patients who apply the rule literally and whose omission of essential links reduces their discourse to an unintelligible fragmentation. In fact, the paradox resides in the fact that while the *sequences* (= the train of associations) have broken the links of logical thought, each sequence nonetheless remains under the control of logic. This is what brought me to speak elsewhere of the dual articulation of analytic discourse (*between* the terms of one and the same sequence and *between* the sequences.)

The analysand's discourse is incorporated by the analyst. By this I mean that the discourse is an object. To this incorporation is coupled—I use the term advisedly-an introjection, that is, processes occurring concommitantly with incorporation. Here I agree with Ferenczi's distinction, so usefully recalled by N. Abraham and M. Torok (1972). In my opinion a distinction must be made between different types of *introjection* of the object: the introjection of instincts by the ego (*instinct introjection*); the introjection of affects and representations by the pre-conscious and the conscious (*imaginary introjection*) and finally the introjection of verbal and perceptual communications. The latter type of introjection I call *symbolic introjection*, in the modern and, if need be, Lacanian sense of the term. It seems to me that what must be emphasised in this distinction is that *verbal, symbolic introjection* is *limited* and *discontinuous*. It is a type of introjection resembling a chain—a *generative introjection*.

While the analysand speaks, the analyst listens. He is working at listening. Now, the patient's discourse progresses along the unwinding of the verbal chain. The function of associative unlinking produces silences, intervals, sighs, gaping holes (*béances*) in the discourse and gaps between parts of syllables, words and sentences; *between* the elements of a sequence and *between* the sequences. Now, while the analysand is speaking, the analyst is working on the patient's associations by means of his own associations. This is the original phenomenon of analytic attention. The analyst's associative work, his symbolizing function, consists in making links. But making links is a process of contradictory transformations. That is to say, the analyst, whose most intimate self is being called upon, must refuse in himself the *temptation of the manifest narrative*, its hypnotic effect (in the strict sense of the word). He must consequently implement contradictory operations of thought. There is never a clear-cut answer to "What is he trying to tell me?" This is ambiguous work. The element must be linked up with some other element, not-A, which can be either -A or A′. This is the ambiguity of analysis. Nobody can come to the aid of the analyst and whisper in his ear the answer, whether not-A is -A (reversal into its opposite) or A′ (turning round upon its own self). In other words, the *negative* not-A (according to the article by Serrus (1968) in Lalande's *Vocabulaire*) is either the product of projection through displacement (for instance: You're behaving with me as you did with your father and mother) or projection through reversal (for instance: You are afraid of it because you desire it). Only the context can decide the matter and the context (that is, the totality of associative sequences) is ambiguous. This leads me to two observations:

1) The model of the psychic structure of the analytic object is the *double reversal*, ending in a double loop

2) As the introjection of associative communication progresses, a function of oscillating transformations becomes centred in the analyst.

An example: When my patient recounted the tomato-rice episode or her anti-dream, I kept wandering off constantly into associations. I thought in the following order (I am reconstructing this after the fact.):

1) Her mother is bad, she is intrusive.

2) Ninon is over-dramatizing with me the way she used to with her mother.

3) It is her mother who over-dramatizes.

4) Ninon has a right not to like tomato-rice.

5) This is already an ulcerative colitis: "her intestines were shedding tears of blood.*

6) Ninon's aggressiveness cannot tolerate the sight of blood or anything that suggests a comparison with it.

7) In fact, she manipulated her mother the way she is currently manipulating me.

8) What a nasty little squirt she must have been!

9) Yes, but what a mother! She is crazy! Ninon fought for her individuation!

10) What homosexuality there was between the two of them!

11) Luckily there was school to act as a buffer.

12) I understand why she rejects my interpretations.

But, after all that, I was still missing the essential point, which only came to me afterwards, when I gave her the interpretation of her "no." That is where the *work of interpretation* was performed. I must confess that when I opened my mouth to begin my interpretation, I did have some vague impression of what I was getting ready to say. But it was in the effort to project it, that is, in the act of formulating my interpretation in the verbal un-

*I am here making a double reference. On the one hand, this sentence was formulated by her doctor during a very painful and intrusive rectoscopy when she had her ulcerative colitis. This reminded me of the intrusion of the tomato-rice in her mouth. On the other hand, I am comparing the tomato-rice to her bloody faeces.

winding of my associative chain that the interpretation was forged in my words without my ever having been able to predict what form it might take. But, as I spoke, I said to myself, "That's it." I had shut my mouth and could have heaved a sigh of relief when it was over. My interpretation was the fruit of analogical thought: I had counterbalanced what had happened in the past and what was happening between these two series.

In the same way, when I decided to write this article, I knew I wanted to speak about the object. Between my idea then and what you are reading today there exists only an homologous connection. The more time went by, the more my first wish seemed to me to have been overtaken by the flow of the theoretical process.

Interpretation is an act of exorcism. It is a means of ridding oneself of what the patient has handed out and giving it back to him so that he may get rid of what has been put in him—or what one has put in him. But in this relation of chronologically successive action that the act of speaking illustrates, due credit must be given to the role of simultaneity in the creation of the interpretation's form and content: simultaneity of the decyphering of what has been heard and of the formulation of attentive thought, in preparation for the interpretation. We surprise ourselves when we interpret .

I would now like to say a word about certain paradoxical forms of introjection of the interpretation, which are the sign of resistance. One type has to do with over-cathecting the interpretation. Just as over-cathecting the patient's discourse has a hypnotic effect, over-cathecting the interpretation amazes and seduces the analysand through the omnipotence projected on the analyst's words. That is one of the dangers of the silent analyst. Everything he says becomes oracular. He is never wrong because he speaks so rarely. On the other hand, what is introjected merely strengthens the patient's narcissism. This voice penetrating you so completely is good, beautiful, marvelous. But it forms a whole that cannot be assimilated.

The second case involves the masquerade of psychic working-out. After I have said something I hear the analysand say, "Let's see, can we go back over what you just said?" And there is my beautiful interpretation all sliced up, fallen victim to obsessionalization. There is a strong tendency to react to this counter-interpretation. It is clear that the effect sought by this dissecting isolation wards off any mobilising of affects and immunizes the patient against them.

More or less complete over-cathexis is negation itself. Thus Wisdom (1961) has spoken of the hysteric for whom the penis is itself a penis-symbol. Things become clearer when one realizes that this penis is hollow and is in fact a vagina that is more greatly feared than the penis. In fact, penis and vagina have been condensed in this contradictory logic wherein coupling is non-coupling since fulfillment is always postponed. Inversely, over-cathecting the analysis as an unlinking-fragmenting process shatters the analyst's words and thwarts any *effect of restarting* through the reappropriation of these words by thought.

One can see from the examples that I have just given that symbolic, verbal introjection cannot claim any monopoly on this. The same pairs of opposites can be found, as well, on the level of the imaginary. Medusa's head can be just as much a mother-figure with penetrating penises as it can be, in Freud's opinion, a figure which wards off danger and has an apotropaic effect on castration. This is an unsolvable question since it depends on whether the matter concerns simple displacement or a reversal into the opposite. Or even a double bind image.

The same holds true for the introjection of instincts. Re-read "Instincts and their Vicissitudes." That is where we see at work in Freud (1915), before any mention of repression, before any reference to the representation-affect opposition has been made, the mechanisms of double reversal (turning around upon the subject's own self and reversal into the opposite) in the coupling or pairing of opposites. In the perverted couple, the partner is the exorcist who takes upon himself a share of the pleasure which escapes the pervert, who gets pleasure from it as in a mirror, through identification. And this can be found even in the solitary ritual of the pervert and even in masturbation, as Joyce McDougall (1973) has so neatly shown. As far as the nature itself of the concept of opposite pairs is concerned, Freud clearly saw its characteristic contradiction. The taking inside oneself of pleasure-giving objects via introjection (he quotes Ferenczi) has as its complement projection, which rids the self of unpleasure. We should not forget, however, that this object which is desired for the pleasure it gives will be consumed and consequently destroyed, after incorporation.

Introjection never ceases to be ambivalent. The fiction of the genital personality belongs to psychoanalytic ideology. At best ambivalence becomes ambiguity. This is what we call subtlety. Our genetic model bears the characteristics of both this ambivalence and of the work of the transformation on the model of primordial relationships. Laplanche (1976) has devoted welcome pages to the introjection of the object. Is it the breast, the milk, the lips (or, we could add, the mother's gaze) which is the object? Laplanche condenses the source, the object and the aim. "*It* (Id) enters through the mouth." From primitive anaclasis emerges the specification of the sexual function. So be it. It seems to me, however, that without being inclined to Kleinianism, one can suppose that the introjection of the "it" is a *discontinuous sequence* (the infant's sucking is, in fact, just that: he establishes a rhythm in his ingestion by swallowing). Without indulging in genetic-fiction, we may still imagine the sequence of affects accompanying introjection. The relation to the breast is not uniformly good when it is there and bad when it is not.

During the process of introjection there occur a series of "thoughts" which I shall translate hypothetically in the following way: "It's good. It's still as good as it was. It's better. It's not quite as good. Will there be enough? I don't want any more. I want more. Is that enough? More. It's not as good. It's not coming through as well. It's getting empty. It's filling up..." We see that introjection is concomitant with the process of projection. We must now direct our attention to this question.

Generalized Projection

Projection, which is not the same thing as expulsion, is the putting outside which is paralleled by the putting inside which characterizes introjection. In my view, projection is limitless, as is introjection. All psychic productions are projective. The field of projection covering the opposite is equally true. What becomes of external reality? What becomes of rational thought? They are not any less projective. All we can say is that there are projective spaces and projective moments which are bound up with differently organized primary and secondary systems.

Here again what matters is the *idea of coupled elements*. An introjection is dangerous when it prevents the simultaneous formation of an introjection. Tausk (1919) had clearly seen that projection is not oriented only toward the outside but also, first of all, toward the inside of the body. Consider hypochondria. The fact is that we are once again confronted with another paradox in which the inside of the body has taken the place of the outside world. When the possibilities of exertion have been exhausted, when the systems of bodily fantasies have been overloaded by the burdens that weigh down the psychic body, it is then that projection turns outward. The internal eye of the persecuted-persecuting organ turns around toward external reality—and now seizes upon the latter in its turn. Dreams are projections—a turning inside-out of that external space into the psychic space of the dreamer, the space bounded by the pole of perception and the pole of motor activity, where everything, in fact, happens as it does in external reality. Thoughts are projections. So are art and science. Projection is production. Transference and counter-transference are projections and productions of the setting.

It is because there is transference that the analyst too, can project non-transferential interpretations, which leads the patient to introject the latter as counter-transference ones. It is because there is non-transference that the analyst can project transferential interpretations, which leads the patient to start up again the process of transferential projections. Transference is that which is the object of an occultation because between what is experienced and what is projected operates the filter of reversal. Thus a patient made remarks to me in an ostensibly hostile tone. As I interpreted this, I came up against her denial. "I wasn't hostile." And I wound up understanding that she truly didn't want to be. But between her wish not only not to be hostile but even to be nice, and its fulfillment through speech, what came out of her at that moment *became* hostile, like the heroines in fairy tales whose mouths give forth only snakes and toads, irrespective of their intentions. The same may happen to the analyst.

The Object and the Circuit

When he distinguished transitional objects, transitional phenomena and transitional space, Winnicott (1971) took a decisive step in the concept of the object in connection with inside-outside, subjective-objective, non-existing–existing and positive-negative relations. Instead of viewing the object as the stake in play between internal and external reality, he brought into action the notion of the *boundary*. By creating the notion of potential space existing at the point of separation between self and object, by making of this space of separation a space of re-union, by describing the creation of the transitional object within it, he allows us to resolve the dilemma. Psychic reality has been transformed. It no longer remains trapped in the unreality-reality opposition; it now defines itself according to the nature of the potentiality which calls forth infinite transformations. In 1971 Winnicott enriched this description by bringing to light the *negative side of relationships*. For some children the gap is the only real thing. In short, the prolonged absence of the mother has resulted in the child's cathecting a dead object, whether the mother henceforth is present or not.

Here I am in agreement with Winnicott over certain positions that I have defended in the past. This is the case, for example, when he writes that the analyst must understand that there could be a blotting out (what I refer to as a "radical decathexis") and "that this blank could be the only fact and the only thing that was real." (*Playing and Reality*, p. 22) Hence, we shall once again have to mention the importance of negative hallucination. Thus *the object is here the non-object*. This negative symbolisation is a contradiction in terms which points out the inevitability of paradox.

The work of the mirror, a product of the logic of opposites, which operates in the analytic setting, is undermined by the realization of this deficiency. It is as though, in these analytic situations, the non-emergence of a living, present object were due to the fact that the interval between the loss of the bad object and its replacement by a good object had been experienced and considered as a fatal desert. Thus, space and time—for it is really a matter of a period of time that was experienced as interminable—are linked. There is no longer any measurable time. There is only infinite waiting, eternal waiting in hopelessness and despair. Whence comes the idea of a "dead Time," as the suspension of all affective and perceptive experience. The subject does not think he can survive this dead time. Consequently the analyst becomes the object of the negative therapeutic reaction because he is the only reliable object, the only one that survives these destructive periods of which he is the no-object. Any other object would run the risk of never reappearing at the other end of the dead time or of never lasting long enough to be experienced as present. Whence the importance for the patient to assure himself at every session that he has perceived the analyst. And sometimes between sessions as well, with a phone call that assures him, by the voice he hears, that this object is still alive, though it remains a bad one.

If perception is so important it is because it alone can ensure the coupling function. Everything then hinges on the double meaning of absence, which can signify potential presence as well as potential loss. Only perception can guarantee that the potential loss has been warded off. There is only one kind of loss that perception cannot ensure against: loss of love. The constancy of the analytic setting, which the patient perceives, must be complemented by his positive cathexis of it. *Perception is a carnal function*. That is why the analyst lets himself be seen only at the beginning and at the end of each session.

I should like to conclude with the idea that the object is neither a form nor an essence but a *circuit of cathexis with shifting and variable boundaries*. This circuit is basically composed of the introjection-projection pair. Freud was obsessed by the representation-perception opposition, which has remained the criterion by which external reality is tested. This has led to Melanie Klein's teratology of phantasies. Bion (1965) has shown that this generalised phantasy structure can be understood only in terms of the O-K pair, that is, in terms of the relationship between infinite truth and finite knowledge, an absolute-relative pair implying a vertex. External reality will remain our cross and our obsession. Freud has given internal reality its conceptual dignity by not shying away from the ambiguities of the concept of psychic reality. But what trouble he encountered when he had to tackle external reality and the problem of perception.

Let us use Freud's example of *fetishism* again. I would like to emphasize two things. The first comes from the 1927 article on fetishism. ". . . the boy refused to take cognizance of the fact of his having perceived that a woman does not have a penis." *Denial*. Freud rejected the hypothesis of scotomization. On the contrary, perception persists and brings with it an energetic action to maintain the denial. Consequently, Freud made use of a temporal concept, namely, successive action in time, "the last impression before the uncanny and traumatic one is retained as a fetish . . . pieces of underclothing, which are so often chosen as a fetish, crystallize the moment of undressing, the last moment in which the woman could still be regarded as phallic." In fact, the regression which reverses the order of events in time "scotomizes" the simultaneity of the two movements of thought, i.e., the one that has to admit castration and the one that denies it.

Similarly, in "Splitting of the Ego in the Process of Defence" (1940 [1938]), when Freud treats the conflict between the instinctual demand and the prohibition placed on it by reality, he offers the solution. Rather than decide between them, that is to say, judge, "the child in fact takes neither course, or rather he takes both simultaneously, which comes to the same thing." Negation and simultaneity are here bound together. The price—splitting of the ego—will have to be paid.

I propose the working hypothesis that primary repression is inaccessible because the repressed subject has not been introjected but rather, repression has taken place in his perception. What has been introjected are the alterations effected on the amputated perception. It is the work on these deformed alterations that will enable us to deduce—through construction—primary repression. The function of phantasy is then only a desperate attempt to rediscover this missing fragment of perception. Any work performed on these phantasies without first having made the hypothesis of a mutilated perception is thenceforth phantasmatic, that is, deceptive. Each order (instincts, representations or language) always has a dual aim. On the one hand, it designates to the ego an order other than its own, that is, another system, and invites it to decipher the relevant absent order. On the other hand, it defines itself, that is, it refers to its own mode of individual structuring, which cannot be reduced to the other orders to which it is nevertheless linked. Thus the analyst is neither a real nor an imaginary object. Nor is he even a symbolic one. He is a *potential* object inducing transformations. He is one of the elements awaiting its complement: an inverse or symmetrical one coming from the analysand in order to form the analytic object, which exists only inasmuch as it is an object *between*, an object relation.

References

Abraham, N. & Torok, M. (1972). Introjecter-incorporer; deuil *ou* melancolic. *Nouv. Rev. Psychan.*, 6, 111-122.

Abrams, S. & Neubauer, P. (1974). Object-orientedness: the person or thing. A paper presented at the winter meeting of the American Psychoanalytic Association.

Arlow, J.A. (ed.) (1973). *Selected Writings of Bertram D. Lewin*. New York: Psychoanalytic Quarterly.

Bion, W.R. (1965). *Transformations*. London: William Heinemann.

Bouvet, M. (1958). Technical variation and the concept of distance. *Int. J. Psa.* 39, 211-221.

Ferenczi, S. (1950). Introjection and transference. IN HIS: *Sex and Psychoanalysis*. New York: Robert Brunner, pp. 35-93.

Freud, S. (1900). *The Interpretation of Dreams. S.E.* 4(1) & 5(2). London: Hogarth Press, 1958.

—— (1905). *Jokes and their Relation to the Unconscious. S.E.* 8. London: Hogarth Press, 1960.

—— (1910). The antithetical meaning of primary words. *S.E.* 11, 153-161. London: Hogarth Press, 1956.

—— (1915). Instincts and their vicissitudes. *S.E.* 14, 109-140. London: Hogarth Press, 1957.

—— (1923). The ego and the id. *S.E.* 19, 11-66. London: Hogarth Press, 1961.

—— (1925). Negation. *S.E.* 19, 235-242. London: Hogarth Press, 1961.

—— (1927). Fetishism. *S.E.* 21, 149-158. London: Hogarth Press, 1961.

—— (1937). Constructions in analysis. *S.E.* 23, 355-270. London: Hogarth Press, 1964.

—— (1940[1938]). Splitting of the ego in the process of defence. *S.E.* 23, 271-278. London: Hogarth Press, 1964.

—— (1950[1895]). *Project for a Scientific Psychology. S.E.* 1. London: Hogarth Press, 1966.

Green, A. (1967). Le narcissisme primaire: structure ou etat. *L'Inconscient*. 1, 127-157; 2, 89-116.

—— (1970). Repetition, difference, replication. *Rev. Franc. Psychanal.* 34, 461-501.

—— (1975). The analyst, symbolization and absence in the analytic setting. *Int. J. Psycho-Anal.* 56, 1-22.

Lalande, A. (1968). *Vocabulaire de la Philosophie*. Paris: Presses Univ. de France, pp. 678-679.
Laplanche, J. (1976). *Life and Death in Psychoanalysis*. Baltimore: Johns Hopkins Press.
Lewin, B.D. (1950). *The Psychoanalysis of Elation*. New York: Norton.
Lyotard, J.F. (1971). *Discours, Figure*. Paris: Klincksieck.
Mao, T. (1937). On contradiction. IN: *Selected Works of Mao Tse-Tung*. Peking: Foreign Languages Press, 1967.
—— (1967). *Selected Works of Mao Tse-Tung*. Peking: Foreign Languages Press.
Marshal, M. (1968). Note on article negat. IN: Lalande, A., *Vocabulaire de la Philosophie*. Paris: Presses Univ. de France, p. 678.
McDougall, J. (1973). Primal scene and sexual perversion. *Int. J. Psa.* 53, 371-382.
Panha, M. (1964). *Milinda's Questions*. London: Luzac & Co., Ltd.
Serrus, R. (1968). Article Negat. IN: Lalande, A., *Vocabulaire de la Philosophie*. Paris: Presses Univ., p. 678.
Spitz, R. (1957). *No and Yes*. New York: IUP.
Tausk, V. (1919). On the origin of the 'influencing machine' in schizophrenia. IN: *Psychoanalytic Reader*. R. Fleiss (ed.) New York: IUP, 1948.
Winnicott, D.W. (1971). *Playing and Reality*. London: Tavistock Publications.
Wisdom, J.O. (1961). A methodological approach to the problems of hysteria. *Int. J. Psycho-Anal.* 42, 224-237.

The "Oedipus" as a Resistance Against the "Oedipus" in Psychoanalytical Practice

Leon Grinberg

EDITOR'S NOTE: *Doctor Grinberg has presented a contribution which gets to the heart of Bion's conceptions of (a) transformations of K → O and (b) the resistance to this transformation as exemplified in the arrogant omniscience of Oedipus, of Adam and Eve, of Palinurus, and of those who were inspired to build the Tower of Babel. The author has conjoined these themes with his own conceptions of projective identification ⇌ projective counter-identification (patient ⇌ analyst) to demonstrate how the patient and/or the analyst may produce resistances* in *K or* to *K which can thwart an evolution in O (truth). For a similar exposition of the oedipal myth as a resistance to "becoming," please also see Thorner's contribution. For another view of the Palinurus legend, please see Paul's contribution*

The "Oedipus" as a Resistance Against the "Oedipus" in Psychoanalytic Practice*

León Grinberg, M.D.

What I am going to set out in the following is the description of my transformation of some of Bion's ideas concerning the Oedipus myth which I am trying to apply to the psychoanalytical process, considering them as much from the analyst's point of view as from that of the patient.

Myths can be compared to a many sided mobile polyhedron which, according to the angle we see it from or the view point from which we observe it, demonstrates different faces, vertices and edges.

Some myths have deeply influenced psychoanalytical thought, particularly the understanding of the early human emotional experiences. One example of this is the Oedipus myth, told with mastery in Greek tragedy, and which was elaborated by Freud and his followers in his theory of the Oedipus complex (Freud, 1913, 1921, 1923). Myth, tragedy and theory are, without doubt, important elements in the understanding of a number of repressed situations, repeated and reactualised in an "undesirably faithful" way in the relationship between the patient and the analyst, and allowing its clarification, the lifting of the repression and filling of the "mnemic lakes" and the modification of symptoms through the analysis of the transference.

It is known that psychoanalysis has placed the Oedipus complex as the central nodule of neurosis and the fundamental basis for the bringing to light of love, hate, jealousy and rivalry as essential aspects of sexual development of the individual. Research into the Oedipus myth has become enriched lately by important contributions which have referred, almost all of them predominantly, to the sexual content of the drama and to the active or passive, sadistic or masochistic, libidinal or aggressive links between the individual and the parental couple. There have also been valuable contributions from the linguistic and semiotic fields.

Bion (1962, 1963), tried to approach the Oedipus myth from a vertex which looks at those other elements which were displaced by the emphasis given to the sexual components of the myth, although it does not exclude the essential importance of the latter. He points out that its different components are linked on a narrative form, and in such a way that none of them can be understood by themselves in isolation. He proposes to study spedifically the elements related to the K link, that of Knowledge (K), so essential in the human being as are also those of Love (L) and Hate (H). The riddle of the Sphinx is an expression of the curiosity of man directed toward himself, but that curiosity is also represented by the determination with which

*I wish to thank Drs. D. Tor and E.T. de Bianchedi with whom I discussed some of the ideas advanced in this paper.

Oedipus pursued his investigations into the crime, against the warnings of Tiresias.

Scientific curiosity is one of the major characteristics of the psychoanalyst's work. (R. Gainberg, 1960) Nevertheless, I feel that his eagerness to search and unravel the secrets of the patient's mind often stumbles against not only the barrier put up by the patient's anxiety, but also by his own anxiety which, in a "tiresianic" way, warns him of the dangers and the high price which he could pay on coming face to face with the "catastrophic change"* (Bion, 1966), and eventually with psychosis. According to Bion, psychoanalytical research has its background in a respectable ancient history, because curiosity regarding the personality is a central feature in the story of Oedipus. Significantly, that curiosity has the same status of sin in the Oedipus myth, in that of Eden and in that of Babel.

The common elements which can be found in the three myths are: an omnipotent and omniscient god who forbids knowledge; a model for mental growth; an attitude of curiosity and challenge; and a punishment related to the awakened curiosity by the prohibitions existing in the myths. The models for mental growth are represented in the myths by the "Tree of Knowledge," the "Riddle of the Sphinx" and the "Tower of Babel." (Bion, 1963).

For Bion the Oedipus myth is an essential part of the learning apparatus in the early stages of development. It constitutes an "Oedipal myth preconception" which operates as a precursor of an important function of the ego for the discovery or knowledge of psychic reality. This preconception will lead to investigations into the relationship with the parental couple whose realization will be evident in contact with the real or substitute parents. Therefore Bion postulates the "private Oedipus myth," formed by alpha elements, and suggests that it is an important factor in the so called "psychoanalytical function of the personality." (Bion, 1963).

This "private Oedipus myth," a foundation for mental growth, can suffer destructive attacks due to envy, greed or sadism stemming from the psychotic part of the personality which opposes knowledge. The consequences of the attack are the fragmentation and dispersing of that preconception, preventing its forming part of a "learning apparatus" and of the attainment of intuition, and preventing the development of the "psychoanalytical function of the personality" and its evolution.

The primitive repressed material belongs mainly to elements of infantile sexuality. The theories of Melanie Klein (1952), contribute with concepts about even more primary levels of mental functioning, analogically modelled on the relationship the baby has with the breast. This model has made it possible to understand, in a clearer way, different situations which arise in

*"Catastrophic change" is a term with which Bion tries to join certain facts characterised by violence, invariance and subversion of the system, elements which he considers inherent to all situations of change and growth. A new idea or a new situation contains a potentially disruptive force which violates the structures of the field in which it appears.

the analytical link. What interests us now is the approach to another level of mental functioning: that of the "psychotic personality" (Bion, 1957). The notion of "psychotic personality," as described by Bion, does not involve a psychiatric diagnosis but rather a modality of mental functioning that manifests itself in the individual's behaviour and language and in the effects it produces in the observer. This mental state co-exists with another conceived of as the "non-psychotic personality" or "neurotic personality."

Freud has already confirmed that more primitive levels of functioning than that of desire, or that of the "pleasure principle," existed; levels which, for lack of binding together, "go beyond the pleasure principle" (Freud, 1920).

At this level, psychotic phenomena are found (not necessarily psychosis), which we understand is as Bion poses them, following Freud. He explains them as states in which the mind acts as apparatus to discharge the increase of stimuli (just as the baby does before the first experience of satisfaction). For this level of mental functioning we are probably lacking more models and myths to make them accessible to understanding. The myth of Narcissus (as well as the concept of narcissism) does not respond to this need, since it refers more to trying to join together in a libidinal way the degree of disorganization, than to explaining the functioning of the psychotic personality.

I suppose that this level of functioning exists not only in psychotic patients but also in all of us (although in small proportions) in a real or potential way. It is possibly the most primitive level of the mind. It is the most "surpassed" by the different levels of organization and also the most difficult to detect and interpret.

Part of the Oedipus myth, and that of Babel, offer the possibility of making more intelligible the phenomena of the "psychotic personality." We can see it in man's attempt to reach understanding or communication, and an omnipotent god who opposes this, punishing with exile or confusion of tongues the attempt to reach knowledge. Also in the Oedipus myth, separating the elements which form the sexual and incestuous part, it is possible to detect in the enigmatic and bizarre figure of the Sphinx, in the plague which destroys Thebes, in the arrogance of Oedipus in following through his investigations, in the warnings of Tiresias, in the omnipotence of the oracle and in the final catastrophe (suicide, blinding and exile), a "constant conjunction."*

I would like now to study the Oedipus myth from the vertex of Bion's theory of transformation (Bion, 1965).

Bion points out that the processes of transformation have, as their point of departure, an experience or initial situation categorised as the O of

*"Constant conjunction" is a term taken from Hume and refers to the fact that certain data observed regularly appear together. Bion uses this term in his hypothesis about the development of thought. A concept or a word are definitions that bind the observed elements that are constantly conjoined.

the transformation. This sign "O" represents the "ultimate unknowable reality," the "absolute truth," "reality," the "thing in itself," the "infinite" or the "unknown." In psychoanalysis we may use the sign "O" for all the unknown in the patient which shows itself by way of the multiple transformations which are brought about. The transformations which are related to "knowing about something" correspond to the transformations of the K link K (Knowledge). These are opposed by the transformation in O, which are related to change, growth, insight or "becoming O." Bion says that reality cannot, by definition, be known, although it can be "been." To this he gives the name "becoming O." The analyst deals with the psychic reality of the patient's personality in a way that goes beyond "knowing something about it," although this "knowing something about it" (transformation in K), is an important part of the psychoanalytical process. The "transformation in O," instead, is something like "being what one is" and that transformation is feared and therefore resisted. The resistential phenomena of the analytical process can be understood as the defence against danger which brings into play "becoming O," in the way that "becoming O" is equivalent to "being one's own truth" with the corresponding responsibility inherent in such a transformation. They are resistances which oppose the transformation $K \rightarrow O$. Only the interpretations which manage to change the transformations of "knowing about something" (K) to "being that something" (O), that is to say $K \rightarrow O$, will have any real effect of change and mental maturation (Bion, 1970).

I have already pointed out the common elements which exist in the three myths. On re-examining the myth of Eden in the light of previously mentioned concepts, it occurred to me that it was possible to find a different interpretation to the importance of the "Tree of Knowledge" and the "Tree of Life." The first, to which Adam and Eve had access and for which they were punished by being expelled from Paradise for having eaten of its fruit, would correspond to the Tree which provides the type of knowledge of the transformation in K, with a tendency toward the type of knowledge of the transformation in O, albeit without reaching O ($K \nrightarrow O$). But the true intuitive knowledge corresponding to "becoming O" is that which is symbolised in the myth by the "Tree of Life," from which one could gain everlasting knowledge O, the "language of achievement" which lasts through the centuries, and the access to which is barred by the "omnipotent and omniscient god" who punishes achievement of Knowledge K and who, in a severe way, prevents all possibility of approaching Knowledge "becoming O." The Bible says literally that "after expelling man from Paradise, Jehova placed cherubims with lighted swords to the East of the Garden, and they moved to and from to guard the way to the "Tree of Life." It is precisely this form of punishment and obstruction to attaining intuitive Knowledge (P) which is repeated in the narratives of the myths of Babel and Oedipus. These myths provide the messages which help us to understand the difficulties which arise as much for the patient as for the analyst in order to tolerate the pain for mental growth. If the mental pain of the "catastrophic change," which leads toward intuitive knowledge (with its characteristics of evolution and language of achievement), is not tolerated, one can fall into the psychopathic or psychotic attitude, with its characteristics of omnipotence and omniscience.

In my opinion, each of the myths shows that it can only reach the stage of transformation in K. But when the possibility arises of approaching the kind of knowledge of the transformation of "becoming O," then omnipotence, omniscience and even "Knowledge K" act as a resistance or barrier to prevent the suffering of the "catastrophic change" which leads toward "Knowledge becoming O."

Oedipus returns to Thebes in order to find out the truth; on solving the riddle of the Sphinx, Oedipus reaches Knowledge K. This searching for knowledge symbolises the "preconception Oedipal myth," precursor of the capacity of learning and insight.

It has already been shown that the Sphinx can not only symbolise Jocasta but, as all mythological monsters, part man, part woman, half human and half animal, represents the image "bizarre object" of the parents whose union gives rise to very primitive persecutory fantasies. On defeating the Sphinx, Oedipus feels that he is defeating the combined couple of his parents, from whom, in his fantasies, he snatches knowledge and, on taking possession of this knowledge (transformation in K), fills himself manically with omnipotence and omniscience which prevents his possibility of developing toward knowledge "becoming O" (transformation in O).

It is here where the negative influence of the psychotic personality appears over the neurotic one.

The theory of projective identification formulated by M. Klein (Klein, 1952), especially that of pathological projective identification formulated by Bion (Bion, 1967), along with the theory of projective counteridentification which I have described (Grinberg, 1956, 1959, 1962, 1963b), are theoretical developments which bring us closer to the understanding of the psychotic phenomena.

Under normal circumstances, the mechanism of projective identification is an integral part of all human relations and lays the foundations of communications. It determines the empathetic link with the object by enabling the individual to place himself in the position of his fellow being and so understand the other's feelings better.

In pathological cases, projective identification consists in an omnipotent fantasy through which unwanted parts of the personality and of internalised objects, together with attendant emotions are split off, projected and controlled in the object toward which the projection was directed. As a result, the object is equated with what was projected onto him. This mechanism operates with utmost intensity during the earliest periods of life. It is important to scrutinise not only the different modalities of the subject's projective identification as conditioned by his varied fantasies and impulses, but also those projective identifications of his parents and the kind of impact they made upon the subject.

The pathological functioning of the patient's projective identification can bring about a specific reaction in the analyst which I have termed "projective counteridentification" (Grinberg, 1956, 1957, 1962). This reaction is not consciously perceived by the analyst; as a result, he is sometimes passively led to play certain roles or functions, or to experience those affects (anger, depression, anxiety, boredom, among others) that the patient actively, though unconsciously, forces onto him. In previous papers I have dealt with different aspects of this phenomenon which should be distinguished from countertransference reactions based upon the analyst's own emotional attitudes, or on his neurotic remnants which have been reactivated by the patient's conflicts.

With a view to making the difference between countertransference and projective counteridentification clearer, I should like to point out that in the analytical situation, the analyst can either be an active subject of introjections and projections, or a passive subject of the patient's projections. In this case, however, two further situations may still develop; his emotional response may be elicited by the reawakening of his own conflicts (Racker's "complementary countertransference") (Racker, 1952), or his affective resonance can be the result of what the patient has projected onto him ("projective counteridentification"). The patient unconsciously stimulates, through this mechanism, the analyst's unconscious identification with a given aspect of an internal object or with certain parts of the patient's self, thus leading him to feel specific emotions or to act in a particular way. To make it clearer still, I would say that different analysts, because of their own countertransference would react in *different* ways to the same material of a hypothetical patient they all might have under treatment; the same hypothetical patient would arouse the *same* emotional response (projective counteridentification) in different analysts. It may take some time before the analyst succeeds in ridding himself of the effects of projective counteridentification. These effects are occasionally quite persistent, thus entailing a number of difficulties.

Projective identification and counteridentification phenomena are frequent in the analysis of narcissistic and borderline personalities, and give rise to a pathogenous interaction between analyst and patient which is not always easy to resolve. One could say that what was projected, by means of the psychopathic modality of projective identification, operates within the object as a parasitic superego which omnipotently induces the analyst's ego to act or feel what the patient wanted him to act or feel, in his unconscious fantasy. I think that to some degree this bears comparison with the hypnotic phenomenon as described by Freud (Freud, 1920): the hypnotiser places himself in the position of the ego ideal and a sort of paralysis appears as a result of the influence of an omnipotent individual upon an impotent and helpless being. I believe the same applies, sometimes, to the process I am discussing: the analyst, being unaware of what happened, may resort to all kinds of rationalizations in order to justify his attitude or his bewilderment, as the hypnotised person does after executing the hypnotic commands.

When the analyst is able to overcome this reaction, he may take advantage of this phenomenon in order to clarify some of the patient's unconscious fantasies and emotions, making possible the adequate interpretations.

Whenever the analyst has to meet such violent projective identifications, he may react in a normal way, by properly interpreting the material brought by the patient and by showing him that the violence of the mechanism has in no way shocked him. Sometimes, however, the analyst may be unable to tolerate it, and then he may react in several different ways: a) by an immediate and equally violent rejection of the material which the patient tries to project into him; b) by ignoring or denying this rejection through severe control or some other defensive mechanism; sooner or later, however, the reaction will become manifest in one way or another; c) by postponing and displacing his reaction, which will then become manifest with another patient: d) by suffering the effects of such an intensive projective identification, and "counteridentifying" himself, in turn. In fact, the response of the analyst will depend on his degree of tolerance.

When this projective counteridentification takes place, the normal communication between the patient's unconscious and that of the analyst will obviously be interrupted. In this case, the unconscious content rejected by the patient will be violently projected onto the analyst who, as the recipient object of such projective identifications, will have to suffer its effects. And he will react as if he had acquired and assimilated the aspects projected onto him in a *real and concrete way*. In certain cases the analyst may have the feeling of being no longer his own self and of unavoidably becoming transformed into the object which the patient, unconsciously, wanted him to be.

In passing, I would like to point out that, after several years of having stated my ideas on "projective counteridentification," I found these were confirmed in Bion's book *Learning from Experience* (1962), where he points out in detail that "the theory of countertransference offers only a partial explanation because it deals with the manifestation only as a symptom of unconscious motives of the analyst and therefore *the contribution of the patient is left without explanation*." Further on he adds: "Thanks to the beta screen, the psychotic patient has the ability to arouse emotions in the *analyst*." (The italics are mine.)

Projective counteridentification will have different modalities according to how the respective modalities of projective identification have been. This mechanism presents qualitative shades which give a determined specificity to its functional modality. Sometimes, it can be expressed through extraverbal communications which cross the analyst's critical threshold producing the projective counteridentification.

It is here where the negative influence of the psychotic personality, with its use of pathological projective identification, appears over the neurotic one. As I pointed out before, we are still lacking mythological models in order to understand the functioning of the psychotic personality, of its effects over the neurotic part of the patient's personality and over the analyst in the psychoanalytical situation. The story of the death of Palinurus, as described by Bion (1970), provides us, in part, with a model for these situations.

In chapter V of the Aeneid of Virgil, it is told how Palinurus captains the fleet of Aeneas and, while he is in command of the rudder, the god Somnus draws near disguised as Phorbas and tries to seduce him and persuade him to go and rest now that the sea is calm. Palinurus does not let himself be convinced saying that one must not be fooled by the appearance of a calm sea. Then the god sprinkles a "lethean forgetfulness" over him and Palinurus is left overcome by an uncomfortable lethargic sleepiness; then he is thrown into the sea, taking with him part of the deck and rudder. When Aeneas realises what has happened, he takes charge of the vessel and he bewails the excessive confidence of Palinurus, which cost him his life and to be lost at sea forever.

This myth is striking and full of suggestions. It is important for its narrative and pictorial quality; it is also important for its language, as is also the myth of Oedipus. I believe it represents also a useful complementary element for the understanding of some of the aspects of the Oedipus myth, especially those which relate to the "psychotic personality," in the resistential manic reaction of Oedipus through omnipotence and omniscience and the ulterior melancholic acting due to the "persecutory guilt" (Grinberg, 1963) seen in poking his eyes out and blinding himself.

The myth of Palinurus allows one to explain better the direct action of the patient's psychotic personality over the analyst's mind and its violent and clouding effect over his analytical function which is so necessary in order to carry out the psychoanalytical task.

We could compare Palinurus with the vicissitudes of an analyst who is carrying out his psychoanalytical treatment in the peace and quietness of his consulting room (with the calmness which the familiar and comfortable surroundings give him), and then, suddenly, he sees himself in danger of being thrown violently from the analytical situation by the elements which appear as a model in the story of Virgil. The effects produced by the "psychotic personality" impair both members of the analytical couple. It is possible to see in the myth the relationship between the analyst and his patient, or between the psychotic part and the non psychotic part of the personality, between the ego allied to fantasy and the ego in contact with reality, between dreams and hallucinations, lethargy and psychic death, etc. We can also see the fate of the analyst if he does not guard himself adequately against the effects of the "psychotic personality" of his patient and/or his own.

The psychotic part of the personality, be it in the patient or in the analyst, acts as a resistential element which interferes with and prevents the achievement of insight. In the narrative of the Oedipus myth one aspect of Oedipus obstructs the determination with which another part of him tries to continue the search. The split aspects of Oedipus, which represent the dissociations and projections which occur frequently in the patient, and even in the analyst, clearly appear represented in the myth. An illustrative example is that of Tiresias who, significantly, was also blinded for seeing the primal scene, and it is he who tries to prevent Oedipus from going ahead with his searching. But Tiresias (who received the gift of prophecy and the privilege of long life from Zeus), not only acted as a "superego," but also, and up to a certain point gets near to Knowledge "becoming O." Tiresias symbolises a split aspect of Oedipus, as also Creon represents it, or his daughter Ismenia, who tells him of the change of the oracle by which the gods, who before brought him down, now extol him and foretell peace and prosperity in the land which will receive him, instead of the plague which destroyed Thebes. The dialogue with Ismenia represents an interior dialogue between two aspects of Oedipus himself. We wonder if the Oedipus myth could not also be categorized as a "dream" in which all the characters represent split aspects of the dreamer, as Freud pointed out.

Freud was able to overcome the "catastrophic change" determined by the hubris of his discovery, because it was Freud. But how many analysts have such a capacity? Usually we do not tolerate exposing ourselves to the danger represented by the new and unknown which can develop in the analytical process. We immediately take refuge in the stockade of known theories so that we may stay with what is familiar to us.

In the analytical couple, the "resistential Oedipus" can be reproduced, because each one of the components takes upon himself the role of an "omnipotent god" who, on the one hand, stimulates curiosity and the search for knowledge and, on the other, obstructs it or sabotages it.

Defensive operations are brought into play in order to face the emergency of whatever material which could liberate anxiety or psychic pain, as much in the patient as in the analyst, among which one finds splitting, pathological projective identification, acting out, omnipotence, omniscience reversal of perspective (Bion, 1963), psychosomatic symptoms and the resistential use of psychoanalytical theories.

Many of the above mentioned defensive processes are sufficiently well known. Nevertheless, I think it useful to say a few words about some of them. Omniscience is characterised by the functioning and influence of a superego which opposes all search for truth and tries to impose itself on a basis of a fantasy of total superiority. Patients who use this fantasy, instead of trying to learn, insist that they "possess" knowledge, trying to avoid the painful experience of the learning process. The "reversal of perspective" consists in a silent and constant rebuff of the interpretive tenets on which the interpretation is based, and this attitude is disguised as an apparent agreement with the analyst. There are patients who react to certain interpretations as if they were a countertransferential confession, misrepresenting in this way the objective of the analysis. What the patient is really doing is denying the dynamic character of the interpretation and its investigatory aspect, which are fundamental preconditions by which the analysis can be capable of furthering change and mental growth. For his part, the analyst can also "reverse" the perspective, taking the associations of the patient as an antidote for his own anxiety in face of the unknown and unknowable of the material. Another way of defensive operation which tends to counterarrest the suffering of psychic pain, consists in the unconscious evacuation of the mentioned pain, along with the conflict which originated it, in the body. Generally, physical pain appears to be better tolerated than psychic pain. In this way, the mental phenomenon is transformed into a sensory feeling which is devoid of the feared emotional meaning or better still, it tries to change that psychic meaning which is intolerable into a sensory experience.

Analyst and patient can also resort to the resistential use of analytical theories because they cannot bear the "catastrophic change" which would lead them toward having to face psychic pain associated with the discovery of a new idea, a strong emotion or insight. On confronting it with the possibility of arriving at Knowledge "becoming O" or with insight, the new idea can provoke in the analyst or the patient a defensive opposition which increases his tendency to remain with the familiar and already known without presenting himself with new doubts. In this way he is flattening or dogmatising psychoanalysis and therefore avoiding the "catastrophic change" and mental growth.

On different occasions I have tried to apply a mathematical model, mentioned by Bion (Bion, 1965), to different situations of theory and clinical experience. It deals with the model represented by the circle crossed by a line at two points ($\ominus$), the circle crossed by a line at one point ($\bigcirc\!\!\!/$) and the circle and the line completely separated without having any point of contact ($\underline{\bigcirc}$). These three variants can represent, for example, the discrimination between the subject and the object, the symbol and the symbolised, reality and fantasy, consciousness and unconsciousness, etc., for the first case; either the state of confusion or of projective counteridentification in the second case; and that of the psychotic personality which is in a world completely separated and without any contact with the neurotic personality, the lack of contact between the patient and the analyst, etc., in the third case.

I think that this model can also be applied to the different types of interaction between the two components of the analytical couple.

If the "analyst-patient" couple functions in a discerning way, facing up to psychic suffering which will allow the "transformation in K" to change into "transformation in becoming O," it would be represented by the secant ($\ominus$). If the "analyst-patient" group is in resistance alliance by means of a mutual idealisation and omnipotence in order to oppose the evolution of "Knowledge becoming O" it would be represented by the tangent ($\bigcirc\!\!\!/$); and when the "analyst-patient" group functions with the predominance of the "reversal of perspective" or of strong feelings of envy, the model which would represent this is that of the line which has no contact with the circle ($\underline{\bigcirc}$).

The patient, by his pathological use of projective identification can evoke a response of projective counteridentification in the analyst which, among other things, leads him to increase the use of his analytical theories (transformation in K), and to utilise them in a resistential way (the Oedipus resistance). In this way the creative part of the analyst can be inhibited and at the same time an increase of his psychotic personality can be stimulated. This leads him to resort to "hyper memory" and omniscience, in a precocious way formulating omnipotent interpretations as if they were the "only possible truth," without admitting doubts or replicas; he may also resort to episodes of acting out.

One could also use Bion's model of the container-contained relationship (Bion, 1963) to represent the existing link between the analyst and the patient. In this model each partner of the therapeutic couple can personify, in an alternating way, the "contained new idea," which requires a group container to allow its evolution. Should anxiety (faced with the achievement of "knowledge becoming O") become predominant in the analytical link, then the "contained-interpretation-new idea," which would potentially promote the evolution of that knowledge could be obstructed (instead of stimulated) by the "group container" made up of the patient and another aspect of the analyst to form a resistential alliance K. Inversely, the "contained-new idea" can be provided by the patient by means of his associations, and instead of being stimulated in its evolution, it is attacked by the "group container" formed by the analyst and another aspect of the patient, resorting to "resistance K."

By way of illustration I want to present a brief clinical vignette where one can appreciate the patient-analyst interaction and its influence in the interpretative formulations.

The patient is an extremely sensitive and intelligent woman. She had excelled in her profession as an architect, but this did not manage to compensate for her depressive state and the role of the victim which she used to put herself in her relationships with others. She felt identified with a self-sacrificing mother who "enjoyed suffering to the limit" but who had never managed to take care of her and to understand her. On the other hand, she felt she had to carry the burden of a father who suffered from manic depressive psychosis and who had been hospitalised on several occasions. At times, she felt an inner emptiness which led to situations of persecution, hostility and rejection; she felt that in this way she was linked to someone, even though it was a link of fear or hate.

She started one session with the following words:

> Patient: "I do not know why, but I find it difficult to speak. I've been very anxious the last few days. I worry about anything, the purchase of the new car, the bank credit; I told my father that if the credit is not granted, he will have to pay the difference himself. Pauline (a friend of hers) paid me a visit yesterday. I thought I'd die. She's such a bore, she is a burden. She keeps making demands that no one can ever satisfy. She asks for advice, but when she gets it she objects, or is always finding faults; she is permanently unsatisfied. On the other hand, I went yesterday with my father to the interview with his psychiatrist; and this made me very anxious too; at a given moment, I felt that the level of

communication between the psychiatrist and me was totally inaccessible to my father."

Analyst: I pointed out her hopelessness in trying to keep safe a part within her which she considers beyond reach and very demanding, and to which she felt that neither she herself, nor I, nor analysis, nor indeed anyone could change. I added that she partly lodged this sector into me and she was afraid that I might demand too much from her.

(I think that this interpretation runs the risk of becoming inaccessible to the patient. Perhaps I should have limited myself to pointing out that she was afraid that she and I could neither speak nor understand each other.)

Patient: "Today we were supposed to open a credit account at the bank, but I remembered that my father once drew some cheques when he had no funds in the account, and as a result we were under an embargo. So, I told him I was not going to open a joint account with him."

Analyst: I told her that she cannot at present join another part of her which threatens to ruin her; besides she is not so sure she ought to join my interpretations because they might fail to offer a guarantee.

(Here I should have included only the second part of the interpretation to avoid the danger of confusion to which personalities of this type are prone. I could have emphasised her doubts more as to whether or not she was going to get anything out of the analysis, and that she does not want to open a "joint account" with me, in this analysis, because she does not understand me well enough nor does she feel sure of herself with me.)

Patient: I felt just like someone who is never more going to change or to improve. I feel hopeless.

Analyst: I interpreted that she was implicitly asking me to rid her of that heavy burden which makes her feel hopeless and skeptical: "never more."

(It is questionable here whether in fact she was asking anything implicitly, or whether this was determined by my projective counteridentification with another part of the patient which was not verbalised. Perhaps it would have been more useful to await her following association.)

Patient: I'm feeling two fears at the same time and I don't know which is the greatest. On the one hand, there is the fear of facing the destroyed, the mad. And there is the greater fear of finding myself confronted with possibilities and not with limitations. If I'm made to face myself just as I am, there are anxiety provoking images which make me aware of my limitations. But if I were to think that I can hope for more, how could I manage to put up with this new reality? It would be catastrophic and terrible. Every time I find myself related to someone else by a tie of understanding and empathy, I just don't know what to do. Giving it up is easier for me than finding that I'm able to wait and change. I couldn't go on living as I do now. I realise that the real load is not what I'm burdened with or what I have. What is really heavy and unbearable to me is what I never had and what I don't have. Perhaps that is why I put a "never again" stamp on me and take it easy. Every time I let myself go into day dreaming or try to regain youth, I feel myself sinking and have to make a tremendous effort to refloat. It's a sensation of physical exertion. I was never able to transmit my day dreaming to anybody, I could never do it. In the course of this analysis I began to feel I might transmit things in a different manner."

Analyst: I pointed out that the fact of trying to transmit things in a different manner could be perhaps still another day dreaming exercise because she was afraid of me and found it terrifying to discover that, through her relationship with me she might get to know and understand the content of her anxiety and depression.

(Here the patient's words appear too sensible and too theoretical. She resorted to intellectualization as a defense mechanism. My interpretation, due to the projective counteridentification, and finding myself allied to the resistance of the patient, overlooked pointing out the use of this defense mechanism and showed a fear of the transferential link, with its threat of drawing her closer to her anxiety. I should have asked her what was the meaning of "to be carried away with her dreamy thoughts," and what were the contents of these fantasies. Instead of doing it this way, I was "placed" in the position of going along with and accepting her intellectual reasonings (knowledge "transformation in K") which was used in order to avoid the authentic insight about the contents of her depression and anxiety ("knowledge transformation in O").

CONCLUSIONS

Resistances which the patient put up during the psychoanalytical process in order to avoid insight and a deeper understanding of his conflicts, because he cannot tolerate psychic suffering, are well known and they constitute one of the great difficulties in clinical practice. But what is less known is the resistance put up by the analyst himself to the evolution of insight and "intuitive knowledge." One of the principal aims of this paper is precisely to point out this kind of resistance of the analyst, which leads him to reinforce the use of his psychoanalytical theories (knowledge K), among other things and, on other occasions, taking onto himself (through projective counteridentification) the resistances of the patient in order to obstruct the development of the treatment and psychoanalytical knowledge. I think that it constitutes one of the most serious dangers which attack the future of psychoanalysis and determines that the work which the analyst carries out with the patients continues to be a "talking about psychoanalysis (K), instead of "being psychoanalysis" (O).

In synthesis, applying the "theory of transformations" to the concepts I have illustrated, I could sum up them in the following way: the final product of the transformation in K utilised by the patient in a resistential context ("Oedipus resistential–patient"), is added to the final product of the transformation in K which occurs in the analyst at a resistential level ("Oedipus resistential-analyst"), in order to obstruct the evolution of the analytical link on its way toward "intuitive knowledge" of the "transformation in becoming O ("Oedipus knowledge-patient-analyst").

References

Bion, W.R. (1957), Differentiation of the psychotic from the non-psychotic personalities, *Int. J. Psycho-Anal.* 38, pp. 266-275.

— (1962), *Learning from Experience*, London: Heinemann.

— (1963), *Elements of Psychoanalysis*, London: Heinemann.

— (1965), *Transformations*, London: Heinemann.

— (1966) Catastrophic change, in *Scientific Bulletin of the British Psychoanalytical Society*, 5.

— (1967), *Second Thoughts*, London: Heinemann.

— (1970), *Attention and Interpretation*, London: Tavistock Publ.

— (1971), *Bion's Brazilian Lectures I*, Imago Editora. Rio de Janeiro. Brasil.

Freud, Sigmund (1913), *Totem and Taboo, S.E. 11*.

— (1920) *Beyond the Pleasure Principle, S.E. 17*.

— (1921), *Group Psychology and Analysis of the Ego, S.E. 18*.

— (1923), *The Ego and the Id, S.E. 20*.

Grinberg, L. (1956), Sobre algunos problemas de técnica psicoanalítica determinados por la identificación y contraidentificación proyectivas, *Rev. de Psic. 13*, p. 4.

— (1957), Perturbaciones en la interpretación debidas a la contraidentificación proyectiva, *Rev. de Psic.* 14, pp. 1-2.

— (1962), On a specific aspect of countertransference due to the patient's projective identification, *Int. J. Psycho-Anal.*, Vol. 43, pp. 436-441.

— (1960), Los significados del morar, *Rev. de Psicoanal.*, 17, 2.

— (1963b), Psicopatología de la identificación y contraidentificación proyectivas y de la contratransferencia, *Rev. de Psicoanal.*, 20, 2.

Klein, M. (1952). *Developments in Psycho-Analysis*, M. Klein et al., London: Hogarth Press.

— (1952), Notes on some schizoid mechanisms, in *Developments in Psychoanalysis*, M. Klein et al., London: Hogarth Press.

Racker, H. (1952), Observaciones sobre la contratransferencia como instrumento tecnico, *Rev. de Psicoanal.* 9, 3.

Who is the Dreamer Who Dreams the Dream and Who is the Dreamer Who Understands It?

James S. Grotstein

EDITOR'S NOTE: *My own contribution is an attempt to comprehend the awesome spatial container and dream generator. In particular I focus on the importance of dream narrative, and narrative generally, as an important component in helping to organize the experience of chaos into time-binding configurations of significance and meaning. Narrative thus appears to be a binding and organizing factor in mental life.* *

* I am especially grateful to Dr. Albert Hutter whose painstaking critique of this contribution I found to be of inestimable assistance.

Who Is the Dreamer Who Dreams the Dream and Who Is the Dreamer Who Understands It?

James S. Grotstein

A Psychoanalytic Inquiry Into the Ultimate Nature of Being [Revised]

In his sleep, Vishnu dreamed the dream of the Universe.

—The Bhagavad-Gita

All life is a dream and the dreams are dreams from a dream.

—Calderon de la Barca

. . . For we know in part, and we prophecy in part.
But when that which is perfect is come, then that
which is in part shall be done away.
When I was a child, I spake as a child: but when
I became a man, I put away childish things.
For now we see through a glass, darkly; but then
face to face: now I know in part; but
then shall I know even as also I am known.
And now abideth faith, hope, charity, these three;
but the greatest of these is charity.

—The First Epistle of Paul the Apostle to the Corinthians 13: 9-13

The Dream

When Freud (1900) bequeathed to us his legacy—the understanding of the dream—psychoanalysis, patients, and laymen generally became so intoxicated with this new unraveling of the content of unconscious communication that the staging of the dream took little notice among scholars and dreamers generally. I believe the dream stage is a very important psychic *container* which has important and intricate relations with its *content*, the dream. Bion's concept of the container and the contained has so wide an application in psychological and biological phenomena generally that I believe it amounts to a new natural law (Bion 1962, 1963, 1965, 1970, 1975). Since Bion himself has not stated it so formally, I myself should like to state it as follows: *all living phenomena can be viewed as content existing in the framework of a container which circumscribes and describes its content, and, reciprocally, the content has great influence in transforming the nature of its*

Grotstein, J.S. ["Who Is the Dreamer Who Dreams the Dream, and Who Is the Dreamer Who Understands It?"] This article first appeared in *Contemporary Psychoanalysis* 15, 110-169, in a shorter version, 1979.

container. In other words, a reciprocal relationship exists between the container and the content of natural phenomena existing in the biological series. I should like to isolate a single instance of this biological vastness, the dream, to demonstrate the importance of the dream framework and its relationship to its container.

When I was a second year medical student I had a dream the night before the final examination in pharmacology which I remember across the years as follows: the setting was a bleak piece of moorland in the Scottish Highlands engulfed by a dense fog. A small portion of the fog slowly cleared and an angel appeared surrealistically asking, "Where is James Grotstein?" The voice was solemn and litanical. The fog slowly re-enveloped her form as if she had never existed or spoken. Then, as if part of a prearranged pageant, the fog cleared again but now some distance away, at a higher promontory where a rocky crag appeared from the cloud bank revealing another angel who, in response to the first angel's question, answered as follows: "He is aloft, contemplating the dosage of sorrow upon the Earth."

The Dreamer Who Dreams the Dream

At the time I had this dream I knew little of dream interpretation. I knew only that psychoanalysis existed, that I was drawn to it, and that dreams had meaning. The meaning of this dream began to unveil itself in subsequent analysis many years later. I do not wish to call attention to the meaning of my dream in this presentation. I wish to call attention instead to the setting, that is, to the framework of it. When I awoke from the dream, I recall having a strange sense of peace (to which I owed a debt of gratitude for having done well in the subsequent examination.) What most arrested my attention then, however, and, I must say, thereafter until the present day, was what I believe to be the beauty and the poetry of the dream. The reader may feel that the lines were "corny" and histrionic reminders of adolescent theater. I can only say that that was not my impression; I was deeply impressed, mystified, and bewildered. I knew that I had experienced the dream, but I do not know who wrote it. I wanted desperately to be introduced to the writer who could write those lines. Across the years I added other wishes to that wish: I wished to be introduced to the producer of the short play (or maybe it was a much longer play, as I now have reason to believe, and I was privileged to see a small portion of it which appeared through an aperture in the cloud bank of sleep). Across the years I also wished to be introduced to the casting director. Where did he find those particular angels? I found that I began to wish to be introduced to the scenic director who chose the Scottish Highlands. He must have known me very well because Scotland had been of enormous importance to me in my youth. The issues of Scotland and dosage were the only aspects of the dream that were familiar to me which belonged to my personal life. Otherwise the dream was phantastic.

As I began to realize all the various people to whom I wished to be introduced, it began slowly to dawn on me that my dream was a play, or a small portion of a larger play: a narrative conceived by a cunning playwright; produced by an economic and dramatic producer; directed by a director who had a sense of timing, the uncanny, and the dramatic moment; staged by a scenic designer who could offset the narrative of the dream with a setting that highlighted it to maximum intensity of feeling; and a casting director who had a flair for the medieval and the romantic nature of theatricality.

In particular, I wished to be introduced to the writer. It was he who intrigued me the most and yet who frustrated me the most because I admired his script but felt frustrated that I felt so alien to him. I experienced the phenomenon which Clifford Scott (1975) has called the "dreamer's envy of himself." The self who wrote that dream was admired, envied, idealized, and unknown to me. So unknown to me was he as a matter of fact that he might just as well have been somebody else.

Years later, I was to encounter patients who were television writers who variously functioned as story editors. It was then that I became introduced to that sophistication of the writing craft which governs the life story of the play from its inception to its first trial response upon the creative mind of the story editor, and then to its modification based upon his criteria of "workability," to the preview prior to the opening night. What makes a dream "workable" appears to be the result of complex artistic and affectual negotiations within the psyche. Little is known about the operation of this or any of the other functions delineated in this presentation. I make special mention of the story editor function because I believe it to be a gauge or function of the dreamer's adaptiveness or resilience to distress as well as a measure of the resourcefulness and creativity of his imagination.

I should like to give a specific example from the external world to show how this "story editor" function may work. A patient who is a television writer functioned occasionally as a story editor for his show. Once, he had to suggest a workable rewrite to an author who was submitting an autobiographical script. The author refused to submit his story to rewrite. In this example we can see an analogy to dream work. The author presenting the autobiographical reality represents raw, uncoded sense data which presents itself to the Dreamer first for "rewrite." "Rewrite" is a way of talking about the transformation of real photographic reality into a narrative which has universal dramatic appeal. An alteration of the story must take place. Censorship would too narrowly define this purpose. Emphases, deletions, and content changes occur in scripts of the external world; whereas in the internal world, the script is mythified and the elements of the narrative are condensed and displaced through the use of metonymy and synechdoche, and symbolization further transforms the narrative into mythic form. It would seem that symbols, both personal and universal, serve as transistors to facilitate the change of the ordinary story into a myth.

In the example above, the writer would not submit his story to "rewrite," therefore, the story would not "work." Might this not be the equivalent of the nightmare? But why must the story be rewritten in order to work, and what does "work" mean? It seems that the human being is so composed and disposed that he believes he must first be able to dream the new reality or, in effect, re-create it in his own mythic way so as to gain sovereignty over it and be able to transfer it over from Bion's first vertical (ordinate) column to his horizontal abscissa (for mental consideration and action). *Thoughts are actions and actions are narratives.* They must first be tried or previewed before thinking is possible.

The universal myths such as the Oedipus complex, Biblical *Genesis*, the legend of Christ, etc., are compressed and condensed narrative prototypes which first emerged in the primal dawn as a man's dream and later conjoined with similar dreams of other men. In the legend of Biblical *Genesis*, for instance, it is important for the God-child, having just been born, to imagine that He created all that His eyes open to before He can allow for the separate creation of His perceptions. Gradually, the composite dream formed and became the myth, and the myth became the prototype *and* palimpsest for all dreams. The myth offers, furthermore, that form of ageless reassurance, known in the law as the principle of *stare decisis* –that there is a precedent to all problems and that the Dreamer, if allowed to dream the problems down Bion's vertical axis, can link the problem to a soluble, mythical problem so as to offer the hope of a solution.

Ultimately, the Dreamer Who Dreams the Dream is that infantile aspect of us who registers changes and transmits this danger as a dream narrative to the Dreamer Who Understands the Dream–for corrective completion. In an analytic hour we can only marvel at the effectiveness of the Dreamer who Dreams the Dream because in this instance (s)he is the one who organizes the schedule of sequence of problems, organized with that stochastic randomness known as free association. This organizational randomness is the highly organized transformational generative syntax of the unconscious; primary process does not quite do justice to the vast sweep of its genius; Bion's alpha function better approximates it. It is my belief that the organizer of associations is the messiah within. I shall return to a discussion of this unique phenomenon when I discuss the Background Object of Primary Identification.

Who Is The Dreamer Who Understands The Dream?

As I continued my inquiry into the mystique of the dream, I began gradually to wonder about even yet another member of the theatrical cast, so to speak: the *audience*. Human beings have been dreaming since the beginning of their existence and are fortunate to be able to remember any portion of their dreams. Although different prophetic meanings have been ascribed to dreams in the past, it was only since Freud that conventional scientific technology was able to be applied to them. Freud believed that dreams were nighttime visualizations of wish-fulfillments. In my later analytic training I came to accept that concept until I discovered the object relations theories of Fairbairn and of Melanie Klein. But even if Freud were right, I began to wonder who discharges the tension—in other words, who watches the dream to know that it is fulfilling a wish, particularly if the dreamer is asleep (and Freud did advise us that the purpose of the dream is to protect sleep).

I reasoned, in other words, that there must be something like an unseen audience in the dream which observes the play, experiences its truths and its messages, and renders an approval—the rubber stamp of continued sleep. It dawned on me that the dream is something like an evacuation of nighttime accretions of mental stimuli arranged as narrative, dramatized in theatrical form and relayed communicatively to an audience who experiences *dramatic communication* in such a way as to undergo the phenomenon of *relief*. This audience must be very literate, articulate, and theater-wise. This audience, moreover, must be a most particular critic and have some hidden, unknown and unknowable, inscrutable knowledge of the rules of human drama and narrative. Certain laws must exist in which the framework of dramatic narrative can be stated and portrayed so that a piece of therapeusis can occur: *The dream is therapy in a dramatic form!*

I began to reason that dreams are arranged by a composite system of subselves—the nocturnal muses—who speak and arrange the language of poetry, narrative, and drama in such a way so as to resonate with a latent story in the audience as if two halves of a mystic symbol who have long ago known each other are rejoining once again after the identifying shibboletic call. When the potential story existing in the mystic Audience-Dreamer's mind is touched by the narrative spun by the therapeutic Dreamer, the two halves of the symbol seem to come together and a therapeutic bowel movement seems to take place. Evacuation is what I believe Freud had in mind by wish-fulfillment in dreams. At the same time the dream narrative, in rejoining its lost ancestral half, seems to lead to solutions of problems, creations (such as the benzene ring dream of the discoverer of aromatic chemistry), and prophecies of the future.

By "evacuation" I mean to suggest that dreams seem to discharge anxiety and tension and allow the dreamer to remain asleep. I began to realize that the problem was more complex than Freud and many of his followers had assumed. It is my belief that the effective"evacuative" function of dreams involves a Dreamer Who Dreams the Dream and a Dreamer Who Understands the Dream. The first corresponds to Bion's conception of the projecting infant and the second to a mother who has the capacity for reverie to "field" the projections for less toxic transformations. Together, they form a "dreaming couple" (to correspond to a "thinking couple").

What emerged from this inquiry into the nature of the container of the dream were the following ideas:

(A) Dreams were dramatic narrations written, directed, produced, etc., by a composite Dreamer, unknown to us, who used the vehicle of narrative as the instrument of phantasy and myth, as well as of neurophysiological perception—namely visualization—to organize the chaotic, fragmented, accretions of mental pain left over as residues of yet one more day of existence. Bion was able to cast additional light on this matter (Bion 1970). What we commonly call the "dream" is the visual transformation of a never-ending pageant of events in the internal world. Their daytime transformation may be free association or whatever manifestations of the unconscious may appear. In short, we never stop dreaming. Dreaming is the absorption and transformation of internal and external sensual data which, after they have been "dreamed," are then ready for mental digestion.

(B) There was an audience who anticipated the dream, required it, and moreover requisitioned it from the dream producer in order to recognize its problems and to resonate with its own hostaged self—a self which is experienced as having been lost like a Sleeping Beauty waiting to be awakened by the Prince Charming dream forged in the smithy of dream work by the Dreamer.

(C) The human being, as we know him, is, as a consciousness or awareness of self, but a pinpoint on the vast surface of Cosmic Selfness and is blessed or doomed—whichever the case may be—never to know his Ultimate Self (Selves?). It is as if the boundaries of the body self do not begin to describe, to circumscribe, or to contain the boundaries of the Sense of Self, or, as I would now more nearly properly like to designate It, the Sense of "I-ness" which seeks Its reflection in Its "Selfness." The images or the representations of a more penetrating and irrupting Sense of Self which is self-transcendent and near infinity-reaching can be contained only as images or representations within the Sense of Self known as ourselves in the flesh. Perhaps another way of saying this is that we are far more, and less, than we realize.

(D) Narrative in dramatic form, as it occurs in dreams, occurs according to certain rhythmic prinicples which allow it to resonate with the lost mystic hostage of the dream audience.

(E) The dream is a passion play insofar as it is the testimonial staging of the performance of and witnessing of the experience of passionate release. In the rhythmic concordance between the dream actor and the dream audience there occurs the preliminary certification of one's emerging authenticity preparatory to a *real* certification via action in the real world. The effect of the audience certification is to have established a boundary to curtail omnipotent performance and passionate penetrations and, conversely, to authenticate those aspects of emerging "I" which are worthy of "Truth" and realness.

(F) The dream is the quintessence of narrative, and narrative is the artistic and awesome arrangement, in a linear, plot-oriented sequential form, of a story which absorbs the passionate outcries of psychic disturbances and perturbations and permits these outcries to "tell their story"in a special and pre-ordained way (according to the laws of narrative) so that the story may be told—and heard. The consequences of this are that the outcries may then be forgotten or acted upon. Experience and traumatic experience especially are not safe until they have been dreamed, upon which they then emerge from the first and second dimension to the third dimension of mind.

The Dreamer Who Understands the Dream is the audience which verifies the passion of the dreamer. In addition to its being requisitioner of the dream, it is also the barrier which contains the dream. It has a mirror function—albeit a porous mirror—to reflect the passions of the dreamer but also to be influenced by them, much like a mother's relationship to a child. I believe this container-audience-mirror function of the Dreamer Who Understands the Dream to correspond to Bion's vertical column two, the function of which is the antipode of the definitory hypothesis in column one and its obligatory complement. It questions truth and accuracy, detects omnipotence, and reduces the raw ore of hypothesis to the elemental thought-grains of substance—unless it has become saturated with the passions of its subject of column one, in which case it can collude, enviously attack, or greedily purloin the passionate hypothesis for its own perverse purposes, thereby precluding the truthful destiny of the hypothesis in the reifying madness which results. Column two, in other words, is the Oedipus complex insofar as the Oedipus complex is a defining barrier which the child must confront in order to know himself.

The audience is the background which helps the foreground hypothesis stay in the foreground until it has defined itself, at which time authentication, correlation, and self-publication are established. The rituals and rites of passage in primitive societies, the requisite ten man composition for a Hebrew religious congregation, the role of the legislature with the president or monarch are but everyday vestiges and derivatives of the powerful authenticating function.

Now that I have established the conception of the Dreamer Who Dreams the Dream and the Dreamer Who Understands the Dream, I should like to suggest a modification in my conception of them. As I have portrayed them so far, they seem more like the static electrons on the rings surrounding an atomic nucleus in a chemist's diagram, rather than the dynamic picture of the physicist's. I actually see an almost infinite number of sorties back and forth between the two of highly coded messages which, in their dynamic reciprocal feedback, finally forge an acceptable dream narrative. In other words, I picture the Dreamer Who Dreams the Dream as being, indirectly, the crying infant who sends projectible messages into the containing mother whose "reverie" catches the ballistic and transforms it. The internalized other container and her reverie become the Dreamer Who Understands the Dream. It is my further impression, moreover, that, subserved in Bion's conceptions of maternal reverie is the maternal capacity to dream or mythify the projections let alone handle them realistically. Thus, *the mother's capacity to put the projected pain to sleep is a testimony to her capacity to dream for the infant. The infant then takes in a dreaming couple to correspond to a thinking couple which can either put feelings to sleep and/or think about them.*

One can see a breakdown in this phenomenon in the poignantly tragic *Denkwürdigkeiten* of Schreber. His delusional system underwent many rapid revisions from being the plaything for sexual abuse by others, to being persecuted by Flechsig, to finally being impregnated by God's rays. Obviously his delusional system underwent multifarious rewrites by his now-chaotic Rewrite Editor, who I believe is a function of the Dreamer Who Understands the Dream in collaboration with the Dreamer Who Dreams the Dream. It is particularly in psychosis that we can see the unsuccessful dream function in the unacceptability of the narrative—or, more to the point, for the narrative finally to become acceptable, the mind must alter itself. *Ultimately, the Dreamer Who Dreams the Dream must find a narrative solution acceptable to the Dreamer Who Understands the Dream, and the two must work in harmony to that end. The failure of their harmony is psychosis, in which case harmony is produced by the alternative of altering the integral structure and coherence of the mind*. A proliferation of "ad libbing" or improvisations then results until a new "psychotic order" is established which submits the Dreamer Who Dreams the Dream and the Dreamer Who Understands the Dream to its new, mad, autochthonous order. The stage of the dream is now in the cursorily restored area of past devastations and is thereafter to be known as the Domain of -K (Domain of Hallucinatory Transformations).

The Dreamer Who Understands the Dream is as mysterious as the Dreamer Who Dreams the Dream. It is the self in relationship to "I." A self in association with a Divine Self seems to be able to experience the Truth of a dream as the Truth within a dream. The advent of the dream constitutes an epiphany of Truth which descends or condescends to intervene and therefore present a rent in its perfection of Truth. Total symmetry transforms to human asymmetrical experience for a moment. The result is continuing peace of mind, solution of a problem, resolution of a dilemma—in short, a sanctuary with a new lease.

The unsuccessful dream—the nightmare—can be seen as an epiphany of a greater rent in the symmetry of Perfect Truth. A war between I and Self—that is, a war between different aspects of the Background Object of Primary Identification, the bastion of Trust and Truth—now seems to undermine the Dreamer. If the background object is thought to have been damaged, then dreams are believed to be too malevolently oracular. This corresponds to what I have termed in another contribution (Grotstein, *1977a*), the Magus Object, one whose language is mysterious, awesome, and foreboding. At the same time, it may be a benevolent Cassandra doomed to be disbelieved by a *Self-self* perversely split-off and at odds with the Dreamer. This is a foreshadowing of psychotic experience. Ultimately, the Dreamer Who Understands the Dream is an arcane representation of the internalized maternal container which "collects" the narrative urgency and modifies the story until dream solution and resolution are possible.

Freud (1900) stated that day residues in the preconscious psychic system are purloined by the instincts which, like devils, constantly seek human form in order to materialize (the metaphor is mine, not Freud's). In so doing, they effectively offer a protective barrier to the day residue. In Bion's terms the day residue are beta → alpha elements which are linked up with inherent and acquired preconceptions. Freud then states that the new-formed amalgam of instinct plus day residue *condenses* in order to achieve sufficient intensity so as to impinge regressively on the projection screen of perception—for discharge. Bion states that this is how sense impression (day residues) and realized preconceptions are *stored*, as in a betamax, awaiting the proper time in the scenario of the unconscious in order to walk onto the stage.

The Dreamer Who Dreams the Dream, in consort with the Dreamer Who Understands the Dream, can normally be thought of as an integrated oneness of purpose which succeeds in allowing the human being to be an individual with a sense of continuing identity, and "at-one-ment" with himself. In the analysis of nuerotics this "oneness" can be seen as the symbolic script writer who writes (determines) the free associations in his/her own inscrutable way. In psychotic illness, on the other hand, it is as if this writer disappears as a single entity, becomes altered, fragmented, and then reconstituted as many disparate, independent "writers" who now create disconnected, loose associations comprising a cacophonic argot of the bizarre. Psychotic illness, in other words, is a testimony to the absence of the Dreamer Who Dreams the Dream and the Dreamer Who Understands the Dream. One might just as well call them dreamers who are trying to dream a dream, dreamers who certainly do not understand the dreams, all of them looking for the lost dream and its dreamer.

From another point of view, the Dreamer Who Dreams the Dream and the Dreamer Who Understands the Dream seem to confirm Steele's (1979) notion that "We all have within the language that constitutes us an unknown partner in dialogue" (p. 394).

THE ACTORS

The explanations of the narrative drama of the dream and its literary counterpart must include a discussion of those who perform the play. In actual plays and novels the characters are created by the author to carry out his artistic intention. They themselves are incidental to the plot unless the focus is mainly on character development. In an actual play a real actor must subordinate his own personality to accommodate to the role and then must "project" artistic emphasis into it. In television plays the conflict of the hapless actor waiting hungrily to be fed his lines by the writer constantly "creating" and "re-creating" him is quite poignant. The actor is absolutely dependent like an infant on his creator and nurturer, the playwright, and the latter is then dependent on the actor to perform his lines. The resentful, envious actor may believe himself to be a fit critic for the playwright's lines and seek to change them so as to assert his defiant independence.

The characters of dreams are cast by an especially clever Casting Director who has especially clever techniques—chimerical ones—to produce a composite figure from all the corners of memory and imagination to be fashioned and honed by the most sophisticated deployment of projective identification and splitting. The finished product is given life. It is as if the dream actors do not know they are actors. We are fortunate if *we* "know" that they are. Once given life, even though imaginatively, they occupy mental space, have lines, agendas, purposes, actions, reactions, responses, and the like. The dream is not a dream without them but we are never the same again because of them owing to their cumulative subterranean effect on our psyches.

I am particularly interested in the fate of the contumacious, unpredictable character created by the Dreamer Who Dreams the Dream and cast by the Casting Director of the Dream Who, once given life, begins to "ad lib," that is, takes matters into his own hands improvisationally and imagines himself to be the Dreamer of the Dream, etc. The depressive forlorn, existential aspects of this capriciously created and perfunctorily dismissed soul were dealt with brilliantly by Tom Stoppard in his play *Rosenkranz and Guildenstern Are Dead*. Pirandello dealt with this theme from another angle in *Six Characters in Search of an Author*, by which title I infer the characters had already "killed" the author by their very birth and were thus orphaned–or, on the other hand, were like "*thoughts without a thinker*" awaiting an author's mind to *realize* them. The "actor" is created or requisitioned by the Dreamer Who Dreams the Dream through his Casting Director function in order to probe a problem which does not easily "go to sleep." By enacting it internally (or even externally), sufficient separation and objectivity occur to allow the dreamer a "second look" at the problem. Dream acting is experimental action which is otherwise known as *thinking*. It constitutes an experimental probe into a random state of affairs in order to achieve plot resolution. It can be likened to improvisational theater despite the fact that there is a script or scenario.

I should like to dwell a bit more on the premise of the dream actor who "ad libs." It is probable that this character had been invested with enormous omnipotence in the first place. In his actual performance I believe he upstages the other actors and seeks to take over the whole stage. In fact, it is my observation that he is trying to break out of the shackles of the "dream" in order, like the Devil Himself, to epiphanize in the real world what his imaginative birth has denied him access to. I think this dream actor's appearance heralds psychosis, and the dream in which he is an actor is a psychotic or pre-psychotic dream.

The new internal objects which have been imaginatively created by projective identification, we must be reminded, have developed agendas of their own. The neurotic and the borderline psychotic believe themselves to be victimized by these new "Frankenstein monsters." The key feature of their fear is that they imagine themselves to be "characters in the plot of someone else's story." At this juncture, there seems to have been a projective identification of the authorship of the dream, re-playing it (the Dreamer Who Dreams The Dream) into an internal object–ultimately the magus, the object which oracularly offers "Ultimate Truth" to the hapless patient. This fate is but another feature of psychotic narrative.

The function of the magus is a particularly interesting one in neurotic and psychotic illness. I am using the magus (singular of magi) to denote a sorcerer figure who casts spells on his victims and compels them to follow an enforced scenario from the magus' life. John Fowles (1966) assigned this function to Dr. Conchis (Conscious?*) in his book *The Magus*. In a personal correspondence with me, Fowles revealed that he had been influenced by Jung at the time he wrote the story. He meant the magus to denote an arcane and archetypal figure who puts his own life story into someone else as the latter's task to master.

It is not difficult to see that the strange task the ensorcelled victim must perform is an estranged and projected element of the victim's life now on its return trajectory. In the meanwhile, the hapless victim believes himself impaled on a strange, inexhaustable, and eerie drama—compelled to play it out–but without its having any personal meaning for him–except for the unconscious guilt which compels him to undertake the journey.

Moreover the victim in analysis, as he seeks to grow, finds himself confronted, I believe, by a "double," a separate personality with a separate agenda which has been created and "given life" by the patient every time he turns his back on awareness and feelings. This double (or doubles) are then believed to be separate human entities requiring an act of their very murder in order for the patient to make progress. In classical literature it may take the form of Orestes' murder of Clytemnestra, Cain's killing of Abel, etc. Perhaps all plots involving parricide, fratricide, matricide, etc., may belong in part to this theme. As such, it may demonstrate the "other side" of the Oedipus complex. Murder mysteries may also fall into this category.

In psychotic illness the authorship of the narrative seems to have been obliterated. Instead of the Dreamer or the magus being the author of the narrative (and being responsible for all the complex integrations implicit in dreams), the dream seems to become a more chaotic, formless series of disjointed tales looking for an author. The characters in them are truly looking for a re-creator, a premise, a director, etc. Now the psychotic no longer fears being abused in someone else's narrative; he now fears being in a narrative which no longer has an author!

---

*Dr. Hutter suggests also that "Conchis" means "shell" and may associate to the oracular function of women.

The Background Subject-Object

I have now come to believe that the human being undergoes a series or sequence of caesuras in which (s)he experiences a sense of separation from the object from whom he emerges, i.e., the Background Object of Primary Identification. This object ultimately becomes God. It was closely hinted at by Freud (1909 [1908]) in his paper on "Family Romances" where he calls attention to a distinction on the part of the child between (a) the remote and romantic parent, and (b) the parent at hand who was more like the caretaker in the gatehouse. I perceive the human infant to experience himself as incompletely separated from a mythical object behind him, his rearing or background object, his object of tradition which rears him and sends him forth. It is the phantasied and mythical counterpart to Erikson's (1959) concept of epigenesis and the sense of tradition which spawns each individual from birth. It is the continuity of the sense of cultural and/or racial identity which ultimately devolves into the personal background of the individual. It is intimately felt as the sense of comfort that someone is behind one or stands behind one in one's effort to face the world.

In another contribution I describe the Background Object of Primary Identification as being intimately identified with the Background Subject of Primary Identification and, together, comprise the primal, inherent self-object, the first of three self-objects, the second of which is the body self as "I's" first object, and the second of which is the interpersonal self-object described by Kohut (1971, 1977). (See Grotstein, 1980a, 1980b). The Background Subject-Object of Primary Identification constitutes a background of safety as defined by Sandler (1960) or Winnicott's (1963) environmental mother as differentiated from the object mother. The Background Subject-Object (Self-Object) of Primary Identification regulates the relationships between "I" and self ("I's" first "external" object) and between "I" and its interpersonal objects much as the placenta did in utero (Beaconsfield, Birdwood, and Beaconsfield, 1980). As we shall see later, the Background Subject-Object of Primary Identification is important not only in instigating the dream, but it is also the mirroring audience which understands it.

The Background Subject-Object of Primary Identification appears to undergo an evolution from a co-participant in the mysterious oneness of primary identification to a "released" and backwardly departing soul or spirit of comforting protection and, ultimately, to a religious, spiritual, or divine essence on one hand and a sense of tradition and background certainty on the other. All this takes place as the infant accepts the gap of separation and finds the confidence to utilize his epistemophilic (K) capacities in coordinated conjunction with the libidinal organization (L) and his inherent undifferentiated defense organization, sometimes known as the aggressive drive or the death instinct (H). The background object helps to coordinate the (K), (L), and (H) focus on all objects of scrutiny so that the sense organs can individually and collectively categorize and conceptualize strange and separate objects so as to make them familiar. We may also see an aspect of the background object as ourselves when we *stand behind* our expressed creations and thoughts, in which case we may now speak of this phenomenon as the *Background Subject of Primary Identification*, a term which designates the greater sense of "I"-ness beyond our reach. It is our organizing, messianic genius who gives us the free associations and the inscrutible schedule of sequence of these associations descending from a greater Truth than we can possibly have access to other than by the oracular ambiguities it chooses to offer us. The background subject-object is the creator and guarantor of our sense of *containment* and constitutes the counterpart to the Object of Destiny.

The background subject-object, in the larger scheme, furnishes the setting of the dream and the setting of thoughts by day as well. In object representations, the symbolic images of objects are the furniture—the tables, so to speak—on which raw thoughts (thoughts without a thinker) are to be placed so as to be examined from multiple points of view. Then, the background object is the housing and container for these object representations. It guarantees the continuity of space and containment through all transformations of dimension and relationships. It is the principle of continuity which, in religious terms, can be called God, and in natural science, the guiding principles of natural laws. In Taoism, it can be seen as the unifying, hovering spirit of Oneness which binds all existence. "A finger flicks and a star quivers!" would be the Tao way of expressing this.

The background subject-object is also important in the integration of the dream. We take this unifying function very much for granted when we presume a patient's dream can be of help in deciphering his/her psyche. We presume, in other words, that the dream represents the product of an intelligent Dreamer who has trusted access to memory and hidden emotions in such a way so as to construct a narrative for the Dreamer and his/her analyst which is capable of meaningful decipherment. For this to be presumed, an "intelligence" must have conceived the dream from the raw, chaotic elements of experience—but with unified purpose and with a unified hand. The unity of the background subject-object vouchsafes this. This unification of function becomes especially apparent when we study the coherences inherent in extended dream associations by the patient. It becomes quite evident that the Dreamer, despite numerous resistances, is trying to give us messages via associative congeners which keep repeating themselves as if to give help and confirmation to our intuitive sorties. In psychotic illness, on the other hand, as we shall see, another condition prevails.

In the sense that the background object is an object, it constitutes the "Other," the object of our experience, whereas, as subject, it expresses our subjective "experience of being connected" with a larger subjective "I"-ness. In Steele's (1979) pivotal paper, he states, in effect, that our hermeneutic relationship to ourselves and to objects is basically dyadic insofar as it is both subjective *and* objective simultaneously. *True empathy is the discovery that our object is also a subject.*

One can visualize mental health as the sense of oneness about oneself in continuity with both the world within and the world without. Mental illness, on the other hand, can be seen from this point of view as a perturbation in the sense of oneness and continuity because of a sense of a defective background subject and object. One does not feel well-launched, does not stand on stable ground, is not well-reared, but rather feels existential dread and is vulnerable to anxiety and/or depression, and so on. Serenity is absent. The sense of continuity is experienced as having been lost or never formed and, in its place, a series of fearful discontinuities forever isolated and estranged from each other takes place. The healthy capacity to be able to tolerate discontinuity can take place only in a dual-track conception where one track is already rooted in continuity. Discontinuity is a phenomenon which emerges from the painful primal pathological splitting of the personality as contrasted with normal, discriminating splitting. Pathological splitting can be seen, in other words, as the descendents of that primal splitting-off of the awareness of being split-off from the primal object. It can be spatially visualized as turning one's back on awareness in lieu of accepting it.

The Background Subject—the Dreamer Who Dreams the Dream—offers the dream to "knit up the ravelled sleeve of care" of the "I" who needs the dream for sanctuary, for repair, for delay, and for resolution. The "I" normally walks in the benevolent shadow of the all-hovering but unknowable, unseeable (ineffable and inscrutible) background subject-object. In psychotic illness, on the other hand, it would seem that the hapless patient believes (s)he has so damaged the background object that, like the commoner version of the Adam and Eve legend, (s)he is exiled from the protective grace of this object's shadow and, instead, must either wander the earth as a derelict without a dream of hope, or hope of dreaming, or (s)he may try to restore the background object by a pathetic recourse to divinity in order to become the producer of the dream—the sorcerer—to restore his/her background object. All this, so that in some future reincarnation (s)he can be restored to the grace of the dream and drink fully once again from its narratives.

I now wish to disclose another dream of mine, a far more recent one. It followed an evening course in Cardio-Pulmonary Resuscitation training at a local hospital. In the dream I was being questioned by an instructor about the procedures I had just learned. Apparently I was hesitant and unsure of some of the techniques, so the instructor first told me where I was in error and then demonstrated faultless technique. Upon awakening I was struck at how I had been able to "represent" the perfect instructor. In short, how could I have been so clumsy—and so perfect at the same time?

The Background Subject could be seen in the first dream as having "produced" the setting and ordered the scenario for a narrative having overtly and latently to do with the religious, idealistic, and philosophical implications of a young Man's acceptance of the role of physician and his awe at the mysterious power implied in "dosage" and in "sorrow." The second dream reveals the background subject as the Knower of Truth trying to epiphanize through an aperture into the Dreamer's mortal awareness as knowledge. Obviously, the "instructor" in the dream understands the techniques of maintaining and restoring life. The student was imperfect and is subject to forgetfulness, apathy, disregard, etc. Idealism renders him vulnerable to the Bearer of Truth. In this function, therefore, the background subject as instructor serves in the role of a stimulating ego ideal, an object which wishes to teach and exhort one to pursue Truth.

The (K) function of the background object (quest for knowledge in the pursuit of Truth) can be seen in many ways. A patient who has come into analysis because of his anguish over learning of his wife's affair with another man has seriously reviewed his past relationships with women. In the course of this "review," he chanced upon a previous girlfriend whom he had known before he was married, and then he had an affair with her. He questioned himself about his own inconsistencies and one-sided morality as a consequence of the affair. In the past he had had casual affairs with women in distant cities where his professional work took him, but he assigned no great emotion to any of these affairs. The affair with his ex-girlfriend was different, however. After the affair with the ex-girlfriend, he pondered the inconsistency of his being able to have an affair when he condemns his wife for having had one. This theme was elaborated by many associations which enabled me to suggest to him that he was moved by himself to become adulterous with a girlfriend whom he once loved in order to bring to his attention a phenomenon which he had long been enacting without experiencing the significance of. For some inexplicable reason I also suggested that, instead of being able to dream about it, he had to commit the phenomenon to action so as to get his attention. He then stated that, indeed, he had had a dream about having an affair with this woman and had been disturbed in this dream. He had forgotten the dream until my interpretation. It is my impression that the background subject aspect of his "I" acted through (K) function in the dream to no avail, so then it acted through a Director of Action function in waking life so as to illuminate the problem.*

I believe the background subject-object aspect of "I" seems to be associated with (O), that aspect of Universal Truth which is unknowable but approachable through (K). The organization of (O) is unknowable, but its manifestations through the apertures of awareness correspond to Kant's and Plato's idea of the "thing-in-itself" casting a shadow from the rear to the *front* where we can then perceive the shadow as a transformation of the "thing-in-itself." The relationship between the "thing-in-itself" and its transformation in (K) can be viewed as a narrative. (O) can be seen as the background subject exhorting or invoking the self, its object, to stimulate it in order to increase its focus and awareness. The exhortation may take the form of symptoms or of spontaneous or determined curiosity.

The awesome, god-like, arcane, mysterious nature of dreams can be seen in the following case example. A young unmarried woman who dabbled

*See Hanna Segal's contribution to this *Memorial* for another explanation of the prophetic dream.

in photography brought a dream as follows: She was in her dark room developing a film. A picture gradually began to form on it. She then turned the film over and realized that another "ghost" image was developing on the other side. She was in awe of it and desired to look at it. As she began to look, the dream ended, but not before dream intimations occurred to her that the other side of the film was replete with marvelous and mysterious knowledge about her. In actual fact, she had been an orphan and was reared by a rich, prominent family. The other side of the film seemed to offer her the answers to all the questions of her origins—and more. The nature of the dream was believed to be "divine revelation" frustrated in its revelation at the ultimate moment. It constituted the "ghost of her analysis."

Dream Narrative and the Origin of Plots

Chomsky (1968) has taught us that the human being is born with an inherent capacity for a transformational generative syntax. In other words, he believes that the human being is born with a capacity for the syntactic organization of the elements of symbolic meaning. The human infant has to wait for the maturity of his symbolic organization so as to master a vocabulary and the rigors of separation which allow him to make distinctions and integrations of symbolic units. Vocabulary and semantics are the content within the framework of his syntactic container. The container, from another point of view, must await the maturity of its counterpart and be patient if it is to be fulfilled in its own sense of mission. I should like to extend the connotations Chomsky has assigned to the inherited deep structures to the concept of the inheritance of the tendency toward an instrumentality of narrative (dream) expression.

Pribram (1971) tells us that the human brain is less a discharging apparatus, as Freud believed, than a communicating apparatus in which the neurons are busily engaged in rapid, computer-like informational sorties between one another so as to establish a continuing informational network acting as a single unit. Language is the medium whereby communication occurs. Symbolism seems to be the communicative requirement of the right brain organization—the organization which functions along holistic, space-orienting, contextual, emotional, and visual cues. The holistic symbol seems to be something like a sending beacon which requires amplification, illumination, and informational fulfillment generally. Semiotics, on the other hand, are the detailed digital content of the left brain organization which functions according to syllogistic, linear modes of content within the spatial organization of the right brain directives.

Dreams can be seen as the containers of content in which the content is communication which is constantly being revised and redefined by the container—the symbol—which is making newer and varying audience demands on the content. The audience of the dream and the producer of the dream are, therefore, but different aspects of the same symbolic unit. When the audience receives the dream from the container-producer, it signals the producer acceptance, modification, censorship, dream-it-again, etc. The two are in very close contact and relate to "I" as subject and self as object. The former organizes and forms the form to be viewed as object (self).

Another way of stating this is that the audience and the writer-producer are identical. *They are merely artificial divisions of the primary sense of "I" in the act of contemplating itself caught in a moment of exquisite communicative intimacy and play, performing the playfully serious task of transforming a hint of a preconception across the transformation gap of understanding into perceptual realization, hoping for ultimate "re-cognition." They are Cartesian fugitives arrested momentarily in flight.*

I should now like to discuss the context of the dream, a phenomenon which is associated with the container. The setting of the dream helps to define the context in which the plot takes place. It is the framework, so to speak. Yet even this framework occurs within the container of another framework, an all embracing one. It can be likened to "New York Theater" or "London Theater." The play is written by a playwright and then cast, produced, directed, etc. Finally, it is staged upon a dramatic stage but the stage itself is in a locale which requires it, anticipates it, and looks forward to it with dramatic glee. The theater-going audience, and the cultural milieu which spawns them, contribute to the background definition and containment which gives the play its purpose, its requisition, and its definition. It is the audience which requires it and which will memorialize it. In terms of the internal world I believe the background of the dream can be as important as the foreground, if not more important, depending upon the vertex of inquiry. Isakower (1938) and Lewin (1950) stated that mother's breast is the screen upon which the dream is projected. Spitz (1965) offered the notion that it is mother's face which forms the dream screen. It was at least noticed by these two contributors that the dream is a piece of action which must be portrayed upon a surface for proper cinematographic projection and perception. If mother's breast or face be the screen for the projected dream narrative, then what is the theater? I suggest that the theater constitutes the ultimate containment of the dream narrative by night, as well as by day, and constitutes the ultimate author of its framework. This ultimate author of framework I propose to call the Background Subject-Object of Primary Identification.

We normally take the dream screen for granted; it is the background which supports our images. But what if the background were our image of a background object which was believed by us to be disfigured or mutilated? The projection on *this* screen would be distorted and even bizarre. But what if the screen disappeared altogether and the "dream" projection just went out into space? Would they not be the "things-in-themselves" apocalyptically at large as psychosis?

The narrative can be seen from the neurophysiological point of view as the summation of all the *communications* transpiring between the "I" and self, whether it be the maintenance of a homeostatic steady state, the contemplative afterthoughts about past events, mental or external, or the anticipation of future events. Maintaining, reflecting, planning, and enjoying (re-creating) all consist of an *infinite set of mental possibilities* which ultimately devolve into the continuity of a narrative.

The narrative can also be seen as a series of universal stories or myths, the "things-in-themselves," which have the capacity to induce the audience into a rhythmic participation with the narrative analogy so as to give the feeling of oneness and reunification, mastery over the chaos, and the restoration of a sense of containment. The fairytale aspect of narrative arrests chaos and allows the audience to gain sanctuary in the two dimensional world of make-believe—but the sanctuary is postponement! The mythic aspects of a narrative grab hold of the catastrophic elements of the mortal condition, organize the chaos, and dilute the intensity via extension into the remote past and the remote future—again postponement—for ultimate confrontation and thinking. If chaos (the "thing-in-itself") can be played with narratively, then it can be thought about. If it can be thought about, then more avenues than one reveal themselves for other options and possibilities.

The narrative then is an organizer or framework which functions via paradigms, that is, analogies. Its framework allows the "thing-in-itself" to undergo a transformation into thought, a phenomenon which takes place in that emptied space of a gap reserved by the infant for his mother in her absence. Once a space can be allowed, then narrative fills it up with all the possibilities which can befall the object—and the "I" in isolation. Yet the fact of narrative itself bespeaks the possibility of options, alternatives, dilution of omnipotent tension and diminution, ultimately, of the Absolute. The narrative allows for the possibility of survival and of surviving (enduring) nonsurvival. When the narrative is properly spun (as decided by the Dreamer Who Understands the Dream), a tangled skein of disturbing meaninglessness seems to become caught up in a mysterious litany—a sacred passion play, where Fate now assumes mastery. The narrative of the dream seems to be a predirected, prestaged, preorganized piece of mysterious pageantry played by actors who, like high priests, are taking part in a splendid sacerdotal pageant. In the first instance, the dream narrative is not unlike the sacred passion plays of medieval times which, in their august ceremonial repetitiousness, layed the groundwork for certainty. This aspect of the dream is the deeper and most archaic version of it, I believe. It is as close as we can come to observing the "thing-in-itself" mastering the "thing-in-itself."

Polti (1916), after Gozzi, Goethe, and Schiller, informs us that all narratives can be classified into thirty-six distinct plots. The plots in turn may be subdivided into congeners, but the number thirty-six still stands, according to Polti, as to the possibility of variations of these. Bettelheim (1975) similarly, although without specifying the number of themes, has tried to call out the various types of myths and fairy tales. I do not know of any related study which has attempted to classify the themes of dreams into indivisible entities although such studies may exist. What would be of more interest to me, however, would be a study of the *relationship* between narrative plots, myths, fairy tales, and dreams. Further, I would be interested in determining the indivisible relationships between objects (the characters of the plot) and the essence of the plot. New relationships would be a function of the universal conflicts between a protagonist and an antagonist with the intercession of the "third Actor," to use Polti's suggestive and mysterious term. The "third Actor" gives dimension to the dramatic narrative whose plot functions around the conflicts spawned by asymmetry between L, H, and K where L can represent love and need but also the desire to remain unborn; where H can represent hatred, aggression, defense, cruelty, or murder but also the concerted efforts of a mother or father to wean or discipline the infant; and K which can represent the quest for knowledge and differentiation. L, H, and K are the keyboard of the pianoforte of plot. Affects and conflict are the players.

I believe my first dream resounded with an august religious cadence. This corresponds to the epic aspects of the dream narrative which exist side by side with fairy tale aspects, the latter granting wish fulfillment. This latter aspect is the vertex from which Freud regarded dreams totalistically. The organization and ritual given by myths and the wish fulfillment given by fairy tales offer a space for the instigator of the dream—the irrupting problem—to be thought about more "realistically." This latter corresponds to a more surface aspect of the dream. By "realistically" I mean the considerations of both internal and external reality. It is as if the narrative cloaks and envelopes the concern with a dressing which can prepare it for internal and external digestion (resolution).

The narrative, at best, is poetic. By poetic I mean the gift of being able to say the irreducible most economically so that meaning saturates and suffuses the conduits of expression to such an intensity that visualization is inevitable. Poetic compression is irresistible to the senses. Poetic rhythm resonates with the fundamental—the never-ending Theme of Themes.

The narrative presents an infinite variety of *plots* in order to organize and unify the data presented to the senses. Plot is therefore an aspect of an inherent structure which is available for application to chaos. Plato's inherent preconceptions (Theory of Forms) can be thought of as the universal, inviolable linkages between preconceptions which constitute universal dream myths, which function as universal preconceptive linkages. The scenarios were there before there were men to know them, to dream them, or to enact them. From the point of view of the dual-track theorem, we, on one track, live out these inexorable scenarios which were written before us, and, on another track, are our innovators anew of our own scenarios. Also, from the dual-track point of view, one can see chaos as the antithesis to contrived plot so that chaos becomes scenarios dialectic insofar as it represents inchoate raw data or data secondarily rendered chaotic through splitting attacks, etc. The data is perceptible to the sense organs of attention of the conscious mind of the left hemisphere (this is "ego" or administrative "I") as well as intuitive awareness of the inner world subserved by the right hemisphere ("id," the emotional "I").

Phantasy is first epiphany of plot and is applied to chaotic data from the mythic reservoirs of inherent structuralistic possibilities. Phantasy functions through splitting the chaotic data into recognizable qualities of separateness (pleasurable and unpleasurable, etc.). The elements are then separated into "objects" of convenience. The establishment of the separated objects constitutes an act of *creation* of essential phantasies. Our senses create human phantoms, no less, and then "direct" them in a narrative to behave in a manner which is destined to subordinate the harmful phantoms to their hegemony of the benevolent ones. All mental illness can be seen as the belief in the life of the phantoms one has created, yet normal happiness may also depend on this ingenuous and awesome origin. Chaos is thus ordered by a process not unlike the "salivation" of food in which the "salivating" mind imparts life to its aliment and thus is able to direct its life according to certain narrative laws. These narrative laws are the themes or plots whereby feelings can surface, be recognized and expressed, and whereby malevolent or painful objects can undergo felicitous transformations under the tutelage of benevolent objects. Phantasy thus is the first organizer by the senses of chaos into a plot which allows for a belief in the mastery of the sensory and intuitive environment.

Once organized by phantasy, the background subject-object is believed by the infantile creator to be reinstated again—"God's in His Heaven and all's right with the world!"—the mastery of chaos by phantasy then allows for the troubles which determined the chaos–and their descendents–to be thought about by the mind, the organ of thinking, so as to remand them to plots and narratives corresponding to the laws of external reality. The premise of each plot, whether phantasy or reality, is the specific organizing motivation of the narrative.

Life is a theme with many subthemes. When we do not feel together with ourselves, the themes are disparate, disjointed, and suffer discontinuities. The narrative is an analogy to the theme. We are all looking for our themes and find them momentarily in the narrative of a dream–or we may have recourse to borrow the narratives of others to resonate with and to locate our own themes. Our life theme, the Theme of Themes, is unknowable to us, like the Background Object. It is analogous to the Order of Things which psychotics have such a penchant to re-establish.

A clinical example of this concept of mythic narrative can be seen in the course of the analysis of a young woman whose dreams seemed to have shown a remarkable continuity throughout the analysis. All her dreams reflected the process of birth in one way or another. The plots of her birth dreams were in the form of sequences of phantasies in which she accounted for her birth in many ways. In her first analytic dream she was on the inside of the "first house she ever lived in, in A________." She was there with other internal unborn children but a man with a knife was on the outside threatening to enter. This appeared to be a pre-caesura dream. Later dreams involved a sequence of phantasies in which she was highborn and special, but had to be raised by ordinary parents. She had been, in fact, raised by her grandparents next door to her parents. The meaning of this dream, however, was to denote her omnipotent associations to a sense of divinity. The other aspect of the dream was her notion she created herself without parents. Later she dreamed she had been born from mother (homosexual women in the dream) but not from father. Still later she was father's child and not mother's. She then imagined she had brought the two parents together to beget her and finally she reconciled with the facts of life, surrendered her illusion of control, and accepted the gift of life with all its legacies and hardships.

The first dream of this presentation (my own) demonstrates the phantasy of birth in which the birth of "I" occurs through the mysterious cloudy vale onto a rugged landscape. The two angels are the first meeting with the breasts of grace. Yet they hint that the sorrow that "I" am to undergo has already been "dosed" as my *moira* . . . (or fate).

The birth aspects of dreams have the function, I have come to believe, to reunite the splits between I and self and between self and selves and to assist the self in striving for a sense of continuity from before the caesura to the present time. The Background Object of "I" is always exhorting it-self to return to "I"-ness after the diaspora which it has undergone to acquire K on its circumspect journey to O.

The specific symbolic constructs in the dream narrative attest to this ambiguity and therefore their own plasticity. The patient with an engineering background dreamed of a Y tube. His associations were such that they led me to suggest to him that he didn't know whether the analysis was helping him to come together or to split apart. Another patient, a psychotic one, dreamed of being Christ on the cross and clearly delineated his outstretched hands. It soon became apparent from his associations that he was being crucified for me. His divine chastity and holiness were the models he would like to impose on my behavior. His crucified, outstretched hands were to keep the analytic couple sexually parted. Indeed other interpretations are certainly possible for either dream element, such is the workable plasticity of dream symbols in particular and dream plots in general.

Still another paradox of dream and narrative generally is the very capacity we have to create characters and give them life. The capacity for projective identification has never been explored sufficiently to account for this phenomenon. Writers are familiar with the realness of the characters they create, and the legend of Pygmalion and Galatea is a monument to this belief. Oftentimes, a very real phantom may be created by us as a double. So frequently, the double originates when the creator is bored, lonely, or misunderstood. The new companion then takes on a more and more powerful role. In one of my cases this imaginary companion became "The Advisor" and took over the direction of the patient's affairs.

In dreams we actually are creating imagos by re-creating the characters of the dreams' cast. In re-creating them we are giving them dramatic power and also psychic power—ultimately maybe even omnipotent power. Characters begin narratively as animations or anthropomorphizations of experience, but, once we give them life, they populate our internal world, occupy mental space, exert influence, and have impact. In the successful fairy tale, a guided dream, we must create plausibly powerful and good characters which can overcome more malevolent ones. We must also harness the ability to deprive malevolent characters of life.

In the more sophisticated dream story we must "create" and "re-create" numbers of characters to solve the narrative plot of the dream. In the unsuccessful dream the Dreamer Who Experiences the Dream may lose contact with his Background Object and become "ensorcelled" by one of the dream characters. At that moment, the experiencer of the dream forgets that the dream is a fairy tale, a myth being spun by the Dreamer Who Dreams the Dream (for a purpose). Instead, the fairy tale or myth becomes a nightmare and the ending of the story is in dark jeopardy. It is our capacity to love which helps us to create beneficent figures of such strength so as to continue our successful dreaming. When we have this benevolent relationship to objects we can trust that the dream is being told by a single person—the Dreamer Who Narrates (dreams) the Dream. Anxiety or tension begins to develop when we realize that the dream may not be told by the Dreamer, but may, instead, be told by a new invading force of disruptive Dreamers. The latter is characteristic of psychosis.

The concept of narrative involves the basic element of plot which, in turn, involves the presence of a dialectic looking for a synthesis. Bion's conception of *definitory hypothesis* and *negation* are basically explanatory themes in this regard. In his grid, definitory hypothesis is the reception and statement of an intuitive declaration (Vertical Column One). Negation (Vertical Column Two) comprises those elements which are *not* definitory hypothesis and which may negate or challenge it. Each constitutes the dialectical complementarity to the other. It is my conception, and I fear space does not allow me the opportunity to clarify this notion, that narrative per se may often times be the projective identification of either definitory hypothesis, or negation, or both into internal or external objects so that action can concretely take place (in Segal's contribution, she hinted at the concept of *concrete symbolic equations*).* The desire for resolution between definitory hypothesis and negation then becomes the motive for the plot.

Projective identification is important in yet other ways in terms of plots. The power of the human imagination has not yet even been accorded

*See H. Segal, this volume.

the significance I believe it deserves. Projective identification borrows deeply from our autochthonous streams to create parthenogenetic images or phantoms which aim at the mastery of chaos. The ultimate Plot–the Theme of Themes–is beyond our meddling–it is the Appointment we all have in Samara–and the course of the scenario of the journey to that Appointment. The Theme of Themes is Truth, Track I of our realistic lives. Track II is our omnipotent, Promethean, authochthonous capacity to be able to imagine that we create our own world and worlds–much like the autochthonous God Infant of *Genesis* whom countless generations have allowed to create his own mother and father, Adam and Eve.

Sooner or later the autochthonous (born from the self) theme of omnipotent self-creativeness runs up against the genital theory of creation–that one was the unwitting result of the sexual intercourse of parents who begot us before we even existed. The oedipus complex, therefore, demonstrates at bottom the ancient, repetitive, inherent resistance to the realization that one did not create oneself, but was created by others. Levi-Strauss (1963, 1969) believes this conflict between the autochthonous and the generative theories to be the most elemental aspect of the oedipus complex and of totemism–kinship relationships.*

The significance of the autochthonous versus genital concept is more far-reaching than just the oedipus complex alone. Dreams and myths are autochthonous resolutions (autoplastic) to realistic problems (alloplastic) prior to the arrival of a non-autochthonous solution. In other words, myths, dreams, and narratives are spun by an autochthonous spinning wheel to bind the chaotic members comprising anxiety prior to "thinking" solutions.

The concept of authochthonous creativeness reveals a birth process other than genital and seemingly more appropriate at first glance to the birth of thoughts, as opposed to concrete babies. Moreover, it is a way in which we can understand the importance of Bion's "C Column" in which visualization, dreams, and myths are located. It is my understanding that Bion's Column C is a way of denoting the mind's tendency to transform sense impressions into alpha elements via alpha function. This alpha function is highly autochthonous, as is the whole Vertical Column, for that matter. We must be able to dream about or mythify inputs in order to achieve a distinction between sleep and wakefulness. This is a more elaborate way of restating Freud's thesis that troublesome day residues are first stripped of their cathexes, and these cathexes are displaced onto less imporant "congeners" of the originally troublesome day residue. This in turn is "marauded" by the instinctual unconscious in its continuous sorties for expression into the world where it desires discharge and/or unconsciousness—not unlike the banished devil who is constantly trying to resurface in human form. The barrier of censorship holds up and drives the unconscious with its new-found booty back into the instinctual labyrinthe of deep repression. Once again the

*I am indebted to Doctor Alfred Silver for this reference.

Devil–in his new amalgam–tries to resurface–once again repressive censorship holds up–and the amalgam "condenses" in order to get sufficient strength once again to emerge. This time it seems to have enough strength to approach to dream screen itself as it regresses to perception for visual epiphany. The visualization upon the dream screen permits discharge and therefore furthers the work of repression by giving a delay to the contumacious impulse. But not only are discharge and repression guaranteed but also there is a "perfection" of the narrative itself against a later moment when the scenario is rightly timed for proper appearance on a proper stage–when it is earmarked for a return of the repressed in order for integration to take place. This integration represents the "solution," not only of the day residue which was not really the main problem in the first place but only the surface expression of the problem–the clothing which the Devil chose in order to appear.

The truer and deeper meaning of the working over the theme and its final appearance is the solution for the unconscious problem–the constant need for the unconscious to become known and integrated with the rest of the self in the ever-expanding sense of "I"-ness in our never-ending sense of self-transcendence. In psychotic illness there is only the apocalyptic epiphany of instinctual "things-in-themselves" and, at the same time, day residues which are not pre-conscious but glaring holocaustal realities. The two converge so rapidly because of the disappearance of ego boundaries in psychosis that the psychotic cannot tell the difference. But it is important to point out, I believe, that reality becomes all the more impinging in proportion as the psychotic cannot dream–that is, cannot produce dream images which can facilitate repressive delay and thematic re-write and development for proper mental digestion. In proportion as he cannot produce the icons and indices of mental images (he cannot re-assemble sensory data to resemble the object he is trying to re-assemble)–or because he believes himself to have so mutilated the dream screen upon which the images are to be projected–that, as stated earlier, he produces chaotic, misshapen, "abortions" of images which are all the more distorted by a misshapen screen–or appear all the more eerie when there is no screen at all upon which to project them. This to me is perhaps the deepest essence of the experience of being psychotic. It is exquisite neurological and emotional "embarrassment" to the unimaginable power.

Bion has intriguingly reminded us that dreams never stop; it is only their visual transformation during sleep that we conventionally call "dreams." Actually we "dream" by day too in order to put some thoughts asleep so as to be able to focus attention (to be awake) to other thoughts, at the expense of the sleep of the otherwise distracting thoughts which are better kept asleep in the background. To pay attention and to concentrate thus involve the complex cooperation of autochthonous dreaming by day as well as by night. In order to repress and/or to put events behind us, that is–to be able to forget about things conveniently–we must be able to autochthonize them to our advantage so as to keep that important boundary between day and night and sleep and wakefulness so that sanity can continue.

In order for any inherent idea, messiah idea, thought without a thinker, etc. (manifestation of "O") to surface, it must first be stimulated by some beta element of sense impression; secondly the scenario or script must be suspended in order to allow sufficient unsaturation for the new thought to have room to be experienced and "hungry" expectation so as to welcome its presence. The question of stimulation by a beta element brings up the important idea of the autochthonous versus the genital theory of the birth of babies *and* of ideas, the autochthonous referring to self-generating and genital referring to dependency on mating with another. The mind which discovers its dependency on mating, through sense experiences, to stimuli from another source soon learns its "oedipal lesson" of the depressive position—that it is dependent for thoughts on stimulation by others. Insofar as one may evade this realization and can pretend that his thoughts are autochthonously self-generating, one is doomed to madness as a way of conducting one's life.

Bion's concept of the alphabetizing process of alpha function is congruent with Freud's concept, as delineated in Chapter 7, of the invasion by the instinctual impulse of the id into the prepsychotic reservoir of day residues in order to find "earthly forms" in order to surface. Because of the censorship imposed by the unpleasure aspect of the pleasure-unpleasure principle, the day residue, which have been "corrupted" by the instinctual impulses, became their kidnapped prey rather than their (the instinctual impulses') ad hoc avenue for reality experiences and discharges and consequently are pulled by them into their deeper unconscious haunts. Freud further believed that at night, while we sleep, the instincts again discharge with their kidnapped preconscious booty but, again because of the perseverence of the agency of censorship, follow a regressive pathway to regression and fall upon the projecting screen of perception so that visualization becomes the final common pathway of this complex process. The visualizations incident upon the regression to perception constitute the screen of imagination which allows reality to be disassembled and then reassembled along with the remitting of inherent preconceptions so that the amalgam of imagery falls upon the psychic screen for a creative and a storage process.

Thus, the normal mind is constantly dreaming while it is paying attention to reality, whether that reality be the reality of wakefulness or the reality of sleep. Attention is thus a bimodal affair and requires the coparticipation of each cerebral hemisphere. Normal being, therefore, is, at best, a harmonious twinship at the very least, as Gazzaniga and LeDoux (1978) have pointed out. And, furthermore, each hemispheric twin relates to its opposite counterpart both as object and as co-subject, as Steele (1979) has so ingeniously pointed out.

The capacity to be psychically healthy must consequently depend upon the ability to disassemble the Gestalten of the outside world, to reassemble them in the internal world and to be able to store them as images in the way they are shown. I believe that psychosis is characterized by the inability to assemble these Gestalten to resemble their external counterparts so that the imagery on the internal screen is disassembled, disjointed, dissymbolic, and in chaotic disarray. The basic problem with psychosis is, not so much that the thinking itself is wrong but that the mythic carpet placed upon the floor of thought is itself defective so that imagery cannot coherently take place and, as a fateful consequence, thought cannot be built upon this imagery. The problem with schizophrenia is dys-symbolism. They cannot paint inner pictures upon their inner screen. Their thoughts therefore lack the essential nutriment and therefore collapse in chaotic disarray. In short, the disordered thinking of psychosis is the result rather than the cause of the incapacity of the schizophrenic to phantasy and to imagine in a way that coheres in depth.

I cannot close the issue of narrative without some reference to the psycholinguistic structural relationship between nouns and verbs. I believe that the dream is an attempt to consolidate chaotic daily action (verbs) into static narrative nouns so as to "store" them. Memory and desire serve similar functions. Psychotics, in my experience, are frightened of verbs—that is—of action, which connotes change and therefore insecurity and object inconstancy—thus their propensity for rigid concretizations and for the tenacity of their perceptual possessiveness. The noun represents an infinite class of objects which seem to be permanent structurally and therefore elude the change which is inherent in action, unless the object can be seen to undergo a spontaneous transformation (e.g. the melting of ice, the development of facial wrinkles, etc.).

I must remind the reader that I am using the term "verbs" and "nouns" in a freely imaginative way. For instance, I choose the term "noun" to denote the "grammar" of that "dream" and narrative function which can "stop frame" an action and transform it into "exctachronic" memory for storage. The "noun", therefore, is the capacity to slow down action into storable memory.

I believe that the dream, by day and by night, has the task of organizing random actions in daily life into "packaged" units after the completion of alpha process. The random action of sense impression then become mythified, dreamed, narrated elements which approach noun status and can be stored, postponed, earmarked for future action, or "triaged" for immediate concern. In the meanwhile, thanks to alpha function, they have become nouns despite the fact that we may conceive of them as narrative actions (verbs). They are stored like a videotape (noun) which contains the recording of the action (verb) but is itself static. It is my further belief that this is what is meant by *repression*. Thus, the purpose of the dream by day and by night is to facilitate the repression of random, intrusive action so as to put it in a package of slumber so that the rest of the personality can either be truly asleep or truly awake.

Dreams which are unsuccessful—that is, disturbing dreams—may, on the other hand, represent *denial* of *action by counter-action*. In other words, denial, unlike repression, represents a constant, continuing counter cathexis which can never cease. The capacity to achieve noun status is bequeathed by the mother with reverie (The Dreamer Who Understand the Dream) to the dreamer by her (its, his) ability to contain the anxiety of the infant by confronting it and then postponing its impact or diluting its intensity. Denial, on the other hand, results when the Dreamer Who Understands the Dream does not approve of the scenario and/or cannot adequately cope with the anxiety and must consequently resort to evasion, a phenomenon which is unmistakably demoralizing and disheartening to the dreamer. The dreamer then enters into a collusive relationship with the Dreamer Who "Understands" the Dreamer which is characterized by that constant action (verb) known as *denial*.

Confidence in the capacity to achieve noun status (*repression*) predicates greater enthusiasm for expression (verbs). The sanctuary of nouns can be more easily relinquished. If noun status be more difficult to achieve, then nouns seem to be more greedily and desperately possessed, and relinquished only with great reluctance if at all, and then with great peril. It is the schizophrenic who is most trapped within his nouns and most disjointed from his verbs which have become his enemy since they spell "change" and "future." Yet the schizophrenic can quickly change to the verb when it means the eschewal of nouns and the future so as to rid the psyche all the more of all the complexities of syntax, whether they be nouns or verbs.

What about the "force" of the dream narrative? Is it due to the pressure of the conflicts in the day residue? Is it due to the compressive force which condensation imposes on unconscious mental elements so that they may "qualify" for sufficient intensity so as to register as illuminated visual images? The Theme of Themes, employing Thoughts Without Thinkers, *is* power looking for words to express them so that they may see the light of day (and night). As Marlowe made his Tamburlaine say:

> Make
> In the mantle of the richest night
> The moon, the planets, and the meteors
> Light!

Marlowe's "mighty line" is but a single example of the power of the birth thrust of creation. May not the power of the birth thrust of the infinitude of thoughts without a thinker trying to achieve illumination—but never finding a thinker to think them—be the underlying source of anxiety? And may not the realization of these stillbirths and abortions of creativity be the underlying source of depression? May not psychosis be the conviction that the thoughts without a thinker have been destroyed and are now haunting ghosts—and may not this conviction so influence realization that only apocalyptic remnants of mutilated, stillborn "thoughts" remain to "represent" the psychotic mind?

Enthusiasm is the rocket-fuel of creation; psychopathology is its perversion, depression is its involution, and psychosis the fragmentation it causes when the mind has defaulted which could contain it.

Alpha Function

It is to Bion's alpha function that we must look for the ultimate, irreducible element of creativity for it unites the Dreamer Who Dreams the Dream, the Dreamer Who Understands the Dream, the Dreamer Who Makes the Dream Understandable etc. (Bion, 1962, 1963, 1965, 1970). Bion believes that alpha function, which corresponds to Freud's primary process but is more extensive, processes the data of experience (beta elements) which confront the sense organs and cause them to undergo an "alpha-betization" in order to become capable of mental digestion as elements of thought. This "alphabetization" also accounts for the transformation of the sense-ible experience into sensual imagery (via image-ination) which then qualify as dream images which can be dreamed and stored. It is my impression that the transformations of the sense impression into imagery are facilitated by alpha function's access to inherent and acquired preconceptions, that is, to archetypes, which are always pressuring to surface but require a sense-ible experience for a vehicle. Alpha function seems able to link up the experience with the archetypes corresponding to it to produce finally a mythic-dream narrative sequence which conveys personal meaningfulness to the dreamer (by day and by night).

Alpha process has at its disposal metonymy, synecdoche, and metathesis. *Metonymy* is the function whereby one element may stand for another (e.g. the *crown* stands for *royalty*). *Synecdoche* is similar to metonymy and allows for a part to stand for the whole or vice versa (e.g. using *London* to designate *England*, or the *army* to designate a *general*). Metonymy and synecdoche roughly correspond to Freud's conception of *condensation*, but they have more variations. *Metathesis*, which includes *condensation* and *displacement*, is the process of the decomposition and transposition of elements from one structure or pattern into that of another (e.g.—in chemistry— $\mathit{Na}OH + H\mathit{Cl} \rightarrow \mathit{Na}\ \mathit{Cl} + H_2O$). It corresponds roughly to Freud's conception of displacement but also accounts for imaginative re-synthesis, both in healthy and in abnormal states. These three sub-functions of alpha function account for the creation of the elements and compounds of imagery in the mythic reservoir and the mythic streams of the unconscious.

If we use the paradigm of the portrait artist, we can say that his model is the experience "O" to be experienced by his visual sense as a beta element to be transformed into an alpha element. His preconceptive archetypes are the pigments on his palate. Perception is his artistry. Metonymy, synecdoche, and metathesis are the ingredients of judgment whereby he selects which pigment to represent whatever feature in shades, colors, and hues via discrete and talented selection.

The completion of the work of alpha function lays the foundation for metaphor. Alpha function imbues personal, mythic meaningfulness to experience and then conveys its product on to comparisons with other experiences. Comparison seems to be the purpose of metaphor. Two tracks, the concrete and the symbolically suggestive, comprise it. Metaphor begins to emerge when the alpha element resulting from alpha function proceeds laterally on Bion's grid to undergo comparison, notation, attention, inquiry, and finally, mental action. All dreams, myths, and narratives develop through these aforementioned processes. They are the instruments whereby the Dreamer Who Dreams the Dream is able to dream "up" the dream; they constitute the criteria whereby the Dreamer Who Understands the Dream can rule upon its credibility; and they comprise the elements whereby the Dreamer Who Makes the Dream Understandable is enabled to make it understandable. All accepted experiences become associated with a dual-track conception as metaphor where one track is the concrete personal *meaning* of the experience and the other is its *significance*.

I believe, however, we must take yet another look at the inherent grid acquired preconceptions for an additional point of view. We ordinarily think of the sense impressions as being primary and as the initiating elements of creation. A case can be made for the stirrings and yearnings of the archetypal preconceptions which, like Wordsworth's "unborn babies" or Michelangelo's "Prisoners," strive and pray for the advent of the experiences which can release them from their immemorial marble to be born. It is as if all our creations are but the re-discoveries which experiences release.

Alpha Function and the Transference Neurosis

Glover (1955) has suggested that a large aspect of psychoanalytic cure resides in the suggestive or persuasive power of the analyst who gives the interpretation to the patient. This is so true, he believes, that inexact interpretations are treacherously pseudo-effective because of the patient's unconscious readiness to accept them in lieu of exposing the truest, most repressed aspects of his neurosis. Thus the transference neurosis, if it is to be a recreation of the infantile neurosis, must depend on particularly accurate interpretations if the displacement is itself to be reasonably accurate. At bottom, however, according to Glover, it is suggestion which facilitates the formation of the transference neurosis.

Now we also know from our clinical experiences as analysts that the development of the transference neurosis (and psychosis) is attended by a withdrawal of symptoms from other areas in the patient's life with a concentration of them instead onto the person of the analyst (the transference neurosis proper). Glover's ideas about the influence of suggestion in this regard conveys the idea that the infantile neurosis (I would now say the *unsuccessful* infantile neurosis because of its continuing activation) needs *suggestion* of a parallel, resonant theme to latch onto, to blend in with, or to be absorbed by in order to facilitate a solution or change. The patient's infantile neurosis apparently seeks narratives, dreams, myths, fairy-tales, etc., as vehicles for this resonance with displacement for imaginative solution.

I suggest that alpha function can treat the infantile neurosis itself as a beta element experience in O, transform it over and over again into mythic, narrative, or dream elements and, thereby, facilitate its *transfer* into parallel, resonant narratives which present themselves in the person's life-long search for the narrative solution. In analytic treatment, however, the patient has the rare opportunity of re-writing his own story so that his infantile neurosis can be *transferred* and *transformed* into a transference neurosis by projective identification of a newly alpha-betized version of his infantile neurosis into the unsaturated network of the transference narrative—all because of suggestion (imagination). The treatment of the transference neurosis thus constitutes a proxy cure for the infantile neurosis. Dreams are, in my opinion, intermediate steps in narrative "metabolism" in the patient's effort to transform his infantile neurosis into a transference neurosis. The dream is merely waiting for the external representative of that function known as the Dreamer Who Makes the Dream Understandable so that the infantile neurosis (and psychosis) can at long last, after so many years of sub-terranean incarceration and torment, find deliverance.

A symbolic translocation of a precipitated incomplete experience awaits for the completion of its experience by this projective translocation into a narrative for organization and solution.

Myths and Fairy Tales

Langer (1942) and Levi-Strauss (1962) believe that myths—and fairy tales—are not only universal but are also inherent. It is my opinion that they are homologous to Chomsky's inherent deep psycholinguistic structures and that the manifest themes of the myths and fairy tales, although manifested in the surface structures, are nonetheless under the guidance and control of the inherent deep structures. I believe there to be a boundary to narrative plots, limitations in the latitude of themes, and some diversity only within a larger uniformity and conformity to the individual scenarios.

Fairy tales—whether *Morte D'Arthur* or *Star Wars*—contain certain invariant characters and certain invariant themes. Almost universally great disaster, plague, or infamy took place long ago. A parent—or both parents—have perished or been captured. The evil erstwhile victor can cast spells on his victims. An old sorcerer, e.g. Merlin, or Obiwan Kenobi, has access to mysterious power which comes from some deep and mysterious fount. It grants power and immunity to its possessor. The sorcerer is privileged to grant the power to his heir-apparent when the latter is finally of age. Purity, honor, and self-sacrifice are demanded of him. With his Excalibur he can slay the dragon, and release his enhostaged and ensorceled loved ones, and restore bliss to the kingdom. It all took place long ago and far away—or in the remote future.

The subsidiary characters include dwarfed or diminutized gnomes, elves, etc., who functions as benign servants. They also offer comical relief. They seem to be little old people who contain (via projective identification) the human fears the hero might otherwise have had—and they also contain his littleness as he mysteriously assumes bigness and power. I believe the problem in some ancient time to have been the actualization of birth which caused in turn the release of Pandora's demons. The release of human feelings at high velocity at birth is probably the source of the feeling that our infantile hero long ago ruptured the Background Object of Primary Identification. This belief in some ancient tragedy or some primitive catastrophe, constitutes one of the elements of the concept of Original Sin. We know it more currently as the hatred, the fear, and the guilt about being born. The desire to repair and restore this Object and Its honor reforges a connection with the Background Object (where the umbilicus used to be), thereby bringing the benign mysterious anchorite sorcerer to bestow the old power to the new hero.

It is my belief that the sorcerer is the true meaning of the term superego. I have come to regard the superego as the repository for the mystery of the infant's future—all the "memoirs of the future" which are "known" to him at birth (and maybe even before) but which have such sensory intensity that they cannot be borne and so have to undergo a projective detour into a warehousing parent until the infant becomes a child and is able to retrieve his lost knowledge. It is the Object of Destiny. The retrieval of this lost knowledge is education, growing, learning from experience, and the pursuit of one's life theme—the Theme of Themes—the scenario of the Dream of Dreams. Fairy tales have a happy ending. The hero manages to acquire—that is—retrieve his mysterious legacy to slay his own internal dragon. The telling of the tale offers relief and postponement. The very background of every fairy tale is faith in a powerful or mighty good Background Object who watches over one and grants perfect immunity. Fairy tales correspond, I believe, to the discharge of immediate tension via the happy ending and the acquisition of postponement. They conform, therefore, to Freud's concept of the pleasure-unpleasure principle.

Myths, on the other hand, may have great similarities to fairy tales thematically, but they differ insofar as they accept tragedy and loss and thereby prepare one for *un*happy endings. They tend to be more existentially fatalistic. They organize and narrate chaos almost like insouciant news commentators at Armageddon. Myths therefore correspond more to a primitive notion of the reality principle perceived "through a glass darkly," on the way to being "face to face" with Truth.

The Themes of both fairy tales and myths deal with evil and tragedy, fear and remorse, all the earthly conditions, and the need for our nursery hero to have enough courage and faith to be able to surmount them. The confrontation with the overwhelming force constitutes the baptism of a sense of competence in oneself in concordance with the faith one has in those who bore one—and those who *fore*bore one—the lexicon of all those who saw to our survival thus far and who have passed the torch of survival to us. The continuity of survival and the repetition of the struggles to reassure it constitute, I believe, the rough draft of the universal dream narrative scenarios.

The dream narrative absorbs some impressive affects, and the knowledge or data which inspires affects, and *dreams* them. The dreaming of them is the first stage in their intermediary metabolism to becoming thinkable about. The dream narrative, by virtue of access to the knowledge of the past, places the new data in contact with all its analogs of memory—similar people, data, events of the past and their past solutions. Freud's analysis of the examination dream corresponds to this idea closely. In that analysis he observed that a recurring dream of failing an examination one took a long time ago and had passed is a way of reminding oneself that one has already negotiated this hurdle in life and therefore is the current reminder that it need not be worried about. A past *known* story and/or mythic story is assigned by the Dreamer of the Dream to carry it further in its mysterious journey. In this way, the "thing-in-itself" is digested down to chewable size and therefore becomes more accessible to solution. One can then think about it, change the circumstances which caused it, evade it, etc. The story narrative induces a state of relaxation and postponement as well as a sense of confidence that the external storyteller—the Dreamer of the Dream—has seen this affair before so there is no cause for alarm—as long as the Dreamer Who Understands the Dream agrees.

The Descent of God

Dreams apparently were considered a secret language between the gods amongst the Assyrians.* In the times of Assurbanipal and Tiglath Pileser III, for instance, Assyrian royal inscriptions were written in places inaccessible to the human eye—there was sculpturing in front, but, behind the sculpturing, were hidden secret inscriptions. These inscriptions were inscribed on clay cylinders inside walls inside buildings. "They were made for the gods. Dreams were the messages of gods to gods," Professor Tadmor states. This secret form of inscription seems to have been taken over by the snake-worshiping Hebrews—perhaps from their Babylonian sojourn—in the form of the secret writings in the phylacteries.

The notion of a divine language has come down to us from the legend of the Tower of Babel. In another contribution I endeavored to demonstrate

*I am grateful to Professor Chaim Tadmor, the distinguished Assyriologist of Hebrew University, for this information. (Tadmor, 1977).

that the omnipotent infant believes himself to possess the god language and resents having to give it up for the earthly language of the mother tongue, the latter of which takes at least a lifetime to gain competence in. In this sense, then, the god language is the infant's imagined capacity to confuse his own baby talk with the "thing-in-itself" and imagine himself to have sway over his cosmos (Grotstein 1977a and 1977b).

Yet there is another consideration which must be adjoined to this view. The infant, in all probability, *is* in contact with a divine language, a language "spoken" by his Background Object to other aspects of the same Object—a divine parental language, if you will—not the language of earthly communication but rather the ambiguous, oracular, language of Truth—O—Infinity, a grammar which is perfect, a syntax which is absolute, a meaning beyond meaning beyond meaning beyond meaning beyond meaning, etc. This "language" is the tongue of infinite dimensionality.

The god language can be seen as the ultimate architecture of the dream by day and the dream by night. It is at one moment the completed connection in the ultimate galaxies of thought—of all the thoughts without a thinker—waiting, like Wordsworth's babies, to be born in thought. Much as in a Picasso painting where the eye of the face in one dimension is also the head of a figure in another dimension, the "thoughts" are posed in infinite dimensions of infinite possibilities. The dream which is experienced is but an infinitesimal portion of this universal holograph. The symbols presented in a dream "talk" to each other, in infinite tongues. The "meanings" are meanings beyond meanings. They are a scaffolding for earthly thoughts to be cast upon for redefinition. When we "analyze" a dream, we get the patient's associations, his day residues, his memories, etc., and we use the latent and manifest dream associations to reconstruct a possibility of inner thinking, an approximation by analogy, if you will. The actual meaning of the dream is unknowable because it contains, at the least, all the possible associations forever backward and forever forward in time. The dream is total language beyond comprehension. Comprehension itself is an embarrassment to the near-perfection of the dream.

Yet the perfection and mystery of the dream are penetrated in yet another way—other than attempts at comprehension—and that is in the very presentation of the dream itself. The divine language seems to intercede on behalf of the person who experiences the dream. The content and staging of the dream reveals the Dreamer's choice of themes, presentations, etc. It is at this point that God descends to intervene and, in so doing, reveals the personalness of His choices. These may correspond to the phenomenon of the "deus ex machina" in Greek plays.

The Dream As Therapy

The process of dreaming constitutes a healing experience as well as an exploratory experience beyond healing. Healing, after all, only restores the injured self to homeostatic symmetry. It is the characteristic of man to desire to explore and therefore to give up his homeostasis and his symmetry for a greater gain. The dream offers epiphanic rents in its own symmetry to lure us like benign Lorelei to self-transcendence. When we explore the dream within and the dream without, we are, after all, attempting merely to recover what we lost when we descended.

A Malayasian aboriginal tribe, the Senoi, have the distinction of having been able to interdict violent crimes and intercommunal conflicts for a period of two to three hundred years because of the insight and inventiveness of *tohats* (shamans) of their various communities. The high degree of social attainment of these "aborigines," in the opinion of Kilton Stewart and H.D. Noone, anthropologists who have studied them, is due to their therapeutic use of dreams (Stewart, 1972). They seem to rely on dream interpretations and dream expressions. Breakfast in a Senoi household is like a dream clinic. The father and older brothers analyze the dreams of the children. The dreams are then discussed by the males in a council elsewhere. Let me quote from Stewart's article:

> . . . man creates features or images of the outside world in his own mind as part of the adaptive process. Some of these features are in conflict with him and with each other. Once internalized, these hostile images turn man against himself and against his fellows. In dreams man has the power to see these facts of his psyche, which have been disguised in external forms, associated with his own fearful emotions, and turned against him and the internal images of other people. If the individual does not receive social aid through education and therapy, these hostile images, built up by man's normal receptiveness to the outside world, get tied together and associated with one another in a way which makes him physically, socially, and psychologically abnormal.
>
> Unaided, these dream beings, which man creates to reproduce inside himself the external socio-physical environment, tend to remain against him the way the environment was against him, or to become disassociated from his major personality and tied up in wasteful psychic, organic, and muscular tensions. With the help of dream interpretations, these psychological replicas of the sociophysical environment can be redirected and reorganized and again become useful to the major personality . . .
>
> The simplest anxiety or terror dream I found among the Senoi was the falling dream. When the Senoi child reports a falling dream, the adult answers with enthusiasm, "That is a wonderful dream, one of the best dreams a man can have. Where did you fall to, and what did you discover?" He makes the same comment when the child reports a climbing, travelling, flying, or soaring dream. The child at first answers, as he would in our society, that it did not seem so wonderful, and that he was so frightened that he awoke before he had fallen anywhere.

> "That was a mistake," answers the adult-authority. "Everything you do in a dream has a purpose, beyond your understanding while you are asleep. You must relax and enjoy yourself when you fall in a dream. Falling is the quickest way to get in contact with the powers of the spirit world, the powers laid open to you through your dreams. Soon, when you have a falling dream, you will remember what I am saying, and as you do, you will feel that you are travelling to the source of the power which has caused you to fall.
>
> "The falling spirits love you. They are attracting you to their land, and you have but to relax and remain asleep in order to come to grips with them. When you meet them, you may be frightened of their terrific power, but go on. When you think you are dying in a dream, you are only receiving the powers of the other world, your own spiritual power which has been turned against you, and which now wishes to become one with you if you will accept it."

It seems that the Senoi are sophisticated about the therapeutic nature of dreams. They respect the fact that dream images may represent dangerous or incestuous situations but are *not* actually what they represent. Not only does relief and psychic growth result from this awareness but it also helps them to use the dream in an experimental manner to conquer anxiety through the "guided dream."

The therapeutic nature of dreams can be understood, I now believe, as the identical effect of the narrative—the very *telling* of the narrative and the *plot* of the narrative. I believe further that the "therapy" involved, like the dream itself, follows Haeckel's Law, "Ontogeny recapitulates phylogeny," in the sense that there seems to be a descending (or ascending, depending on one's point of view) hierarchy of communications involved. The most primitive level of communication is the "god language" which speaks oracularly and ambiguously. The dream is awesome and constitutes commandments for the recipient of the dream to follow. This is the first of a variety of solutions to problems offered in the dream and in the holy narrative. All problems can be seen primarily as being due to our wandering away from God's will. Resolution is absolution: a return to the Word of God.

A variation of expression on this primitive, arcane level is the phenomenon of "showing," which has the connotation of magical induction of corresponding behavior in all the witnesses to the "showing." This phenomenon is otherwise known as hypnotic trance or brain washing via induction by magical gestures. It is a form of pregenital or psychotic manipulative exhibitionism. The dramatic action of awesome primitive godheads is believed to contain a secret message for the dreamer to divine, ultimately leading to an induced change in the dreamer's thoughts and behaviors. When Hamlet said, "The play's the thing wherein I'll catch the conscience of the king," I believe he had this phenomenon in mind. The dream is indeed the play which can catch the conscience of us all. I extend this to include the capacity of the awesome "god dream" to "show" to the dreamer and, likewise, the capacity of the dream to unmask powerful internal objects which behave as if they have moral authority, but unjustifiably. The revelatory dream is a bid for their abdication and the end to perverse, corrupt, addictive, and evil morality. The showing is thus an inductive unmasking.

A more common version of this dramatic "relationship through showing", as Fairbairn (1954) called it, is the phenomenon of psychic "defenses." We commonly depart from animistic language when we talk about defenses and, instead, use the more formal (and sterile) language of process. It is my experience that "defense" is a phenomenon in the first instance in which an infant dramatizes his distaste about a feeling or an awareness and so comports himself as to suggest imperiously that the awareness should disappear. Defenses first take somatic form—spitting up, defecating, muscular aversion, etc. Denial, after all, is psychic murder and must originally have involved the then appropriate musculature to effect. Posture became the prototype for defense. Its very posture was to *display* the power of the subject's response to the awareness and to induce the enemy (awareness) to obey its sign and depart.

The next level of solution is the mythic. It is more sophisticated than resolution through absolution and "awesome showing" and allows for sufficient descent of omnipotence so that Fate is constructed as being above the gods and does not intercede or absolve. In this stage tragedy is accepted. When we say "God's will," we are on the verge of meaning inexorable Fate. The mythic-epic solution prepares us to withstand the inevitability of tragedy and loss. It avoids being nightmare through mobilizing *pathos*, which I believe alternatively can be seen as *empathy* for the tragic hero. This phenomenon comes close to the all-too-human "feeling sorry for oneself," an important dramatic agent which rescues us from tragedy. When extreme, it becomes martyrdom, thus giving tragedy a holy cause and seemingly reversing the loss implicit in the original tragedy. Fairy tale dreams and narratives, on the other hand, romanticize the probability of tragedy and then offer a happy ending—which postpones confrontation with the real problem which inspired the dream.

The next level of dream-narrative sophistication is in the sophistication of plot—it can be called "modern drama" in any age. Here the construction of plot is more immediately brought to bear on the problems. First, the problems are "universalized" for dramatic presentation in order to facilitate disguise *and* credibility at the same time. This is to accomplish universality for purposes of dilution of feelings of aloneness and uniqueness of one's plight. The plot is then so constructed along the lines prescribed by dramatic possibilities so as to produce a universally credible conflict which then lends itself to that limited variety of solutions alluded to earlier. The climax of the narrative or dream is the catastasis, at which point the dramatic propensities of the dream network or storyteller have achieved optimum concentration of dramatic involvement preparatory to discharge of tension and to plot solution, whether by catastrophe or successful resolution.

Participating in the therapeutic enterprise is the faculty of dreams and narratives which can be called the "guided dream" or the "guided daydream." These are skillfully constructed ad hoc alternative narratives which offer ways around the conflict. The capacity to envision alternatives may seem like escape from reality on one level but really can be the preparation for *thinking* on another. It is, after all, the very capacity to offer alternative solutions which instigated the need for thinking in the first place and which constitutes one of its most compelling annuities in the second place.

Oftentimes we find that dreams seem to be continuous for several days because a proper solution was not found or was only tentative. I should like to demonstrate this phenomenon with the following case example:

The patient is a divorced playwright to whom I referred in another context earlier. One of his main presenting complaints was depression over his wife's leaving him. Many months of analysis were spent in analyzing his difficulty in accepting the finality of the situation. Finally, he narrated the following dream: He was walking outside on the street by a large building when he heard the shots of firearms and then saw a man falling to the ground from the top of the tall building. He awoke in terror. His associations led to the building's being associated with my office and also to his "falling off" in respect to his wife, by which he meant his acceptance of the fact of the severance of their relationship.

The next night he had another dream: He was standing on a high bluff with a beautiful view of the ocean. The bluff and the view from one angle looked like his native New York State but, upon looking down on the surface of the ocean, he was reminded of a Polynesian paradise in which there were many young men and women swimming joyfully together. He "felt" that the ocean was cold down below yet it looked warm. He stated, "My eyes said one thing and my skin said another." He also saw an awesome African mask lying on the floor of the ocean. The black mask was oval-shaped—"like a vagina," he stated, and also had a spear which was penis-shaped. Suddenly he was pushed off the bluff into the ocean by someone he could not see.

His associations were to his awareness of being "pushed" by his wife, to the scary aspect of the African mask, and to the confusion of his senses about whether the sea was really warm or cold. After many other associations I was able to interpret to him that this dream was linked up with the previous dream and that he was searching for a solution for the falling off. I suggested to him that it was a birth dream and one in which he was pushed off a promontory by the spear of father's mask, the penis inside of the womb telling him he was taking too long in paradise and now had to be ejected. In other words, his "bluff" had to be called. At this same time the black mask reminded him of a black colleague whose "bluff" he had called, making him feel very good about himself and allowing him to feel free and separate. The pushing-off-the-bluff also was his feeling of being ejected by his wife into accepting cold separation and reality. His longing to get back into paradise having been coldly rejected, caused him to throw coldness onto the paradise, a "sour grapes" phenomenon, as it were. The confusion between the warm and the cold had to do with his desire to be "back inside" where it was warm but he felt "cold" for having been pushed out and believed furthermore that the world down below in the Polynesian paradise was heaven, his mother's womb with all the frolicking unborn children—a paradise which his birth and his analytic rebirth excluded him from.

The first "falling" was a nightmare for which he was unprepared. The second "falling" fitted into the pattern of his progress in analysis and he was able to experience my "pushing" into awareness in a dramatic narrative, epic, myth form which was acceptable to his Dreamer Who Understood the Dream.

The issue of the Shaman-psychoanalyst archetype in the dream organization suggests another important parallel between psychoanalysis and dream narrative—the induction of a state of dramatic tension which mobilizes the keen attention of the audience's consciousness. Psychoanalysis, for all its appearing to be tedious, always seems to demonstrate and dramatize the hidden truth of our being to our attention so as to give it optimal recognition. The revelation of truth is always dramatic: in fact, the failure to experience the drama of truthful revelation in the face of irrefragable truth constitutes that formidable and characteristic routine known as lying to oneself. The drama of the acceptance of truth is therefore a shield for transformation and for evolution. Its purpose is to beckon our attention. It is still a mystery when dreams seek to dramatize *without* calling their truths to our attention on some occasions and when they seek to dramatize *by* calling our attention to them on other occasions. This mystery may very well be at the center of the dilemma of whether or not the "I" experiencing the dream is desirous and capable of "knowing" the dream or whether the omnipotent Dreamer Who Understands the Dream purloins it for itself so as to rid consciousness of it. Who, after all, is the Owner of the Dream, the one who does not allow us to remember it?

Insofar as the subject of the Dreamer may feel, like Oedipus, omnipotently curious about the dream, then it may become a nightmare. The nightmare effect can only chasten the receptive self so as to discourage it from attuning itself to any further "leaks of Truth." Whether or not the Dreamer Who Understands the Dream or the "I" who can remember the dream gain sovereignty over the dream is thereafter a matter of the confidence of the latter to disengage the poser of the former over conscious control of dream reception.

Anyone who has experienced psychoanalysis either as analyst or analysand cannot fail to be impressed by the drama inherent when these two reagents come together in this unique medium. The setting for drama is built-in. The analyst seeks to harness it for dramatic exposure of those portions of the analysand's personality which are in his shadow and thereby unseen. Drama releases them to be visualized, then experienced. Dosage and timing of interpretation, the "artificial" abstinence of the analyst, the use of lying down, etc., all conspire to induce the surfacing of latent dramatic episodes on the scenario of the analytic chronicle. The dramas may get out of hand, eventuating in defensiveness, regression, psychosis, fear, and abandonment of the analysis. But, all in all, drama is the instrument of the analysis and seeks to facilitate revelation of the arcane, the recondite, the elliptical, and the shadowy. *Drama* knocks on the door of *Revelation* so that Revelation may be transformed into *Experience*.

The Dreamer Who Makes the Dream Understandable

Up until this point I have been assuming in this presentation that the deepest, and most arcane level of the dream is omnipotent, that is, the language of gods. I now wish to rectify that notion. It was transiently useful for presentation of a point of view but now must be modified. I wish, consequently, to introduce another missing link in dreaming, the Dreamer Who Makes The Dream Understandable. He is the one who makes use of the dream narrative to explore himself and the dilemma which stimulated the dream.

Bion pointed out in his paper "On Arrogance" that there are certain borderline or psychotic individuals who have experienced "infantile catastrophe," the fallout from which devolves into a triumvirate symptomatology: arrogance, stupidity, and curiosity (Bion, 1957). He believed that this triumvirate developed as a result of an infantile perceptuual catastrophe. Due to the early development of the epistemophilic instinct and its association to the libidinal instinct and the death instinct, the desire to know becomes greedily sucking and enviously mutilating of the first object of curiosity, mother's body. This was Klein's contribution. Bion added to that the idea of inherent preconceptions, by which I infer he means those inherited prototypes which anticipate experience so as to achieve a realization when the experience confirms the preconception. The ideas of inherent preconceptions, which have their origin in the philosophy of Plato and of Kant, offer a whole new perspective from which to gauge the unconscious.

Inherited preconceptions correspond to the "things-in-themselves," not representations. They are the experiences of REALITY knocking at the doors which do not exist in the schizophrenic's unwalled mindlessness. To turn the things-in-themselves into a representation requires a mind which can allow for postponement and transformation.

In his paper "On Arrogance" Bion called attention to the omnipotence of the desire to "know" and its consequences of *stupifying* the *arrogant* "knower" into a state of *arrogant stupidity*, the obverse of arrogant curiosity, which is now characterized by disburdening the mind of its thoughts or even of disburdening the self of its mind which thinks the thoughts—through abnormal projective identification. The blind Tiresias and the blinding of Oedipus in the Oedipal tragedy are examples of this phenomenon.

I take this to mean that the infant is confronted by a perceptual storm of sensory stimuli from without and within (biological urges such as hunger) which "release" the "things-in-themselves" or inherent preconceptions into stark apocalyptic epiphany. The capacity to mute this epiphany and to postpone its debut is the faculty both of mother's capacity for *reverie* and the infant's capacity to utilize this rèverie (autistic children cannot). In all probability the infant—and his adult counterpart—has to undergo the complex task of allowing the "thing-in-itself" to be released in gradual, sequential dosages of experience. He achieves this, thanks to mother's reveries, by believing himself to be *omnipotently* capable of willing away the "things-in-themselves." This is done by omnipotent mechanisms such as splitting, projective identification, idealization, magic omnipotent denial, and manic defenses. Paradoxically, the omnipotent mechanisms confer omnipotence on the "things-in-themselves," thus my assumption in the first part of this presentation. Now, however, this fiction must be exposed. The things-in-themselves can be thought of, I believe, as the agents of ultimate, unknowable Truth (Bion's "O") attempting an entrance through the apertures or sluices of the self in its forward, progressive developmental sweep.

As I adumbrated earlier, I believe the infant dreamer to utilize his "sender," the Dreamer Who Understands the Dream, to convey the autochthonously imaginative creation known as the dream narrative to the Audience Who Understands the Dream, an arcane representation of an internal containing object. Together they form a "C" Column of differentiation between sleep and wakefulness which facilitates the alpha barrier Bion refers to as being necessary for the maintenance of sanity as well as between the perceptual functions of background and foreground.

If the personality of the dreamer is such that he has the confidence, thanks to reverie and his use of reverie, that he can *postpone* his rendezvous with the "things-in-themselves," he then believes himself to contain an internal object pair, an omnipotent mother container and an omnipotent ego ideal sender which corresponds to an omnipotent "*thinking couple*," not unlike Hermann Hesse's archetypes delineated in *Demian* (Hesse, 1925). The one is the Dreamer Who Dreams the Dream and the other is the Dreamer Who Understands the Dream. Ultimately, the infant develops a confidence in his capacity to "know" his internal and external reality. This tendency normally comes at the expense of the gradual dissolution of the hegemony of the omnipotent thinking couple in favor of a real thinking couple. The "things-in-themselves" are at the same time denuded of omnipotence but not of significance.

Gradually there develops the appearance of a function which corresponds to the intrinsic analyst within us all. This, I believe, is the Dreamer, the Joseph who makes the dream understandable. He understands that the "things-in-themselves" are *not* omnipotent but *are* significant and offer necessary perspectives of Truth ("O"). As a consequence he tries to utilize the dream narrative to explore the perspectives it casts upon the dreamer's daily internal and external mental life for "re-cognition." The "name" of this figure must archaically, like the Tetragrammaton, seem to be ineffable and inscrutable but in recent times has been called the *analyst*. I do not know his dream name or his mythic forebearers. He seems to be the Observer who oversees the unfolding of the Scenario, who keeps a steady and continuous vigil on the scenario and the agents which seek to interrupt, obstruct, or alter it. By his vigil and his grasp of the scene of conflicts, feelings, etc., he makes computations or narrational alterations which become the ever-changing directives of the scenario. He is the guarantor of its future. He performs many functions but his commonest role is the Dreamer Who Makes the Dream Understandable. His presence and his development is also synchronously reciprocal with the Dreamer Who Dreams the Dream and the Dreamer Who Understands the Dream, by which I mean that the apparent omnipotence of their functions (the God Language) tends to reduce the state of respect for Truth and its agents, the "things-in-themselves." The Dreamer Who Makes the Dream Understandable—and his Partner, the Dreamer Who Is Willing To Have His Dream Understood—form a coalition which seems to mitigate the omnipotent powers who speak the God Language. The psychoanalyst today, as well as his close counterpart in ancient Greece, the playwright, the novelist, and the artist generally, are the external correspondents to this archetypal function (Entralgo, 1970).

A young female analytic patient once dreamt that she was in my office and was staring at the ceiling. Suddenly there appeared a frightening and eerie shadow of an enormous falcon on the spot where she had been staring. She realized that the falcon itself was near but only observable by its shadow. Then she found herself in the middle of my office sitting on the floor with several close friends while I myself seemed to have disappeared. The group she then found herself in indulged in a religious exorcism of her "possession." Her associations to this dream led me to the conclusion that she had come close to experiencing the "thing-in-itself," which was here represented as a shadow, much like the shadow in Plato's immortal Cave. The point of dreaming of this shadow of the falcon was that it might not have been the shadow at all but rather "it itself!" the most frightening of all apparitions. The dream was repeated in many different transformations in the following several weeks. One notable transformation was the appearance of a sinister snake which ultimately became her friend and guide. This was associated with the symbol for the medical profession (her husband was a doctor, as am I). Further analysis was able to link up the imagery of the falcon with deadly predatory curiosity on one hand and her lifelong persona of apparent superficiality on the other. This particular dream of the falcon's shadow seemed to perforate her pretense as a persona and precipitated her involvement in a truer attempt on her part to come to grips with her invasive curiosity and her fear of it.

Imagination

The capacity for imagination to soar offers us the benign and delightful opportunity to transcend the third dimensional limitations of our body frontiers and the infinite. When used in artisitc creation, imagination amounts to the power to perform an act of birth. Writers have long been familiar with this fantastic and unique element of creative power. The characters in a novel, play, or dream seem to have separate life systems and interact naturally with the other characters. It is difficult to "imagine" that the characters are not real.

When we speak of pathological imagination we generally use the term "phantasy." Actually, we are referring in this instance to that capacity of imagination to "imagine away" painful impression. Perhaps we could call this phenomenon "negative imagination." Negative imagination corresponds inchoately to the infant's turning his back, so to speak, on these painful impressions and putting them behind him—hopefully. We have known from Melanie Klein's concept of projective identification that the phenomenology of this is to project bad feelings into a "toilet breast," an object which seems to comply with our desire to be rid of the pain. What has not been understood, however, is that the infant not only believes himself to have created a transformed internal object, he also believes himself to have given birth to a twin, a negative self, whose content is all that he wished to evade. Bion (1950) described this phenomenon in his paper "The Imaginary Twin." He also alluded to it in a recent address to the Los Angeles Psychoanalytic Institute as "the ghost of analysis." This negatively imagined self (a transformation in hallucinosis, as it were) becomes associated as the fetal infant who is associated with being unborn. It is almost completely split off from the more obvious creator twin and has its own separate life and separate agenda.* It seems to exhort, importune, and coerce the hapless creator twin to do its bidding. Extortion and blackmail are its instruments. A separate life system is its power. If the patient seeks to cooperate with the analyst in analysis, the negative twin responds as if real murder is being committed. On the other hand, this twin silently and chronically "suicides" its creator twin much like a cancer through trying to ensorcell it to keep in supply—that is, to maintain—the illusion that it is unborn and therefore safe. Let me describe three examples:

The first example is that of a forty-year-old surgeon who entered analysis because of depression and then developed a drinking problem. Interpretations about his alcoholism were of no avail until I realized his "twin"

*I am indebted to Doctor Bernard Bail for helping me with these conceptions.

was seeking alcohol in order to preserve a feeling of being unborn and was inveigling the patient to believe its entreaties—at his expense. This interpretation had a powerful and corrective effect.

The second example is of a beautiful, thirty-year-old woman who had a traumatic family situation which she chronically recites as the cause of all her problems. She depends deeply on the analysis but seems unable to make progress or get relief from it. One day recently she mentioned that she feels "murdered by her life." This inspired in me a series of thoughts which culminated in the following interpretation: "My interpretations to you are understood but ineffective because of your other self, the one who deadens you in order to evade and erase disturbing experiences, acts as an "evidence collector" (the patient is an attorney) and therefore misconstrues my interpretations as confirmations of how bad you are. Ultimately, this twin convinces you *she* is the proper analyst–not I. Yet you have to come to me in order to "cure" her. If she had been effective, you would not have had to come into analysis in the first place. As it is, her promises are empty but you wish to believe them so you bring *her* here, not you, in order for me to plug the holes in her imperfections so that she can be reempowered to ensorcel you and to discredit me."

The patient was shaken by the interpretation as she left the office. The next day she reported to me that, upon leaving my office, she crossed the street against the light in very heavy traffic without being aware. She was nearly killed. Only then did she really believe that she contained a murderer who is afraid of being murdered.

The third example is that of a single professional woman in her forties who entered analysis because of depression. She was in a previous analysis for many years but became severely negativistic toward her therapist and quit the treatment. Her interpersonal relationships were precarious both personally and professionally. It gradually became apparent to me that she was relating to me and the analysis in such a depressively manipulating way so as to coerce me to give her advice about her life situations. It turned out that her previous analyst, although interpretive in most respects with her, had latterly begun to indulge in advice. In the background of the patient is the "awareness" of having been taken by mother to her grandmother's on the other side of the country by train at three weeks of age. Although a loud, almost raucous person herself, she is most highly sensitive to noise and interruptions.

Because of the above and other associations and dreams, I was able to give her the following interpretation: "Your pre-train ride self seems always to wish to reassure yourself that she is still unborn and seeks to coerce you to reinforce this notion by avoiding any progress. When your former analyst tried to analyze you, your "unborn" twin self convinced you that the analyst was trying to show you how bad you are. When he tried to be helpful to you in terms of advice, he then became a convenient target for your bad advice-giving "unborn" twin self to convince you that the analyst is your bad adviser, not you." The interpretation was received with enormous surprise and credibility. She immediately lay down on the couch (she generally sat up on the couch) and began to work in a new and enthusiastic way.

The "twin" is the product of an act of birth by the imagination pressed into the service of denial of Truth. The return of the evaded Truth is felt to be like a cross to a vampire—it means its very death. Whether we create the fictitious characters of our planned plays and novels consciously or unconsciously or whether we create unconscious characters in our own inner novel and then assign them to real people in the real world, the effect often is the same—the character, once created, lives forever—unless killed. Then it becomes a ghost. It is my impression that this is what Bion had in mind about the ghost of analysis, for instance. Duerenmatt emphasized the continuing nature of these characters in his novel *The Pledge*.

The capacity for imagination to bestow life is the instrument for creative Truth on one hand, but also, in its reciprocal function, it parallels this truth-inspiring function by its negation—Falsehood, the ultimate antecedent of which is the presentation of the illusion of the unborn state. *All defenses and resistences can be seen as perversions of imagination*.

In psychotic restitutions the patient may find himself once again involved in a Kafkaesque plot—one in the first spatial dimension—in which he is caught as a character in someone else's novel and without flexibility, margin, or escape. Absolutism seems to characterize the patient's fictional plight. Yet it can easily be discerned, upon scrutiny, that the writers of the diabolical novel which pre-empts our hero's life are *fictitious characters given life by the patient's perverse imagination*. The irony of psychotic illusion is that its persecutors do not exist and have to be invented in order to play their roles. *Once given life, they ad lib*!! Tom Stoppard's play, *Rosenkranz and Guildenstern Are Dead* poignantly deals with this aspect of character manipulation by playwright-creators who resort to peremptory creation and dismissal of characters at will.

The "ad libbing" of these characters brings forth another important point alluded to by Bion, the concept of *shifting perspective*. This concept has a number of meanings, and applications. I should like only to hint at one which I believe to be appropriate to the present discussion. When we dream of a number of characters in a dream, we are detailing reference points of perspective. The first dream could very well have been told from the vantage point of the first angel, or the second, etc. This conception begins to bear fruit when we consider the idea of good and bad internal objects. *Does a bad internal object know that it is bad*? Does it have a rationale or a belief system for itself so that it can effectively attempt to discredit what the dreamer might call a good object? The concept of *Rashomon* seems to govern the shifting perspectives of the inner narrative, in other words. The real dream is a composite of all the dreams that could be told from each vantage point—and more. In psychotic illusion this multiple viewpoint of a single narrative degenerates into split off, disparate stories without connection.

With these views in mind, we can thus postulate that psychopathology is a bad novel or a bad dream which does not "work." We are caught in a plot conflict and cannot escape. The myth of the Labyrinthe may well encompass this feeling. In the course of dreaming our story, we may have gotten caught inside a dilemma (projective identification) and forgot how we got in and therefore, without an Ariadne's thread, cannot get out until some analytic Theseus frees us.

The Laminations of Awareness

Throughout this presentation I have been using the dream as a specific instance of a consciousness or of an awareness within us which is greater than what we have hitherto called consciousness of self. And that the dream is a vent in the shield which separates our two worlds, the outer world of conscious, asymmetrical experience and the inner world of infinite symmetry and inner cosmic vastness. Freud (1900-1901) himself recognized the "dream connection" when he stated, "There is often a passage in even the most thoroughly interpreted dream which has to be left obscure; this is because we become aware during the work of interpretation that at that point there is a tangle of dream-thoughts which cannot be unravelled and which moreover adds nothing to our knowledge of the content of the dream. *This is the dream's navel, the spot where it reaches down into the unknown*." (p. 25).*

The term "unconscious," the proper name for this system of inner cosmic vastness which contains a wealth of "myriad consciousnesses," is therefore an unfortunate term because it belies the awarenesses implicit and inherent in this system. The truth of the matter is that what we call the unconscious is really unconscious *to* us but is itself never unconscious *of* us.

I have therefore come to believe that consciousness occurs in laminations of awareness and that these laminations extend in a spectrum from "unconscious" symmetrical awarenesses through preconscious awarenesses, and incude conscious awarenesses. I also believe that consciousness itself has a bipolar or a bimodal distribution, to use a term coined by Deikman (1971). By bimodal consciousness I mean that our conscious self may have its own conscious awareness, let us say of the external world and, to a certain degree, of the internal world; whereas the internal world may have many laminations of consciousness, that is, of itself, of other structures, thoughts, and feelings within the unconscious, etc. Moreover, when we focus attention in the act of concentration we are giving active conscious awareness to the object upon which we are focusing and are suspending the

*Italics mine.

background awareness which acts in the manner of a background-foreground or figure-ground manner. In other words, when we focus attention, we are lifting the object from its background into the foreground of our attention but there is still a background attention that is being partially suspended. We encounter this phenomenon for instance when we are listening in an analytic hour to patient material and experience two forms of consciousness, a loose background consciousness and a focused foreground consciousness. This phenomenon is easily demonstrable, for instance, when we are driving in our car, listening to the radio, thinking our thoughts, and preconsciously watching the traffic without being directly aware of some of these procedures.

Gazzaniga and LeDoux (1978) have discovered that the human being has two consciousnesses, one for each of the cerebral hemispheres, but that they are experienced as a single consciousness. In creative work and in analysis, we strive to suspend the consciousness of the dominant hemisphere in order to permit the expression of the consciousness of the non-dominant hemisphere, the latter of which is the awareness of the *personal meaning* of experience (a consequence of alpha function). After this can be gleaned, the suspension of the consciousness of the dominant hemisphere can be lifted, and a "binocularization" or stereoscopy of both consciousnesses can then take place in a non-anatomical third brain in order to achieve the ultimate consciousness of *significance* (Grotstein, 1978).

I believe that if the phenomenon of consciousness be carried to its logical extreme we can begin to redefine consciousness as an attribute of an organism or even of a cell which is a property of the living organism's vitality and sense of purpose. I do not think it too wildly speculative, therefore, to attribute something like prototypical consciousness to the sperm cell which is "conscious" in a way of its purpose in its trajectory toward the uterus—or even of an egg cell in its descent down the fallopian tube. Consciousness then would be a statement of the proprioceptive sense of awareness between I and self in the human organism and of the reflection upon oneself in lesser units of human existence. The monitoring function of the reticular filtering formation would be a proprioceptive consciousness of sensation in the somatosensory system. This would be a specific demonstration of consciousness of consciousness.

Erikson's (1959) concept of *epigenesis* connotes the consciousness of purpose of an inherent template or ground-plan which organizes the future development of the parts and the whole of all organisms including the human. Epigenesis can therefore be seen, in its consciousness of the future of the organism, as a "memoir of the future" to apply Bion's term (Bion, 1977). It is a memoir of the future insofar as the concept of epigenesis represents both an anatomical-embryological conception which has been hewn and programmed with the coding of phylogenetic eons. It becomes the "immortal software" of animal and plant phylogenetic consciousness. Bailey (1978) has reminded us that the concept of phylogenetic regression is explicit in Freud's theory of regression and that it has suffered an eclipse in popularity amongst analysts. Our whole life progression is a continuation of ontogeny which ineluctably "recapitulates phylogeny," so that the development of the species and the hardships it had to survive are programmed into an epigenetic template as "inherent software." We have learned and continued to learn from species–racial–mythical–historical–and current experiences.*

I therefore believe that our innate behavior coordinators, or inherent preconceptions, or apparatuses of primary autonomy, or whatever eponym they go by, constitute the inherited software of consciousness which is the biography of the existence of life for all time and is programmed into the capsule of the double helix for immortal projection. Every component descending from the epigenetic groundplan has its own consciousness of purpose. What we loosely call integration, development, maturation, etc., are but gross or molar terms for molecular, atomic, and subatomic consciousnesses which ultimately, like the "rogue wave" of the sea, unite resonantly into a single wave of consciousness known as the human experience of being aware on whatever level.

In general, I believe there is always a tendency for the rogue wave of consciousness to take place, that is, that there develops a unification of all consciousnesses in a resonant form to give specific awareness. Condensation in the dream for instance gives it dramatic intensity, according to Freud, and therefore presents a picture of the quintessence of dream consciousness. However, we are not able to tolerate the consciousnesses in what we commonly call the unconscious because of the difficulty our perceptual apparatus has in being able to contain so much consciousness, not only because of the danger of perceptual overload, but also because of the limitation of the human capacity to assign meaningfulness and significance to perceptions. Matte Blanco (1978) has described the difficulty in perception between asymmetrical consciousness and symmetrical unconsciousness at length elsewhere in this volume. The breakdown of consciousness because of the meaningfulness of perception is otherwise known as the oedipus complex, and the perceptual catastrophe emanating from it, as epitomized by Oedipus' enucleation of his eyes, has been beautifully delineated by Bion and is described in Bahia's article which is also in this volume.

Earlier I spoke of bimodal consciousness and its existence in the routines of our daily life. I mentioned that it contains focused attention when we are concentrating on an event and background attention which does not intrude into focused attention but seems to be located in the back of our minds in some kind of loose awareness. I mentioned also how analysts try to suspend a focused attention in order to tap into the background consciousness only to return to focused attention to reap the harvest of this altered

*I am grateful to Dr. Michael Paul for his stimulation and contributions of thought in this area. It was he who first presented the idea of the phylogenetic precursors to consciousness to me.

attention. Thus, the foreground-background consciousness dichotomy would represent an aspect of bimodal consciousness and this in turn, that is, the foreground-background consciousness of our overt awareness in our asymmetrical world, is itself antipodal to the myriads of subordinate "consciousnesses" which comprise our nature, our development, our history, our ontogeny, our phylogeny, and in general, the history of living cells.

The ultimate nature of consciousness is, therefore, the sum of all these consciousnesses plus the potential consciousness that is possible from the realization of all the possible significances of all the possible thoughts and feelings in consciousnesses which are comprehensible to our mind.

Matte Blanco (1980), as adumbrated above, has advised us in his own conception of the narcissism myth that when Narcissus looked into the River Styx he saw on the other side of the veil of water his unconscious self, his symmetrical twin. Matte Blanco believes that a conscious mind lives in the third dimension of asymmetry, asymmetry being the characteristic of development in real life. Symmetry in the mathematical sense characterizes the unconscious and seems to occupy dimensions approaching the infinite. He believes therefore that a barrier between the asymmetrical field of normal living and the "unreal" symmetrical world of the unconscious had to be developed in order to preserve the sanity of the asymmetrical mind. The symmetrical world of the unconscious, therefore, constitutes something of a reservoir of potentiality and of creativity allowing thoughts to emerge into asymmetry whenever the subject is able to tolerate them.

Regression

I should now like to say a word about the psychoanalytic concept of regression from the point of view of awareness or of consciousness, that is, from the topographical point of view. In ordinary parlance we think of regression as a descent of consciousness from a surface level to a deeper level within the structure of the psyche, constituting a retracing of our development in reverse. I should like to suggest that the whole psychoanalytic concept of regression suffers from a perceptual distortion. When we use the term *regression*, we really mean *progression* of primitive awarenesses to the surface rather than the other way around. After all, it is not our capacity to perceive the primitive (our perceptual apparatus) which regresses. Structures do not regress. Perceptual content may, under certain circumstances, find access to the surface of awareness and therefore rise to meet the sense organ receptors of the perceptual apparatus—and of intuition. This "progression" takes place in terms of the return of the repressed in mental illness but also occurs normally on an ongoing basis. Creativity is but one normal facet of it—but there is another, and I should like to discuss that now. It constitutes perhaps the ultimate meaning of my first dream:

On The Ultimate Nature of Being

The Dreamer Who Dreams the Dream and The Dreamer Who Understands the Dream comprise the arcane "thinking couple" who produce, and "comprehend" the dream. They originally are the Gods Who Understand the Language of Gods. Ultimately the God Language becomes translated by an internal Shaman known as the Dreamer Who Makes the Dream Understandable. His (Her) involvement constitutes a significant milestone in the experience of dreaming. Thereafter, the dream becomes less and less the language of gods and more and more the untangling skein of highly coded human experience becoming decoded for relegation according to significance and ultimate being. This evolution predicates the development of a mind which can produce dreams and a mind which requires them and appreciates them. As this maturation proceeds, the Dreamer Who Dreams the Dream and the Dreamer Who Understands the Dream undergo mature modifications which permit dreams to become the idiom of experience rather than to that of omnipotence.

These "Dreamers" seem all-in-all to constitute a monumental presumption of a phenomenon not unlike an umbilicus to the mysterious and the divine. Bion has helped decipher this enigma by postulating inherent ideas as things-in-themselves which press with messianic zeal toward apertures of expression through the dream by day and the dream by night. Matte Blanco (1975) has also made a significant contribution in this area by demonstrating to us that the unconscious exists in the null (0) dimension and is therefore (a) syncretistic and concretistic; (b) all "ideas" in the unconscious conveyed to infinite sets that is, each idea is part of another group of ideas which is part of another group of ideas, etc.; (c) infinite symmetry exists in unconscious processes as compared with the limited asymmetry of human experience externally. The consequence of the above postulates, according to Matte Blanco, is the creation of an invisible barrier between the symmetrical and the asymmetrical experiences. A barrier must be created in order to filter out the intelligence from a symmetrical infinite which pours like the Flood of Yore into the sluices of a human, therefore limited, asymmetrical fountainhead. The hint we have of our symmetrical infinite—always unreachable, unseeable, ineffable, inscrutable—the very Tetragrammation itself—constitutes the quintessence of our connection with the Background Subject-Object of Primary Identification and is our closest claim to something *like* a Divinity or an inspiration within. Adonai, the ineffable and inscrutable name of the godhead of the Hebrews, literally means "I am!" When once we dream, we are as an audience to the Gods. Now the dream is a revelation of our unknowable capacity for thinking and remains but a brief glimpse into the ultimate nature of our unfathomable being. The greatness of our being stands behind us; we can exist only in the shadows it casts into the caves of our experience.

As Jung (1944) says, "We are connected to the gods." At the utmost, however, it is the nature of the *relationship* between these inner beings and the relationships to their counterparts in the outer world which constitutes the ultimate nature of being. The Dreamer Who Dreams the Dream, the Dreamer Who Understands the Dream, and the Dreamer Who Makes the Dream. Understandable are but the inner aspects of a relationship to the analyst on the outside who is helping to stimulate the mental activity of dreaming in the first place—or witness his equivalent maybe with the dreamer who is not in analysis. The Dreamers are part of a transaction into their requisite counterparts in the outer world. Being human is but a facet of being together with another. The first transaction is the relationship with the Background Subject-Object of Primary Identification. All further relationships are with the descendents of primary identification—those who are meaningful to us throughout our lives. The dreams constitute, I therefore believe, a residue of an umbilical connection with the Background Object and an umbilical shadow of connection to those who are chosen by us as worthy enough to occupy our mental lives today.

The Dreamer Who Makes the Dream Understandable is a statement of the function of the desire of the personality to individuate, to expand its psychic space, to seek its future, and to make itself known to itself. In this regard it fulfills Bion's postulates for self-publication which, in effect, are continuing redemptions by the self of the hostile self which wants to be born but which is incarcerated by the "never-to-be-born" self, the omnipotent dreamer. The latter might correspond to the "excluded middle" in all self-rescuing operations.

Earlier I have referred to the Background Subject-Object of Primary Identification and its counterpart the Subject-Object of Destiny. I believe that the Subject-Object of Destiny, known in its earthly role as the ego ideal in association with the superego, is the container of the Future, as is the unconscious the Object of the Past. The psychic apparatus, in other words, even though unfortunately named, connotes a vector of change from the past through the present to the future. We are always moving in our scenarios, therefore, from the Subject-Object of the Past in connection with the Background Subject-Object of Primary Identification into the direction of the Subject-Object of Destiny, which is, like the ever-receding and always distant city of Samarkand, always vanishing on the horizon as we approach it. I believe that the ego ideal and, what I should now like to call the Instinctual Object, are but points of view from which ego, ego ideal, and Instinctual Object can view a common object from different points of view so as to achieve a common binocular focus. In other words, the importance of the relationship, for instance, between the ego and the ego ideal is not so much their conversation between themselves about themselves but rather about what they are perceiving as a common focus—their points of view. The same is true of the Instinctual Object. Thus the instinctual (or the past), the moral (or the future) and the here and now confer together to have that kind of conversation which must occur all the time in the tegmental area of the mid-brain when the eyes converse with each other about what they see in common on the outside. The ultimate sense of "I"-ness rests therefore in that middle area of binocularization—the mental representation of the mid-brain's tegmentum in which significance and meaning are associated to the perception by a superordinating, non-anatomical third brain which harvests the yield of the left and the right brain—or the ego ideal and the ego—or the ego and the id, etc., so as to gain that binocularization to achieve correlation and transcendental growth—thus, *tertiary process*!

Psychosis is characterized by the inability to allow this common focus. The conversation between one eye and the other in themetaphoric tegmentum is disjointed and attacked, therefore no resolution or fusion takes place. Correlation and transcendental experience are negated. It is as if the psychotic, instead of having two eyes to focus upon a common object, is two cyclopian eyes staring at the same object but not talking to each other. There is no communication and therefore there is no growth. Yet that is the victory of psychosis—the arrestment of progress and the forfeiture of the future because of the dread of the past. For the psychotic the past and the future are the same. What he projects behind him is indistinguishably confused with his future. He destroys his future in order not to keep his rendezvous with his past. The psychotic has no intention of keeping his appointment in Samara. He defeats death by forfeiting life.

Our Ultimate Nature of Being (0) spans the crevasse between the Background Subject-Object of Primary Identification and Its Shadow, the Subject-Object of Destiny, our Future. They are linked by the Theme of Themes and propel us *to and from* our once and future excellence. Our daily human lives are brief vignettes in this scenario and are like evanescent eddies in a relentless stream of change. The dream is the organization of the continuing mythic narrative which orders our chaos along our way.

The Dosage of Sorrow

I believe there to be a regular traffic between the symmetrical unconscious and asymmetrical consciousness. I believe, furthermore, that the "repressed" is comprised, not so much of instincts or drives, as Freud suggested, but rather of infinite myriads of potential awarenesses and/or preconceptions as Bion has suggested. The repressed, both primary and secondary, contains an infinite galaxy of potential *meaningfulnesses* which await *realization* in order to be assigned *significance*. The unconscious is the sum total or the reservoir of all the significances that are conceivable. The realization of meaningfulness which significance imparts to unconscious knowledge (Bion's "thoughts without a thinker") occurs in the depressive position. Meaningfulness occurs in the shadow of the inescapable sadness of growth and separation from one's previous self. As knowledge of oneself can be tolerated, it is experienced as being "dosed" by our capacity to bear the sorrow of loss and insecurity in order to allow our psychic space to expand commensurately. The dosage of sorrow denotes our capacity to bear truth. The young medical student who dreamed the dream of the dosage of sorrow was to realize decades later that that dream was the forewarning, like the Oracle at Delphi, about the fate and fatefulness of his odyssey into his future. If his mind was to allow for the truths gleaned from this odyssey, he would have to suffer the sorrow which Truth administers and, thereby, transcend himself with each dosage of sorrow.

The Dream as an Act of Creative Thinking

Heretofore, I have dealt with the alleged purpose of the dream as a special function (Bion's alpha function) which alienates, mystifies, and mythifies the sense data of emotional experience so as to suspend them in a narrative which allows for postponement. Bion's conception of alpha function is a mythical mechanism which accounts for our ability to concentrate attention by day and by night (to be able to concentrate on being attentively awake and focussed by day and "attentive to sleep by night"). The dream therefore helps us to handle stimuli which is quantitatively *and* qualitatively excessive so that a membrane of alpha elements can separate sleep from wakefulness, unconsciousness from consciousness, etc.

We must now enter into a whole new realm of dream functioning, creative *thinking* and *planning*, not just creative narrative alone. Perhaps one of the clearest examples of this function, which Freud parenthetically hinted at but did not amplify, was the famous dream of August Kekule von Stradonitz. While puzzling over the chemical structure of benzene, he dreamed that he saw six snakes entertwining, thereby discovering the hexagonal structure of aromatic compounds. A more commonplace analogue to this creative dream phenomenon is that of cryptically physically ill patients who may dream of the neoplasm or fistula they have inside which has not yet been discovered by their physicians. Even more commonly, in psychoanalysis itself, we have frequent confirmation of this creative phenomenon when the patient's dream is able to illuminate an important but darkened area which had been difficult or even impossible to ferret out via usual free associations. We are dependent on the dream creator for these hints in most instances.

This creative, exploratory aspect of the dream bears testimony to the "thinker" behind the dream, the Dreamer who Produces the Dream and the vastness of the epistemophilic organization at his/her disposal if we are only able to accept its functioning. The dream, and its production agency, alpha function, are, as it were, the earthly or personal representatives of Eternal Truth "O." Alpha function is like the Krebs Cycle of Carbohydrate Metabolism which can allow the transformation of the image of this Truth "O" as knowledge (K) so that we, the dreamer, can allow our transformation by this experience of → K so that we evolve (transcend) from K → O. The dream facilitates this transformational transcendence. But then the question must be asked: Do we evolve, transcend, transform via an unconscious experience in which the dream has conveyed its O → K message? Or is it necessary to be conscious of the dream's harvest so as to experience the experience with full awareness? While I do not think that an answer is readily available, I should suggest that it might be possible for some evolution of self to occur unconsciously, but I also believe that the Dreamer may repeat his dream narrative in many different ways successively until the Truth "O" becomes known in K.

Thus, I envision dream functioning as not only producing a continuous membrane of separation between psychical reality and external reality via narrative, but also, as a creative thinker and explorer in its own right. This conception is very much in keeping with Bion's notion of alpha function but is at serious odds with the narrow strictures Freud placed upon his own primary process as the regulatory mechanism of instinctual functions. I would now go on to suggest that alpha function is a closer approximation than is primary process to the quality of mental activity which happens beneath consciousness. Insofar as alpha function is the agency which allows us to know O by its shadow, K, we are approximating Kant's conception of the relationship between the noumenon, the thing-in-itself, O, and its shadow derivative, K. We cannot know O, but we can know something about O through K. As such, that K by which we know something about O becomes an intermediary between it and us. I now wish to discuss the importance of the function of this intermediary.

It is at this point that I wish to invoke Peirce's (1960) concept of thirdness and its relationship to the linguistic function of semiology, the study of signs. Peirce believes that language is composed of three different functions, one of which is the interpretant "I" (the subject), the second of which is the object, and the third is the sign by which the object is to be interpreted. The sign or semiotic designates and/or indicates the objects to the interpretant.

In this respect it is a revelatory function. Yet we can also see that this sign also does the opposite—that is, it does not reveal all the truth about "O." The sign can therefore be likened to a fuse which allows electricity from a source but also keeps some electricity back. It is a regulatory threshold which acts as an active membrane allowing some revelation and disallowing others. Of utmost importance in the phenomenon of communication is the ability for the sign to have a good equilateral relationship between interpretant and object. As Silver (personal communication) has pointed out, psychotic communication begins to approximate when "I" (interpretant) approaches "O" (object) at a distance from the sign so that the triangle of the thirdness becomes narrower between "O" and "I" and longer between

"O" and "S" and "I" and "S." This describes the psychotic's tendency to bypass the delay imposed by the sign and to get to the object directly so as to fuse with it and become it. On the other hand, after invading the object and becoming it, a psychotic state of confusion exists, the restitution of which is the confusion by the now psychotic "I" of the sign with its object. According to Freud (1911), the verbal representation (the sign) has now become used as the thing representation ("O"), deep structure, which has disappeared.

Thus, the purpose of alpha function is to keep the equilateral regularity in the triangle of thirdness between the three involved members and to allow "I"-ness to be able to get outside the triangle so as to be able to understand the meaning of the relationship between the sign and its object and the significance this meaning has for oneself. Perhaps dreams function as creative thinkers when this thirdness is maintained. Dreams which occur when thirdness begins to diminish may be more troublesome and defensive and less explanatory. Ultimately, thirdness is a way of talking about the relationship between, not only "I," "O," and "S," but also between the Dreamer who Dreams the Dream, the Dreamer who Understands the Dream, and the Dreamer who Makes the Dream Understandable, the latter in relationship to a perceiving "I."

Dream Access and Retrieval

Since the dream has access to the functional primary process (alpha function), it has at its disposal an intriguingly complex capacity for memory storage—the timelessness and spacelessness of the zero dimension (See Grotstein, 1978). Thus, an infinitude of memories can be stored holographically, that is, each memory byte (to use a computer term) can be stored in the same place as if an infinite number of ghosts occupy the same body. Dream memory storage therefore avails itself of the vast reaches of its synchronic capacity. As the dream unfolds, it *seems* to be *diachronic*, that is, sequential. The non-dominant hemisphere has synchronic capacity, but the dominant hemisphere, in recognizing the dream, experiences it sequentially because it has only three-dimensional space-time capacity (diachronic). The translative distortion of the retrieval from one mode to the other is enormous. Witness the frustration we all have when we try to remember, let alone repeat, a dream.

"Siamese Twins" and the Importance of Ambiguity

When the infant proceeds from the practicing sensory-motor period into object constancy (transformation from the symbiotic stage of the paranoid-schizoid position to the depressive position of separation-individuation with object constancy), the object of the senses seems to be surrendered for a spiritual portraiture or image of the object in the object's absence—much like the great achievement of the Hebrews in foreswearing tangible idols for the ineffable and inscrutible god without a name. Yet psychoanalysis has helped us realize that the sensory-motor "grasp" of the object is not entirely foresworn as we mature; we merely subordinate our claim to the reassurance of tangibility to the overlordship of re-presentability of the image of the non-tangible object which is now newly tangible but only to our memory and our imagination. I am suggesting that the sensory-motor tangible object and its re-presentational image comprise a *metaphor couple* which can be pictured as a "siamese twin" in which there are two heads, one for the object and the other for the image, and a fusion between them. This siamese twin model constitutes not only the basis for *metaphor*, but also of *ambiguity*; the two of which are but different ways of expressing the capacity that words, thoughts, and expressions have to offer in terms of possibilities of meanings far beyond their concrete (tangible) properties.

I arrived at the conception of the siamese twin model when I tried to reconcile Klein's conception of the infant's being separate from the beginning of life with Mahler's insistance that mental "hatching" did not occur until at least five months—and, for all intents and purposes, not really until fifteen to eighteen months of postnatal life. I was able to reconcile the dilemma by invoking the dual-track theorem in which both investigators were right: Klein's infant and Mahler's infant occupy the dual-track, one track of which represents separation, and the other track represents the continuation of primary at-one-ment with the primal mother (Background Object of Primary Identification). I then reasoned that the image which best pictures the relationship between an infant and its mother in the autistic phase is one in which the infant is sitting on the mother's lap. The heads are separate, but the bodies are fused; mother is unseen. In the symbiotic phase proper (I say "proper" because I believe the autistic phase is an early form of symbiosis) the heads are facing, but the bodies are still fused. Thus the symbiotic paradigm appears to be a siamese twin bonding.

It was only a short step to link this image with psycholinguistic and communication theory. The siamese twin relationship allows for an inherent preconception to be able to locate its counterpart in the external world by first trying to locate its homologue (exact duplicate) and, failing that, to locate an object which corresponds enough to it to *resemble* the homologue (track one of continuing primary at-one-ment) and yet to be different enough to be unfamiliar or separate (track two of separation).

In dream memory access and retrieval, *homologues* of day residues are searched for in the synchronic, holographic memory file, and, failing that, *analogues*, similar and different, are utilized. These analogues are plastic and are subject to the complex refinements of metathesis (vida supra) for imaginative recombinations.

I now must introduce yet another aspect of siamese twin symbolism in addition to the homologue—analogue twins. The new one is that of opposition–corresponding to the relationship of Bion's Column One to Column Two: definitory hypothesis confronting the challenge of its negation. Negation represents one kind of opposition to a definitory statement; thus, the opposite of love could be thought of as hate. Yet there is another opposite to love, influence, the intercession of which allows Bion's grid to become three dimensional. It also paradoxically unites the former opposites, love and hate, by "reminding" them that they share passion in common. In short, every definitory statement evokes (a) its homologue, (b) its analogue, (c) its opposite, and (d) its negation, the last two being ambiguous relative to each other. These four definitory evocations constitute a series of siamese twinships (or really siamese quadruplets composed of component siamese twins) which allows for the optional manifestation of ambiguity, which represents the storage, retrieval, conduct, and expression of all mental phenomena–and combines the workings of the digital *and* the analogue computer. The dream *is* ambiguity and takes full advantage of the esthetic, communicative, and dramatic capacity which ambiguity offers us so economically.

Dream Action

Finally, the siamese twins and quadruplets, those chimerical androgynes of ambiguity are gathered together by the Ballet Master of the Dream to progress through the highly stylized choreography of the scenario. This "choreography," the planned steps of the piece, involves the intricacies of expanded and contracted time. This shrinking and expanding of time–often experienced as if Father Time were "playing" us like an accordion is accomplished by the employment of the instruments of dimension. Whereas we dwell merely in the third dimension–knowingly–in our dominant consciousness (by day), we dwell in the zero dimension by night (Grotstein, 1978). The Dream Accordion can "play" us through both its scales on the dual tracks of consciousness so that we can experience the logic of the dream in sequential three dimensionality on one scale, and can experience the flattened, "molasses" slowness of the second dimension, the violent speed of the first dimension, and the infinity–and infinitesimal–of the limitlessness of the zero dimension.

Postscript

My newer vision of "I"-ness and its embrasure of "I"-"Self" in all the Cartesian artifactual perspectives are offered as a replacement for what I now believe to be the current, outmoded psychic apparatus (ego, id, superego) of classical analysis. "I" is always unitary, phantasies otherwise notwithstanding. Yet "I" can be dual as in twinship: "I" → "Self" (subject to object), "I" → "I" (subject to subject), etc. Every aspect of ourselves is

"I"; there is no not "I." "Id" is *not* "it" but "I." Of all Freud's errors, this to me was one of the most serious and fateful.

Furthermore, "I" emerges as a greater and less known and knowable entity than has hitherto been thought. My contribution suggests that dreams, *ph*antasies, *f*antasies, thoughts ("thoughts without a thinker") are fashioned by an inspired scenarist who seems to "cut" the primal picture of Truth into carefully partitioned puzzle pieces and then disperses them for our curiosity to retrieve. The coherence implicit in their dispersal is predicated by a "selected fact" which gives them significance and meaning—and this selected fact is itself fore-ordained as the puzzle of Truth is cut—and is known to the Dreamer Who Dreams the Dream.

One further point is worthy of mention. Bion has pointed out that the basic myths of mankind, for instance, the myths of Eden, Babel, and Oedipus, all include two important functions amongst many: (a) a compunction by a demon to be curious; and (b) an injunction by a god against the fulfillment of curiosity. This injunction against curiosity has oftentimes been analogized to states of resistance in analysis and are derived from manifestations of the repressive barrier. I believe that the status of the repressive barrier and the injunction against curiosity have a profound meaning. There is a natural divide between the functioning of the left brain-mind and the right brain-mind. They are two different ways of processing the data of experience. The corpus callosum can be thought of in model form as a metaphoric bridge which conveys messages between the two. The repressive barrier is that aspect of the metaphoric function of the corpus callosum which keeps certain messages from getting across. It conducts selected information and filters out other information. Otherwise, each would destroy the other.

What used to be called the id needs as much protection against what used to be called the ego as the reverse. The natural barrier between them has much to do with the different dimensional worlds they occupy. Matte Blanco (1975) has demonstrated a difference between symmetrical logic and bi-logic as being components of two different hemispheric modes of thinking. In short, the non-dominant hemisphere functions in the zero dimension with synchronic immediacy (like an infinite vertical orchestra score); whereas the dominant hemisphere functions in linear, diachronic sequentiality—in the third dimension. The two time-space worlds are incompatible and must be kept apart. Curiosity, particularly analytic curiosity—especially that analytic curiosity which penetrates dreamwork, is always in danger of perforating the Gossamer veil which protects the integrity of the other cosmos, the internal world. Thus, the course of our curiosity and investigation must go between Scylla and Charybdis in purusing the dispersal of Truth's puzzle-fragments on one hand and not penetrating the Innocence of the boundaries of the other world on the other. We must never know its functioning; we are entitled only to its data.

This is the intercourse which is so sacred that it must not be known; it must always remain inscrutable. The act of psychic creation involves the most arcane, most mysterious union **between** two modes of "being" and of "valuing" the data of inner and outer experience. Their intercourse creates "thoughts." It can never be penetrated.

Summary

The dream, in it evolution from the *Dream* to the *dream*, is a palimpsest upon which is written, rewritten, and again overwritten the mythic pageant of existence. It is produced by the Dreamer Who Dreams The Dream, a composite of many smithy roles and functions, and is understood by its requisitioner, The Dreamer Who Understands The Dream. The Dreamer Who Makes The Dream Understandable translates the dream for our "understanding" which we make use of for delay and avoidance of confrontations or for solutions. All three of these Dreamers are functions of "I-self" in its ultimate, unknowable quintessence and awesome excellence. We are fated never to know them—only to be their clients and to walk in their shadow.

The dream is the epiphany of "divine conversations" between the Background Subject-Object of Primary Identification and the Subject-Object of Destiny and constitutes a "reading" of our existence while we are in transit between our once and future excellence.

Narrative is the skilled, artistic, and awesome arrangement of psychic moments into a syllogistic, linear, plot-oriented sequence of events which gather the outcries from all corners of the psyche and lure them to be dreamed—so that their story may be told—and forgotten—or acted upon—whatever, for experience generally and traumatic experience specifically are not safe until they are dreamed.

The dream ultimately is a narrative and narrating window into our inner cosmic vastness, and our capacity for self-transcendence is ultimately due to the dosage of sorrow our minds can tolerate in the gradual appreciation of the significance of the unfolding contents from this vastness.

> . . . Our revels now are ended. These our actors,
> As I foretold you, were all spirits, and
> Are melted into air, into thin air;
> And, like the baseless fabric of this vision,
> The cloud-capp'd towers, the gorgeous palaces,
> The solemn temples, the great globe itself,
> Yea, all which it inherit shall dissolve
> And, like this insubstantial pageant faded,
> Leave not a rack behind. We are such stuff
> As dreams are made on, and our little life is
> Rounded with a sleep . . .

References

Bahia, A.B. (1977). The theories: their influence and effect on psychoanalytic technique. *Int. J. Psycho-Anal.* 58, 345-364.

Bailey, K.G. (1978). The concept of phylogenetic regression. *J. Am. Acad. Psychoanal.* 6(1), 5-37.

Beaconsfield, P; Birdwood, G. & Beaconsfield, R. (1980). The placenta. *Sci. Am.* 243(2), 94-102.
Bion, W.R. (1950). The imaginary twin. IN HIS: *Second Thoughts*. London: William Heinemann, 1967, pp. 3-22.
—— (1957). On arrogance. *Op. Cit.*, pp. 86-92.
—— (1962). *Learning From Experience*. London: William Heinemann.
—— (1963). *Elements of Psychoanalysis*. London: William Heinemann.
—— (1965). *Transformations*. London: William Heinemann.
—— (1966). Catastrophic change. *Sci. Bull. Brit. Psychoanal. Society*. Volume 5.
—— (1970). *Attention and Interpretation*. London: Tavistock.
—— (1975). *A Memoir of the Future, Book One: The Dream*. J. Saloma (ed.) Rio de Janeiro: Imago Editoria, Ltd.
Duerenmatt, F. (1964). *The Pledge*. Richard and Clara Winston (trans.). Middlesex: Penguin Books.
Entralgo, P.L. (1970). *The Therapy of the Word in Classical Antiquity*. L.J. Rather and John M. Sharp (eds. and trans.). New Haven: Yale Univ. Press.
Erikson, E.H. (1959). Identity and the Life Cycle. *Psychol. Issues* Vol. 1, No. 1, Mon. 1. New York: IUP.
Fairbairn, W.R.D. (1954). *An Object Relations Theory of the Personality*. New York: Basic Books.
Fowles, J. (1966). *The Magus*. Boston: Little Brown and Co., 1965.
Freud, S. (1900). *The Interpretation of Dreams. S.E.* 4 & 5. London: Hogarth Press, 1958.
—— (1909 [1908]). Family romances. *S.E.* 9, 235-244. London: Hogarth Press, 1959.
—— (1911). Psychoanalytic notes on an autobiographical account ot a case of paranoia (dementia paranoides). *S.E.* 12. 3-84. London: Hogarth Press, 1958.
Gazzaniga. M.S. & Ledoux, J.E. (1978). *The Integrated Mind*. New York: Plenum Press.
Glover, E. (1955). The therapeutic effect of inexact interpretations: A contribution to the theory of suggestion. IN: *The Technique of Psycho-Analysis*. New York: IUP, pp. 353-367.
Grotstein, J.S. (1977a). The psychoanalytic concept of schizophrenia. I. The dilemma. *Int. J. Psycho-Anal.* 58, 403-425.
—— (1977b). The psychoanalytic concept of schizophrenia. II. reconciliation. *Int. J. Psycho-Anal.* 58, 427-452.
—— (1978). Inner space: its dimensions and its coordinates. *Int. J. Psycho-Anal.* 59, 55-61.
—— (1980a). *Splitting and Projective Identification*. New York: Jason Aronson. In press.
—— (1980b). A proposed revision of the psychoanalytic concept of primitive mental states. Part I: Introduction to a newer psychoanalytic metapsychology to comprehend psychoses, borderline states, and narcissistic disorders; Part II: The borderline syndrome: disorders of autistic relatedness in which there is a failure in the quest for safety; Part III: Self (narcissistic) disorders disorders of symbiotic relatedness in which there is a failure in the quest for self-affirmation. *Contemp. Psa.* In press.
Hesse, H. (1925). *Demian: The Story of Emil Sinclair's Youth.* Michael Roloff and Michael Lebeck (trans.). New York: Harper and Row, 1965.
Isakower, O. (1938). A contribution to the psychopathology associated with falling asleep. *Int. J. Psycho-Anal.* 19, 331-345.
Jung, C.G. (1944). The symbolism of the madals. IN HIS: *Collected Works of C.G. Jung*. Bollinger Series II. New York: Pantheon Books.
Langer, S.K. (1942). *Philosophy in a new Key*. New York: Master Books
Levi-Strauss, C. (1962). *The Savage Mind*. George Weidenfeld and Nicholson, Ltd. (trans.) Chicago: Univ. Chicago Press.
—— (1963). *Structural Anthropology*. Claire Jacobson and Brooke Grundfest Schospf (trans.). New York: Basic Books.
—— (1969). *The Elementary Structure of Kinship*. Boston: Beacon Press.
Lewin, B.D. (1950). *The Psychoanalysis of Elation*. New York: Norton.
Matte Blanco, I. (1978). *The Unconscious as Infinite Sets*. London: Duckworth Press.
Peirce, C. (1960). *The Collected Papers of Charles Peirce*. Cambridge, Mass: Harvard Univ. Press.
Pirandello, L.D. (1969). *Six Characters in Search of an Author*. London: William Heinemann, 1954.
Polti, G. (1916). *The Thirty-Six: Dramatic Situations*. Lucille Ray (trans.). Boston: The Writers, Inc.
Pribram, K. (1971). *Languages of the Brain*. Englewood Cliffs, New Jersey: Prentice-Hall, Inc.
Sandler, J. (1960). The background of safety. *Int. J. Psycho-Anal.* 41, 352-356.
Scott, S.C.M. (1975). Remembering Sleep. *Int. Rev. Psycho-Anal.* 2(3), 253-254.
Spitz, R. (1965). *The First Year of Life*. New York: IUP.
Steele, R.S. (1979). Psychoanalysis and hermeneutics. *Int. Rev. Psycho-Anal.* 6, 389-412.
Steward, K. (1972). Dream theory in Malaya. IN: *Altered States of Consciousness*. Charles Tart (ed.) New York: Doubleday and Co., pp. 161-167.
Tadmor, C. (1977). Personal communication.
Winnicott, D.W. (1963). Communicating and non-communicating leading to a study of certain opposites. IN: *The Maturational Process and the Facilitating Environment*. New York: IUP. 1965, pp. 179-192.

The Aims of Psycho-Analytic Treatment

Elliott Jaques

EDITOR'S NOTE: *Professor Jaques' essay aims at a reassessment of the values held by analysts in doing psychoanalytic treatment and, in particular, of the values their interpretations place upon the patients' associations and behavior. He utilizes Klein's distinction between the life and the death instincts and Bion's distinction between the psychotic and non-psychotic personalities to arrive at an overall reappraisal of the psychoanalytic moral value system. Normalcy, in contrast to abnormalcy, Jaques believes, is associated with the capacity of the life instinct to insure our survival adaptively and creatively, whereas abnormalcy can be thought of as the contradiction to our survival, to our adaptation, and to our environment. This contribution is a most interesting re-statement of what distinctions the analyst must make in his daily work.*

The Aims of Psycho-Analytic Treatment

Elliott Jaques

I

Wilfred Bion has been among those writers who have been most clear and explicit about the differences between normality and abnormality, a difference he has expressed so sharply in his distinction between each person's psychotic and non-psychotic personalities (1957). It is this distinction which is essential for the formulation of the aims of psycho-analytical treatment and of the criteria for the termination of treatment. This theme may, I hope, be a suitable contribution for this occasion of recognising Wilfred Bion's long and distinguished contribution to psycho-analytic theory and practice.

II

It has always been easier to say what is abnormal in human behaviour than to say what is normal; easier to specify or diagnose symptoms of illness than to specify the signs of health. The difficulty is that as soon as we turn to normality it is hard to avoid producing a long list of moral and ethical values—such as being capable of work and of love. And when we do produce these values, it begins to seem as though to be normal is to be filled with goodness and virtue. It then becomes impossible to know whether our conception of normality is merely a relative protestant, or capitalist, or socialist, or bourgeois, or some other kind of religious or political ethic, or whether we are considering something more fundamental in human nature.

This problem is rather more than material for a philosophical debate. It concerns some very practical questions indeed. What are our diagnostic criteria? What are our objectives in psychological treatment? Are we trying to help individuals to become more amenable to the ethical mores of their time? Or even, perhaps, to become more conformant to the dominant political ideology of the society in which they find themselves. Can deviant behaviour be normal? Most societies tend to behave as though it were not.

But how can we be sure? If deviance is treated as abnormal, then social change is inhibited and made more difficult. And yet, if all deviance is accepted as normal we are equally in trouble, for something is wrong somewhere with that idea too. How do we judge and decide which kinds of deviance might be normal and which abnormal? How do we avoid imposing upon everyone the value system of the dominant group, whether that group be an elite or the majority—or, indeed, our own personal values?

This same problem besets legal theory and jurisprudence. There it is encountered in the form of what constitutes lawful behaviour. These questions lie at the heart of what we mean by psychological treatment. Every time a psycho-analyst decides to make an interpretation it is because he judges that he has seen or heard or otherwise observed some evidence of abnormal behaviour. More than that, he believes he understands some of the unconscious psychic mechanisms—the motives and conflicts—which are causing the individual to behave in that abnormal way. He thus draws the attention of the patient to the abnormal behaviour, and sets out the evidence, in the form of connections between associations, symbolic contents, and manifestations of splitting, repression, projections, concretism, and defences of various kinds.

But what is the psycho-analyst's evidence for abnormality? Here he is probably on firmer ground than anyone else in making his judgments. He is on firmer ground because of the way he has structured the analytic situation. He has set himself up as a neutral screen, as a target for the patient's projections and introjections, and false perceptions, in which the unconscious transference effects can be isolated. He can show the patient *in vivo*, in the analytic situation, how he brings his personalities—psychotic and nonpsychotic—into the living relationship with the analyst. He can show him how these personalities are a reliving or acting out of more primitive unresolved conflicts, whether pubertal, or oedipal, or early childhood relationships with the parents; or of early infantile relationships with part objects such as the breast and penis based upon concretistic types of projective identification and introjection in which the analyst as an unconsciously perceived very primitive object becomes filled with bits of the patient's mental life and a source of introjected bits with which the patient in turn gets filled.

But the question still remains as to why such projections and introjections and distortions of reality are abnormal. Should not the goal of psychological treatment be the reinforcement of acting out and distortion, and the elimination and overcoming, once and for all, of reality-based perception? We could then bring about the final victory of the pleasure principle over the reality principle, and establish the permissive Dionysian society as against the more severe Apollonian one—to let Orpheus and Narcissus reign, and to banish the Promethean view of life forever.

There have always been loud voices lifted in favour of this Dionysian and Narcissistic view of life, and it is not sufficient for analysts to say that we do not agree with it on some vague and unformulated psychological or moral ground. All who are involved in therapeutic work with human beings—psychiatrists, psycho-analysts, psycho-therapists, social case-workers—have this problem of determining where they stand. Otherwise we are in danger of remaining in a circular argument: normal behaviour is the behaviour which results from psychological treatment; abnormal behaviour is that which calls for such treatment. But it is our initial unstated assumptions which colour our whole framework of thinking—and one of the major critiques of psychoanalysis at the present time is that we are engaged in turning out individuals who simply conform to society as it is.

To take a current example: if a patient displays intensely anti-coloured, or anti-semitic, or anti-capitalist, or anti-nazi feelings: is that neurotic or realistic? If a patient is intensely religious, believes in God, goes to church, goes to confession, and prays: is that neurotic or realistic? Or conversely, if a patient does not believe in God and does not do all these things, is that a failure in reality sense?

III

This question of criteria of abnormality is part of the more general question in psycho-analysis of the criteria for termination of analysis. The criteria divide themselves into two categories. There are, first, the surface criteria—such as the ability to work or to endure frustration. Then there are the psychic or depth criteria—such as mending of ego splits.

The striking thing is that the literature on the criteria for terminating analysis is full of descriptions of surface criteria but contains little enough reference to the deeper psychic processes. These surface descriptions serve to give a picture of what psycho-analysts consider to be a normal personality. As Menninger and Pruyser (1963) put it, the criteria for termination contain the implicit philosophy and ethic of psycho-analysis. There is a wide range of views under this heading such as the view that love is the greatest thing on earth: it is kind, does not envy, is not vain, seeks the welfare of others, rejoices in truth and not in iniquity; the philosophical view which takes the goal of psycho-analysis to be free patients from whatever is trivial, chance, accidental, or misleading from earlier conditioning, and to replace it by the more significant and the more universal.

These philosophical views, while interesting enough in themselves, nevertheless state personal outlooks which might or might not be acceptable to others. Freud (1923) himself stated a number of criteria, which are of the surface but with some reference to underlying psychic processes. Along with his dictum that analysis should make the unconscious conscious, so that where id was there shall ego be, he added that the main criterion for a successful outcome in analysis would show in the patient's ability to love and to work—a view that is reflected in all his writings.

Then there are a number of criteria of what might be said to be the normal personality, which include such states as: gratitude without submissiveness, independence without rebelliousness, hatred without projection and persecution, love without idealisation, independence of thought, capacity for sublimation, capacity to endure frustration, elimination of over-emotionality and emotional shallowness.

Such criteria are to be found in many writers in such common phrases as: greater freedom; capacity for joy; cessation of compulsion; diminution of tendency to depression; ability to be a parent; improved social relationships; using persons as ends and not as means; balance of work and play, and success in both; sportsmanship; pleasure in others; satisfaction without guilt; and so on. These characteristics are reinforced by the familiar criteria of sexual maturity including, for example, non-narcissistic genital or mature sexuality, heterosexual potency and capacity for orgasm, genital primacy and the achievement of a genital character.

These criteria—which are the most common types of indicator described in the psycho-analytical literature—are impressive for the extent to which they resemble views on morality rather than systematic or technical scientific criteria. They are perhaps best summed up by the writer who says that somehow with his clinical acumen and his sense of what is important, the analyst finally arrives at a decision that the criteria for termination have been sufficiently fulfilled to justify the next move.

This intuitive judgment is a real and substantial judgment, as every analyst knows. But clearly it is difficult to pin down in words. The attempts to do so take us closer to a deeper conception of normality. These below-the-surface criteria take the form of such statements as: removal of resistances so that there is a greater degree of awareness of the unconscious (Hoffer, 1950), and thus in Freud's (1923) terms the unconscious becomes conscious and id becomes ego; removal of the oedipus complex; re-experiencing of traumata of the early weeks of life; overcoming of splits in the ego.

Reviewing these criteria for termination of psycho-analysis leaves one with the impression that what we have is a familiar picture of normal man as seen in our own society, with the additional point that somehow if unconscious processes can become more accessible to consciousness, then the behaviour seen as normal or ethical will occur. That connection cannot be taken for granted. It calls for examination.

IV

To carry the analysis further I should like to turn to one set of criteria in depth for the termination of analysis—the criteria set out by Melanie Klein and elaborated by Wilfred Bion. Mrs. Klein stated them as working through the anxieties of the first year of life; that is to say, the resolution of infantile persecutory and depressive anxiety. If we look further into these views they lead to certain interesting conclusions with respect to our theme.

By infantile persecutory and depressive anxiety, Mrs. Klein was referring to what she called psychotic anxieties. But if we consider the rest of her work it becomes clear that she considered no other kind of anxiety but anxiety arising from psychotic processes. That is to say, like Freud, she distinguished between fear based upon the reality-based perception of true danger, and anxiety based upon unrealistic projections of the person's own phantasies into the external world or into vaguely defined situations in his own internal world. In short, all anxiety is psychotically based upon processes of projective identification and reintrojection. It is all delusional.

We begin then to get a definition of normality as that type of personality functioning which contrasts with psychotic functioning, a distinction made explicit by Bion. The normal person is one who is largely free from psychotic parts, or at least has the psychotic parts well under control. The neurotic person is one in whom the psychotic parts are not wholly under control. They tend to suffuse personality functioning, producing distortions and disturbance and sometimes breaking out in full force in anxiety attacks and emotionally debilitating defences and regressions. The psychotic person is one in whom the psychotic parts are dominant, and eventuate not in anxiety and regression but in the use of projective identification to rid himself as far as possible of all awareness of reality, and eventually of life itself. It is this threat to life that I think holds the key to the question of normality.

It was Mrs. Klein's frequently stated view, a view shared by many analysts, that for the infant to remain alive is a minor triumph in each case. The early infant ego, ill-formed and weak, is repeatedly overwhelmed by discharges of love, under the impact of innate loving impulses and of gratification resulting from external love and care; and discharges of rage and hate, under the impact of innate hating impulses aggravated by external frustrations and separations. This duality, or instinctual bi-polarity, is conceptualised in the model of the life and death instincts formulated by Freud. Violent conflict arises continually, as the infant becomes stimulated from both literally and in the sense of degree of freedom from anxiety even if the major struggle is decided in favour of life rather than of death.

Survival for the human being—as indeed for all forms of life—is not easy. Living existence is far from guaranteed. Indeed, it is the continued survival of life on earth that is the wonder. Certain it is that only those organisms with strong provisions for living will survive.

In its process of survival, the young infant has recourse to a major defensive process. It splits its love and its hate—dealing with only one at a time. And equally it splits its objects into all good and all bad objects. Bion has vividly described how the infant uses the breast and mother as a container into which hate and destructive objects are projected, and under dominantly loving circumstances container and contained can be reintrojected to reinforce loving impulses, good objects, and life itself in the infant.

If hate reinforced by bad external circumstances outweighs the loving and life impulses, the infant will die. If they are more evenly balanced, the outcome is an attempt to retain absolute splitting and projective identification, and the result is psychotic personality development. If love and good experiences predominate, it becomes possible for the developing infant to begin to give up absolute splitting and projective identification, and with maturation to begin during the second half of the first year to achieve some integration of itself and its objects and to come to terms with ambivalence.

The capacity to experience ambivalence, if the infant succeeds in developing it, is the big step toward contact with reality, and potentiality for life. The same object can now be recognised as both good and bad, sometimes gratifying and sometimes frustrating, never perfect or ideal, but equally not a continuous and hostile persecutor. The emotional experience is that of hate mitigated by love, a state achievable only if the infant's loving impulses in fact are stronger than its primal hate, envy and destructiveness.

With the experience of ambivalence comes the experience of guilt arising from intermittently hating the very objects you love. If love is able to mitigate hate, this guilt becomes tolerable and life and development carry on. If love and the feel for life are less able to cope with the hating impulses, then regressions occur—to the division of the world into two separate worlds of good and bad, or love and persecution, by means of the splitting and projective identification of the primitive infantile situation—the paranoid-schizoid position. Not only is development impaired, but contact with reality is undermined. Moreover, to the extent that withdrawal from reality occurs, so psychotic anxieties—or persecution and of overwhelming guilt—enter the scene. Sanity comes into question, and in the final analysis, life itself is more and more at stake.

I have described these processes in order to illustrate a particular point of significance in our attempt to explore just what is meant by normality. The phenomena which we in psycho-analysis—in common with the philosophers, moralists, lawyers and social scientists—call normal are precisely those characteristics of human behaviour which happen to accompany the dominance of the unconscious will to live. To put it another way, they are the characteristics of behaviour when the life instinct dominates over the death instinct, or when hate and destructiveness are mitigated by love, or—more simply—they are what a person is like when he has decided to live rather than to die.

It is these phenomena which are directly observable in psycho-analysis in the meanings to be interpreted from the patient's associations, dreams, behaviours in terms of the realities of his or her working relationship with the analyst. One of the outstanding qualities of Bion's clinical descriptions has been the concentration upon the immediacy of the patient's behaviour—upon how that behaviour expresses the meaning of the analyst and the analytic work to the patient throughout each session.

From this point of view the criteria for interpretation and for termination lose their normative content. What the patient's behaviour outside the analysis might be like becomes clinically irrelevant—for the analyst can in any case never really know. What the analyst is left with is whatever evidence he can piece together of the extent to which, on the one hand, he is engaged in a relationship in which he is being used as a container of projected bits of thoughts and mind which the patient is unable to digest and is striving to eliminate (and at depth a container of bizarre objects), and to what extent, on the other hand, he is engaged in a relationship in which his insights and observations are being sought by those parts of the patient striving to undo the splitting of unresolved paranoid-schizoid processes which threaten life.

The questions of the objectives of psycho-analysis, of the criteria for termination of analysis, and of the related criteria for the making of interpretations, are thus questions to be asked and answered exclusively in relation to the patient and his or her activities in the consulting room. They are strictly clinical questions, in the limited and narrow meaning of clinical as having to do with the patient's living attitudes and behaviour in the situation of two people located in a room for specified periods of time within the particular conditions of free association. The objective treatment in these terms is to aid the patient to reduce the functioning of the psychotic personalities by the analysis and mitigation of psychotic anxieties particularly in the paranoid-schizoid position—as these appear in the actuality of each unique session.

To adopt this limited clinical view is not, of course, to argue that psycho-analysis has nothing to do with the patient's behaviour in everyday life. There is most certainly an assumption about the meaning of normality which can be stated in more general terms as the reduction of psychotic parts of the personality. This definition is a condition for survival value not just for the individual but for the human race. This conclusion is indeed suggested within the structure of our language: for if we consider the word "good" we find that etymologically it comes from the root "gad" which simply means whole. The integrated, the whole, the product of the successful working-through of the depressive position is what is good. It is the opposite, the product of splitting and fragmentation, which gives us the "bits" which are the etymological root of the word "bad."

Normality, then, is that behaviour which accompanies life and racial survival; abnormality is that which accompanies death and racial destruction. The normal is not necessarily the conformant statistical Mr. Average Man; the abnormal is not necessarily the deviant. The possibilities for particular behaviour patterns are infinitely variable, depending both upon prevailing social conditions and upon the originality and creativeness of the individual.

Against this background, a number of other conclusions follow. Psycho-analysis can be related to the goals of morality and of law in the sense of finding those precepts and those legal limits which can reinforce the chances of survival of the reasonable man—the survival-oriented man—and the human race. Just what those precepts and laws might be may vary depending upon the circumstance obtaining. Thus, for example, the laws and moral attitudes toward families, reproduction, abortion, euthenasia, homosexuality, are likely to vary considerably in different societies or in the same society at different times, depending upon the density of population, the degree of affluence of the economy, and a host of other possible factors.

Our objectives in psycho-analysis may thus be emptied of all social and moral values—except one. That one value is that the individual should be aided to understand his unconscious motivations and conflicts, particularly those which give rise to psychotic anxieties—persecutory and depressive—as these appear in the actuality of the on-going working relationship between patient and analyst. For the evidence is that with the resolution of those anxieties and the defence mechanisms they induce, and the psychic processes which give rise to them, the individual's capacity to survive is markedly increased. At the same time, it may be observed that his love of others is also increased.

Psycho-analysis thus leads to an ethic which may slightly modify the categorical imperative of Immanuel Kant. The sign of normality is that the individual wills not only his own survival but the survival equally of all mankind. A society whose political, legal and social institutions were based upon such a precept would in turn reinforce the psychological health of its members.

References

Bion, W.R. (1957). Differentiation of the psychotic from the non-psychotic personalities. *Int. J. Psycho-Anal*. 38, 266-275.

—— (1962). *Learning from Experience*. London: William Heinemann.

—— (1963). *Elements of Psycho-Analysis*. London: William Heinemann.

—— (1965). *Transformations*. London: William Heinemann.

—— (1970). *Attention and Interpretation*. London: Tavistock.

Freud, S. (1920). *Beyond the Pleasure Principle. S.E.* 19. London: Hogarth Press, 1957.

—— (1923). *The Ego and the Id. S.E.* 19. London: Hogarth, 1961.

Hoffer, W. (1950). Three psychological criteria for the termination of analysis. *Int. J. Psycho-Anal.* 31, 194-195.

Klein, M. (1950). On the criteria for the termination of analysis. *Int. J. Psycho-Anal*. 31, 78-80.

Langer, S. (1967). *Mind: An Essay on Human Feelings*, Vol. I. Baltimore and London: John Hopkins Press.

Menninger, K. & Pruyser, P. (1963). *The Vital Balance*. New York: Viking.

Philosophical Issues in Bion's Thought

Melvin Lansky

EDITOR'S NOTE: *Doctor Lansky comes to psychoanalysis from a background in philosophy. I am grateful to him for his acceptance of my invitation to "find out what Bion is all about philosophically and put it down on paper." Bion was one of the greatest philosophers, albeit "amateur," writing in psychoanalytic literature in our time. His sweep was from Plato through Kant to Ezra Pound–and beyond. I implored Doctor Lansky to be my detective to scout out Bion's philosophical sources. This contribution is the rich harvest of that request. All of us in psychoanalysis have had the opportunity from time to time to regret that Freud did not make better use of the frameworks of philosophy that were open to him at the time, e.g., Plato's theory of forms, Kant's noumenon-phenomenon dichotomy, Berkeley's and Hume's rationalism, Locke's empiricism, etc. We know already that Freud fell into a Cartesian trap of dividing id, ego, and superego and could actually maintain that there were portions of the self that were not "I" (ego)! Psychoanalysis is badly in need of a good philosophic scrubbing, and Bion seems to have the soap and the brush to do it.*

Philosophical Issues in Bion's Thought*

Melvin R. Lansky, M.D.

I

Any inquiry into the philosophical significance of Bion's work requires some explanation because Bion does not consider himself a philosopher, nor his works as a philosophical system. He is not trained philosophically in any formal sense and sees his major philosophical debt to Kant and to Paton, with whom he had conversations about Kant in his years at Oxford. Any thinker, a theoretical one especially, may be looked at philosophically; and Bion, who deals with abstractions, essences, discussions of knowledge, reality, and the passions, is more philosophical in style of thought than almost anyone writing, in English at least, of the psychoanalytic theorists. Nonetheless, there are more specific reasons for considering Bion's work philosophically. These include his work on the fundamental ideas of psychoanalysis; his similarity to analysts who were also philosophers in seeing the basic issues of analysis in terms of the analytic process itself; and his refinements and theoretical extensions of Melanie Klein's contributions to analysis that serve to clarify major philosophical currents in the so-called Freudian-Kleinian dispute. These will all be seen to converge and the last named, that is, Bion's work in the light of the Freud-Klein controversy will be the major focus of this discussion.

II

Although Bion may be considered a Kleinian—he was analyzed by Melanie Klein and works with Kleinian concepts—his work is quite distinct from that of current exemplars of Kleinian clinical research and theory, for example, Hanna Segal (1973) and Herbert Rosenfeld (1965). Bion is more metatheoretical in the same basic school of thought. He does more than extend the clinical conceptual apparatus developed by Melanie Klein to convey the results of her observations and extend her discoveries beyond the work of Freud and Abraham. Bion concerns himself with the philosophical essences involved—the processes such that projective identification becomes more than a phantasy of relocation and control and a notion of relevance to the theory of treatment. Bion's work deals with how we are to understand the issues theoretically in the context of the evidence from the treatment setting, whether this be the nature of thought, projective identification, the con-

*Several conversations with Dr. Bion have enabled me to develop the thoughts in this paper. Needless to say, the responsibility for any inaccuracies in them remains mine.

tainer-contained relationship, or the mutual relationship of the paranoid-schizoid and depressive positions.

Bion's is always a Kantian (1788) look at Kleinian concepts. Notions subsumed intuitively to phantasy become enlarged, systematized and categorized but always the fundamental unknowability of the thing in itself (beta element) is kept in mind.

Bion's task is to get at the foundations, the most universal notation and language for the essence of psychoanalytic data. Here his work is philosophical as much as psychoanalytical in the same sense that Whitehead and Russell's *Principia Mathematica* (1925-1927) is philosophical as much as mathematical. In exactly comparable ways, Bion is metapsychoanalytical as Whitehead and Russell are metamathematical in looking for the foundations of mathematics rather than an actual system of mathematics. Bion's choice of the problem of the foundations of analysis is reminiscent of Frege's "Foundations of Arithmetic." (1968) Indeed, he is only one of the few writers in English to cite Frege and show some sensitivity to the importance of Frege's thought for any work on the foundations of theoretical systems that transcends the statements made within the system.

Behind the task of looking at the foundations is the immense philosophical task of asking, "What is it that is known; what about the known; what is the knowable; and in what sense?" Here Bion's sensitivity to the epistomological issues draws heavily from Kant. Things in the material world and in the mental apparatus are fundamentally unknowable in themselves. It is only through primary and secondary properties that we apprehend them. This makes for constant uncertainty about the essence of the material world apart from our sensory world. Bion's Kantian touch to the internal world, as understood from the data of psychoanalysis, adds to and deepens fundamental Freudian and Kleinian discoveries and divests them of unnecessary philosophical difficulties so that they can be understood in a systematic way. So Bion addresses the problem of thought in an attempt to get to the foundations of what sort of thought is capable of usage in the process of thinking, that is, memory, storage, and transformation to dream thoughts, concepts and ideas. Here, philosophical clarity is crucial. That which is capable of memory, storage, and transformation is not in itself knowable, apart from the primary and secondary qualities in which it appears as transformations. That which undergoes thinking has been rendered usable by what Bion (1962) chooses to refer to as alpha function. That which is in itself knowable, the thing in itself (beta elements), may be shared as sensory or emotional experience only if it is incapable of metabolism by the process of thought and must be evacuated by projective identification or hallucinosis. Having grasped the epistomological significance of the fundamental unknowability of anything capable of alpha function and transformation and the untransformability of anything known in itself (beta elements), Bion can then approach the foundations of thinking in the analytic setting (the elements of psychoanalysis and the grid) (1963).

The grid can be used to conceptualize the data of psychoanalysis only because its philosophical tasks have been accomplished. It is clear what is knowable, thinkable and transformable and what is not. With this in view, the elements of psychoanalytic data can be conceptualized in a way perspicacious enough to lead to other formulations based in the analytic setting that have to do with the process of thinking. All of this has to do with the expansion of Kleinian notion of projective identification from a simple phantasy to the process of analysis and to the process of transformation. By the process of transformation one has not only a theory of thinking but also an elaborate theory of defense against awareness (much more elegant than the impulse-defense model developed by ego-psychological "Freudians"). It is based on "The Two Principles of Mental Functioning" (1911) to which Bion so often refers—what is psychotic (and what must be evacuated in the service of evasion of reality) as compared to what can be thought or adduced to modify reality (the normal or non-psychotic transformable part of the personality) constitute the same distinction as that between the pleasure and reality principles. Bion expands Freud's paper into a fundamental theory of thought.

These foundations are predicated on well thought out notions of what is thinkable, knowable and transformable within the analytic setting itself. No other route to the direct foundations gets directly to the atoms and molecules of what goes on. This is, for example, missed entirely in the so-called "Freudian" metapsychological writings of Rapaport (1967), Hartmann (1939) and others that do not start from the analytic setting itself, do not portray an epistomological sensitivity to strictly analytic data, and are peppered with philosophical assumptions that are not recognized as such and, accordingly, are not dealt with. I will deal with the philosophical assumptions in Part IV below. In terms of theory formation, Bion's work, no matter how abstract and mathematical it may seem, always deals with the concrete.

The elements of psychoanalysis are formulations about the actual data from analyst and analysand. Alpha function is that which is to be studied as the concrete function of containment in the dyad. Beta elements are those that are experienced as evacuated parts from the patient, and so forth. The work of Hartmann and Rapaport are also theoretical but they do not theorize using concepts referable to the data. Their work is currently beseiged with what seems, from a theoretical view, to be insurmountable difficulties (See Leites [1971], Basch [1976], Gill [1976], Schafer [1976], Holt [1975] and numerous others), difficulties which may be likened to theoretical difficulties in attempting a science of chemistry without first having a periodic table. There is no straightening out theoretical problems because there is no central notion of what the data are. Bion's grasp of the importance of the elements and his elaboration (however tentative) supply an attempt at a periodic table for strictly analytic data. Without some such attempt at getting to the data and thinking about them, no really satisfactory theory can emerge—indeed, it is a notorious difficulty with psychoanalytic training that "theory" and "technique" often have nothing to do with each other.

Bion's philosophical sensitivities have enabled extremely minimal and elegant fundamental formulations that go from strictly analytical data to a conceptualization of psychopathology, technique, defensive operations, and the possibility of cure. This is understandable in terms of his examination of the role of thinking in the psychotic part of the personality; the role of the two principles of mental functioning; and the full appreciation of the significance of projective identification. Briefly put, psychotic elements of the personality cannot be metabolized by the same process of thinking that is used to modify reality in the non-psychotic part of the personality. Rather they must be evacuated by projective identification; the mental apparatus may only be relieved of accretions of mental stimuli by evacuation. That which is evacuated is direct sensory or emotional data that constitute the thing in itself (beta elements) incapable of transformation by the process of thinking. Beta elements may be experienced by the analyst but they are not communicated directly. This is best conceptualized not simply as a phantasy of split off parts of the self put into the analyst but as indicative of the failure of alpha function (Bion, 1962, 1963). The attempt to repair such failure involves the elaboration of the concept of projective identification to emphasize the role of the object who receives the evacuated parts—the container. Bion's reformulation of projective identification, to go beyond the unilateral phantasy (as Klein's literal statements, albeit not her intent, would have it), allows for detailed examination of the place of the container and the process of projective identification within the analytic setting.

By his theoretical expansion of projective identification within the clinical setting to include the entire contained-container relationship, Bion is able to grasp the fundamentals of therapeutic work and account for learning from experience and the influence of environment in ways that are not entirely clear in Klein's original formulations in terms of phantasy. The essence of the difficulty is that "phantasy" is a unilateral notion and "projective identification" is basically dyadic. By grasping the philosophical significance of stating projective identification phenomena in terms of container-contained, Bion is able to locate the task of analysis of the psychotic part of the personality with the internalization of the alpha (container) function provided by the analyst in receiving beta elements evacuated by projective identification. Working with a minimum of presuppositions, Bion is able to focus clearly on the therapeutic effect of the process of interpretation. This is the process of internalization of the analyst-patient relationship as a container-contained relationship that allows for transformation and the dominance of the reality principle, as opposed to evacuation by projective identification (or the dominance of the pleasure principle). This renders entirely intelligible the possibilities of previous failure of "reverie" (or alpha function) by the mother and any other environmental influences contributing to the failure of alpha function. It is not so much a departure from as a philosophically sound version of the insights developed by Melanie Klein.

III

Psychoanalysis has tended, for the most part, to adopt Freud's antipathy to the philosophical enterprise. Freud had a tendency to equate philosophy with some philosophers of his time who equated the knowable with the contents of consciousness and, hence, were antagonistic to the very idea of the unconscious. There has also been a generalization of the psychoanalytic suspiciousness of the use of rationalization in the analytical process. The technical stance with such patients has, unfortunately, generalized to reasoning outside of the analytic situation. This has been much to the detriment of the development of the philosophical foundations of analysis and the use of philosophical analysis in the spectrum of analytical thinking. There has been surprisingly little influence on analysis by philosophers and very few philosophically trained analysts. Some of Bion's views have similarities to those of some philosophically trained analysts. I will mention, in particular, Otto Rank (1923) and the lesser known Helmuth Kaiser (See Fierman, 1965). Some of the themes are striking enough in common to warrant consideration and comparison with Bion's contributions.

Otto Rank's conceptualizations of analysis led eventually to his breaking off ties to strictly psychoanalytic considerations and developing the theory and practice of what he called "psychotherapy." Rank's notion of therapy recognizes the centrality of separateness exemplified metaphorically and actually, according to Rank, in the trauma of birth. Rank's views have been soundly criticized, by Freud among others, not so much for the appreciation of separateness and aloneness but for the devaluation of everything else. Contrariwise, Rank's contribution may be viewed not so much in terms of the things that it de-emphasizes but in view of its central preoccupation with process of analysis and how it reflects the fundamental psychopathological feature of the patient's attempts to deny the experience of separateness and aloneness within the context of the therapy. This is not to say that other issues are not important, only that they are not central and primary in terms of the therapeutic process. Rank's technical posture is based on time limited therapy entirely based on the interpretation of separateness of the therapist in the here and now.

Helmuth Kaiser, another philosopher, much influenced by Wilhelm Reich's (1949) early notions of analyzing character armor before id content, began to think systematically about the theory of technique based on character analysis. Kaiser raised the question of whether character analysis, with the emphasis on transference and resistance in the here and now, was not the essence of effective psychotherapy without the use of genetic reconstructions or interpretations of the id content. Kaiser's process-oriented therapy is organized around interpretation of transference and resistance with attention to the attempts to evade responsibility for one's thoughts and actions by phantasied fusion with the therapist. At first blush, this does not seem to be very similar to Bion's work but if it be understood first that Kaiser's notion of the evasion of responsibility has a good deal of kinship with the notion of the inability to tolerate the depressive position and, second, that he emphasizes phantasied fusion with the therapist in the attempt to avoid separateness, then his views become quite similar to a number of points emphasized by Kleinians: the interplay between the paranoid-schizoid and the depressive position; the use of fusion by projective identification; and the neglect of (or relegation to secondary importance of) genetic reconstructions.

What these two philosophically trained thinkers have in common is the emphasis on the essence of the curative process within the therapeutic situation in the dyad itself. The essence of the talking treatment between two people is that such treatment effects change. The thrust with Rank and with Kaiser is the penetration of the philosophical essence of the circumstance of successful therapy. Bion, remaining in a strictly psychoanalytic framework, has much the same philosophical concerns. His work goes for the essence of the problem of how interpretation can be of help. The analytic situation as a learning situation is seen as a situation where one is enabled to learn from experience by the analytic process itself. With Bion there is a clearer view of the process than portrayed, at least in the written works, of Freud and Klein. Bion's work on thinking clears up ambiguities in the Kleinian and, indeed, Freudian notions of phantasy that suggest reconstructions of genetic material as essentially curative elements. Bion keeps the theoretical emphasis on the innateness and the agency of the patient's productions without entering into the irrelevancies of either the task or specific content of collaborating with the patient over reconstructions. The idea of an innate (unsaturated) preconception mating with a realization to form a concept which may be named does not depend for its theoretical solidarity on the same things as do, say, the idea of a specific phantasy about the breast or of parental intercourse or the contents of mother's body or the timing of the paranoid-schizoid or depressive positions. The latter presumes specific content at a time when there is considerable doubt about the ability of the psychic apparatus to form and be guided by specific propositions. Bion avoids this pitfall by sticking to the notion of preconception not formed by experience but awaiting an experience before it eventually becomes usable as a concept.

Accordingly, Bion is not saddled with a debatable theory of concept formation nor one of reconstruction of the specific conceptual contents of the infant's mind, as Klein seems to be. Nor is the process of analysis to be confused with a reconstructive task. This is, in essence, the same philosophical move toward the examination of the analytic process itself in the here and now, that Rank and Kaiser undertook. None of them is unclear about the influence of the past, defensive structure, development or impulses—

memory and desire as Bion would say. But with each the central and primary focus is the here and now of the therapeutic dyad. This is the same philosophical movement accomplished by Bion's analysis of projective identification in terms of the dyadic container-contained relationship and the therapeutic function as the internalization of the alpha function performed in the analytic session. Like his philosophically-minded predecessors Bion is concerned with essences, not reductionistic oversimplifications or simple schemata. There is in all three a recognition of the centrality of the sense of loneliness and separateness and the avoidance of that sense of separateness by the phantasied fusion. Bion (1963) writes:

> No matter how good or bad the cooperation may turn out to be, the analyst should not lose or deprive his patient of the sense of isolation that belongs to the knowledge that the circumstances, that have led to the analysis and the consequences that may in the future arise from it, are a responsibility that can be shared with nobody. Discussions of technical or other matters with colleagues or relatives must never obscure this essential isolation.
>
> Opposed to the establishment of a relationship yielding experiences of a sense of responsibility is the drive to be mean and greedy.
>
> The sense of loneliness seems to relate to a feeling of the object of scrutiny; that is, it is being abandoned and, in the scrutinizing object, it is cutting itself off from the source or base on which it depends for its existence. (pp. 15-16)

Bion's notions read more like Kleinian clinical ideas mixed with Rank's, or the lesser-known Kaiser's philosophical sensitivities than simple derivatives of the writings of Klein or other of her less original followers.

Bion's emphasis on the analyst's attention unsaturated with memory and desire make more explicit Freud's injunction to the analyst to enter the analytic situation with "freely suspended attention" and Klein's basic understanding of projective identification as attempted fusion to avoid the awareness of separateness and personal chaos. Again, this sharpens the philosophical essence of both Freud and Klein and makes clear that the central focus in the conduct of the analysis is less an academic laying bare of memory (gaps) and desire (wishes, impulses) than an attempt by the analyst to free himself from the constraints of memory and desire so that he can face the reality of the present and by so doing free the patients from the noxious influence of memory and desire that keep him in the past and future rather than in the present (Bahia, 1977).

IV

I will turn now to the significance of Bion's thought insofar as it clarifies issues, mostly philosophical in my view, in the so-called Freudian-Kleinian controversy. That controversy has been stated to evolve around many types of issues. The most confusing is perhaps the designation "Freudian" to signify developmentalist and ego-psychological aspects of Sigmund Freud's thought as selectively taken, expanded upon, and added to by such thinkers as Anna Freud, Heinz Hartmann, Erik Erikson, and David Rapaport. To varying degrees, these thinkers represent the point of view that psychoanalysis is a general psychology and that material from the analytic situation has been added to by nonanalytic observations and reformulations of structural notions (ego, id, and super ego) so that the observational study of and establishment of lines of development of these structures is possible. There is a tendency to see the drives instead of the unconscious, to see dreams as no different from other mental productions, to see defenses as against drives rather than awareness, and to see the ego as the organ of adaptation, not including the experiential self, and to see the knowable expressed in terms of the observable. Thus, the analytic situation is supplemented by direct observations, for example, related to child development. There is a definite empirical strain of Sigmund Freud's thinking from which this point of view derives, but, basically, Freudian (in terms of the Freudian-Kleinian controversy) may be understood to mean derived from Anna Freud and her followers rather than the mainstream of the thinking of Sigmund Freud.

There is a tendency to ignore the fact that most so-called Kleinian tenets also derive directly from the work of Sigmund Freud and this is explicitly acknowledged by Kleinians themselves. It tends to be more overlooked by their critics who also tend not to see in Freud the non-mechanistic side, the one that he himself struggled against—the side that talked about phylogenetically inherited castration anxiety (Freud, 1912), innate sexual theories (Freud, 1905), primal repression (Freud, 1915a) and the dual instinct theory involving the death instinct (Freud, 1920). These Freudian ideas, so unsavory to so-called Freudians, all involve innate ideas and tendencies not derived from experience and smack of vitalistic tendencies that the more mechanistic ego and developmental psychologists find opprobrious.

I am presuming that the basis of the protracted Freudian-Kleinian controversy devolves around philosophically disparate tendencies inherited from Freud himself, that these philosophical tendencies have been poorly recognized or not seen as at all philosophical, and that this confusion has been the basis of innumerable pointless discussions past the central issues involved.

Some of Melanie Klein's ideas have been so solidly based clinically that they may now be said to be out of the realm of controversy and in the mainstream of psychoanalytic thinking. These include her observations on the severity of the primitive conscience (preceding the super-ego consolidation at the end of the oedipal period [Klein, 1934]); the importance of early aggression and the vicissitudes of aggression, defensive operations associated with splits in the ego, and intense envy that differentiate these schizoid mechanisms from higher level neurotic organization (Klein, 1946). Other Kleinian views, particularly her dating of the onset of the paranoid-schizoid and depressive position and the oedipus complex are debatable and, it seems to me, peripheral matters.

What is central seems to me to involve the Kleinian notion of phantasy. Klein posits phantasy present from birth or before, not derived from experience and fully explicit in terms of the breast, the contents of mother's body, parental intercourse, and other notions. Phantasy has been a cornerstone of psychoanalytic theories since Freud abandoned exclusive reliance on the seduction hypothesis in 1897 and especially since his formulation on infantile sexuality in *Three Essays on Sexuality* in 1905. What is hotly contended centers around the notion of whether unconscious phantasy was once conscious and then repressed (developmentalist) or whether it is innate and primally repressed (Kleinian; see also Freud's metapsychological essays). Developmentalists' evocation of arguments, that the mental apparatus cannot cogitate in the way posited by Kleinians at or before birth, betray an ignorance of the fact that the dispute over innate ideas is the battleground for a philosophical controversy that has been unrecognized as such and, hence, not dealt with in an intelligible way. Specifically, developmentalist arguments presuppose an empirical view somewhat like that of John Locke (1690), namely, that ideas are built up based entirely on experience and corresponding to generalizations derived from percepts in an infant that starts life with a mind that is basically a *tabula rasa* and, basically, all learning is from experience. The fundamental philosophic assumptions that go unrecognized and, therefore run the risk of being somewhat smugly assumed, is that the mind is a *tabula rasa* from birth and depends entirely on generalizations from sensory knowledge to form increasingly complex ideas about human and non-human external world to which these ideas correspond. It is Locke's correspondence theory of knowledge and the *tabula rasa* assumption about the infantile mind that is surprisingly close to the philosophical underpinnings of developmentalists and ego psychologists. It is an observationalist epistemology that does not see itself as grounded philosophically but only in the observation of fact.

Locke's appeal to observationally oriented English empiricists (some of whom like Newton have little idea of what philosophical assumptions were inherent in their own methods) did not succeed in sustaining the objections of his philosophical critics, Berkeley (1710) and Hume (1739), who pointed out early that it makes no sense for an idea to be thought of as *corresponding* to an external event or material object but only as cohering with other ideas. In the work of Kant more clarity is attained with the notion that the thing in itself (*ding an sich*) is unknowable apart from its primary and secondary qualities and that knowledge can be conceived only through the apparatus of the mind which superimposes categories on the contents of experience that are really prior to the data. Both these Kantian ideas have bearing on the clarification of the Freudian-Kleinian disagreements, as will be seen below.

The writings of Melanie Klein, too, are rife with philosophical assumptions or neglect of philosophical clarification. Most threateningly to empirically minded developmentalists is the possibility that the innate ideas smack of vitalism, the irreducible flow of a life force in a realm different from sensory experience and natural law. Vitalism is seen by some to be a threat to anything scientific and, indeed, a loss of the great area of the unconscious reclaimed by Freud for scientific scrutiny. I cannot, in the present discussion, elaborate notions of vitalism with the sophistication suitable for a really adequate discussion, but it suffices to say that such vitalism is associated within the minds of its opponents with occultism and anti-scientism, if not downright obscurantism. Klein herself and some Kleinian thinkers are certainly guilty of theoretical sloppiness particularly as regards epistomological matters and philosophy of science, that is, theories of how one comes by knowledge and how one concludes that a candidate for knowledge has validity. Prior to Bion, there is no real philosophic method in Kleinian thought and a seeming contempt of epistemological issues.

The Freud-Klein controversy then, if it is seen to concern the innateness or experiential derivation of ideas about the world, has ancient philosophical counterparts with the developmentalists and Kleinians polarized around issues that are, respectively, Aristotlean as opposed to Platonic; empiricist as opposed to rationalistic; and mechanistic as opposed to vitalistic.

It is a major advantage of Bion's work that he, like Kant, to whom he is so indebted, avoids the pitfalls of both philosophical extremes. In Bion's work on thinking the notion of preconception and realization mating to form a concept which can be named is crucial in clarification of the problem of the origin of ideas. Phantasies, in the sense of *concepts* about the world—the breast, the contents of the mother's body, parental intercourse, etc.—are not innate. However, there is a phylogenetic preparedness to receive information for theories. This Bion calls a preconception. Only after the preconception becomes partially saturated by experience does it become a namable concept for explicit phantasies. Preconceptions, like Kantian categories speak to the innate disposition of the mind to receive experience. Presuming that the predisposition (preconception) is not itself derived from experience, Bion like Kant avoids pitfalls of rationalistic and empiristic extremes by granting a certain validity to each point of view as part of a more perspicacious synthesis that is elaborated in the relation of the disposition of the mind to utilize sensory data of increasing complexity as more and more abstract ideas develop. Bion's notion of preconception will be thought to add little unless it is realized how much must already be in the mind to utilize comparatively scant empirical data into the elaborate and well formed sexual theories which, as every psychoanalyst knows, are formed by even very young children. Such ideas are not formed by collecting ideas as though they were in a scientific laboratory and arriving at elaborate conclusions based on qualified empirical generalizations. One cannot, for example, really explain castration anxiety by castration threats. A little information (realization) goes a long way in theory (phantasy) formation. The phantasy, then, is the concept, not the preconception, and what is innate is not necessarily the formed product that is the underpinning of unconscious mental life. Furthermore, the unconscious is, in itself, unknowable except in its transformations (or evacuations by projective identification or hallucinosis). We are not bound, therefore, to interpret *the* phantasy, only to locate the invariant structure evident in the process of transformation, projective identification or hallucinosis that only partakes of properties or structures of the thing in itself. The thing in itself is only knowable through saturated beta elements evacuated by projective identification or indirectly by transformations using alpha function. Bion, like Kant, is clear about what can be clear and what cannot, so there is no question of sensory generalizations *or* innate ideas but always in some measure both.

Bion's conceptual apparatus has changed the dispute over innate ideas to a new level in the same sense that Kant's Critical Idealism changed the empiricist-rationalist controversy to a new level. In his insistence on definite structures that are unknowable, except through their transformations, Bion moves out of the realm of philosophic vitalism into the realm of structuralism. As an analytic method, structuralism can be applied to many fields of knowledge—language, mathematics, anthropology, among others. Jean Piaget (1970) (also very much influenced by Kant and also considering himself an empirical Kantian) has defined structuralism as follows:

> As a first approximation, we may say that a structure is a system of transformations. Inasmuch as it is a system and not a mere collection of elements and their properties these transformations involve laws: the structure is preserved or enriched by the interplay of its transformation laws which never yield results external to the system or employ elements that are external to it. In short, the notion of structure is comprised of three key ideas: the idea of wholeness, the idea of transformation, and the idea of self regulation." (p. 5).

Piaget's succinct formulation may be applied to much of Freud's work which will be seen to have structuralist aspects usually not appreciated by writers in English (See Lacan, 1977). Freud's (1900) structuralism is seen most clearly and centrally in *The Interpretation of Dreams*. The basic idea of dream interpretation involves an understanding of a process of transformation. The day residue stimulates the dream thoughts which are transformed by the dream work to the manifest content of the dream. This is the first and still the most central emphasis on transformation from unconscious to conscious. There has been an unfortunate tendency (especially by Rapaport and his followers) to see the essence of *The Interpretation of Dreams* in Chapter 7—"The Psychology of the Dream Process." This is the most "metapsychological" part of the book (in the American sense) and overemphasis on this aspect has led not only to insurmountable theoretical difficulties (impossible to review within the scope of this paper) but also to a failure to appreciate the structuralistic import of the theory of transformation (The Dream Work) taken up in Chapter 6. The idea of structure then, does not involve the knowledge of the structural "thing in itself." In psychoanalytic terms, the unconscious is not the same as the content of the phantasies.

They are all on a level of transformation of it (Note Freud's (1915b) wavering use of instinct as the impulse itself or the mental representation of the impulse, for example, in "Instincts and Their Vicissitudes.") Transformation, a central notion in Bion's work moves from the more ambiguous and burdensome language of impulse or wish and defense to transformations of unconscious structures unknowable in themselves but understandable in terms of invariance of the transformation process. Bion is perhaps the only writer in English sensitive to the philosophical advantages of thinking in structural terms. His formulations enable development of basic Freudian and Kleinian discoveries freed from the trappings of ancient philosophical difficulties.

References

Bahia, A.B. (1977). New Theories: their influence and effect on psychoanalytic technique, *Int. J. Psycho-Anal.*, 58, pp. 345-364.

Basch, M.F. (1976). Theory formation in chapter VII., *J. Am. Psa. Assoc.*, 24, 61-100.

Berkeley, G. (1710). *Treatise Concerning the Principles of Human Knowledge*, ed. M.W. Calkins, New York: Scribner and Sons, 1929.

Bion, W.R. (162). *Learning from Experience*, London: Heinemann.

—— (1963). *Elements of Psychoanalysis*, New York, Basic Books.

Fierman, L.B. (ed.) (1965). *Effective Psychotherapy: The Contribution of Hellmuth Kaiser*, New York, Free Press.

Frege, G. (1968). *The Foundations of Arithmetic (Grundlagen der Arithmetik)*. Tr. J.L. Austing. Evanston, Northwestern Univ. Press.

Freud, S. (1900). *The Interpretation of Dreams, S.E. 4&5*. London: Hogarth Press, 1958.

—— (1905). *Three Essays on Sexuality, S.E. 7*: 123-245.

—— (1911). Formulation on the two principles of mental functioning, *S.E. 12*: 213-226.

—— (1912). *Totem and Taboo, S.E. 13*.

—— (1915*a*). The unconscious, *S.E. 14*: 159-217.

—— (1915*b*). Instincts and their vicissitudes, *S.E. 14*: 109-140.

—— (1920). *Beyond the Pleasure Principle, S.E. 18*.

Gill, M. (1976). Metapsychology is not psychology, *Psychological Issues Monograph 36*, Chapt. 3.

Hartmann, H. (1939). *Ego Psychology and the Problem of Adaptation*, (D. Rapaport, trans.) New York. Int. Univ. Press.

Holt, R. (1975). The past and future of ego psychology, *PsAn. Quart., 44*, pp. 550-576.

Hume, David (1739). *Treatise of Human Nature*, Oxford, Claredon 1888.

Kant, I. (1788). *Critique of Pure Reason*, New York: Bobs-Merrill, 1956.

Klein, M. (1934). The early development of conscience in the child, in *Contributions to Psychoanalysis* 1921-1945, London: Hogarth Press, 1948, pp. 292-320.

—— (1946). Notes on some schizoid mechanisms, in *Developments in Psychoanalysis*, London: Hogarth Press, 1952, pp. 99-110.

Lacan, J. (1977). *Ecrits*, (tr. A. Sheridan), New York: Norton.

Leites, N. (1971). *The New Ego*, New York: Jason Aronson.

Locke, John (1690). *An Essay Concerning Human Understanding*. (A.C. Frasier, ed.) New York: Dover, 1959.

Piaget, J. (1970). *Structuralism*, New York: Basic Books, Chapter 1.

Rank, O. (1923). *The Trauma of Birth*, New York: Harper Row, 1973.

Rapaport, D. (1967). *Collected Papers*, (M. Gill, ed.) New York: Basic Books.

Reich, W. (1949). *Character Analysis*. New York: Noonday.

Rosenfeld, H. (1965). *Psychotic States*, New York: Int. Univ. Press.

Schafer, R. (1976). *A New Language for Psychoanalysis*, New Haven: Yale Univ. Press.

Segal, H. (1973). *An Introduction to the Work of Melanie Klein*, New York: Basic Books.

Whitehead, A.N. and Russell, B. (1925-1927). *Principia Mathematica to Fifty Six 2nd Ed.*, New York: Cambridge Univ. Press.

Some Communicative Properties of the Bipersonal Field

Robert J. Langs

EDITOR'S NOTE: *Robert Langs' prodigious publications are having a growing impact on the practice of psychoanalysis and psychoanalytic psychotherapy by practitioners throughout this country and abroad. More than any other classical psychoanalyst I know of, he has been able to utilize many key concepts of Klein and especially of Bion for practical clinical use. Dr. Langs conceptualizes that psychoanalysis and psychoanalytic psychotherapy comprise a "field" between two human beings, a patient and a therapist, and that this "field" is a bipersonal one, one in which each has an influence on the other. This composite makes it mandatory that the therapist considers, not only the free associations of the patients in their own right as factors for analysis, but he must also consider the moment-by-moment impact his own interventions and presence are having on the patient's associations. His bipersonal field comprises a special practical instance of what I have otherwise termed the "dual-track theory." He describes three fundamental field theories to delineate the modes of communication and/or non-communication in these fields.*

The original manuscript was prepared for the Memorial *in 1977, but, because of the long delay in its publication, the present contribution was pre-published in 1978 in his book,* The Listening Process.* *In the meanwhile, however, Dr. Langs has penetrated even more deeply into Bion's conception of the lie which the latter dealt with in* Attention and Interpretation. *The outcome of that penetration is an addendum to this manuscript which ingeniously incorporates "lie theory" into psychoanalytic technique.*

*Robert J. Langs (1978). *The Listening Process*. New York: Jason Aronson, Inc., pp. 549-616.

Some Communicative Properties of the Bipersonal Field

Robert J. Langs

When a psychoanalytic investigator is struggling to develop a new perspective on disquieting clinical observations, there is often a most constructive interplay between his ill-formed ideas, his ongoing clinical observations, and his reading of the literature. Preoccupied with clinical data that momentarily defy organization, he searches for the *selected fact* (Bion, 1962) that would synthesize and properly link together his still divergent conceptions and observations. The analyst may actively sift others' contributions in the hopes of discovering clues to the missing integrating elements. More often than not, however, such active efforts do not bear fruit; the problem lies fallow or repeatedly frustrates efforts at resolution, until either a moment of clinical insight develops or, through serendipity, reading undertaken for a quite different purpose provides catalytic insights that allow for the elusive solution.

This proved to be the case in regard to my efforts to conceptualize the communicative dimension of the patient-analyst interaction. In the course of many years of struggle, bits of insight, new uncertainties, further understanding, new dissatisfactions, further clinical observations, and minor clues from reading generated a seemingly endless cycle in which fragments of resolution alternated with additional clinical observations that raised new and pertinent questions. Along the way, it was the reading of Bion's *Learning from Experience*, and especially his discussion of alpha functions and of alpha and beta elements–supplemented by a study of his later works (see Bion, 1977)–that provided me with a critical selected fact that finally helped to organize my experiences and ideas in a somewhat stable manner. This presentation offers a broad outline of the crystallizations that followed: it describes some basic communicative properties of the psychotherapeutic and psychoanalytic bipersonal field* and suggests a major means of categorizing the overall qualities of these fields. The implications of these conceptualizations for the understanding of the analytic interaction and for the technical approach of the analyst will also receive special emphasis.

Langs, R. ["Some Communicative Properties of the Bipersonal Field"] This article was prepublished in: (a) *The International Journal of Psychoanalytic Psychotherapy*, 7, 89-136. New York: Jason Aronson, 1978; and (b) as "Appendix A" in *The Listening Process*. New York: Jason Aronson, 1978, pp. 549-616.

*In this paper, I will not attempt to distinguish between the psychoanalytic and psychotherapeutic situations. Although in large part the ideas that will be developed have equal applicability to both modalities, I will allude primarily to the analytic experience, since most of the relevant literature is so focused. I wish to apologize for the personal historical approach I have adopted in developing the themes of this paper: to the extent that they represent discoveries, the ideas presented here have had a very personal development and I have found no other means of doing full justice to my subject. I do, as well, offer full acknowledgement of the contributions of others (see also Langs, 1967c).

The Development of Background Concepts

In outlining the developments that have led me to a basic type-classification of communicative therapeutic fields, I will sketch historically some of the major observations that contributed to these formulations. My own training as a psychoanalyst and my recent study of the psychoanalytic literature related to the analytic experience (Langs, 1976c) have indicated that, on the whole, classical psychoanalysts assume the psychoanalytic experience to take place in a single type of communicative field. With few exceptions (see below) analysts in general—Freudians, Kleinians, the middle group who have followed the lead of Winnicott, and others who have attempted an integrated approach—have written an enormous number of clinical papers related to the psychoanalytic interaction and psychoanalytic technique with the inherent assumption that there is a single basic analytic model. As a result, little or no attention has been paid to the communicative style of the patient (and still less, to that of the analyst) except to suggest that certain patients who do not develop a so-called transference neurosis are essentially not analyzable (see Greenson, 1967). Such a suggestion implies that the patient is unable to fit into the analyst's stereotyped communicative model and is therefore unanalyzable (for another relevant example see Angel, 1971). Not all, however, of these difficult patients, generally viewed as having borderline syndromes or psychotic reactions, have been considered unsuitable for analysis, while many have been so considered, for a variety of reasons, with seemingly less severe disturbances (for a similar discussion of this trend see Giovacchini, 1975).

The type of communicative field which these analysts accepted and found workable can be characterized as one in which the patient readily and verbally free associates, conveys analyzable derivatives of his inner mental world—his unconscious fantasies, memories, introjects, self-representations, and the like—and in which the analyst in response interprets relevant contents, defenses, and dynamic constellations as they have a bearing on the patient's intrapsychic conflicts and psychopathology. Disturbances in this flow and analytic work generally appear in the form of interference with the communication of derivatives (primarily those related to the analyst) and as those readily identifiable behaviors which have been termed acting out, or as I prefer, either *living out* or *enactments* (see Langs, 1976c). These serve primarily as resistances, although they do simultaneously communicate, in some sense, unconscious contents and dynamics.

Inevitably every analyst experiences exceptions to this model. In fact, it is my current clinical impression, based on experiences directly with patients and in supervision, that exceptions are far more common than the rule. Quite early in my analytic work I was confronted with analysands whose associations did not appear to be readily interpretable. I was also struck by patients, both in therapy and in analysis, who seemed relatively uninterested in the acquisition of cognitive insights, but who, it eventually turned out, remained in treatment for a variety of other reasons: to gain direct support against a spouse, to spend large sums of money as a means of harming a spouse or parent, to provide a cover for directly destructive intentions toward another person, to gain in the therapist a gratifying companion in an otherwise empty life, or to find a target for unbridled expressions of aggression and sexuality. (This latter type of patient has been described in the literature on erotized and aggressive transferences; see Langs, 1976c.) Such analysands challenged for me the generally accepted image of analysis and the tenet that the role of the analyst was to create a secure analytic setting and therapeutic alliance within which the derivatives of the patient's transference constellation (his unconcious transference fantasies) could unfold and be analyzed.

Although I observed much of this well before Bird (1972), in a relatively isolated contribution, dramatically stated that at times patients attempt to harm their analysts, Searles (1965) was writing during this period of such matters as patients' efforts to drive their analysts crazy and the realistic impact that patients have on their analysts–including the much delayed discovery of the patient's therapeutic intentions and efforts toward the analyst (see especially Searles, 1959, 1975, and Langs, 1975b, 1976a, 1976b). At this time, I was painfully aware that the overidealized and unrealistic world-of-fantasy model of analysis and therapy was something of a myth, a point expressly made in the second volume of *The Technique of Psychoanalytic Psychotherapy* (1974). My understanding of the problem, however, was limited to an awareness that patients enter analysis with deviant motives and to the technical recommendation that these needs and intended or actual misuses had to be discovered, analyzed, worked through, and resolved before other analytic work would be feasible.

My perception of this aspect of the analytic situation began to change gradually as a consequence of the development of several new clinical concepts. Largely because *The Technique of Psychoanalytic Psychotherapy* (Langs, 1973, 1974) was empirically derived, I had approached the study of transference within an adaptive framework, thereby reformulating aspects of the influence of the patient's unconscious transference fantasies and stressing his exquisite, unconscious sensitivity to the therapist's errors. Having already written on the relationship between day residues and dreams (Langs, 1971), I found this model quite serviceable in considering the patient's reactions to the therapist, since it stressed the precipitants of these responses as one key to their understanding. I pointed out that transference responses do not occur ex nihilo, but are consistently prompted by life events, especially by occurrences within the therapeutic or analytic interaction. Recognizing the presence of many reactions in the patient derived primarily from the countertransference-based errors of the therapist, I described a series of iatrogenic syndromes (Langs, 1974).

This adaptive, interactional approach crystallized while I was completing the *Technique* volumes, and I embodied it in the concept of the *adaptive context* (Langs, 1972, 1973)–the internal or, more usually, the external reality stimulus for the patient's intrapsychic responses. The discovery of a reality precipitant for every intrapsychic reaction consolidated the adaptive dimension of my approach to understanding the patient and led to an extensive consideration of the nature of these adaptive stimuli, especially as they pertained to the therapist's interventions and failures to intervene. Many new perspectives followed from the principles that all of the patient's associations subsequent to an intervention bore on the analyst's communication and that the patient's responses were always a mixture, on the one hand, of valid perceptiveness and commentary and, on the other, of distorting fantasies. It was then feasible to extend these concepts to the therapist's management of the ground rules—a position that led to a number of additional discoveries.

I soon realized that the patient was, unconsciously, exquisitely sensitive to the analyst's errors and I could trace the vicissitudes of his responses. I found that the clinical data readily reaffirmed and extended Searles's concept (see 1965, 1972, 1975) that the patient not only unconsciously perceives the analyst's errors, but also unconsciously introjects dimensions of the analyst's maladaptive inner world and functioning as they are unconsciously communicated through his errors. This led to studies of the patient's unconscious curative efforts toward the therapist, an insight first described by Little (1951) and then specifically elaborated upon by Searles (1965, 1975), and was counterbalanced by investigations of the positive effects of valid interventions.

While I was developing an appreciation of the complexities of the analytic interaction and of the extent of the analyst's continuous involvement and conscious and unconscious communication with the patient—aspects of the interaction which I once again found Searles (1965, 1972, 1975) especially sensitive to—my reading and clinical work prompted me to consider more carefully the analyst's demeanor, his basic attitude or stance, toward the patient. In this respect, Balint's *The Basic Fault* (1968) was especially important in that he suggested that certain types of patients require both a different than usual mode of listening by the analyst and a distinctive manner of relating. He referred to patients suffering from what he termed a *basic fault*, an ego defect or sector of inner mental damage derived from such disruptive preoedipal experiences as acute traumas and faulty mothering. These analysands required a response from the analyst that created a sense of *primary love*; the analyst essentially became the medium through which the patient could regress, discover his basic fault, mourn it, and then progress once again. He drew an analogy to the oxygen we breathe and the water through which the swimmer swims: neither the oxygen nor the water asks anything of the recipient and yet offers essential support. For Balint, this therapeutic carriage was essential with patients for whom two-person interactions were far more important than those at a three-person level.

Here was an important indication that in addition to his interpretations, the manner in which the analyst created the analytic situation and related to the analysand could have a significant influence on the analytic work and outcome. Winnicott (1958, 1965), who stressed the *holding* qualities of the analytic setting and of the analyst's stance, had suggested as early as 1956 that with certain patients the holding environment, of which the analyst is a part, would have to do all the essential therapeutic work for long periods of time. It is no coincidence that Winnicott's metaphor of the maternal-like holding functions of the analyst bears a striking resemblance to Bion's metaphor (1977) of *the container* and *the contained* which he too applied, in part, to the analyst's functions (see below, and also Langs, 1976a, 1976b, 1976c). Khan too (1963, 1964), in writing of the *maternal shield*, offered a metaphor for certain inherently protective, and yet noninterpretive, aspects of the analyst's relationship with his patient.

It had, then, become increasingly clear (a) that many patients did not confine themselves to the largely verbal communication in an analyzable form of derivatives both of unconscious fantasies and of other inner contents and defenses, and (b) that the analyst's functions extended beyond his development of a safe setting and the use of verbal interventions geared toward neutral interpretations. He had an additional responsibility to create a special setting and hold for the patient, to manage the ground rules, and to maintain his hold as long as necessary. It had also become evident that there was an ever-present interaction between the patient and the analyst, much of it on an unconscious level, with continuous pressures toward both health and regression on both sides–though hopefully in different proportions for patient and analyst (see Searles, 1965, and his concept of *therapeutic symbiosis*). Finally, with the development of the concept of the adaptive context, it was possible to study more carefully the communications from the patient and to recognize that at times his associations provided interpretable derivatives, while at other times they did not: either there were many apparent derivatives and no adaptive context in which to dynamically organize and understand them, or the adaptive context was evident, but clear-cut and meaningful derivatives were lacking (see Searles, 1973b for a related discussion). Further, the production of these derivatives was not solely a function of the intrapsychic balances, contents, and state of the analysand, but was continuously influenced by the analyst as well (Langs, 1975a, 1975b, 1975c, 1976a, 1976c).

I had begun to develop clinical material for a new book, and intending a rather comprehensive investigation of this area, I decided to review very carefully the relevant literature. Among many, for me truly remarkable, discoveries (Langs, 1976c), I was especially drawn to a paper by the Barangers (1966) in which they discussed the development of insight in the analytic situation–the *bipersonal field*, as they termed it. While I can remember vividly my initial, utter confusion in response to their discussion of projective identification as the major mechanism within that field–my first exposure to the term–I nonetheless found their conception of the analytic relationship in terms of a bipersonal field not only extremely attractive, but soon quite productive of additional personal insights.

The field concept led me to intensify my investigations of the ground rules of analysis, since it was evident that these tenets were, in part, the delimiting determinants of the field—both as its internal and external boundaries and, as a key factor in the very nature of the transactions within its confines. The field metaphor was supported by Milner's analogy (1952) between the ground rules of analysis and the frame of a painting: each sets off the world within its confines from the rest of reality and gives that inner world its special qualities and rules. In analysis, for example, the frame makes the transference illusion possible. In these two ways, the ground rules of analysis took on three-dimensional qualities and a reexamination of their functions became vital. I soon saw that since they could be viewed as the framework of the bipersonal field, their establishment and maintenance were perhaps the major factors giving the analytic field its therapeutic qualities and communicative characteristics—a point suggested by Bleger (1967) and explicitly elaborated upon by Viderman (1974).

Among the many important ideas to which the bipersonal field concept led, several are most pertinent to this presentation. The metaphor suggests that every point in the field—every communication, interaction, structure, and occurrence within and between the two members of the dyad—receives vectors from both participants, albeit in varying proportions. Thus, every communication from the patient is influenced to a greater or lesser extent by the analyst, and vice versa. Further, every point in the field is layered and thus requires equal consideration of its realistic and fantasied components. Each content and communication, with its conscious and unconscious elements, must be scrutinized for its veridical core (primarily its nontransference layer for the patient and its noncountertransference layer for the analyst) as well as for its intrapsychically distorted aspects (primarily transference for the patient and countertransference for the analyst). In addition, both intrapsychic and interactional processes and mechanisms must consistently be considered.

One can hypothesize an interactional interface along which the communications from patient and analyst take place, and then consider the vectors that determine its position and qualities: its location vis-à-vis the respective pathologies of patient and analyst; the extent to which it is fixed or mobile, in terms of the relative contributions of the patient and analyst; the degree to which its primary qualities are related to unconscious fantasies, memories, and introjects, or to projective and introjective identifications; and the degree to which it embodies what I have termed the *me-not-me* property—the manner in which the communications from each participant allude both to the self and the not-self. (In other words), the patient's associations consistently refer to both himself and the analyst, in terms of both valid perceptions and distorted fantasies; see Langs, 1976c).

The bipersonal field concept also directs the analyst to a consideration of the nature of the communications that take place within the field: the extent to which verbal communications prevail and maintain their intended meaning; the degree to which symbolic and illusory verbal and behavioral communication is present; the openness of the interactional flow; the presence of projective identifications; and the use of language and behavior for discharge and direct gratification rather than for insight (Langs, 1976a, 1976c). The concept also encourages a study of the defenses that exist within the field, stressing the contributions of both participants, thereby supplementing the strictly intrapsychic viewpoint of both defenses and resistances. Thus, while the Barangers (1966) had described *bastions* of the bipersonal field (shared sectors of the communicative field that are split off, repressed, and denied by both participants), I delineated various sectors of *therapeutic misalliance* (Langs, 1975b, 1976a, 1976c) which involves unconscious collusion between the patient and analyst directed toward noninsightful symptom relief and other inappropriate, shared defenses and gratifications. Similarly, I delineated *interactional resistances* that were created and shared by the two participants. This line of thought led to the recognition of *interactional syndromes*: symptoms in either participant to which both patient and analyst contribute in varying proportions—a notion that provides an interactional addendum to the concept of the intrapsychically based transference and countertransference neuroses (or syndromes).

Work on the bipersonal field interdigitated with studies of the nature of the unconscious and conscious communication between the patient and analyst—the unconscious communicative interaction. For the patient, the stress was on a balanced appreciation of his valid functioning, as compared to his pathological responses, so that both unconscious perception and unconscious fantasy received attention. The former, while most often valid, could also be distorted—*unconscious misperception*. Such perceptions form the core of the patient's introjects of the analyst—realistic nuclei which may then be surrounded by pathological, intrapsychically-founded distortions. Unconscious perceptions and introjections of the therapist's countertransference-based behaviors and their underlying psychopathology may, on the one hand, be misappropriated by the patient to reinforce his own psychopathology and may, on the other, evoke both unconscious retaliation and unconscious efforts at cure (Searles, 1965, 1975, Langs, 1975b, 1976a, 1976c). Valid interventions by the analyst, however, not only generate cognitive insight and the related resolution of intrapsychic conflicts, anxieties, and distorted fantasies and introjects, but they also inherently provide the patient with positive and curative introjects based on the analyst's sound functioning.

For the analyst, his manifest interventions—interpretations and managements of the frame—were seen to extend beyond their direct contents into a wide range of unconscious communications. Erroneous interventions and mismanagements of the frame were found, since they were not in keeping with the patient's communications and needs, to convey aspects of the analyst's pathological unconscious fantasies, memories, and introjects, and to constitute the projective identification into the patient of aspects of the analyst's own pathological inner mental world. Here too

Bion's unique investigations of project identification, and his specific development of the metaphor of the container and the contained (1977), facilitated the understanding of this dimension of the unconscious interaction between the patient and analyst. While heretofore the stress had been on the patient's pathological projective identifications into the anlayst and on the latter's capacity to contain, metabolize, and interpret these contents (see for example, Grinberg, 1962; Bion, 1977; Langs, 1976a, 1976b, 1976c), the bipersonal field concept prompted an equal consideration of the analyst's pathological projective identifications into the patient, and his use of the patient as a pathological or inappropriate container for these contents (Langs, 1976a, 1976c).

In this connection, I also recognized that projective identification could range from primitive omnipotent fantasies with almost no effort at interactional fulfillment to more mature, structuralized interactional efforts to place contents into the dyadic partner. I suggest the use of the term *interactional projection* (Langs, 1976a, 1976c) to stress the actuality of the projective effort in projective identification and to contrast it with projection which I—and others— defined as an essentially intrapsychic mechanism. Finally, by making extensive use of Wangh's concept (1962), the *evocation of a proxy*, I was able to recognize uses of projective identification beyond its usually described role as a means of getting rid of bad inner contents, placing good contents into an object for safekeeping, and externalizing one's troubling inner representations in order to better manage them from without (Segal, 1967). Wangh's work implied that projective identification also serves the subject as a means of evoking adaptive responses in the object which can then be introjected by the subject.

One final clarification helped to set the stage for the main subject of this paper—the identification of major types of communicative bipersonal fields. This took the form of clarifying the types of communications from the patient and the ways in which the analyst could organize and conceptualize this material (Langs, 1978b). In essence, it was suggested that on the first level, a patient's associations could be organized around their *manifest contents*. This approach, which is essentially nonanalytic since it totally rejects all notions of unconscious process and content, confines itself to the surface of the patient's communications.

On the second level, the analyst organizes material from the patient by attending to the manifest associations, isolating various segments of this material, and inputing to each a specific unconscious meaning; I term these inferences *Type One derivatives*. Here, the manifest content is addressed in relative isolation, and the latent content—the unconscious communication—is determined by the recognition of obvious displacements, the use of symbols, the intuitive understanding of underlying meanings, and a knowledge of a given patient's communicative idiom. By and large, the distinction between unconscious fantasy and unconscious perception is ignored, and Type One derivatives are conceived of primarily in terms of the former.

A third level of organizing the material from the patient is feasible through the use of the *adaptive context* as the dynamic organizer of the patient's associations; this yields *Type Two derivatives*. The model here is that of the day residue and the manifest dream, the latent content of which is fully comprehended only with the knowledge of the dream's precipitant and related associations (Langs, 1971, 1978b). Each adaptive context itself has both manifest and latent meanings. Further, most crucial adaptive contexts for the patient in analysis stem from his interaction with the analyst; as a result, a true understanding of the nature of an adaptive stimulus and of the responses it evokes (associations and behaviors) is founded on the self-knowledge of the analyst—his sensitivity to the conscious, and especially, unconscious meanings and projections conveyed in his verbal interventions, silences, and efforts to manage the frame.

Type Two derivatives, then, are always viewed dynamically and as responses to adaptive stimuli. As a rule, they imply that virtually all of the communications from the patient must, on this level, be appended or related to the analytic interaction—those representing perceptions and introjections, as well as fantasies and distortions. At this level, many seemingly divergent and relatively undecipherable associations accrue significance in the light of the recognized adaptive context.

In all, then, my investigations of the bipersonal field had, at this point, provided me with the following tools: (1) the concepts of the adaptive context and of Type Two derivatives, means through which it became feasible to determine whether the communications from the patient constituted analyzable derivatives of unconscious fantasies and perceptions, (2) an understanding of basic interactional mechanisms and of the unconscious communications and projective efforts of both patient and analyst, (3) a comprehension of the essential role played by the framework of the analytic situation in determining the communicative properties of the therapeutic field, and (4) a conception of the dimensions of the bipersonal field itself, as created and continued by both patient and analyst.

At this juncture, there was evident need for a basic conceptualization of major types of therapeutic or communicative bipersonal fields. In continued clinical observations, I experimented with a number of possibilities, but a satisfactory classification seemed to elude crystallization until a point at which a reorganization of my clinical observations coincided with a rereading of Bion's writings, especially a series of comments in his 1962 book, *Learning from Experience*. Much later, after the necessary concepts had been developed, I found independent confirmation of aspects of my ideas in an important paper by Khan (1973). At the time of writing this paper, I restudied a series of additional ideas in Bion's writings (1977) that, on the one hand, suggested an unconscious influence on the delineation of these fields that I had not previously explicitly recognized and that, on the other, helped to further refine my understanding of the concepts I was attempting to define. Finally, I have just now become aware of efforts by Liberman (in press) to study styles of communication in patients.

The Three Major Bipersonal Fields

For some time, I had developed, as I have described, considerable evidence for distinctly different types of bipersonal fields. In the course of struggling with these clinical observations, I found that Winnicott's (1965, 1971) conception of the analytic setting as a type of transitional or play space within which the capacity for illusion plays a central role seemed pregnant with meaning. I could see that, in my terms, this implied the presence of analyzable Type Two derivatives, and I was aware that certain bipersonal fields possessed this quality, while others certainly did not. This, however, seemed insufficient for a full classification; the crucial variables had not emerged. Still, I had made a number of fascinating clinical observations along the following lines: as a rule, when the analyst modified the framework of the bipersonal field, the transitional-play qualities tended to diminish or disappear. This could be seen in the flatness of a patient's subsequent communications and in the relative absence of interpretable derivatives (see Halpert 1972, for an illustration). Often, under these conditions the patient would eventually make such comments as "I can no longer write or paint," or, "My child's school does not have a playground."

These observations provided further evidence of the importance of the analyst to both the patient's communicative style and to the overall communicative qualities of the bipersonal field, and placed special stress on the role of a secure framework in creating a transitional-play-illusory comunicative space. Still, they did not facilitate an understanding of those fields in which these qualities were more or less absent. Under the latter conditions it was evident that patients and perhaps analysts tended to overuse projective identification, denial mechanisms, and acting out on gross and far more subtle levels but these findings still lacked an organizing element.

In *Learning from Experience*, Bion (1962) postulates the presence in the mind of an *alpha function*, which operates on sense impressions and raw emotions to create *alpha elements* that are suitable for storage and dreaming–that is, for symbolic usage (see also Khan, 1973). This function is essential for memory, conscious thinking, and reasoning. It is developed in the infant through an interaction with a mother capable of *reverie*, who subjects a young child's projective identifications to her own alpha functioning and returns, into the child, detoxified projective identifications which were formerly terrifying and morbid. When alpha functioning is disturbed, either because of innate factors or by attacks based on hate and envy, the infant is left with *beta elements* which are things-in-themselves, suitable for projective identification and acting out, but not for dream thoughts; nor can these elements cohere into a *contact barrier* that will enable the mechanisms of repression, suppression, and learning to occur. Beta elements essentially are objects that can be evacuated to rid the psyche of accretions of stimuli and to eject unwanted contents.

Perhaps most crucial to the development of alpha functioning and elements is the capacity of the infant to modify, rather than evade, frustration. Thus, thinking may remain at a level modeled on muscular movement and may function as a means of unburdening the psyche, largely through projective identification; here, the infant does not attempt to actualize his omnipotent fantasies of projective identification because he has an undeveloped capacity to tolerate frustration. This type of projective identification, primarily a flight from reality, is quite different from that used excessively to have the mother or analyst experience the inner contents of the child-patient. In Bion's discussion, the mother's capacity for reverie was seen as comparable to the analyst's hold and to his receptivity to the patient's projective identifications (see also Bion, 1965, 1970, and Langs, 1976a, 1976c).

While these basic concepts are subjected to extensive elaboration by Bion, the outline presented here is sufficient for the purposes of this paper. Most relevant is his thesis that there are two types of communicative elements: *alpha* and *beta*. The former are suitable for symbolic usage and creative communication and may readily be seen as comparable to what I have termed "analyzable derivatives of unconscious fantasies, memories, and introjects"–Type Two derivatives. They are one of the major organizing elements of the Type A field that I will soon describe. In contrast, beta elements are not utilized symbolically or for the purposes of communication and cognitive understanding; they are primarily discharge products, largely projective identifications designed to lessen inner psychic tension. This concept relates to the finding that patients may free associate verbally without producing analyzable derivatives organized around meaningful adaptive contexts and without permitting valid interpretations in terms of their unconscious contents and functions. These elements are an important factor in the Type B field (see below). It seems evident that these discharge products require a particular type of analyst intervention, either in the form of appropriately holding and containing the patient and his projective identifications or of interpretations based on the *metabolism* (Langs, 1976a) and understanding of the relevant projected contents and processes. In Bion's terms, such holding and intervening may foster the development of alpha functions and elements in a patient previously blocked in this regard and are the expression of the analyst's capacity for reverie.

One additional group of interrelated concepts almost exclusively developed by Bion (1977) pertain to the static, noncommunicative Type C field that rounds out the classifications to be presented here. These brilliant and original ideas are scattered throughout Bion's (1977) four major works and may be briefly organized around four basic concepts: (1) the -K link (Bion 1962), (2) the functions of column two of the grid–the psi function (Bion,

1963, 1965), (3) the phenomenon of reversible perspective (Bion, 1963), and (4) his discussion of lies and the thinker (Bion, 1970).

In brief, Bion (1962) postulated three types of links between objects: K (knowledge), L (love), and H (hate). The K link is "commensal" in that it involves two objects (persons) who are dependent on each other for mutual benefit without harm for either. It is growth promoting and permits both particularization and abstraction. In contrast, the -K link tends to be infused with envy and to be parasitic in that it may be destructive to both objects and may interfere with growth. It is characterized by not-understanding (misunderstanding or misrepresenting) and it functions to defeat the analyst and to denude and strip of meaning all interactional elements, thus generating a worthless residue. This link destroys knowledge, has a primary quality of "withoutness," converts alpha elements into beta elements, and creates a feeling in the patient of being surrounded by the bizarre objects that represent in part his thoughts stripped of meaning and ejected.

Although Bion's (1977) development of a grid with horizontal and vertical axes designed for the classification and comprehension of the elements of psychoanalysis cannot be fully detailed here, several of its aspects are relevant. The horizontal axis provides "the definitory function of a formulation" (Bion 1963, p. 65)–that is, the use of a communication. Communications are placed into column two of this grid, the psi function, when they constitute hypotheses known to be false and maintained as a barrier against anxiety lest any other theories take their place. These communications are utilized to inhibit thought; they constitute ideas used to deny more accurate, but more frightening, ones and serve as barriers against turbulence and psychological upheaval. At times, in the form of common sense facts, they are used to deny expressions of fantasy; their manifestations pertain to the patient's defenses and resistances. This language function cannot, however, be interpreted until the column-two dimension is apparent and has evolved. Bion (1965) suggests that the criterion for intervening relates to the analyst's capacity to experience resistances in the patient that would be evoked if an interpretation were given.

To explain reversible perspective, Bion (1963) draws upon the familiar line drawing which may be seen either as two profiles or as a vase. Through this metaphor he suggests that in the area of sensibility–the experience of the lines per se–there may be agreement between two individuals, while in the area of insensibility–the conception of what is seen–there may be disagreement. Applying this to the patient and analyst, Bion describes analytic situations in which both appear to agree on the facts, while the patient conceals an important level of disagreement that relates to the basic assumptions of the analytic relationship and situation. The patient's glib agreement is designed to conceal his lack of conviction; even when painful emotions are evident, the patient has a facile explanation for them. Basically, the patient's responses, designed to disguise the real nature of his experiences, invite interventions regarding contents that will not be confirmed. This occurs because the patient accepts interpretations on the surface, while secretly rejecting the premises on which they are based. The analyst may comprehend, but the patient does not, and views the analyst's premises as false. The debate, however, is unspoken; it derives from the patient's maintaining a point of view that is different from that of the analyst. The patient's agreement, then, serves -K and column-two functions in that it is a barrier against pain and a defense against change. Such analytic situations are stalemated; they lack real progress and are quite static. Splitting is arrested, as is the evacuation of beta elements, and action is unnecessary. The conditions are similar to those under which the patient uses an hallucination as a substitute for reality. There is a no engagement on the issues; rather than agreeing or disagreeing, the patient simply reverses the perspective and shifts his point of view. For Bion, the main factor here is the patient's impaired capacity to tolerate pain.

In his comments on "Lies and the Thinker," Bion (1970) extends and elaborates upon many of the earlier ideas outlined here. He investigates the lie and demonstrates its frequent column-two function, while noting that, at times, it may fall into his column six–an action-oriented group of communications–as well. In the former function, the lie serves as a barrier against statements that would lead to psychological upheaval, while in the latter, it may actually generate that upheaval. The lie is also studied in terms of its -K function, and its role in preventing catastrophic change. Bion notes that the patient tries to induce the analyst to accept and work with the lie in order to prevent the experience of inner disruption. The patient in analysis will often experience a conflict between the need to know and the need to deny, and the problem is complicated by there being no absolute value to either truth or lie. Bion suggests the need to investigate column two in order to see in what respects its pains compare with those of other systems. He notes that this category involves conflicts with impressions of reality. When the conflict between needing to know and to deny becomes acute, the patient may usher in attacks on linking in order to stop the stimulation that has led to the conflict; however, with some liars, such an aim is not detectible and they do not betray a pattern of this kind. In general, the relationship between the liar and his audience is parasitic, and the lie functions as a means of denudation.

While this highly condensed résumé of Bion's ideas has undoubtedly generated some degree of confusion in the reader, I trust that the main themes are evident: (a) that certain communications may function as barriers, lies, forms of concealment, attacks on interpersonal links, and attempts to destroy rather than generate meaning, and (b) that there are many patients who attempt to maintain a static and stalemated analytic situation through extremely subtle and difficult to detect means–this, largely in the service of preventing a dreaded psychological upheaval. The relevance to the Type C field to be described below will soon become evident.

Before completing this final introductory survey, I must openly express certain misgivings in the context of the present discussion. I have been quite concerned that the concepts of beta elements and the discharge qualities of projective identifications draw upon an economic model of the mental apparatus that is open to serious theoretical and clinical questions (see the recent discussion by Wallerstein, 1977). This economic view of the mental apparatus is a throwback to Freud's earlier, topographic model, much of which is now no longer serviceable according to most writers. It may well be that such metaphors are more descriptive than theoretically meaningful, but despite repeated efforts to search for a different type of conception, I continue to find the present delineation eminently useful for clinical conception, prediction, and interpretation. I am well aware that many analysts will believe that these descriptions of column-two functions (efforts at destruction of meaning) are merely restatements of familiar concepts related to our present understanding of defense and resistance. It is beyond the scope of this paper to establish the important distinctions and their clinical implications that I believe to be pertinent here, although I will offer initial clinical observations and ideas in this respect in my discussion of the three communicative fields. These vital clinical and theoretical issues are all unsettled, and I would welcome revision and refinement based on additional clinical observations and conceptual rethinking.

In all, then, the insights provided by Bion's discussions and my own continued clinical observations finally led me to a tripartite classification of communicative fields. While I will stress this point less here, these styles of communication seem also to be descriptive of individual propensities. I will now identify each major type of bipersonal field, and describe its principal characteristics. Although, in actual clinical situations, one finds intermixtures, my own observations indicate that a particular group of characteristics do indeed tend to predominate. Each field will be described as bipersonal and communicative, under the influence of both patient and analyst.

The Type A Field

In the Type A field of symbolic communication, analyzable derivatives and symbolic interpretations of inner mental contents and mechanisms predominate. The patient's associations and behaviors convey workable derivatives, and the analyst offers valid interpretations of their functions, contents, and meanings. This is the communicative field in which transference as an illusion (a complex concept in itself, see Langs, 1976c), the use of symbolic communication, and the broader use of illusion prevail. It has been described as an analytic play space (Winnicott, 1971) or as a transitional space (Khan, 1973). The patient's verbal and behavioral communications are readily organizable around significant adaptive contexts, thereby yielding derivatives of his unconscious fantasies, memories, introjects, perceptions, and self-representations (aspects of id, ego, and superego) expressed in a form that lends itself to verbal interpretation. In addition, the patient is prepared to understand the symbolic meaning of the analyst's interventions, which are themselves conveyed in this idiom. It is this type of field, as I indicated previously, that is implicitly the ideal of the classical psychoanalyst, who expects to work under these conditions and who may view patients who are unable to comply as unanalyzable—that is, because their associations seem uninterpretable or because they are prone to what is viewed as intractable acting out.

In this type of bipersonal field, the communications from the patient organize primarily around adaptive responses, analyzable derivatives of unconscious transference fantasies and perceptions, and the verbal and nonverbal resistances to their expression. It is to be stressed, however, that when resistances and defenses predominate, the unconscious derivatives relevant to their nature and to the material being defended against are, in general, available in the communications from the patient. It is possible to establish the adaptive context and precipitant for these resistances. Ultimately they are analyzable in terms of unconscious meanings and defenses.

In the Type A field, a secure frame is an essential and silent element, consistently maintained while the analyst interprets the patient's communications. It therefore requires an analyst capable of securing and managing the framework—one who, in addition, has the capacity to think symbolically and utilize the transitional space as a place both for understanding the patient's derivatives and for their synthesis into valid, sensitively timed symbolic interpretations. The patient must be capable of symbolic communication, must have a tolerance for the regression and anxiety invoked by a secure frame (Langs, 1976a, 1976c), or must possess an ability to use illusion and derivative expression, and must have a capacity to understand and utilize the analyst's interpretations on that level. It is my impression that Searles's description (1970, 1971, 1973a) of a workable therapeutic symbiosis refers to this type of field.

Not all analysts are capable of synthesis and symbolic communication at this level, nor are all analysts capable of securing the framework needed for a bipersonal field characterized by these communicative qualities. As will become evident, virtually all previous so-called training analyses have taken place in a field under consistent pressure to deviate from this Type A form to either the more discharge-oriented field (Type B) or the more static, noncommunicative interaction (Type C). Such analytic experiences tend to occur within bipersonal fields whose frames are modified, often extensively so since so-called training analysts are prone to nonillusory and nonsymbolic communication toward their analysands. They may use language or mismanage the frame in order to projectively identify into their analysands their own inner disturbance, thereby fostering Type B communication, or they may make cliché-ridden, stereotyped interventions, unconsciously designed as falsifications and barriers, which promote the development of a Type C field. As a result, an analyst's own analysis has tended to reinforce his own greater or lesser need for either the discharge or the nonmeaningful modes of communication characteristic, respectively, of Types B and C interactions. Either outcome, of course, greatly influences the communicative interaction with his own patients. Often, these propensities are outside the analyst's awareness and are expressed despite his manifest intentions to secure the ground rules of each analytic situation and to create opportunities for interpreting. His actual, unconsciously determined communicative style and use of language may deviate significantly from the optimal Type A mode.

There are strong, inherent needs within both patient and analyst to shift away from a Type A communicative field toward the more direct and inappropriate gratifications that are relatively absent in the symbolic mode. It has been assumed in the classical psychoanalytic literature, so far as I can determine, that all analysts attempt to create a Type A field and that they are capable of doing so and of offering relevant interpretations within such a field. If I may be permitted a well-founded, but undocumented, thesis, I would suggest that, to the contrary, there are many classically trained analysts who are quite incapable of consistently maintaining this Type A field, and it is quite likely that this is even more the case with therapists with other backgrounds.

In brief, the analyst may be the prime mover in modifying a Type A field into Type B or C, or he may accept the latter types when patients attempt to create them. He does this through inappropriate silences, erroneous verbal interventions, and alterations in the framework of the bipersonal field that are, almost without exception, quite inappropriate. This latter is the single most overlooked vehicle both for countertransference expressions and as a means of detrimentally altering the communicative properties of the bipersonal field (see Langs, 1975c, 1976a, 1976c, 1978a). In one sense, all such technical errors tend to express failures in the analyst's holding capacity, containing functions, and use of alpha function; they therefore reflect the nonsymbolic use of language and behavior for pathological projective identification and to express beta elements and thus rid the analyst of accretions of inner tension. They may also serve as Type C barriers (see below).

Characteristically, patients will respond to such efforts in kind. They will shift away from the use of alpha elements, and away from derivative and symbolic communication if this has been their communicative style, and move either toward holding the analyst and containing his projective identifications or toward the discharge of projective identifications and beta elements on their own part. Alternately, they too shift to a Type C idiom. In addition, patients who suffer from inadequate alpha functioning and are blocked in their use of symbolic and derivative communication will tend themselves to maintain Type B and Type C fields and be refractory toward any possible shift to a Type A field. Under these conditions, verbal interventions are virtually useless. The analyst must first *rectify* the altered frame and shift to symbolic communicating; only then will his interventions have their consciously intended meanings and effects. Clearly, both self-awareness and the resolution of the underlying countertransference problems are a vital part of such work.

In this context, it should be noted first, I have not suggested that a Type A field is characteristic of patients at the more neurotic end of the psychopathological continuum, nor will I later suggest that Type B and Type C fields are necessarily characteristic of those with more severe psychopathology—that is, borderline, narcissistic, and schizophrenic patients. While in general, it may well be that this is the general trend, I have noted many exceptions to this rule and leave the matter open to empirical study. Secondly, implicit in these ideas is the suggestion that the analyst move the patient toward the utilization of a Type A communicative mode through his appropriate management and maintenance of the framework and his valid verbal, symbolic interpretations. These are essential for the Type A field itself; however, I do not wish to suggest, as implied in the classical psychoanalytic literature, that the Type A field is the only viable therapeutic field. While Khan (1973) has suggested that what I term the Type A field is optimal and has indicated that it requires a high level of maturation, my own clinical observations suggest that communicative styles are genetically and intrapsychically determined and that effective analytic work will tend more to create interludes of symbolic communication in Type B and Type C patients, rather than, as a rule, to effect a shift to a fundamentally Type A mode (see below). In any case, it is evident that effective analytic work and adaptive, insightful and structural inner change can accrue to a patient in types of fields other than the Type A. It is therefore my belief that further clinical research will be needed to identify the advantages and limitations of analytic work within each of the three types of fields described here.

One final point: while the Type A field is most efficacious for cognitive insight, it is also the field in which the patient and, to a lesser extent, the analyst most intensely experience their pathological and primitive inner mental contents and the related anxieties and temporary mental disorganization. While this is an aspect of a therapeutic (or analyzable) regression (Langs, 1976a) with great curative potential, it is a quite disturbing experience that prompts major defensive reactions. In part, then, a shift to a Type B or C field initiated by either participant has an important defensive function.

The Type B Field

The Type B field is an action-discharge field in which projective identification predominates. In it, either the patient or the analyst makes extensive use of projective identification designed to rid the psyche of disturbing accretions of inner stimuli, to make use of the other member of the dyad as a container for disruptive projective identifications, and to evoke positive proxy responses. Major contributions to the development of this type of communicative field may come from either the patient or the analyst, and often come from both.

There are patients of all psychopathological types who show deficient alpha functioning and impairment in the use of illusion and symbolic communication—failures in the expression of analyzable derivatives of inner contents and dynamisms. Such patients make extensive use of projective identification, largely as a means of denying reality and utilizing the analyst as a container for their disturbing inner contents, endeavoring to transform the analytic situation into a place of discharge and action.

In a Type B field either participant may also seek inappropriate, direct gratification of pathological, instinctual drive needs. In the patient, this usually takes the forms of direct demands for alterations in the frame and of subtle or gross efforts to obtain a variety of noninterpretive satisfactions. Should these be gratified, his use of this mode of communicating—and functioning—is reinforced.

Despite the relative absence of a contribution from the analyst that would shape the field along Type B lines, patients so inclined tend to adhere to this type of communication for long periods; their fundamental use of this mode is, perhaps, essentially unmodifiable. This suggests that this form of communication is a long-standing, basic personality attribute and mode of interaction. While the matter should be left open in that it may well be feasible analytically to modify the pathological aspects of Type B communication to where the patient will shift to a basic Type A mode, an equally constructive analytic goal appears to be to develop longer, more effective use of alpha functioning with more usable alpha elements and modify the pathological use of projective identification and efforts at discharge so that the Type B communicative mode is maintained in a less pathological form. Such a modification also implies the analyst's development of nonpathological defenses and capacities to manage his own inner mental world. Analytic experience supports Bion's (1977) concept that it is essential that the analyst have the capacities to hold the patient, to maintain a state of reverie, to think symbolically, and to contain and metabolize the patient's projective identifications toward symbolic understanding. In this way, he creates an interaction in which the patient is able to introjectively identify with these attributes of the analyst, to incorporate detoxified projective identifications, and to develop his own alpha functioning.

In a Type B field, there are actually few analyzable derivatives of unconscious mental contents, and interpretations of contents and defenses along usual symbolic lines are virtually never confirmed by the patient, either on the cognitive or introjective-interactional levels (Langs, 1976a, 1976c, 1978b). The analyst must work within the communicative medium of the patient, in which projective identification and the excretion of tension producing stimuli prevail. He must therefore contain these projective identifications, metabolize them toward understanding, and offer interpretations of these interactional efforts, holding the frame steady all the while. Only the maintenance of a secure frame and interpretations of the unconscious functions of the Type B communicative style will adaptively modify its pathological meanings and uses.

As for the analyst, any alteration that he makes in the frame will express his own propensity for a Type B communicative field and pressure the patient in that direction. His own use of pathological projective identification and discharge as reflected in his verbal interventions and other behaviors will have a similar influence. All of his communications to the patient, therefore, must be scrutinized in depth for such expressions. The development of a Type B communicative field calls for *rectification* of an altered frame and a resumption of symbolic-interpretive work by the analyst. It is characteristic of patients who tend to communicate along Type B lines to momentarily shift to the communication of analyzable derivatives in response to the analyst's unneeded alterations in the framework. Such associations, however, are only relevant to the impaired frame and tend to be quite fleeting; these patients will, as a rule, return to action-discharge and projective identification soon after initial efforts to convey their unconscious perceptions and introjections of the erring therapist—their unconscious efforts to cure the therapist. In general, however, it is consistent analytic work in keeping with the attributes of the Type B field, undertaken in a secured framework, that promotes the gradual shift toward a greater use of Type A communications and a lessened use by the patient of pathological projective identifications and other interactional mechanisms. Finally, it appears to me that the Type B field has many of the characteristics of the pathological symbiosis described by Searles (1971).

The Type C Field

In delineating this static, noncommunicative field I would stress at the outset that while the Type A and Type B fields reflect modes of positive communication and are designed to convey derivatives of inner mental states, contents, and mechanisms, the Type C field is designed for noncommunication, for the destruction of meaning, and for the absence of derivative expression. To the extent that such efforts do indeed destroy meaning, relevant interaction, relatedness, and positive communication, they have a negative function and meaning; in this restricted and unusual sense, then, the Type C field reflects and conveys a meaningful mode of relating and ineracting.

The Type C field is characterized by the pervasive absence of interpretable derivatives of unconscious fantasies, memories, and introjects and by the presence of massive defensive barriers. As a rule, the patient's communications are on a manifest content level, and there is a remarkable sense of flatness and emptiness to behaviors and associations. When an adaptive context is evident, the patient's associations do not meaningfully organize around its conscious and unconscious implications; similarly, when the patient's associations seem filled with potential meaning, there will be no adaptive context to serve as the essential organizer. Typically, these patients ruminate emptily for long periods of time or tend to report detailed, extended narratives in a form that renders their possible unconscious meanings indecipherable—the "Type C narrator." Occasionally, there is a circumscribed sense of depth and metaphorical communication; at such times, these patients tend unconsciously to represent the static, noncommunicative, walled-off qualities of their communicative style and the bipersonal field within which it is embedded. Without interpretive efforts directed toward these massive defenses, the therapist or analyst almost never has material available for interpretation. The most common exception occurs only occasionally, when the patient responds to an erroneous interpretation or an unneeded modification in the framework with derivatives related to the unconscious perceptions and introjections of the therapist's communicated and projected pathology, and briefly works over these pathological introjects.

In a Type C field, patient behaviors and associations are essentially intrapsychic and interpersonal barriers, falsifications, and lies (in the nonmoral sense) designed to seal off meaningful mental contents and to maintain the therapeutic interaction and work in a stalemated state. These massive barriers differ in important ways from the defenses utilized by patients in the Type A and Type B communicative fields, and are, I believe, significantly different from the defenses described in the classical psychoanalytic literature.

For example, in a Type A field, defenses and resistances are communicated in both manifest and derivative forms; eventually the unconscious fantasies and memories on which they are based and the sector of unconscious, anxiety provoking material against which they defend are communicated indirectly by the patient and become available for interpretive analytic work. While there are moments of flatness and emptiness in such a field, the patient consistently and spontaneously shifts to derivative and indepth communication that permits symbolic understanding and intervention.

In contrast, in a Type C field, the patient's massive defenses are, most of the time, essentially amorphous and impervious to any possible underlying meaning and derivatives. They are impenetrable barriers whose own essential meanings tend not to be communicated by the patient. Although from time to time he will indeed represent more metaphorically the nature of these defensive walls, he reveals little of the quality of what lies beyond them. Type C patients typically speak from time to time of things being meaningless, of huge brick and concrete walls, of empty vacuums and abysses, of death and coffins and graves, of entombment in metal containers such as army tanks, and of similar representative images. Most of the time, they destroy not only the positive meaning of their words and behaviors, but the basic links between themselves and their objects, including the therapist, and between their conscious awareness and their unconscious inner mental world. Their associations are filled with clichés, the commonplace, and that which is already known, and they turn the analyst's previously meaningful interpretations and formulations into noncommunication, repeating them in endless and empty detail.

Except for the remarkable studies of Bion (1977), the systematic identification of the Type C field has tended to elude analysts. Certainly, analysts in general have been aware of major difficulties in working with certain types of patients and in generating validated interpretations to them. More specifically, it seems likely that some of the narcissistic patients described by Kohut (1971, 1977) and Kernberg (1975), patients who treat their analysts as seemingly nonexistent and who generate intense boredom in these analysts, are operating within a Type C communicative field. Still, the analyst's commitment to search for truth and meaning, plus his possible need to deny his own propensities toward Type C communication, seems to have defensively delayed the delineation of this type of communicative field. Similarly, it may well be that in addition to the patient's own inherent propensities toward this type of communication, those of the analyst play a significant role in the creation of a Type C field. In the main, the analyst mismanages the framework and intervenes on a manifest content level, or he may even use Type One derivatives (specifically, through not working with Type Two derivatives) that actually constitute psychoanalytic clichés, falsifications, and barriers, rather than meaningful interpretations.

It is, I believe, the Type C field in which reversing perspective, as described by Bion (1963), often occurs. Under these conditions, both patient and analyst are aware of the behaviors and words exchanged, and yet the analyst may attempt to ascribe meaning to communications which for the patient are meaningless and function as barriers. At times, of course, the reversing perspective may occur in the other direction: the patient actually communicates in derivative form while the analyst experiences defensiveness and an absence of meaning. Communications in this field often resemble the figures embedded in a field of multi-colored dots used to test individuals for color-blindness. In a Type C field, the analyst or patient may well see the numbers because he is not "colorblind," while the other is only able to see a series of meaningless dots.

Another way to conceptualize the flat and elusive quality of this field is to think of the patient's communications as reflections in a mirror. To treat such unreal images as actualities and attempt to touch them or to experience them in depth would be to fail to recognize the function of the mirror. In such a case the mirror itself is a barrier to reality, actuality, and substance. There is a significant sense of deception and invalidation when the analyst treats as actual the falsified and unreal communications of the patient. In this field the distinction between language and communication becomes evident: while language may indeed serve as a means of conveying meaning, it is evident that its main function may also be the destruction of meaning and the creation of impenetrable barriers to such meaning—that is, noncommunication.

Initial observations suggest that the Type C communicative mode constitutes a massive defensiveness against what may be variously termed a psychotic core, excessive psychic pain, inner mental catastrophe, and inner disorganization. These patients—and therapists—are often quite able to function socially and within work situations as long as they can utilize these massive defensive barriers. Often well-defended latent psychotics and depressives, they may appear to have narcissistic character disorders and to be severely depressed or paranoid-like. As a rule, there are isolated clues to the massive underlying disturbance: either in the reported history of the patient or in an occasional early session during which there is a momentary, and as a rule quite limited, breakthrough of the underlying turmoil. The extremely guarded and suspicious patients destroy the sense of meaning in any effort by the analyst to interpret unconscious contents, doing so because they dread the inner core and need to maintain their rigid, impenetrable defenses. On the other hand, because of wishes for cure and relief, they will accept and work with interpretations related to their massive defensiveness, as long as these are well timed and affectively meaningful; it is at such moments that these patients are likely to meaningfully communicate derivatives of their chaotic, pathological inner mental disturbance, thus permitting momentary periods of deeper interpretive work.

In a Type C field, the interaction is characteristically static and immobile. Very little projective identification and few analyzable derivatives are available from the patient. The field is characterized by its holding qualities. However, while the analyst's main function for long periods may well be that of securing the framework and holding the patient, these patients often show little appreciation of being held (in the analytic sense) and seem instead disconnected and detached because of the destruction of their links to the analyst on so many levels. By distinguishing these holding functions from the analyst's containing capacities, which relate to the introjection of the patient's projective identifications and other communications, we can see that there is also little for the analyst to contain and metabolize. These patients often endure long unproductive analyses or periods of psychotherapy and often generate stalemated treatment situations. Because of these qualities of the Type C patient, the analyst often feels bored, empty, unrelated, and poorly held by the patient as well. It may well be that these patients fall into the group described by Searles (1965, 1970, 1971, 1973a) as in the autistic phase of analysis. In addition to often disregarding the presence of the analyst, the patient will treat him as part of the nonhuman environment.

While I have characterized the Type C field largely in terms of the patient's needs and characteristics, it should be stressed that many analysts and therapists have comparable needs and communicative propensities that contribute significantly to the development of the Type C field. These propensities are manifested in unneeded modifications in the frame which function as massive barriers to meaningful communication in derivative form, and which serve to generate interactional defenses within the patient. Through failing to interpret and through a variety of erroneous interventions, especially those that fail to utilize the adaptive context and derivative communication, these analysts express clichés and false premises. Their ultimately nonmeaningful communications unconsciously invite and encourage Type C relatedness in their patients. Such analysts wish to be held inappropriately by the patient. They fear placing destructive projective identifications into the patient and wish instead to maintain a static field that will reinforce their own massive barriers against the chaotic and unresolved inner mental worlds of both themselves and their patients. As Bion (1977) noted, the container may fear the contained, and the contained may fear the container: each dreading attack, denudation, and destruction. The analyst may therefore dread both containing the patient's pathological mental contents and projecting his own disruptive inner mental world into the patient. Immobilization and noncommunication are rigidly maintained as the only seemingly safe harbor.

Technically, in a Type C field the analyst must wait patiently for unconscious communications from the patient that represent the massive defensive barriers and falsifications characteristic of this mode of communication. When such material appears, often accompanied by some suggestion of the dreaded underlying derivatives, the analyst is in a position to help the patient understand the presence and nature of these massive barriers and to provide hints as to the nature of the underlying contents that they serve to so massively seal off. In general, such efforts are validated largely through the additional revelation of dreaded unconscious derivatives which may then be interpreted cognitively, introjected, metabolized, detoxified, and reprojected in less disruptive form. While efforts to interpret unconscious contents directly are, by and large, doomed to failure, an approach that understands the true nature of the communicative mode of these patients and concentrates on the interpretive modification of these defensive barriers will prove effective in modifying their psychopathology and the aspects of that pathology reflected in their communicative styles.

To carry out such work, however, the analyst must be capable of managing his responses to the patient's barriers and falsifications, his destruction of links, his forms of nonrelating, and his use of falsifying chichés. He must control propensities to modify the frame, to intervene erroneously based on an inappropriate need within himself to suggest meaning in its absence or to jar and stir up the rigid and stalemated Type C patient. The analyst must also be capable of full use of the validating process, lest he continue to intervene in terms of manifest content and Type One derivatives, considering the clichéd and unmeaningful responses of his patient as validation. Such interactions are characteristically filled with self- and mutual-deception, and produce no true insight or inner structural change. In addition to being capable of symbolic communication, such an analyst must be able to tolerate the anxiety and dread related to experiencing the intensely primitive and horrifying inner mental world of these patients and to the threats to his own defenses against surprisingly similar inner contents. He must also analyze and resolve his dread of containing his patient's underlying, destructive projective identifications and his fear of being driven crazy by the patient—an anxiety studied by Searles (1958, 1959). He must master his dread of being attacked and even annihilated by the patient's noncommunication and negative projective identifications, which create a void in which his capacity to think, formulate, and organize—to function meaningfully and relatedly—is being destroyed by the patient's Type C style.

Additional Relevant Literature

In his quite original and creative contribution, "The Role of Illusion in the Analytic Space and Process," Khan (1973) studied the constitution of the analytic space and interaction. He did this initially in terms of the analytic framework as defined by its basic taboos–motility, sight, and touch. These taboos facilitate the patient's expression of his incestuous and parricidal wishes through the word. For Khan, these taboos–in my terms, the ground rules or framework–create an area of illusion in which language may explore and express wish systems beyond mere humiliation and remorse.

Noting the importance of the increment of affect which the area of illusion provides through transference, Khan suggests that Freud (1914), in his basic study of repetition and action as compared to remembering, had stressed the distinction between (a) action as converted into language and affective expression and (b) action that involves muscular and behavioral expression. The former requires a degree of growth and a stability of personality organization for both parties, so that they may work in the area of illusion through symbolic discourse. Acting out is therefore defined as behavior that transgresses symbolic discourse and seeks concrete expression and need fulfillment. Within this framework, Khan offered two clinical vignettes–patients either unable to develop an area of illusion or with whom it was precariously held.

With one patient, he felt that he had been eliminated from the analytic space and had become a passive witness whom the patient victimized with her excruciating pain and inexhaustible demands. He found her unable to relate to her own self-knowledge or to his interpretive interventions. In a dream, the patient observed a stained-glass ceiling of a cathedral crumbling and disintegrating, a communication that Khan saw as a warning of what she was going to do to the illusional space of the analytic situation–disrupt and destroy both the illusion and its structure.

This patient had been involved in direct physical contact with previous analysts and had actually seduced one of them. Khan felt that she was perpetually either acting into language, which he noted was not symbolic discourse, or acting upon life, which constitutes the total negation of any positive experience of relating that might take place in her analysis. Her language failed to assimilate her experiences on the intrapsychic and interpersonal levels, just as her body personalized her instincts and her affects. He soon referred this patient to another analyst. In his discussion of this patient, Khan stressed her total negation of his presence, her negation of herself as a person, and her invention of the fetishistic object of her psyche with which she provoked the analyst in order to destroy rather than be cured. These factors did not allow the space of illusion in the analytic situation to crystallize; instead, the patient seemed to live in a delusional reality that she wished to shed.

The second patient described was unable to respond to the demands of a previous analyst that she should verbalize her feelings and unconscious fantasies; instead, she had traumatized her analyst, pulling her hair, and breaking up the furniture in her consultation room. Khan was able to sympathize with her incapcity to use language as an idiom either to express herself or to relate to him. He permitted open motility and limited touching of his books, and he felt that his capacity to her in the analytic space gradually led her to tolerate him as a separate person, distant but related. He described the development of some distance between himself and the patient and the gradual creation of an illusional space in which the patient could begin to explore language as playing. Her incapacity and rage were valid to Khan as existential facts. Crucial in the developments described in this analysis was the fact that he had not tried to intrude upon these two areas of her experience with interpretations.

Khan discussed his findings in terms of Winnicott's paper (1951) on transitional objects and phenomena, in which the concept of illusion was first introduced to psychoanalysis. Khan stressed the importance of a period of hesitation, as related to playing and transitional phenomena, which provides the matrix for the emergence of the area of illusion. He noted that the concept of resistance in classical analysis takes for granted the capacity to operate in such an area, while his concept of a period of hesitation, borrowed from Winnicott (1951), connotes the emergence of a capacity which is as yet far from established as an ego function. Following Winnicott (1945), Khan also wrote of the importance of the maternal holding environment for the development of these ego functions, noting that moments of illusion develop as mother and child live and experience together.

In concluding, Khan suggested that his first patient had made of language and mentation a frenzied existence that had a momentum all its own; neither vehicles of self-knowledge or relating, they had functioned to negate the reality of the analytic space and the analyst, as well as that of emotionality. This was seen as a usurpation of the legitimate functions of the bodily organs; illusion breaks down and fantasy generates into mentation, while language usurps the functions that belong to organs of experience and discharge—a pathogenic distortion of the ego. Khan stressed the importance of recognizing that with certain patients who have not established this area of illusion, the analyst must technically endeavor to curtail his hypermentation to facilitate the emergence of this area of illusion in the period of hesitation.

It may be seen, then, that Khan has described here, to use the terms developed in his paper, his own recognition that not all patients are able to create a Type A communicative bipersonal field. The particular patients that he described appear to have developed Type B and Type C communicative fields respectively, possibly, however, in part because his own responses had qualities that fostered their specific development. His clinical observations vividly define some of the qualities of these two communicative fields, and his discussion serves to clarify aspects of their genetic basis and the distinctive analytic techniques required by each.

In a separate series of studies, most of them published in Spanish, Liberman (in press) has attempted to delineate styles of psychoanalytic dialogue that he identified in terms of both the patient's ways of offering his material and the analyst's manner of receiving and interpreting it. These styles are correlated with specific ego states, anxieties, and mechanisms of defense and are classified in terms of clinical diagnostic entities, modes of communication, and linguistic styles. The latter are described as occurring in persons looking for unknowns without creating suspense, lyrical, epic, narrative, seeking unknowns and creating suspense, and dramatic with esthetic impact. Each requires a distinctive interventional response by the analyst.

It is beyond the scope of this presentation to further describe the typology developed by Liberman and to compare it with the classification offered here. Perhaps most important for the moment is the recognition that this analyst is attempting to explore a dimension of the analytic interaction that is comparable to the area under investigation in this paper, and that his particular contribution attempts to investigate the interrelatedness of clinical diagnosis, style of defense, mode of communication, linguistic usage, and interpretive response—an endeavor that points to the rich complexities and extensive clinical importance of these studies.*

Clinical Vignettes

Because of my unmodifiable commitment to the total confidentiality of my own therapeutic and analytic work, it will not be feasible for me to present material from this work, even though such an approach would, due to the interactional emphasis, prove especially meaningful. I will instead offer a series of highly condensed clinical segments drawn from supervisory experiences and trust that they will orient the reader sufficiently to discover and elaborate personally the basic concepts presented here. I do plan to offer far more elaborate and specific clinical vignettes in a series of future publications.

Case 1

Mr. A was in psychotherapy with Dr. Z, who had also treated his brother. The early phase of this treatment was characterized by occasional family

*After completing this paper, I found a study by Fiumara (1977) of the development of the symbolic function in infancy and in analysis. Many of her ideas overlap with and extend basic concepts discussed here. Fiumara's work indicates, as does that of Khan (1973), that the Type A field and mode of communication is, indeed, the most mature and optimal. Fiumara is sensitive as well to the roles of the framework and interpretations in creating conditions for possible symbolic communication and alludes to the use of pseudosymbols and falsifications that are protective but inimical to growth.

sessions, contacts with Mr. A's parents, a wide variety of noninterpretive interventions by Dr. Z, and frequent modifications in the basic ground rules. At one point, an emergency arose and it was necessary for Dr. Z to take an extended vacation. Dr. Z explained the details of the illness in one of his parents that had necessitated the trip, and the patient had responded in a rather chaotic manner with a multiplicity of questions; he missed the last session prior to the therapist's trip and two of the three initial sessions when therapy was resumed.

In subsequent sessions, the patient was rather directly demanding and provocative of Dr. Z, who attempted to interpret these reactions as a reflection of Mr. A's anger over the unexpected interruption. There was no sense of validation of these interventions: the patient tended to deny hostile feelings regarding his therapist's trip and instead behaved quite provocatively at home—to the point of evoking urgent telephone calls from Mr. A's mother to Dr. Z. This situation remained chaotic until Dr. Z began to refuse to talk to Mr. A's parents on the telephone and interpreted directly to the patient that he seemed involved in efforts to either destroy the treatment process itself or to so disturb Dr. Z that he would feel inordinately frustrated, angry, or disorganized. To this, the patient responded by remembering how just prior to the session, he had fought with his mother over a petty issue, refusing to allow her to offer any possible compromise and refusing to even understand what he now recognized were her rather sensible arguments. He had virtually driven her up a wall.

As a tentative thesis, I would suggest that through a variety of noninterpretive interventions and inappropriate modifications of the framework, this therapist was utilizing his patient as an inappropriate container for his own pathological projective identifications (Langs, 1976a) and that his own propensity to create a Type B communicative field had reinforced the patient's tendencies in this direction. As a result, this bipersonal field was characterized by unconscious exchanges of projective and introjective identifications, and pathological reprojections, without insight or control in either participant. Efforts by the therapist to treat the patient's behaviors and associations as symbolic communications, based on the mistaken implicit hypothesis that a Type A field prevailed, were met with nonconfirmation and the intensification of disruptive behaviors and projective identifications by the patient. There is evidence too that while this therapist considered his interventions themselves to be symbolic communications, they actually constituted a vehicle for pathological projective identifications on his part—a means of discharging inner tension rather than offering true cognitive insight.

Under the influence of supervision, the therapist undertook extensive efforts toward self-analysis and toward rectifying the frame. Further, by limiting his interventions to the symbolic interpretation of the patient's pathological projective identifications, he found derivative, symbolic validation, as illustrated in the patient's recollection of his quarrel with his mother. In addition to offering cognitive insight, this interpretation provided the patient with an opportunity (a) to experience the therapist's capacity to metabolize and understand his potentially disruptive projective identifications and (b) to receive a reprojection that had been detoxified. Subsequent associations alluded to a teacher who was able to handle another instructor's class when it got out of control and included references to the calming effect on all concerned. This positive introject also helped the patient better manage his own inner impulses and propensities toward pathological projective identification. With additional working through, his behavior calmed down considerably both in the treatment situation and at home.

The patient began a session some months later by wondering if his mother had again called the therapist. He had been anxious in a restaurant while eating with his parents, and for the first time his mother was tolerant; Mr. A felt that this reflected the direct influence of the therapist. The patient had two oral presentations pending and wanted the therapist to tell him how to manipulate his professors so that he would not have to present in front of the classes. One of the teachers might understand, but the other would be very destructive. When the therapist remained silent, the patient kept asking what he should do and demanded an answer. The therapist then intervened and noted that the patient appeared to have assumed that he, the therapist, had spoken to his mother and had told her how to handle him, and that on this basis, Mr. A felt that he, the therapist, should advise him about the school problem as well.

The patient now alluded to past telephone conversations between the therapist and his mother and said that on the one hand, the therapist did not like to be rude, but on the other hand, he would not violate his patient's trust. The patient had spoken to a friend (a peer with whom he had an evident latent homosexual relationship) rather extensively about his own therapy and about his fantasies of collusion between his therapist and his parents. He thought of his mother and father as weak and incompetent fools.

The therapist pointed out that the patient had very intense feelings regarding the prior contacts with his parents and seemed quite infuriated by them. Mr. A then insisted on his trust of the therapist, but after some elaboration in this direction, he suddenly indicated that these conversations had indeed been a violation—something like his parents coming into his room and opening his drawers but finding nothing. He turned to the onset of his symptoms, which included intense anxiety when speaking in class and when eating, and wondered if he could now understand what had really happened.

In this hour, we can see continued efforts by the patient to create with the therapist a Type B field in which the discharge of tension and immediate gratification would prevail. When the therapist did not respond in kind, and implied as well that the frame was now secure in regard to the confidentiality of the treatment, the patient shifted to symbolic communication and the bipersonal field took on characteristics of a Type A field. In the adaptive context of the previous alteration of the framework and its present rectification, the patient offered Type Two derivatives that implied an unconscious perception of the deviant therapist as one who was gratifying unconscious homosexual fantasies and defending himself against them as well, whatever additional homosexual gratification and defense the arrangements and qualities of the interaction had for Mr. A himself. The patient also communicated his unconscious perception of himself and the therapist in this context as foolish and incompetent. With the further effort at interpretation, the patient modified his massive denial regarding the therapist's violation of his confidentiality and conveyed this realization through a simile. This constituted a symbolic representation of a type previously quite unusual for this patient. Thus, there was a growing change not only in this patient's behaviors, but also in his mode of interacting and in the form of his communication. I would view the patient's return to his initial symptoms and his renewed search for understanding as a reflection of his hope for more insightful resolution of the relevant unconscious fantasies, memories, conflicts, etc.—a hope based on the growing development between himself and his therapist of a Type A communicative field.

I would make a particular point of the patient's comment that the violation in confidentiality was something like his parents' searching his drawers and finding nothing. In addition to extensively exchanging pathological projective identifications, this patient and therapist had created interactional interludes which were quite static and empty. These occurred despite the therapist's efforts at intervening. The patient's unconscious communication here seems to stress the extent to which pathological projective identification and mutual acting out, as well as clichéd interventions, are designed on one level to create voids and absence of true meaning.

Case 2

Mr. B was in psychotherapy with Dr. Y. During the initial months, his sessions were characterized by lengthy and detailed narratives with no apparent adaptive context. He would talk of both major and sometimes seemingly insignificant problems on his job, of the details of his sexual exploits, and of a variety of problems with his male peers. Efforts by the therapist, based largely on Type One derivatives, to suggest general unconscious hostility, sexual and bodily anxieties, and competitiveness with his peers, and additional attempts to relate these themes and anxieties to the therapeutic relationship, generated both responses that were flat and nonvalidating, and new lengthy tales.

Soon, the therapist became relatively silent. When the patient hinted at a possible source of anxiety, Dr. Y suggested concerns about treatment and anxieties about becoming involved. In general, the patient rather flatly acknowledged such worries, but had little more to say. In one session during this period, the patient began his hour by describing his sense of invincibility and how readily he gets past dangers and problems: he had once been suspended from his job and had neatly manipulated his reinstatement. He had nicely evaded serving in the armed forces. After describing in some detail the relevant experiences, he alluded to an address before a meeting of the tenants in his apartment house. He was the vice president of the tenant organization, but the president, frightened because a tenant had been killed in the building, had turned the meeting over to the patient. Under these pressures, Mr. B felt weak and forced to reveal himself. Although that night he had had some kind of homosexual dream, he denied homosexual fears and went on in some detail regarding his preference for women, noting, however, that he had had many strange fantasies about them. He concluded this hour by stating that he wanted to get to know himself better, but somehow it all seemed so pointless.

In the following session the patient went on in great detail about his job, about games and roles, about not knowing what to believe and about how disturbed he was with his way of life. His parents had never helped him discover himself and he had had to learn how to meet his own needs. Again in some detail, he described a sexual relationship with a girlfriend who seldom talked to him and who had been shocked when he revealed his own secrets, including his fears of impregnating her. Sometimes he liked women that he could dominate even when he was afraid of them. The next few hours were similarly ruminative.

In assessing this clinical situation, there was evidence that both patient and therapist had initially created a Type C field in which the patient generated extended narratives without a relevant adaptive context or meaningful bridges to the therapeutic relationship. It seems likely that his use of language in these hours was designed as a barrier and falsification with which he covered underlying homosexual fantasies and perceptions pertinent to his relationship with the therapist. Unconsciously, the therapist had attempted to give these manifest associations pertinence and meaning, without, however, alluding to the underlying homosexual problems. His interventions had proved to serve as clichés that reinforced the patient's own facade and intensified the Type C qualities of the bipersonal field. The patient felt disillusioned and even bored at times, while the therapist felt somewhat confused and distracted, finding little to grasp in the patient's long tales.

Under the influence of supervision, the therapist became relatively silent and intervened occasionally in respect to the patient's needs for defensive obstacles. While these interventions did not sufficiently utilize the various metaphorical representations of these barriers communicated by the patient, unconsciously they sufficiently conveyed the therapist's willingness to modify the Type C field into a Type A mode so that the patient responded with the main session described here.

In this particular hour, unconsciously the patient described the false sense of invincibility that one can derive from impenetrable Type C field barriers. He implied, however, that such manipulations leave one vulnerable and proceeded to talk of the tenant's meeting—a situation with a background of violence in which he was forced into the spotlight. This appeared to be, in part, the patient's experience of the therapist's recent interventions, and it conveyed the therapeutic anxiety characteristic of a Type A field. Compromising but endeavoring to communicate, the patient then referred vaguely to a homosexual dream, but immediately denied homosexual anxieties. He turned to fantasies of women and yet recognized that something was awry. He went on in some detail, indicated his wish to get to know himself better, and when the therapist failed to intervene, he became disillusioned. In the following hour, there was a static and flat quality, some indirect, Type Two derivative allusions to the therapist's failure to help the patient discover himself and to an unconscious perception of Dr. Y's dread of containing Mr. B's primitive inner mental world—a dread undoubtedly shared by Mr. B as well.

In the adaptive context of the therapist's silent listening and interventions regarding the patient's undue defensiveness, this session conveys in Type Two derivative form the patient's fear of revealing himself within the therapeutic situation and the underlying violence-related and homosexual fantasies, perceptions, and anxieties. The patient had offered a bridge to the treatment situation, and the therapist should have interpreted that Mr. B was experiencing pressures in the treatment situation to reveal himself and that he—the patient—sensed the background of violence and homosexual fears which he tried to obliterate through vagueness and a shift to thoughts about women. In this way, the therapist would have responded with a cognitive symbolic interpretation of his own to the patient's shift toward a Type A mode of communication. In the communicative realm, this would have reinforced the patient's development of a Type A field and conveyed the therapist's capacity to contain and metabolize the patient's primitive inner mental fantasies and perceptions, his valid unconscious perceptions of the therapist's anxieties, and the symbolic mode of communication. Based on what we must postulate as his own need for massive defensiveness and noncommunication, the therapist failed to intervene, and the patient responded with relatively embedded or concealed derivatives—centered for the moment on the therapist's inappropriate anxieties and failures to contain. When the therapist was unable to understand the meanings of those latter communications, the patient shifted back to the Type C mode for several sessions.

Case 3

Mrs. C was a fifty-eight-year-old woman in treatment with Dr. X. For some months therapy had been based on a so-called supportive approach, filled with such alterations in the framework as last-minute changes in the hours, self-revelations by the therapist, and extensive use of noninterpretive interventions. There had been, however, no sense of progress, and the patient's difficulties with an insensitive husband and a drug-addicted daughter continued to plague her and to generate repeated episodes of depression.

Under the influence of supervision, the therapist, over several weeks, rectified the frame and initiated efforts to intervene, primarily on an interpretive level. The patient's sessions, which had been quite disorganized and seemingly meaningless to the therapist, became filled with affect and a unique sense of meaning.

During one hour at this time, the patient tearfully spoke of her drug-addicted daughter and her need for proper limits. She had visited another daughter and for the first time had spoken meaningfully to her and experienced a sense of warmth. The patient had felt a great sense of relief, but there had been something disquieting and strange about the experience. Together with this daughter, the patient for the first time confronted her husband regarding his drug-addicted child and he became disorganized and wanted to leave. When this daughter had been ill as a child, her husband had been unavailable. During the pregnancy with this child, the patient had nearly suffered a miscarriage but her obstetrician had put her to bed and changed her medication, thereby saving the situation.

At this point in the session, the patient asked the therapist if she should take medication. He answered that the patient was now expressing feelings she had previously suppressed and which both she and her family feared, and that now, in response, she wanted to run away from them again. Mrs. C then said she had been thinking of a vacation, but was afraid of leaving her addicted daughter in the house, since she and her friends would wreck it. The patient recalled a similar discussion early in treatment and remembered the therapist as saying it would have been better for everyone if the house had caught fire when the daughter was in it. The therapist responded that the patient was becoming quite afraid of the feelings she was now experiencing in treatment and that she had a need to generate an image of him as unfeeling and destructive. The patient ended the hour by saying that she had been afraid that the therapist would give up on her and was relieved that he hadn't; she felt that she would be able to make it someday.

In the adaptive context of the rectified frame, we may sense the therapeutic regression and anxiety developing in this patient as she shifted from a Type C to a Type A communicative field. Prior to the corrective efforts of the therapist, Mrs. C and Dr. X had used language primarily for noncommunication, and the bipersonal field had a distinctly static quality. The therapist's seeming kindnesses unconsciously were designed to help cover over his patient's inner destructiveness and, in all probability, parallel problems within himself. They were part of an effort at creating falsifications that could conceal far more painful truths.

In a sense, then, it is no coincidence that the patient responded to the securing of the frame with the communication of Type Two derivatives related to her unconscious perception and introjection of the therapist's initial stance and its alteration. Her reference to her husband's fear of the truth and wish to flee, along with her request for medication, contains in derivative form both (a) her dread of her own inner mental world and a Type A communicative field, plus related efforts to shift back to the Type C field through the use of medication as an obliterating agent, and (b) the therapist's previous dread of these same inner contents and his reinforcement of the patient's massive defenses.

The patient's validating responses to the therapist's initial interventions, however lacking in specifics, demonstrates how the interface of the bipersonal field shifts significantly toward the pathology of the patient in the absence of countertransference-based inputs from the therapist. In derivative form, the patient now communicated both her dread of inner devastation and her fear of her uncontrolled destructiveness toward her addicted daughter. It is no coincidence that the patient attempted to project and projectively identify these impulses into the therapist and that, in addition, she communicated these anxieties in the form of a fabrication (however destructive the therapist's attitude had been toward both the patient and this daughter, he was certain that he had never consciously expressed a blatantly murderous wish toward either of them).

It appears that the patient wished once again to utilize the therapist in creating a misalliance and bastion through which the truth might still remain unknown. In this situation, however, it is quite evident that the patient's defenses are no longer in the form of amorphous and impenetrable barriers, but instead quite clearly reveal both the underlying nature of the defense itself and the fantasies and impulses that are being defended against. It is, as I said above, the presence of such derivatives in the face of the patient's defensiveness, and their analyzability as Type Two derivatives within a specific adaptive context, that characterizes resistances in the Type A field. Showing some appreciation for the symbolic qualities of the patient's communications, the therapist interpreted aspects of the patient's defenses and anxieties, and, despite the fact that his intervention once again fell short of the specificity and depth required in this situation, the patient responded with a sense of appreciation for the therapist's perseverance and, by implication, for their shared capacity to modify the Type C field into a more hopeful, however painful, Type A Mode.

Case 4

As a final illustration, I will turn to the psychotherapy of Mr.D, who had been treated some years earlier in a clinic for what had appeared to be an ambulatory schizophrenic syndrome with multiple obsessions, phobias, and depression. He was now in twice-weekly psychotherapy with a private therapist who essentially had offered the patient a secure frame and hold, occasional general interpretations based on Type One derivatives, and a sense of tolerance for the patient's anxieties, along with some capacity to contain Mr. D's disruptive projective identifications—although these were seldom metabolized toward interpretive insights. Over many months, the patient's symptoms had gradually improved to the point where he appeared capable of confronting his dreaded phobic situations and his obsession seemed no longer horrifying, overintense, or disruptive to his functioning. It seemed evident that termination was somewhere invisibly in the air, although neither patient or therapist had as yet suggested it.

During one session at this time, the patient meticulously detailed a journey that he had taken recently by railroad in connection with his job as a salesman. He described the experience several times over and emphasized how fine he felt and how different it was from years ago when he would panic and fear being overwhelmed as the train moved along, or even worse, getting upset that it might suddenly break down and get stuck. His girlfriend of several years had been surprised that he had handled this particular trip so well, and the patient spent much of the final part of the session asking the therapist what he thought about what his patient had accomplished.

During the next hour, Mr. D described another trip in some detail. On this occasion, the train had been stuck in a tunnel, and the patient had been momentarily frightened, but then felt quite well. For a moment, he felt that it was not himself who was on that train, but this passed, as did another transient feeling that the train was not really stuck–that nothing was happening. He then ruminated at length over earlier episodes in which he had been stuck on trains and elevators, and the type of panic and anxiety that he had experienced. He stressed the extent to which this was not present now and how this characterized him in the past, not in present. In response to continued inquiries as to the therapist's thoughts about all of this, Dr. W suggested that the patient seemed to have mastered his bodily anxieties and fears of disintegration. The patient felt quite reassured and repeated his therapist's formulation in several different versions.

During the next hour, the patient ruminated in some detail about how well he was feeling. He recalled a dream in which a young man, E, who had recently been fired at the patient's place of business, invited Mr. D to undress and get into bed with him. He suggested that they perform fellatio on each other. The dream reminded him of homosexual fantasies and anxieties that he had had some years back, although, he said, he had none of these feelings in the present. He had enjoyed working with E and would miss him. E was very good at making up stories and at hiding from the boss, and all this reminded the patient of times when he would lock himself in the bathroom at work in order not to be disturbed. After ruminating about his job, the patient asked Dr. W what he thought about the dream, and the therapist remained silent. The patient ended the hour by ruminating further about his job.

During the next session, the patient described a battle with his girlfriend and his rage at her for always changing the subject and not facing issues. He spoke in some detail again about the firing of E and his own concerns about suddenly losing his job. For him, it would be an unreal experience, and he would just disappear for a few weeks if it were to happen. On the other hand, he might want to come to his sessions; he would be afraid of losing the therapist's support. Here, the therapist intervened and suggested that the patient was concerned about the eventual termination of his treatment and that he had a need to put such a possibility at a distance and create barriers to the anger and turmoil it would create for him. The patient stated that he had had a strange thought that the therapist might want to end the treatment. He had had a fleeting image of going berserk but had then gotten himself under control and really didn't feel worried about it. Besides, it was too soon to end treatment, and he really didn't think that the therapist would just kick him out.

In the next hour, the patient reported a dream about a man who seemed to be chasing him out of his own apartment. There was some sense of a sexual threat, something like the danger of rape, but then the patient had found himself in an empty vault with the door closed and he felt safe and protected. The patient ruminated about a man at the bank that he mistrusted and about details of his job. He had had thoughts of changing his bank because he no longer felt appreciated as a customer, but he had really put the matter quite out of his mind. Often, when he felt conflicted, he could make his mind a blank and feel relief. The therapist pointed out that the patient had a tendency to seal himself off from dangers and to seek safety in voids; he suggested that this was reflected not only in his dream but in the way in which he was communicating in the session. The patient responded by recalling childhood fears of bombs and explosions, and by remembering fantasies about attacking his boss for firing E—fantasies that he had forgotten until that moment. In a rather tentative way, he wondered if all this had something to do with the possibility of his treatment's ending; he did feel much better and perhaps it was time to think about it after all.

This material illustrates the development of a Type C communicative field, largely based on the patient's intense need for unmodifiable barriers, an impenetrable container for his psychotic core. While the therapist appears initially to have contributed to the Type C field by attempting to interpret contents that had been communicated by the patient largely as a means of denying any difficulty and creating an impenetrable obstacle to the underlying anxieties and fantasies, we see in the sequence that Dr. W soon recognized that such interventions were not being confirmed and seemed to have little effect on the patient.

In the adaptive context of anxieties regarding eventual termination, this material initially served as a distracting fabrication designed to avoid this subject and its ramifications for the patient. Perhaps in part because the therapist introduced bodily anxieties which the patient introjected as Dr. W's unconscious homosexual difficulties, Mr. D did report an overtly homosexual dream. However, despite a few fragmented derivative associations—e.g., the firing of Mr. E—the material remained quite flat and was without a clearcut adaptive context (the day residue related to Mr. E's loss of the job actually represented in derivative form and covered the more significant concern about termination which the patient essentially avoided). The subsequent associations did not generate derivative meaning. In this session, the patient represented the Type C field symbolically through the references to hiding and locking himself in the bathroom, but the therapist failed to intervene. As a result, the following hour was quite ruminative, although the patient did eventually produce rather remote and thin derivatives related to possible termination. When the therapist intervened in this regard, the patient responded with initial validation and then denial.

During the following hour, there was a shift toward Type A communication, especially after the therapist interpreted the patient's use of denial, emptiness, and barriers. The dream itself appears to represent fantasies and anxieties related to the possible termination of the treatment, as do the additional associations prior to the therapist's next intervention. Following that comment, the patient found a means of representing his dread of losing control of his explosive and primitive inner mental world; he then quickly reconstituted.

This sequence reflects, first, the type of underlying material that tends to be revealed by patients in a Type C field when their massive defensiveness and use of fabrication to generate nonmeaning are pointed out to them. Secondly, we see that in a Type C field dreams are quickly sealed off and that even when there are some derivative associations and a meaningful adaptive context, the patient remains rather constricted and fearful. Through the therapist's proper intervening, it appears that this patient was able to express aspects of his dreaded inner mental world and that he felt capable of managing these disruptive contents. Subsequent sessions suggest that this was not a return to rigid Type C barriers, but instead, that it represented a greater degree of flexibility, a softening of his defenses, and a capacity to better manage the inner contents experienced when he momentarily modified these defenses. Earlier in treatment, such breakthroughs of explosive content were followed by repeated ruminative sessions and intense efforts at noncommunication and barrier formation, including rather striking use of denial and projection. At this point in treatment, the therapist felt that these efforts had been considerably modified in a positive direction.

Earlier in treatment, this patient had repeatedly objected to the therapist's interventions on the grounds that he—the patient—made it a practice to conceal his most important communications from the therapist for several weeks at a time. As a result, since every effort at interpretation undertaken by this therapist was actually based on accepting the patient's ruminations, which served essentially as fabrications or lies designed to cover the painful underlying truths, his comments were met with ridicule and refutation. The therapist soon became aware of the significance of this mechanism, and began to interpret its function, no longer endeavoring to interpret content. In a manner that cannot be detailed here, these efforts to deal first with the patient's communicative mode significantly modified this defense to the point that the patient was able to significantly alter its use. During the period within which the patient maintained this mechanism, the therapist felt enormously frustrated: he was working with images that the patient would immediately make disappear by telling him that these were not his important associations, and he experienced himself as if he were under a vicious attack designed to destroy his integrity, his capacity to interpret, and perhaps even his own sanity. While I will not attempt to further document this therapeutic interlude, I refer to it in concluding these clinical vignettes in an effort to characterize the underlying envy and destructiveness that prevails in a Type C communicative field, the truly deceptive qualities of the patient's associations as they function to destroy meaning and relatedness rather than to generate it, the ungraspable mirror image quality of these associations, and the absurdity of attempting to interpret such contents in light of their true nature and functions.

Concluding Comments

It is my impression that the delineation of three major communicative styles and fields has extensive clinical and theoretical ramifications. Investigations of the communicative properties of the bipersonal field not only shed light on the intrapsychic and interactional realms, and their interplay, but also generate an additional level of conceptualization that extends beyond these two familiar spheres. I shall therefore conclude this presentation with a brief listing of some of the major implications of these concepts.

1. Basic to the conceptualization of communicative bipersonal fields is the listening process. In this respect, consistent efforts must be maintained to identify the adaptive context for the patient's associations and behaviors, and it is essential to organize this material in terms of manifest content and Type One and Type Two derivatives. In addition, one needs sensitivity to interactional mechanisms and a capacity to experience, metabolize, and understand the patient's projective identifications, validating all such experiences through the patient's verbal associations. These listening, experiencing and organizing abilities must be applied not only to the patient's communications, but also to those of the therapist as well. In this manner, it becomes feasible to monitor fluctuations in the nature of the communicative field and to identify the main instigator for such shifts.

2. While it appears evident that the Type A communicative mode is essential for the therapist or analyst, and represents the greatest degree of maturation for both patient and therapist, insightful therapeutic work is feasible in each communicative field. Such endeavors, however, require a symbolic interpretive capacity in the therapist, without which he will be unable to interpret the patient's unconscious fantasies, memories, and introjects as they appear in a Type A field related to the patient's intrapsychic conflicts and anxieties; neither will he be able to properly metabolize and interpret projective identifications in the Type B field nor the negation of meaning and use of amorphous barriers in the Type C field. Inherent to such an interpretive approach is the generation of positive, ego building introjective identifications that occur quite unconsciously in the course of the therapeutic interaction. Insight and positive introjection go hand and hand, and are the essential basis of adaptive structural changes (Langs, 1967a, 1976c).

3. The intrapsychic and interactional nature of defensive formations

are distinctive to each communicative field. In a Type A field we find the array of defenses described in the classical psychoanalytic literature—repression, displacement, isolation, and the like. However, in addition to their intrapsychic basis, they are open to interactional influence in that both pressures toward, and models of, defensiveness and resistance may be offered to the patient by the therapist, generating what I have termed *interactional defenses and resistances* (Langs, 1976a, 1976c). In the Type A field, the patient characteristically expresses these resistances in a form that includes the communication of Type Two derivatives related both to the unconscious meaning and functions of the defense-resistance itself and the unconscious fantasies, memories, and introjects which are being defended against—most often in relation to the analyst. There is a sense of depth to the patient's resistances and they are essentially analyzable over a reasonable period of time.

In a Type B field, the major defenses will be interactional, with intrapsychic underpinnings. They will take the form of defensive utilization of projective identification as a means of disburdening the psyche of anxiety and placing intolerable fantasies and introjects into the object—here, from patient into therapist (or the reverse). However, these defensive projective identifications have in common with the resistances seen in the Type A field that they serve a positive communicative function, so that the patient's behaviors and verbal associations tend ultimately to reveal the unconscious nature, meaning, and function of the defensive projective identification and the underlying contents that the patient wishes to externalize.

In a Type C field, however, the patient's defenses and resistances have a distinct sense of flatness and emptiness and are in themselves basically designed for noncommunication, absence of understanding, falsification, and impenetrable barrier. For long periods in such therapies, there are few, if any, interpretable derivatives related to these defenses and the disturbing contents that they seal off. At best, the Type C patient will communicate occasional metaphors—usually Type One derivatives—with which they represent the nature of their communicative style. It is therefore not feasible to interpret these defense-resistances in depth or, as a rule, in terms of a specific adaptive context and Type Two derivatives.

4. The therapist's basic interventions are also distinctive for each bipersonal field. In the Type A field, his basic tools involve the maintenance of a secure framework and the use of interpretations and reconstructions derived largely from Type Two derivatives—unconscious fantasies and perceptions—related to the therapeutic interaction, in terms of both transference and nontransference. Such work will center upon the analysis of defenses and resistance on the first level, and core unconscious fantasies, memories, and introjects on the second.

In a Type B field, the basic tool is the acceptance and containment, metabolism and understanding, and interpretation of the patient's projective identifications in terms of their defensive and core meanings. In this field, the maintenance of a secure frame is also essential; the work proceeds from resistances to core contents as it does in the Type A field. However, while Type Two derivatives are the main material for interpretation in the Type A field, in the Type B field much of the analytic work is based on the patient's projective identifications. These interactional projections can, however, be organized around meaningful adaptive contexts and thus permit dynamic and genetic interpretations, much of it once again related to the therapeutic interaction in terms of both transference and nontransference.

In the Type C field, specific adaptive contexts are rare, as are Type Two derivatives. Much of the therapeutic work is based on the patient's projective identification into the therapist of meaninglessness, and his use of falsifications, noncommunication, and opaque barriers. The interpretive work must therefore utilize Type One derivatives in the form of metaphors from the patient related to these defensive barriers and the efforts at noncommunication; the effective interpretation of these resistances will also permit periods of interpretation and reconstruction of the emerging material.

5. It follows from this discussion that we can no longer maintain the unitary model of the course of a satisfactory psychoanalysis or psychotherapy, of the indications for termination, and of the definition of *cure*. To date, the classical psychoanalytic literature has delineated these factors in terms of the Type A field, correctly suggesting that with such patients the analytic work concentrates on the analysis of transference (and nontransference) in terms of resistances, core fantasies, memories, and introjects, current dynamics, and reconstructions of significant past experiences and responses to them. True structural change is defined accordingly and derives primarily from the cognitive insight accrued from these interpretive and recontructive efforts, and secondarily from the positive introjections of the analyst that occur spontaneously and unconsciously in the course of such work. Termination is indicated at the point of symptom relief based on the working through of the relevant areas of conflict and disturbance, and on the establishment of stabilized insight and other inner adaptive changes. Such accomplishments imply a diminution in the use of pathological defenses and an improved capacity to manage one's inner mental world.

In a Type B field, much of the analytic work is done through the metabolism and interpretation of the patient's pathological projective identifications, efforts that include the interpretation of their defensive and unconscious content dimensions. In the course of a successful treatment, there is a modification in the extent to which the patient utilizes pathological projective identifications. This is accomplished in part through the interpretation of their nature and function and in part through the introjective identification by the patient of the constructively modified projective contents as they are validly reprojected by the therapist into the patient. This interactional process generates constructive introjective identifications based on therapist introjects, process introjects, and the reception of detoxified reprojections. Overall, the therapeutic process may be seen as achieving a diminution in the use of pathological projective identifications and a modification or detoxification of the contents and inner states so projected. In addition, from time to time, there will be opportunities for the interpretation and reconstruction of symbolic communications and Type Two derivatives as well.

In all, then, the goal of analysis or therapy with these patients is symptom relief based primarily on insightful and structuralized modifications of their use of pathological projective identifications and secondarily on alterations of the related pathological unconscious fantasies, memories, and introjects. With some Type B patients, it may be feasible to shift their basic mode to Type A communication, while with others, the outcome may take the form of more frequent use of Type A communications along with a less pathological use of the Type B mode. It is to be stressed that the pursuit of cognitive insights and symbolic interpretations of the patient's use of interactional mechanisms is a *sine qua non*; it is fundamental to the constructive cognitive and identificatory changes that take place within this field. My initial impression is that both definitive reconstructions and specific interpretations of unconscious fantasies, memories, and introjects, will be feasible somewhat less often than with Type A patients.

In the Type C communicative field, the goal is to analyze and work through the efforts by these patients to destroy meaning, relatedness, and communication, and to maintain their impervious barriers against a highly disturbed inner core. Interpretive efforts concentrate on the metaphors of these defenses and the patient's interactional projections of nonmeaning. From time to time, as the patient begins to modify the rigidity and destructiveness of these defenses, the primitive underlying contents–unconscious fantasies, memories, and introjects–will be expressed in derivative form and will lend themselves to interpretation and reconstruction. However, as one would expect, such interventions are less common with these patients than in the other two communicative fields. Termination with Type C patients is based both on the gradual modification of their rigid defenses plus their needs to destroy meaning and falsify, and on the periodic interpretation and reconstruction of the underlying contents and processes. Both cognitive and identificatory factors are involved, but an initial impression suggests that most of these patients maintain this communicative mode throughout their treatment, albeit in a gradually less pathological form. Occasionally, there may be a major shift to the Type A form.

6. We may briefly consider the interaction between patient and analyst, or therapist, based on their individual preferred communicative mode. A Type A therapist will feel adequately held and stimulated by a Type A patient and should work well in developing interpretations and reconstructions of the patient's Type Two derivative symbolic communications. Potentially, such a therapist should be capable, with a Type B patient, of containing, metabolizing, and interpreting the patient's projective identifications, though there is a danger of countertransference-based defensiveness and other inappropriate reactions. At times this type of therapist may feel

and be somewhat overwhelmed by these interactional pressures. A common countertransference problem in this symbolically functioning Type A therapist takes the form of a failure to consciously recognize the patient's interactional projections and a related tendency to disregard the interactional sphere.

Finally, with the Type C patient there may be a strong sense of boredom, and a possibility of failure to understand the true nature and functions of the patient's associations. A Type A therapist may have difficulty in empathizing with a Type C patient and may have problems in recognizing the need of such a patient to destroy meanings and to erect impenetrable barriers. Such therapists may be inclined to attribute and interpret meaning where none is intended, experiencing the reversing-perspective and embedded-figure types of phenomena referred to earlier in this paper. There may be countertransference-based hostility and seductiveness in Type A therapists with Type C patients, as well as efforts unconsciously designed to rupture their most frustrating defensive alignment. The implicit envy and destructiveness in the Type C form of communication may evoke countertransference-based reactions of various types within a Type A analyst. If such a therapist comes to terms with the patient's communicative mode, he can then become capable of patient and meaningful interventions when indicated.

The Type B therapist will tend to be bored by a Type A patient, will have difficulties in interpreting and reconstructing, and will tend to use language as a means of discharging his own anxieties and as a form of interactional projection into his patients. The therapist's communicative mode will exert great pressures on the Type A patient to shift toward a responsive Type B mode or a defensive Type C form. Because virtually all therapists maintain an ideal of Type A functioning, it is often difficult to recognize one's own tendencies toward Type B communication through the discharge use of language and mismanagements of the framework that are consciously intended and mistaken as validly therapeutic. In particular, the development of a Type B mode of communication in a patient should direct the therapist toward the possibility of similar propensities within himself, although in general, each therapist should undertake an extensive self-examination to determine his own communicative style and its fluctuations.

With the Type C patient, the Type B therapist is likely to feel quite bored and empty. He will tend to be prone to traumatic sexual and aggressive and other projective identifications into the Type C patient in an effort to rupture his defenses and to evoke responsive interactional projections.

A Type C therapist will be threatened by both the Type A and Type B patient. The former, with his symbolic communications and therapeutic regressive anxiety, will constitute a threat to the Type C therapist who dreads the inner mental world of both his patient and himself. These patients generate meaning and communication, and the Type C therapist will unconsciously intervene in a manner designed to destroy such meaning, to falsify, and to evoke amorphous barriers. Similarly, with a Type B patient who is generating meaningful and anxiety provoking projective identifications, the Type communication, and anxiety required for effective analytic work in such a field.

These are but a few of the implications of the present formulations, many of which deserve extensive clinical investigation. In this context, I am reminded that there are those who feel that psychoanalysis is in a state of basic consolidation or even stalemate (see Rangell, 1975), and others who find analysis to be in a state of considerable flux and creativity (see Green, 1975). In addition to hoping that I have prompted the reader to take a fresh look at his interaction with his patients, I hope also to have demonstrated that there are many original and imaginative thinkers in psychoanalysis today—some of whom have been mentioned in the course of this presentation. Psychoanalysts should master their propensities for the Type B and Type C modes of communication, not only with their patients, but in their work at large, and should be capable of maintaining a Type A field in which they welcome new and even strange ideas and concepts, and the growth-promoting anxieties and potential reorganization so contained (see Stone, 1975). It is on this note that I conclude with the following:

Medium is message;
Medium determines message;
Medium must be analyzed before message.

Postscript

Clinical investigations which have followed this contribution have lead to additional insights. For the sake of completeness, I will briefly list the most salient of these;

1. There are *two* basic communicative styles, Type A and Type C. Thus, there are truth tellers and liers, each defined in terms of the way in which they respond to activated adaptive (intervention) contexts. The Type A patient works over these truths in a meaningful manner on a derivative level, while the Type C patient fails to do so and instead creates barriers and falsifications. However, it should be understood that these two basic communicative styles are on a continuum. Thus, the highly defended Type A patient, who shows meaningful derivative resistances, is often difficult to distinguish from a Type C, non derivative-defensive-resistant patient who is beginning to make efforts at minimal meaningful communication.

2. On this basis, Type B communication has been divided into two types: (1) The Type B-A patient who engages in pathological projective identification within the framework of a meaningful communicative network; and (2) the Type B-C patient who engages in pathological interactional projections in the absence of meaningful communication (i.e., a directly represented adaptive context and a coalesceable derivative network). With the

Type B-A patient, containing and interpreting is carried out relatively easily by the therapist, while the Type B-C patient appears to wish unconsciously to basically parasitize and destroy the therapist and the therapeutic situation. These patients, who often suffer from certain types of borderline and schizophrenic syndromes, are among the most difficult to engage in psychotherapy or psychoanalysis. They wish only for a pathological symbiosis or parasitic relationship with the therapist, and continuously destroy meaningful relatedness.

3. Through the communicative approach, truth has been defined as the actualities of the unconscious communicative interaction. Thus, the truth as it pertains to the patient's neurosis involves his derivative responses to activated adaptive contexts based on the interventions of the therapist. Those patients who work over these truths in a meaningful manner may be termed *truth patients*, and they correspond to those who use the type A communicative style. In contrast, those patients who wish not to work over the unconscious communicative truths of the therapeutic experience may be termed *lie patients* or *lie-barrier patients* in that they falsify these truths or create impenetrable barriers to their realizations. This type of patient corresponds to the Type C communicator.

In similar fashion, the therapist who begins his interpretations with the unconscious implications of his interventions (the adaptive context) and then identifies the patient's adaptive derivative responses as they illuminate the indicators or therapeutic contexts which represent the patient's neurosis, may be termed *truth therapists*. All other efforts constitute responses as *lie* or *lie-barrier therapists*, in that they are designed to either avoid or falsify the essential communicative truths within the therapeutic interaction as they relate to the patient's emotional illness. While there is only one type of truth therapist, there are several kinds of lie therapists. This includes the therapist who makes use of psychoanalytic clichés, the framework changer who alters the ground rules, and the genetic reconstructionist–styles of intervening which do not take into account activated intervention contexts, but which instead treats the patient's material in isolated, nondynamic, and nonadaptive fashion. There is much evidence that psychoanalysis, as it is now constituted, is largely a form of lie therapy.

4. More specific distinction can be made between the patient's style of *sending* messages and his style of *receiving* them. The Type A receiver will respond with Type Two derivative validation to the therapist's interventions, and then subsequently work over, both consciously and unconsciously, the insights so derived. The Type C receiver will initially validate a correct intervention by the therapist, only to subsequently seal it off behind Type C or lie barriers. As a result, there is no subsequent working through of the initial insight, and instead, there is an obliteration of its implications. Finally, the Type B receiver will initially validate a correct intervention by the therapist, but will then follow this insightful response with a series of pathological projective identifications which virtually destroy the insight so gained.

5. We may conceptualize five basic maturational modes of relatedness: the *autistic*, in which there is essentially nonrelatedness; the *healthy symbiosis* which is designed for growth and individuation; the *pathological symbiosis* which is designed for inappropraite merger; the *parasitic relationship* which is designed for the destruction of one or both members of a relationship dyad; and the *commensal mode* of relatedness which provides the two relationship partners with equal shares of satisfaction. Psychotherapy should be constituted as a healthy symbiosis since the patient's therapeutic needs are uppermost, and the gratification of the therapist is secondary. In terms of communicative fields, it is the Type A field which is constituted as a healthy symbiosis, and which can produce true insight, growth, and individuation. The Type C patient tends to effect a pathological symbiosis with the therapist, as will some Type B patients. However, the Type B-C communicator wishes to parasitize the therapist and destroy him.

Similarly, it is the Type A therapist who truly offers the patient a healthy form of symbiosis, while the Type B and C therapists wish to effect either a pathological symbiosis of a parasitic mode of relatedness with the patient.

6. There are two kinds of Type C patient. The first involves patient's whose basic communicative style is Type C in nature, and who will tend to utilize lie-barrier systems in the presence of activated adaptive contexts. The second is basically a Type A patient who, in the middle phase of psychotherapy, has a need to *lie fallow* and therefore to make use of the Type C communicative style in the absence of an activated intervention context. This is done as a means of engaging in self-analysis, much of it in the form of Type One derivative and lie-barrier efforts, which, when undertaken in the context of a secure holding environment, enables the patient to modify the pathological qualities of both his derivative and nonderivative defenses. Thus, this particular phase of Type C communication is a necessary aspect of the curative process, and should not be interfered with by the therapist.

It is felt that these additional insights attest to the vitality of the delineation of communicative styles in patients and therapists. In actual clinical practice, these distinctions have proven to be a highly useful means of enhancing our understanding of the therapeutic interaction and the techniques which it requires.

References

Angel, K. (1971). Unanalyzability and narcissistic transference disturbances. *Psychoanalytic Quarterly* 40:264-276.

Balint, M. (1968). *The Basic Fault: Therapeutic Aspects of Regression*. London: Tavistock.

Baranger, M. and Baranger, W. (1966). Insight and the analytic situation. In *Psychoanalysis in the Americas*, ed. R. Litman. New York: International Universities Press, pp. 56-72.

Bion, W. (1963). *Elements of Psycho-analysis*. In *Seven Servants*. New York: Aronson, 1977.

—— (1965). *Transformations*. In *Seven Servants*. New York: Aronson, 1977.

—— (1970). *Attention and Interpretation*. In *Seven Servants*. New York: Aronson, 1977.

—— (1977). *Seven Servants*. New York: Aronson.

Bird, B. (1972). Notes on transference: universal phenomenon and the hardest part of analysis. *Journal of the American Psychoanalytic Association* 20:267-301.

Bleger, J. (1967). Psycho-analysis of the psychoanalytic frame. *International Journal of Psychoanalysis* 48:511-519.
Fiumara, G. (1977). The symbolic function, transference and psychic reality. International Review of Psycho-Analysis 4:171-180.
Freud, S. (1914). Remembering, repeating, and working-through. (further recommendations on the technique of psycho-analysis, II). *Standard Edition* 12:145-156.
Giovacchini, P. (1975). The concrete and difficult patient. In *Tactics and Techniques in Psychoanalytic Therapy*, ed. P. Giovacchini. New York: Science House, pp. 351-363.
Green, A. (1975). The analyst, symbolization and absence in the analytic setting (on changes in analytic practice and analytic experience). *International Journal of Psycho-Analysis* 56:1-22.
Greenson, R. (1967). *The Technique and Practice of Psychoanalysis* Vol. I. New York: International Universities Press.
Grinberg, L. (1962). On a specific aspect of counter-transference due to the patient's projective identification. *International Journal of Psycho-Analysis* 43:436-440.
Halpert, E. (1972). The effect of insurance on psychoanalytic treatment. *Journal of the American Psychoanalytic Association* 20:122-133.
Kernberg, O. (1975). *Borderline Conditions and Pathological Narcissism*. New York: Aronson.
Kohut, H. (1971). *The Analysis of the Self: A Systematic Approach to the Psychoanalytic Treatment of Narcissistic Personality Disorders*. New York: International Universities Press.
—— (1977). *The Restoration of the Self*. New York: International Universities Press.
Khan, M. (1963). The concept of cumulative trauma. *The Psychoanalytic Study of the Child* 18:286-306.
—— (1964). Ego distortion, cumulative trauma, and the role of reconstruction in the analytic situation. *International Journal of Psycho-Analysis* 45:272-278.
—— (1971), pp. 19, 23, 36c.
—— (1973). The role of illusion in the analytic space and process. In *The Privacy of the Self*. New York: International Universities Press, 1974, pp. 251-269.
Langs, R. (1971). Day residues, recall residues, and dreams: reality and the psyche. *Journal of the American Psychoanalytic Association* 19:499-523.
—— (1972). A psychoanalytic study of material from patients in psychotherapy. *International Journal of Psychoanalytic Psychotherapy* 1 (1):4-45.
—— (1973). *The Technique of Psychoanalytic Psychotherapy*, Vol. 1. New York: Aronson.
—— (1974). *The Technique of Psychoanalytic Psychotherapy*, Vol. 2. New York: Aronson.
—— (1975a). Therapeutic Misalliances. *International Journal of Psychoanalytic Psychotherapy* 4:77-105.
—— (1975b). The therapeutic relationship and deviations in technique. *International Journal of Psychotherapy* 4:106-141.
—— (1975c). The patient's unconscious perception of the therapist's errors. In *Tactics and Techniques in Psychoanalytic Therapy, Vol. II: Countertransference*. ed. P. Giovacchini. New York: Aronson, pp. 239-250.
—— (1976a). *The Bipersonal Field*. New York: Aronson.
—— (1976b). *The Therapeutic Interaction*, Vols. 1 and 2. New York: Aronson.
—— (1976c). On becoming a psychiatrist. *International Journal of Psychoanalytic Psychotherapy* 5:255-280.
—— (1977). Validation and the framework of the therapeutic situation. *Contemporary Psychoanalysis*.
Liberman, D. (In press). *Dreams in the Bipersonal Field*. N.Y.: Aronson.
Little, M. (1951). Countertransference and the patient's response to it. *Int. J. Psycho-Anal*. 32, 32-40.
Milner, M. (1952). Aspects of symbolism and comprehension of the not-self. *International Journal of Psycho-Analysis* 33:181-195.
Racker, H. (1957). The meaning and uses of countertransference. *Psychoanalytic Quarterly* 26:303-357.
Rangell, L. (1975). Psychoanalysis and the process of change: an essay on the past, present and future. *International Journal of Psycho-Analysis* 56:87-98.
Searles, H. (1958). The schizophrenic's vulnerability to the therapist's unconscious processes. *Journal of Nervous and Mental Disease* 127:247-262.
—— (1959). The effort to drive the other person crazy—an element in the aetiology and psychotherapy of schizophrenia. *British Journal of Medical Psychology* 32:1-18.
—— (1960). *The Nonhuman Environment*. New York: International Universities Press.
—— (1965). *Collected Papers on Schizophrenia and Related Subjects*. New York: International Universities Press.
—— (1970). Autism and the phase of transition to therapeutic symbiosis. *Contemporary Psychoanalysis* 7:1-20.
—— (1971). Pathological symbiosis and autism. In *The Name of Life* ed. Bernard Landis and E. Tauber. New York: Holt, Rinehart & Winston.
—— (1972). The functions of the patient's realistic perceptions of the analyst in delusional transference. *British Journal of Medical Psychology* 45:1-18.

—— (1973a). Some aspects of unconscious fantasy. *International Journal of Psychoanalytic Psychotherapy* 2:37-50.
—— (1973b). Concerning therapeutic symbiosis. *The Annual of Psychoanalysis* 1:247-262.
Segal, H. (1967). Melanie Klein's technique. *Psychoanalytic Forum* 2:197-211
Stone, L. (1975). Some problems and potentialities of present-day psychoanalysis. *Psychoanalytic Quarterly* 44:331-370.
Viderman, S. (1975). Interpretation in the analytic space. *International Review of Psycho-Analysis* 1:467-480.
Wallerstein, R. (1977). Psychic energy reconsidered: introduction. *Journal of the American Psychoanalytic Association* 25:529-536.
Wangh, M. (1962). The "evocation of a proxy:" a psychological maneuver, its use as a defense, its purposes and genesis. *The Psychoanalytic Study of the Child* 17:451-469.
Winnicott, D. (1945). Primitive emotional development. In *Collected Papers: Through Paediatrics to Psycho-Analysis*. London: Tavistock Publications, 1958, pp. 145-156.
—— (1951). Transitional objects and transitional phenomena. In *Collected Papers: Through Paediatrics to Psycho-Analysis*. London: Tavistock Publications, 1958, pp. 229-242.
—— (1956). Primary maternal preoccupation. In *Collected Papers: Through Paediatrics to Psycho-Analysis*. London: Tavistock Publications, 1958, pp. 300-305.
—— (1958). *Collected Papers: Through Paediatrics to Psycho-Analysis*. London: Tavistock Publications.
—— (1965). *The Maturational Processes and the Facilitating Environment*. London: Hogarth Press.
—— (1971). *Playing and Reality*. New York: Basic Books.

EDITOR'S NOTE: *Professor Matte-Blanco graces the Memorial not only with his years of experience as a psychoanalyst but also as a keen student of mathematical logic. Those of you who have not read his* The Unconscious as Infinite Sets* *are in for a very great treat. I hope I do not harm Professor Matte-Blanco's presentation by offering a few explanatory remarks. His concept of a bi-logic and bi-modal thinking refers to the logic of symmetry and asymmetry respectively. The unconscious, which is comprised of entities in* infinite sets *(a* baby *is part of the set of* family, *which is part of the set of* humanity, *etc.), is also characterized by a mode of "thinking" which Matte-Blanco designates mathematically as symmetrical; this* symmetrical *nature of infinite sets is in contrast to the* asymmetrical *limitations* within *sets (finite sets) and of sets in "rational" thinking. Perhaps a way of demonstrating the illusive nature of symmetricality is to imagine a fetus surrounded by a cushion of amniotic fluid. Any pressure against that sack would be symmetrically distributed around the periphery of the fetus so that, if the points of pressure were to be charted on polar-coordinated space via projective geometry, then all the points would devolve into one point on the graph, thereby demonstrating the symmetry of the experience. By contrast, separation is an asymmetrical experience where some points of contact are felt more than others and are localized.*

In this presentation Professor Matte-Blanco is setting forth eighty propositions which characterize Bion's contributions and is subjecting them to the rigorous comparison of mathematical logic. It is a tour de force of critique by one of the very few people I know who can grapple with the more advanced ideas Bion has proposed.

Let me quote from The Unconscious as Infinite Sets: an essay in bi-logic:

"A bi-logical system is a system formed by two logical systems. *The first is simply bivalent logic, which we observe in its*

*Matte-Blanco, Ignacio (1975). *The Unconscious as Infinite Sets: an essay in bi-logic*. London: Duckworth Press.

> *'pure' state in many pieces of thinking (Aristotelian thinking) . . . . The second component system is . . . . anaclitic logic, in which the principle of symmetry makes its appearance . . . .* Anaclitic logic would *then be the conjunction of the principle of symmetry with simple bivalent logic . . . .*"

Reflecting With Bion

Ignacio Matte-Blanco

–0.* Foreword

From the ocean of Dr. Bion's golden harvest I have gleaned a few grains. Beyond them as well as in them there is the homogeneous indivisible unity.** I have looked at them with my humble eyes, and tried to express the multiplicity in my own way; and also tried to translate the unity into transparent words. This is the result.

I take it for granted that the reader is familiar with Dr. Bion's contributions; I must, unfortunately, add that unless he has some familiarity with my own efforts he may find that whatever transparency I may have succeeded in achieving may appear to him dark and impenetrable. In order to facilitate understanding I have made some hints as to where there is something in my writings which may help at certain moments.

1.

Where to begin? Where to follow? The early Bion is perhaps better known. The later Bion–that from the Brazilian lectures to the "Memoir" to the Roman lectures . . . and God only knows where to: the future Bion . . .– seems to me a realisation of the first. We no longer hear much of projective identification, of bizarre objects, alpha- or beta-elements, of K or the grid. At times he even seems impatient with the restrictions that such notions put on the understanding-of, and fusing-with, his present self-whole: the drama of the difference and at the same time the identity between part and whole.

Yet the early Bion is the father of the later Bion. The son, however, has gone farther than the father and has, lovingly, become the father of the father, as befits a venerable patriarch.

Decisions: As a gleaner I shall follow no chronological order by only my own spontaneity.

2.

My intention: to learn from Bion, to soak myself with "*his*" personal impersonality. I cannot do this, however, if I do not keep my own authenticity, "*my*" personal impersonality. The result of these two premises: at times the discovery of an isomorphism between him and me; most of the time a

*See 75.

**For the conception of the two modes of being in man, see I.M.B., 1975, ch. 28.

development of my own authenticity. Father-mother Bion, like Virgil, will lead me by the hand and I shall go with him, next to him.

My hope: just as in this pilgrimage Bion has shown for me, may my reflections be useful to help others to focus on some of his brilliance.

Put otherwise: to see whether my reflections in-with with-in Bion help me, and perhaps others, to get into the depth of Bion, a function similar to that performed by the lights which from hidden corners of an ancient medieval square try to illuminate various perspectives of a noble monument, venerable, present and evolving to the future: a memoir of the future; and, in this process, to become more myself and realise both what I was and what he has helped me to be.

3.

Some "bionians" strike me as mechanical. From the way they employ them, alpha- and beta-elements, K, O, etc., appear at the same time so crude and so wishy-washy! Perhaps they are lazy and prefer to repeat words which have become devoid of meaning. Their laziness would spring from their fear of thinking, and therefore of facing catastrophic changes and facing *alone* the horror of deicide in order to be God, i.e., to fulfill the secret hope of any and all human beings. No one can comfort us in such a plight because, if he does, our own creation is no longer ours, but somebody else's. No wonder that many prefer to cling to concepts transformed into stereotypes.

4.

Let me, from the beginning, clear up a possible misunderstanding. The rebellion or aggression against the breast, mother, penis, father is "infinitized" at the deeper levels of the mind (we shall later see something of the why and how of this process). A breast, penis, father or mother felt-seen as infinite is isomorphic to the notion of God of more developed thinking. As the deep levels, where everything is infinitized, are always active in all of us, it seems more faithful *to these levels* to refer to the abstract structure of which senicide, . . . parricide and deicide are representatives, and, therefore, to speak of deicide and not of senicide, penicide, matricide, parricide: this is in keeping in more than one way both with bivalent logic and with the principle of symmetry, which rules the unconscious (I.M.B., 1959 and 1975 ch. 3). For instance: a) according to this principle no distinction is made either between deicide, parricide, senicide or between any of these elements and the whole set or class of them; b) any of the elements of the class, according to this principle, has all the potentialities of the class in question. c) On the other hand, according to bivalent logic, deicide is in this case a greater deed than senicide or parricide: it is the greatest deed of all the possible deeds included in the class. This being so, if bivalent logic is applied at this point, then it is understandable that deicide should be the "most natural" representative of this class or structure. In a similar way, though for other reasons, 1/2 is the "most natural" representative of the equivalence class {1/2, 2/4, 3/6 . . . 50/100 . . .}. Of course, this procedure creates contrasts with conscious thinking. We shall see some of them. To have them ever present in our meditations is fundamental for a proper understanding of man. It creates problems but it yields insights.

We may now consider one of these problem-insights. The strange, surprising, pathetic thing is that, after all, deicide does not exist in either of the two modes: it is an impossible absurdity in bivalent logic (: the concept of God is that of an immortal being) and is outside the homogeneous indivisible reality for which no individual, no life or death exists. Yet it is a daily, most present bi-modal* reality in our life: though it does not exist-is in any of the modes, it is in any and all of us. How? A puzzling suspended animation in midair, somewhere, nowhere, yet *there*.

So, after all, not only *those* bionians but everyone of us is frightened. There are, however, ways and ways of being frightened. We cannot escape fear and tremor and, theistically or atheistically, somehow, we pray: "Father, if it is possible take this cup away from me, not my will but thine be done."

5.

Bion speaks of ". . . a stylized description of emotional experience" and points out that "the falsification that is introduced by such a method of presentation is immeasurably less than . . . The photograph of the fountain of truth may be well enough, but it is of the fountain after it has been muddied by the photographer and his apparatus;" (1962 p. XI). In other words: the problem of the falsification of emotion by its (re)presentation.

One asks: is this falsification inevitable, whatever the presentation? The answer: yes. The reason: the nature of emotion: divisible *and* indivisible, i.e., formed *and* not formed of parts; spatial *and* spaceless; temporal *and* timeless. To represent one must think, i.e., affirm something of something else: divide.. Dividing, however, muddies the indivisible aspect of emotion which is alien to thinking and truth, but *is* the fountain of truth, the mother of thought.

6.

Confronted by the homogeneous indivisible reality, man is like Narcissus—I mean that of Ovid, not his psycho-analytical version:

> There are no mountains which divide us,
> no walls with closed doors, but only a
> small drop of water
> keeps one of us so far away from the other"

*I employ the term "bi-modal" to mean something in which both modes of being (asymmetrical or dividing and homogeneous indivisible) are present. This is a more comprehensive concept than bi-logic, of which bi-logic is only a sub-concept. (For the concept of bi-logic see I.M.B. 1975 ch. 3 and 1976a.)

But man does not resign himself to die away like Narcissus. He wants to cross the desperate abyss between both modes, which are so distant, yet so near. Prometheus has come to his help by taking the fire of thinking from heaven and giving it to him who has gladly accepted it. Man has consequently been able to conceive the infinite. From above, however, Jupiter punished him by having Pandora open the jar which contained the evils—envy, spite, revenge: all bi-logical structures,* deicidal irreverence of thought daring (to try) to think the unthinkable, know the unknowable, divide the indivisible. And even thought itself became muddied: the real number system, the purest expression of the dividing-thinking mode of man turned out to be riddled with (bi-logical) paradoxes. So man was condemned to *live* with his dual nature, not to die away like Narcissus.

Hope, however, was left to him: a bi-logical structure, which remained inside the jar to save him from being overwhelmed by Jupiter and sacrilegious thought.

7.

"This state contrasts with the animism in that live objects are endowed with the qualities of death." (Bion, 1962, p. 9)

May we say: life = death (and, from the context) = inanimate object = lack of "awareness of all feelings" (op. cit., p. 10). In short: presence of indivision.

8.

Indivision: something primary, a mode of being. Division: something primary too, also a mode of being. Therefore, presence of indivision is not the same as lack of division.

9.

". . . hate would not exist if love were not present." (Bion, 1962, p. 10).

I would develop this idea in the following way: "initially" there is only one thing in which nothing is distinguishable, hence, neither love nor hate; "then" the same thing is divided in two opposites, love and hate. The two are, however, inseparable.

Is this final state the same as the initial one? My guess: the second is a translation (I.M.B. 1975 ch. 8 and25) of the first and as such a failure, notwithstanding the fact that it is a development of Logos.

*For the concept of bi-logical structure see I.M.B., 1976a.

10.

"The term alpha-function is, intentionally, devoid of meaning . . . a counterpart of the mathematicians' variable . . " (Bion, 1962, p. 3)

May we add: or the propositional function, which, according to logicians, has no meaning so long as the x of the function is not replaced by a concrete value: until then there is no statement, hence no meaning.

I believe, however, that this truth should be completed in the following way: anything susceptible of having a meaning, just by the sole fact of being susceptible of having a meaning already *has* a meaning, even if it is not a concrete one. Take the function $y = 3x$. I know *beforehand* that the meaning of y that will emerge when I give a value to x will be totally different from the meaning of y which will emerge when I give a value to x if $y = 3x\sqrt{-1}$: a real number in the first case, a complex one in the second.

Put otherwise, syntaxis is, in a sense, filled with meanings, which "incarnate" in semantical statements. Furthermore, one syntactical meaning leads into another and another and another, either in a straight line into infinity or into infinity in a circular line: the set of triads* (I.M.B. 1975, p. 330), is like the set of rational numbers, which has no lower or upper bound (I.M.B. 1977 Verona). If we pass from one triad to another, in the end we find ourselves in an ever expanding universe of triads (extensive infinite) or in the intensive infinite net-mesh of "syntaxis become semantics," a seamless net and a mesh made of infinite "full" holes. The total is in bi-univocal correspondence with Jesus' seamless tunic, which itself is an image of (: a bi-univocal correspondence with) indivisible God, Jesus himself being an "incarnation" (as man) of the homogeneous indivisible reality which is neither finite nor infinite, in which–for thought–potentiality is identical to actuality.

. . . and the drunkenness of thinking sinking into feeling . . .

11.

The conception of bizarre objects clearly stands on the firm ground of Freudian and Kleinian conceptions: it is inconceivable without the characteristics of the system unconscious, especially identity between psychical and external reality, condensation and displacement; it is equally inconceivable without the Kleinian notion of part object. But the bizarre object obviously is a new development, for the particle "felt to consist of a real external object which is incapsulated in a piece of personality that has engulfed it" (Bion 1956 [1967, p. 39]) is neither a Freudian nor Kleinian conception but, on the contrary, a Bionian one. It illuminates strange spaces of the schizophrenic mind and also of the mind in general.

*A triad: a structure formed of something, something else and the relation between them.

The study of the relation between the concept of the bizarre objects and that of the two modes of being could, in my opinion, lead to interesting new developments. This would be a vast subject and I shall not tackle it here. I shall, instead, only put forward the following statement: the bizarre object must be considered to be a bi-logical structure. The reason: the very fact that it is an object or particle that is and moves in ("normal" or usual) space clearly shows that in many of its aspects it is submitted to the laws of bivalent logic. In the midst of a chain of bivalent-logical happenings, however, we find aspects or links which obviously show the workings of symmetrical logic. A part of the personality is "cut up, split into minute fragments" (loc. cit. p. 38); on the other hand the patient's "sense of imprisonment is intensified by the menacing presence of the expelled fragments within whose planetary movements he is contained" (loc. cit. p. 39). Furthermore,

> If the piece of personality is concerned with sight, the gramophone when played is felt to be watching the patient . . . The object, angered at being engulfed, swells up, so to speak, and suffuses and controls the piece of personality that engulfs it: to that extent the particle of personality has become a thing . . . leads the patient to feel that words are the actual things they name and so adds to the confusions, described by Segal, that arise because the patient equates, but does not symbolize." (Bion, 1957 [1967, p. 48]).

If we look at these quotations from the point of view of the two modes we find:

–the piece of personality behaves like a whole personality as is shown in that it is active, engulfs, controls. This entails equal cardinality between part and whole: application of the principle of symmetry.

–the piece of personality becomes a thing and the controlled or engulfed object becomes angered and controls the piece of personality: it becomes a piece of personality. This is, again, an obvious symmetrization. It looks as though a complex situation which is described in terms of a series of operations such as expressing anger, controlling, menacing, etc., is treated in such a way that each element of this structure may play any of the roles: the part has as equal cardinality as the whole and as any other part. This is obviously a series of symmetrizations which results, we may say, in the fact that what happens in the whole situation also happens in any one of its single aspects: a curious copresence of heterogeneity and homogeneity. This also entails a real frenzy of epistemological seesaws (see 13.).

–the symbolic equation is clearly a symmetrization: no difference exists between the elements of a class, be they primitive or symbolic objects.

In other words, there are obviously both logico-bivalent and symmetrical links in the conception of the bizarre object. Hence, this latter is a bi-logical structure. It is fascinating to observe that the relations between these two types of links are not always the same but, on the contrary, vary greatly.

The result is a very complex structure. Futhermore, the logico-bivalent *as well as the bi-logical* reactions of the whole patient to that particular, extremely complex bi-logical structure called bizarre object, greatly adds to the complexity of the situation.

A detailed study of this question from this point of view could yield various new insights.

12.

Physical sciences as well as biological sciences move comfortably (so far) in the realm of bivalent logic. The movement of a body, chemical reactions, cell reproduction and physiological processes are described in terms of this logic. But when we come to study the intimacy of mental life, as psycho-analysis does, there are moments when the mind violently defies and rebels against bivalent logic. At this point our study no longer conforms with the usual scientific canons. For instance, how could a bizarre object be studied only in terms of bivalent logic?

So far psycho-analytic language is not sufficiently precise, and this is due (at least partly) to the fact that, when it comes to describe the strange behaviour of the unconscious, it uses a language which is more adapted to describe material reality. Now, the Freudian conception of consciousness and the unconscious (and, consequently, that of the ego and the id), can be reformulated in logico-mathematical terms with the help of the principle of symmetry. This leads to the conception of the two modes of being which, in its turn, is intimately connected with the mathematical concept of the infinite. So we arrive at what we might call bi-modal psycho-analysis, which enables us to reach to the very core of mathematics.

If one or more generations of mathematically trained analysts were to tackle thoroughly all the numerous aspects of the question of both logics in the mind and of the mathematical concept of the infinite, ever present in mental manifestations, some new and deep insights about the mind could, I feel, be reached, as well as some new and deep insights about the foundations of mathematics.

Will such generations ever come to be?

13.

"CAPT. BION I stared at the speck of mud trembling on the straw. . . . Wot 'appened then? 'E fell on 'is arse. And 'is Arse wuz angry and said, Get off my arse! You've done nothing but throw shit at me all yore life and now you expects England to be my booty! Boo-ootiful soup; in a shell-hole in Flanders Fields. Legs and guts . . . must 'ave bin twenty men in there—Germ'um and frogslegs and all starts!" (1975b. 63).

As I see it, this piece—which recalls, with an amusing Cockney humour, a grim experience—expresses subtleties worthy of an erudite treatise on mathematical bi-logic. The humour of the first part seems connected with the fact that the object is treated in the same breath as part of the body and as a whole person (in this latter case it becomes the *A*rse). The subject of the story is felt and treated as one and indivisible but his body can be seen (*thought* of) as formed of parts: two ways of experiencing reality, i.e., as indivisible homogeneous *and* as divisible, heterogeneous. When the arse, one *part*, is singled out, isolated, a new relation is established between the individual and the part, which is seen, unexpectedly—and here seems to be the clue to the humour—no longer as a part but as a whole, as a person. In other words, the mode of being which treats reality as indivisible, suddenly comes forth and claims its right to "undivide." But the heterogenic mode does not give way and the result is not one but two: the undivided unity has been divided into two undivided wholes, i.e., unities! This is an example of what I have come to call the epistemological seesaw: when one mode gains the upper hand, the other mode butts in and gains, in its turn, the upper hand, and then the first mode butts in again . . . and so on indefinitely: an example, out of many different ones, of infinite circular regress, a manifestation which is co-extensive with the condition of being human.

The second round won by the heterogenic mode is seen when the Arse speaks of *his* arse: a symmetrical piece of logic in which the part is equal to the whole, yet it is a part. In other words, the heterogenic thinking mode is not dislodged: both modes are confluent and express themselves in *the very same* piece of reality.

The next round of the homogeneous mode is seen when from "booty" it passes on to "boo-ootiful" (a typical onirical homogenisation of things so widely different) to the mess-soup of Flanders Field . . . and here the legs and guts are heterogeneous . . . but Germ'um and frogslegs are again homogeneised in the earthland.

In conclusion, we see here the ups and downs of an epistemological seesaw which continues till the end of the chapter. The result of this seesaw in action is a bi-logical structure (I.M.B. 1976a, 1976b).

14.

The story is told by Captain Bion in the midst of the war in circumstances of great stress, in which so many memories come to his mind: tension leads to regression and (formal) regression expresses itself in terms of a deeper level of interaction or co-presence between both modes (I.M.B. 1975, ch. 14).

15.

Why did Bion make Capt. Bion tell this story in this book? It seems that to show his reader some peculiarities of oneiric experience. I conclude that Bion avails himself in his description (through *his* Captain) of the intricacies of the epistemological seesaw, and decides, here, not to tackle the task of explaining what he is doing.

Science gliding-into and fusing-with Art?

16.

What is an oneiric-like experience or expression? The answer is by no means easy. A simple dream may show, not only successively but also, perhaps, contemporarily, various depths of co-presence of both modes of being. At times, and this is one extreme of the range of variation, the dream is structured almost like the stream of conscious thinking in waking life, whereas at other times, and this is the other extreme, it is more hazy, with no clear asymmetric delimitation of one part or concept or object from another. Between these two extremes we find a great variety of bi-logical and other bimodal structures (I.M.B. 1977) in which certain links of the dream process are homogeneised while others remain, as in waking life, sharply defined.

17.

I dreamt last night that I was plunging into the water. The plunging itself was, as a sequence, like a real life plunging. But the course followed a curve which, though possible in itself in the physical world, was not real for a man who plunges into the water. This and other details showed that this piece of the dream was a meeting point of several things, some of which could not be represented in a real life plunging: there was no isomorphism between the real and the oneiric experience. This latter was, in this aspect, a condensation and, as such, a homogenisation of asymmetrically distinguishable notions: a link of a bi-logical structure and, therefore, a bi-logical co-presence. The laws of space, among other things, are respected at times and not respected at other times in this co-presence. The result: a space behaving in strange ways makes its appearance.

The path chosen by Bion in the "Memoir" is obviously an artistic one: to *convey and make alive* the strangeness and the mystery of this mysterious world of man in which, among other things, the future and the past melt, *at times*, into each other and disappear. Putting this disappearance in dividing terms: a memoir of the future. And space also fades, *at times*, into homogeneity.

I, on my part, believe that something of that rich experience told by Bion can be understood in terms of the notions of modes and their co-presence. To study the *structure* of the dream in the light of these notions may lead to new insights.

18.

Whatever the bi-logical structure visible in the dream is, there is also in every dream, so it seems to me, *a sort of hazy mantle which wraps every aspect of*

the representation and gives an oneiric quality even to the most asymmetrical, rational aspects of it. However m:.thematical a piece of a dream may be, it always has the seal or the stamp of a process which happens in a special state of consciousness. This would be a case of a non-bi-logical but still bimodal co-presence.

19.

We must remember, however, that in our waking life we frequently pass through experiences which are dream-like. They may last only seconds and we may not be aware of them. They come over and again innumerable times every day, so that, from the point of view of presence or absence of such experiences, there is not much difference between dream and waking life.

For a scientific study it is important to succeed in describing them accurately. I put forward the above reflections as an attempt in that direction.

20.

We now return to 13. Does Captain Bion tell a dream-like experience? His story actually isolates and puts into a sharp focus some aspects of the co-presence of both modes as well as some bi-logical structures seen in dreams. Is that dream-like? I believe not, but this is a long story and a difficult subject . . .

As for Dr. W.R. Bion, he has chosen to illustrate his point with a story and let the reader draw the conclusions. Art or Science? I only know that the haziness of dream is not visible to me in the story and this would point to science; and that the description has a freshness and suggestion proper to Art. Anyway, the approach put forward by our author provides more flexible possibilities for the study of man.

I fear there is another alternative: I haven't understood what Dr. Bion is doing. I hope this alternative is not true: it would save me anxiety.

21.

What *is* alpha function? Is it really a term devoid of meaning, as Bion insists throughout his writings? Maybe I do not understand him, but I must confess that I am not convinced that it is.

I would see alpha function in two ways: a) something like a mathematician's variable, as Bion explains. In this case it seems to me to have a meaning, at least in the sense explained in 10.: b) as an activity of the intellect: to translate the stuff of life and of the world into sets of triads of something, something else and the relation between them, i.e., the activity of the heterogenic mode, which sees reality as divided *and unites its parts* by means of the relation. The alpha function would, therefore, be the activity of the mode which only knows the discrete. Even if it may, perhaps, be argued or doubted that in itself this activity *is* a meaning, I think it is undeniable that it is meaningful, i.e., *it has* a meaning. In other words, an activity, *inasmuch as it is activity*, is probably something which *is* no meaning, because action and meaning are two different concepts. But an activity may be random, meaningless (may not have a meaning) or, alternatively, meaningful (it may have a meaning). If alpha function is an activity, my feeling is that it belongs to the class of meaningful activities. At this point the reflections of 10. seem pertinent.

22.

Meaning, we may say, is one of the fundamental modes of being of man . . . and of the world. In the essence of the asymmetrical mode, meaning lies, is at home, in its own abode. We and the world are fully meaningful but not only meaningful.

I wonder what would Bion think of these reflections.

23.

See 1962, ch. 5, number 3, p. 11-12. I see this paragraph as an extremely condensed account of many observations and formulations: typically Bionian. If I were to follow my own inclination I would analyse it into a good number of intersections of a good number of propositional functions, but here I shall only comment: he is (among other things) describing one *type* of co-presence of various levels of depth between both modes of being. The alpha function the patient lacks would be, in this case, fairly developed asymmetrical thinking. The greedy and fearful taking of "one beta-element after another" also appears to me a way of describing an irresistible inevitable plunging into symmetry-undifferentiation, in spite of the asymmetrical evaluation of the situation; and, at the same time, an irresistible tendency to "heterogenise," in order to conquer the mystery outside thinking. This latter would represent a desperate attempt to treat as asymmetrical what is symmetrical, to "conquer" and understand the un-understandable: an *essentially* unsuccessful mental tenesmus. It is a *fearful* taking in, in order to master fear.

The fact that interpretations are taken as "contributions remarkable for what they are not rather than for what they are" (loc. cit. p. 12) suggests a presence, in the same "piece" of psychical reality, of two levels of different depth, inseparable in actual experience, but separable conceptually, which are contemporarily lived as one: an impossible thing for our thinking, an easy reality in our life. The patient, in fact, "does ultimately grasp some of the meaning of what is said to him" (loc. cit. p. 12): some success, which shows, after all, that the effort was not wasted. A step toward the cure, i.e., a better co-existence of both modes.

24.

I do not succeed in being at peace with the beta-elements. I cannot integrate them into what experience and reflection have led me to think: I cannot digest them. To discuss all the various aspects of this conception (1962, 1963, 1965, 1970, 1974, 1975a) would be a long and difficult task. I shrink from it just now. I shall, therefore, limit myself to a few reflections.

An initial comment: at first sight the *concept* of beta-element might be considered similar to that of symmetrical or homogeneous mode of being. I myself contemplated for a time the possibility of an isomorphism between both concepts; several other people have also thought of this possibility. Upon reflection, however, it seems to me that it must be entirely ruled out. The question is far more complex and multifaceted.

25.

> If alpha-function is disturbed, and therefore inoperative, the sense impressions of which the patient is aware and the emotions which he is experiencing remain unchanged. I shall call them beta-elements." (Bion, 1962, p. 6).

This is *one* aspect of the conception. The word "element" seems perfectly appropriate here: it points to *some thing*, quite definite, which remains unchanged. When he adds that beta-elements are stored and that they are "not so much memories but undigested facts" (loc. cit. p. 7), such comments are quite in keeping with the above quotation. So, one begins to think that beta-elements, however obscure they may be, are limited things. In other words, they belong to the realm of the discrete, of things that can be differentiated from other things. Put in my own terms: they refer to some aspect of the heterogenic mode. However, a doubt slips in when one considers that a beta-element may be an unchanged emotion, for emotion, as I see it, is a meeting point of both modes.

26.

When Bion says that "In contrast with the alpha-elements the beta-elements are not felt to be phenomena, but things in themselves" (loc. cit. p. 6) then, it seems to me, we are, this time, fully confronted with a conception which I am unable to reconcile with the one just discussed. Personally I feel that any *thing* is knowable because there is always an aspect of things, any and all things, which entails the concept of triad. To say that the term "things-in-themselves" refers to *objects* that are unknowable *to mankind*" (Bion, loc. cit. p. 100, my italics) suggests that such objects, i.e., things, may be knowable to beings who are not human. So far as I am concerned this sentence raises formidable problems (see 49, 65, 67, 68, and 69).

Bion also says that beta-elements are "not thought" (Bion 1970, p. 11 and 131). This suggests to me that they are outside the realm of the thinkable and, hence, of the knowable. But in that case, as I see the question, they could not be things. If they are not things then they would, as I see the question, be the homogeneous indivisible reality, which, according to the view I have tried to put forward, would not be *a* thing. Judging from the way beta-elements are described, however, this alternative should be ruled out.

In short, it seems that the conception of beta-elements, if viewed against my own frame of reference of reality, is self-contradictory. On the other hand it does not appear to belong to the realm of bi-logical structures, which at times do not respect the principle of non-contradiction.

I wonder what Bion would think of these reflections.

27.

My puzzlement increases or at least is not solved when I consider other aspects of Bion's conception of beta-elements. The beta-element as a bad breast, not distinguishable from an evacuation; the distinction between a beta-element, which seems an abstraction, and the *concept* of a beta-element (1965, p. 108): all this is very obscure to me. Much could be discussed, for instance, about the relation, *in our discourse*, between a thing which is an abstraction and the concept of this thing.

Still more obscure to me is the idea that the beta-element may be made into an alpha-element (1963, p. 27). There are, furthermore, various other aspects of the question that I would like to understand. It seems to me quite possible that these difficulties may be due to the fact that I have simply not understood Dr. Bion's formulation of the beta-elements.

Conclusion: from my own vantage point, the beta-element appears to me something rather like an open wound.

I would, however, like to point out that, so far as I am concerned, I feel that Bion's conception could stimulate the development of my own thinking and lead me to vistas which would be new to me while also, I suspect, different from Bion's.

28.

In 23. through 27. I have been changing (perhaps distorting) Bion's thinking. This type of activity is inevitable because one cannot jump out of one's skin. But it is also a good thing, though a fearful one. This is the activity observed in learning to be a disciple. We assimilate the master, become him and make him disappear and come back as well, but in a new way, within us: deicide, self-deification, deification of the master in the midst of the deicide, but a deification which remains deicide because the master has become a part of ourselves, which we use and express, i.e., he has ceased to be a master.

But the master does not die. Therefore, no deicide has ever taken place! And yet *it has*, and so we must start this chain all over again and repeat it endlessly, infinitely: an infinite circular regress, the utter misery of thinking, its abyssal finitude which makes it "fall" into infinity which, *nevertheless*, is a genuine way for thinking to think: the infinite only exists for thinking.

. . . And the fear that He may annihilate us . . . Oh God! We must start all over again another annoying-frightening chain of infinite circular regress: annihilation, non-annihilation, annihilation, non-annihilation . . . : the (infinite) power of the denumerable but *not* the power of the continuum (according to present-day mathematics) because thinking, so far as I can see, i.e., the set of triads, can only be put into bi-univocal correspondence with natural or rational numbers but not with the set of real numbers. However, I suspect that (present-day) mathematics is wrong on this point, and this might be due to its fear of killing the principle of non-contradiction: a deicide again. A more serene bi-modal attitude would perhaps see that the paradoxes of the infinite really are (logico-bivalent) antinomies . . . and would serenely accept bi-logic.

29.

But love still remains. And love implicitly contains the deification of the master as well as of ourselves, without deicide. What a wonderful thing love is.!

30.

However, it is not so easy to get away completely, i.e., all the way of human depth. At more superficial levels love is in conflict with hate and we therefore fall into the infinite regresses just described. But there are deeper strata in which love = hate. We need not worry, however, because at such depths neither love nor hate mean either love or hate. (This is only a paradox, not an antinomy.)

31.

28. furnishes a good example of the utterly strange, impossible and even inconceivable (for thinking) nature of man. The wringing pains of towering self-deification, the terrifying panic of annihilation, *together* with the incon-

ceivable absurdity of *both* deicide *and* non-deicide; and annihilation *and* non-annihilation. And all this also goes *together* with the hieratic* admirable *au dessus de la melée* essence of the homogeneous indivisible unity. Furthermore, when thinking gets to thinking about deicide and its absurdity and its reality, thinking falls into infinite sequences of alternating opposites, as shown in 28.

Perhaps we should, in contrast-agreement with Hamlet, say: To be *and* not to be: that is the question. And we should add: not just *one* to be *and* not to be but an infinite set of them, a set which has, perhaps the power of the continuum.

Human nature: how terrible how beautiful; how miserable how sublime!

32.

If 30. is true, then we seem to have solved nothing and are back where we started: in the midst of anguish. Does conflict between love and hate remain, and with it all our anguish? It certainly does, and we cannot escape the anguish of being human, of suffering from ambivalence. However, ambivalence, while still remaining at the "thinking surface," disappears at the deeper levels, and this is a fountain of serenity.

33.

If we reflect about what is said in 28. we may conclude that every time we affirm something we are affirming it, at some level, against somebody; put in terms of the infinitization of the translating function: a deicide. The paradoxical and pathetical fact is that we do it in order to save our skin.

34.

*Dios no muere.*** In other words, He whom we think-feel we have killed does not die at all: He is alien to the concepts of life and death. A class is neither mortal nor immortal. So is a triangle. So is the homogeneous indivisible reality. What a simple yet strange realisation this is! Maturation helps us to live it, but somewhere in us deicide and its horrors remain alive until *we* die.

*For lack of a better term I am using a Spanish meaning of the word hieratic: extremely solemn; and I am using solemn to mean, with the Shorter Oxford Dictionary: 4b. "Of great dignity or importance. 7. Impressive, awe-inspiring." I intend all these meanings together, but still something more, which the reader must, himself, expand, if not complete, because it cannot, asymmetrically) completely complete.

**God doesn't die: Words pronounced by Gabriel Garcia Moreno at the moment of dying from murder.

35.

I see 28. through 34. as the expression of a fundamental misunderstanding which is constitutive of our own human structure: the abysses that are opened and into which we fall when we try—and simply cannot avoid doing so—to understand what is outside understanding because it is outside thinking.

36.

This is, I feel, the real meaning of the concept of the infinite: an attempt at understanding what is outside understanding, at reconciling two modes which cannot ever quarrel between themselves because the homogeneous mode is outside *from*, or alien to, the "zone of quarrel," whatever quarrel.

Pathetic, isn't it? Yes but also dramatic, solemn, beautiful . . . and source of suffering.

37.

> . . . the difference between a true thought and a lie consists in the fact that a thinker is logically necessary for the lie but not for the true thought. Nobody need think the true thought: it awaits the advent of the thinker who achieves significance through the true thought. The lie and its thinker are inseparable. The thinker is of no consequence to the truth, but the truth is logically necessary to the thinker . . .
>
> . . . Descartes' tacit assumption that thoughts presuppose a thinker is valid only for the lie." (Bion, 1970, p. 102-103).

It seems to me that this quotation expresses clearly one aspect, but only one, of Bion's conception of "thought without a thinker." We may say that this aspect is nearer to a view which might be called "classical," which is also more easily understandable. I believe it means that the relations or systems of relations implicit between things or world events can be put in bi-univocal correspondence with statements, which are triads or systems of triads formed of something, something else and the relation between both. A true statement, therefore, corresponds bi-univocally (or is isomorphic) to the "objective" nature of things or world events. When somebody utters or thinks (thinking, if viewed only in its physiological happening, is at heart the same as uttering*) a statement, he is only explicitating (in thought or verbal expression) something which existed in the world before he explicitated it: a system of implicit relations. If we call the abstract structure which com-

*It is known that thinking entails activity of the muscles employed in speaking.

prises both this system of relations and the statement isomorphic to it by the name of thought, then we may say that a thinker is not logically necessary for the true thought. Thoughts would be the logical aspect of the world. The set of all thoughts, if understood in this way, would correspond to Logos or the asymmetrical mode.

A lie does not correspond to *things* and Bion is convincing when he affirms that lies are the only thoughts that need a thinker. One must, however, ask why people lie. The answer obviously is that something in themselves, shall we call it a state of mind, leads them to lie. The exact structure of a given lie has a quite precise bi-univocal correspondence or isomorphism with a mental state of the liar: it is the expression of this state. In this sense a lie is a lie or a falsity with respect to world events which are external to the thinker, *and also* is a true statement of a world event in that particular part of world events which we call, for instance, "John" i.e., the man who is telling the lie.

So, lies are always, in some way, profound truths, that is, truths of the deep unconscious. This leads to the serious question of what truth is and whether for any world event there may be, theoretically, *one* logico-bivalent truth *and an infinite number* of bi-logical truths.

Considering that, if carefully examined, a lie seems to imply an underlying bi-logical structure, we may then conclude, paraphrasing Bion, that a thinker is necessary for the lie, and a thing, but not a thinker, is necessary for a true thought, which is itself a thing. Both things and thinker, however, are, if viewed from this angle, world events.

38.

Another aspect of Bion's conception of thought without a thinker, and, I feel, his most creative contribution to this argument as created by him, is clearly seen in the last three paragraphs of "Second Thoughts" (1967, p. 164-166). These paragraphs present a profound intuition behind which there is a subtle and rich experience. If I look at it from the angle of my own evolution I would comment that it seems true that "the idea of infinitude is prior to any idea of the finite" (loc. cit. p. 165); and would add that the idea of the infinite is, in its turn, the expression of the attempt at thinking the unthinkable, the homogeneous indivisible reality: the attempt, similar to that of Narcissus looking at the fountain, to bridge the gap between both modes. As in the case of Narcissus, it is a failure: the homogeneous mode is outside any notion including that of the infinite; when thinking creates the infinite, it, like Narcissus, only succeeds in "seeing" itself.

Furthermore, as we all are *also* the homogeneous indivisible reality, then any thought anybody has is also ours. The patient's interpretation that "papers or books were really filched from him" (loc. cit. p. 165) seems to be the result of *experiencing* the homogeneous indivisible reality and *observing it or describing it* with heterogeneous (heterogenic?) eyes. The result is a logico-bivalent falsity which points to some inexpressible reality.

The co-presence of both modes is always in us. A source of deep insights as well as of colossal misunderstandings.

39.

". . . a mental life in which his universe is populated by inanimate objects." (1962 p. 14).

A reflection about this question: "inanimate" is usually used as equivalent to "immobile," just as life is usually associated with some form of movement. But inanimate matter has also turned out to be full of movement and energy. In the end the only "thing" that does not move is that which is indivisible. But neither is *that* "that" at rest: it is not even a thing, it is outside both the notions of movement and non-movement, (it is alien to *any* notion), even if we tend to confuse "rest" with "outside the notion of movement." Example: *requiescat in pace*. A dead man is neither moving nor at rest even if his soul, according to Catholic theology, is either in heaven, purgatory or hell. It would seem that these "places" are not outside the *notion* of movement if this notion is understood to mean something not merely physical, because joy and suffering are not outside this notion. All this, however, does not apply to the dead man; similarly, if one burns a piece of paper which was lying on the floor, one cannot say where this piece is now, because it is nowhere, neither on the floor nor in mid-air or anywhere else.

We also seem to tend, erroneously, to translate "indivision" as "at rest." Movement, however, seems really to have, as such, an aspect of indivision which, paradoxically, does not seem to be the same as the homogeneous indivisible reality. What is it?

40.

Perhaps Bergson was *both* right and wrong in what he said about movement and Russell rightly criticized him where he was wrong but (possibly) missed those aspects about which he was right. In the end we seem to find ourselves with no clear idea of what movement is. Bergson's criticism of the physical analysis of movement (the description of movement makes use of an infinite sequence of immobilities. How can such a sequence really picture movement?) is convincing but his account of movement does not seem to convince (me, at least). Maybe I don't understand him.

If we knew what movement really is, perhaps we could better understand the mind and the world. I guess that the two modes of being could help us in this fix. But how? Beyond the concept of bi-logic or, perhaps, outside it, even if, anyway, not by means of a "non-bi-modal" concept?

41.

"It appears that our rudimentary equipment for "thinking" thoughts is adequate when the problems are associated with the inanimate, but not when the object for investigation is the phenomenon of life itself." (1962 p. 14).

Coincidence–in this–with Bergson. Could it not be said: the dividing aspect of life is accessible to thinking, the undivided is not? We have tried to explore that aspect and have coined bi-logical structures; there is a potentially infinite number of them. Our nature also seems to express, spontaneously, other ways of co-existence of both modes which are neither logico-bivalent or multi-valent nor bi-logical.

Let us try to define and explore them. A convergence of various approaches to the same problem–Bergson's, Bion's and that of others–might succeed in demolishing the barrier to understanding. It is, however, necessary to remain aware that this is not an easy task.

42.

I feel that I can define the alpha-element in my own terms. I would call alpha-element each triad or set of traids which are the formulation of an inner experience or of a piece of the world, in short, a world-event.

The set of all possible triads, together with all its subsets (i.e., the power set of the set of all possible triads) together with all "things," which in one way or another are isomorphic to any subset of it, or at least can be put into bi-univocal correspondence with it,* forms the heterogenic-dividing mode (I.M.B. [Verona] 1977). Considering that it can be put in bi-univocal correspondence with the set of rational numbers, the set of triads has the power of the denumerable; considering, furthermore, that a power set of a denumerable set has the power of the continuum, we can say that the heterogenic dividing mode is a set which has *at least*, the power of the continuum. Considering, once more, that all sets which have a power superior to that of the continuum are describable in terms of triads and are, therefore, elements of the heterogenic dividing mode, we must conclude that the heterogenic-dividing mode has at least the power of the set of the highest conceivable power.

Science deals with the discrete: it creates heterogeneity and then unites the discrete elements in never-ending associations of triaids: the heterogenic mode. Note that, as already said, even in those aspects which are not triads but "things" the heterogenic mode is triadic.**

*Can they? Yes, they can, because all "things" have (implicitly) an aspect of Logos, susceptible of being made visible by means of "triadic descriptions," which, after all, are bi-univocal correspondences. See also 37.

**The above is a development of a formulation (I.M.B. Verona 1977) which, starting from man, extends the heterogenic mode to the whole world: the world in its meaningful (triadic) aspect. Which is not the only aspect of the world.

43.

It will be seen that 42. is a transformation of a (set of) concept(s) of Bion into a (set of) concept(s) of mine: an isomorphism. But that part of Bion's thinking which I have tried to transform into my thinking has come to be only one part of my formulation, just as on other occasions my formulation fits in with only one part of Bion's formulation. This is, I think, an example of what I said before: Bion's formulation, which I tried to put into bi-univocal correspondence with (transform into) mine, made mine grow and in the end what I was trying to transform became a part of a total.

This reflection may serve as a reassurance for us, deicides—who, after all, are all of us, because all of us are aspirants or would-be Gods. When we assert ourselves as God and (try to) occupy the whole of space we find that the same space may also be occupied by another god: in fact an infinite number of them. So Bion's creation may comfortably co-exist—in the same subject—with that of any of his disciples or of those who are not his disciples, for that matter. Put in other words: there is space for an infinite number of unique gods. This strange absurd formulation must, however, be coextensive with the clear realisation that we are smaller than anything conceivable: points (which are so small as to have no dimension). Because they have no dimension, points are homogeneous indivisible: the image of *that* which is expressed as infinite. A point, any point, is the unreachable "meeting point" of both modes. Imperfectly expressed: the meeting point of God and nothing.

We live in the midst of this tissue of profound sense and nonsensical nonsense: we are this tissue. And we cannot escape from this fate. Oh! the inadequacy of thinking when it comes to facing being!

44.

(Reflections about 43.) I (we) am (are) so much limited (biologically limited) that, confronted with something, I (we) tend to have an allergic reaction to it, unless I (we) succeed in metabolising it and re-synthesising it into my (our) own protein: the way of all flesh. Put in psychological terms: fear of being annihilated. Some Kleinian-prone analyst suffering from bigotry would possibly say: "what you have is just envy," thereby using (or mis-using) the Kleinian notion of envy, which is itself a restricted version of envy. I would not deny this assertion, but I do not think it is the whole explanation.

45.

The conception of the two modes of being is full of problems which, I feel, are fruitful and stimulating. I should like to comment on two of them.

At the end of 10. a serious question is raised. Is God an "incarnation" or a representation of the homogeneous unity or is He the homogeneous unity? If the last of these alternatives is right, it creates colossal problems, for the concept of homogeneous indivisible reality, *which springs from psycho-analytic observation*, refers to any one of us and to any "piece" of the world. If God is this unity then, considering that psycho-analytic observation has led us to the conclusion that one way of seeing man is as a homogeneous indivisible unity, we must conclude that man is God, i.e., we are controlled with a form of pantheism, which is quite different from self-deification. But we must beware of words and of established meanings, because they may be misleading; in this particular case, furthermore, "God" and "pantheism" probably have more than one established meaning. Personally I feel that the concepts theism and atheism as well as the frontal antithesis between them, as these three concepts are usually understood, amount to a colossal mis-formulation of strange and obscure realities which are not at all conveyed by such terms or concepts in their everyday meaning. As for the other alternatives ("incarnation," representant), they also lead to paradoxical or antinomical and, anyway, incomprehensible formulations. However, the temptation to escape from such difficulties by rejecting or ignoring the results of observation and reflection is, I feel, childishly anxious. The only possibility open, and a frustrating as well as a fascinating one, is that of arduous and humble ulterior reflection and effort toward clarification.

A second problem: we have considered various cases of infinite regress. I feel that these cases again confront psychoanalysis with serious problems, in fact as serious as were the paradoxes at the turn of the century for mathematics. It is gradually dawning upon us that psycho-analysis is always dealing with the mathematical infinite, even if psycho-analysts are, on the whole, not yet aware of it. Psycho-analysis may become the science which will have the greatest opportunity for developing the concept of the infinite and its "relations" with the homogeneous indivisible reality. If and when it does, it will have performed a great service to mathematics.

46.

What is that which is actually transformed into alpha-elements? Dr. Bion points to the difficulty of this problem when he carefully tells us that alpha-function "operates on the sense impressions, *whatever they are*, and on the emotions, *whatever they are*, of which the patient is aware." (1962 p. 6, my italics).

What is a sense impression? A sensation seems different from a perception (I.M.B. 1975, ch. 21). But the fact of *becoming aware* of a sensation changes a sensation into a perception, and this is impregnated with formulations-triads, that is, already with alpha-elements. So, I would think, alpha-function *may* operate on sense impressions we are aware of but *not in those aspects of the impression we are aware of.* We try to translate into triads something which actually is outside the realm of the thinkable: we may (provisionally) say that we "thinkate" the unthinkable but the unthinkable itself is *not* in the product of our effort (the alpha-element): the unthinkable cannot be thought.

47.

To "thinkate": the activity of trying to think the unthinkable by treating it (unsuccessfully) as though it were thinkable; in short: trying to think the unthinkable, which is absurd. Forgive me for the ugly neologism but I know of no word in any language which can convey this meaning; perhaps we shall later find a nicer word. To explain further: "thinkate:: would be the essential, unfulfillable, *intention* which has resulted in what I have called the translating function (I.M.B., 1975 ch. 8 and 25): to make the "indivisible-unthinkable" thinkable, hence divisible. Only that instead of thinking the unthinkable we only succeed in thinking what is thinkable, thinking endlessly. In this way, however, we get an important result: we conceive the mathematical infinite and the mathematical notion of limit. Would this be a territory of contact betwen both modes, a barrier in Bion's sense? If we try to reply we realise first, that the "distance" between the two modes is infinite and however much we try to make it smaller it always remains infinite. But even this description is misleading because there is no possibility of contact, not even of neighbourhood, between something which *is* approachable, contactable (the dividing mode) and something which is wholly outside these notions and any notion; hence there is no distance, just as no distance exists between, say, $(a + b)^2$ and the city of Rome. We here see the self-deception into which, without realising it, we have fallen in the creation of the important notion of (mathematical) limit: we were, *without realising it at all*, trying to come near to the homogeneous indivisible reality, but we did not realise that there is no distance between the two modes, so, there is no possibility of approaching the homogeneous mode. In the end, however, we got the important notion of approaching something (a number for instance) and of coming "as near to it as we wish" (as mathematicians say) without ever reaching it. Fundamental though this notion is in logico-bivalent mathematics, it is a complete failure with regard to the homogeneous indivisible reality. This would be an example of "thinkating." And we must recognise that for us, poor thinking beings, this thinkating gives us a rather satisfactory illusion of reaching the unthinkable.

48.

It would be a serious mistake, however, to think that alpha-function or the translating function—which *by the very essence of their nature are unsuccessful*—are a complete failure. In fact, from one point of view they are an impressive success. Though one can never succeed in making the homogeneous-unthinkable thinkable, the activity of the translating function (and I believe there is a vast zone of intersection between this function and Bion's alpha-function—see 50). results in something very valuable for man: it gives him the opportunity of expanding toward infinity the possibilities of understanding. *The hieratic unreachable homogeneous indivisible reality turns out to be the most powerful stimulus for the expression and full realisation of the potentialities of the heterogenic-dividing-synthetising mode.*

If we look, in particular, at the process of synthesis and generalisation, we may say that it is a great success if seen from the point of view of widening the territory of the heterogenic mode; it is instead a failure, a form of "thinkating, if it is looked at as an attempt at translating the homogeneous mode: it results in a mimicry of the mode, for to be a unity in the midst of multiplicity is not the same as to be *just a unity*, i.e., undivided, homogeneous, indivisible.

But it is a most fertile failure.

The homogeneous mode may be said to produce "induced current" in the heterogenic mode.

49.

I should like to put forward three thoughts. First: the least we can say about the relation between thought and knowledge is that for any given piece of knowledge there is a thought that is in bi-univocal correspondence with it and, most likely, also is isomorphic to it in one or more ways. I believe we can say more than that. Most probably thought and knowledge are simply two ways of looking at the same reality; I shall, however, not discuss this.

Second: any and all thoughts are a form of knowledge and hence of truth. Note that this is not saying the same as in the previous paragraph. This assertion leads to the fundamental question of what truth is, which I shall not discuss in detail here. I shall limit myself to pointing out that what is true in a system may not be so in another system. For instance, according to Euclidean geometry from a given point only one line can be traced which is parallel to a given line. This is not true in non-Euclidean geometry. Another example: Psycho-Analysis has furnished ample evidence which shows that a given action, such as stealing, which is generally considered to be bad is, in certain cases and for certain patients, a good action. In other words it is true that stealing is a bad action for "objective" morality and it is true that stealing is a good action for a given "subjective" morality.

Third: I submit that if we stick to the current ideas of what knowledge is, we can say that anything that is knowable is knowable to man. At first sight this might not seem true, for it is conceivable that the complexity and subtlety of a certain knowable structure is so great that it is beyond human capability and not beyond super-human capability. But, if he has patience and *human* ingenuity, man can get around this difficulty. A mathematician friend once told me that if the theory of relativity were formulated in words, it would take about thirty pages to develop it and then it would be, practically, incomprehensible to most people. But if formulas are employed, then man can circumvent the obstacle and understand. In other words, formulas are like titles of subjects which can be understood. Working with these titles man can get to understand realities which would be beyond his reach if he were to have present in his mind all there is under the title.

This is an interesting subject to develop. (Also see 26., 67. and 69.).

50.

42., 43., 46. and 48. provide an opportunity for peeping at *the notion of relation between two concepts*. Is the translating function the same thing as the alpha-function? The answer seems to be: no. But obviously they have much in common. How much? A first answer: just as the set $\{3, b\}$ is the intersection between the sets $\{a, b, 3, 5\}$ and $\{17, 3, 19, n, 5555, b\}$ we may say that alpha and translating functions have a zone of intersection. To discover what the intersection is, amounts to defining the sets of the elements in common between them; and we discover that words or verbal expressions have so many potential meanings that the effort to explicitate them would soon confront us with the problem of the infinite.

So we use other methods: "I *feel* that so and so is saying something similar to what I say; and this other concept, I feel, points toward . . ." When people follow this road, in the end they decide they are "of the same school of thought," shake hands and become great friends if something the other said struck a "good" chord in them; or they disagree and conclude they "belong to different schools" and even feel hostile if the other struck a sound that did not please them. A psycho-analytic example: Kleinians and A. Freudian-Hartmannians. Research becomes in this way a mixture of thinkingemotionemotionthinking:

thinkingemotion↘ . . . . ↗emo . . . kingthinking . . . onemoti . . .↘etc.:
emotionthinking↗ ↘ingemotionemotionemo . . . .↗.

the infinite net-mesh of bi-logic. However, if one indulges in a "measured" amount of bi-logic one finds that friendship-fusion may stimulate research. In the present case I believe that the study of the concept of alpha-function may stimulate the development of the concept of translating function, and vice versa. In the end one may arrive at a more comprehensive view of reality.

51.

The epistemological question seems hopeless, a Babel. Think of the fights between political groups, between nations, inside nations, in the family, between religious creeds, between analysts ... They are all due to, or at least connected with, differences of opinion: an epistemological question.

In spite of it all, we may be hopeful. It is possible that analysts may one day succeed in producing some healing light for human nature. Am I wrong in feeling that hearing Dr. Bion one breathes that hope? At least I do.

52.

May I suggest one concrete hopeful programme: to realise and explore the meaning of "one each question, at each point, there is not one truth but an infinite number of them, all with equal rights." It s very hard to accept that this sentence is true and to resign oneself to this predicament: it goes against the grain. Yet ... we would do well if we tried to see what it means and entails.

53.

A better understanding could take place if we became fully aware that psycho-analysis leads us into the ways of Parmenides and Zeno *and* into the ways of Heraclitus. Each reality can be seen *with equal right* as being homogeneousindivisible and as being potentially-infinitely-divisible: as a concrete thing (a breast, a penis, etc.) *and* as the set of all things that this thing is symbolised by, or symbolises; in the deep unconscious a breast, a book, a teacher are not different things, but the same thing, just "breastness": they are homogeneous-indivisible. The fact that in our interpretations we use one representant, for instance, the breast, to refer to the whole class, is a question of our (bi-logical) thinking, not of our symmetrical thinking.

Both ways *are true*. I do not see why and how I should choose one and reject the other as, it might seem (I am not sure), the three gentlemen just mentioned did. On the other hand I also find it hard to accept both alternatives: it confuses me, it leads me into anxiety. But I have not succeeded in avoiding from accepting them both.

54.

Once we have accepted both modes we realise that, for thinking, they are utterly incompatible between themselves. At the same time, as psychoanalytic observation shows daily, they are always co-present: bi-modal copresence, one type of which is bi-logic.

Once this awareness is reached, the possibility of infinite truths at each point becomes clear and inevitable. Strange, anxiogenous but inevitable. One must reflect more on its exact meaning.

55.

Even if one questions whether a sensation is a sense-impression, one may, I believe, apply to these latter the same reflections of 46. We may, therefore, conclude that if a sense-impression, *whatever it is*, is already conscious ("the patient is aware") it contains triads, because consciousness, light, presupposes heterogeneity, unless it is so vivid as to be dazzling and then it becomes triad-less but it is no longer consciousness . . . , unless we decide to call by the same name two different things. And so we come to a paradox (or are there two?): the alpha-function operates on the alpha-elements and the translating function of the heterogenic mode operates on itself! *However*, its work (their work?) is *induced* by the homogeneous indivisible reality (which is "lodged" in the "inducing coil") whereas alpha-function (translating function) *moves* in the *induced coil** . . . and tries to give an impressionistic impression of the homogeneous reality.

56.

What about "the emotions, whatever they are"? I believe something similar holds here. I see emotions as bi-logical structures (I.M.B. 1975, ch. 22 and 25); 1976a, 1976b). If we have an emotion we are aware of, ulterior work of translation may reveal a great many new aspects of it, formulate a great many new triads. This is not a useless or redundant but, on the contrary, a most useful and creative work. (Note that the last but one sentence is at least strange, perhaps paradoxical.)

57.

A closer look at some of what precedes enables us to approach a new insight:

The never-ending translation is a never-ending increase of triads. Suppose we have 3/8 and 4/8. Between these two rational numbers there are no eighths. But if we write them in an equivalent way we then realise that between 3/8 = 6/16 and 4/8 = 8/16 there is 7/16. We have another triad: 7, 16 and the relation between 7 and 16: 7/16. If instead we write our original numbers as 12/32 (= 3/8) and 16/32 (= 4/8) then we have 13/32, 14/32 and 15/32 between them: three new triads. Generalising: in the open interval between 3/8 and 4/8 (written according to the mathematic custom: $3/8 < x < 4/8$) there is an infinite set of rational numbers and this set has the power of the denumerable. And each number is different from any and all others.

The same holds for the set of triads. *We can increase our understanding of any*, however small, *piece of reality we have already understood*; we can

*The reader may see that I put "lodged" and "inducing coil" between brackets and "*moves*" and "*induced coil*" in italics. For a further understanding of this, see I.M.B. 1975, p. 349 (footnote).

increase it infinitely, and the minimum power of the set of our possibilities of further understanding that piece of reality, is the power of the denumerable.

58.

I must confess: that the set of triads does *not* have the power of the continuum, is not at all clear to me. Neither is it clear that it must have this power. (See also 42.). This question leads to a very difficult problem: the possibility that the set of rational numbers may have the power of the continuum *and* that of the denumerable: an absurdity in bivalent logic, but perhaps not (I believe) in the paradoxes of the infinite, which would be at the "frontier" (if there is one) between bivalent logic and bi-logic.

Mathematicians would probably smile with protective irony at who-ever takes this possibility seriously. However, I think this is subject for future arduous reflections concerning the possibility of a bi-logical foundation of mathematics.

59.

Would 57 be another way of expressing (a transformation of) Dr. Bion's remarks in the Brazilian Lectures 2, that the more we know the greater the territory becomes of what we don't know?

My guess: what Dr. Bion says and 57 are not the same thing, but 57 would *contain* a transformation *of a part* of what Dr. Bion says, and would also express more than what Dr. Bion says, just as what Dr. Bion says would, in its turn, contain more than 57.

Put in simple mathematical terms: Dr. Bion's remarks and 57 study two subjects which are different to a certain extent while having a large zone of intersection. It is only the respective formulations of this zone that can be made the subject of a bi-univocal correspondence or of a transformation or isomorphism. Note, however, that it is is an isomorphism, then the intersection is not that between two unstructured sets but between two abstract structures. If we look at this last question we are actually led to conclude that the zone is, in this case, not an unstructured set; we are, therefore, not dealing with a bi-univocal correspondence but rather with an isomorphism.

60.

Is Bion a Kleinian? Is he a Freudian? Is he a Bionian?

Analysed by M. Klein, in the atmosphere of Freud, his early writings have a distinctive flavour of M. Klein's last writings (projective identification, paranoid-schizoid position, envy) and, I believe, not so much of her early ones. M. Klein's beginnings are marked, in my opinion, by a constant reference to the overwhelming intensity of the child's feelings. She clearly pointed toward the concept of the infinite but stopped short of it, possibly because her intuitive nature did not show signs of a proclivity for mathematical analysis. In her later years the infinite which at first was transparent in her researches (only now transparent to me) became more dissimulated, though, perhaps, always hinted at. It seems to me that the infinite was also present from the beginning in Bion but it was only gradually that it became more obvious: the reverse of what happened in the case of M. Klein. Also in his case, and in spite of Bion's mathematical tendency, it is, on the whole, not presented in its more specifically mathematical aspects. Furthermore, it has, I believe, gradually given way in his thinking to the thing for the translation of which the infinite was (in my opinion) created by man: the homogeneous indivisible reality. Again here, he chose a highly personal way: instead of an explicit formulation of that reality he veiled reality "with-in" poetry: a highly Bionian way of being both modes, his seal and coat of arms.

61.

More reflection, a great deal more of it, is needed in order to see whether one may eventually succeed in discovering the distinctive traits of Bion's thinking. If and when this is achieved, I feel we shall have formulated a new way of co-existence between the two modes of being in man; because at least part of Dr. Bion's originality can, I believe, be seen in terms of the unique co-presence of both modes which he incarnates.

62.

Melanie Klein was profoundly assimilated by Bion and she gradually outwardly disappeared from him. But Bion's structure contains the elements of Kleinian presence. Just as our adipose tissue tends to have the proportions of fatty acids of the fat of the animals which we have actually eaten and not of that of other animals which we might have eaten. To put it more poetically:

> "Comme le fruit se fond en jouissance
> comme en delice il change son absence
> dans une bouche ou sa forme se meurt
> je hume ici ma future fumée
> et le ciel chante à l'âme consumée
> le changement des rives en rumeur."
> (Paul Valery, "Le Cimitière marin")

63.

I would, therefore, say, with Parthenope Bion (1973), that Bion is a post-Kleinian. But he is also a Kleinian.

Bion has eaten and assimilated Freud and seems to be still eating and assimilating him. He is, therefore, a post-Freudian and a Freudian. For the same reason he is a post-Bionian and a Bionian.

Does that answer the question put in 60?

64.

What are *we* to be? Bionians? In Rome Dr. Bion urged us earnestly, almost dramatically, to think by ourselves, to be ourselves. Is that possible if we are Bionians? I believe that depends on how we are so. In order to be ourselves we must assimilate him all the time and in so doing make him—in terms of a frequent but unsatisfactory "blend" of homogeneity with logico-bivalent thinking—disappear, and therefore face the horror of deicide. We become Bion-ourselves: post-Bionians. But after he is "bi-logically dead" we find him again alive and creative; and we drink again from his source: we become post-Bionians who have become, again, Bionians: we are only doing what he himself is doing. And so on: the incomprehensible mystery of communion.

Bionians, ourselves, post-Bionians, Bionians, ourselves . . . : creative evolution.

65.

(Reading Grinberg, 1975, p. 63) Is the ultimate reality of the object unknowable, forever unknowable?

a) If we accept that thinking-knowledge is or entails division, the expression of the heterogenic-dividing mode, then we may say that the heterogenic-dividing mode of being in us *and in the world* is, itself, *most naturally* knowable. *There is no unreachable—theoretically unreachable—territory of this mode*. We must immediately add, however, that (as I have put forward at Verona (I.M.B., 1977) the set of triads (: of knowledge-thinking), like the set of rational numbers* is an infinite set with no upper or lower bound. We

*I have chosen the rational numbers and not the natural numbers because , just as between any two rational numbers (the so-called density property), so "between" any two triads of knowledge we may place an infinite number of triads of knowledge. This is not the case with the set of natural numbers. As for the set of real numbers it also shares the density property with the rational numbers. We must, however, consider in this case the subset of irrational numbers; so far, I have not been able to see that there is a subset of triads in bi-univocal correspondence with it. This problem, however, as I see it, remains open. (See also 42.)

cannot, therefore, as individuals, ever have all possible knowledge. Is this a practical and not a conceptual impossibility? Remember here that the infinite is something radically, *essentially* different from whatever finite set of numbers, however great.

b) On the other hand there is the unknowable unthinkable indivisible homogeneous reality. It is unknowable and unthinkable because it is indivisible homogeneous, has no parts, and knowledge-thinking presupposes parts of aspects. Is this the Kantian thing-in-itself? I don't know. I only know that this reality (thing) is *the thing-in-itself-unknowable*.

Is what is described in a) an outcome or aspect of b) or a way of looking at b)?; or is it "incommensurable" with or of a different nature from b)? I don't know. So far, this is a riddle to me.

66.

"PRO-LOGUE . . . a fictitious account of psycho-analysis . . ." (Bion, 1975b, p. 7-9). It makes me think of the following implications and equivalences:*

1. [Nothing is seen in total darkness, something is seen in twilight, much is seen in "good" light, nothing is seen in dazzling light]

$\Rightarrow$

[for purposes of seeing, total darkness = dazzling light]

$\Rightarrow$

[*p*. not-*p*]   (*p and* not-*p*)

$\Leftrightarrow$

2. [the arse becomes the mouth *and* the mouth becomes the arse].

$\Leftrightarrow$

3. [nothing is distinguishable, there is only a homogeneous indivisible reality.]

However, if the principle is applied, as in 2, and if its application is "wrapped" in bivalent logic (the result is, in this case, bi-logic), then we can even get to know something *about* or "*around*" the thing-in-itself; I mean we can get familiar with it by studying its presence in bi-logical or other bimodal manifestations. Otherwise "the thing in itself is unknowable" (loc. cit. p. 8).

67.

"The thing in itself is unknowable." One may call it a "thing," a "noumenon" or, like Bion, simply "O," or "reality." All such names are inadequate

*Note the meanings of the signs employed: a) "$\Rightarrow$" means "implies"; b) "$\Leftrightarrow$" means "is equivalent to"; c) "." means "and"; d) "iff" means "if and only if."

because they are nearer *to our concept* of the "thing," "noumenon" . . . etc., than to the noumenon itself. Because, if it is a thing, i.e., something separate from other things, it belongs to the realm of the discrete, hence it is knowable; and if it is unknowable it is not a thing: it is homogeneous indivisible.

Is the formulation just put forward an opening toward another way of looking at this question, which has been oppressing all of us, admirers of Kant, for two hundred years plus a lifetime (our lifetime)? I may say that, so far as I am concerned, with my little torch of the two modes to take me by the hand, I am beginning to discover new meanings in the question. Though I feel like remaining reflective and silent before greatness and poetry-philosophy, I have, with fear, taken upon myself the task of communicating my reflections.

68.

I wonder what Kant would think if he heard Bion, who has meditated for years about the (Kantian) unknowable noumenon, talk now in a way reminiscent of Buddhist wisdom and let us suspect that the unknowable is unknowable because it is unthinkable.

69.

Could it be said that Kant implied, as is put forward in 67, that in some way reality is untranslatable in terms of thinking—because it is homogeneous indivisible, and thinking divides—but that thinking tries all the same to translate it into its own terms? Was he aware (in his own way) that the concept of the infinite, which is present in all men and which finds its most perfect expression in the mathematical infinite, is actually the expression of the attempt of the intellect, of the heterogenic-dividing mode, to translate the untranslatable homogeneity, at thinking the unthinkable?

Or did Kant mean something entirely different? I don't know.

Does Bion mean something else? What I can say is that Bion, who has been thinking and understanding all his life, also seems to feel quite at ease in thought-lessness,* i.e., indivisibility.

70.

Sometimes some people speaking of alpha- or beta-elements seem to give the impression that they are handling little round stones or little pieces of sheep's dung: it seems to me they are implying a colossal misinterpretation of the fluid-non-fluid-solid-non-solid-gaseous-non-gaseous and also indivisible

*Thought-lessness is to be understood literally, i.e., as devoid of thought.

and non-material quality of the human mind. And they seem to throw these little objects against the "uninitiated" eyes, trying to dazzle them and show how brave they are and how stupid those people are who don't understand them. Oh, how human this game is! But it is also irritating. It seems an inharmonious way of compensating the fear of annihilation by means of self-deification. (See also 3). This fear could be dealt with in better ways.

71.

I shall first make four quotations and then discuss a question that is implicit in them.

1. "So, at the two extremes. I can either be easily comprehensible and misleading, or truthful and incomprehensible" (Bion, 1974, p. 24).
2. "For this purpose I have used two things which are entirely meaningless; beta-elements which do not belong to the domain of thinking, and alpha-elements which are reserved for the domain of thought . . . These words are useful if we want to talk about things, even if there is no reason to believe they are facts . . . that . . . exist, except by a kind of metaphor . . ." (loc. cit., p. 28-29).
3. "The analyst . . . must be able to tolerate this expanding universe which expands faster than he can think" (loc. cit. p. 32).
4. That intense anxiety, that "state of mental agony" experienced, as reported, during Dr. Bion's lecture in Rio (Bion, 1975a, p. 8).

These four quotations show the difficulties and vicissitudes which one encounters in the "total" understanding of reality. One realises, in the first place, that understanding cannot ever be total. The first and third quotation make this very visible. In the second place (as the second and fourth quotation show), one also realises that when we seek deep understanding we find ourselves, willingly or unwillingly, in the midst of something "which do(es) not belong to the domain of thinking." The report of the Rio lecture strongly conveys this impression, i.e., of a condition or state of mind in which one finds oneself, of being, so to speak suspended in midair, between being-only-one-and-whole-only-thing, and feeling at the same time that, with our intellect, we grasp every *thing* in one fusing, life-death embrace. There is also the desperate awareness that we have grasped nothing. Every understanding is a misunderstanding. Furthermore, when light becomes so vivid as to be dazzling, it amounts to total darkness.

I believe schizophrenics have at times this same anxiety, and sometimes they seem to get out of it by coining a new word which is for them the alpha and omega of knowledge *as well as of indivision*. The patient who said he was an "orcopedian" and explained that this meant "the world-center-piece," is probably an example. But schizophrenics fool themselves, and their wonderful experience is unsatisfactory. In the midst of our limitations, those of us who do not reach their ecstasy are, after all, better off.

In short, a bi-modal experience in which the intellect, tired of translating, tired of bi-logic, attempts a deicidal becoming: becoming the unity, but *through the intellect*: light, only light, after all, with no homogeneity-indivision. It leads to dismay and sometimes to a "state of mental agony." Perhaps Dr. Bion succeeded in conveying and creating an experience of this kind in Rio. To have this, together with *some* awareness of it, may lead to maturation.

72.

The last sentence just written, in some way allays my anxiety and seems to make more tolerable the dazzling light-darkness, by making it of an intensity which does not blind. But it also leaves a feeling of dissatisfaction because it is a silent humble witness of the ungraspable whole of the two modes "fused" in one: a bi-modal experience become super-uni-modal: the individual-and-non-individual. However, if we avoid looking at the sun and humbly choose to stay in the twilight that befits the intellect, then we need not feel discouraged when we are confronted with the limitations of the intellect. For, though it is an important truth that every partial intellectual vision is a falsification—and every human thought *is* a partial vision—we may draw comfort if we look at the question from the other side, not that of falsification but that of revelation, and be content that, after all, thinking does reveal to us a bit of the truth: twilight truth or twilight knowledge, which is nothing in front of the knowable, but anyway some truth. An ideogram is false in that it is incomplete but it is true so far as it is a reflection of nature: some truth, not total truth.

73.

Throughout 2500 years Western thinking has avoided seeing the meaning of the concept of the infinite, the basis of the real number system, which is itself the foundation of mathematics. When Zeno almost forced them to think, philosophers and mathematicians were frightened, and did not seem to know they were, at the possibility of reaching certain insights, such as viewing the infinite as thinking's attempt at translating the homogeneous indivisible reality: this is precisely what Zeno's paradoxes pointed to. They reacted, called him a sophist and thought they had unmasked his fallacies. Zeno's arguments, however, are like "los muertos que vos matasteis," who "gozan de buena salud."* True, there were some exceptions (like Bertrand Russell), but these did not seem to go sufficiently far.

*"The dead you killed are in good health."

Another important opportunity was missed when Newton and Leibniz discovered the basic concepts of infinitesimal analysis. For two hundred years the best mathematical minds were at work until they clarified, in an admirable collective effort of thinking, which culminated in the transparent work of Cauchy, a great deal of the mysteries of the concept of limit. Once again, in the midst of this new admirable development of *thinking* which had taken place, mathematicians were blind to the fact that the homogeneous mode was "subterraneously" co-present and most influential. In fact, though everything that they found is true, it belonged to a realm of being which is *parallel* to the homogeneous mode. Their findings, however, did result in making mathematicians ignore the homogeneous mode. But they did not prove that there was no such mode; in other words, their admirable translating work was also a form of "thinkating."

Subsequently the studies of Cantor threw new light on, and made the problem provoked by the paradoxes of the infinite more urgent. How is it possible that the set of points of a segment of a straight line, however small the segment, has the same number of points (the same power or cardinality) as an infinite line or an infinite tri-dimensional space? Why should we affirm that even numbers are as many as the natural numbers, but not say that though this is true, that it is *equally* true to affirm, as common sense does, that they constitute only half the natural numbers? How is it possible that we must conclude that the union of one denumerable set with another denumerable set is still a denumerable set; and also conclude that the union of two sets with the power of the continuum has also the power of the continuum, but we have no right to say that 5 + 5 = 5! Are we so sure that everything is so clear? Do we have to fear so much the principle of non-contradiction that we cannot do without it at times? Are you, mathematicians, so sure that all that I am saying here is just a stupid misunderstanding? On the other hand, may it not be possible that there exists a way of *being outside the principle of non-contradiction without violating or denying it*? I *know* there is.*

Mathematics has, so far, closed its eyes to these problems or, in a better way, it has not opened them sufficiently to find a new way toward a more ample understanding of nature. In the meantime Psycho-Analysis has come in with a bunch of new disturbances-opportunities. Freud has discovered that processes in the unconscious are timeless, that psychical and physical reality are treated by the unconscious as though they were the same thing; and he has also discovered the basic unity and interchangeability of primary objects and their symbols. These discoveries have paved the way for the concept of homogeneous indivisible reality, and for that of bi-modal co-presence and bi-logic.

What will come out of all this?

*In fact, in a bi-logical mathematical structure I have put forward, it is perfectly legitimate to say that 5 + 5 = 10 = 20 = 1.066 = any other number. (See I.M.B. 1976 b.)

74.

I am now looking again at the ocean. There are many things that I can go on learning from Bion. I want to learn from him and don't want to learn from him. I am afraid of being drowned in food and this fear is biologically sound: we eat to exist and grow, and we don't exist and grow in order to eat. This is true not only for our body. Eat, yes, but be yourself. This entails moderation in eating, otherwise you deform yourself by developing fat which should not belong to you, and by inhibiting your creative possibilities. I, like many people, cannot learn from anybody unless I go through a slow process of reflection and assimilation.

Some analyst might say that I am a prey to voracity and aggressive envious wishes against the breast. My reply: what I say in the previous paragraph is true; what you say is also true but not relevant just now. To make it a stereotyped interpretation, which after so much use becomes a platitude, is a sign of inertia as well as an abuse.

75.

In mathematics $-0 = +0 = 0$; and between -0 and $+0$, that is, between 0 and 0 there is only 0. So $\{1, 2, 3 \ldots 80\}$ does not exist between -0 and $+0$. Similarly, what is divided does not exist for what is undivided, i.e., the homogeneous indivisible reality. Vice versa, the undivided reality is not grasped by thinking, cannot be thought. The translating function is a form of thinking which, however, is *not* thinking the homogeneous indivisible reality but trying to think *about* and only succeeding in thinking "outside" this reality. If we were *to look without thinking*, (a logico-bivalent or "dividing" absurdity) i.e., to look from the "point of view" of the homogeneous indivisible reality, we should have to conclude that the translating function, which from the point of view of thinking can actually be said to be thinking (and sometimes excellent thinking), is not good or correct thinking if it pretends to convey the homogeneous reality: so far as this pretension or intention is concerned, it is a complete failure, a pitiful babbling. Out of respect for thinking and out of respect for the indivisible reality we must not call this babbling thinking. For want of a better term, let us *provisionally* call it "thinkating."

76.

(Starting from 75.). One side of the coin: the concept of the infinite has every right to be called the supreme, most intrepid creation of the intellect. Its most precise expression is the mathematical infinite. Mathematics moves in its atmosphere. But the infinite also pervades human life. It is at the core of theism and atheism and hence of theistic and atheistic religions; at the core of the structure of society, of love and hate, envy and all strong emotions. Every time we *speak* about all these things we make some clear or occult reference to the infinite.

The other side: the concept is riddled with what mathematicians call its paradoxes. This last word hides, I feel, the gravity of the problem: insoluble contradictions. The deep cause of these contradictions is, as I see it, that the infinite is the attempt at thinking the unthinkable.

Conclusion: as an expression of thinking, a supreme achievement; as an attempt at thinking the unthinkable, a babble, a complete failure.

Meeting point of both outcomes: the paradoxes of the infinite, a most intelligent babble. We must try to get into their core and transform it into an articulate whole. My guess is that, so far, only bi-logic can achieve this aim.

77.

A distinct impression from the Rome lectures is that Dr. Bion, to put it in my own terms, has gone wholeheartedly into a bi-modal co-presence of an original kind. In order to understand it, I personally feel I must reflect more about it and him. I realise that this co-presence is not bi-logic. I find his public thinking free of bi-logic, as befits scientific thinking (no private thinking is completely free of bi-logic), and is at the same time highly and originally bi-modal. One gets the impression that each "grain" of his understanding is also (in my terms) homogeneous indivisible. I personally find it fascinating. I also believe that this is one of the reasons for Dr. Bion's impact on people.

May we succeed in understanding and formulating his bi-modality. Note that this task would not be the same as the translating function because we are in this case dealing with bi-modality and not just with the homogeneous indivisible; and bi-modality seems to be not alien to the possibility of isomorphism or bi-univocal correspondence.

78.

A poem may be single or double acrostic. Dr. Bion's thinking is frequently a multiple acrostic. Reality is infinitely acrostic. To explain: the letters a, b, c, d can be arranged in 4 x 3 x 2 x 1 = 24 different ways (permutations). Of all possible permutations of the letters of a poem, a single acrostic privileges only two of them to be meaningful: the overt and the hidden one. Any piece of reality, however small, can be conceived as being formed of an infinite number of elements (triads), hence the possibility of an infinite acrostic, all of the meanings of which are logic-bivalent. Frequently Dr. Bion's thinking is a multiple, logico-bivalent acrostic. This fact confers a puzzling, disquieting, stimulating quality to his thinking, a quality which many of us have enjoyed. At times it just touches on the humourous as, for instance, when he gives a sharp answer to a question in such an acrostic way that it may at first sight seem he hasn't answered it at all.

79.

Before reflecting about Bion I had not thought of the existence of the acrostics of the mind. Now I feel it is a fascinating subject which helps our understanding. Consider the following:

–There are logico-bivalent acrostic thoughts. These, like all logico-bivalent thinking (I.M.B. Verona 1977), are bi-modal. Hence any thought of this type is acrostic in two ways: bi-modal and logico-bivalent.

–There are logico-bivalent thoughts which are not logico-bivalent acrostics. These are, necessarily, bi-modal, and as a consequence, bi-modal acrostics.

–Schizophrenic utterances frequently produce a strange disquieting impression. Upon examination we find that they are *bi-logical acrostics*.

–All the acrostics of the mind are disquieting: they tend to provoke the sense of the uncanny. As an extreme case we may consider the paranoid delusion that some patients have when they think that people are making references to them on the radio or in the newspapers. From a logico-bivalent point of view this is false, but not from a bi-modal point of view, for any bi-modal acrostic—which means every one of the thoughts and utterances of the world–makes a reference to any one of us, individuals, so far as we *are* the homogeneous indivisible reality. Viewed from this point of view we may say that a delusion always has an aspect of truth. What makes it a delusion is the fact that the "blend" between both modes that is expressed in it does not respect completely the heterogenic mode. A most interesting subject for further research.

–One may defend oneself against Bion's acrostic thinking by saying it is strange, unpredictable, cock-eyed or even schizophrenic: a defence against the emergence of a catastrophic reaction which, in this case, never arrives at exploding but always remains painfully tenesmic.

Instead of all the just mentioned adjectives, would it not be better to try to understand and assimilate him?

80.

(To complete 43). If somebody is authentic and creative, then he feels, symmetrically, that he is God. If and when he discovers the creativity-divinity of another, he feels annihilated. Then he tries deicide. If *that* God does not die there is no alternative but to accept his existence. A form of politheism is then born in the depths of one's entrails. Maturity means accepting that one is god and at the same time a point, i.e., so small as to have no dimensions, and that the others are also gods and points as well. This is a very difficult achievement; most people remain at the level of self-deification and annihilation of the other. Maturity contains and implicity expresses the long and detailed story of self-deification, deicide, annihilation, self-deification, birth of two (or more) gods. But the point itself (see 43), an O-dimensional space, is mysteriously, in its turn, the "meeting-point" of both modes: the extensive-dividing one, and the indivisible. The point is a wonderful intuitive creation of the human intellect; perhaps mathematics has only begun to explore it.

Anybody who approaches Bion with authenticity and respect for the other, goës through this maturational experience.

Is this reflection acrostic?

+0*

I have gleaned a few grains: ever so few! I must now stop my gleaner's harvest. The ocean of Dr. Bion's golden harvest remains untouched. I cannot even claim to have looked at his most important contributions. (My intention is to continue to draw inspiration from him.) I can only claim to have tried to look with the eyes of nature (my nature) and to have tried to keep these eyes untainted by nurture, which frequently deforms us, humans; this holds true in particular, and especially, for psycho-analytic nurtures of whatever brand: Freudian, Kleinian, Anna-freudian, Hartmannian, Jungian (Freudians, please forgive me) and also Bionian.

> Dear Doctor Bion,
>
> Looking at you as one looks at an elder brother or father, may I say that, just as I feel (and believe my reflections show) that your longing search completes and stimulates the development of my longing search, I hope that, after reading these pages, you may also feel that my longing search may help to complement yours.
>
> And may you live long to continue to give us your bread of understanding, of mysterious acrostic understanding as well as indivision in the unity beyond understanding. Thank you and God bless you.**

*See 75.

**[Editor's Note:] As the reader must have surmised, this tribute was written to Dr. Bion while he was still alive.

A Note on Bion's Concept "Reversal of Alpha-Function"

Donald Meltzer

EDITOR'S NOTE: *Doctor Meltzer has taken up the enlightening theme of studying Bion's concept of "reversal of alpha function" and employs it to discriminate between Klein's concept of mutilation of objects and Bion's concept of the formation of bizarre objects. A pithy clinical example is used to demonstrate Meltzer's theme that Bion's concept of the reversal of alpha function amounts to a particular kind of mutilation in which the patient's ego* and *superego are projected into the image of an object, thereby rendering the self denuded of mind and the image bizarrely distorted (unnaturally changed). Meltzer then discusses the significance of this for psychoanalytic practice.*

A Note on Bion's Concept "Reversal of Alpha Function"

Donald Meltzer, M.D. (Oxford)

When a new theory is proposed in psycho-analysis it can be said to undertake two functions: one is to organize the clinical phenomena that have already been observed, in a more aesthetic (beautiful?) way; the other is to provide a tool of observation that will open to view previously invisible phenomena of the consulting room. Wilfred Bion, beginning with his papers on schizophrenia, sought to amplify the model of the mind which we employ in psycho-analysis so that processes of thinking and disturbances in this capacity could be investigated. The first systematic presentation of this effort, *Learning from Experience* (1962) formulated an "empty" concept of alpha-process by means of which the "sense impressions of emotional experiences" were converted into elements, building-blocks for dream thoughts, which could be used for thinking, might be available for storage as memory, and whose continuity formed a "contact barrier" that separated conscious from unconscious mental processes.

The "emptiness" of this model was stressed over and over by Bion, along with the caution against over-hasty attempts to fill it with clinical meaning. He himself has been almost single-handedly exploring its possible meaning in the series of books which followed, namely *Elements of Psycho-analysis* (1963), *Transformations* (1965), and *Attention and Interpretation* (1970). It is with a certain trepidation that this paper is offered as a tentative exploration of his fascinating idea that alpha-process can perhaps work backwards, cannibalizing the already formed alpha-elements to produce either the beta-screen or perhaps bizarre objects. It is probably best to quote rather than to paraphrase. He writes (page 25, *Learning from Experience*) in evaluating the analyst's and patient's separate contributions to the situation in which the beta-screen is being formed:

> The analysand contributes changes which are associated with the replacement of alpha-function by what may be described as a reversal of direction of the function.

And here he adds a note:

> The reversal of direction is compatible with the treatment of thoughts by evacuation; that is to say, that if the personality lacks the apparatus that would enable it to "think" thoughts but is ca-

Meltzer, D. ["A Note on Bion's Concept of Reversal of Alpha Function"] This contribution was originally prepared for the *Bion Memorial* but was first published as "Appendix" in *The Kleinian Development*, Part III: *The Clinical Significance of the Work of Bion*. Perthshire: Clunie Press, 1978, 119-126.

> pable of attempting to rid the psyche of thoughts in much the same way as it rids itself of accretions of stimuli, then reversal of alpha-function may be the method employed.

He continues,

> Instead of sense impressions being changed into alpha elements for use in dream thoughts and unconscious waking thinking, the development of the contact-barrier is replaced by its destruction. This is effected by the reversal of alpha-function so that the contact barrier and the dream thoughts and unconscious waking thinking, which are the texture of the contact-barrier, are turned into alpha-elements, divested of all characteristics that separate them from beta-elements and are then projected, thus forming the beta-screen.

Further,

> Reversal of alpha-function means the dispersal of the contact-barrier and is quite compatible with the establishment of objects with the characteristics I once ascribed to bizarre objects.

He further points out that there is an important difference in his conception of the beta-element and the bizarre object; the latter is "beta-element plus ego and superego traces."

Before we can embark upon the clinical material through which meaning may be poured into the "empty" vessel of thought, it is necessary to remind the reader of an historical item. Bion has amplified Melanie Klein's concept of sadistic and omnipotent attacks upon internal objects and the structure of the self to include also attacks on individual functions of the ego and upon "linking" in general as the basic operation in thought, its prototype being the link between infant and breast. To test the usefulness of Bion's formulations it is necessary to demonstrate that they make possible an integration of observations not possible by previous formulations. The particular question that will arise in connection with the material to follow is this: does the formulation of alpha-function and its possible reversal extend the range of psycho-analytic observation and thought beyond that made possible by Mrs. Klein's formulations regarding sadistic attacks, splitting processes and projective identification with internal objects?

CLINICAL MATERIAL—A 35-YEAR OLD MAN

The session begins perhaps two minutes late: no comment. He has had a horrible dream, which it takes him some considerable time to tell against strong resistance, in the form of a "what's the use" attitude. The background of the dream collects before the dream is actually presented, including some material of previous sessions which had dealt with his feelings of ingratitude to his mother's friends whom the two of them had visited in Germany in the summer. He had never sent a thank-you note but yesterday received an invitation for Christmas.. He hates ingratitude in himself or others and yesterday's material had centered on a fellow of the college (his initials D.M.) whose furniture he had helped to move; D.M. has never thanked the patient nor invited him to dinner. Today's material then veers off into a description of his sensitivity to his surroundings and how he will lose his room in college next year and have to find one in another which he hates. It is connected with the institute in the U.S.A. where he spent two miserable years and he also feels at loggerheads with X. who tried to bully him into accepting the "great honour" of being a fellow at his college. In the dream there is a huge L-shaped room like one at the American institute but also, by virtue of the grey lino, like his present room as it was before he had bullied and cajoled the authorities into carpeting and decorating and had exchanged all the horrible furniture for a rather nice settee and chairs. Yes, he realises that this excessive dependence on external comfort implies a defect in his internal sense of security. In the dream someone was talking about an old woman who had been dreadfully deformed by an accident. Then she seemed to be there on the floor, alive but so deformed she was hardly recognisable as a human. One extraordinary and somehow particularly horrible feature was that originally she had had extremely long fingernails, extending not only outward but also up her fingers, and under the skin of the arm. These seemed to have been struck and driven up her arm so that their ends stuck out near her elbows. The point seemed to be that she was suing for compensation but this was refused on the ground that she was so completely deformed that one could get no idea at all of what had been her original state. This applied particularly to the fingernails, for, although they did not protrude from her fingers but only from her elbows, the intervening nails did not show through the skin. The impression of horror did not seem to be accompanied by any emotion other than aversion.

I suggest to him that the background of the dream indicates that the problem is one of guilt and reparation, neither of which can be set in motion unless the mutilated object can be recognized and connected with its former undamaged and perhaps young and beautiful state, i.e., his mother as a young woman in his childhood as compared with the old woman, equated with her friends in Germany, who kept being generous to him despite his ingratitude, thus becoming old and empty. In order to get rid of this tormenting sense of guilt it is necessary to so attack the old mother that her disfigurement defies connection with the original object, thus becoming "some old woman" rather than "mummy." But is there not a mathematical technique that he mentioned yesterday, called "transpositional equations," connected with analytical geometry, whereby, if the distortion of the grid of reference can be demonstraed, two objects which seem grossly different can be shown to be basically identical but projected on to different grid systems like distortions in a picture on a piece of rubber? He agreed; his work deals with the mathematics which makes such crude analogies unnecessary. (I am thinking of the pictures of fish and skulls in D'Arcy Thompson's "Growth of Form" and he confirms this reference.) The long fingernails therefore represent the lines of the grid and if they can be made visible and the grid rectified to its basic axes, the image of the beautiful young mother can be rediscovered in the dehumanized old woman. The motto of the defence would be, "If you damage mummy and the sight of it causes you guilt and remorse, smash her beyond all recognition until you feel only horror and revulsion."

DISCUSSION

We were approaching the first holiday break of this man's analysis, which had been arranged at an interview just prior to the previous summer holiday when he was expecting his mother to come all the way from Australia to visit him and take him to see some aristocratic friends of hers in Germany. The patient had not seen his mother for some years and was disturbed, not only at finding her looking much older than his image of her, but also at finding his prior devotion much cooled. He is the eldest of her children and the only "successful" one, having been rather arrogantly independent since early childhood.

From the Kleinian point of view it is a rather ordinary dream that illustrates the thesis that retreat from depressive anxiety referrable to damaged internal objects follows a route whereby the depressive pain is felt as persecutory depression and opens the way to further attacks on the damaged object as a persecutor. The parallel material of his associations suggests that the room in college which he had made cosy by "bullying and cajoling" the authorities to carpet, hiding the old lino which reminded him of the "two miserable years" in the United States, was to be taken away: that is, that the analysis was threatening to return him to a state of misery (the analyst being from the U.S.) as revenge for his not feeling "honoured" at being accepted for analysis (as with X's invitation). The analyst, like the fellow with the same initials (D.M.), is to contain the split-off attribute of ingratitude.

But what could a Kleinian formulation make of these fingernails which, instead of growing out, had been driven in the reverse direction until they stuck out at the old woman's elbow? What could it make of the refusal of compensation on the grounds that the old woman was so horribly deformed that no idea could be established of her previous state? Perhaps we can assume that the imponderable nature of the deformed old woman is exactly the quality that makes her a bizarre object in Bion's sense rather than a mutilated object in Mrs. Klein's. In the courtroom of the dream no-one seemed to doubt that she had been a human, that there had been an accident, that her fingernails had been driven up her arm. But somehow the *frame of reference of thought* had been destroyed, a frame having a particular connection with the patient's overriding professional preoccupations. One might say that his work has to do with getting at the truth about problems of analytical geometry through formulae which would be far more precise than the "crude analogies" of grid-distortion.

Not only could Kleinian formulations before Bion have made no headway with such a problem; they would not have been able even to state the problem itself: namely the attack on thinking. They could approach only the attack on feeling, where, of course, they go quite some distance. In contrast a Freudian formulation would probably get hung up on the castration anxiety which is most certainly an element in the dream (are the woman's nipples the remnants of her penis, smashed up and driven inward and upward until they stick out of the breasts?).

BIONIC RECAPITULATION

The patient is facing the first holiday break of his analysis and feels that his jealousy of the other analytical children is going to drive him to attack his internal analytical mother with a view to lessening the devotion and its consequent separation pain. But the return to analysis would hold him to a state of mind of misery about these attacks, hating himself for ingratitude, perhaps even reducing him to having to beg, rather than bully, the daddy-authorities to redecorate the mummy and make her cosy once more. That would be unbearably humiliating to such an independent baby. Although he has spent years developing a mode of thought for seeing the truth with precision in such situations, he is prepared to destroy that mental capacity (alpha-function of a particular sort) by making it run in reverse (instead of growing outward to form the lines of a grid of reference, the fingernails are driven backwards to disappear under the skin, appearing only at the elbows). The consequence is a beta-element "plus ego and superego traces" (the distorted old woman, having only traces of the mother and of his discarded ego-capacity for thinking with transpositional equations). She is now a bizarre object, uncontainable in thought, suitable only for evacuation.

IMPLICATIONS

Let us take the "crude analogy" of a geometric grid on a piece of rubber as a model of a piece of mental equipment, a particular bit of alpha-function apparatus. Place on it a picture of an old woman and pull the rubber in various ways until the picture of a beautiful young woman appears. Take this as a model of alpha-function operating on "the sense impressions of an emotional experience." Such a bit of apparatus may be essential for the creation of an image that makes it possible to connect the old woman who visits you from Australia with the young beautiful mother who insisted on having other children against your sage advice.

POSTSCRIPT

The analysis progressed very well through the next term bringing forward memory after memory of the catastrophic reactions to the births of his next siblings, reactions which progressively relegated his father to a position of negligible importance in his life and consolidated his status as mother's little husband and adviser. As the second holiday break approached he became rather restive, left early to go to Australia to visit his family on the grounds that his next sibling (who had the same Christian name as the analyst) needed his help and advice. While there he did a group-therapy "experience" during which he developed a manic state, thought he was the Messiah, and returned late to break off the analysis, full of "gratitude" that the analysis had laid the background for his total cure in the group. He was, however, willing to see the analyst once a week to help him to understand how this transformation of the patient had come about. Over the next two months he gradually slipped into a state of depression after breaking off completely in a rage at the analyst's "stupidity." He finally returned to analysis in time to make a more satisfactory preparation for the long summer break. It was of interest that he could not bring himself to pay his fees until the last day, by which time the four months of work came to almost the precise amount he had paid for the five-day group "therapy."

Dr. Bion wrote me a kind and interesting note when I sent him the paper:

> 'aesthetic (beautiful?) way'–Now I would use as a model: the diamond cutter's method of cutting a stone so that a ray of light entering the stone is reflected back *by the same path* in such a way that the light is augmented–the same 'free association' is reflected back by the same path, but with augmented 'brilliance.' So the patient is able to see his 'reflection,' only more clearly than he can see his personality as expressed by himself alone (i.e., without an analyst).

References

Bion, W.R. (1962). *Learning From Experience*. London: Heinemann.
—— (1963). *Elements of Psycho-Analysis*. New York: Basic Books.
—— (1965). *Transformations*. London: Heinemann.
—— (1970). *Attention and Interpretation*. London: Tavistock.

EDITOR'S NOTE: *Roger E. Money-Kyrle has brought his natural science training to bear on psychoanalytic problems over the years (he was educated as a biologist and has backgrounds in epistemology, logic, and philosophy). He was analyzed both by Freud and by Klein.*

Man's Picture of His World* *is but one of his later summaries of his ideas. Money-Kyrle is, like Bion, a Kleinian and post-Kleinian metapsychologist. Like Bion, he is interested in how we learn to think and, more to the point, how we learn* not *to think. This contribution, which was originally printed in* The International Journal of Psycho-Analysis *in 1968, represents a clear and succinct account of Money-Kyrle's ideas about mind. He has updated the article with a postscript specially written for the Memorial.*

The main thrust of the author's ideas, after accounting for the change in analytic orientation from sexual inhibition, through unconscious moral conflict, to unconscious misconceptions, is to conceptualize that basic mental health invokes the capacity for "re-cognition" of the inherent class (note Matte-Blanco in this regard) of an infant's pre-conceptions about a breast, his capacity to "recognize" its realization with a found breast, and to preserve this "re-cognition" against undermining and replacements by misconceptions. It is the dominance of permanent "mis-conceptions" which characterize mental illness. Thus mental illness, rather than being merely a sexual or moral difficulty, is now, thanks to Bion and Money-Kyrle, a defect in thinking, a defect characterized by a mind which either does not contain a "thinking couple" (a projecting infant plus a mother whose "reverie" can effectively transform the infant's projections into less toxic forms) or is so saturated with "mis-conceptions" that the capacity for "empty thoughts" to become properly developed is forever impeded. Bion and Money-Kyrle have thus done for psychoanalytic phenomenology what Piaget had been more superficially attempting for "descriptive" or "anthropological" psychology. Cognition and "re-cognition" are the essence of human experience, in short.

*Money-Kyrle, R.E. (1961). ***Man's Picture of His World***. New York: Int. Univ. Press.

Cognitive Development*

R.E. Money-Kyrle

Introduction: Three States in the Approach to Mental Illness

As perhaps often happens, I became preoccupied with a problem–in this case the problem of cognitive development–without knowing why it was of such interest to me. I subsequently discovered some of the reasons, and by way of introduction will outline what seems to me the most rational one.

Briefly then, and with a good deal of oversimplification, I think I became preoccupied with cognitive development as the result of reaching the third of three stages in my approach to mental illness–stages which very roughly reflect successive attitudes which were fairly common in the psychoanalytic movement as a whole.

In the first stage, 40 or 50 years ago, my dominant assumption would have been that *mental illness is the result of sexual inhibitions*. This may be profoundly true; but naively understood can lead to very superficial analysis. Moreover, in a subtle way, it can encourage a patient to adhere to the unconscious belief that, instead of giving up his Oedipus complex, he can realize it with the analyst's help and so be master of the world.

In the second stage, 20 to 25 years ago, my dominant assumption would have been that *mental illness is the result of unconscious moral conflict.* This supplements, rather than contradicts, the earlier view, and implies a better understanding of Freud's concept of the superego with Kleinian additions about the complexity of the early ego-superego relationship. In particular, a harsh superego is thought of as the result, less of a harsh upbringing, than of an "intra-psychic paranoia" (if I may coin the word). The receipt, therefore, is to try to get the patient to reintegrate the projections which distorted his superego–a process which precipitates what Klein called the depressive position, and provides a motive in depressive guilt for curbing attacks on improved internal figures.

In the third and recent stage, my dominant assumption is that *the patient, whether clinically ill or not, suffers from unconscious misconceptions and delusions*. As before, this assumption supplements rather than supersedes the other two: the patient's inhibitions are a product of his misconceptions, and his harsh superego is itself a misconception. But it is not the only one. I now often get the impression that the deep unconscious, even of apparently normal analysands, is simply riddled with misconceptions, particularly in the sexual sphere. Where, for example, I would formerly have interpreted a dream as a representation of the parents' intercourse, I would

*This paper was read before the British Psycho-Analytic Society at a meeting on 6 December 1967.

Money-Kyrle, R. ["On Cognitive Development"] This article originally appeared in *The International Journal of Psycho-Analysis* 49, 691-698.

now more often interpret it as a *misrepresentation* of this event. Indeed, every conceivable representation of it seems to proliferate in the unconscious *except the right one*.

Such misconceptions of the primal scene used to be attributed to the external impediments put in the way of the child's sexual curiosity. But I am now convinced that, like other animals, he is innately predisposed to discover the truth, and that the impediments are mainly emotional. Indeed, these impediments are by now much better understood. I think, too, we are on the edge of understanding the innate process of cognitive development against which they operate—often with fantastic strength. (See, for instance, what Bion [1962] has written on the conflict between K and –K.)

My aim has been to outline a theory of this interaction (between our perception of truth and the will to distort it). In doing so, I found I could widen its scope to include unconscious (non-psychotic) delusions—in particular, disorientations—as well as misconceptions. But all I have really done is to suggest two new "hooks" to hang a lot of existing theory on, and even this work is very incomplete. The two hooks relate to the two mental tasks any newborn animal has to perform if it is to survive: the acquisition of a few, I believe innately predetermined, concepts (or class notions), and, what is not innately predetermined, the location of their members in a space-time system. I will now try to explain what I mean by this.

Concept Building

As my starting point, I take from Bion (1962, 1963) the notion of an "innate preconception mating with a realization to form a conception"; and from Schlick (1925) the view that acquiring knowledge consists, not in being aware of sensory-emotional experience but in *recognizing* what it is. If this means recognizing something as a member of a class, or subordinating it to a concept, Schlick's and Bion's approaches seem to be similar—except that Bion starts with concepts (or preconceptions) which are in some sense innate.*

Of course there are enormous difficulties. The 2,000-year-old problem of universals, that is, general notions, is involved. On the one side are the nominalists to whom a class is no more than the common name we give to a number of similar objects or events, or perhaps a convenient logical fiction. On the other, are the realists, descendants as it were of Plato, to whom a class is an ideal laid up in heaven, which we are reminded of whenever we see an imperfect copy. Plato's *Ideas*, then, would seem to be the mythical forerunners of Bion's "Innate Preconceptions."

The difficulty in accepting their existence springs, I think, from the impossibility of imagining them. We can imagine a particular dog, we can

*Whether these are thought of as the product of some kind of racial memory or of cerebral variation and selection is perhaps psychoanalytically irrelevant. Personally, I think of them as products of variation and selection.

imagine a mongrel having qualities taken from many particular dogs; but this is no more than a kind of visual symbol, or name, for the concept "dog in general which we cannot imagine.

An innate preconception, then, if it exists, is something we use without being able to imagine it. I think of it as having some of the qualities of a forgotten word. Various words suggest themselves to us, which we have no hesitation in rejecting, till the right word occurs which we recognize immediately. I think this is what Bion means by an "empty thought." It is also something which, though it cannot be imagined, can be described as analogous, say, to a form waiting for a content. We may assume its hypothetical existence, develop a theory from this assumption, and see whether the theory so developed fits, and helps to clarify phenomena observed in psychoanalysis.

So far as our present knowledge goes, the first innate preconception to operate in a new-born baby is presumably one of a breast or nipple. Or rather, since the opposite emotions of love and hate may be supposed to colour the preconception from the beginning, of a good breast and a bad one. The two classes, defined negatively as excluding what does not frustrate on the one hand, and as what does not satisfy on the other, cover a wide range: a number of objects could be *recognized* as members (or in Bion's terms, could mate with them). But whatever is first recognized as such—a particular breast or bottle given in a particular way—would seem to have the effect of narrowing the class. A memory image of the first member to be recognized acts as a kind of name for the class; but being analogous to an onomatopoeic name, it limits what can be recognized as members to objects that resemble it fairly closely. At any rate, the baby can now be satisfied only by the good breast it has had before, and not by an alternative which would have satisfied it if this had been offered in the first place. A class represented by a memory image functioning as a name is a concept. It differs from an innate preconception in that it results from the mating of an innate preconception with a realization (Bion), or what is the same thing, from the primary act of recognizing a member of an innate class. The process would appear to be the same as that observed behaviouristically by ethologists and called "imprinting" by them.

Side by side with the development of a concept of a breast, or more specifically, of a nipple, we may suppose the development of a concept of something which receives, or contains, the nipple, that is, a mouth—though the "psychic flow" can be felt to be in either direction. From these two concepts, it would seem that all, or almost all of the vast number of concepts we employ are ultimately derived by processes of division and combination (splitting and integration).* Moreover, I have the strong impression that the next steps in the construction of a set of basic concepts does not depend solely on external experience, but is itself innately predetermined. The original innate preconception of the good and bad breast or nipple seems

*In taking "nipple" and "mouth" as the two most primitive concepts I do not wish to exclude the possibility that they may themselves be derived from still more primitive ones, or that we may eventually be able to reconstruct the psychology of the developing foetus.

itself to undergo a spontaneous differentiation and to bud-off, as it were, other innate preconceptions—in particular, those of a good and a bad penis. If so, the mouth concept is correspondingly differentiated into mouth and vagina. Or it may be that a mouth preconception differentiates into preconceptions of mouth and vagina, and precipitates a corresponding differentiation in the nipple concept. The exact procedure must be extraordinarily complex; but the experience of seeing a patient, who has failed to achieve such differentiations in infancy, begin to make them in dreams occurring in analysis—penis differentiating from nipple; vagina from mouth and anus, and so on—has convinced me that what I am trying to describe does, in some form, normally take place in the first few months of postnatal life.

Assuming as I do that further innately determined differentiations within the two basic innate preconceptions occur in the first few months of postnatal life, and that even a civilized environment provides objects to be recognized as members of the several classes so formed, a baby must be assumed capable of quickly learning to understand the basic structure of all the essential facts of life. In particular, he should be capable of understanding—though not of course in a fully adult way—the relation between his parents, and the way in which other rival babies may be made. Indeed, I believe that, if he does not preconsciously begin to understand this by the time he is about six months old, he never will, nor will his adult sexual life be normal—at least not without the help of prolonged analysis.*

Bion has described psychotic mechanisms which attack concept building at its source, so that the "thought" of an absent object—originally, the breast—is not formed and thinking is impossible. I am concerned here with the lesser disturbances which distort concepts rather than prevent their formation altogether and which distort them mainly for the purpose of evading the Oedipus complex. What actually seems to happen is that, while part of the developing personality does learn to understand the facts of life, suffers the pains of an Oedipus complex, discards it from guilt, becomes reconciled to the parental relation, internalizes it and achieves maturity, other parts remain ignorant and retarded. Quite often, no part achieves this kind of cognitive maturity. An individual in whom all parts have achieved it exists only as a standard of cognitive normality which no one quite achieves.

The reasons for the partial failure are to be found in Freud's "Two Principles of Mental Functioning" (1911). The infant, or some part of the infant, fails to *recognize* what is intolerable to him. There may be a primary failure to recognize a member of an innate class, in which case the corresponding concept does not form. A vital term in the vocabulary of thought is missing. In this way, primal envy of the kind described by Klein (1957) may prevent the formation of the concept of a good breast. (The concept of a bad one always seems to form). Or if the concept is formed, envy may

*The exact dating of early stages reconstructed in analysis is made more difficult because parts of the self, e.g., an oral part, which are split off and do not undergo emotional development seem to be yet capable of acquiring knowledge belonging to later periods, e.g., the oedipal one. This may retrospectively intensify the oedipal element in the oral stage.

prevent the subsequent recognition of its members. So a patient may feel that good analysts (breasts) exist, but the analyst (breast) he has is almost never it. The recognition, or re-recognition, of a good penis seems to be a commoner failure, presumably because of the pain of jealousy as well as envy which the recognition would arouse. This, however, can be evaded if the child deludes himself into the belief that this object is given to him and not to his rivals. A similar difficulty seems to impede the formation of the concept of a good vagina; though there is always a concept of a bad one endowed with cannibalistic aims and/or "sphincter sadism."

Psychoanalytic observation of the way a patient, who is "cognitively retarded," begins to develop missing concepts in dreams—penis and vagina separating themselves from nipple and mouth, further developing into a concept of parental intercourse etc.—can be recognized as fitting the theory fairly well. But the theory has to be extended to fit another observation. Such patients do not suddenly become aware of these concepts in a form available for use in catching up on their own retarded sexual development. This may come later. In my experience, the new concepts are likely to be noticed first in what may be called "dream ideographs." But these ideographs themselves often seem to have forerunners in physical manifestations, which are sometimes hypochondriacal. For example, a transient series of slight jaundice attacks occurred in a patient each heralded by a physical sensation suggesting a psychosomatic constriction of the bile duct, and seemed to alternate with, or be replaced by dreams which suggested oedipal attacks, by constriction, on an early part-object representation of parental intercourse. The evidence was at first more convincing to the patient than to myself, but it certainly looked as if the jaundice had represented, in a concrete way, the same oedipal fantasy as was later represented ideographically in the dreams. The whole episode seemed to me to be a physiological expression of the rule, discovered by Segal (1957), that "symbolic equation" precedes the use of symbols, especially in dreams, as a primitive form of representational thought—that is, in the use of images to represent objects and situations which are not at the moment present to the senses.

To fit such observations, the theory of conceptual development has to be extended to include, not only growth in the number and scope of concepts, but also the growth of each single concept through at least three stages: a stage of concrete representation, which strictly speaking is not representational at all, since no distinction is made between the representation and the object or situation represented; a stage of ideographic representation as in dreams; and a final stage of conscious, and predominantly verbal, thought. (I think these stages have some affinity with Bion's [1962] much fuller list of stages in sophistication. But the shorter list is meant to stress stages, not so much in sophistication, as in degrees of consciouness.)

Going back to my primary assumption that *recognition* is the basic act in cognitive development, successful development would now seem to depend on two types of uninhibited recognition: first, the recognition of members of innate preconceptions, and second, the recognition of emotional experiences at one level of consciousness as members of concepts already formed at a lower level. In other words, given an object, say father's penis, of which a thought has to be formed if conceptual maturity (and normal sexuality) is to be achieved, I am suggesting that the development of this thought normally goes through three stages: concrete identification, unconscious ideographic representation, conscious, predominantly verbal representation. If the last stage is reached as it were theoretically, without going through the other two, the resulting concept would seem to be unserviceable for emotional development.

But the same sort of emotional impediments which operate against the formation of a concept in the first place also operate against its development from one mental layer to another. When a concept is not available to complete an act of recognition, its place is usually taken by a misconception.

I will try to illustrate some of these points from an example already quoted in a previous paper (in the British Psycho-Analytical Society's Scientific Bulletin). A woman who had always maintained that her mother was "warped in mind," by which she meant "frigid," dreamed that "she was upstairs with her mother and in a happy frame of mind till she suddenly realized that the woman in the flat below, who was "warped in body" (through illness), was receiving an attractive lover. From that moment everything went wrong. Murders of an old woman and a little girl were committed or impending. The attractive lover was suspected of these; but a cat masquerading as a baby was felt somehow to be responsible." If scanned in terms of conceptual theory, the following conclusions seem to follow: the dreamer's baby self had, at the ideographic level, a concept of a good breast and was capable of *recognizing* herself as enjoying it (upstairs with mother and in a happy frame of mind). She had never had, or had lost, a concept, at the same level, of a good parental intercourse, or if she had, she had refused to *recognize* her own parents' intercourse as an example of it (the woman in the flat below, that is, the lower part of her mother, was "warped" or frigid). But, in the dream, this devastating *recognition* momentarily occurs (to her astonishment the woman in the flat below receives an attractive lover). She has a concept of murderous jealousy, but is unable to *recognize* herself as in this state. Instead, she projects it into her father (the attractive lover who is thought to be murdering the old woman and little girl, her mother and herself). In this way, a misconception of the parents' intercourse as a murderous assault takes the place of the correct conception.

It is very clear that it is this projection of murderous jealousy, much more than the evidence of any actual quarrels between her parents, that had prevented her from either forming a concept of a good parental intercourse, or of recognizing her own parents as enjoying one. In fact her parents appear to have been happily married, so the misconception is formed in the teeth both of an innate preconception and of experience. Yet there is a part of her that does recognize the murderer correctly as her baby self, the cat. But this is immediately split off and projected—as a defence against the depressive position.

System Building

Coming now to the second of the two new hooks to hang old theory on, the baby has not only to form a number of basic concepts in terms of which he can recognize the "facts of life," but also to arrange their members in a space-time system. Now a system is itself a complex concept but it seems reasonable to treat the two tasks separately since there appears to be a fundamental difference in the role instinct plays in each of them: if basic concepts emerge from innate preconceptions, only experience stimulated by innate curiosity, can locate their members in a space-time system.

There are two main systems to consider, one to represent the outer world in which we have to orient ourselves, the other, originally an internalization of this, develops into an unconscious system of religion and morality.

Again Bion (1965) has described psychotic mechanisms which attack the sense of time, so that a space-time system cannot begin to form. I am concerned with lesser disturbances which give rise to various kinds of "disorientation"—a term I use to cover a fairly wide range of phenomena. Essential to the sense of orientation in either system is that it has a base, the O of coordinate geometry. This appears not to be normally the body-ego, but something to which the body-ego orients itself as its "home." The first base, from which all others would seem to be derived, is the first object to emerge from the new-born infant's sensory confusion, namely the breast or perhaps specifically the nipple. The first space-time divisions to develop are threefold: a period of enjoyment (being fed), a period of remembrance (having been fed) and a period of expectation (going to be fed). For this can be inferred from the way so many patients orient themselves in exactly this threefold manner to their daily session.

From the beginning, the capacity to retain a latent memory of the external world system seems to depend on a capacity to internalize the base, at first in a very concrete way. A patient who wished to forget the analytic breast, dreamed that "she was going to have an operation to remove a small nipple-shaped lump on her head." That is, to forget it, she had to have the internal nipple concretely removed. I suppose the sense of concretely containing the lost object to be a necessary forerunner of its unconscious ideographic, and finally its conscious verbal representation. In the dream, the concrete stage is itself represented ideographically. Though much is still very obscure and the exact dividing-line is difficult to mark, the division between the inner- and the outer-world systems must be related to the division between concrete pre-representational thought in terms of "internal objects" and some stage of representational thought.

What is easier to follow is the development of the base, both internally and externally, from breast or nipple to mother as a whole person, to the combined parents, to the idea of a home, a country one belongs to, and so on. So long as the inner and outer relation to these is preserved, we are never disoriented, and to this extent are preserved from acute anxiety attacks. But orientation to the base is easily lost in several ways. I am not concerned at the moment with the ways in which the good base can turn "bad" by the infant projecting his own aggression into it so that it is misrecognized as bad. Apart from this, the orientation to the good base can be lost in at least three ways: the baby can get into it by total projective identification, either out of envy or as an escape from a persecuting outer world; he can get oriented to the wrong base, in the sense that it is not the one he really needs; or he can become confused in his orientation because his base is confused with a part of his own body.

I will try to give examples of each of these in turn. As to the first—the delusion that one is the base—Rosenfeld (1965) and others have explored its extreme forms in psychosis where the patient becomes totally confused with the analyst. In less extreme forms, the same mechanism is recognizable in those "egocentric" or "geocentric" states which result from a partial failure to outgrow the delusion of primary narcissism. The normal, or sane solution involves a humiliating recognition of one's littleness, followed by a grateful dependence which ends, after weaning, in the internalization of the lost good object.

Some people, however, especially if their actual abilities and real success enable them to give substance to their delusion, retain it all their lives. These are the narcissistic men or women who live in projective identification with father's idealized penis or mother's idealized breast. Far commoner, in patients (and to some degree in all analysands) is the sense of having lost, through actual failure, this blissful state. Their unconscious analytic aim is, not to outgrow, but to restore it. For example, a woman dreamed "that she was lying on a couch (as if in analysis); but that (instead of having an analyst) she had a patient, lying at right angles to her with his head close to hers. Then he annoyed her by trying to snatch the pillow." Assuming, as I think we may, that her "patient" in the dream was really her analyst, the position of the dreamer's head and mouth, close to the head of the analyst-patient lying at right angles, strongly suggests that the experience of being analysed revived a memory of her infant self feeding at the breast. But the experience is painfully humiliating, and is reversed. It is she who is feeding (analysing) the analyst. In other words, the dream is an attempt, under the dominance of the pleasure principle to deny the reality which, nevertheless, threatens to break through the unconscious delusion; for the analyst claims the pillow—that is, claims to be the breast. Similarly, another patient dreamed "of an Indian woman exhibiting herself in a very sexy way on the top of a hill." There seemed little doubt that the Indian woman represented the seductive brown nipple. But the patient recognized her as a repudiated aspect of herself, that is, it is she who is the nipple. Or again, yet another patient dreamed that "she is holding forth and paying no attention to the little Professor who should be giving the lecture." She has taken the place of the nipple, and relegated it to an inferior position. (I know this interpretation without evidence must seem unconvincing. But my assumption that I was the "Little Professor" ultimately standing for the nipple was based on my general impression of the patient built up over a long period. For example, we were already both convinced that she had been very well fed as a baby, but had resented what she felt to be her mother's dominating way of feeding her. In most relationships, she resented not being the "senior partner," and had, I felt sure, resented it in her first relationship to the breast.)

Closely related to the delusional projective identification with the mother's breast or nipple, is the delusional projective identification with the father's penis. A man dreams, for example, that "an admired senior is performing a difficult feat on a stage which consists in standing at an angle of 45 degrees and producing fire from his head. To his embarrassment, the dreamer notices the tip of a child's penis showing through the performer's trousers. Fire is produced with an immense effort, but it is felt to be inadequate." In other words, the baby boy has projected his baby penis into father's to perform the feat of intercourse. But in fact the projection degrades the performance into an inadequate urination.

Elsewhere (1965), I have argued that the whole human race has suffered, in varying degrees, from delusions of being projectively identified with their mothers or fathers, as whole- or part-objects, ever since they began to wear clothes, not for warmth or modesty, but to ape their animal gods by putting on their skins. Robes of office, uniforms, clothes expressing status, and status itself as an invisible garment, still serve the same purpose of maintaining the fiction that we are identified with what we unconsciously feel to be our betters, that is, parents (at part- or whole-object level) who are so much admired and therefore envied.

But it is clinically important to distinguish other motives for projective identification. For example, a patient who used to do it from envy, began to do it from fear as soon as she had accepted her littleness. She had become frightened of a senior colleague whom previously she might have treated with contempt, and then dreamed "she was crawling into a sleeping bag (associated with myself) to protect her from the fall-out in an atomic war (associated with the caustic criticisms expected from this senior colleague)."

Coming to the sense of being oriented to the wrong base, since this can be "wrong" in the epistemological as opposed to the "moral" sense only if the choice results from a confusion between what is needed and what is sought, "wrong orientations" are not easy to distinguish from confused ones. But the patient quoted earlier, whose dream of apparently wanting to have an operation to cut out a nipple-shaped lump on her head was interpreted as a wish to have her memory of the nipple taken away, did seem at that time to be predominantly oriented to her father's penis. This was shown for example, in her claim that what she wanted was a husband and not an analyst who stood for a breast—although her dreams and symptoms constantly betrayed her deeper longing for this first object. In other words, she was predominantly oriented to the wrong object.

Orientation to a confused object is the main theme of Meltzer's paper, "The Relation of Anal Masturbation to Projective Identification" (1966) in which he describes the state of mind of the baby left on the pot after a feed, feeling resentful with his mother and becoming confused with her in the following manner: in trying to find a substitute for the breast, with which he is angry, he unconsciously identifies his own buttocks with it, and himself with his mother, so that he unconsciously does not know which is breast and which is bottom and whether it is his or hers. Preoccupation with the contents of his own rectum (whether faeces or finger) may lead to the sense of getting inside, as in envious projective identification with the breast, but this time it is inside a confused bottom-breast. Then the final outcome is likely to be a claustrophobic feeling often expressed in dreams of being lost in a hostile town or building menaced by enemies, and desperately trying to find a way out, and back to some refuge (the lost breast). An example, in which, however, a misunderstanding of the mother's wishes is blamed for the confusion, appears in another patient's dream that "she sees a woman on a balcony (sees the breast) and asks her how to get there. The woman makes a gesture which she thinks means that she will find a door behind her. She does, but gets lost in this back building." In other words, she misunderstands her mother's invitation to reach up to the balcony-breast, and gets lost in her own bottom, also confused with her mother's.

In discussing the spatio-temporal system, I have so far only referred to the relation to the base. But of course it is also something into which all other orientations to secondary figures, whether as parts of the self or siblings, have to be fitted. Confusion with such secondary objects are also common. Moreover, the system, though primarily a space-time one, also gives the mechanical and psychological qualities of the objects in it. But errors here belong to the theme of misrecognitions allocating the wrong objects to the wrong categories which I have already outlined.

Before leaving the subject, however, I would like to say a word about the inner-world system of religion and morality. The base here, of course, is the superego, or more often a number of not very well integrated superegos, themselves in different stages of development from very primitive to fully sophisticated figures. Now the same mechanisms which produce misconceptions and delusions in the outer world also operate in the inner. In particular, aggression can be projected intrapsychically from the ego into the superego, to create the archaic figures. That is, they are the product of an "intrapsychic paranoia." And the ego can project itself totally into an admired and envied internal figure to produce an "intrapsychic megalomania." Alternatively, there can be the sense of grateful dependence on a good and wise internal mentor. Each of these, and others, are associated with a characteristic morality. Ethical relativists seem to me to have overlooked one reason, other than prejudice, to prefer the last alternative: it is much less under the influence of mechanisms which distort the truth.

In conclusion, I would like to give you my own assessment of the theory I have tried to outline. As I said at the beginning of this paper, it is not in itself a new psychoanalytic theory, but a couple of theoretical hooks to hang a lot of existing theories on, and so to co-ordinate these and make them more accessible to memory. I know it is very incomplete. Parts of it are muddled and perhaps self-contradictory. But already it is of some help to me, in sessions in recognizing what is analytically important: first, a patient's orientation to myself as base in his inner and outer world, and secondly, the degree of truth with which he is able to recognize, or misrecognize, all the objects in *his* space-time system. I therefore envisage the possible development of a kind of psychoanalytic geometry and physics with which to represent a patient's changing true and false beliefs about his relation to objects and their nature, in *his* inner and outer worlds. Analysts, as Bion rightly reminds us, should learn to tolerate the anxiety of contact with the unknown. But the better their theory, the easier it is for them to come out of confusion by recognizing, and helping the patient to recognize, his departures from truth.

The development of such a thoery to the limit of its usefulness, is obviously a long-term project. I do not know how much further I can get with it at present, but I would like to persuade others to work on it.

References

Bion, W.R. (1962). *Learning from Experience*. (London: Heinemann.)
—— (1963). *Elements of Psycho-Analysis*. (London: Heinemann.)
—— (1965). *Transformations*. (London: Heinemann.)
Freud, S. (1911). "Formulations on the two principles of mental functioning." *S.E.* Vol. 12.
Klein, M. (1957). *Envy and Gratitude*. (London: Tavistock.)
Meltzer, D. (1966). "The relation of anal masturbation to projective identification." *Int. J. Psycho-Anal.* Vol. 47, pp. 335-342.
Money-Kyrle, R.E. (1965). "Megalomania." *Amer. Imago*, Vol. 22.
Rosenfeld, H. (1965). *Psychotic States*. (London: Hogarth.)
Schlick, M. (1925). *Erkenntnislehre*. (Berlin: Springer.)
Segal, H. (1957): "Notes on symbol formation. *Int. J. Psycho-Anal.*, Vol. 38.

Cognitive Development

Post Script

The above paper, published in 1968, was in the main clearly inspired by Bion's theory of Innate Preconceptions. In this post script, I would like to add something about his theory of the role of a mother's capacity for "reverie" in aiding her child to overcome some of the first impediments to normal cognitive development.

To start with what Bion would call a "myth," that is, a Theory in Narrative Form: Suppose a very young baby is becoming increasingly aware of the absence of something unknown but necessary to its peace of mind (or the presence of something unknown and intolerable, or both, if e.g. the need is to be given the breast and have the hunger taken away) and that his awareness reaches the level of acute anxiety. His mother may have one of three possible responses; she may fail to become aware of her baby's panic (even if she is near), she may become panic-stricken herself, or in her reverie, she may respond with the feeling that the poor baby is unnecessarily terrified in perfectly safe situation. In the last case, her sympathetic lack of anxiety is almost certain to communicate itself to the baby who may then get back the sense of a need to be given or relieved of something, without the panic, and the mother's subsequent behaviour in feeding, dewinding or potting may help her baby to discover what his panic had been about. One may suppose further that a few repetitions of this kind of sequences will help him to perceive what he needs to be given, or to have taken away, instead of projecting panic.

What is more, I think the baby will soon begin to internalise a containing "breast mother" to contain and think about any crises, so that he may learn to think about and deal with them rationally instead of "flat-spinning" in them as some of us are in danger of doing all our lives.

It may be worth mentioning, too, that apart from what other character traits may play a part in enabling a mother to aid her baby's first steps in thinking, a major role may be allocated to the degree of her own mother's past capacity to help her in this when she was a baby—and so on *ad infinitum*.

Although Bion does not want his α- and β-element concepts to be saturated with meaning, it may be worth enquiring how far they can be fitted into the above "myth." To begin with, the panic which is projected is a β-element fit only for projection, while the α-element awareness of a need is the same element tinged with security instead of panic so that it can be stored and remembered. The final knowledge of what is needed may, or may not, be aided by an innate preconception. If it is the need to be fed, there is almost certainly an innate pre-conception of a breast and nipple to mate with the realisation of an actual one. But if the need is to be potted or dewinded it is doubtful whether there is any more specific pre-conception than a general one of a being, a breast-mother, to satisfy all needs.

Now to test the theory against a clinical experience: A patient of mine (who may have heard of Bion's theory though not from me) dreamed that she was trying to sweep up prickly pine or fir needles, and put them in a box. But the box leaked and the needles would not stay in. Then an older woman (a mother figure who had recommended her to come to me for analysis) gave her a bag to put in the box after which the needles stayed in. The mother figure then said: "now you can feed with the others." In interpreting, I thought the pine or fir needles stood for painful prickly tears fit only for projection. The box which I thought was her baby self could not hold them; but the motherly lady had given her a bag (me as a psycho-analytic breast) which did. I may in some sense have been felt to convert β-element persecuting tears about the bad breast into α-element depressive tears about the absent or injured "no-breast." For it was after this that she could feed from it like the others which probably meant from a breast "remembered" as having satisfied her before and not only momentarily experienced.

It will be noted that the dream also seems to give an account of primal introjective-identification; for the breast bag which could hold the painful tears is internalised and put in this leaky box-self. And if I am right, this is what happens in normal development: The infant finds a breast to cry into, and in turn gets back from it his distress in a detoxicated form which is capable of being stored and recalled, if necessary, as an element in thought. Moreover, the container, originally the breast which returned the β-elements as α-elements, is internalised too.

It may be, in the case just described, that the leaky box in which the bag was put represented the real mother's breast which in Melanie Klein's view is the first introject as the core of the ego. For there is some evidence that the real mother was depressed when my patient was an infant and may have been internalised as a breast which could not contain sadness or any painful emotion very well. In any case, I think the bag in the box given by the motherly lady was myself as analyst who, of course, works under much easier conditions.

If for any reason—the baby's envy of a good breast or his greed or the mother's incapacity for "reverie"—the early projections are not received into a container that can contain them, and return them together with its containing self, all the effects which Bion has described come into being. The projections become more bizarre, and surround the psychotic like a prison.

But if the first step is successfully accomplished, I would suppose that the baby internalises a breast with a double function: The feeding-breast which Melanie Klein has made us familiar with, and a kind of lavatory-breast which contains what is projected. When internalised, this may later develop into what Freud called the pre-conscious which contains what is not needed at the moment, but which remains accessible. The difficulty we sometimes experience in finding it is a neurotic problem.

It will be observed that the above argument is mainly influenced by Bion's work. I am by no means sure that what I say is consistent with what Bion means or even whether it is consistent with itself. Indeed it is pretty certain that it is not; for I have discovered that the attempt to be too precise does soon land one in contradictions. But I am quite sure that the attempt to build a theory about the precursors of what one can perceive about thinking is as justified as it was in physics to build a theory about the invisible and intangible molecules, atoms and electric particles of which the tangible universe is thought to be composed.

In conclusion, it may be worth pointing out that work such as Bion's may incidentally help to solve such problems as whether psychosis, or intelligence, is inherited. As to psychosis, if Bion is right, the innate factor is greed and/or envy, and not any specific defect in the construction of the mental apparatus as such. And as to intelligence, no one brought up under the influence of the *Origin of Species* and *The Descent of Man* can have any serious doubt that in some degree intelligence is innate. But again if Bion is right, the child's mother plays a fundamental role in his learning to think and the good or bad effects of this are probably well nigh unalterable, and so could be easily thought to be innate.

A Mental Atlas of the Process of Psychological Birth

Michael Paul

EDITOR'S NOTE: *Thanks to Bion's questions about the "primeval" mnemic residues of mental birth which Freud's earlier adumbrative remarks stimulated him to think about, the concept of the "caesura" of existence is now being investigated by Kleinian writers as they leave the ground of past explorations in the oral period to the Freudian newcomers such as Mahler, Spitz, Kohut, and Kernberg. Doctor Paul in his other life was a distinguished biochemist whose principal medium consisted of such entities as cyclic AMP (cyclic adenosine monophosphate). His current area of interest is the linking of the constituents of archaic, elemental thought processes and in the active but unborn state to experiences in the post partum condition, albeit based upon the reconstructive inferences of clinical practice. Doctor Paul, in short, has accepted the challenge of attempting to forge a link between pre-caesural and post-caesural experiences using psychoanalysis as his instrument. The reader can also see yet another aspect of the Palinurus story from the* Aeneid, *to which Doctor Grinberg has also made reference.*

A Mental Atlas of the Process of Psychological Birth

Michael I. Paul

In his *Inhibitions, Symptoms and Anxiety* (1926), Freud was concerned not only with the relations between anxiety and symptom formation, but with certain aspects of the process of birth which had been primarily introduced by Otto Rank's consideration of the birth trauma. Rank (1929) was concerned, as was Freud, not with the elements of a birth process as revealed by the analysis of unconscious phantasy, but rather with the "traumatic" aspects of birth in relation to the development of a theory of anxiety. It is clear, however, that Freud was aware of exceedingly primitive mnemic residues which could be ascribed to birth traumata, but was critical of Rank's attempt to simplify the theory of anxiety to a singular aetiology in the birth trauma.

"Anxiety is not newly created in regression, it is reproduced as an affective state in accordance with an already existing mnemic image. If we go further and enquire into the origin of that anxiety—and of affects in general—we shall be leaving the realm of pure psychology and entering the borderland of physiology. Affective states have become incorporated in the mind as precipitates of primaeval traumatic experiences and when a similar situation occurs they are revived like mnemic symbols." He continues, "We cannot possibly suppose that the foetus has any sort of knowledge that there is a possibility of its life being destroyed. It can only be aware of some vast disturbance in the economy of its narcissistic libido. Large sums of excitation crowd in on it giving rise to new feelings of unpleasure and some organs acquire an increased cathexis, thus foreshadowing the object's cathexis that will soon set in. What elements in all this will be made use of as the sign of a danger situation? It is easy to say that the baby will repeat its affect of anxiety in every situation that recalls the event of birth. The important thing to know is '*what recalls the event and what is it that is recalled*' " (Freud, 1926).

It is in reference to this last point that I wish to begin the consideration of how we can recognize elements of these "primeval" mnemic residues which are preverbal and contained in sense channels which are unrecognizable to ordinary communication. I wish to elaborate certain connections between a life which I believe is a representation of a prenatal experience and the postnatal world taking as a point of inspiration Freud's statement, "There is much more continuity between intra-uterine life and earliest infancy than the impressive caesura of the act of birth allows us to believe" (Freud, 1926).

We are familiar with the experience of being exposed to certain aspects of obsessional "thinking" which has a cyclic quality. There is no forward motion of a train of thought developed on a "track."

The individual feels subjected to "painful thoughts" or rather thoughts which cannot be thought through and are associated with severe mental pain more or less depending upon the content. Patients will refer to "dwelling" on their thoughts, "ruminating," "worrying," and mean a repetitive circularity which continues and is associated with increasing emotional pain. This "pain" is so important that one realizes that a good deal of modern drug habituation to tranquilizers, sleeping medications and alcohol addiction results from attempts to reduce or abate the pain. The thought cycle may take a variety of forms but several definable features can be noted: repetitive quality, lack of progression to a higher level of abstraction, lack of linking capacity, concreteness, peremptory quality, a tendency to impel to action and profound intrusiveness. This last point is of extreme importance as patients often begin to anticipate with dread the sudden intrusion of the painful pattern of thoughts which then "think" them or rather control their minds such that little else is felt to occur. When patients experience these "thoughts," they complain often of insomnia and complain that they cannot stop the process. An action is necessary in order to put a stop to this state of mind which may be any of a variety from self-induced narcosis to physical violence. One often hears the expression, "I can't get these thoughts off my mind," "They won't leave me alone," etc. The "thoughts" are felt to possess the thinker and often are felt to be experienced as holding or grasping tenaciously. This process is accompanied frequently by anxiety and agitation. Attempts are made at this time to disburden the mind of these unpleasant experiences which frequently results in massive projective identification (Klein, 1957; Bion, 1962).

I have noted in several patients powerful attempts to put a stop to my communications at certain key points in a session as they are felt in advance to be quite dangerous and are defended against with great force. These patients behave as though any further communication would certainly lead to a catastrophe and instigate something which would seem to be irrevocable.

Mrs. X, a 47-year-old mother of two, suffers an incapacity to work, extreme anxiety, marked agitation, alcoholism and extreme obesity. She has marked insomnia and experiences her "thoughts" as visual images of varied content but "knows" that there are certain forms of these thoughts which are far too dangerous to verbalize. Sometimes she feels that if she were to "say what she sees," whatever it is would "happen" and resolutely refuses at that point to continue. She is aware of categories of thought which she divides into categories such as "I'm too tired to talk about them," "I can only talk about them sometimes," and "These can *never* be verbalized." When these "thoughts" emerge into her conscious mind, she can be seen to shudder and often begins to weep uncontrollably. She squirms on the couch and has intense pain. No attempt at interpretation has been successful in leading to any further flow of material at these times. Often she is mute and if an interpretation is "close to the mark," she will become enraged and has an attitude that states that I don't realize what I could do to her if in fact I were to continue. At that time I am felt to be stupid or utterly cruel. "How could you?" is her response, which may remain weeks to months in her mind. She is virtually unable to let go of the phantasy that I may have induced this response.

This woman, highly articulate, well-educated, and a skilled writer, realizes that these episodes involve intense superstition, understands the massive degree of irrationality she experiences and is utterly ashamed of her inability to dare to cooperate under these circumstances. At these times she is in profound despair, utterly hopeless and convinced that nothing she nor I can do will produce a change. She frequently calls herself stupid and dumb with intense force, and describes herself as a perpetual "fool." She utilizes these epithets as a means of producing psychic closure and the flow of material stops abruptly. She is then "caught between," as it were, her realization that her despair stems from her failure and inability to cooperate, and her intense fear that cooperation will lead to catastrophe. She is functionally unable to make distinctions in time. The past, present, and future are confused, and she predicts the future entirely based on her past despair, which compounds the hopelessness.

This is quite similar to the "no exit" situation which Sartre depicts in his play. She is "stuck" as she describes and portrays very well the concept of therapeutic impasse.

At this mental location she typically states, "There is no point to this; I can't see the point in continuing, but I'm too terrified not to come to analysis." Why is she "stuck"? Where is she "stuck"? one might ask. What is the point she is seeking?

An important analytic "fact" is evidenced in that these attempts at closure are most obvious at the end of the session, the end of the week, and holidays. When this patient gets up, she complains of a feeling of dizziness and profound disorientation and often remains in the exit portion of the office for several minutes after leaving the consulting room. The patient demonstrates an obstruction in her thinking process in that she cannot come to the "point" she is attempting to reach as a result of what she feels is a "blanking" of her mind. Often she feels there is no point either in what I say or what she thinks. She is never sure whether she "really" thinks what she says, and makes reference to the possibility that even though she might not mean it to be, she could be fabricating parts of the material. She does not lie as far as she can tell, but neither is she certain that what she says is the truth.

I have noted this "doubt" of the truth of her narrative to occur subsequent to her having stopped the flow of her speech. After this "stop," there is often a change of vocal tone which I can notice, followed by her "doubt" of the truth of what she says. This patient states and has demonstrated that this process is very different from purposive lying, as she would simply refuse to talk consciously which has been amply demonstrated throughout the analysis.

Bion (1970) distinguishes between true thoughts and lies, in that "a thinker is logically necessary for the lie but not for the true thought." He continues, "The lie and the true thought are inseparable. The thinker is of no consequence to the truth, but the truth is logically necessary to the thinker." Further, "The lie gains existence by virtue of the epistemologically prior existence of the liar. . . . Whether the thoughts are entertained or not is of significance to the thinker but not to the truth. If entertained, they are conducive to mental health; if not, they initiate disturbance.

The process of emergence of thoughts inseparable from the thinker as a function of the lie then must be considered in the clinical description given above. Are the thoughts we are referring to emerging "true" thoughts which seem to erupt spontaneously from the infinite Galactic void of mental space which create a disturbance associated with their arrival? Psychoanalytic evidence suggests that the means by which these "thoughts" are processed are inadequate to transform them to thinking the thought through. These thoughts are then subject to ejection in phantasy since the "mind" of the patient in question has not the equipment for effective transformation of thought. One distinction between the lie and true thought in Bion's terms may relate to the difference between "conjury or invention" versus spontaneous emergence without effort. In the analytic session, there is a difference between the "thought" emerging through directly, and the divergent pathway of the thought going around an obstruction. The former affords penetration to awareness, while the divergent route is essentially an evasion. One version of the "lie" then in this context may refer to this divergent pathway as an evasion.

To return to the case being considered . . . in her fourth year of treatment she dreamed that she was in an autopsy room watching the end of a post-mortem which then transformed into an embalming scene. She saw the circulatory hookup and as the process was begun, she awakened screaming from her dream but could not shake off the hideous sensation of being flooded and engorged with fluid as the embalming began. She stated she could feel the fluid flooding every element of her being and at that time had a resurgence of a previous active symptom, a choking phobia which had been intensely limiting of her activities.

Phantasizing being inside mother immediately preceded this dramatic example taking the form of her replicating in the transference relationship between herself and myself the phantasy of the ability to know everything I was thinking, what I would interpret next, and so forth. She has been dominated by these forms of omniscience especially developed in her relation to her mother as a model. Mother was described as intensely critical with an unerring eye for the perception of the bad. The patient's history suggests a mother who was unable to contain her child's infantile anxieties and responded by abrupt separation. My patient learned to "track" and telemeter mother's mental meanderings in order to ward off the abrupt experience of pain upon intense, scathing criticism.

The themes of crisis, criticism and hypocrisy were evident not only in this patient's analysis but in the analyses of each of the eight patients of this type with whom I have had experience.

Crisis in Greek means to separate, whereas criticism has as a main definition the process of distinction which also is associated with separation. Hypocrisy I reasoned means, literally, below criticism or beneath the divide and refers to not making a distinction with a pejorative connotation. These themes revolve around phantasies associated with the prenatal state—hypocrisy with cowardly nondistinction and crisis especially with the experience of impending psychological birth. Criticism employed in a destructive hostile manner can be seen by the moral approach to make the boundary between the inside and outside.

The patient has been a chronic alcoholic who is "soused," in her own terms, and thus far has been unable to stop. She drinks to stop separation anxiety and shows what could be interpreted as excessive greed noted by her extraordinary anxiety. In the dream mentioned above, she associated to drinking and being "pickled," but there were clear references to prenatal experience. Greed seems to me to be a moral term and, although descriptive, has a profoundly negative connotation. Is the extreme sensitivity of a quasi-foetal-infantile state of mind still operating on the model,or a placental feed a mental state which can brook no separation from a continuously feeding object another way of describing greed? Are we witnessing the phenotype of a primitive, perhaps foetal, mental state in the adult world? In this way, the presence of the moral approach denoted by the transition in linguistic usage from descriptive-phenomenological to moralistic quality of language is a marker for the appearance of the gap between pre- and post-natal experience. This concept bears close relation to addictive states, as well as the general conception of narcissism which will be explored in other works.

To return to Mrs. X's dream, it is possible to consider it as a representation of a prenatal experience having achieved representation associated with a severely dysphoric state. Upon interpretation of this dream, the patient questioned her mother and discovered that she indeed had a toxemia of pregnancy which was exacerbated just prior to birth.

Another patient likened his relationship to the analyst to an experience with a renal dialysis machine without which he could not live.

A series of phenomena, both non-verbal and verbal, have become significant across a group of at least eight patients who have severe narcissistic disorders.

1. The consulting room is felt to be markedly different from the external world. Disorientation and/or severe dizziness often accompany entering and/or leaving. Upon entering, often the patient avoids contact with me directly and often finds great difficulty leaving. In phantasy, the consulting room is experienced as "inside the mother's body." Often I am incidental or mostly felt *not* to be present.

2. These patients show evidence of long-standing, rather complete projective identification and show extreme sensitivities to the perception of heat and cold as a constant. By projective identification, I mean to convey a

quality of deep psychic fusion with an internal phantasy of being-in-the-mother's body. This state of mind is predominant and rather fixed, any deviation from which is immediately attended by a sense of impending catastrophe. This is to be distinguished from an oscillating quality in which other patients move in and out of a state of being "inside." The patients experiencing projective identification behave as though they were hermeneutically sealed in a world never to be exposed to the air. One such patient in previous analysis for twenty years wore long winter underwear at all times to protect himself from the "cold" which he "might" experience. Upon successful interpretation of a state of psychic fusion with "mother's" body, the patient will suddenly note the presence of sudden "cold." A rapid change in temperature within a split second of the interpretation is experienced, and piloerection is grossly observable as an accompanying phenomenon. Two of these patients have given histories of a special supersensitivity to cold, in that they state that they can distinguish between one degree Fahrenheit up or down and talk about temperature very frequently as a general analytic theme.

In both patients who are specifically sensitive to cold, neither has had any demonstrable physiologic reason and both have had repeated, thorough endocrinologic studies. In addition, both are subject to frequent "colds" and the "flu," which makes them extremely wary of draughts, night air, etc.

3. Interpretation of the stages of projective states leads very rapidly to changes in the perception of sound, temperature, visual acuity, visual clarity, and will produce disorientation and dizziness, often with severe temporary vertigo as the boundary between inside and outside is crossed in phantasy. Sudden changes in perception then signal the shift from inside to outside, and vice versa. Warmth, stuffiness and an uncomfortably enclosed sensation are well-known markers for the "inside" experience. The dizziness and disorientation distinguish a level of primitiveness which links to the representation in phantasy of the birth process. In my experience, the shift in perception of temperature and the sudden onset of dizziness are the most reliable indicators of a change in state of mind which related directly to the experience of birth.

4. Sudden onset of headache, often frontal and rhythmically pounding, is an associated phenomenon noted in the context of this change in state of mind from inside to outside. Pain of a band-like pressure quality across the forehead and usually bilaterally symmetrical is a common finding. If the pressure is not felt intrinsically, often the patient will press hands quite forcibly against the forehead and the top of the head associated with phantasies of moving back from outside to inside. The pounding headache does *not* have a vascular periodicity and is not regular or in synchrony with the heartbeat, but occurs as an indefinite, unpleasant sensation occurring "within the head" at a frequency of several times a minute. The force of speech in rhythmical patterns with a periodic repetitiveness may be noted clearly to precede the actual physical sensation even though the pounding speech pattern may exist without the physical quality and vice versa.

5. A sensation of "pressure" usually felt about the head is frequently

associated with a stoppage of the "sinuses" and has been noted in several patients as "waves" over the body passing from the head to the feet in rhythmic force. Often this pressure sensation and upper respiratory partial obstruction is associated with the patient putting at least a temporary end to communication and is noted to be a form of grammatical "period." This is a transitional phase from inside to outside and is often accompanied by terror → panic. I have noted that at this point there is associated a profound splitting of sense modalities, for example hearing from vision which seems to uncouple the transitional process of movement in psychic space (Paul and Carson, 1977).

The respiratory phenomena include in some patients a sudden gasping for air or in smokers the holding of smoke inside their lungs to the point of pain. Upon questioning, the internal "outlining" of the respiratory passages so that the internal aspects of the lungs could be felt was the salient feature in several patients, *not* the feeling of air hunger. Breathing is often "held" fixed for long pauses during which all activity stops and the consulting room atmosphere "feels" dead. Profound tightening of the throat musculature and intense fear of choking may ensue in selected cases.

6. In a single case of this type I noted the presence of oedema which had been diagnosed as idiopathic associated with phantasies of fusion with the mother's body, which specifically and progressively remitted upon interpretation of these phantasies. This analysand has been addicted to a powerful diuretic for a number of years which she took for "depression."

I shall present an additional case example to demonstrate a series of phenomena which are important for the development of understanding of the pre-verbal phenomena linked to elements of the postulated pre-birth and birth experience.

As the patient enters, she hunches and averts her eyes so as to avoid any emotional connection between us. She moves to the couch and sits on the edge and settles for a moment as if in deep reflection. Silently she swivels toward me with her body maintaining a downcase eyes-half-shut-mien. Suddenly her head snaps to a position on direct confrontation to mine and glares. This movement is stereotyped and evokes a quality of tension which is so powerful that she quickly averts her eyes and communication is at a halt. It is as if the scene has been set for expectation of an emotional explosion which has been the usual sequel for the past two years. A gradually increasing crescendo of complaining begins in a demanding, whining voice which has a piercing resonance. The rhythm picks up speed as does the intensity although the volume remains approximately the same. Attempts at interpretation even after ten minutes or longer of steady repetition are ignored, cut off, and attempts are made to stop the analyst's speech. Any attempt to persevere meets with an increase of voice force and intensity meant to keep the analyst's position fixed to silence. The grating quality picks up again with increasing repetitiveness and intensity which fills the consulting room with a tension that is palpable both in patient and analyst. I am aware of an increasing sense of intense pain which evokes in me an experience of emotionally wanting to shut down, or yields a powerful quality of annoyance, isolation, and suddenly I become aware of hatred which threatens to lead to action. I have noticed a desire to strike out, to shout her down, to get rid of her in any way possible. Introspection upon this phenomenon reveals the pattern of vocal qualities mentioned above, brought forward in a rhythmical, repetitive, increasing crescendo grating which evokes intense feelings in the analyst.

The content of the material continually has to do with expectations of disaster, and how nothing can help her. She feels trapped, encocooned, irrevocably damaged; time has passed her by; the future will bring only disaster and terror. She wonders what will she do, and feels she must do something, as I or no one else can help her return from having reached the point of violence she intuits. Then as if she were at the end of a cadenza, she returns to the beginning again, "D.C. al Fine," with increasing percussiveness, so that the verbal material is more *felt* than heard, and the piercing resonance mentioned above increases. This I have dubbed "repetition percussion," as it heralds the experience which, if continued, leads to blinding dizziness, loss of orientation in space, terror, and such intense blaming hatred that she avows that mere contact with me has produced the experience which is so frightening she cannot continue it and yet cannot stop until either she has reached a limit at which point the dysphoric state will be interrupted by a violent mental event signalled by the sudden presence of dizziness.

In the second year a specific timing of these rhythmic patterns began to emerge. When she would be expecting her menses, which were highly irregular and usually delayed often by two to three weeks, she would experience increasing irritability, intense frustration about minor issues and would begin the haranguing diatribe mentioned above, leave the session in utter frustration, usually weaving and staggering out the door after having almost lurched into me, which was always out of her way to do. She would say, "I don't know where I am," appear to be drugged, linger at the exit, and finally leave in disgust after having attempted to instill me with a sense of my utter cruelty. The dizziness was so severe, there was question as to her ability to walk. She would apologize about "what I am doing to you," but persist with repeated phone calls two to three times an evening during the week before a period. She had dreams of herself as a shrimp exposed to the world without a shell and in utter danger. During this period she had on her own recognizance a complete medico-endocrinologic study including a neurological workup, which was negative. She was terrified that she was hemorrhaging to death although she had awareness that her menstrual flow was within her usual limits. Similar events such as these gave rise to her breaks from treatment with two other analysts, both of whom had treated her five years each.

Associated with these intense "attacks" she would "look for a fight" with fellow employees, negate anyone who attempted to approach her, and demonstrated especial hatred for her mother, whom she could not forgive for giving birth to her. She had lost many jobs because of this behavior and stated that both her previous analysts terminated treatment with her because of it. It was only a matter of time before I would do the same because she felt that she was at an "impasse" which would not "give." Either she would die, end up in an institution, or I would be severely damaged, according to her.

It became increasingly evident that there was a sharp contrast between her feeling in the room the "instant" she entered compared with her experience outside. She felt she could be relatively calm, but take one look at me and be struck with hatred, confusion, and gradual numbness. I interpreted to her that her menstrual periods were experienced as if she were giving birth to a damaged baby which had been pounding against the uterine wall again and again attempting to emerge, but at an impasse. Her repeated rhythmical attempts to break out were repetitious of her experience at birth which led to her mother's exhaustion and the patient's increasing sense of "terror." These interpretations over a period of several months appeared to "take" and the violence diminished although aspects of the above experience were repeated with every period. *She discovered upon questioning her mother that such an event as reconstructed analytically actually did occur with her mother developing a secondary uterine inertia which resulted in caesarian section. Thus the pounding rhythm, the bloody phantasies of damaged children, parts of the body scattered over the streets, phantasies of violent accidents transforming to the shrimp dreams, and sudden confusion and disorientation corresponded to the particular discrete events associated with parturition.*

The transition from a watery environment to a gaseous medium has been studied in great detail by embryologists. Anatomical and physiologic adaptations to the sudden shift from water to air involve massive changes in circulatory dynamics as the umbilical cord is clamped with the well-known closure of the shunt through the foramen ovale and the subsequent sudden initiation of flow through the respiratory circuit which had been dormant. As the amniotic membranes rupture the pressure of the amniotic fluid which had suspended the foetus in flotation suddenly decreases, although while in utero the foetus must be subject to an experience of increased pressure relatively evenly distributed over its body through direct contact. Although we do not know directly, the foetus may experience sensations received from the mother's body either by direct approximation (i.e., uterine contractions) or through her circulatory system via the placenta. It is entirely likely that affective states such as anxiety which are mediated by humoral agents (i.e., epinephrine) reach the foetus as a passive recipient. Recent studies with premature infants have suggested that the foetus perceives sound in utero coming from borborygmi and from the maternal circulatory system. Sound travels four times faster in water than in air and would depend for its reception upon the foetus being able to transduce the "pressure waves" of sound in a fluid medium to a form of auditory trace.

Bion (1975) has reminded us that if one closes one's eyes, pressure on the globes will result in seeing lights. This can be confirmed by the reader.

Thus it is likely that some form of input from outside the foetus' anatomy comes in and is received through a form of vision and hearing, but mediated through a pressure modality. This feature of sensory input via a pressure system may be an important reference for the "dating" of the experience of pressure when it becomes an important analytic theme.

With the birth process in physical form, the blood flow is cut off from the mother and the foetus must undergo a rapid shift from a gill-like form of respiration to the use of the lungs. The external fluid pressure on the skin is suddenly reduced and the organs of sensation from the skin to olfaction, vision, and hearing must undergo a fundamental change in the threshold of stimulation. The foetus as it is born is suddenly subjected to intensities of sound, light, temperature, and touch, which is entirely different from its intrauterine experience.

Even though the reader is familiar with the elements of the birth process, consideration of each of the issues mentioned above shows that nothing less than a major stage in evolution which required millenia in the history of phylogeny occurs regularly with every human birth in a matter of seconds.

I have noted a number of unchanging phases in current linguistic usage that refer to the phases of the transitional process from inside the mother in phantasy to birth (Paul and Carson, 1976).

The experience of psychic movement toward psychological birth is attended by what seems to be severe mental pain. Terror and severe intense anxiety are frequently described. "I can't make ends meet," "I'm under extreme pressure," "I'm up against the wall," "I've gotten in over my head," are frequent references to the instigation of the shift to the outside. In the intermediate process, one frequently hears, "I'm out on a limb," "I've overextended myself." References to the outside state include vertigo, "I'm out in the cold," etc. The experience of separation from an object which is used as though it were expected to be placental is extremely traumatic. The term placental-object describes the nature of the form of psychic attachment to the analyst and delineates the expectations which are placed upon him by the patient. Bion (1967) has described psychotic transference as "thin and tenacious." These patients show a similar tenacity and adhesiveness. The patients conform in description to the grown-up version of the children described by Meltzer (1975) in his *Explorations in Autism*. The patient feels he cannot afford to allow the analyst time separately simply because he will die if separated. He feels "cut off," "ripped off," as in umbilical cord and placenta and cannot tolerate independent existence without the presence of a nourishing object.

These patients treat the analyst as if he were present only in a very undifferentiated form. They experience the analysis as a place to *be*, but do not have a conception of taking something in. A profound hatred is evidenced for anything which reminds them of the feeding situation. Two of the these patients gave histories of failure to thrive in infancy and one had severe celiac disease associated with chronic diarrhea from earliest infancy through the age of one-and-one-half years. Severe colic was evidenced in three others, lasting a full year with marked inability to sleep, and they gave histories of pronounced screaming throughout the night which could only be soothed by the presence of a parent rocking them through the night. They evidence a wish to be held about which they are very guarded and interpret the analyst's intervention as an attempt to force feed them which they ward off as if a catastrophe would occur if they were to listen or try to understand. If the patients do listen, they experience "pressure," feel "pressured," and there is a sudden ushering in of a delinking process so that the analyst's constructions are rendered meaningless. This "pressure" has similarity to the patients' experience when mentally located in utero just prior to birth in phantasy. It is almost as if any intake would destroy their delusion of being in a state of uterine sanctuary.

We do not have the methodology to specifically demonstrate the exact developmental links of intrauterine life in symbolic form through the development of infancy and childhood which would satisfy the scrutiny of strict scientific validation. How does the foetus and even the infant "remember" the events described above? The foetus and infant would have to be capable of registering the experience in memory and then retrieve it in a symbolic form enough to even verbalize the phantasies as have been described. The development of symbolic communicative skills does not develop at least until 12-18 months (Mahler, 1968), which then leaves us with a mystery. It is convenient, as many including myself have done, to deny prematurely the validity of such formulations. If, however, when the child gains communicative skills, the verbal forms which are linked to invariant deep structural patterns (Chomsky) are capable of containing the code locked in the soma, the succeeding development of complexity of language better enables the person to transcribe and translate a primitive language which requires the symbol for further transformation. The development of language would then bridge the gap between a primitive somatic experiential language and what we understand as symbolic phantasy. That verbal forms can be utilized for transcribing primitive body language after birth has already been amply demonstrated by Melanie Klein (1961) and extended by Hanna Segal (1956) in her description of the development of the symbolic equation. I mean to extend these important discoveries to include an even more primitive state in order to postulate the existence of a form of experience in utero which is registered by the foetus and which is capable of translation at a later time into a symbolic form.

Further, Mrs. Klein describes "phantasied onslaughts on the mother following two main kinds: one is the predominantly oral impulse to suck dry, bite up, scoop out and rob the mother's body of its good contents. The other line of attack derives from the anal and urethral impulses and implies expelling dangerous substances (excrements) out of the self and onto the mother." She continues, "These excrements and bad parts of the self are meant not only to injure, but also to control and to take possession of the object" (Klein, M., 1975). In her pioneering description of projective and introjective mechanisms, she defined the earliest object relations after birth and made mention briefly of the sources of primary anxiety as being related to the trauma of birth (Klein, M., 1952). In the above description, it appears to me that the attempts to forcefully gain nutrients and locate waste in the maternal object not only relate to oral and anal aggressive phantasies, but also relate to the attempt to maintain a functioning placenta as a primary expectation which has never been worked through. In the intrauterine state, there is no oral feeding or anal excretion as all of these functions are perfectly handled by the placenta as intermediary between the mother and foetus. Might this not relate to the frequent expectations of perfection rigidly maintained in schizoid patients? Birth is then literally a rip-off (as defined in current parlance) which is experienced as a violent robbery, battery and attempted murder on the part of the mother and vice versa.

A frequent finding in these patients has been a form of drug addiction or habituation from alcohol through hallucinogens. The drug is phantasied to put them in touch with the experience of being inside a mother by means of taking a psychoactive agent which can be "felt" to act within them. A striking finding has been the lack of specificity of the drug used for the most part as long as the experience of the "feel" of the drug acting inside them is evident (Paul, M.I., 1977). Regardless of major pharmacologic differences in the drugs utilized, several patients described no ability to discriminate between these drugs even those thought to be widely different in activity on a spectrum between alcohol, barbiturates, and tranquilizers on the one hand and stimulants on the other. The experience they seek in common is the "rush" from the perception of the feel of the drugs beginning to take effect and the dose is self-adjusted until this experience is reached. The experience of diminution of anxiety or the ablation of the "birth" symptoms of pressure, etc., is not the main target, but rather the maintenance of a feeling of something active inside them which they can control. Even if on a very potent drug, such as Ritalin or amphetamine in relative naive users, the effect on the mental process is denied unless they can continue to feel the "rush" and then continue to increase the dose until "psychological tolerance" is reached.

Often several patients have been in various states of obvious narcosis, but have denied perceiving any such state of mind unless the drug's activity is felt as the driving force of the "rush." Within the drug culture, a very clear discrimination is made between those habitues who use drugs orally versus those who "mainline" or inject by vein. The "mainliners" are felt to be those who are true addicts with a difficulty in contrast to those who use the oral route. Is the "mainline" a version of the umbilical circulation and the "rush" the acting-out of a primitive experience of the reception of chemical substance coming in through the placenta to the foetal circulation? This main line situation would most clearly be the nearest approximation to a return to overt womb phantasies with the idealized perceptions of warmth, comfort and oceanic bliss that are well-known parts of the experience of naive uses of opiates. The threshold of perceived drug activity changes markedly with temporary resolution of states of massive projective identification with the dosage for intended activity being much lower when partial separation has been achieved.

In each patient Dracula phantasies emerged as a transitional state between inside and outside as identification with the baby who was in the womb (coffin) in the mother (Transylvanian soil) and parasitized the woman victim (analyst mother) by direct entry of fangs into the blood supply. References to black magic included those parts of the black mass which involved the ritual eating of the placenta after the devil-possessed baby is born. These phantasies have in common a direct contact with the blood supply of the mother and come up in close approximation to material relating to intolerance to the frustration of separation from the mother. Although there are clear examples of oral sadism, I believe they represent transitional phantasies attempting to maintain a version of placental connection outside the mother's body by direct attack. These activities are all known to occur at night and seem to correlate with alarming dreams and/or state of insomnia.

According to the shorter edition of the *Oxford English Dictionary*, the word "pressure" derives both from Middle English and Old French "pressen," "presser," in several contexts:

> I. *Literal and directly connected senses.* 1. To exert a steady force against (something in context); 2. To press to death: to execute the punishment of "peine forte et dure" upon a person arraigned for a felony who stood mute and would not plead. To compress, squeeze, extract juice.
>
> II. *Figurative senses.* 1. To bear heavily on; to reduce to straits; to beset, harass. To oppress, crush. To distress, afflict. To weigh down, burden (the mind, feelings, spirits). 2. To produce a strong mental or moral impression. To urge on, compel, force.
>
> III. *Senses connected with the notion of a throng, or of pushing one's way in a throng.* 1. To crowd. 2. To push or strain forward. 3. To push one's way into a person's presence, or into a place boldly, presumptuously, or insistently. 4. To venture, obtrude or intrude oneself.
>
> IV. *Combined.* Compacted or moulded by pressure.

I have found these definitions illuminating in that there is a continuum suggesting different phases of the experience of birth relating to phantasies of patients who have located themselves in the birth canal experiencing a powerful mental force suggested by the above-mentioned definitions. Experiences ranging from an uncomfortable sense of pressure to torture have been frequently observed. These patients feel themselves to be victimized by a force which is out of their control and experience themselves to be passive recipients of intolerable pain which they feel is a crushing force, oppression, a torture which is frequently experienced in the transference as the violent percussive, tyrranical, violence I have previously described. Under these conditions, thinking is severely impaired as far as the capacity to develop abstract modes.

Is there a state of mind which represents the emerging active experience of an encapsulated foetal aspect of development which contains a mental process which is a primitive form of thinking? If there is a pressure-vision as hypothesized previously, the form of thinking evolving from these primitive anlage would likely be mediated through the medium of pressure. In more developed forms, pressure is related to exceeding the threshold of a sense organ, for example through hearing or vision, at which incoming sense data can be adequately discriminated. When this threshold is reached (which would be subject to individual sensitivities), there is noted a form of psychic pain. An impression is made upon the mind which impels to action. This foetal level of experience would have been developed for use in a watery environment in which threshold levels of stimulation would have to be reached by pressure as an activating principle. A patient experiencing these phenomena would likely disburden his mind of such stimuli by means of projective identification which would account for the transference phenomena which are so constant in these individuals. Is this the obtruding experience of a form of "thoughts without a thinker," in Bion's terms, which gives rise to both the phenomena of worry and the lie as a means of avoiding this painful experience of pressure?

Worry would involve those repetitive cycles of reverberating circular patterns of thought arising from primitive foetal derivation under the influence of a pressure modality. The lie in one form would involve veering off from these primitive affectual experiences emerging from this foetal aspect of the mind. Psychic pain as a determinant of the inability to tolerate frustration has long been considered indefinable, mysterious, and has been intuited to be among the most important elements leading to the evolution of psychotic mental process (Bion, 1967).

In the patients I have described in this presentation, psychic pain has been the most dominant feature in the treatment and the greatest source of complaint. It is as though catastrophic feelings which seem to be imprints of the experience just before birth emerge and threaten the patient with the feeling of impending doom. The theme of death is very close in phantasy in these individuals to that of birth, and to them indistinguishable. These catastrophic expectations are mediated by a "foetal mental set," so to speak, and as they emerge, having been stimulated by sense input from the outside, there is a form of mating which occurs between the emerging foetal experience coded through pressure as an integrating medium and the incoming sense data which may not be coded for pressure if it has been integrated at a more advanced level of development. This mating of two different levels of sense experience must be subject to a set of rules which remain to be discovered. A singular feature of the mating of a foetal pressure level with an element of experience which has had exposure to the air, as it were, is psychological turbulence which contributes to psychic pain. This mating is a kind of "poor fit," a bringing together of a mismatch, and leads to concretism of thought.

If the analyst communicates in articulate speech, the patient doesn't understand, but experiences the speech as if it were meaningless sound which may be subject to fragmentation. Unless this level of experience is investigated, such interpretation of significance will be lost and the analysis will be superficial. Does understanding increase if pressure is approximated to pressure? If the tonal qualities and percussive elements of the voice are matched, there seems to be a facilitated communication, but this must be taken as a beginning speculation, the rules for which beg to be researched. Rascovsky (1960) described "foetal levels" of experience and put forward the hypothesis that these experiences were part of the emerging transference experience and would be amenable to interpretaton; however, the consideration of the nature of the language utilized to communicate to the foetal level was not developed. "Ploye (1973) reviewed considerations of prenatal mental life and put forward the assumption that symbol formation may well operate at levels far earlier than those usually thought to be possible, and with sufficient reason for one to be able to infer not only the nature but also the date of the reconstructed event." Dr. Ploye confined his elucidations of prenatal mental life to imprints of toxaemia of pregnancy, early and late threats to pregnancy, and felt he could identify these states in dreams with anatomic precision. I have confirmed his observations and wish to extend them to the theory of thinking which evolves through the work of Klein and Bion.

In *Elements of Psychoanalysis*, Bion (1963) demonstrated a method by which a myth could be utilized as receptor for transformations of experience both in sensory and affective qualities. By segmenting the Oedipal myth into individual themes, he hinted at a structural organization which integrates a set of sensory interconnections in a coded form. This template may act as a kind of filter which links sensory representation according to a set of rules which act as a pre-conception, making possible a specific quality of thought. Incoming sensa would then mate with retrievable mnemic residues according to the structure of the mythic template which bears analogy to the molecular approximation of reactants at the active site of an enzyme. The mythic structure would impart a mental counterpart of stereospecificity. This is the subject of a further study.

He has further drawn attention in a paper delivered to the Los Angeles Psychoanalytic Society on "The Grid," To the Death of Palinurus, as an example of visual phantasy. I have quoted the relevant section of the Story from Dryden's translation of Vergil's *Aeneid* and have divided this section into eleven main elements, as the form of this story has seemed to me to be useful as a model to illuminate a series of mechanisms, including sensory phenomena, takeover by the psychotic part of the personality, projective identification, the experience of drug narcosis, deamonic possession, delusion formation, and the re-entry to the mother's body representing the transformation from an air to a watery environment, each of which has been noted to exist in the material of each patient mentioned.

> Now smiling hope, with sweet vicissitude, within the hero's mind his joys renewed. He calls to raise the masts, the sheets display; the cheerful crew with diligence obey; they scud before the winds, and sail in open sea ahead of all the master pilot steers; and, as he leads, the following navy veers.
>
> The steeds of night had traveled half the sky, the drowsy rowers on their benches lie, when the soft God of sleep, with easy flight, descends, and draws behind a trail of light. Thou Palinurus art his destined prey to thee alone he takes his fatal way. Dire dreams to thee and iron sleep he bears, and lighting on thy prow, the form of Phorbas wears.
>
> Then thus the *traitor* god began his tale: "The winds, my friend, inspire a pleasing gale; The ships without thy care, securely sail. Now *steal* an hour of sweet repose: and I will take the rudder and thy room supply." To whom the yawning pilot half asleep: "Me dost thou bid to trust the treacherous deep, the *harlot-smiles* of race? Shall I believe the *siren south* again, and, oft betray'd not know the *monster main*? He said: his fastened hands the rudder keep, and fix'd on heaven, his eyes repel invading sleep. The God was wroth and at his temples threw a branch in Lethe dipped and drunk with stygian dew: The pilot vanquished by the power divine soon closed his swimming eyes and lay supine. Scarce were his limbs extended at their length, the God insulting with superior strength, fell heavy on him, plunged him in the sea, and, with the stern, the rudder tore away. Headlong he fell and struggling in the main, cried out for helping hands but cried in vain. The victor daemon mounts, obscure in air while the ship sails on without the pilot's care."

The elements of this story which these patients demonstrate in common include:

1) hope, bliss and clear weather
2) the falling of night, descent of sleep
3) dire dreams
4) the deception of Palinurus through the wiles of the traitor God
5) recognition of Somnus' lie and the fight
6) overpowering of Palinurus by Lethe and stygian dew
7) the ocean as smiling harlot-monster
8) awakening before drowning

9) the daemon mounts obscure in air

10) the ship sails on without a pilot

11) the moral element

In the analytic work there is evidenced a dread of the night and falling asleep because of the fear of nightmares. The ubiquitous experience of numbness and sleepy deadness ranging to mindlessness can be mimicked with a drug (stygian dew) or lethe (forgetfulness) which often involves an attempt to fight against the temptation to use a drug leading to "giving in" to the siren south, a voicelike temptress promising bliss and relief from pain. The feminine nature of the smiling harlot-monster is shown by a powerful infantile maternal transference with penetration in phantasy into the mother's body giving rise to feelings of drowning, choking, in addition to painful respiratory sensations and oedema. There is always a powerful negative maternal relationship in which a dread fear of dependency upon an individual is frequently replaced by drug dependency. After the takeover phenomenon the ship does sail on without a pilot noted by disorientation in space, loss of judgment, mindlessness and loss of perception. The story above describes a movement from air to water in terms of the maternal prenatal state and may be a clearer representation of what is meant by the "death instinct."

I have made use of a variety of theoretical formulations to describe a process which can be summarized diagrammatically to demonstrate more clearly the cyclic process of transformation of phantasy elements as mentioned earlier. This diagram is by no means complete or fixed, but is rather meant to serve as a tentative atlas of mental location and to put into coherent form the series of phenomena which have been individually detailed up to this point. The designators "in," "canal," and "out," refer to discrete locations in phantasy which correspond to anatomical sites inside the uterus before instigation of the birth process, during, and after. Many of the phenomena have been detailed by other authors (Freud, 1926; Rank, 1929; Bion, 1967; Ployé, 1973; Klein, 1952; Laing, 1976; Winnicott, 1949).

The letters A, B, C . . . designate locational configurations which move through sequential transformations or remain fixed depending upon the dynamic interplay of the analytic work. These cohesive units represent states of mind as well as levels of development and serve to cohere what hitherto has seemed to be disparate experience. What are the instigators for the transformations between A, B, C . . . and what determines the direction of cyclic flow? These are important questions for psychoanalytic research in both theory and technique which affords us the awe and pleasure of exploration in the future.

References

Bion, W.R. (1963), *Elements of Psycho-Analysis*. London: Heinemann, Ltd.
—— (1965), *Transformations*. London: Heinemann, Ltd.
—— (1967), *Second Thoughts*. London: Heinemann, Ltd.

INDICATORS OF MENTAL LOCATION

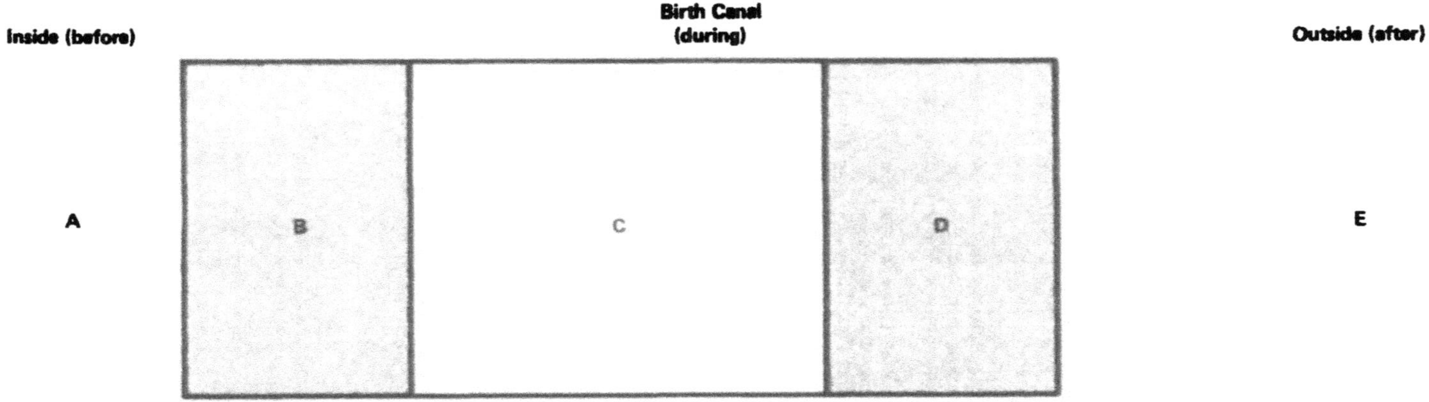

A	B	C	D	E
Intense visions Dream-like colour Timeless	Sensation of heat Claustrophobia Trapped Sensation Deadened Pointless Hopeless Despair	Turbulence Pressure "Squeeze" Physiological symptoms . . . a) Headache b) Pounding sensation c) Waves over body Intense anxiety --- Splitting of sense modalities	Cold chills Dizziness Vertigo Disorientation Heightened colour sensation Hypersensitivity to sound and light Disappearance of memory for event while "inside" Eerie sensation	Awe Wonder Strangeness Dimension

—— (1970), *Attention and Interpretation*. London: Tavistock Publications, Ltd.
—— (1975), Lecture, Los Angeles Psychoanalytic Society, June 4, 1975.
Chomsky, N. (1968), *Language and Mind*. New York: Harcourt, Brace & World.
Freud, S. (1926), *Inhibitions, Symptoms and Anxiety, S.E. 20*. London: Hogarth Press.
Klein, M. (1952), Notes on some *Developments in Psycho-Analysis*, ED. BY: M. Klein, P. Heimann, S. Isaacs and J. Riviere; London: Hogarth Press.
—— (1957), *Envy and Gratitude*. London: Tavistock Publications.
—— (1961), *Narrative of a Child Analysis*. London: Hogarth Press.
Laing, R.D. (1976), *The Facts of Life*. New York: Pantheon Press.
Mahler, M. (1968), *On Human Symbiosis and The Vicissitudes of Individuation, Volume I. Infantile Psychosis*, New York: Int. Univ. Press, Inc.
Meltzer, D. (1967), *The Psychoanalytical Process*. London: Heinemann, Ltd.
Meltzer, D.; Bremner, Jr.; Hoxter, S.; Weddel, D.; and Wittenberg, I., (1975), *Explorations in Autism*. Perthshire: Clunie Press.
Paul, M.I. (1976), The sense of strangeness, *Int. Rev. Psycho-Anal*. 3, 435-440.
—— (1977, in preparation), Transformational aspects of phantasy under the influence of marijuana.
—— and Carson, I.M. (1980), A contribution to the study of dimension, *Int. Rev. Psycho-Anal*., 7, 101-112.
Ploye, P.M. (1973), Does prenatal mental life exist? *Int. J. Psycho-Anal*., pp. 54, 241-246.
Rank, O. (1929), *The Trauma of Birth*. London: Routledge and Kegal Paul, Ltd.
Rascovsky, A. (1960), *El Psiquismo Fetal*. PAIDOS: Buenos Aires. *Shorter Oxford English Dictionary*, Ed., C.T. Onion, Oxford Univ. Press.
Virgil (1887), *The Aeneid*. John Dryden Translation, 3rd Ed., London and New York.
Winnicott, D.W. (1949), Birth memories, birth trauma, and anxiety, in *Collected Papers: Through Paediatrics to Psycho-analysis*, London: Tavistock Publications, 1959, pp. 174-193.

The Development of the Analysands' and Analysts' Enthusiasm for the Process of Psychoanalysis

W. Clifford M. Scott

EDITOR'S NOTE: *Dr. Scott's contribution constitutes a cogent penetration into and through the seeming mechanisticness of the "mechanisms" which circumscribe Klein's paranoid-schizoid and depressive positions with the end result of locating the vitality of enthusiasm—enthusiasm for analysis and enthusiasm for life itself. He traces the developmental course which enthusiasm must take in order to emerge. This course begins in the primitive, hard-won battle to separate off true danger from feelings of persecution and terminates in the achievement of mourning in the depressive position.*

The Development of the Analysands' and Analysts' Enthusiasm for the Process of Psychoanalysis*

W. Clifford M. Scott

Analysis leads to an increased ability to work and to love. This statement has almost become a cliché. The affect that best describes this increased ability is enthusiasm or zest. Zest only develops slowly. The vicissitudes of its development are the content of this paper.

To describe what eventually becomes what we call the normal enthusiasm in the analyst and analysand for the process of analysis it is necessary to outline the vicissitudes of pleasure from its simplest form through subsequent stages:

First, through the split between persecution and megalomania.

Secondly, through ambivalence.

Thirdly, through sadomasochism.

Fourthly, through envy and admiration.

Fifthly, through grief, mania and mourning, with its resolution in reparation.

All of these stages are subject to *regression* and, hopefully, later, to *progression* to a more or less stable ability to tolerate working through the same sequence again:

First, alertness to danger (or, as a patient said: "You don't need to be paranoid to see they are out to get you.").

Secondly, excitement without being megalomanic.

Thirdly, ambivalence and multivalence.

Fourthly, tolerating pain in oneself and ability to inflict pain without becoming sadomasochistic.

Fifthly, suffering loss and developing efficient mourning realizing that, the more one hopes for, and attains, the greater the loss one is risking.

Sixthly, confidence that mourning leading to reparative enthusiasm may be accomplished without manically denying unaccomplished or *postponed reparation* to lost objects and opportunities, by being able to seek new objects and new opportunities.

---

*A paper read before Division 39 of the American Psychological Association, Montreal, Quebec–September 1, 1980.

Thus enthusiasm and zest for continuing love of people and work develops.

To reformulate in more detail what I have already said, the roots of zest lie in the earliest aspects of pleasure we remember, or observe, of the pleasure-pain sequence in the infant. This sequence we call narcissistic, since any distinctions between what becomes ego and object are not yet present. Nevertheless, there is plenty of consciousness and change or transformation. Such sequences when remembered, or repeated later while awake or in dreams, seem magical. The changes range from bliss to pain, including Freud's "oceanic feeling," William James's booming, buzzing, confusion, and what I have called cosmic bliss and catastrophic chaos. This is the time of the earliest splitting and confusion; the time of persecution and megalomania.

Some more or less stable boundary and container develops. This we call a body with its distinction between outside and inside. Gradually differentiation between parts; e.g., lips, tongue, saliva, etc., and nipple, milk, breast, etc., and differentiation between functions, e.g., breathing in and out, sucking and swallowing, drooling and vomiting, etc., emerge.

Eventually more and more complete differentiation of the body's rhythmic activities (instincts), its cognition and its affects, develops. Eventually in consciousness sensations, perceptions, memories and anticipations, etc., are differentiated. Memory, anticipatory and eidetic images, become differentiated and interrelated. Eventually, poised or active ambivalent states develop in which good and bad attitudes of a continuing body to a continuing object arise.

Ambivalence is soon complicated by sadomasochistic relations in which more than tolerated ambivalence is present. Pleasure is ruthlessly sought regardless of desiring to produce pain as well. This is sadism. Pain is tolerated, or in fact desired, as part of pleasure seeking. This is masochism.

During this ambivalent sado-masochistic development, projection and introjective mechanisms have been active in creating the continuity of the ego and the world of external and internal objects. Eventually envy emerges. The envied object with its self satisfaction may be an object of love and projective identification with consequent loss of aspects of the ego. The envied object may be attacked with hate and spite. With its destruction, any part of the ego which had been projected into it is destroyed as well. When the envy is overcome, any projected love and hate may be reintrojected, and admiration becomes possible as development continues. Regardless of any damage to development which results from envy of objects, or self-envy of parts of the ego, the damage is rarely enough to prevent the emergence of new complicated and crucial affects. Eventually there develops some realization of the way hate may destroy good opportunities, or good relations to objects, or the objects themselves, and some realization of the way objects may destroy opportunities or good relations to the ego or to parts of the ego. The effect of this realization is emergent sadness. The sadness may be without hope.

Subsequently, there appears some realization that all objects and the opportunities they present have not been destroyed, and that all parts of the ego and its relationship to objects have not been destroyed. The re-establishment of good relations to a good object leads to hope for a better future. Such hope may be unstable.

The pain of emerging hopeless sadness may lead to regression either to a pre-sad type of gladness or badness; namely, to a persecutory or megalomanic state. Normally development is to progression to the work of mourning, to making good, to making reparation in new opportunities with new objects, or in new relationships to old objects, instead of making attempts at restitution of some status quo ante. The difference between progression to mourning and reparation, and regression to a previous state is of the utmost importance. Disappointment and sadness in the same situation which previously resulted in frustration and anger, become tolerated without regression to frustration and anger. Mourning work begins, leading to a change from hopelessness to hopefulness. The work of mourning leads to reparation, to a new object and situation, or to an old object in a new situation, of the damage done by previous aggression by the object or by the subject. With mourning, the realization emerges that a new beginning becomes possible, linking losses to a new found object and opportunities. The stability of such new relations may nevertheless be endangered by more or less completely repressing the work which was needed to reach these new relations. The greater the repression, the less the preparedness will be for resolving new losses, and the less efficient will learning to mourn be. Eventually, during mourning, gladness at sadness becomes tolerated, with the hope that new objects will tolerate this gladness at hopeful sadness, without being made sad themselves. More or less continuously zest emerges, as gladness at sadness changes from gladness at gladness, as new relationships of mutual satisfaction develop. Nevertheless, the enthusiasm of successful mourning must be free from repression of the work done to achieve it.

Such a summary of development from infantile excitement to eventual zest should also include the story of changing balances between different zonal activities and gender differences, and their derivatives, which lead to the differences in personalities. All the vicissitudes of respiratory, oral, anal, urethral and genital drives, as well as the general motor drive to explore the world, all in their relation to the identifications with the same or different genders have much to do with the difference of character. All these factors are important but I will not elaborate them since they have been before us much longer than the factors I am emphasizing. Neither does analytic work as a sublimation need to be elaborated here.

I have emphasized the balances developed between frustrations and disappointments, and the acceptance of sadness, and mourning, and the lifelong struggle to increase mourning's efficiency, and consequently the zest for progressive development. We must accept the risks of new development leading to new opportunities and new zest, knowing that the more we risk the more we may lose. I have done so because I am convinced that regardless of how much has been accomplished due to our understanding of instincts and their vicissitudes, much more can be added by increasing our understanding of the crucial stages of ego development through the paranoid and megalomanic positions or aspects, to the depressive, manic, mournful and zestful positions or aspects. In recent decades much has been written about borderline phenomena. In my experience the most neglected borderline is when unconscious anxiety about facing grief or equal intensity of the love and hate previously present, prevents progressive development to being able to mourn the past and to make-up for past losses in the future. Classical and current textbooks of psychology say little about normal mourning.

Now I will follow my remarks about theory with clinical and technical material. With patients from two years of age to the eighties, the analyst's recurrent presence, his minimal interference with free play or free speech, his curiosity about everything shown or said to him, his sympathetic understanding shown by his attitude and his speech, even at the early age when his speech can be understood long before the analysand's speech, can be a competent method of expression in its own right. All these lead eventually to the analyst and the situation he provides being accepted as new, as different and as more useful than anything previously experienced. The analyst will be attacked with love and with hate, he will be idealized and he will be trusted, he will be envied, and he will be admired, especially by students and even by patients who want to be analysts but never can be. At times he will, and at times he will not, be considered sympathetic or understanding. More than sympathy and understanding will be demanded. What the analyst gives may be too little and too late. What the patient accepts may not be from the right person, or in the right situation. But eventually the work of analysis will be accepted and valued, and indeed enjoyed. With the enjoyment of analysis, dreams of analysis become more frequent. Eventually self-analysis begins by talking to one's self including talking about the difficulties in talking, as a substitute for the session with the analyst.

The dream of analysis may lead to a silent self analysis. Like a patient who says: "I am thinking of analysis." The fuller understanding of self-analysis results in being able to talk out loud to one's self in a suitable place. Listening to the action of talking to one's self is very different from inner speech, even the inner speech of talking to one's self about oneself and the world about. The inhibitions which prevent talking to one's self go back to the early years, when babbling to one's self alone began to be replaced by talking in one's mother tongue out loud to a fantasy of one's mother, more or less identified with one's own self. The loss of the mother by absence at such times, followed by the mourning of the loss, and establishing a good mother or parent in fantasy, has much to do with being able to repeat this later in developing an ability for self-analysis. Talking alone is usually first done by the infant either before going to sleep or on waking up or during both. Later, talking to one's self may occur at any suitable time, but the adult has to overcome much difficulty before becoming able to do so with zest. Edward Glover often referred to self-analysis as "the analytic toilet," but it may become much more zestful than such an activity.

Much more has been written about the work of analysis than about the work of self-analysis, and about the transition from one to the other in the terminal stages of analysis. The more the possibility of self-analysis is accepted, the more the loss of the external analyst is mourned, and the more a useful internal analyst, more or less identified with the self, is established the more the zest for self-analysis. Zest for self-analysis will also be related to the analysand's belief in some good role he plays in the analyst's self-analysis.

To sum up and conclude I will again emphasize our need to keep the derivatives of libido before us always, and to keep the model of successful mourning before us always, so that we may become ever more enthusiastically at ease in trying to cope with pathology, especially pathological mourning.

Analysis began with young and middle-aged adults. Eventually, children and late-aged adults learned the value of analysis. Recently older and older adults are learning that they can learn and are valuing analysis.

So often the analysand wants to be told, or shown, what to do, rather than become conscious of the fantasy of what he wants. He finds it painful to mourn the past, and to look to the future to find the substitute with which reparation can be made. Those who have been most deprived, and are most hopeless, and helpless, and persistently angry in the present, may continue to be defensive against ongoing analysis and against the hope that the unconscious will provide new fantasy that can be matched by a newly recognized reality so that new development can ensue.

Regardless of what our fantasy or belief is of the beginning of thought, we often realize that we think we thought but have forgotten. We call the forgotten and unrememberable, the repressed. We only need to forget reflexively once for the forgotten to disappear. As soon as I forget I have forgotten, it is as if I never knew. The problem of separating the repressed unconscious, from the unconscious which has never yet become conscious, is with us daily. Our curiosity about the beginning of consciousness, about the earliest symbols and their derivatives, about our earliest and simplest use of noise, and later of speech in its most complex forms, is often related to our having destroyed some possible stage of development. Any destruction or primary inhibition has wide ranging effects on many aspects of development, and plays its part in subsequent frustrations and disappointments. Any sign that a frustration may be of unaccomplished grief at the loss or destruction of a potentiality, may alert us to a potentiality which may become conscious. Such a potentiality may be exploited if, and only if, the grief at its previous destruction, or inhibition, is adequately mourned, and adequate reparation is made by using this new potential in development with zest.

Hopefully, the younger can learn from the older throughout life, even in preparation for death by preparatory mourning so that the death-bed-scene may become, not feared, not a scene of guilt, but a part of natural development which can be valued better by all concerned. Analysis of the dying is for future research, but already the enthusiastic, sympathetic, understanding of some analysts is beginning to have good effects on the dying and those who care for them.* Successfully mourning the inevitable before it happens leads to maximal enthusiasm for life as it is. Learning to make the best of a bad job on the part of the analysand and analyst will enhance enthusiasm for curiously seeking what can still be done. This can happen without either, the analysand's, or analyst's, enthusiasm being spoiled by mania, or by regression.

Much of our work contains the wish to accept responsibility for continuously trying to separate truth from error, and to accept no plateau of learning, or of affective or motor development, and to accept the sequence of dilemmas and paradoxes of life with enthusiasm.

Resolving the anger and disappointment at the finiteness of affect, motility, cognition, competence, and eventually of life itself, leaves us with our ignorance and our attitude to the unknown, both in ourselves and in others. Hopefully, we may resolve our hate and sadness about the unknown and become able to love the unknown with zest. We can woo the unknown since from it all new good, as well as, bad and sad states, will come. As a philosopher colleague said to me: "We had better love the unknown—there is so much of it."

Finally I return to my beginning when I referred to analysis enhancing love and work. I wish to add enhanced ability to recognize enemies from whom one reserves hate, enhanced ability to grieve disappointment instead of hating frustration, and enhanced ability to mourn with zest and accept new beginnings.

References

Bion, W.R. (1962). *Learning From Experience*. New York: Basic Books.
—— (1963). *Elements of Psycho-Analysis*. New York: Basic Books.
—— (1965). *Transformations*. London: William Heinemann.
—— (1970). *Attention and Interpretation*. London: Tavistock Publications.
Freud, S. (1957-1974). *The Standard Edition of the Complete Psychological Works*. London: Hogarth Press.
Klein, M. (1975). *Love, Guilt, and Reparation and Other Works, 1921-1945*. New York: Dell Publishing Company.
—— (1975). *The Psycho-Analysis of Children*. New York: Dell Publishing Company.
—— (1975). *Envy and Gratitude and Other Works*. New York: Dell Publishing Company.
—— (1975). *Narrative of a Child Analysis*. New York: Dell Publishing Company.
Scott, W.C.M. (1960). Depression, confusion, and multivalence. *Int. J. Psycho-Anal*. 41, 497-503.
—— (1963). The psychoanalytic treatment of mania. American Psychiatric Association, *Psychiatric Research Report*, No. 17 (November).
—— (1964). Mania and mourning. *Int. J. Psycho-Anal*. 45, 373-377.
—— (1966). The mutually defensive roles of depression and mania. *J. Canadian Psychiat. Assoc*., Vol. 11, Special Supplement.
—— (1975). Remembering sleep and dreams. *Int. J. Psycho-Anal*. 2, 253-354.

*[Editor's Note: Dr. Bernard Bail's contribution in this volume is an example of this laudable development.]

EDITOR'S NOTE: *Doctor Segal is herein re-exploring some intriguing notions about dreams and dreaming. In employing Bion's conceptions about alpha and beta elements (and functioning) conjoined to her own discovery of the symbolic equation aspect of concrete thinking (in a state of projective identification) the patient confuses (a) himself with the object to be symbolized and (b) the object to be symbolized with the symbol for it. With these tenets Segal seeks to advance from Freud's simple notion of dreams as formations to a more sophisticated notion that dreams are veritable "bowel movements" in which painful states of mind can be dreamed away by evacuation, provided the elements of the experience have been "alphabetized" by alpha function. Elements which resist alpha function become beta elements (to use a Bionian term) and are suitable for prediction of future acting-out. Thus the predictive dream is part of a more elaborate procedure in which the undigested beta elements must be dreamed* and *acted-out in order to achieve ultimate evacuation.*

The Function of Dreams

Hanna Segal (London)

Jones tells us that to the end of his life Freud considered *The Interpretation of Dreams* his most important work. This is not surprising. Whereas his studies on hysteria revealed the meaning of symptoms, it was his work on dreams that opened up for him and us the understanding of the universal dream world and dream language. The structure of the dream also reflects the structure of personality.

To recap briefly the classical theory of dreams, repressed wishes find their fulfillment in the dream by means of indirect representation, displacement, condensation, etc., and by use of symbols which Freud puts in a slightly different category from other means of indirect presentation. Dream work is the psychic work put into this process. By means of dream work a compromise is achieved between the repressing forces and the repressed and the forbidden wish can find fulfillment without disturbing the repressing agencies. Freud did not revise much the theory of dreams in the light of his further work. For instance, he did not tell us how his views on dreams were affected by his formulation of the duality of instincts and the conflict between libidinal and destructive dreams. He also, at the time of his basic formulations about the dream, did not yet have available to him the concept of working through. I myself, feel rather uneasy about the dream being conceived as nothing but a compromise: The dream is not just an equivalent of a neurotic symptom, dream work is also part of the psychic work of working through. Hence, the analyst's satisfaction when, in the course of analysis, "good" dreams appear.

The classical theory of dream function takes for granted an ego capable of adequate repression and of performing the psychic work of dreaming, which, to my mind, implies a certain amount of working through of internal problems. It also takes for granted the capacity for symbolisation. Now, when we extend our psychoanalytical researches, we come more and more across patients in whom those functions, on which dreaming depends, are disturbed or inadequate. The function of symbolisation should be investigated further. Freud took the existence of symbols as given and universal and, I think, unchangeable phenomena. This, of course, was particularly so before he broke with Jung and the Swiss School of analysts. Jones, in his paper on symbolism, which denotes the main break with the Swiss School, implies already, though he does not explicitly state it, that symbolisation involves psychic work connected with repression—"Only the repressed is symbolised—only the repressed needs to be symbolised." (Jones, 1916). Melanie Klein made the next big step forward. In the analysis of an autistic little boy described in her paper 'Symbol Formation and its Importance for the Development of the Ego' (Klein 1930), she gives an account of the analysis of a child who was incapable of forming or using symbols. In her view, symbolisation occurs by a repression and displacement of interest in the mother's body so that objects in the external world are endowed with symbolic meaning. In the case of Dick, the autistic child, a phantasised, sadistic and projective attack on to his mother's body gave rise to a paralysing degree of anxiety so that the process came to a stand-still and no symbol formation occurred. The child did not speak or play or form relationships. I investigated further those phenomena describing the psychic dynamics of the formation of what I called the symbolic equation or the concrete symbol characteristic of psychoses and the symbol proper suitable for purposes of sublimation and communication (Segal 1950). Briefly stated, in my view, when projective identification is in ascendance and the ego is identified and confused with the object, then the symbol, a creation of the ego, becomes identified and confused with the thing symbolised. The symbol and the object symbolised become the same, giving rise to concrete thinking. Only when separation and separateness are accepted and worked through does the symbol become, not equated with the object, but a representative of the object. This, in my view, implies a full depressive elaboration; the symbol becoming a precipitate of a process of mourning. The disturbance of the relationship between the self and the object is reflected in a disturbance in the relationship between the self, the object symbolised and the symbol. I define the term 'symbolic equation and symbol' in the following way: "In the symbolic equation, the symbol substitute is felt to be the original object. The substitute's own properties are not recognized or admitted . . . the symbol proper available for sublimation and furthering the development of the ego is felt to represent the object. Its own characteristics are recognized, respected and used. It arises when depressive feelings predominate over the paranoid-schizoid ones, when separation from the object, ambivalence, guilt and loss can be experienced and tolerated. The symbol is used, not to deny, but to overcome loss. When the mechanism of projective identification is used massively as a defense against depressive anxieties, symbols already formed and functioning as symbols may revert to symbolic equations"—as, for instance, in a psychotic breakdown.

To Jones'—'only what is repressed needs to be symbolised,' I added, 'only what can be adequately mourned can be adequately symbolised.' Thus, the capacity for non-concrete symbol formation is in itself an achievement of the ego—an achievement necessary for the formation of the kind of dreams covered by Freud's theory.

We know that in the psychotic, the borderline, and the psychopathic dreams do not function in this way. In the acute psychotic, often, if not always, there is no distinction between hallucinations and dreams. Indeed, no clear distinction occurs between states of being asleep or awake, delusion, hallucination, night-time events, which could go by the name of dreams, and they often have the same psychic value. In nonchronic states, but when psychotic processes are in ascendance, dreams may be experienced as real and concrete events. Bion reports on a patient who was terrified by the appearance of his analyst in the dream, as he took it as evidence of having actually devoured the analyst. (Bion, 1958). Dreams may be equated with faeces and used for purposes of evacuation or when minute, internal fragmentation occurs, they may be felt like a stream of urine and the patient may react to having bad dreams as to incidents of incontinence. (Bion, 1958). A patient can use dreams for getting rid of rather than working through unwanted parts of the self and objects and he can use them in analysis for projective identification. We are all familiar with patients who come and flood us, fill us, with dreams in a way disruptive to the relationship and to the analysis.

I had the opportunity of observing this type of function of the dreams particularly in two borderline psychotic patients both of whom dreamt profusely, but in whom it was the function rather than the content of the dreams that had to be paid attention to. In these patients, often dreams were experienced as concrete happenings. This was particularly clear with my woman patient. This woman, who is very quarrelsome in a paranoid way, can bring a dream in which she was attacked by X or Y, or sometimes myself, and if one attempts to understand some aspect of the dream, she will say indignantly "But it is X or Y or you who have attacked me," treating the event in the dream as a completely real event. There is apparently no awareness that *she dreamt* the dream. Similarly, an erotic dream in which, say, a man pursues her, is felt practically as a proof of his love. In fact, her dreams, although she calls them dreams, are not dreams to her but a reality, and in this they parallel another mental phenomenon in her life, in which she uses a similarly misleading word. She experiences most weird and bizarre sexual phantasies and she freely speaks of them as 'phantasies,' but if one enquires into them more closely, it becomes apparent that these are not phantasies but hallucinations. They are felt as real experiences. For instance, she walks very awkwardly because she feels she has a penis stuck in her vagina; and mentally, when she phantasises a sexual relationship with someone, she uses the word 'phantasy,' but in fact, she believes and behaves as if it were a reality. For instance, she accuses me of being jealous of her sexual life, busting her relationships, etc., when, in fact, she has no sexual life or relationships. So what she calls phantasy and what she calls a dream are, in fact, experienced as a reality though she thinly denies it. These so-called dreams constantly invade the external reality situation. For instance, she will complain about the smell of gas in my room and it will transpire later that she dreamt of bursting a balloon or exploding a bomb. The evacuation that happens in the dream seems to invade the perception of the reality.

These concretized dreams lend themselves particularly for purposes of expulsion. This was especially clear in my male patient, who used to write his dreams extensively in a little notebook. He had volumes and volumes of them. For instance, following his mother's death, he had dreams of triumph over her, aggression, guilt, loss, but in his conscious life, the mourning of his mother was conspicuous by its absence. It was interpretations of the kind—'you have got rid of your feelings for your mother in your dream'—that were more effective in bringing about some conscious experience of his affect than any detailed analysis of the dream. He was using the dream to get rid of that part of his mind which was giving him pain and later discharged the dream into his notebook. He deals similarly with insight. An insightful session is often followed by a dream which seems to be closely related to it. In other patients, this kind of dream is usually a step in the working-through. In his case, however, more often than not, such a dream means that he got rid of all feeling about the previous session by making it into a dream and getting rid of it from his mind.

In the woman patient, similarly, the dream is part of an expulsive process. For instance, when she complains about the smell of gas in my room, she mentally expels the gas into the room.

Their dreams were characterised by very poor and crude symbolisation and one was struck both by the concreteness of the experience and the invasion of reality, as though there was no differention between their mind and the outside world. They had no internal mental sphere in which the dream could be contained. Khan, elaborating Winnicott's concept of transitional space, describes it in terms of dream space. (Khan, 1972). For myself, I found most helpful in understanding those phenomena, Bion's model of mental functioning, particularly his concept of the alpha and beta elements and his concept of a mother capable of containing projective identification. (Bion, 1963).

Bion distinguishes between alpha and beta elements of mental functioning. Beta elements are raw perceptions and emotions suitable only for projective identification—raw elements of experience to be gotten rid of. Beta elements are transformed into alpha elements by the alpha function. Those are elements which can be stored in memory, which can be repressed and elaborated further. They are suitable for symbolisation and formation of dream thoughts. It is the beta elements which can become bizarre objects or concrete symbols, in my sense of the word, that I think are elements of the psychotic-type dream, and alpha elements, which are the material of the neurotic and normal dream. This elaboration is also linked with mental space. In Bion's model, the infant's first mode of functioning is by projective identification (an elaboration of Freud's idea of the original deflection of the death instinct and Klein's concept of projective identification). The infant deals with discomfort and anxiety by projecting it into mother. This is not only a phantasy operation. A good enough mother responds to the infant's anxiety. A mother capable of containing projective identifications can elaborate the projections in her own unconscious and respond appropriately, thereby lessening the anxiety and giving meaning to it. If this condition obtains, the infant introjects the maternal object as a container capable of containing anxiety, conflict, etc., and elaborating them meaningfully. This internalized container provides a mental space and in this space alpha function can be performed. Another way of looking at it would be that it is in this container in which alpha functioning can occur that primary processes begin to be elaborated into secondary ones. The failure of the container and alpha functioning results in the inability to perform the dream work and therefore, the appearance of psychotic, concrete dreams.

I would like to give an example which shows, I think, the function of dreaming and its failure, resulting in concretization. The material comes from an unusually gifted and able man who has a constant struggle with psychotic parts of his personality. We ended a Friday session with the patient expressing enormous relief and telling me that everything in that session had a good resonance in him. On Monday, he came to his session very disturbed. He said he had a very good afternoon's work on Friday and Saturday morning, but he had a dream on Saturday which had disturbed him very much. In the first part of the dream, he was with Mrs. Small. She was in bed and he was either teaching or treating her. There was also a little girl (here he became rather evasive)—well, maybe a young girl. She was very pleasant with him—maybe a little sexy. And then quite suddenly, someone removed from the room a food trolley and a big cello. He woke up frightened. He said it was not the first part of the dream that frightened him, but the second. He felt it had something to do with a loss of internal structure. On Sunday he could still work, but he felt his work lacked depth and resonance and he felt something was going very wrong. In the middle of Sunday night he woke up with a dream, but he could not hold on to it and instead he became aware of a backache low in his back—maybe the small of his back.

He said the "Mrs. Small" part of the dream did not disturb him because he could quickly see through it. In the past, Mrs. Small, whom he does not think much of, represented a belittling of Mrs. Klein (Klein-Small) and he understood that and he supposed she represented me changed into a patient and also into a sexy little girl. He supposed it was an envious attack, because on Friday he felt so helped by me. He then had some associations to the cello—his niece having one, his admiration for Casals and a few other associations which led me to suggest tentatively that it seemed to be a very bisexual instrument; but that interpretation fell rather flat. What struck him more he said was that it is one of the biggest musical instruments around. He then said that I had a very deep voice and another thing that frightened him was that when he woke up from the dream, he could not remember what we were talking about in the session.

It seems to me that the whole situation, which in the first night is represented by the dream, in the second night, happens concretely. By changing me into Mrs. Small, he had lost me as the internalised organ with deep resonance. The cello represents the mother with deep resonance, the mother who can contain the patient's projections and give a good resonance; but with the loss of this organ, there is an immediate concretization of the situation. In his dream on Saturday night he belittles me by changing me into Mrs. Small. This leads to the loss of the cello—"one of the biggest musical instruments there are." He wakes up anxious. The function of the dream to contain and elaborate anxiety begins to fail. The next night, instead of a dream, he has a pain in the small of the back. Hypochondriasis, much lessened now, had at one time been a leading psychotic-flavoured symptom. The attack on the containing functions of the analyst represented as the organ with the resonance resulted in the patient losing his own resonance (his depth of understanding), and his memory–he cannot remember the session. When this happens, he can only experience concrete physical symptoms. The belittled analyst, who, in the dream, was represented by Mrs. Small becomes a concrete pain in the small of his back.

My attention has been drawn recently to a borderline phenomenon exhibited markedly by the two borderline patients whom I have mentioned earlier. They both frequently presented what I have come to think of as predictive dreams. That is, their dreams predicted their action–what has been dreamt, had to be acted out. Of course, up to a point, all dreams are acted out, as the dream expresses problems and solutions carried out also by similar means in life, but in these patients the acting out of the dream was extraordinarily literal and carried out in complete detail. For instance, my male patient is often late and, not surprisingly, often dreams of being late. What drew my attention to the predictive character of his dreams was the extraordinary precision with which a dream predicts his lateness to the minute. For instance, he will come 2, 6 or 45 minutes late and give me a plausible, to himself, reason, but later in the session he will report a dream in which he was late for a meal or a meeting for exactly the number of minutes which he actually was late on that day. I do not think it is a post hoc interpretation he puts on his dreams since he writes them down carefully first thing in the morning. I have also become aware that a Thursday or Friday dream containing phantasies of acting out at the weekend, is by no means a dream *instead* of the acting out but often a dream containing a plan for acting out, which is often then carried out in precise detail. This, of course, could be a failure of my analysis of the dream preceding the weekend. Other patients sometimes bring a similar plan for acting out in order to warn the analyst and get help and effective analysis obviates the need to act out, but I have a feeling that there is something so powerfully automatic in this patient's compulsion to act out the dream that analysis seldom moves it. Often he would not report the dream until the weekend.

In the woman, these predictive dreams particularly relate to paranoid dreams. There is a kind of row that I have become familiar with now that is characterised by an extra-ordinary automatic progression, apparently totally unaffected by my response. The session can go something like this–she will say in an accusing voice "You frowned at me." There can be any number of responses and I have tried various ones at different times. For instance, I could interpret "You are afraid that I am frowning at you because you slammed the door yesterday"; or I could say "What do you think I am frowning about?"; and here she might answer "You frowned at me because I slammed the door"; or I can be silent and wait for developments, but my silence is taken as a confirmation that I am terribly angry with her. Then it will be, "not only do you frown, but now you are silent, which is worse." I never say, "I did not frown," but I did try pointing out to her that it did not occur to her that she may have been mistaken in her perception. This could only make the row worse, because now, not only do I frown, but I accuse her of being mad. In either case, I have a feeling that my response is completely irrelevant and the row, the quarrel in which certain roles are assigned to me, will continue in a completely automatic fashion. At some point, however, usually when an interpretation touches on some fundamental anxiety, she will tell me a dream and then it will appear that the row we were supposed to be having in the session, is an almost word-for-word repetition of the row she has actually had in the dream, either with me or her mother or father or some thinly veiled transference figure like a teacher. This response to an interpretation–telling me a dream–only happens, however, when the row has run its course, at least for a time. Other similar interpretation, given earlier in the session, would be ignored or woven into the row. Now, I have come to recognise the particular feeling in the counter-transference. It is like being a puppet caught in someone else's nightmare and totally unable to do anything else but to play the allotted role, usually the one of the persecutor. So now, when the row begins in this particular way, I sometimes simply say "you have had a quarrel with me or someone like me in the dream" and sometimes this obviates her need to act out in the session. It is as though in those predictive dreams of both patients, dreams act as what Bion calls a "definitory hypothesis." (Bion, 1963). They define in detail how the session is to happen.

I was wondering in what ways the predictive dreams differed from the evacuative dreams, whether of the kind I described that my male patient experiences, or the kind that the woman patient experiences as happening, when they spill over, as it were, into reality. I think they are somewhat different. I think that the evacuating dream actually successfully evacuates something from the patient's inner perception. Thus, when my patient dreams of mourning his mother, he does not need to mourn her. The predictive dreams, however, seem to be dreams which do not entirely succeed in the evacuation and they seem to remain in the patient's psyche like a bad object which then the patient has to dispose of by acting the dream out. The evacuation does not seem to be completed until the dream has been both dreamt *and* acted out. This is very marked with the woman patient: going through the row, telling me the dream, getting the interpretation, gives her enormous relief, but I am seldom convinced that the relief is actually due to an acquired insight. It seems more to be due to a feeling of completed evacuation.

In conclusion: We can say that we are far from having exhausted the possibilities of understanding the world of dreams opened up by Freud, but our attention is increasingly drawn to the form and function of dreaming rather than to the dreams' content. It is the form and the function which reflects and helps to illuminate the disturbances in the functioning of the ego.

References

Bion, W.R. (1957). The differentiation between the psychotic and non-psychotic personalities. *Int. J. Psycho-Anal.* 38, 266-275.

—— (1958). On hallucination. *Int. J. Psycho-Anal.* 39, 341-349.

—— (1963). *Elements of Psycho-Analysis*. London: Heinemann.

Jones, E. (1916). The theory of symbolism. IN: *Papers on Psycho-Analysis*. Boston: Beacon Press, 1961, 87-144.

Khan, M. (1974). The Privacy of the Self. IN: *Papers on Psychoanalytic Theory and Technique*. New York: IUP, pp. 306ff. ALSO IN: *Int. J. Psa. Psychother.* 1972, Vol. 1, 31-35.

Klein, M. (1930). The importance of symbol formation in the development of the ego. *Int. J. Psycho-Anal.* 11, 24-39.

Segal, H. (1957). Notes on symbol formation. *Int. J. Psycho-Anal.* 38, 391-397.

Notes on the Desire for Knowledge

Hans Thorner

EDITOR'S NOTE: *Doctor Thorner, like Doctor Grinberg and Doctor Bail, has addressed himself to the strictures against the acquisition of knowledge about truth which are inherent in our culture, in our myths, and in our personalities. Thorner seems to be reaffirming the belief, first adumbrated by Freud and Abraham, later by Klein, and still later, in its fuller flowering, by Bion, that thinking, rather than sexual discharge, is the principal line of departure of the phenomenon of human existence. Moreover, he reaffirms, we are fated at best to get a glimpse of truth but never to know it. We can only pretend to know it through our arrogance, in which case we call it an idol.*

Notes on the Desire for Knowledge

Hans A. Thorner

Und sehe, das wir nichts wissen können!
Das will mir schier das Herz verbrennen.

Goethe, *Faust* I.

The desire for knowledge, as one of the fundamentals of the human situation, is bound to play a great part in psycho-analysis. The early workers in psycho-analysis showed a deep interest in the theme. But then, surprisingly, the subject seems to have disappeared from the analytical literature, until it was taken up again by Bion. The first papers concerned themselves with the origin of research, as it is observed in children and in cultural life. Freud considered the subject important enough to insert a special section in the Three Essays on Sexuality, which he entitled "Sexual Researches in Childhood" (Freud 1905). He even called the desire for knowledge an instinct, instinct for knowledge or epistemological instinct, although he was quite clear that this desire is not an instinct proper. As the first researches of the child were concerned with sexual matters, particularly with the birth of children, where they come from and the sexual relations between the parents, it was clear from the beginning that the instinct for research was related to the sexual instinct, although it could "not be classed exclusively as belonging to sexuality."

In his paper on Leonardo da Vinci Freud (1910) followed up this trend of thought and related the desire for research in Leonardo with a weak sexual drive for which there is evidence in Leonardo's biography. This posed a certain problem. As the repression of the sexual instinct may lead to intellectual inhibition, Freud made the point that in rare cases, as in Leonardo, some repression may occur without succeeding "in relegating a component instinct of sexual desire to the unconscious. Instead the libido escapes the fate of repression by being sublimated from the very beginning into curiosity and by becoming attached to the powerful instinct for research as a reinforcement . . . but owing to the complete difference in the underlying processes (sublimation instead of eruption from the unconscious), the quality of neurosis is absent."

Other workers in the field, of whom I shall only name three, followed Freud in this exposition. Abraham (1924) said "the displacement of the infantile pleasure in sucking to the intellectual sphere is of great practical significance." Abraham connects this with digesting the collected facts and the wish to give them back. The capacity in intellectual production can be disturbed and inhibited in some while others produce too quickly. "It is no exaggeration to say of such people that they have scarcely taken a thing in before it comes out of their mouth again." Very soon Freud (1913), examining obsessional neuroses, emphasized the sadistic instinctual component in obsessional thought processes and said that "the instinct for knowledge can actually take the place of sadism in the mechanism of obsessional neurosis. Indeed it is at bottom a sublimated off-shoot of the instinct of mastery exalted into something intellectual and its repudiation in the form of doubt plays a large part in the picture of obsessional neurosis."

Melanie Klein, who developed the psycho-analysis of children, brought her experiences with them to the study of the intellectual development. Melanie Klein (1921) stressed the marked omnipotence amounting to a form of megalomania with which the child tries to cope with the new problems and the child's resistance to accept biological explanations for the subjects of his researches that were offered to him. In her early papers she also stressed the libidinal origin of the instinct for knowledge, but later, when she laid greater stress on the aggressive components and the death instinct, she linked the desire for knowledge with mastering anxiety (Klein, M. 1923).

Mary Chadwick linked the instinct for knowledge with the oral component instinct and with the wish for a child. The desire for knowledge is the equivalent of the desire for a child. But the desire for a child is quickly and thoroughly repressed. It is replaced by the desire to know, which is the remaining trace of the original wish. The desire for possession of the object is replaced by the desire to know the object. The child's desire for knowledge is directed to the world that surrounds the child, the world of sense impressions. This forms also the basis for Freud's study of the origin of thought processes. In his paper on "Formulations of the Two Principles" (Freud 1911) Freud developed the idea that, when the pain-pleasure principle can no longer fulfill its purpose through hallucinatory satisfactions of the instinctual needs as it cannot give real satisfaction, particularly as the mother becomes increasingly less available to supply real satisfaction, the reality principle is forced on the individual. What was the unco-ordinated motor discharge of the accretion of stimuli (expressions of emotions) becomes a co-ordinated action with a purpose to alter the external world in order to achieve need satisfaction. This implies frustration through the lack of instantaneous hallucinatory satisfaction and through the delay by the co-ordination of the motor discharge into action; this gap is bridged by the act of thinking. Thinking is seen as an action with minimal energy quantitites.

Since then psycho-analytical interest has gone to different subjects, the super-ego, the structure of the personality, the work of Melanie Klein, the psycho-analysis of small children and the psycho-analysis of psychoses.

Looking back at the work of Freud from the point of view of today's scientific climate, different from that in which Freud discovered psycho-analysis, we can recognize a change in analytical thinking. So far as knowledge is concerned one could say that the classical work of Freud is an attempt to establish a biology of knowledge, a theory of how knowledge came to exist in nature. In his pre-analytical work Freud wanted to create a psychology which is a natural science, as physics and chemistry. Natural processes in the nervous system are unconscious, therefore Freud found himself in a position, in which he had to explain "consciousness." In "The Interpretation of Dreams" when he had given up this early approach, he found himself in almost the opposite position. Unconscious processes were still the basis of psycho-analysis, but they had to be justified alongside consciousness. The concept of the unconscious became a major problem and in the course of time it had to be clarified in the light of new discoveries, for instance, the structure of the personality, parts of which were partly conscious and partly unconscious.

Under the impact of modern science, which has pushed its frontiers into new dimensions, a reappraisal of causal relationships could not be without influence on psycho-analysis (Thorner, 1963). Bion's work is part of this new position. Bion, building on the work of Freud and Melanie Klein, based his concepts on his work with psychotics, as Freud, in his time, based his on his experience with neurotic patients. Bion's aim is not to give a biological theory of the origin of thought based on sense impressions of the outer world, as Freud did in his "Formulations." For Freud the external world had to supply instinct satisfaction. Bion is concerned with the awareness of the personality, of emotional experiences within the personality. His theory of thinking takes thoughts as existing. For both, thinking is forced on the organism by the needs of reality: for Freud, reality forces thinking on the organism in order to achieve instinct satisfaction. Thoughts are the products of thinking. For Bion (1962a), who starts with the existence of thoughts, thinking is forced on an existing apparatus which has to be adapted to its new task of coping with thoughts. However different Bion may be from Freud he does not refute or contradict Freud, as both deal with different problems and use different conceptual frameworks (Bion 1962). Freud is firmly based on biology, hence the existence of thoughts has to be explained; while Bion takes the existence of "thoughts" (as pre-conceptions) as given and uses the conceptual framework of mathematics and logic to elucidate the problems of the mind. Both have the concept of truth. For Bion truth is a factor of the inner reality. It is the ultimate reality which may be approximated but never be reached. It belongs to the emotional world and not to the world of things. For Freud, who set himself the problem of knowledge of the external world—instinct satisfaction by the external world—truth is part of the external world. Freud starts with sense perception, but he is also fully aware of the limitations of sense perceptions. When it comes to emotional events, which cannot be communicated by sense perceptions as external events are, he takes "consciousness" as the sense organ of the emotional world (Freud, 1900). Bion, who is primarily concerned with the self-awareness of the personality, lays greater stress on non-sensuous impressions. By postulating the existence of thoughts, he eliminates the necessity to develop a theory of the nature of thoughts and the underlying processes of thinking. He postulates the existence of a function (alpha-function) which modifies sense perception into alpha-elements, which then can be dealt with by the thinking apparatus (which is modelled on the alimentary apparatus). The alpha-elements can be stored and, dependent on their position with reference to a contact barrier (Bion 1962), they are either conscious or unconscious. Hence there is not a fundamental difference between conscious and unconscious and Bion can therefore present a state of mind which is conscious and unconscious at the same time. In order to comprehend an emotional element it is necessary to "see" the conscious and the unconscious part at the same time. As Bion calls it, the emotional element can be seen in a "binocular" way on the basis of his theory of functions. If the alpha-function fails beta-elements appear, which are precursors of thoughts and are somewhere between an alpha-element and a sense perception or between thoughts and real things. They also can be stored but not as thoughts, as Bion says, but as "undigested facts." As these undigested facts have retained the character of concrete objects they do not lend themselves to verbal formulations, but to communication by projective identification.

Freud tried to deal with a similar difficulty on the basis of a biological framework. He differentiated between ideas and feelings. He employed concepts from his research in aphasia, thing-presentation and word-presentation, for the differentiation between conscious and unconscious presentation; an idea—in the pre-conscious form—links up with its word-presentation in order to become conscious. In contrast feelings are either conscious or unconscious, "the distinction between Cs and Pcs has no meaning where feelings are concerned"; the expression of "unconscious" feelings is, according to Freud, only a short cut and loose formulation (Freud 1923).

Knowledge—Bion calls it, for short, "K"—is a particular form of object relation, which Bion calls a link, just as love and hate are links. They are emotional links, they are not static but dynamic. Knowledge therefore is for Bion somthing that concerns itself primarily with sense perception, that is object relations. "K" is not a piece of knowledge but the process to get to know. A patient comes to analysis to get to know himself and the analyst's presence promotes the development of this link. Side by side with the desire for knowledge there is a resistance to knowledge. Getting to know inevitably brings the individual into contact with objects that arouse displeasure. Hence tolerance to pain and displeasure is a pre-condition for the ability to think. In fact a thought which is a replacement of an object by its non-material character is in itself a frustrating experience. Only if it is possible to tolerate that frustration the individual is able to maintain a thought. Otherwise the thought turns into an absent, that is to say, a bad, frustrating object.

Bion recapitulates this theoretical formulation in more concrete terms as a model, or, as he calls it, in C categories. The model is the baby/breast relation. The baby has severe anxiety such as a feeling of dying; it cannot communicate this verbally because it has no language. The nature of its consciousness, which is very rudimentary, is not known to us. The baby which has no verbal communication communicates by projective identification of beta-elements. The mother/breast acts as a recipient or a container for the projection. The projected objects will remain in the container (breast) so that the mother can work on them by her reverie, which is a more pictorial word for alpha-function, until enough alpha-elements have been produced that can be communicated to the child. The undigestible facts (beta-elements) of the child become (digestible) alpha-elements through the reverie of the mother, which the child can accept and use, for its development and growth.

Here is an example from my analytical practice. A schizophrenic boy, who was a patient in a psychiatric hospital where I worked, was the only son of very hard-working parents. They were prepared to do anything that would restore their son's sanity. My desire to help this boy and his family made me involved in the patient's problem and was not a promising background for any analytical work. The other handicap was my lack of experience and the lack of psycho-analytical equipment available at that time, some forty years ago. Mrs. Klein had not yet written her paper on schizoid mechanisms, the concept of projective identification did not exist, and Bion had not yet written any of his psycho-analytical papers. The boy, who was acutely hallucinated, was not an easy object for psycho-analysis, but I felt I should try what I could do for him. He wandered about the room and in one of the analytical sessions, he opened his trousers, showed me his penis, and wanted me to touch it. I was not prepared for such an event. I was trained to give interpretations of verbal communications, dreams, etc., but the situation I was faced with was quite of a different nature. The concept of acting out did not help me, nor the concept of unconscious wishes, because the patient was apparently conscious of what a neurotic patient would have repressed into the unconscious. The only thing I knew was that I was embarrassed and did not know what to do, so the analysis came to an end before it had begun.

Now I can understand what had happened. This schizophrenic had no words because he had no, or very little, alpha-function. Instead of alpha-elements he was left with beta-elements, which have a concrete character, something like a penis or like "doing." I avoid the word "action." By his doing he violently projected into me an emotional situation for which I should have acted as the container, but I was unable to contain it and to use my alpha-function on it. Instead, the strong emotional reaction, my embarrassment, broke the container/analyst. In this case I was the breast that was unable to turn this event by my psycho-analytical reverie into alpha-elements which, as interpretations, the patient might have been able to digest.

The emotional impact the patient made on the analyst prevented the K-link to develop because the emotional experience destroyed the container. This was true for the psycho-analytical container but also for the patient himself. He was not able to cope with *his* anxieties. For his own reasons, he either never developed alpha-function, or, what he possessed of it, he was unable to use. That his alpha function failed him we know from the fact that he had been hallucinated. Instead of alpha-elements he was left with beta-elements which could only be expelled by hallucinations or acting out. If the analyst had been able to receive the beta-elements, the patient might have become able to digest them in the course of time. The overpowering force of this emotional experience was of a purely emotional character and my lack of psycho-analytic equipment at that time made me defenceless, and so the analysis could never make a start.

Owing to the nature of the psycho-analytical objects, that is to say, the subject of psycho-analytical study, psycho-analytical theories are different in structure from scientific theories which deal with concrete objects, which are measurable. Freud recognized this difference clearly. In "The Psycho-genesis in a Case of Homosexuality in a Woman" (Freud, 1920), he said that psycho-analysis can only explain a development retrospectively; it cannot predict events because we do not know the quantity of each factor involved.

The K-link, as an object relation, is restricted to knowledge of sensuous objects; but psycho-analysis deals with objects that cannot be experienced by the senses. Bion (1962a) describes this powerfully: "The sense data may be able in a state of fear or rage to contribute data concerning the heart-beat and similar events peripheral, as we see it, to an emotional state. But there are no sense data directly related to psychic quality, as there are sense data directly related to concrete objects. . . ." These non-sensuous objects belong to the domain of "O" which represents for Bion the ultimate reality. This ultimate reality is the world of "things-in-themselves" (Kant) which epistemologically are a priori concepts and as such unknowable. They are not the "things" but contained in the "things" and as things (phenomena) can be perceived by the senses. These sense-perceptions are worked on by alpha-functions producing alpha-elements which establish the K-link.

Scientific theories which concern themselves with concrete objects and events are abstract and any particular event to which the theory is applicable shows that this event follows the course outlined by the abstract formula of the theory. Psycho-analytical theories concern themselves with "O" but can only be formulated in terms of the K-link, that is, as a relationship of sensuous objects. Therefore psycho-analytical theories consist of a narrative of particular events which contain a pattern applicable to other events of similar configuration. These conditions are satisfied in myths, which have proved their significance for human emotional life. Their truth-value is not due to their antiquity but their antiquity is due to their "truth." The central psycho-analytical theory is the Oedipus myth. Similar to scientific theories it can be used to study new events. This corresponds to the prediction of natural events on the basis of an existing theory. Interpretations of the myth lead to new abstractions which are open to verification by psycho-analytical observation. Originally the Oedipus myth was exclusively interpreted from the sexual point of view, but very early Freud (1905) pointed to the link with the desire for knowledge.

Here is an illustration by a clinical case. The patient is a man who had a schizophrenic breakdown many years ago. He still retains some persecutory ideas and feelings.

He reported an apparently insignificant event. In the course of a conversation with an acquaintance at a sports club he said that he was going to make a cup of tea for himself, to which his friend replied with the suggestion to come over to his house, which was not far from the club, to have tea there. The analysis turned round his reaction to the invitation which frightened him. As an association he told me that he was afraid of being buggered. I pointed out to him that he had been very quick with this explanation of his fear as there was no evidence in the incident to indicate that he expected such an attack. Although it is true that he has homosexual fears, this response appeared to me as a cliche without emotional conviction. He became angry with me and accused me of rejecting his association when he looked for a reason for his anxiety. Then he changed his imagery: he may be eaten up or be devoured. This was more closely related to the structure of the incident. In his first association he said that he was afraid of being penetrated, while in the second suggestion he was the one who penetrated the house by entering it. The fear of penetrating was a fear of which he had frequently complained: he had dreams in which he entered a tunnel or suchlike without being able to extricate himself; at other times he was afraid of marriage which he called "collar and chain." The next day he produced a dream of a similar configuration in which he could not stop a car because the brakes had failed.

When he received the invitation his fear had the character as if something had really happened. The concrete nature of his thinking was familiar to us. So far as I can tell he never had true hallucinations but something very close to it. Objects used to change their appearances and took on a threatening character, i.e., lamp-posts turned into phalluses and nails became instruments of torture and murder. It was a step toward improvement when one day he could say: "Nails are nails again."

The events of this session could be understood in terms of the development of the K-link. The patient was faced with the emotional experience of fear—"O"—which he had to transform into a sensuous experience. He mentioned the fear of being homosexually attacked. Rightly or wrongly I felt that this was a premature explanation, for which I could not see any evidence in his material. This suspicion was confirmed in a later session when he gave more details: he mentioned the wife of his friend and that he arrived in his car before his friend so that he had some time with his hostess alone. This appeared to be nearer an Oedipal anxiety.

I suggested that his first association was a defence (in terms of Bion's Grid, a column 2 category) against coming in contact with the fear of entering the house and being devoured. When he received the invitation he had only a feeling of anxiety. What is the idea of being eaten up? It did not appear to be a thought (alpha-element); it had the character of a beta-element which was only suitable for evacuation. In this way he turned an internal anxiety into an external fear which offered the defence of evasion. In this case he did not evade the invitation, as he often did. In fact he leads the life of a recluse who does not want to leave his house to meet reality.

Kant's thing-in-itself is not so far removed from Plato's concept of an idea. The idea of a chair has no sensuous form; yet it is contained in every chair but only as a particular chair does it become a "phenomenon" and, as such, recognizable by the senses. To apply this to the patient: his fear is felt as something inside him–"O"–but in order to transform it into something that can be formulated it must be applied to a special event. On the other hand this fear arises in many circumstances (in his dreams of entering a tunnel, at this invitation, at a prospect of a marriage, etc.). By observing the pattern of these circumstances–i.e., what they have in common–one can say that "O" is the idea or the thing-in-itself that is contained in these instances and could be formulated as an approximation "being imprisoned in something." According to Bion you come nearer to "O" when among other conditions you are able to exercise patience to allow "O" to evolve. If the analyst succeeds in doing that, then he evolves the K-link which then becomes capable of being dealt with by the thinking apparatus. The patient himself did not evolve the K-link as "O" was not transformed by his alpha-function, which failed to generate alpha-elements (thoughts). Instead he was left with beta-elements which are experienced as an accretion of stimuli in his mind and only capable of being evacuated by projective identification (Thorner, 1955).

What is the driving force behind the desire for knowledge? Freud saw it as an elementary force which he classed among the instincts although it was not an instinct proper. Abraham named the infantile pleasure in sucking as the driving force and linked it up with the alimentary apparatus. Mary Chadwick saw it in the desire for a child; "knowing equals possessing." Melanie Klein also accepted the libidinal source of the desire for knowledge but in her later papers on this subject, in which she laid greater stress on the destructive instincts, she considered the drive for research as a means of mastering anxiety as a reassurance against the fear that the object (the mother's inside) had been damaged.

In Bion's work the impetus for knowledge is the desire to grasp what, in fact, is unknowable–the truth. The ultimate truth exists, whether it is discovered or not; the awareness of its existence is one of the elementary experiences of the mind. Truth is autonomous and part of the Faith of man. The search for truth is as elementary as Freud's concept of the instinct for knowledge. As Bion says, truth is essential for psychic health. Yet there is an awe that separates man from truth. Children look for an answer to their sexual questions but, when they are given a rational biological answer, they are reluctant to accept it; they cling to their own magical and omnipotent mythology. Truth exists whether there is a questioner or not. Truth requires from the thinker modesty to accept something outside his powers. If the thinker takes an omnipotent attitude, truth is no longer what he must accept, but what he has created: truth becomes dependent on the questioner. Bion said that truth does not need a thinker, but the liar is necessary for a false thought, a lie.

Looking at myths as potential psycho-analytical theories we may well ask why there are so many myths, such as the Fall of Man, the Tower of Babel and the Oedipus myth, that seem to say that knowledge is forbidden. God forbids Man to eat from the tree of knowledge of good and evil, in the myth of the Tower of Babel human ambitions to reach the sky are thwarted, and in the Oedipus myth Tiresius warns Oedipus against the pursuit of his quest. What does this mean? Why is man prevented from acquiring knowledge? In a verse on the Fall of Man God says: "Behold, the man has become as one of us, to know good and evil; and now, lest he put forth his hand, and takes also of the tree of life, and eat, and lives for ever."* The objection to man's knowledge is that he is becoming "one of us," the fathers. This leads us back to the Oedipus myth. The sexual desire of the son to be like his father has its intellectual counterpart in the desire to participate in the truth, that is to be like God. This is most powerfully portrayed in the Riddle of the Sphinx. Oedipus's discovery of the solution of the riddle leads to the death of the Sphinx. The Greeks would call the desire for knowledge carried to the extreme hubris—but Socrates said: "I know that I do not know."

Bion (1957) brought the seemingly unrelated curiosity, arrogance and stupidity together as a Triad. The desire for knowledge demanding the possession of everything without concern for the object is greed and arrogance and its self-destructive results lays open the stupidity that is behind the desire for knowledge at all cost. This notion is very close to Freud's remark "that the instinct for knowledge can actually take the place of sadism . . . a sublimated off-shoot of the instinct of mastery. . . ."

The concept of knowledge is not the same as that of truth in Bion's writing. The desire for knowledge is a search for truth, which may be approximated without being reached. Bion describes the mystic as one who claims to have direct access to God. Just as the mystic cannot be contained by the group, so the "messianic idea," which is the ultimate truth, cannot be contained by the mind. The messianic idea brings about what Bion calls the "catastrophic change." As Bion says, "O" cannot be known, as it breaks the bounds of the container. "O" can only be lived. What the alpha-function does by transforming sense perceptions into thoughts (alpha-elements) the interpretations of the analyst do to "O." It particularizes and makes it manageable to be thought by the thinking apparatus. If, on the other hand, the messianic idea is not transformed into thoughts, but becomes a beta-element, then we are no longer faced with "O" but with an idol (Thorner, 1973)—the golden calf.

* The Elohist uses have the grammatical form of plural for God—one of us. Reading this verse gives the impression that the antiquity of this verse reaches to the pre-monotheistic phase of Jewish history.

References

Abraham, K. (1924), The influence of oral erotism on character formation, *Selected Papers*. London: Hogarth PRess, 1948, pp. 393-406.
Bion, W.R. (1957), On arrogance, *Second Thoughts*. Heinemann, London: 1967, pp. 86-92.
— (1962), *Learning from Experience*. Heineman, London: 1967, pp. 53/54.
— (1962a), A theory of thinking, *Second Thoughts*. Heinemann, London: pp. 110-119.
Chadwick, M. (1925), Uber die Wurzel der Wissbegierde, *Int. Zeitsch*. 11, pp. 54-68. (English abstract, *Int. J. Psycho-Anal*. 6, 468/9).
Freud, S. (1900), *The Interpretation of Dreams S.E. 5*, pp. 615.
— (1905), Three essays on the theory of sexuality. S.E. 7, pp. 194.
— (1910), Leonardo da Vinci and a memory of his childhood. S.E. 11, pp. 80.
— (1911), Formulations on the two principles of mental functioning. S.E. 12, pp. 215.
— (1913), The disposition to obsessional neurosis. S.E. 12, pp. 324.
— (1915), The unconscious. S.E. 14, pp. 177.
— (1920), The Psychogenesis of homosexuality in a case of a woman. S.E. 18, pp. 168.
— (1923), The ego and the id. S.E. 19, pp. 23.
Klein, M. (1921), The development of a child. II. Early analysis. I. pp. 25 ff.
— (1923), *The Psycho-Analysis of Children. Writings*, 2, pp. 173/5.
Thorner, H.A. (1955), Three defences against inner persecution. *New Directions in Psycho-Analysis*. ED. M. Klein, P. Heimann, R.E. Money-Kyrle 1955; Maresfield Reprints 1977, pp. 298 ff.
— (1963), Urasche, Grund und Motiv. *Psyche* 16, pp. 670-85.
— (1973), Das Idol. *Psyche*, 27.

Metapsychology After Forty Years

J.O. Wisdom

EDITOR'S NOTE: *Professor Wisdom, a logician and a philosopher, has been a long-time friend of psychoanalysis and has observed with active interest the development of the Kleinian and Object-Relations fields of psychoanalysis in England.*

His contribution is an in-depth critique of Bion's work as presented in his first metapsychological book Learning from Experience *and does* not *go into his subsequent work on* Elements, Transformations, *etc. As such, it constitutes the most exhaustive critique of any one work to date. By choosing this avenue he is according central status to Bion's conceptualizations on metapsychology and, thereby, to Bion as perhaps the greatest contributor to it since Freud. His contribution in some ways parallels the equally exhaustive critique of Matte Blanco's. He carefully sifts out the ore of Bion's early diggings, questions the deficiencies without compromise, and then gets to the achievements they represent for psychoanalytic metapsychology. He believes, first of all, that Bion's formulations are beyond Freud's* and *Klein's but also lift both to firmer status. He especially cites the importance of alpha function as an improvement over primary process; the newness of the concept "no thing" as the prerequisite for thought, the importance of the psychotic model for infantile development in lieu of the neurotic one, the origin of thinking in projective identification into a maternal container, the role of dreaming in preserving the contact barrier between sleep and wakefulness, etc. Wisdom leaves no doubt that the impact Bion has made and is making on psychoanalysis may very well be the most considerable of any person since Freud—and all this from the critique of only one of Bion's books!*

Metapsychology After Forty Years*

J.O. Wisdom

1. Introduction

Freud constantly developed his metapsychology, but his major addition could be assigned to 1923, with the coming of *The Ego and the Id*, or perhaps to 1925, when he radically altered his theory of anxiety. Since then, much less attention has been given to metapsychology. The growth of ego-psychology, and the hands of Freud himself (even when over 70), of Melanie Klein, of Anna Freud, and of Fairbairn, had to do largely with clinical processes. Thus the concept of transitional object (Winnicott, 1951), to mention one of the best known additions, though it has metapsychological overtones, is clinical. A certain number of metapsychological concepts have indeed made their appearance: phantasy created by the death-instinct (this Kleinian idea is clearest in Isaacs, 1952); primary love (Balint, 1937); neutralised aggression (Hartmann, Kris & Loewenstein, 1949); conflict-free sphere (Hartmann, 1939); body-scheme (Scott, 1952); tripartite division of the ego (Fairbairn, 1944); centralised role of object-relations (Balint, 1935; Fairbairn, 1941). All would have in common the role of throwing light on the neuroses. It is true that some are intended to cover the psychoses as well, but only on the basis of a different fixation-point without taking into account any specific difference in clinical manifestations. None started from a purely psychotic phenomenon.

A new departure has been made by Bion (1962) precisely because of tackling a problem arising out of a phenomenon peculiar to schizophrenia.

Bion's problem, I think, concerns thought disorders in schizophrenia. Why does the problem arise? Because he listens to schizophrenics on the couch ostensibly producing thoughts, but he cannot understand these thoughts as communications about the world at large and he cannot understand these thoughts in terms of the theories that he has learnt. So he is driven to try to look for some new way of understanding these thoughts. One sees at once therefore that he is concerned with twin problems: one is schizophrenia and the other is thought disorder. Naturally the second one leads to the question: what produces thought disorder and also what is it that produces the thought process to be disordered? That, in effect, is how

*A large part of this paper consists essentially of one entitled "Dr. Bion's Theories of Function and Thinking," given to the Imago Group (London), 14 April, 1964, and (with slight alterations) to the British Psycho-Analytical Society, 7 October, 1964. In opening the discussion to that Society on the (pre-circulated) paper, I dwelt solely on certain metapsychological problems. That metapsychological discussion, rewritten from a tape-recording (together with some introductory remarks), forms the rest of the present paper. Long as this paper is, it is confined to Dr. Bion's *Learning from Experience* published some 15 years ago, and does not take account of his numerous subsequent contributions.

I see his problem arising, and what has given rise to his quite elaborate metapsychology.

It is worth emphasizing that this metapsychology of Bion's is not a clinically based theory but a clinically stimulated theory—no theories are based on observations, but only stimulated or provoked by them, and this is not a theory that he has erected upon observations of schizophrenics but one that he has invented as a result of ruminating about the schizophrenic problems.

Bion's programme might, I think, be epitomized as "Back to Dreams," because one of his most interesting and fruitful and central ideas is the idea that a schizophrenic, at any rate in some phases, is neither asleep nor awake because the schizophrenic cannot dream. Now this gives perhaps a pointer that dreams may in the end be something that will require to be looked at once again. Freud said that dreams were the royal road to the unconscious, and I think that Bion's work may be saying this again in a new way. It is not of course that analysts have downgraded the importance of dreams; but as a key to research or further development of theory, dreams have not figured in recent times as they used to do.

It is essential to relate the metapsychology in Bion's work to the classical or post-classical ideas of metapsychology, principally those of Freud and Melanie Klein, since his view is most closely related to theirs. Before entering upon this undertaking, however, we shall need a detailed statement of his ideas as they appear in his book *Learning from Experience* (1962).*

*This is no ordinary book written, if he does not mind my saying so, by no ordinary man. The present work (like the previous one on Groups) is likely to become a classic, but because of the difficulty of its ideas it is unlikely to be widely read, so before discussing the wider aims and implications of the work I shall attempt in this paper to give a careful statement of its contents.

A word may be said about the nature of the actual writing because it is common knowledge that Dr. Bion's writings are difficult. What can be promised to the reader is that if he wishes to make the effort there is something quite specific in Dr. Bion for him to grapple with; the reader need have no fear that having made a considerable intellectual effort he will find in the end that there is nothing there. There are many common defects that his book does not suffer from, that is, vagueness, verbosity, pomposity, pretentiousness, long-windedenss, and lack of content. His own writing is short, terse, and whether his views are right or wrong , pregnant with meaning; perhaps most important of all, it is largely understandable. But its understandability is that of a difficult work expressed (for the most part) with clarity and precision which require intellectual effort to take them in. When a schoolboy is faced with learning geometry he has to make considerable intellectual effort; though if he does so the thing is inherently extremely simple. Naturally Bion does not reach this level of clarity (and there are some obscurities) but he goes some way toward it. There is, I think, one defect—one of degree—in that the treatments of the various themes do not stand out sharply from one another: it is not always clear when one has left one theme and entered upon another; threads have to be picked up at various places; and one sign of this difficulty is that, on seeking to check a point in this small book, it is often hard to locate the place. Against this criticism should be set the opposite: that, despite some degree of this defect, the writing has an extraordinary degree of clarity—and last but not least the author was up against an inordinately difficult task. What I am saying in crude metaphorical terms is that he succeeded about eighty percent.

The book consists of twenty-eight chapters, most of which are only three or four pages long. The new metapsychological theory is set out in Chapters 1 to 12, 18, and part of Chapter 26, the basis of thinking and learning occupies Chapters 11, 12, 19, 20, and 22; Chapter 26 is the most overtly devoted to the application to clinical phenomena (many readers may find the application a little hard to discern). Lastly Chapters 13 to 17 and 27 and 28 are devoted to a notation and how it may be applied. It should be added that this division of the book does not correspond to the summary of contents given at the beginning; perhaps the author has given an obscure description of his

2. Contents

Bion is concerned with three main themes: (i) the development of a new metapsychology (for the present I am adhering to this expression because of its widespread use); (ii) the application of this new metapsychology to the problem of thinking and learning, that is to say to offer a theory of what thinking and learning consist of or how they can originate; and (iii) the application of this metapsychology to the phenomena of the consulting room. It may be added that there is a connecting link between (ii) and (iii); for the stimulus for the work obviously lay in the thought disorders of schizophrenics, hence the phenomena of the consulting room and failure to think and learn arose in the same context. Derivatively it could be said that Bion aimed at increasing our knowledge of the mind (and therefore of neurotics) by exploring psychosis. The author could of course quite well have developed his metapsychology independently of these practical problems in a purely thoeretical setting. But it is a common procedure, and indeed an excellent one, for an author putting forward a new theory to develop it in the medium of one of its applications.*

3. Bion's Metapsychology

There are two main parts: (i) one is the function of consciousness and (ii) the other is the dynamical theory; in addition there is (iii) the relation of these to one another.

(i) Bion adopts Freud's later view that consciousness is a sense-organ for the perception of psychical qualities. Bion rejects the idea that consciousness has the function of comprehension. He says that this leads to contradictions, but I have not been able to find out what these are.

Bion's metapsychological theory may be described in the following way.

(ii) There exists an alpha-function—a first cousin to the classical pri-

own book or I have misunderstood him, but I think the explanation is that themes reappear in different chapters unsegregated and that the boundaries of chapters were not always well chosen. One short chapter in particular is peculiar in this connection. Chapter 21, consisting of two pages, is said to concern the Kleinian theory of depressive and paranoid-schizoid positions. I have not found that the chapter has anything to do with these, and indeed I wondered whether this was a misprint [I understand from Dr. Bion that something of this kind happened], whether the reference should be to some other chapter, such as Chapter 10 which might merit such a description. So despite my early remarks to do with clarity and simplicity there are certain features of the book that are puzzling.

I have made a deliberate attempt to criticise this work. In non-academic circles criticism is often confused with antagonism. Antagonism, however, means finding mistakes *without* understanding, while criticism means finding mistakes *with* understanding, so that it can be a constructive enterprise. There are few works that are worthy of criticism.

*In addition there is, so to speak, a postscript consisting of an attempt to devise a terminology for recording and handling all these ideas, though primarily the material of the consulting room. I doubt if Dr. Bion would accept my classing the parts on terminology as a postscript, as he probably intends them to be an application of his theory in a rather special form, enabling analysts to learn more things more easily.

mary process—which operates on sense-impressions and on emotions (pp. 6, 8). Alpha-function may be successful or unsuccessful. When it is successful it produces alpha-elements out of the sense-impressions or emotions; alpha-elements may be stored for further use, for example in constructing dreams. When alpha-function is unsuccessful the "raw" sense-impressions or emotions are unchanged and no alpha-elements are produced. In their unchanged state they are called beta-elements; these elements are not amenable to storage or for use in dream thoughts. They can however be projected. Beta-elements may nonetheless be stored in a different sense, that is they can form lumber of which their owner is unaware. One consequence of these hypotheses is that if an emotional experience cannot be transformed into alpha-elements there is no material with which the person can dream. He cannot transform raw material into manifest content.

The most immediate consequence is that failure of alpha-function, in leading to failure to dream, ipso facto means that a person cannot sleep; this is because the function of a dream is to preserve sleep, and therefore if there is no dream there is no sleep. This incisive conclusion might need to be changed, in view of later research on sleep without dreams.

On the other hand objects of consciousness are not raw sense-impressions but derivatives of the operation of alpha-function upon them. Hence if alpha-function is totally unsuccessful there is no object of consciousness. In this case a person cannot be conscious and therefore cannot be awake. In the extreme position, therefore, a person who has no successful alpha-function and therefore no alpha-elements can neither sleep nor be awake.

Obviously this is an extreme position that could never be reached, but it could hold in great degree, and Bion remarks that clinically psychotic patients sometimes present themselves as if they were precisely in this state.*

(iii) The question now arises how we combine the two ingredients of the theory. In order that alpha-elements can operate there must be consciousness of one or other of the two fields—impressions or emotions. It is for this reason that Bion requires the theory of consciousness, namely that it is a sort of sense-organ for apprehending psychical qualities.**

*Dr. H. Stewart, in discussion, pointed out that Bion's theory could be tested by recording the EEG's of schizophrenics, to see whether they lacked the rhythms associated with dreaming.

**There would appear to be a minor inconsistency here; one part of the theory asserts that there can be no object of consciousness until alpha-function has operated upon raw material; the other asserts that consciousness must be focussed on raw material; and these two contentions cannot easily be combined. But it should not be too difficult to repair this defect. I presume we should require two layers of consciousness, one very primitive, analogous to a sort of sense-organ, and the other analogous to perception of objects. I think Bion has a perceptual model in mind in which there is a dichotomy between consciousness of sense-impressions and consciousness of physical objects, as, for example, consciousness of an appearance of a brown patch of colour and consciousness of a thing that possesses such an appearance. It is important to bring out the assumption embedded here because it is not a priori, and not the only one possible. There are some who hold that unintegrated sense-impressions are a myth; at any rate it is an important issue to come to grips with, whether all perception is perception of some object from which we can detach or abstract an impression or whether there are such things as sensory-impressions prior to the perception of objects.

4. Consequences of the Theory

(i) One consequence, Bion claims, is that if there is a destructive attack on alpha-function, this can destroy conscious contact between the person and himself or between him and others; as a result animate objects cease to be represented or are treated as inanimate (p. 9). His explanation is interesting. According to Bion, an infant's love is inseparable from envy (one reason he gives for this is because the love arouses envy and jealousy in an excluded third party). Next he makes the point that an infant receives both milk and love from the breast; because the love arouses envy the infant strives to do without the breast. But avoiding envy runs the infant into fear of starvation, which ultimately drives him to further feeding. In order to avoid the positive feedback that increases this envy unendurably, a split occurs between material and psychical satisfactions offered by the breast, that is to say, the love is denied and what is accepted from the breast is material comfort. Further, material comfort is thus obtained without having to acknowledge its source (this type of splitting has nothing to do with the type that the depressive position has to meet).

However, the craving for love remains unsatisfied and constitutes the dynamism for continual greed for material comfort. In this state, Bion remarks, the infant is at once insatiable and implacable in its pursuit of satiation. In other words, when feeling a lack the infant attempts to make good the deficiency by searching for something lost and ends up in extreme dependence on material comfort. "Quantity must be the governing consideration, not quality" (p. 11).

At this point Bion links the process with the incorporation of beta-elements. (It is not clear why food is a beta-element. When the love component of the food has been eliminated, it does not follow that the material quality of the food is not appreciated as such, that is, it would not be just a sense-impression but would be a material object. The fact that it continues to disappoint and is not the object sought does not alter the fact that it is an object and not merely a beta-element. Let us, however, tentatively grant the slight jump involved.) Bion illustrates the position by means of a patient who renders all the interpretations given to him inanimate, as so much hot air. Thus Bion gives a theory of comforts which would apply to life generally but which he applies particularly to those in the consulting room, their function being to escape the conseqences of envy. When this attitude is dominant the personality can have relationships only with those aspects of itself that resemble an automaton.

(ii) There is another interesting consequence of the hypothesis that without alpha-function a person can be neither asleep nor awake if he cannot dream. In order to conduct everyday affairs, which involve being awake, it is necessary to be asleep to other elements in the personality. A consequence of this is that a person must be simultaneously having a dream to represent these elements; in short, without dreaming with one part of his personality a person could not conduct rational discourse with someone with another part of his personality (p. 15).

(iii) This leads to a further development of Bion's theory. It follows from what has just been said that a dream forms a barrier between two parts of the personality, namely formation by alpha-function and the use of what is formed. Without the barrier, either part might swamp the other. It is worth drawing attention to a comparison between this theory and the classical one. In the classical theory, a dream defends itself against attempts to penetrate it, that is, penetrate its latent contents, and the present theory offers an explanation of this. The present theory has the counterparts of censorship and resistance, and these counterparts provide an explanation of the split separating conscious and unconscious. *The dream virtually preserves the personality from entering into a psychotic state*. Hence Bion remarks on the tenacity with which the dream protects itself against being penetrated. (His comment here is not wholly different from Freud's; after all, Freud's reason why the dream would not yield up its secrets was the shock of the concealed wishes that the dream contained. Bion adds, however, that these involve psychotic states, which is a good deal stronger: *the function of the dream is to preserve sanity* (p. 16), and the psychotic fears loss of the capacity to dream at all.)

(iv) Bion now considers another aspect of the barrier which he calls a contact-barrier. It not only helps in keeping things apart but also helps to bring them together or to communicate. To be explicit, the alpha-elements formed by the activity of alpha-function constitute in particular a dream and in general a contact-barrier.

There is, however, a clinical phenomenon which is at variance with the idea of a contact-barrier. With severely disordered schizophrenic patients Bion found that the usual interpretations were ineffective, and then at last he hit on the idea that the torrent of dissociated ideas displayed a defective alpha-function, so the patient could not use his consciousness, nor when this consciousness was projected into the analyst could the analyst use it either. However there was no resistance to the passage of elements from one zone to the other, so he conjectured that, instead of a contact-barrier, what he saw was a beta-barrier, which presumably is a cluster of beta-elements passing freely from the patient to the analyst but clustering fairly densely between the two, thus forming a beta-screen. This suggested specific interpretations: the purpose of the beta-screen is to evoke the kind of response from the analyst that the patient desires.

According to classical theory there is a process whose function is to unburden the psyche of accretions of stimuli (p. 24). Bion is able to give a new interpretation of this. He notes that schizophrenic remarks resemble this process more closely than they do speech.* The classical idea was non-

*When Bion speaks of a screen of beta-elements being manifested clinically by an outpouring of words, lacking objective reference, content, or thesis, he may be on the track of an explanation of a certain kind of writing, which is common enough in the theoretical field generally and even in psycho-analysis and which is characteristically verbose, tortuous, and vacuous.

object-relational; Bion's interpetation is, so to speak, semi-object-relational, in that this process is to control the analyst and to make him a repository for these accretions, to that extent making him a personal object but no more than that. He is not regarded as a person in his own right.

(v) Bion considers that the replacement of a contact-barrier by a beta-screen is equivalent to a regression from the depression position to the paranoid-schizoid position. Such a regression amounts to a reversal of the direction of alpha-function with destruction of the contact-barrier. The ingredients of the contact-barrier, instead of being alpha-elements, are divested of nearly all their characteristics and are rendered into beta-elements. This, however, is not an exact transformation into beta-elements because the reversal from alpha-elements back into beta-elements carries with it traces of ego and super-ego activity. Bizarre objects are the nearest to being a realisation of the concept of beta-element. Bion considers further that the beta-element, which consists only of sense-impressions, is nonetheless viewed as if the sense-impressions were part of the personality on the one hand and formed a thing-in-itself on the other.

5. Thinking and Learning

Bion now makes a further application of his theory of functions to the theory of thought processes (p. 28).

(i) He starts from Freud's idea that thought fills the gap between tension and its discharge when there is a delay, that is, thought is an experimental way of acting. Now Freud's idea clearly involves intolerance of frustration, hence tension, hence its relief through thought, which thus delays the unburdening of the psyche of the accretions of stimuli. Bion remarks from clinical evidence that no distinction can be made by the infant between the material and the psychological, but he holds that this is not so important as the decision by the infant whether to evade frustration or to modify it. If evaded, the attempt is made to unburden the psyche of the accretions of stimuli, which Bion links with projective identification. This does not involve unrealistic phantasy alone, because there are actions that are more or less a counterpart of this phantasy, i.e., realistic ones. Hence Bion revises the theory of the reality-principle to operate contemporaneously with the pleasure-principle rather than to follow upon it. The fact that one can realise the phantasy in reality implies some degree of contact with reality. Bion says, "The patient's ability to gear his omnipotent phantasy of projective identification to reality is directly related to his capacity for tolerance of frustration. If he cannot tolerate frustration the omnipotent phantasy of projective identification has proportionately less factual counterpart in external reality" (p. 32). What I think Bion is leading up to here is that, since thinking involves toleration of frustration, if projective identification dominates, it prevents thinking from arising. We come back to this later.

(ii) Bion holds that projective identification cannot occur without introjection, the one to evacuate bad, the other to accumulate good objects; he therefore takes up this subject.

Using once more the fact that the infant ingests both love and food at the breast, and noting that the stomach is a repository of the milk, he asks what is the repository for the love. Since this has no obvious answer, he appears to give a hypothetical answer that the breast is not a physical breast purely but a psychosomatic breast, and that the infant possesses a psychosomatic alimentary canal. Now a mother can discern a state of mind in an infant before the infant can become conscious of it, e.g., needing food. In such a situation the need for the breast is a feeling, not just a physiological contraction.

At this point Bion makes a categorical statement of profound significance, which presumably is intended to be an explicit hypothesis or interpretation. He says that *the feeling of "need for the breast" is itself a "bad breast*," and he goes on to add that the infant does not feel it wants a good breast but does feel it wants to evacuate a bad one (p. 34). (This is a fundamental and important conjecture and it is to be regretted that, along with one or two isolated examples, Bion states an important new theory as if it were a fact.) From this he develops the following consequence. In the hunger-situation, taking in food may be indistinguishable from evacuating a bad breast. He then says that sooner or later the wanted breast is felt as an idea of a (good) breast missing and not as a bad breast present, and he makes some attempt to explain how this fundamental transition occurs. He says, "Is a 'thought' the same as the absence of a thing? If there is no 'thing,' is 'no thing' a thought and is it by virtue of the fact that there is [exists] 'no thing' that one recognises that 'it' must be thought?" (p. 35). (This may strike the reader as somewhat tricky, but it is perfectly expressed, though to understand it one has to watch the inverted commas carefully.) Perhaps it would be easier if we express the process thus: felt hunger = present bad breast → (by reality testing and having a mother capable of receiving a projection of the bad breast) a breast is not actually present → {breast absent = 'bad breast present' is a thought}. (I would query whether Bion's bold reconstruction, in resting on discriminating a feeling from external reality, does not presuppose the existence of a thought rather than reveal the process of a thought coming into existence, and at the same time presuppose awareness of the existence of external reality.)

Bion develops this line of enquiry further with the case of an infant fed but feeling unloved. Here the infant is aware of a need for the good breast, but again he equates need-for-a-good-breast to a bad-breast-that-needs-to-be-evacuated. Now of the experiences of the good and bad breast, the material component of milk-satiation or deprivation can be an immediate sense-impression and therefore enables us to assign chronological priority to beta-elements over alpha-elements. Intolerance of frustration, if very strong, might be dealt with by immediate evacuation of beta-elements, thus short-circuiting the formation of alpha-function. What I think Bion is suggesting is that if the beta-elements can be successfully evacuated into a suitable receptacle (which he goes on to discuss), this fact might serve (if I render him correctly) to bring about the discrimination between the phantasy of a bad breast and the reality of there being no breast present. However this may be, in some way or other an *absent breast must become recognised as an idea.* In other words, absence of a thing has to be transformed into a thought.

(iii) Bion now returns to his question about the receptacle for the love-component of the food given to an infant: he suggests the hypothesis (p. 36) that the love absorbed by the infant is expressed by a mother's reverie. We may then conjecture what sort of receptor-organ is required for the infant to profit from reverie.

By raising the question of the factors underlying the mother's capacity for reverie, Bion is able to expand his answer on the preceding topic. For he suggests that projective identification* of a need for a breast felt as a bad breast, which would allow the idea of an absent breast to emerge, becomes possible subject to a certain condition: namely provided the mother's reverie is capable of accommodating the projective identification; and that a mother's reverie may do so he puts forward as a hypothesis. (The objection arises that Bion is explaining the discrimination between phantasy and reality by hypotheses that presuppose a channel of communication between them and therefore presuppose that phantasy and reality are already discriminated; although his idea is an attractive one, the way it is developed looks fallacious, because without the prior existence of a method of communication, the projective identification could not find a home.)

This concludes Bion's answer to the question how a need of a breast felt as a bad breast is replaced by the thought of an absent breast. We have now to connect all this with the theme of thinking.

(iv) An infant capable of tolerating frustration can permit itself to have a sense of reality, according to Bion, and presumably, therefore, to be capable of thought. If not, omnipotence mechanisms come into operation, notably projective identification. If the mother is able to accept the projective identifications, the frustration can be borne more easily. If she is unable to indulge in reverie, or if the reverie does occur but is not associated with the child or its father, Bion assumes that this would be communicated, however incomprehensibly, to the infant; and thus a further burden is thrown on the child's capacity to tolerate frustration, and presumably, therefore, on its capacity for thought. Hence inability to tolerate frustration, and therefore the inevitability of projective identification, would short-circuit thinking. Yet projective identification, according to Bion, is an early form of the capacity for thinking (p. 37). What I take him to mean is that, although projective identification in certain conditions undermines thinking, at a more primitive level it promotes a rudimentary form of thinking, because it leads

*In some of the places where Bion speaks of "projective identification," he should presumably have spoken of projection, e.g., when what is projected is an orbital or when projection takes place before alpha-function has found an integrated emotion.

to the discrimination between an absent breast and a bad breast present, i.e., between phantasy and reality.

In short, Bion explains thinking as the result of tolerating a need for a breast felt to be absent, and this as the result of tolerating a need-for-breast, *not felt* as a bad breast and evacuated; so that the need becomes recognised as referring, not to a bad-breast-felt-to-be-present, but to the absence-of-a-breast, and hence to a thought.

Further, Bion has the idea of a "pre-conception," which is not yet a conception. It probably belongs to the present context, but this is uncertain, so it will be more convenient to discuss it later on.*

6. Further Elucidations

In the course of expounding the theory, I put some queries or rudimentary criticisms in brackets to register a difficulty without side-tracking the reader's attention too much. I shall now deal with the main ones together with one or two minor weaknesses not yet mentioned.

(i) Bion has taken some trouble with logic and methodology, and I want to make the point that his procedure of inventing an undefined concept, such as alpha-function, whose attributes emerge from the use to which he puts it, so far from being unscientific, is a well-recognised device of basic importance in the higher reaches of science. Do you find a definition of gravitational force at the beginning of a work on celestial mechanics? Do you

**Notation and Presentation*. Many chapters are devoted to the question of a notation for recording sessions and for facilitating our thinking about them and about psycho-analytic theory. In contrast to the chapters devoted to the new theories, I found these rather incomprehensible in the sense that they seemed to have no focus. One can appreciate the need for recording in a simple way, and methodologically for distinguishing between "levels" such as what a patient says and conjectures about his underlying motives. This in fact is highly important and commonly overlooked. But it can be met by means of existing tools—all that is lacking is the will and skill to use them. But clear thinking is not as a rule produced by notation; a good notation is produced by clear thinking. As things are at present, it would be simple enough to record, say, manifest themes, preconscious attitudes, preconconscious manifestation of transference, conjectured unconscious object-situation, conjectured unconscious anxiety, conjectured unconscious defence-mechanism. A mathematical notation is almost wholly useless for such purposes. Some people prefer words written in full, others prefer Unc. for unconscious or for beta-element, but this is a matter of personal preference. A symbol is not clear if the idea it represents is not clear. The sole justification for symbols in mathematics is that they make *mathematical inferences* easier to carry out, i.e., make theorems easier to arrive at. There is no sign that Bion hopes to find theorems in this way. If this had been his aim I would have sympathised but thought it premature. It should also be recognised that a mere mathematical looking description has a grave disadvantage: it makes people think they have accurate knowledge when they have not, and it gives a deceptive impression of being scientific. Take Gödel's theorem in modern logic, one of the most difficult and important ever discovered. A vast symbolism is used in the proof. Yet recently a beautiful treatment was given of it without technical terms and yet with high precision—it was not popular in the sense of being loose.

I appreciate (what I think is) the point in Bion's excursion into mathematical-type symbolism. He is concerned not only with the most rudimentary process of thinking, occurring say at three days old, but with developments from this to abstract thinking, and he rightly holds that theoretical science, notation, and so on are extensions of this, so he wanted (I think) to use his new theory of thinking to promote new thinking. I do not think he has succeeded. And I think it is a pity he tried, because the attempt seems to me to spoil the presentation of his masterly new theories. [I understand Dr. Bion has had second thoughts about his excursion into notation.]

find it anywhere in the work? It is of course vaguely related to the force you are familiar with when you pull a door open—but not closely related. When Maxwell introduced his concept of "displacement force" into his electromagnetic equations (electromagnetics is virtually synonymous with these equations), did he define it? It stands for something like a backfire. But his very name for it is an admission that, like Bion, he had little that was specific to say about it. In quantum mechanics, is the fundamental concept of a wave defined? What is given is a mathematical expression that in simplified cases describes a wave in water. Freud, equally legitimately, did the same sort of thing when he introduced the concept of libido. Such concepts cannot be objected to on methodological grounds, but only on scientific grounds, namely if the theory they are part of fails to do what it was intended to do, namely explain something, or if it turns out to be untestable.

Whether one thinks metapsychology a good thing or a bad thing, for what it is worth Bion has made the only large-scale addition to it since Freud. Bion's addition—whether right or wrong—is more powerful in its scope for it purports to explain the basic processes of mental functioning.*

(ii) What does alpha-function operate upon? The raw material, before being integrated into an object by alpha-function, consists according to Bion of sense-impressions and emotions. It is not necessary to identify sense-impressions with what philosophers have called "sense-data," about which there is a fair degree of consensus that they do not exist. But if there are impressions of some sort before the operation of alpha-function they would consist of vague assortments of colours (having none of the spatial definiteness attributed to sense-data); I will call this experience a "perceptual kaleidoscope." Such a kaleidoscope ceases to exist once operated upon by alpha-function, for it is transmuted into the perceptual appearances of spatial objects. What, then, corresponds to this in the emotional sphere? An emotion is a formed entity with a structure and manifestations. A perceptual appearance is not. Yet Bion treats them as parallels. What he needs is a *manifestation* of an emotion as a parallel to a perceptual appearance regarded as a manifestation of an object. These are presumably sensory pleasures and pains: what Ryle has aptly called "pangs" (belonging to an emotion), referring, for instance (as a manifestation of anger), to a peculiar, specific indescribable feeling, of which an inept description might be a churning burning feeling (possibly located in the stomach). To complete this account I would add the idea of an "emotional kaleidoscope," which when operated upon by alpha-function becomes emotions plus their manifestations.

Alpha-function, then, is brought to bear on the perceptual kaleidoscope, to create perceptual objects and perceptual appearances, and to bear

*While on methodological matters, I do not wish to imply that Bion's methodology is wholly above reproach. There is one serious error, which has not, as it happens, led to any ill consequences. He speaks on a few occasions of "deducing" results from observations. Nothing can be deduced or inferred from observations. Conjectures can be made and that is all. The point is crucial to scientific thinking.

on the emotional kaleidoscope to create structures consisting of emotions and their sensory manifestations, i.e., the emotional kaleidoscope becomes transmuted into pangs forming the frontage of emotions.

Thus in each domain, perception and emotion, there are three entities: the perceptual kaleidoscope, then (after integration) a view (as Woodger puts it) of a spatial object (and a view of a spatial *object*): and, corresponding to kaleidoscope, view, and object, we have sensory pleasures and pains, *pang* of an emotion, and pang of an *emotion*, or sensation, pang, and emotion. Once alpha-function has failed to operate, the kaleidoscope and sensory pleasures and pains cannot be experienced (though an attempt may be made to approximate to them by artificial devices): they are what Bion calls, after Kant, things-in-themselves.

Bion does not develop this subject; I have done so because it, or some such development, seems to be needed to understand this thoery adequately, but more especially in order to grasp the nature of beta-elements.

(iii) The meaning of "beta-element" is innocent enough—the intake of experience when alpha-function has failed to operate. Now Bion illustrates an alpha-element by a dream image, but he does not actually illustrate a beta-element. This is because it is a thing-in-itself, which cannot be perceived or described, since only the results of operating with alpha-function can be communicated. But in terms of the preceding subsection (if it renders Bion reasonably well) we can say that "beta-element" denotes elements of the sensory kaleidoscope or are sensory pleasures or pains.

Bion's thesis is that, if these are unworked-over by alpha-function, there is nothing that can be done with them except evacuate them by one or other means of projection; projection is the only psychical process available for doing anything with them at all.

There would be no difficulty about this, were it not that Bion regards material milk (i.e., milk from which the love-component has been removed) as a beta-element (p. 11). This seems to me to be plainly wrong. For it is true of reality that there is such a substance as material milk made of protein, carbohydrate, fat, water, etc., but containing no psychical component.

The split in all our personalities that enables us to recognise this is an indispensable asset: it enables us to recognise a purely material substance, which is nonetheless integrated—or worked over by alpha-function.

It is not easy to amend this part of the theory, but an attempt may be made.

It is not certain that Bion really meant to equate material comforts with beta-elements—the reference could be an uncorrected typological mistake or a looseness in the writing. For he also equates material milk or comforts with "bizarre" objects (also on p. 11); indeed he says, "Clinically the bizarre object which is suffused with superego characteristics comes nearest to providing a realization to correspond with the concept of beta-elements" (p. 26). Bizarre objects are evacuated beta-elements that are reintrojected and endowed with superego characteristics. Evidently, although pure beta-elements can be subjected only to projection, re-introjected beta-elements can be subjected to a process that endows them with superego characteristics, and this process would seem to be some factor in alpha-function, on Bion's account of this function. Yet this conclusion, though not necessarily wrong, is against the spirit of his theory.

Possibly his account of bizarre objects was not sufficiently considered. Why, incidentally, did he not give them a more or less meaningless name, such as "beta-superegoised"? It would have been useful to reserve the name "bizarre" objects for clinical realisations of beta-superegoised-elements. An alternative idea suggests itself, using one of Bion's own ideas, involving not beta-elements with a minute quantity added but alpha-elements with an enormous amount subtracted: if there is some failure of alpha-function, alpha-elements would become distorted, or poor in properties. Such a concept, of what might be called "betafied-alpha" element, would also be realised in clinically bizarre objects, and would be more in the spirit of the theory.

Can such a concept be connected with material comfort? We might construct steps in a hypothetical process as follows: alpha-element (e.g., psychosomatic milk with love and material components), then interference by envy → material milk = unified object (not a split off component) when affective component is *not* specially wanted, but = betafied-alpha-element when affection *is* wanted.

In this way, it might be possible to account for recognition of the reality of milk as a material substance and its being apparently treated as a bizarre object.

7. Deficiencies

So far, the main aim has been to elucidate ideas rather than to discuss the import of Bion's theories or whether they are true or false.

(*a*) The whole theory is one of alpha-functioning and its disturbances. Bion gives no clue whatever to what produces dysfunction and how it happens,* but possibly he connects it with intolerance of frustration. Presumably he could tack on any of the existing theories, e.g., a clash between the two, sexuality and aggression, or what I have elsewhere called "nuclear strain" between positive and negative attitudes. In this connexion, Bion does not apparently consider whether alpha-function grows, develops, matures, or occurs in varying degrees. Is it fully-fledged at its inception, or could dysfunction be attributed to lack of maturation? His theory does not necessitate such an idea, but is susceptible of being extended in this way. Some further theory of dysfunction, however, is needed.

*Making use of the mother-child relationship, the projection of beta-elements by the infant on Bion's account would diminish if the mother were able to accept the projections, but this would not explain why the beta-elements arose in the first place, i.e., why alpha-function failed.

(*b*) I have mentioned already that, in giving an account of the origin of thinking and also of communication, Bion does not seem to me to have quite hit it off, although he was working in the right direction, because his account *presupposes* thinking and communication. I shall return to this later.

(*c*) I have failed to understand how Bion's theory of the "no breast" origin of thoughts presupposes his theory of functions. It would seem that his theory—or one that I would substitute—could be held independently. Yet the book was intended to reach a theory of thinking based upon the metapsychology of functions.

8. Achievements

Bion's theory of functions deals with a gap left by existing theory between libido and perceptual objects. Put this way, his theory might seem to be a rather small link, but it is astonishing how much he gets out of so little. And it is a measure of the power of a theory when a small amount of theory is rich in consequences.

Bion's theory leads to a number of results consisting of (in some cases) improved explanations, as compared with classical theory and to some extent Kleinian theory, or of new explanations where the classical and Kleinian theories provided none. Among the newly explained are: (*a*) repression, censorship, and resistance, (*b*) nightmares in the ordinary sense (not restricted to the hysteriform kind discussed by Ernest Jones), (*c*) the intensity of repression by the idea that the underlay is a cauldron better understood as psychotic than neurotic, (*d*) explaining lack of repression in schizophrenia, (*e*) a new explanation of torrents of accretions of stimuli, (*f*) equating a thought with a "no thing," (*g*) thought taken to be the result of tolerating the need to evacuate and the need for projective identification, (*h*) rudimentary thought as projective identification, (*i*) an idea (though perhaps more a question than an answer) about the site of the love-component of milk. To these I think, I would add that the theory contributes to the solution of the problem of the compulsion to repeat; for the attempt to form alpha-elements must go on and on, even though the only gain is to be the recipient of betafied elements, despite their being unwanted and frustrating. These consequences are incidental in that they are not the main aim of the work; they are nonetheless of great significance, because such possibilities always constitute a test of a new theory.

Bion would seem to have aimed mainly at explaining certain clinical phenomena that run counter to existing theories, for without a correct explanation he could not satisfactorily handle patients to whom he attributed these phenomena. The phenomena are: (*a*) regarding interpretations as meaningless/bad/useless yet wanting more and more of them (p. 11); (*b*) using language not to communicate but to convert the analyst into a receptacle for unwanted waste products (pp. 13-14); (*c*) states in which a patient seems properly speaking to be neither asleep nor awake (p. 7); (*d*) states where the patient seemed to deposit his consciousness in the analyst and to be only an unconscious that could not function (pp. 20-21).

9. Relation to Freudian and Kleinian Theory

It is important to specify what theories these clinical assessments conflict with. (*a*) Kleinian theory might seem to imply that good objects are sought and bad objects not sought. Melanie Klein was fully aware that this is not so, but she did not elaborate her theory sufficiently to cover the point. Bion's clinical finding is not in conflict with the spirit of her work, but does with her theory so far as it has been explicitly formulated. (*b*) His clinical finding conflicts with the fundamental assumption that all striving is object-relational. Bion's finding requires that this assumption should be given at least a nuance of modification. (*c*) classical and post-classical dream theory implies that a person is aways either asleep or awake; Bion's findings (quite apart from trance states) requires this to be slightly modified. (*d*) Classical and post-classical theory implies that the unconscious is submerged below consciousness; Bion's finding is that in schizophrenia this is not necessarily so (and in other ways this has long been recognised, in that schizophrenics may display notably phenomena that according to the classical theory ought to be repressed).

Bion is thus not strongly at variance with the classical theory, and he is only very slightly at variance with the Kleinian theory. But he is sufficiently at variance with both to lead him to seek a new theory to deal the various discrepancies, and this theory gives the impression and fulfills the promise of genuine newness. Whether it can be judged to have the hall-mark of a "five-star" theory depends on whether it leads to new consequences (even false ones).

10. Undesigned Consequences

Where do we look for independent results in the sense of unsuspected phenomena following from the theory which may be found if specifically sought? One possible answer might be the discovery of ebb and flow in the psychopathology of a person varying with the type of reverie dominating his partner from time to time. Another might concern groups: cohesions and splinters in groups might be explicable in terms of degree of tolerance of beta-elements, leading to new discriminations of types of group-solidarity founded on mutual support of alpha-function or on (? gangster groups) mutual acceptance of beta-projections with no regard for the partners concerned; by finding the group situation that would betafy, it might be possible to anticipate the onset of a fight-flight situation. By means of EEG investigations, it might be possible to tell when a patient in analysis, connected up to give simultaneous EEG reading, was having a preconscious dream or not while giving his associations. To mention such general possibilities, however, does not amount to much; what is required is to think out in detail how one of these possibilities might go, and then it could be looked for; still, even without this, the theory must be esteemed in that it holds out such possibilities at all.

Having completed the exegesis of Bion's theories in some detail, together with a comparison of his conclusions with those of Freud and Melanie Klein, an estimate of what is novel, and an assessment of significance, I turn now to broad questions of metapsychology in order to consider the basic relations betwen Bion's metapsychology, that of Freud, and that of Melanie Klein, and in this connexion to discuss some fundamental questions. This task can be conveniently tackled within the framework of the question: what is a baby's mind like at the age of nought days, at the first cry? This is a fundamental question for psychoanalysts, but there is no official answer to be found in any paper, even a tentative one. There are such things as perceptual impressions and sensations of pleasure and pain, but no analyst would hold that the mind at the age of nought is like a wax tablet, a Lockean *tabula rasa*, and is only a receptacle of such impressions. There would have to be some sort of structure. What sort of minimum structure is one tempted to postulate? For example, has the mind at the age of nought got an unconscious or not? And how is one to try to answer that? I would guess that, according to Freud, the mind at the age of nought does have an unconscious for the following reason. Freud held that every human being has instincts. Now instincts are biological, and therefore one would presume they do not arise suddenly, but are in the organism from the beginning. The instincts are represented by the libido as a psychical representation, and there is no reason to doubt that the psychical representation is a concomitant of the instincts from the beginning. Hence an important part of the unconscious, as Freud understood it, would be there at the age of nought.

I would say further that, if there is no unconscious at the age of nought, then the child would have no mind when it was asleep.

What other constituents is one likely to want to install into the infant mind? Let us make a list of possible candidates:

instincts,

drives and libido,

primary processes,

phantasy,

internal objects,

an entity described by Freud as the "body ego,"

alpha-function, and factors in alpha-function.

Let us ignore instincts because they are biological and are represented psychically by drives and libido. Drives and libido are simply different facets of one thing. And primary processes are simply modes of their operation. We shall return to this group in a moment. What is the relation between phantasy and internal objects.

Phantasy in the Kleinian sense I understand to be the working of the mind on the internal stage, that is to say it is what the person does with or to his internal objects. We thus seem to discriminate between a phantasy and an internal object; but may not an internal object *be* a phantasy? In reviewing Guntrip's recent work Rycroft has credited Guntrip with making a simplification by reducing both these two conceptions to one (Rycroft's discernment is accepted by Guntrip as his intention). I would say that this is a mistaken policy. Certainly the processes of phantasy might create internal objects first of all, and secondly use them. But these would be two different entities or processes; and, if we were to call them both phantasy, we should have to distinguish them as two kinds of phantasy. So we might as well call the first an object, and preserve the convenient distinction between an internal object and phantasy.

Let us now consider how these might be related to libido. Libido is non-object-relational, and yet it attaches itself in the end, when it gets out of a primary narcissistic phase, to objects, so there is a problem of relating libido to objects. It seems to me possible to regard phantasy as a vehicle that carries libido. In the Kleinian theory, the concept of something libidinal is certainly used but it is not the same as the classical concept of libido because in Freud libido is non-object-relational. As a way of relating the object-relational to the non-object relational, I am suggesting that libido may be regarded as a fluid pulsating through the veins of phantasy. It should, however, be recognised that such a concept of libido would differ in some significant respects from Freud's. Laws of primary processes would then become laws not of libido but of phantasy.

So far we have the possibility of having a combination (without being committed to it) of sensations, libido, phantasies, and internal objects at the age of nought. Nothing has been said about whether the new-born baby has an "I" or an ego, is a "self" or a person. Though phantasy and internal objects suggest some such entity, neither sensation nor libido does. Nonetheless Freud's conception of a "body-ego" suggests at least some rudimentary integration of sensations. At least a rudimentary communication-centre would seem to be required. And, if so, might not a simple one suffice to link sensations and phantasies?

Such would be more or less in accord with the unarticulated picture of the infant's mind provided by psycho-analytic theory as we have it from Freud, Melanie Klein, and Fairbairn. Where, if at all, do alpha-function and alpha-factors fit into it?

Alpha-function has all the look of being a primary process or a general form of all primary processes. To recall what they are, they include the classical ones from the theory of dreams, namely condensation, displacement and symbolisation, perceptualisation ("dramatisation"), and secondary elaboration, to which must be added Silberer's anagogic symbolism, projection, projective identification, introjection, and splitting, and possibly new ones. These are all characterised as feeling processes that operate without a realistic knowledge of physical realities. What is alpha-function? It means integrating sense impressions into sensory objects, and also integrating sensations of other kinds into emotions. Until alpha-function has done its work there are no alpha-elements, and therefore nothing for the mind to operate *with* at all; so it has to be basic. The question now arises whether alpha-function has to operate and create alpha-elements for primary processes to use or whether primary processes have to occur before alpha-function can come into existence. It might look as if alpha-function had to do its work first and make a few objects in the world for the baby, physical objects or emotional objects, before displacement could operate, on the grounds that the baby could not displace its emotions from one object to another until there were emotions and objects. But suppose the baby is confronted with its mother, perhaps full face, and then side face, but has not learnt to integrate these two views into one head. Now if the baby reacts to these two views with the same emotional pang, it might then be in a position to displace its feelings from the one sensory-impression to the other. This might be a process by which the baby becomes able to integrate these two views of the face, or the breast or anything else, into one object. Now if this sort of account could hold, then displacement would be a factor in alpha-function. On the other hand, the account just given might be said really to presuppose the integratedness of e.g., the side face, and of the emotion felt toward it. Further introjection and splitting, for instance, seem to presuppose the integratedness of certain emotions. Hence, it would seem, alpha-function must be prior to primary processes. The answer might, however, be that integration and laws of process arise together; or perhaps the inconclusiveness of our discussion is due to an insufficiently specific problem—the answer might come more readily after other issues have been cleared up.

Let us next consider the relation of alpha-function to internal objects. Here it is plain that even a rudimentary internal object presupposes some integration. Now the use of internal objects by phantasy in its turn presupposes the existence of internal objects. Hence alpha-function would seem to be prior to all the ingredients of the infant's mind, except sensations and pangs.

Since the formation of an internal object by phantasy is one of the most primitive integrations, we might call the primary internal objects "alpha-introjects." And it might be convenient to denote the most primitive use by phantasy of alpha-objects by "kappa-function." Put in these terms, the reader will recognise that Melanie Klein's basic work had to do with kappa-function; and that Bion is concerned with the further question of how alpha-introjects are formed.

It is therefore fitting to turn to this most fundamental question, and ask how the first internal object is produced.

Bion gives an answer in terms of thought-processes. According to him, when there is frustration and hunger, for example, which cannot be stood, projection of discomfort ensues, and the hunger can be borne if the mother can accept the projection by means of her reverie. More specifically, a breast that is actually absent and wanted is felt to be a bad breast present, to be got rid of by projection. There thus (somehow) arises the sense of a "no thing," which is a rudimentary thought. As an account of producing thoughts, this seems to me to suffer from circularity; for the account explaining the existence of a first thought presupposes the existence of a mother of whom there is already a thought as an object. Nor can this account be adapted to explaining the formation of the first internal object, for the process presupposes the discrimination of a receptacle (external) to receive the projection, while the receptacle presupposes an internal object. Bion also leaves the transition from a present bad breast to a breast absent somewhat mysterious. So I think that Bion's attempt, though in the right direction, does not quite come off, but that the difficulties may be met by an alternative account, in the same spirit (which I gave to the Imago Group, 22 January, 1963).

A mind could not be aware of an external object without an apparatus for conceptions. A mind could exist without internal divisions involving internal objects. How could the first internal object or, as I have called it, "orbital introject" be formed? Not by introjection since this presupposes awareness of an external object. But a discomfort such as hunger could be experienced phenomenologically as something being torn away. Thus if you pinch a piece of your flesh and pull, you will get an immediate experience of this kind. My hypothesis is that hunger feels something like this, and I call the feeling a hunger-hole.* Thus the first orbital would be, not a bad breast present but an absence—like the positive sense of "the Nothing" made famous by Sartre.

I would not disagree with Bion that an attempt may be made to get rid of this by projection, and an attempt at muscular eviction might reduce the pang for a time, but after a while the hunger-hole will return or even feel worse. When fed, however, the phenomenological sense would be one of the self being recharged, rather than of the hunger-hole being filled up directly: in other words the effect of feeling recharged would be the sense of the hunger-hole being dissipated from within, i.e., filled by projection from the central core of the self. This experience could simultaneously be associated with attempts at projecting the hunger-hole, and would make it possible for such attempts to feel successful. The sense of passing a hunger-hole out across the boundary** of the self would produce the conception of an object

*This cannot be immediately equated with a "bad breast," for to do so would presuppose the conception of a bad breast before any thought had come into existence.

***Pace* Kant, I think one could phenomenologically have the sense of a boundary without presupposing the conception of something on the other side of it.

outside the self. On this account a primordial thought becomes the sense of "disappearance of a bad hunger-hole through the boundary of the self." It would be an emotional object, projected at the vague perceptual kaleidoscope and thus form a perceptual object. (To begin with, they would naturally be felt to be animated.) It is then a relatively simple matter to build up subsequent developments notably about introjection, but this is not needed here. I think such an account may avoid the basic difficulties in Bion's.

At this point perhaps Bion's idea of a "pre-conception" may be brought in. It means an expectation as yet unmatched by the experience of a real thing corresponding to it. There is no doubt that Bion is on to something significant here, but his account is not very concrete. His idea seems to be a mixture of something primitive or not matured by real experience and of something sophisticated, for he likens a pre-conception to a mathematical variable. Thus a pre-conception seems to be at once thin and abstract. Now the idea of a primordial object, described by the feeling of a hunger-hole, may make Bion's idea specific: for the "hunger-hole," though highly concrete, is a pre-conception in the sense that it owes nothing to a counterpart in the external world; and though concrete, it needs some time to be matched against the real experience of a bad breast, thus becoming modified and therefore enriched by experience. The very first pre-conception would be the experience of a hunger-hole departing through the body-boundary.

I would add further that thought-formation by means of the thinking machinery involved in the transition from "hunger-hole" to thought of an absent breast presupposes a distinction, which is to be found in Bion's more recent book (*Elements of Psycho-Analysis*, 1963, p. 35), between thinking as a process that develops thoughts and thinking that manipulates already existing thoughts.

Harking back to the question of priorities, a hunger-hole would not be a product of integration. Thus the first orbital introject, a bad object, would itself create integration, i.e., would give rise to integration by coming into existence. The sense of becoming recharged and the concomitant vanishing of the hunger-hole would give rise to a further integration. So we answer our question, not by assigning priority to the primary processes over integration but to certain primary operations to do with hunger, projection, and being recharged. Only then would sufficient integration develop to permit the primary processes such as the dream-work to occur.

In my view, then, alpha-function is not present in the mind at birth but is preceded by certain other activities for a few days. We, therefore, have to go back on the plausible idea that alpha-function precedes phantasy, for phantasy comes into being with the first efforts to cope with the first hunger-hole.

We turn now to a different topic—the breakdown of alpha-function, with consequential formation of beta-elements.

In a certain way the idea of beta-element seems to be more important than the idea of alpha-function, the latter being simply something designed to introduce the other. Seeing that beta-element is the result of dysfunction, one could generalize Bion's problem as follows: what are the ways in which mental dysfunction can occur? The question may not be new, but the classical answers have been few. The chief one was that dysfunction is due to repression, and later came others, e.g., splitting. Bion's work suggests asking whether there are not many ways of producing dysfunction, more than we have thought of (and this is one of the reasons why Bion's kind of theorizing is of fundamental importance, for it may show where new phenomena are to be found).

Now Bion himself has depicted a new sort of splitting, typified by a person who is always collecting gadgets, thus resembling the infant who is getting milk but no love. The milk and the love components are separated, and for various reasons that Bion then elaborates the infant has to become more and more greedy and to get more and more milk, which never satisfies, because it always lacks the love component. (This is a form of splitting that produces an approximation to a beta-element in his system; it produces a split between the love component and the material components to make up objects.) Now it struck me that there might be a great many other ways in which splittings might occur, as I will illustrate.

Suppose we invert Bion's process. If the external object has a sensory outside like the mother's face or a chair or what-not, and an emotional inside possessing it, suppose this time the desired object is the emotion while its sensory manifestations are discarded, *i.e.*, a situation where only emotional objects form part of a person's life and sensory objects do not enter, we should have a very bizarre form of schizoid process—in fact such a person would be somebody who treated all their everyday objects from pieces of chalk to microphones as if they were elements in a dream, with purely emotional significance and no physical part to play.

Now this suggests investigating dreams anew for possible dysfunctions. According to Bion there is a contact barrier between the unconscious and the conscious, which consists of dream elements. The schizophrenic person of the kind he especially describes, who is neither asleep nor awake, cannot dream. So external events have an immediate impact upon the unconscious. This raises in my mind the question whether it is something to do with primary dream processes that has gone wrong. The great residual question of dreams that Freud discussed and left unsettled was in connection with the repetition-compulsion where the *dream-work*, as he put it, *fails to operate*. So this idea of dream processes failing to operate is not entirely new. What one might therefore ask is whether there are several parts of dream processes that fail to operate, or whether the dream-work can fail to operate in various ways. Conceivably the sort of schizoid states that arise might depend on which primary processes were failing; therefore it might be worth looking to see what possible primary processes were failing to operate.

A connected question would be this: is the present list of primary processes complete? If there are undiscovered primary processes, this would be highly important both generally and also for schizophrenia. Here is an example which may be a primary process; I would describe it as an exchange principle, illustrated by ball games with no aim of winning or losing, where a ball is hit backwards and forwards from one person to another, *i.e.*, exchanged; this might indicate a primary process of exchanging a feeling or exchanging part of the personality with another person.

The outcome of all this is that dysfunction of alpha-processes might occur in an unexpectedly wide variety of ways, producing approximations to beta-elements or bizarre objects each characteristic of a different form of schizophrenia.

The final problem I wish to consider concerns how integration comes about at all. Bion gives no explanation of dysfunction, nor for that matter of what produces alpha-function. It is totally unplausible that the mind at the age of nought is an integrated whole, which then suffers splitting. More plausible is the idea that pleasurable and unpleasurable experiences are unrelated to one another to begin with. Assuming this, there can be no question of splitting until integration occurs. What would require explanation would be the integration. What is to bring it about at all, especially if it is distressing? Further, when a certain level of integration has taken place, say by four months, to be followed under stress by a split, it seems to have escaped notice that the split-off components have to remain in some sort of remote contact, otherwise therapy could never overcome a split. How is this possible?

For convenience unintegrated experiences and split-off components of the personality may be called "segregates." We are faced with twin problems: how segregates come together; and what sort of tenuous linkage they retain when cut off.

The idea of a split is too harsh conceptually, for it suggests an on-or-off contact or communication. What is wanted is a different model for a silent though real contact—not so much a switch as a foggy medium that permits of a just discernible image but too vague to arouse unrest. Then, if the fog lifts slightly, strain begins to make itself felt—which would thicken the fog sufficiently to relieve the strain. For the fog to lift at all, some attractiveness of the vague image would have to be postulated or else some tendency to dissipate unless specially checked.

Such postulates would serve to deal with abandoned projective identifications. A projected piece of oneself, according to this model, would attract the core of the personality, but the complementary segregate would be obscured by fog. We have here something analogous to the opposite of autoscopy, namely a denial of oneself, which might be called "acutoscotomy." The process is, of course, just as important or more so when it concerns purely intrapsychic factors, as when there is "nuclear strain" between two segregates within the nucleus of the self.

Remote from the patient as this may appear to be, it offers the possibility of interpreting dysfunction in terms of autoscotomising a segregate of the personality because of inability to disperse the fog surrounding it.

Casting a backward glance over the metapsychological problems discussed, we could say that the recent contribution to it by Bion might be characterised as "back to dreams," though not only, as heretofore, to well functioning dreams as the clue to the workings of the personality, but also to the ways in which the dream-work may fail to operate.

References

Balint, M. (1935), Critical notes on the theory of the pregential organisations of the libido, in *Primary Love and Psycho-Analytic Technique*. London: Hogarth Press, 1952.

—— (1937), Early developmental states of the ego. Primary object-love, in *Primary Love and Psycho-Analytic Technique*. London: Hogarth Press, 1952.

—— (1952). *Primary Love and Psycho-Analytic Technique*. London: Hogarth Press.

Bion, W.R. (1962). *Learning from Experience*. London: Heinemann.

—— (1963). *Elements of Psycho-Analysis*. London: Heinemann, 35.

Fairbairn, W.R.D. (1941), A revised psychopathology of the psychoses and neuroses, *Psychoanalytic Studies of the Personality*. London: Routledge and Kegan Paul, 1952, pp. 28-58.

Freud, Sigmund (1923). *The Ego and the Id. S.E.*, Vol. *19*.

—— (1933), Revision of the theory of dreams, *New Introductory Lectures on Psycho-Analysis. S.E. 22, 7-31*.

Hartmann, H. (1937). *Ego Psychology and the Problem of Adaptation*. London: Imago, trans. 1958.

Hartmann, H., Kris, E., & Loewenstein, R.M. (1949), Notes on the theory of aggression, *Psychoanalytic Study of the Child, 3-4 9-36*.

Isaacs, Susan (1952), The nature and function of phantasy, *Developments in Psycho-Analysis*, Ed. Riviere. London: Hogarth Press, 1952, pp. 67-121.

Scott, W.C.M. (1952), Patients who sleep or look at the psychoanalyst during treatment: technical considerations, *Int. J. Psycho-Anal.*, *33*, pp. 465-469.

Winnicott, D.W. (1951), Transitional objects and transitional phenomena, *Collected Papers*. London: Hogarth Press, 1958 pp. 229-242.

CONTRIBUTIONS ON GROUPS

Contributions on Groups

EDITOR'S NOTE: *The contributions in this section deal with the author's understanding of the application of Bion's theory of group process. Bion's conceptions of the dynamics of groups remain novel and even arcane to most psychoanalysts. Many have wondered, for instance, whether Tavistock groups (the current name for the Bion-inspired study groups) are therapeutic in aim or merely heuristic. Doctor Robert Gosling, Chairman of the Professional Committee of the Tavistock Clinic and a leader in the application of the Tavistock group process, has been gracious enough to offer a summary of his views of the relationship of the Tavistock group method to psychoanalytic theory. Let me quote Dr. Gosling:*

It is futile to speculate on what Bion had in mind concerning groups at such and such a time in the past; indeed he himself was often perplexed by what he had written some time before. The best I can do is to describe the influence of Bion's writings on my understanding of the present scene of group work.

In the first place he wrote from the position of an analyst who had deliberately and self-consciously exposed himself to the emotional turmoil of becoming a member of a group. In this way he was different from Freud and others who wrote about group phenomena at a distance. In the second place the stance he tried to adopt toward this emotional experience seems to me to be very similar to the one he tried to maintain when exploring the emotional events taking place between the psycho-analytic pair.

At this point I should point out that unless we are careful this reference to psycho-analysis is likely to cause as much confusion as it is clarification. The kind of psycho-analysis I have in mind is the kind that tries to take into account what both parties to the interchange are up to even though what the analyst says to the analysand is framed chiefly to meet the latter's urgent need for enlightenment. This implies that there are other parts of the interpretation that are not expounded to the analysand, either because they have not yet reached the stage of being adequately formulated or because they appear at the time to be of more moment to the analyst than to the analysand. It is the kind of analysis that searches for clues of understanding as much in the counter-transference as it does in the transference—or almost, the kind that supposes that the sense of "a blank screen" is more common, even if fleetingly so, in the experience of the analysand than it is in that of the analyst, the kind that requires the analyst to pay close attention to the interpretations he is prompted to give during or after a session even if he does not actually get round to giving them. It is the kind in which when an interpretation is given by the analyst that purports to describe what is going on in the analysand's mind a need is at once exposed to search for a further interpretation (even though it may be held in reserve) that would account for how such a strange belief that such a thing is possible can seem at the time to be so convincing, that is to say, that would account for what these two people are doing to each other and the illusions they hold about themselves and each other.

Such an activity as this is obviously concerned with more than the business of symptom removal, promoting adaptive behaviour or medical cure. To the extent that it has anything to do with doctoring at all it is probably closest to the implicit and unspoken hermaneutic aspect of a doctor's work, and to an explicit examination of what Balint has called the "doctor's apostolic function."

The groups that Bion concerned himself with directly were groups of 8 to 10 individuals who met together to try to understand the tensions the individuals composing them were experiencing. Obviously the tensions that were immediately present for examination were those experienced by the particular individuals concerned by virtue of their being drawn together as members of a group devoted to this undertaking. The examination was in the here-and-now; it was existential.

Anyone who has attempted to assist such a group in the role of a consultant will know only too well that what Bion has called "an emotional storm" going on between the psycho-analytic pair becomes a veritable blizzard in a more populous group. The input is profuse and unordered, and at times about all that the consultant is in a position to articulate is a statement that tries to communicate to the other members where he seems to be at in his experience of the events. Indeed to be a member of a group whether as consultant or in some other role seems to be characterised by being a participant in a crossfire of multilateral projective identifications, and it is from that position that he can speak—if indeed he can speak at all.

It is true that Bion did his seminal work on groups in relation to individuals who had got themselves into the role of patient;

first, battle casualties who were in the throes of rehabilitation (rehabilitation to what?); and then to patients seeking relief from neurotic suffering (were any of them cured of an illness by his efforts?). His ideas have certainly had an influence on many group workers in the field of psychotherapy after having been adapted and extended according to experience in this field. But his book "Experiences in Groups" is most certainly not a textbook on group psychotherapy, no more than his later works are textbooks on psycho-analysis.

His ideas have also had a great influence on group workers in the educational field of the kind that in the United States flourished in the university "laboratories" for the exploration of group dynamics and in the activities of the National Training Laboratory. The fact that many of these activities have now expanded into the quasi-religious field of the encounter movement etc., and the humanistic psychology movement and then on to Zen and who knows what, is another matter.

At the Tavistock these ideas became married to another set of ideas that seemed to bring with them great illumination, namely, systems theory, and the resultant progeny are often known as Tavistock Groups (usually sponsored in the United States by the A. K. Rice Institute of Washington, DC). They are educational in aim (i.e., they are not a prescription for ill people) and they afford a useful bridge between psycho-analytic theory and systems theory. This is possible because a radical psycho-analytic object relations theory purports to describe the interrelationship between an endopsychic sub-system of objects and an external sub-system of actual objects (what in ordinary parlance is called a group or an institution). Psycho-analytic theory of a predominately ego psychology kind cannot do this—though it can do many other things.

What relevance has this to psycho-analysts? Exposure to such group work could, in my view, greatly enhance a psycho-analytic training. (We certainly insist that all the trainees in psycho-analytic psychotherapy at the Tavistock Clinic attend them from time to time.) But it would not increase his knowledge of psycho-analysis as such, whether as a body of theory or as a therapeutic technique. What might be expected of it are three things:

1. He might understand better some of the conscious and unconscious forces impinging on the psycho-analytic pair and the extent to which these are contributed to by the members of the pair themselves. This might assist him to make a better evaluation as to whether a one to-one psycho-analytic approach is more appropriate than one that includes a wider inter-active system, such as a marital pair or a family, or not.

2. He might come to know more about the kinds of psychological fields his patients are living in and therefore able to detect more hidden elements in their material; and

3. He might be able to judge better how to contribute understanding derived from the work of the psycho-analytic pair to other social situations with the hope that such understanding will play a useful rather than a futile part. In my view, most psycho-analysts are deplorably ignorant and inept at these things. The trials and tribulations of most psycho-analytic societies are clear examples of it.

In considering whether psycho-analytic institutes should promote such training activities, I am led to ask what such institutes are for: are they for teaching psycho-analysis or for training psycho-analysts? In my view it is principally the former, as to become an effective psycho-analyst in any given social context requires a great deal more to be taken on board than a familiarity with psycho-analytic theory and practice and a great deal more than any one institute can teach, from competence in financial and political affairs to an ability to make valid applications of psycho-analytic knowledge and skills in other settings, as in psychotherapy. Maybe a psycho-analytic institute should provide tutors to help trainees to gain the education they need to become practising psycho-analysts wherever it may be found over and above a strictly psycho-analytic one.

This view of mine has arisen in London where we are fortunate enough to have besides the Psycho-Analytic Institute such other and related training enterprises as the Tavistock where it is possible to concentrate on certain applications of psycho-analysis, as in group psychotherapy, child psychotherapy, adult psychotherapy, the leading of professional support groups, etc., as new professional skills, and where it is also possible to become sensitive to group and intergroup processes in a general or generic way in such training events as these so-called Tavistock Groups. I suppose that under different circumstances I would alter my view.

As to the relation between an Internal Object and a Basic Assumption, let me state the following: an Internal Object is a psychic structure inferred by someone who has observed a series of interpersonal events taking place, even if the event is an attempt to communicate an ineffable experience such as a dream (and I take it for granted that the observer of such events is often a party to them as well). Under certain circumstances these interpersonal events may lead the observer to assert that a group is present and to infer that the members share certain convictions about the group but remain unaware of them. These convictions tend to cohere round certain archaic notions, such as the need for succour, the dangers posed by predators, the ubiquitousness of sexual attraction, etc. In so far as a group seems to be possessed by such shared preoccupations it may be said to be a Basic Assumption Group. Though the convictions are held by individual members of the group, it is the fact that they are shared by members that gives them their special characteristics, i.e., their power to determine social behaviour.

The two terms come out of two different vocabularies: one arises from efforts to construct a psychology of the individual from observing his social behaviour, and the other arises from efforts to account for the behaviour of individuals in groups. They seem to me to be parallel activities with correspondences but are not exactly overlapping. Would I be right in saying that from one activity to the other there is, to use another of Bion's ideas, a shift of vertex?

A Study of Very Small Groups

Robert Gosling

EDITOR'S NOTE: *From the Tavistock Clinic, from which Bion's "Tavistock Method" took its name, comes Doctor Gosling's contribution about "very small groups" (VSG), which number from five to six people. It seems to be a unique size in which to discuss group characteristics which are denuded of the comfortable rituals and cliches of small groups and large groups. Since the discovery by Bion of forces within a group structure which he outlined in his* Experience in Groups, *his protégé has become better known as a vehicle for the engendering of knowledge about authority and leadership in group situations generally, and the group experience has become a training ground for awarenesses in this direction. It is a human relations laboratory method of learning about people. Doctor Gosling is here reporting about his experiences as a consultant for a very small group at the Leicester Conference. Behavior which can be characterized as due to splitting and projective identification, movement from the paranoid-schizoid to the depressive positions, and notation of the oedipus complex can be observed.*

A Study of Very Small Groups

R. Gosling

Introduction

In 1948, or thereabouts, after some years as an Army Psychiatrist, Wilfred Bion had the disconcerting experience of finding himself surrounded by a small number of patients expecting treatment from him in the setting of a Psychiatric Clinic that had a reputation for harbouring some experts in psychotherapy. Furthermore, Bion had been made to realise that the Professional Committee of the Clinic held to the idea that he had become something of an expert in "taking" groups, though just what the Committee members thought his "taking" them would consist of he had no means of knowing. It goes without saying that they had also made the assumption that these groups that he was to "take" would have a therapeutic effect on the patients that composed them. To be caught up in such a nexus of expectations and to feel stimulated to see what can be made of the situation is a not uncommon experience. What was uncommon, however, was to have such an alert and thoughtful man as Bion to do it and then to describe some of his experiences.

His open-eyed and somewhat startled approach has had a widespread influence on the understanding of the social dynamics of small groups, particularly to the extent that the dynamics are the product of powerful fantasies that have become shared by those composing the groups as a result of various kinds of communication that to a large extent go unnoticed or unacknowledged. The fantasies that have become shared in this way are experienced as self-evidently reasonable assumptions. As each member's contribution to their formation has been made anonymously, no one seems to be responsible for them.

The stance that Bion tried to adopt in relation to his experience of being a "staff member" amongst a small number of "patients" in a clinic was similar to the stance that a psychoanalyst might try to adopt in relation to the events taking place in his consulting room. In trying to articulate his experience, however, he was careful not to slip into using the images and metaphors of infancy and childhood that abound in psychoanalysis, but turned instead to the language of wider social experience, namely, history and mythology.

This approach, particularly insofar as it gave pride of place to unconscious processes, gave a particular emphasis to the work done subsequently by his colleagues in the Tavistock Institute of Human Relations in the fast developing field of Group Relations Training. Following the seminal work of Kurt Lewin, the study of small group dynamics flourished in a variety of ways in the USA under the auspices of the National Training Laboratory until it exploded into a veritable shower of adventures of the present day encounter movement and beyond. The preoccupations of a small number of Tavistock workers, following in the direction first suggested by Bion, led them to develop the human relations laboratory method of learning along a somewhat different channel. This resulted in a series of experiential conferences held at Leicester, England, by which name they are widely known. Their design and the thinking that lies behind the design have been described by Trist and Sofer (1959) and by Rice (1965).

Over time the central preoccupation of these conferences has shifted considerably. For instance, in 1960 the conference was entitled "A Training Conference in Group Relations" and its stated task was "to provide members with learning experiences which can enable them to become aware of the main problems of leadership and especially of the deeper and frequently unrecognised forces at work in modern organisational life and inter-personal relations." By 1971 the title had changed to "Authority and Leadership-a Working Conference" and the task was "to provide members with opportunities to learn about the nature of authority and the interpersonal and inter-group problems encountered in its exercise." Five years later the title had come to be "Authority, Leadership and Organisation–a Working Conference" and the task had come to include opportunities to learn about "the institutional problems encountered in exercising authority within the conference organisation."

For such undertakings conference members are recruited from a wide variety of backgrounds, professions and disciplines: industrialists and social workers, psychiatrists and educators, clerics and social administrators; both sexes and all ages. The aim of the conference is reflected in its setting, namely a university hall of residence. The aim is educational and not therapeutic; members come to study and learn and not as patients to find treatment; such therapeutic gain as there may be is a chance by-product, though an acceptable one. The design of the conference and the tone of the various meetings reflect a belief in the value of learning from experience; any teaching in the conventional sense is provided only incidentally; the aim of the staff is to help the membership to come to grips with its own behaviour in the "here and now" through the offering of interpretations of that behaviour. Some of the experiences commonly encountered in such conferences in the setting of small groups (numbering about ten members and one consultant) and large groups (numbering from 40 to 80 members and two or three consultants) have been described in detail by Turquet (1974) and (1975).

This approach to learning has been elaborated further as a result of working in conjunction with other similarly interested organisations beside the Tavistock Institute of Human Relations, in particular, the Grubb Institute for Behavioural Studies in London, the Department of Education of Bristol University and the A.K. Rice Institute in Washington, DC. It is a pleasure to acknowledge my indebtedness to colleagues in all these institutions. To anyone who has read Bion's book, "Experiences in Groups" (1961), my great indebtedness to him will be obvious. Fundamentally, however, I am indebted to the various conference members whose uncertain capacities for co-operation have been linked to my own in exploring the phenomena of very small groups (numbering five to six members and one consultant); it is they who have provided me with the raw material for the reflections that I can now present.

Before doing so, however, my position within the sequence of these conferences should be made clear so that my reflections on the very small groups may be put into their context. For some years I had taken the role of consultant to a number of different events in these training conferences, in particular, the small groups set up to study their own experience as the conference proceeded. In 1975 it bore in upon some of us that many members coming to these training conferences spent much of their working lives engaged in groups consisting of five or so people, and that although the conference offered them opportunities to explore the phenomena occurring in small groups of about 10 members and large groups of from 40 to 80, they did not do so for groups of the size they most commonly encountered in their work settings.

Consequently, at the next conference, in parallel with the on-going examination of small groups (SG's) and large groups (LG's), members were offered an opportunity to study the events in groups consisting of only five members and one consultant (VSG's), the members being selected in such a way as to avoid so far as possible their coming together with either members or a consultant from their small group experience. Naturally, as the large group experience included all the membership they had inevitably met each other during that event. Furthermore there were other concurrent formal training events, to say nothing of numerous informal meetings of a "social" kind, in which members were free to choose their own companions, such as an event to study inter-group processes and another to study the impact of the institution of the conference itself on the individual and of the individual on the institution. Although members of the very small groups (VSG's) might therefore have relations with each other of their own making outside the group, the conference management in its design of the programme had kept them down to a minimum.

During the conference the consultants working in their first VSG's had opportunities for comparing notes, refining some of their emerging ideas and sharpening their awareness. It was commonly known that this particular experiment had not been carried out before in such a conference and so in their temper they had a needle of excitement to them that sometimes verged on a point of outrage. Believing there was ever only one first time, I was glad to be able to test out some of my first impressions in a second series of VSG's scheduled for a conference in the following year. It is from my experience of this second conference that most of my reflections are drawn.

It should be recognised that just as members of such a conference move from one episode to another, sometimes dragging with them hang-overs of feelings and expectations, sometimes determined to differentiate one event from another and to let bye-gones be bye-gones, and very frequently suffused with such a sense of déjàvu that the whole series of events seems to be one long drawn out relearning of what has always been dimly known, so too the staff members are inevitably caught up in analagous trajectories through the experience of the conference, a conference that in some respects is unlike any conference that has ever gone before. My reflections on the VSG's, therefore, are an aspect of my own particular trajectory through this particular conference (following upon the particular conference that went before it and so on). The VSG's that I refer to took place concurrently with a series of SG's and LG's, as well as some other training events, according to the programme given below. With the SG's and LG's they shared certain features: as well as being events that depended strictly on studying the "here and now" experience of the group, they were in addition groupings that had been designated by the conference management and were bounded in their work by this membership and by a designated place and duration. In the other training events there were more options open to the membership as to how they went about their learning.

Characteristics of the Psychological Field

The simplest way for members of a VSG to dispose themselves so as to study the group's behaviour is to arrange themselves in a circle. This means that for each person present the others fall within his field of vision. No turning of the head is needed to take in a neighbour's facial expression, gestures or posture as is usually the case in an SG of ten or so members. Even less is it like an LG in which it is virtually impossible to take in what most of the other members are up to. There is therefore, in comparison, a plentiful and detailed non-verbal feed-back. Members less commonly get confused with other members, and statements are only rarely attributed to the wrong member. When a member starts to tilt his chair backwards and to balance on its back legs, to the other members it speaks loudly of his momentary anxiety, his wish to take up a mid position in the matter that is being considered, his wish to be half in and half out of the group, or whatever else; in an SG although the same event would certainly have an impact, its precise message might, as it were, be just out of hearing. In an SG opportunities are plentiful for conducting transactions that escape some members' notice and that quickly produce an atmosphere of not knowing what is happening or quite where one is in it all. Although recall of recent events is often inaccurate and statements are often wrongly attributed, there is usually a not too remote possibility of putting them right and so reconstituting for the members concerned a boundary to their own individuality. In an LG, by contrast, the depersonalising processes are continual and are often only countered by differentiating oneself from one's neighbour or by engaging actively with the consultants.

PROGRAMME: SEPTEMBER 1976

DAY TIME	Thurs 9th	Fri 10th	Sat 11th	Sun 12th	Mon 13th	Tue 14th	Wed 15th	Thurs 16th	Fri 17th	Sat 18th	Sun 19th	Mon 20th	Tue 21st
8:15 Breakfast													
9:00-10:30		SG	SG	SG	SG	–	–	LG	LG	LG	LG	LG	P
10:30 Coffee													
11:00-12:30		MG/ VSG	MG/ VSG	MG/ VSG	MG/ VSG		LG	SG	SG	SG	IE	OG	OG
1:00 Lunch	P 2.00												
2:30-4:00*	OG	IG	IG	–	2.3.30 IG	–	SG	–	IE	–	IEP	–	
4:00 Tea*					3:30 Tea								
4:30-6:00*	SG	IG	OG	IG	4-5:30 OG	–	IE	IE	OG	IE	OG	P	
6:30 Dinner													
7:30-9:00	SG	MG/ VSG	–	MG/ VSG	–	–	IE	IE	–	IE	–	OG	

P = Plenary Session
OG = Orientation Group
SG = Small Group
MG = Median Group
VSG = Very Small Group
LG = Large Group
IG = Intergroup Event
IE = Institutional Event

Note: At this conference members were given the option when applying to take part in either a VSG or an MG–a Median Group of about 20 members.

In the VSG each member can give roughly an equally personal account of all the others; it is relatively difficult to hide behind another member successfully or to remain virtually anonymous. In an SG inevitably there are prominent characters at any one time, and opportunities abound for others to remain hidden while yet having an effect on the group. If a member is absent from a VSG his or her identity is instantly recognised by all the others; in an SG it may take a moment or two to work out who the empty chair belongs to; in an LG it is often impossible to know for sure whether anyone is absent or not and if so who it is. In this sense the boundary of the VSG in respect of membership is easily perceived and feels firm. This firmness is further attested to by the way a sense of familiarity soon builds up that stands in contrast to the uncertainties of the other conference events; indeed the reality of these past and future other events gets very attenuated indeed and the VSG can spend long periods absorbed in its own experience as if nothing else in the world existed.

This intense personalisation of each member of a VSG, as well as of the consultant, precludes some of the adventurous splitting, stereotyping and unashamed use of other members as vehicles for projection that wax and wane in an SG. In a VSG it is as if some other thread of experience of a member demanded recognition before the previous one had been fully grasped and shared; no sooner have the members identified the consultant's behaviour, say, as the cause of their present disarray than someone remembers that he made quite a useful remark only a short while ago. It is therefore more difficult to encounter and explore in a VSG some of the enormities of archaic convictions that soon become apparent in an SG, let alone what happens in an LG. A further feature of this brake on splitting tendencies in a VSG is that the very prominence of the non-verbal communications keeps them perpetually linked to what is being said in words; a member tends therefore to be experienced as someone sending a complex, even contradictory, message, but one representing a relatively whole and ambivalent person. In an SG, however, there often grows up a culture that pays almost exclusive attention to what has been put into words and does its best to ignore all that is being expressed by other means. This tendency is doubtlessly reinforced by the consultant's behaviour as he is seen struggling to put into words his impression of what the group is up to. The extreme form of this culture occurs when a group colludes in propounding the view that you only need to be silent to be sure you communicate nothing.

Another prominent characteristic of the psychological field is related to the physical proximity of members to each other, i.e., to all of the other members, not just to one's neighbours. This characteristic is manifested in the self-consciousness of members about how close their hands are to those of their neighbours, whether their feet are likely to touch those of a member opposite, how big a shift backwards of their chair they can make without appearing notably hostile. Your neighbours' breathing becomes a prominent feature of your awareness; if you want to cough you must do it into someone's face unless you make a deliberate manoeuvre not to. Eye contact is telling when present, awkward when absent and always under keen surveillance as to its intensity and duration. It would seem that in this way the VSG is constantly faced with the problems of intimacy, particularly intimacy as a danger to be avoided, as if the bodily proximity of other members were sexually so exciting as to threaten an explosion. Although at the start of the series of meetings members may comment on their sense of safety and the promise of intimacy, as time goes on revealing or forthright statements are prominent by their absence. Members' behaviour suggests that intimacy is an impending danger which must always be guarded against. Open recognition of sexual feelings for each other, for instance, that at some point is a common event in an SG, is embarked on in a VSG with great caution. My impression is that in an SG it is felt that all that might take place is a sexual orgy with little personal commitment, whereas in a VSG it is felt as if it could alter the whole course of one's life, like wife-swapping. But this remains little more than a personal hunch and I find myself not at all well informed about the nature of the menace that intimacy is felt to have in a VSG.

Yet another characteristic of the psychological field that influences events is related to the number of people present and to the nature of the mental work that this requires of members. I suggest that for most of us it is possible to have simultaneous relations with several people at once, allowing each person moderately full recognition, provided the number is small. Empathy, or coenaesthetic perception (Spitz 1965) is effected by putting oneself in the other person's shoes, i.e., by splitting one's self into a part that stays at home and another that is exported imaginatively to feel out what the other person is experiencing. Now splitting one's self up into parts is obviously potentially damaging to one's sense of integrity; exporting these parts, furthermore, is obviously potentially depleting. To recognise another person fairly fully requires the exported part of the self to be a sizeable segment of one's own self, containing a fair mixture of both good and bad objects and a coherent sub-ego that experiences them. Although people vary in the number of simultaneous fairly full relationships they can sustain, I suggest that at some point the splitting and projective processes required become more threatening to the individual than the advantages experienced from the multiple relationships.*

To engage affectively with the membership of a VSG therefore, though it does not promise plain sailing, is not immediately felt as a divisive and impoverishing undertaking. An SG, however, at once poses questions of alliances, the prospect of being rejected by everyone else, a mass attack, the strong and the weak, the parts and the whole, fragmentation and homogenisation and so forth. The individual's sense of his own identity can come in for some fairly rough handling through being set up to play a part on behalf of the group or being used as a vehicle or repository for impulses that are

*It may be that this faculty for having simultaneous multiple relationships without raising persecutory anxiety to a serious level is related to the personality characteristic termed Capacity by Jaques (1961).

generally unwanted or deplored. Engulfment, disturbing and intrusive attributions and scapegoating are in the forefront of the picture when joining an SG, whereas in a VSG more benign expectations can be entertained. As one member put it, the interchanges of the VSG felt less "grabby" than those in her SG. Threats to an individual's sense of his identity are even greater and more perpetual in an LG (See Turquet 1975).

Finally, a fifth characteristic of the psychological field is that of perceived symmetry. With only six or seven people in the room pairing continually reappears. Another member is nearly always experienced as being either next to you or opposite you. Although remarks may be made by a member as if they were addressed to the group as a whole, within a short time the responses tend to be coming from one other member. For a while some issue may be tossed around as of general concern, but before long it seems to get captured by a pair of members. Whereas in an SG this capturing of a theme by a pair is usually tolerated for a long time and even enjoyed as a vicarious experience, in a VSG the pairing quickly becomes exclusive and the fact that the theme being developed does not tally with the experience of one of the other members becomes obtrusive. The pairings are therefore short-lived but continually recurring, often with a sense of surreptitiously continuing something that had had to be abandoned prematurely or at least carrying overtones of what had taken place earlier. Indeed, the simple dyadic gestalt that seems to be hard to resist puts distinct limitations on what takes place in a VSG. One member remarked on the fact that in the VSG he missed the "power politics of the SG and all the attendant archaic and crazy events."

Psychological Models

Within this field, some characteristics of which have been adumbrated above, the members of the VSG have a variety of experiences. In an attempt to give meaning to these experiences various psychological models are offered using memories of analagous experiences of the past. Of course, none fits exactly and the work of the group in coming to grips with the uniqueness of its experience lies in bringing into conjunction fragments of memory in a novel, apt and suggestive way. No one person is in a position to do it all, though for periods of time the belief that there is such a one may take root. In fact it is a never ending interactive process in which the search for meaning itself creates new conditions that in turn require new meanings to be found for them.

Nevertheless, as each member has limited experience to draw upon and a modest capacity for inventiveness, I have so far been able to identify only four clusters of past experience from which psychological models appear to be drawn:

1. The Confessional. On entering a VSG ideas about greater intimacy, getting to know people "better," confession, letting one's hair down, dropping one's facade, honesty etc. usually abound. In such states I, as

the consultant, have been experienced as some kind of bishop, a psychotherapist or a somewhat oversized friend acting as host.

2. The Family. In the shifting configurations of the group, notions concerning the nuclear family return time and time again. Morevoer these notions are usually expressed with pleasure as if something reassuring had been discovered and this despite the fact that it later transpires that at least some of the members have had anything but reassuring experiences in their actual families. In this state I tend to get cast in a parental or grand-parental role, adoptive or generative, or as an enfant terrible, or occasionally as a suitor from another family.

3. Negotiation. The ebb and flow of individual differences and the commonalities of membership, of what is private what is public, of what is idiosyncratic and what is shared are sometimes construed as negotiations. The notion of negotiation, however, touches on a wide spectrum of experience from political negotiations of power, to commercial negotiations of value, to the kind of negotiation of personal realities that takes place in a marriage or in a therapy group. Here I tend to get cast in the role of a negotiator with an unfair advantage, an adjudicator or a landlord.

4. The Balloon or Lifeboat. The fourth model that I think I have identified is related to an experience few of us have had in actuality but which seems to be very familiar in psychic reality; it is that of a balloon in which someone has got to be jettisoned and who is it going to be? This model is so scaring that it appears only momentarily and I am not at all sure of its validity for anyone but myself.

By contrast, in an SG the culture of dependency is likely to be more like that met with in the body of a church or an evangelical chapel than in a confessional, and more like that of a classroom than a tea-party. If it comes to be felt as a safe place to return to from other exciting and divisive events in the conference, it is likened to a home rather than a family, defined by territory, rules and a tradition rather than a set of relationships. The roles created from the matrix of an SG resemble the figures of the Comedia del Arte more than they do members of a nuclear family. In an SG there are frequent periods of preoccupation with issues of control over threatening explosions or rivalrous chaos; these are not prominent in the VSG and may be represented more by issues concerned with having to regulate a threatening intimacy.

A particular manifestation of the characteristic of VSG whereby the members are highly personalised is that when some member is mobilised to perform an important group task, such as to stand up to the consultant's authority, the person's known outside role may be taken into account in his selection. In one VSG it was a parson set up to embroil me in a "psychoanalysis versus religion" conflict; in the other it was a family therapist to embroil me in arguments about individual versus family therapy. My experience in SG's suggests that selection for such an important role usually gives greater weight to relevant personality characteristics such as a notably argumentative, authoritarian or courageous person, than to his actual role in the outside world. Similarly a member who is to carry bewilderment and incomprehension on behalf of the group, the dunce or the ingenue, can come from quite a range of candidates in an SG. In both the VSG's of my experience an actual difference of cultural background and native language was used for much of the time.

No sooner had these thoughts of mine got to the stage of being expressed as above than I was confronted with the experience of yet another VSG to which what I thought I had learned so far seemed to have only the vaguest relevance. This was a VSG experience in 1977 provided for members of a Training Group numbering 13 in conjunction with a Working Conference membership of 45 and a Conference Staff Group of 12. Training Group members had each had experience of being a member of a Working Conference on at least two occasions before. The aim of the Training Group was to provide them with the experience of assuming the role of consultant to groups of Working Conference members later in the conference. In this setting the two VSG's, one of six members and the other of seven members, remained firmly sub-groups of the 14; it was the Training Group as a whole that held the predominant sentience.

There was much nostalgia for the raw experiences of the SG's of yesteryear; there was some pressure to demonstrate expertise in identifying some small group phenomena that had become familiar; notions of "doing things on behalf of the group" were so quickly mobilised and so firmly ensconced in the orthodox jargon of the group that there was little room left for testing things out in the light of members' personal experience. For my part I had, by accepting a staff role in relation to the Training Group, come to put a premium on the fact that I had worked in two VSG's before and so was more "experienced" than most others. I was constantly hoping that some of the psychological models that had seemed to be fruitful in the past would turn out to be so again. It is unclear how much time was wasted by us all trying to recreate circumstances that would have vindicated the idea that we all had "experience." In fact the salient affective issues in the VSG were of a depressive kind, in particular how one is one's own most dangerous saboteur and how one's public stance on the side of learning turns out to be a determination to repeat what one already knows and to learn as little that is new as possible. This was affectively related to the "middle age" position of one's life-span and the members' experience of being in the middle of a sandwich between the Working Conference members and the Conference staff.

This experience left me with two vivid realisations:

1. How much the events I was trying to get to grips with were defined, predicated or determined by their social context and therefore how empty of meaning it was to refer to VSG's, SG's or LG's as if they were reproducible objects or even that there was such an identifiable category as what I have heard referred to as "conference learning." The initials VSG refer to events that have a certain amount in common,

such as number of participants and the fact that they take place in a tradition of exploration called the Leicester Conference, but that are profoundly influenced by what is going on round them in time and place. So much is this the case that any generalisation about VSG's that can fairly be made is likely to be so modest as to be of very little use or interest.

2. How quickly a formulation, a concept or a theory loses its enabling quality and becomes a barrier to the possibility of making further observations. This is a topic that has been greatly enriched by Bion of recent years. An experience of a VSG is deepened or led on to a further and new experience only at the moment that a theory about it is being fashioned. The theory may then lie around for a while to be applied occasionally and enjoyed in a way that is neither productive nor harmful. Sooner or later, however, it becomes a barrier to new experiences, a Procrustean bed and a downright blight. Psycho-analytic practice is also replete with this phenomenon. Using Bion's (1970) notions of the *container* and the *contained*, the relationship between them is either symbiotic, commensal or parasitic: productive, uneventful or destructive. Perhaps the most that can be hoped for is that this cycle of degeneration, if there is one, is accomplished in as short a time as possible

At this point I am reminded of the fact that the theory of the Oedipus Complex remains for me a recurrently enlivening one. It is a theory that I seem constantly to have forgotten only then to have to discover it all over again and each time as if I were doing so with great originality; the shock of the event confronts me with my rivalry and hatred of Freud and is something that my patients quite often don't get over all that easily either. It occurs to me therefore that the theory (and set of images) of the Oedipus Complex must lie for the most part (for good and obvious reasons) just on the boundary of what I must repress and what I can acknowledge. This instability of what is known, or thought to be known, seems to be required if it is to be rediscovered repeatedly always in a new context and so always for the first time.

I am therefore led to think, and reluctantly to believe, that while any reader or any author of an essay entitled "A Study of Very Small Groups" might reasonably search its pages for some clarity of exposition and firmness of conclusion, to the extent that he claims to have found it he may be headed for disaster. It seems that the most he can expect are a variety of suggestive comments any one of which can become an albatross hung about his neck if it is taken at its face value. It is as if learning has always to take place on the edge of exasperation. In these matters there can be few authors more stimulating to one's inclination to re-examine one's experiences yet once again than Wilfred Bion. His writings are rich in suggestiveness. At the same time there are few authors whose obliquity is more exasperating—unless the present author has unwittingly outdone him!

References

Bion, W.R. (1970). *Attention and Interpretation*. London: Tavistock Publications.
Jaques, E. (1961). *Equitable Payment*. London: Heinemann, pp. 185-187.
Rice, A.K. (1965). *Learning for Leadership*. London: Tavistock Publications.
Spitz, R. (1965). *The First Year of Life*. New York: IUP.
Trist, E.L. & Soffr, C. (1959). *Explorations in Group Relations*. Leicester: Leicester University Press.
Turquet, P.M. (1974). *Leadership: the individual and the group. IN: Analysis of Groups*. Gibbard et al. (eds.), San Francisco/London: Jossey-Bass, pp. 349-371.
—— (1975). Threats to identity in the large group. IN: *The Large Group: Therapy and Dynamics*. Kreeger, L. (ed.) London: Constable.

The Individual in the Group: On Learning to Work with the Psychoanalytic Method

Martha Harris

EDITOR'S NOTE: *Martha Harris, who in private life is Mrs. Donald Meltzer, is Organizing Tutor for the Programme of Training in Psychoanalytic Psychotherapy with children, parents, and young people at the Tavistock Clinic and is, consequently, in a position of great responsibility in regard to the curriculum. In this contribution she outlines the Tavistock training curriculum and demonstrates those aspects of Bion's thinking which the curriculum and program reflect.*

The Individual in the Group: On Learning to Work With the Psycho-Analytic Method

Martha Harris

This paper attempts to convey some of the ways in which I see Dr. Bion's work as raising questions and throwing light upon problems of organizing training in psycho-analytical method and attitudes. His thoughts on this topic are most cogently but, as always, often obliquely stated in "Attention and Interpretation." There he pursues further his ideas about the relationship between the container and the contained; the nature of the transformations affected by the quality of their interaction; the subtle proliferation of mythology and lies which in differing degrees obstruct the search for truth. There he continues the preoccupation which runs throughout his writings, with the relationship between the individual and the group, and, as befits a historian, the relationships between different groups.

It is hardly possible to be complacent about the history of psycho-analytic groups or of psycho-analysis in groups. The tension between the pressures of the group and the thrust of the individual for development is a theme which runs throughout Bion's work: between man as a social animal dependent upon, and with obligations to society, and man as a developing individual with a mind that grows through introjecting experiences of himself in the world, impelled to think in order to retain internally relationships with needed and valued objects in their absence.

Those of us who are concerned with training and establishment of psycho-analytic work cannot afford to neglect his ideas. The vertex from which I shall be speaking is that of one who has been concerned for over twenty-five years with the practice and training in psycho-analysis in public institutions as well as privately, and in particular with the expansion of the Tavistock training in Psycho-analytical Psychotherapy with Children, Parents and Young People. This is a four-year training upon on-going work and is divided into two parts. Part I is concerned with the development of psycho-analytical observation and attitudes in various settings, while Part II is specifically concerned with learning to apply the method of psycho-analysis to treatment, ranging from once weekly to five times weekly.

This training qualifies people to become members of the Association of Child Psychotherapists and to join what was initially a somewhat nebulous and almost unrecognized profession which has now expanded to achieve a salary and career structure within the British Health Service. This professional respectability carries with it the necessity of conforming to certain minimal criteria changeable only by the agreement of the appropriate committees. These are by definition bound to be fairly conservative in their operation and undoubtedly inimical to "catastrophic change." And yet change and expansion needs to be facilitated so that psycho-analytic ideas and attitudes can travel and take root among workers who are ready to receive them, so that their usefulness may find homes in which to flourish.

So how does one keep the mystical idea of psycho-analysis alive within such a formal structure? How can a structure remain adaptable and be used to protect, perhaps even to promote the development of the individual worker within it? How can one create a group of professionals, of psycho-analytic workers who are able to function with and among other groups of professionals in a way that reduces interference, is "commensal" in Bion's terms, and may even be beneficial?

To quote from "Attention and Interpretation": "In the symbiotic relationship there is a confrontation and the result is growth-producing though that growth may not be discerned without some difficulty. In the parasitic relationship the product of the relationship is something that destroys both parties to the association. The realization that approximates most closely to my formulation is the group individual setting dominated by envy. The envy cannot be satisfactorily ascribed to one or other party; in fact it is a function of the relationship. . . ."

In the symbiotic relationship the group is capable of hostility and benevolence and the mystic contribution is subject to close scrutiny. From the scrutiny the group grows in stature and the mystic likewise. In the parasitic association even friendliness is deadly. An easily seen example of this is in the group's promotion of the individual to a place in the establishment where his energies are deflected from his creative destructive role and absorbed in administrative functions . . . the dangers of the invitation to group or individual to become respectable, to be medically qualified, to be a university department, to be a therapeutic group, to be anything in short, but not explosive."

The institutionalizing of words, religions and psycho-analysis—all are special instances of institutionalizing memory so that it may contain the mystic revelation and its creative and destructive force. The function of the establishment is to take and absorb the consequences so that the group is not destroyed."

Perhaps one could transpose this into a lower key and say that the function of the psycho-analytical training group or establishment is to provide a sufficiently protected and organized place in the world within which students are given the opportunity, facilitated by their own personal analysis, to study and to experience development and change, in themselves and in their patients; to study and to work with the elements and configurations which impede that process. If psychoanalytic work, transcending the urge to cure, has an appeal for them, this will be prompted by the emotional impact of the close scrutiny of the children and adults with whom they are concerned.

As described by Bion in "Elements of Psycho-analysis," the evolution of the transference in the psycho-analytic relationship, involving passion rather than violence (as e.g. in the form of action by either analyst or patient) is essentially creative-destructive for both: destructive of existing states of mind and constantly creating others. It may not always be apparent whether the new state of mind is—so to speak—a step in the right direction. It is hard for the teachers and establishment of any group that begins to meet with some success in the world, to bear in mind that they may not know the right direction, that there may not be a right direction, without being formless and disintegrated. It is difficult to allow the individual workers to find their own style and voice in a language and in a setting which enables them to carry on some meaningful discourse.

Some of the applicants for the Tavistock Course have already sought analysis for their own personal problems. They may be motivated to become psychotherapists themselves partly through projective identification with their analysts, fundamentally still children who believe that to have children/patients, will make them grown-up like mummy and daddy. This is a ubiquitous phenomenon and we all probably retain vestiges of it within our personality. Others, however, may wish to learn to work with patients, following some more genuine introjection and appreciation of the attention and understanding from which they have benefited and which they would like to share with others.

Observation as a Prelude to Analysis

As Part I of the course is concerned, not with the application of the psychoanalytic method to patients, but with the development of psycho-analytic modes of observation and thinking in varied settings, students are not required to have had some experience of analysis themselves before they begin.

We attempt to give them a disciplined experience of close observation of the week by week development of an infant in a family, of a young child or children. Such detailed observation has inevitably an emotional impact upon the observer which is likely to disturb complacency and to lead to the kind of self-questioning that evokes an interest in personal analysis in those whose desire to get at the truth of themselves is likely to be stronger than their wish to preserve the status quo. The same kind of closer observation of the details of interaction and the responsibilities involved in the work with children, families or young people which students are also doing in this first part of the course, also alerts them to the mental pain as well as to the developmental thrusts in their charges. It enables them to be more receptive of the projections of this which come their way and to see that personal analysis leading to self-analysis is a method of being able to bear this better.

These infant observation seminars were initiated by Esther Bick in 1949. They now form part of the curriculum of the British Psycho-analytical Society and have proved to be one of the best preparations for developing those qualities of perception which Bion describes as essential in the psychoanalytic consulting room. The mother-baby couple, initially the baby-breast, can be perceived as a model for the psycho-analytic couple, exemplifying the relationships, for instance, which he categorizes as parasitic, symbiotic or commensal. The discussion of these observations within a small group in which theoretical preconceptions are relegated as far as possible to the background, can be a model for the essential work group where the task is to study the aspects of material described and to look at them from different angles until some pattern emerges which speaks for itself. The discussion relates to a situation in which the observer has no responsibility other than to notice what there is to be seen while remaining unobtrusively friendly and receptive. As the impulse to action has to be noted and restrained, the task of the group is to follow, imagine and think about the observations including the role and effect of the observer, and noting the difficulty sometimes in refraining from taking action to "improve" the situation.

Thus one has the leisure to note how relationships develop and change without interpretation or formal intervention. This helps toward the orientation described by Bion in which the analyst realizes that he is observing phenomena from which it is possible to construe mental processes. If one is truly observing configurations which are there and is describing them well enough, unimpeded by theoretical preconceptions, other people with a different theoretical background may, if they can also free themselves from their preconceptions, make similar findings.

As it is difficult to free oneself from one's background and the expectations and modes of thinking established by that, it is a help in seminars which focus on detailed observation to have members who come from different backgrounds. There is no university course which prepares one for psycho-analytical thinking and observation. People may be facilitated, but are also limited, by the vertex from which they begin to describe human behaviour and interaction. To have in a seminar people who approach it from different vertices is an enrichment, even if at times one has to reckon with those whose previous training may have positively blocked their spontaneous vision.

Let us assume that detailed observation, and that the increase in awareness of the children's emotional life in their work settings which ensues, brings the student into greater contact with mental pain and the devices used to avoid experiencing this. He may feel the urge to understand the turmoil and disturbance evoked in himself, a state of mind which is likely to prompt him to seek analysis for himself. This may be necessary for his training and is essential for those who wish to proceed to Part II. The link between analysis and training is, however, an unfortunate one. Experience indicates that the more the former can be seen as an entirely private matter, a process which will hopefully give the analysand a new experience of hitherto unapprehended parts of himself, the freer he is likely to be to have such an experience, which will incidentally add to the equipment he can bring to his work.

If the analyst is required to make judgements about his progress, this undoubtedly encourages the analysand to keep an eye on the expectations of analyst and teachers, to make transformations in K (learning about) rather than in O (becoming). It is difficult enough to become the person one is without positive encouragement from the establishment toward conformity and deception.

Relationship Between Student and Teaching Group

To recount a personal recollection of Dr. Bion when confronted with the anxieties of a candidate with a first training case: "What do I do if the patient asks me if I am a student?" "What *are* you when you *cease* to be a student of psycho-analysis?" Every teacher must be continually learning or he has no immediate experience to share. Every therapist must be learning something in the heat of every session or he has nothing of interest to say. One of the ways in which senior practitioners can continue to learn, apart from their own direct experience, is by trying to share the experiences of younger people and by trying to look at material from their vertices.

In a psycho-analytically oriented framework, the work must be done by the individual on his own, whether he be concerned with the meaning of the behaviour of another individual in an intimate individual, family, or small group setting. In order to work well, to think about relationships involved, most people for a while do need the support of some group of colleagues as well as of teachers and supervisors, who are learning with them.

According to Bion's premises, all groups are subject to basic assumption activity which interferes with the capacity of the members to work severally and together. We must assume that no training group or society of psycho-analytical workers is going to be free of these phenomena, or that one can ever afford to relax one's vigilance in trying to spot their recurrences. Perhaps the pairing groups produce the messianic hopes whether substantial or false, which tend then to become invested in a dependent group or groups relying on these new or apparently original messages. Then in turn these are inclined to become the fight-flight groups ready to flee from or to attack enemy ideologies. The dependent group structure so often manifests itself in the reliance upon a crystallized selection of the theories of Freud; the original Messiah; sometimes pitted against a similar extrapolation from Melanie Klein: a latter day saint. Bion is unlikely to escape the same fate. Their theories in such a climate of polarization are suitably selected and presented to eliminate the essential questioning, contradictions and progressions inherent in the formulation of pioneers who are constantly struggling to conceptualize more comprehensively the clinical observations they are making. Bion's postulation about the impossibility of knowing or describing truth, about the existence of thoughts which do not require a thinker (and of psycho-analysis as one of these thoughts) may help us to try to relinquish the idea of owning our own particular brand of psycho-analysis.

One can hope to promote a relationship between fellow workers, students and teachers which might be described by Bion as symbiotic for some, and for the rest at least commensal: co-existent if not mutually profitable. Thus the therapist's relationships with his patients, objects of study, may take place within a framework of teachers or colleagues who are all dedicated to the task of enlarging their field of observation and of self scrutiny. In such an atmosphere, hopefully, senior colleagues instead of being content to rest upon positions earned by past achievements, or longevity, may be able to continue or to allow others to continue that process of mental and emotional growth whose infinite possibilities are released according to Bion by putting aside memory and desire in order to have a better apprehension of the present moment.

Recruitment for Training

A group or training is kept alive or ossifies by virtue of the quality of the new members it recruits. These may be attracted by the power or status which membership is supposed to confer upon them; they may be attracted by the possibility of participating in some interesting learning experience connected with the work which they are already doing or which they would like to do. The senior members forming the establishment which selects the new trainees tend to become increasingly exclusive as a training acquires a reputation and attracts more applicants. Sheer numbers may make exclusion necessary. The tendency in a genuinely well-meaning establishment concerned with preserving standards of work is to use experience of past mistakes to play safe. The establishment of a group in which envy predominates, as described by Bion, may tend, under the guise of protecting standards, to proliferate regulations which do the choosing and end up by including a preponderance of people who have come to join an élite profession which they have a vested interest in restricting.

If one has to limit recruitment, how can this be effected without producing an élitist atmosphere? The best way of selecting would seem to be to give candidates an experience analogous to the work which they wish to do, which will also allow them an opportunity for self-selection, and place the decision as far as possible in their hands. The most obvious course is to encourage prospective students to have a personal analysis. If they find they can stay with that and with the revelations of themselves which unfold in its progress, then hopefully they should have a better basis for supposing they may be able to help others to undergo a similar experience. This is the usual procedure in most psycho-analytical societies and in principle can hardly be bettered as an initial method of selection.

One must allow, however, for the likelihood that some analysands will return having fairly successfully resisted a real experience and grasp of their more unpleasant parts (the unwanted O), perhaps having learned *about* them and become cleverer consciously or unconsciously in disguising them. These may return filled with enthusiasm about analytic work and training, having achieved some sort of collusion of mutual idealization with their analyst, enthusiasm about analysis for others, not for themselves.

If one can sometimes deceive one's analyst and go on deceiving oneself, one can surely also deceive one's tutors and teachers. It seems necessary throughout training to allow work and study experiences which as far as possible encourage students to test the results and capacities which they have. It seems important not to collude in the idealization of being a psycho-analyst or a psychotherapist. For that reason we hope that students in Part I will already be working professionally with children, families and young people in a job that may be seen as valuable in itself and potentially more interesting and rewarding as the worker's perceptions increase. The aim is to make it easy for students to leave after the first part of the training, or to develop more satisfactory roles and methods of working in the fields where they are already employed. The basic aim of the course is not to create a certain number of trained professionals, labelled "child psychotherapist," but to offer an education in psycho-analytical attitudes and ideas which will speak to some people learning to practise the psycho-analytical method, and to others learning to practise these attitudes and modes of thought in related fields: as in social case work, or in pastoral care in schools and colleges. The present Part II of the course is likely in the future to be one alternative, alongside others which may be devised to try to meet the need for further development in related fields.

Teaching Methods and Continued Self-Selection

Students who do proceed to the second part of the course; (the application of the psycho-analytic method in the playroom and consulting room) need support to bear the exigencies of the work, but also sometimes toward selecting themselves out of it if the burden seems likely to be greater than the pleasure and profit derived from it. The attitude of the teaching group can surely do much to promote or discourage honesty in the individual.

If seminars are used too much for monitoring and judging the progress of cases or of the students presenting the cases, their potential usefulness can be obscured by the evocation of feelings of inferiority, defensiveness and the urge to produce less than honest work: to bring to a seminar, for instance, only those sessions in which the therapist thinks he appears to advantage. The primary function of a seminar leader, as of a supervisor, is surely to help the therapist after the event to think about the experience of clinical interaction which he is describing, and to recapture imaginatively the events described. Thus he may be able to think about them better and become more able to shoulder the burden of clinical responsibility and more open to receiving the patient's projections. This, I imagine, is an aspect of what Bion is describing when he talks of experiencing O, involving always a further penetration in the direction of the unknown. I would be inclined to think that the most fruitful seminar or supervision is one in which participants are left, not just satisfied with a piece of good work done, dazzled by the brilliance of pupil, teacher or patient, but with the impetus for further exploration in their own work and may be encouraged to persevere in face of difficulties.

In supervision (surely one should try to discard the name and concept of "control"), the tendency of the non-omnipotent student who is anxious to learn and who respects his supervisor, is to look for explanations, clarifications and good interpretations which he is sure the greater expert can offer. Bion has repeatedly emphasized that however inexperienced and uncertain the candidate, no knowledge and experience on the part of the supervisor can equal the actual experience of being with the patient in the session. The supervisor is always working with the student's reports.

This perhaps brings us to the usefulness of Bion's advocacy of the abdication of memory and desire. It is a difficult concept for the inexperienced student to grasp. When one is conscious of having so little information about psycho-analytic theory and personality development to remember, it is particularly difficult to put that aside rather than to cling tenaciously to the scraps that one has. But it seems to me essential to proceed and to encourage students to proceed on two fronts: they need to acquire and evaluate information which I suspect must mean in earlier learning days the writing of some very detailed notes on cases and observations as an exercise in remembering and in producing something which can be studied sufficiently closely in seminars or supervisions to throw into relief what is *not* there. But yet the encouragement toward the putting aside of memory and desire, that "willing suspension of disbelief" as described by Coleridge, would seem to me a state of mind essential to try to cultivate in the psycho-analytic sessions. When achieved it can, for instance, relieve the boredom and frustration of apparently interminable unchanging sessions with a latency child who sits everlastingly drawing similar geometric patterns. The recollection that so it was yesterday and the desire—somewhat hopeless—that it should not be thus tomorrow, can so cloud one's perceptions that they are unable perhaps to receive some intimation of anxiety or emotionality peeping out from the confines of the pattern today.

It is perhaps especially difficult for people working analytically in clinics to achieve the necessary state of sequestration to direct the beam of darkness on the here and now, to put aside expectations arising from yesterday's session together with whatever information may have percolated from some other worker about the family or crises at school. It is helpful as an exercise in studying what may be drawn out of the immediate session to concentrate occasionally in clinical seminars upon the presentation of a session in detail without any history, to work in the dark to find out how much food for thought there is when not flooded with information.

If one has to guard against institutionalising psycho-analysis, one must beware of using past experience in training to limit future as yet un-thought-of developments. Bion's comments on the limitations of relying upon memory and desire have some applicability to the field of training as well as to the consulting room; to one's wish for instance to keep up standards which may alas tend toward reproducing paler copies of oneself. The more one has to delegate to committee judgements the more one is likely to flatten out into a group of socal and well-adjusted banality consisting of those who have learned to adapt successfully to the system.

However, as a tutor or supervisor one cannot abdicate entirely the responsibility which greater experience confers, both to the patient and to the student for trying to see that some reasonable match of capabilities takes place between a particular case and a particular student with regard to his stage of development. Experience is likely to bear out the fallibility of these assessments and certainly one cannot judge from the apparent progress of the treatment alone the capabilities of the worker who is undertaking it. Some patients have such an urge to grow and to understand, that they do well with attention but limited comprehension on the therapist's part. Others need infinite patience and test to the limit the therapist's capacity to bear negativism and the projection of frustration and pain.

It seems to me that during training one must allow situations which give students the opportunity to test and live through some of the stresses to which they must inevitably be subjected sooner or later in psycho-analytic work, to find if they can struggle with them and even enjoy that struggle. As Dr. Bion once remarked: one may not necessarily have to be outstandingly intelligent to be a psycho-analyst, but such intelligence as one has must be available to use under fire, and this is especially true in work with certain children. Baptism under fire at some point is an essential part of the development of a child psychotherapist, and it can be a help toward recognizing the same configurations occurring in a subtler form in the adult.

If we cannot and should not protect our students from difficult and frustrating experiences, and should probably be loath to rescue them too soon even when the going becomes very rough, support may be necessary and required: of the kind that shares the burden of thinking and worrying. This may alleviate but can never remove the loneliness in difficult clinical situations for no supervisor can relieve one of the burden of deciding how to respond in the immediacy of the session.

As obviously in this field teachers must continue to be practitioners, continued experience with patients, especially when these are not all aspiring analysts or psychotherapists, keeps one closely in touch with the pains and unpredictabilities in becoming an individual, and more able to empathize with the problems of fellow practitioners who are less experienced in years. The humility which this should engender is the only way of hoping to create a profession that will not be idealized as an élite, and of hoping that it will not attract recruits for this reason.

Written Work

In the Tavistock training we have found that it helps students to think about what they are doing and learning, by writing accounts of their work at different stages. We seem likely to extend this as an additional method of self selection, to ask for descriptions and distillations of sequences of observations, work experiences, case presentations and comprehension of theory. Encouragement to present honest accounts of experiences rather than scholastic essays including references to all the right authorities may contribute to producing a group of workers who do not proliferate the kind of theories described by Bion as characteristic of the lying group dominated by envy. Probably one of the ways of mitigating the envy of the achievements of others, the passively dependent attitude which sees the strength and expertise in others, and which is moreover unable to discriminate between true and false achievement, is the attempt at least to do and to take stock of what one is managing to do oneself, to use language as a prelude to further achievement.

Theory

There is a question as to how to teach theory in a course which aims to encourage students to learn from a genuine experience of themselves in close contact with others. The collection, the manipulation, the evaluation of theories are traditionally used in the field of mental health as bulwarks against disturbing uncertainties endemic in the work. But yet one needs theories and "models," to use Bion's term, as a notation or mythology to bind constant conjunctions. They are necessary as tools to help one to organize thinking about experiences in order to proceed further. "Theory not as a solution but as a model which may prove convenient and useful" (Attention and Interpretation).

Over the years with the help of Donald Meltzer, a selection of reading has been evolving which aims to orient students to the study of psychoanalysis as a developing art-science of a descriptive kind, essentially useful as it illuminates the experiences and furthers the method of working with the transference within the consulting room. It is studied from a historical point of view as a series of pioneering adventures in the mind. We begin with Freud's attempts to free himself from a nineteenth century physiological view of the mind, to evolve theoretical models which could account for the phenomena he encountered in his patients. We follow the development of his theories of psychopathology as he attempts to reconstruct from his patients their childhood neurosis and to account for what went wrong. The work of Melanie Klein centering round *The Narrative of a Child Analysis*, is studied from the point of view of her attempt to observe how the child builds up from infancy, his inner world and the way in which this influences the kind of adult that he will become. Finally Bion's work is studied as an attempt to evolve a model of the mind providing a method of studying linkages between emotionality, truth and lies, which is in the vanguard of psycho-analysis.

Working in Institutions

The emphasis in all of this has been on how the establishment may foster the development of individuality and individual responsibility. Yet we are training people to work in institutions that are likely to contain rival groups and forces that are inimical to psycho-analysis. We must hope to create a friendlier climate in some of these institutions.

The practice of the pscho-analytic method requires a degree of sequestration so that the patient may be protected from the impingement of unnecessary external intrusions which could interfere with the evolution of the transference. The therapist himself needs to find a place in his institution so that he too can deploy his attention during the treatment in a relatively uncluttered way.

This sequestration and preoccupation lend themselves to being perceived by other less psycho-analytically involved colleagues as a mystique and as a claim to special consideration and position. Therapists in a clinic can attract to themselves only too readily an ambivalent transference, as to parents who evoke curiosity by obtruding evidence that they are engaged upon some mysterious intercourse, but who tantalize by performing it behind doors. They may take refuge from the attacks of the critical by forming a close-knit little group, a mutual protection society which, however much in possession of the truth it may feel, is bound to be essentially persecuted at core; or they may try to deal with these transference phenomena by denial and placation of differences. The tendency to revert to basic assumption behaviour tends to enter into and between every group formation in an institution or clinic which can readily split itself, give up the task in hand in favour of defending respective positions or ideologies. The most pervasive basic assumption perhaps in work with children is the dependency one. Close work with children in pain, and accountability to rivalry with their parents, tends to bring out feelings of inadequacy and unresolved infantile dependence in ourselves. If we cannot manage to deal with those by introspection, and introjective identification with valued internal parental figures, how can we manage to deal with them in the children we treat? Surely there must be someone who can provide a better answer than we can? Our supervisors, our analyst, or supporting these some excellent theoretical formulation into which all clinical data must ultimately fit. There are tendencies even (perhaps particularly) in the most progressive groups to rely upon the latest findings and formulations to provide the answer for every problem. Hence the polarization in so many psycho-analytical groups between adherents to different psycho-analytical theories, rival loyalties to the different flags where unresolved hostility and envy underlying the dependence is split off on to the rival group. There is something to be said for working in an institution which contains a section of workers who are simply ignorant of or hostile to psycho-analysis. This gives one an impetus to have another look at essentials.

Dr. Bion's studies of group behaviour have continued to be the germinal impulse for the recurrent group relations conferences held by the Tavistock, an impetus to institutional groups to study themselves and their behaviour to one another. There is one psycho-analytical tradition that regards the study of a group behaviour as almost disloyal to psycho-analysis which is concerned with the internal world, the internal grouping. Yet the study of the transferring of this internal grouping to the therapist in the psycho-analytic couple is surely complemented by the study of the behaviour of the individual in a group, of the impingement of group pressures upon him. The departure from analytic attitudes occurs when the study of group behaviour becomes the kind of group therapy when a cure is effected through an abdication of responsibility, by fragmenting and losing parts of oneself in the group, by a regressing to proto-mental activity, carried along by the stream of unconsciousness or the mythology jointly engendered.

Work Groups and Establishments

I should now like to return to that early distinction made by Bion between the basic assumption and the work groups. Without continual and rigorous examination of the group activities in the realm of training and of practice with colleagues the activities of the establishment group are only too easy to talk about but to overlook when one becomes it. *Knowing about* groups and being aware of the nature of one's emotional participation in a group activity are two different things, again instances of the distinction between transformations in K and *becoming* O, where experience is transformed into growth and learning through experience takes place.

In order to prevent oneself from becoming the spokesman of some "advanced" psycho-analytic group perhaps one should consider the following quotation from *Attention and Interpretation*: "The individual himself must be able to distinguish between himself as an ordinary person and his view that he is omniscient and omnipotent. It is a step toward recognition of a distinction between the group as it really is and its idealization as an embodiment of the omnipotence of the individuals who compose it. Sometimes the separation fails and the group is not only seen to be ideally omnipotent and omniscient but believed to be so in actuality. The individual's realization of a gulf between his view of himself as omnipotent and his view of himself as an ordinary human being must be achieved as a result of a task of the group itself as well as in individual analysis. Otherwise there is a danger that a state of mind is transferred (by projective identification) to the group and acted out there—not altered."

Despite all the emphasis upon training people to be as far as possible individuals within their group it seems likely that for most of us the continuance of a group or an establishment within which we can work is a necessity.

"The function of a group is to produce a genius: the function of the Establishment is to take up and absorb the consequence so that the group is not destroyed." The International Psycho-analytical Association is the Establishment within which the work of psycho-analytic geniuses, rare as always, but including surely Bion, must be preserved and utilized. But when an establishment becomes too vast and monolithic the tendency is to increase committees and legislation in ways that do not allow for individual developments and eccentricities. "Dislike of the onus of decision, or awareness of responsibility for the decision, contributes to the formulation of selection procedures by which selection, like dogma and laws of science, is made to act as a substitute for judgement or a scapegoat for the guilt attendant on overtly acknowledged exercise of responsibility" (*Attention and Interpretation*).

There is room and it seems to me necessary to allow for a number of establishments within which the psycho-analytic ideas of genius are contained and within which students may become acquainted with them and learn to apply them from different vertices. The vertex from which one looks when nourished by close observation of child and of infant development would seem to be a fruitful one for discerning later on the presence of the child within the adult, an essential nucleus of analytic work with adults.

How does a parent who wishes to have his child psycho-analysed or a person who wishes to have a psycho-analytic experience himself know how to set about it? Bion in "Experiences in Groups," indicates that in this field the label on the bottle can be no guarantee of the contents. "Psycho-analyst" like "psychotherapist" is a trade name; the former more exclusive than the latter and carrying with it probably the guarantee of a more formal training. But neither name is any guarantee as to whether the individual in the role designated has some competence and capacity to go on struggling to improve that competence by practising the psycho-analytic method. Prospective clients or patients will have to continue to use their other known professional advisers, their friends, the grapevine, and sometimes–if available–their own intutition in the last resort when they wish to find their way to have psycho-analytical treatment. But a variety of training establishments which are attempting to cultivate a psycho-analytic attitude and to follow the psycho-analytic method must hopefully make this more available to patients who exist everywhere, and not only in our capital cities. To quote Bion's comments about the growth of the personality, applicable also to institutions which are concerned with this: "What is required is not the decrease of inhibition but a decrease of the impulse to inhibit; the impulse to inhibit is fundamentally envy of the growth-stimulating objects."

References

Bion, W.R. (1959). *Experience in Groups*. London: Tavistock Publ.
—— (1963). *Elements of Psychoanalysis*. London: Heinemann.
—— (1970). *Attention and Interpretation*. London: Tavistock Publ.
Klein, M. (1961). *The Narrative of a Child Analysis*. New York: Basic Books.

Bion's Contribution to Thinking About Groups

Isabel Menzies Lyth

Isabel Menzies Lyth's contribution examines Bion's group theories from a different vantage point. She highlights Bion's use of the group as an entity for study within its own sense of unity, not just as a collection of individuals. In so doing, he was enabled to pinpoint the development of psychotic phenomena in a subgroup within the group which manifested itself as if it were sane but which would inevitably become disruptive to the group itself. These psychotic disruptions corresponded to Klein's theory of the paranoid-schizoid position for the individual infant. Bion is revealed, moreover, as a person who believed in the social and political nature of man and who emphasized his "need for a partner."

Bion's Contribution to Thinking About Groups

Isabel Menzies Lyth

I have found it unexpectedly difficult to separate Bion's work in groups from his work in psycho-analysis. The consistency is more striking than the difference: the development is continuous, not disparate. His relationships with psycho-analysis began in the 1930's and continued throughout his work with groups in the Army and later. The two areas of his work seemed to grow closer and to have an even more creative interaction when he went into analysis with Melanie Klein and found her theory and practice so enlightening. Still, it was through his work in groups that his thinking first began to have an impact on a wider audience with his papers in "Human Relations" (1948-51), later re-published in "Experiences in Groups" (1961). These made clear his extraordinary clinical acumen. Many people have remarked on his superb powers of observation. But, in some ways, that seems an understatement. His observation was backed by an equally striking capacity to make sense of his observations. As we know, it is almost impossible to make "pure" observations, a fact of which Bion himself was only too well aware. It was the "mix" in Bion that was so extraordinary.

A companion point about his work is perhaps less familiar, but most obvious to a member of one of his groups—his remarkable capacity to be observed. His papers show that he was aware of being under constant scrutiny and that he experienced considerable turmoil, the effect of massive projection by the group, his own doubts and uncertainties, the pain of waiting for insight to evolve, the frequent unwelcomeness of his interpretations. He remained apparently unmoved and imperturbable. His colleague and friend, A.K. Rice, said of him: "Bion can sit farther behind his own face than any other man I know." This was an invaluable asset to the clinician in groups, giving the group freedom to pursue its own course uncontaminated by inappropriate messages from the leader. Those of us who have tried to emulate him know how difficult this is.

I will now discuss some points about Bion's work with groups which, for me, are definitive. Firstly, his insistence on the use of the group *per se*, the dynamics of the group in the here and now, as the instrument of therapy and learning. Group therapy, he said, should not be a debased form of psycho-analysis. It is essentially different. Reflections of this can be seen in his group papers where he uses language and concepts specific to groups, although acknowledging his debt to Kleinian theory. And the reader can himself make the links, noting, for example, the constant operation of projective identification. It is only in "Group Dynamics: A Re-View" (1952, 1955, 1961) that he makes explicit the close connection between his group theories and Kleinian theory.

Menzies Lyth, I. ["Bion's Contribution to Thinking About Groups"]. This article originally appeared in *The Bulletin of the British Psycho-Analytic Society*; it is also scheduled to appear in *The International Journal/Review of Psycho-Analysis*.

His insistence on the use of the group *per se* was critical at a time when other workers were either not of the same opinion, or were less skilled or determined in practising it. There was a good deal of debased psycho-analysis, as I know from experience. But the use of the group *per se* is the true derivative of psycho-analysis. I suspect that this view has not yet been fully accepted in group work or in therapeutic communities which only too often fail to make appropriate use of the group or community as the therapeutic instrument, viewing the individual and his disturbance in isolation rather than as a nodal point in a group dynamic, both contributing to and reflecting group tensions. One may compare Bion's own use of the community in the Northfield Experiment (1961).

My second point concerns his elucidation of the psychotic elements in groups. Previous references to psychotic group behaviour had almost exclusively described gross phenomena, akin to diagnostically psychotic disorders. The subtlety of Bion's intuition was in pinpointing the less obvious but immensely powerful psychotic phenomena that appear in groups that are apparently behaving sanely, if a little strangely, groups that are working more or less effectively and whose members are clinically normal or neurotic. He described clusters of these psychotic phenomena as the three basic assumptions in groups about how to achieve their objectives, the basic assumptions of dependency, fight-flight and pairing. They have in common massive splitting and projective identification, loss of individual distinctiveness or depersonalisation, diminution of effective contact with reality, lack of belief in progress and development through work and suffering. Once one's eyes have been opened, one cannot but be impressed by those aspects of groups and institutions whose individual members are sophisticated, intelligent and capable of learning from experience. They are reminiscent of Melanie Klein's descriptions of the infantile psychotic positions. Bion himself compared them, saying: "The adult must establish contact with the emotional life of the group in which he lives; this task would appear to be as formidable to the adult as the relationship to the breast appears to be to the infant, and the failure to meet the demands of this task is revealed in his regression." (1952, 1955, 1961).

Thirdly, Bion regarded the human being as essentially a group or political animal. He said that the human being was a group animal, at war both with the group and with those aspects of his own personality that constitute his "groupishness," yet unable to exist without groups, even if it be only the group he asserts he does not belong to or the internal group with which the solitary individual is in a dynamic relationship. Bion regarded the individual and group psychology as different ways of looking at the same phenomenon, group psychology illuminating aspects of the individual that may seem alien to individual psychology. He makes many references to this duality and the dilemma it creates for the individual. These clearly demonstrate his humanity; his sympathy, tolerance and compassion for the human being in his dilemma.

The last point in my list is more general. It concerns the quality of the man, his wisdom and erudition combined with his capacity for speculative and creative thinking and his perception of the relevance of findings in one situation for others. He carried his insights from groups and psycho-analysis into an incredible variety of other areas, many in which he was well-read and knowledgeable, others in which he capitalised on personal experiences. These included religions, the Army, the Church, the aristocracy and economics. His remarks about monetary systems now seem prophetic in our society, dominated as it is by primitive group phenomena, the anti-work basic assumptions of dependency, fighting and pairing, a society whose monetary systems seem to be going mad.

This picks up another quality shown in his writing and in personal contact. His work on groups has often been described as seminal. It is evocative and inspiring, albeit also often shocking and hard to assimilate. His work has been carried farther and into many other areas by other creative thinkers and men of action. One discovers and rediscovers his findings in one's own work. This seems to stem partly from the generous way he shared his pioneering struggles with groups. He knew what we would experience because he experienced it himself, even if he made more of his experience than we can, thus helping us, however, to make more of ours. If one tries to follow him, there is no let-up. Like Freud, he knew that the task of being a psychoanalyst or a group leader was no easy one. It demands constant training and vigilance and the ability to stay with ignorance and uncertainty "without any irritable reaching after fact and reason" (Keats in Bion, 1970). Every fresh discovery leads to further awareness of ignorance and the need to continue the painful search. We follow him at our peril. But if one *can* be in touch with his thinking, one also fails to follow him at one's peril.

People often ask why Bion gave up working with groups to concentrate on psycho-analysis. He replied in *The Dawn of Oblivion* (1979): "I had more pressing problems which could be adequately dealt with only by psychoanalysis–or something better"; i.e., pushing further and further into the primitive in the individual. He seemed compelled by these problems and his work on them has certainly contributed to making psycho-analysis "something better."

But Bion did not entirely give up groups. He followed up in psychoanalysis some of his group findings, notably the importance in normal and neurotic individuals of the psychotic elements and the need to deal with them in psycho-analysis or in the group. There are many references to groups in his psycho-analytical writings that imply there is more work to be done. When he wrote about groups again at length and in depth much later in *Attention and Interpretation* (1970), the continuing development of his theories was clear. His presentation of group theory here was not, however, intended for use basically as such but as a "fable, constructed in terms of the group" to be regarded as "a dramatized, personified, socialized, and pictorialized representation of the human personality." He brought psychoanalysis and group theory close indeed here. He was concerned with the processes of change, the way the creative idea is handled, and what may happen to it, our need for it if vitality and growth are to be sustained and our fear of disruption by it, change being experienced as catastrophic.

I will conclude by discussing what he said about groups in this context, because it demonstrates the development in his thinking, because it seems to stem from his personal experiences–at times it seems almost autobiographical–and because it now relates to his future. I select only one aspect, his exploration in various contexts of the relationship between three entities–the genius, mystic or messiah, the group and the Establishment. The mystic produces the creative idea, scientific, artistic or religious. The group needs the mystic, "a continued supply of genius" (1970) if it is to remain vital and grow. The mystic needs the group to provide conditions in which his genius can flourish and be propagated. But the relations between them is fraught with hazards; the mystic is always potentially disruptive to the group whether a declared revolutionary or not. Inevitably his contribution challenges the existing state of the group and its coherence and seems to threaten catastrophe. This arouses tensions and emotional drives appropriate to the primitive group, drives which are directed to destroying the mystic and preserving group coherence at all costs, even at the cost of growth and vitality.

The resolution of this dilemma is crucial for the mystic *and* the group and brings in the Establishment, the sub-group that exercises power, responsibility and containment on behalf of the group. Hopefully, the Establishment will manage the situation in a way that Bion describes as "symbiotic." This implies both hostility and benevolence; the mystic's ideas are subjected to critical scrutiny which benefits both the mystic and the group. The Establishment can then develop laws or techniques that help the ordinary member to use the mystic's ideas. The alternative relationship Bion calls "parasitic"; the mystic and the group destroy each other. "Even friendliness is deadly." The establishment may promote the mystic to a position which deflects him from his creative and destructive role and absorbs him in administration. Bion writes him an epitaph. "He was loaded with honours and sank without a trace." (1970). Or the Establishment may try to deny the mystic a place in society where he can deploy his powers.

This configuration is universal and Bion gives convincing examples of its appearance in groups and in the psycho-analysis of the individual. We need look no further than our own Society to find repeated occurrences of the pattern. The hazards are daunting but Bion is hopeful. Truth will ultimately triumph and though truth may not give much consolation, it makes for growth. The forces in the group orientated to growth and development will also ultimately triumph through work in spite of the hindrance of basic assumption phenomena and although it may take a long time.

Bion experienced this personally. After six weeks of exciting work in the Northfield Experiment, he was removed from his post. The creative idea did not die. He continued his work in War Office Selection Boards and at the

Tavistock Clinic and Institute and it was taken up by many others. Speculating, I have wondered how far the danger of being made "respectable" influenced his decision to leave London. He had been successively the Director of the London Clinic of Psycho-Analysis, the President of the British Psycho-Analytical Society and a member of its Training Committee. The hazards were perhaps greater for Bion than for some mystics, since his understanding of group processes contributed to his having a flair for that kind of role.

What of the future? The tasks and the problems remain with us. The death of the mystic does not necessarily mean the end of his creative and destructive influence, as Bion vividly describes in relation to both the religious mystic and the scientist. The need continues for the symbiotic relationship to facilitate critical scrutiny of his work, to develop ways in which it can be used by more ordinary workers, and to foster conditions for the "continued supply of genius" in psycho-analysis and group work.

References

Bion, W.R. (1948-51). Experiences in Groups. *Human Relations*, Vol. I-IV.

—— (1961). *Experiences in Groups*. London: Tavistock Publications.

—— (1952, 1955 and 1961). Groups Dynamics: A Re-View. *Int. J. Psycho-Anal.* 33. In Melanie Klein, Paula Heimann, R. Money-Kyrle (eds.) *New Directions in Psycho-Analysis*. London: Tavistock Publications and in *Experiences in Groups*. London: Tavistock Publications.

—— (1970). *Attention and Interpretation*. London: Tavistock Publications.

—— (1979). *The Dawn of Oblivion*. Perthshire: Clunie Press.

The Influence of Wilfred Bion on the A.K. Rice Group Relations Conferences

Margaret Rioch

EDITOR'S NOTE: *Doctor Rioch has contributed an article which explains the relationship between Bion's Tavistock Group Method, as described in* Experiences in Groups, *and the work of A.K. Rice whose "Authority Training Groups" seem now to be their latter day derivative in part. She points out that Rice, who* was *at the Tavistock and had been in a group with Bion, developed group concepts which complemented those of Bion. Particularly, he emphasized the role of authority in respect to the right of participation of each constituent in a group enterprise. Doctor Rioch points out how congruent their respective theories are in reference to the dialectic between rational and instinctual forces. She then adds an insightful yet ironic twist by suggesting that both Bion's and Rice's concepts of groups were "work" groups, not "play" groups. She ends with a regret that the concept of group "play" was not included, her point extending to the concept of the playful or esthetically "irrational" forces which are beneficial to indulge in. If Rice be the complement to Bion, then Rioch is the supplement to both of them.*

The Influence of Wilfred Bion and the A.K. Rice Group Relations Conferences

Margaret J. Rioch
Professor Emeritus in Residence,
The American University, Washington, D.C.

It is difficult to overestimate the influence that Wilfred Bion has had on the A.K. Rice Group Relations conferences in the United States and on the conferences developed in England under the leadership of A.K. Rice, Pierre Turquet and E.J. Miller. Even those who have not read his famous "Experiences in Groups" are familiar with his concepts and use them, perhaps superficially, but perhaps also usefully in their work as consultants to groups. Even inexperienced consultants know what is meant by a fight-flight group or a dependency group. They know too what is meant by a basic assumption group and even a work group, though they may not have seen the latter in action. Still the concept is there. One might well speculate that without the thinking of Bion, especially the thinking which went into "Experiences in Groups," Rice might not have developed the group relations conferences with their emphasis upon leadership and authority.

I think that the work of the A.K. Rice Institute has a firm basis in theory, which has given it a solid foundation and has endowed those of us who work in this area with a sense that we know what we are doing, as well as with a sense of unity. Wilfred Bion provided a way of looking at groups which makes it possible to use constructively A. Kenneth Rice's concepts of primary task, of authority, leadership, boundaries, and the various concepts which have to do with groups as open systems, exchanging products with the environment. It also makes it possible to see a number of groups functioning together to form an institution, whether that be the institution of a Group Relations Conference, or a business, or a university or a church.

Bion's thinking, strongly psychoanalytic, strongly Kleinian, as it is, forms a basis for the more sociological thinking of A. Kenneth Rice. It is not strange that Rice was influenced by Bion since they were at one time both at the Tavistock in London, and since Rice was a member of one of Bion's first study groups. (Rice, 1965, p. 4) It is striking, however, that the concepts which Rice used in his various works on organzations and which are basic to his development of the conferences as educational events so neatly dovetail with the concepts of Bion and form such a perfect complement to Bion's work. This is not to say that Rice's work is simply derivative. To the extent that it, like all work, is derivative, it derives from many sources, not the least of which was Rice's own wide experience as a consultant in various parts of the world, including Africa and India, as well as Europe and the United States.

Bion makes the point that a group is a unity, different from the sum of its parts. "Time-keeping is no function of any part, in isolation, of the mechanism of a clock, yet time-keeping is a function of the clock and of the various parts of the clock when held in combination with each other. There is no more need to be confused by the impression that a group is more than the sum of its members than it would be to be confused by the idea that a clock is more than a collection of the parts that are necessary to make a clock." (Bion, 1959, p. 119) Rice's concept of the primary task of the group or institution as that task which the group must perform in order to survive as a group is meaningless if the group or institution is not more than the sum of its parts. For what otherwise is this entity which has a primary task? The primary tasks of all the sub-groups in an institution do not simply add up to the primary task of the institution as a whole. Rice is as clear on this as Bion is. The tasks of the sub-groups may be very disparate. One may be feeding the members of the institution. One may be providing shelter. One may be providing opportunities for learning. One of the tasks of the sub-groups may sometimes conflict with another or with the primary task of the institution as a whole. This is one aspect which an organizational consultant must keep in mind in viewing the whole, especially from a diagnostic point of view. And conference consultants must constantly ask themselves whether they, as consultants to sub-groups, are perhaps subverting the task of the whole.

Bion's concept of the "basic assumption" group as distinguished from the "work group" is a psychoanalytic concept. Identifying the irrational aspects of the group as distinct from the rational aspects makes possible a distinction between a regressed and a more maturely functioning group. Bion, however, emphasizes that in *every group* there is one aspect which functions on an "as if" basis, i.e., on a basic assumption basis. There is only a question of whether the basic assumptions function in the service of the work group or whether they run away with it. This is the question of whether a hospital, for example, can use the tendency to dependency in the service of its task of caring for the sick, or whether the tendency to dependency on the part of both patients and staff gets in the way of doing useful work and interferes with the primary task, namely the return of the patients to the community as able bodied and well functioning members of it. Rice was also keenly aware of the mischief which could be caused in an organization when the various individuals who compose it, and especially the leaders, are not sufficiently in touch with reality. They may act, for instance, as if they had all the time in the world when in reality a decision, on which survival depends, must be made immediately. He was also aware of the satisfactions to be had when an organization carried out its task effectively and rationally.

Rice, in developing the group relations conferences, was at pains to offer members opportunities to explore the irrational aspects, that is, the basic assumption aspects of groups. He thought it essential that leaders and managers should be aware that irrational behavior occurs in groups, that people who are, as individuals, mature and rational, may under group pressure succumb to irrational, primitive impulses. Leaders should also learn, he thought, how irrational, primitive forces can be mobilized in the service of task performance.

The central opportunities to learn, provided by Rice in his group relations conferences have come to be concerned with authority. In his book ("Learning for Leadership") Rice does not develop this concept, but is still talking about leadership. Toward the end of his life, however, and in the last conference brochures for which he was responsible, he talked about authority. The American conferences have followed him in this ever since. Authority is seen by most consultants simply as the right to do certain work or to perform certain tasks. A lawyer has the right to practise law; a physician, to practise medicine; and a hair dresser, to cut hair. It is obvious, however, that the members of a conference see the authority of the consultant as something much larger than life, as something like the way in which a child perceives his parents. This is the way in which Bion describes the basic assumption leader. The group thinks it has met to be sheltered by his all-powerful might. He may also be a fight-flight leader and the group then assumes that they are met so that he will lead them victoriously in battle or will take them safely into retreat. It seems clear that groups project their needs first and foremost on Bion himself. Only when he clearly refuses the role by his behavior as a work leader do groups search for a more suitable receptacle for their projections, or perhaps they give up the basic assumption under which they had been operating.

Although Bion does not speak much about authority, and although indeed the word is not listed in the index at the back of his book, he shows a clear sense of the limits of his authority as the person "taking" the group. He usually refers to himself as a "member" of the group and speaks of the difficulties which the group has of which he is a "member." All the time it is obvious that the group is preoccupied with him and has probably come together because it was made known that he would "take" the group. The irrational elements in the attitudes of the other members toward authority, their dependence, their rebellion (fight), their escape from the task for which they have supposedly met (flight), their hope for an as yet unborn Messiah (pairing) could scarcely be clearer. These attitudes, together with the contrasting rational, work group, which is reality- and task-oriented are, I think, the elements which Rice wanted to make clear in the group relations conferences which he developed. Rice always wanted members to see that by sheer force of numbers, if by nothing else, the power was theirs. They also, and they only, had the authority to decide what they would and would not do. But they could also learn how bitterly they struggle against taking authority into their own hands and how they much prefer to leave the authority with the staff. At the same time, of course, they complain loudly about the way in which they are treated by the staff.

I remember vividly an argument between A.K. Rice and a staff member who was maintaining that a person with very little power to wield, for example, a private in the Army, could find little or no profit in the conferences. Rice, on the contrary, thought that he could, because he could learn how much authority he had over his own behavior, and that it mattered not at all that he had little power to wield over others. As I read Wilfred Bion, and from my knowledge of him, I think he would agree with Dr. Rice.

One of the important concepts developed by Rice and used by him and by those who have learned from him, both inside and outside of group conferences, is the concept of boundaries. A boundary should not be and need not be a barrier across which no transactions can take place. A boundary is more like a membrane, like the skin, for example, across which many transactions and many communications take place. Rice was concerned that the boundaries around institutions should be firm but optimally permeable. People and material must come into the institution. That is the import system. And people and products must go out. That is the export system. There must also be boundaries around the institution as a whole and around the sub-systems. They too must be firm, but optimally permeable. The study of the Small Group must not be confused with the study of the Large Group and vice versa.

Without making a great fuss about it and without making rules that this or that is prohibited to group members, Bion seems to have been able to create a group culture in which boundaries naturally existed. When group phenomena took place in actuality or in fantasy, this was all that mattered. Bion worked at interpreting the group. It was a bit different with Rice. His task and his situation were also different. He wanted members of conferences to learn about boundaries and he, therefore, drew them clearly and explicitly. The staff sat and sits separate from the members in conference openings, for example. When there is a separate members' lounge, no staff consultant enters it. This emphasizes the staff-member boundaries. The staff begins and ends all sessions promptly. This emphasizes the time boundaries around such exercise. Rice thought that in institutions, boundaries should be drawn which were functional. They should be drawn at places where one task ends and another begins. Boundaries can also be drawn which are not functional. A great deal of thought can profitably be given as to where they can best be drawn. In a university, for example, are the traditional departments the best way to divide up the faculty in order that work shall be done? Or might there be a better way? In his book on The University, Rice addresses himself in detail to this question.

Rice often made his teaching clear in conference openings, brochures, and in his published works. But members of conferences still lived and live in basic assumption life and continued or continue to find the consultants a convenient receptacle for their projections. Rice taught his staff members not to collude with these projections, but to be work leaders as consistently as possible. It was surely a stroke of genius on Bion's part that it seems never to have occurred to him to behave like anything else. He is constantly, as he describes himself in "Experiences in Groups," working, trying to understand and to make clear what the group is doing, and in particular what it is doing to him.

Both Bion and Rice are in the psychoanalytic tradition. Bion is himself a Kleinian analyst. Rice, as befits a member of the Tavistock staff, is as familiar with psychoanalytic concepts and methods as many an analyst, though he constantly made clear that this was not his specialty. But both men, as good twentieth century post-Freudians, are trying to explain, make clear, and make manageable the dark, irrational, primitive forces in man. Freud called them instincts. Some religious people, especially Christians, and also the self-actualizers, think it is in the nature of things that man is headed for a great destiny, and they have no problem of reconciliation of the rational with the irrational. But those who have been bitten by psychoanalysis, of whatever variety, have the problem of reconciling the egotistical, irrational trends which they have learned to uncover in their patients, and which they also recognize in children, with the quite extraordinary accomplishments which they also recognize in the human race, in spite of its wars, its plagues, its greed, and general ornariness. Bion managed the problem by assuming a double aspect in man, especially man in groups, the rational scientific, and the irrational, primitive, lost in fantasy. Rice follows him in this and is involved not only in finding ways of illuminating the two aspects, but also in finding ways of making the primitive more manageable. Bion assumed that the two aspects of man are always there, but that in effective groups, the basic assumptions are subservient to the work and are harnessed in the service of work. Rice was also concerned with how to help organizations to work more effectively to accomplish more of what they set out to do. It has indeed been the impression of many, many people, to judge from what they have reported about themselves, that they do learn each time they attend a conference, as members or as staff, to function a little better, a little more effectively.

For both Bion and Rice, the question is the same, as it must be for every serious thinker since Freud. How can man, while preserving his primitive, animal instincts, yet develop great civilizations and produce great works of art and literature? In fact, how can he live with serenity in view of the uncertainty with which he is faced?

The concept which seems to me to be lacking in both their works is the concept of the activity called play. They have surely not been unaware of this. Their theories allow for a basketball team or a chamber music orchestra which are groups met to "play." The work of such groups is in fact their play. That is their primary task, to speak in Rice's terms. But neither Rice nor Bion has given a great deal of thought to the purely esthetic aspect of life. It may be significant that the activity of composition, in music, literature, or painting, is seldom very satisfactory as a group task, though in architecture at least one and often more than one group is necessary for carrying out the architect's plans. In composing, a group is often necessary to perform the composer's work and a group is surely necessary to publish and read a writer's work.

Neither Rice nor Bion was trying to write a treatise on esthetics. And it is as foolish to complain that they have not done so as to say that a work on biology should also be on history. But it is not without significance to note this omission. Perhaps the War was such a serious matter for those living in England that the thought of play could not seriously enter their heads or be found to lodge there. Perhaps it is characteristic of the Protestant ethic that the ideal group for both Bion and Rice is a "working" group. The way one deals with the irrational is to keep it subservient to the rational. It is possible, however, that at another time and another place a man might find in the concept of play a true synthesis of mature, scientific and primitive, fantasy elements without the one being subservient to the other.

However that may be, and however he may have attained it, Wilfred Bion embodied serenity and courage in himself in a way which is rare in people of the last half of the twentieth century. He knew well all the tortuous horrors of sick individual souls and all the international madness of a world at war. And yet he lived from a deep center of quiet which those who met him could not fail to sense and to receive from him.

References

Bion, W.R. (1959). *Experiences in Groups*. New York: Basic Books.

Rice, A.K. (1965). *Learning for Leadership: Interpersonal and Intergroup Relations*. London: Tavistock Publications.

PUBLICATIONS BY WILFRED R. BION

(1943). Intra-group tensions in therapy; their study as a task of the group. *Lancet* 2, 27 November.
(1946). Leaderless group project. *Bull. Menninger Clinic* 10.
(1948). Psychiatry in a time of crisis. *Brit. J. Med. Psychol.* 21.
(1948). Experiences in groups. *Human Relations* 1–4, 1948–1951.
(1950). The imaginary twin. In *Second Thoughts*, 1967.
(1952). Group dynamics: a re-view. *Int. J. Psycho-Anal.* 33. Also in *New Directions in Psycho-Analysis*, 1955.
(1954). Notes on the theory of schizophrenia. *Int. J. Psycho-Anal.* 35. Also in *Second Thoughts*, 1967.
(1955). Language and the schizophrenic. In *New Directions in Psycho-Analysis*. Reprinted Maresfield Library 1977.
(1956). Development of schizophrenic thought. *Int. J. Psycho-Anal.* 37. Also in *Second Thoughts*, 1967.
(1957). Differentiation of the psychotic from the non-psychotic personalities. *Int. J. Psycho-Anal.* 38. Also in *Second Thoughts*, 1967.
(1958). On hallucination. *Int. J. Psycho-Anal.* 39. Also in *Second Thoughts*, 1967.
(1958). On arrogance. *Int. J. Psycho-Anal.* 39. Also in *Second Thoughts*, 1967.
(1959). Attacks on linking. *Int. J. Psycho-Anal.* 40. Also in *Second Thoughts*, 1967.
(1961). *Experiences in Groups*, London: Tavistock Publications. (Reprint of the papers from *Human Relations* and *Int. J. Psycho-Anal.*)
(1962). A theory of thinking. *Int. J. Psycho-Anal.* 43, Also in *Second Thoughts*, 1967.
(1962). *Learning from Experience*. London: Heinemann. Reprinted Maresfield Library 1984.
(1963). *Elements of Psycho-Analysis*. London: Heinemann. Reprinted Maresfield Library 1984.
(1965). *Transformations*. London: Heinemann. Reprinted Maresfield Library 1984.
(1966). Catastrophic change. *Bull. Brit. Psycho-Anal. Soc.* No. 5, 1966.
(1967). *Second Thoughts*. London: Heinemann. Reprinted Maresfield Library 1984.
(1967). Notes on memory and desire. *Psychoanal. Forum*, 2.
(1970). *Attention and Interpretation*. London: Tavistock Publications. Reprinted Maresfield Library 1984.
(1973). *Bion's Brazilian Lectures*, 1. Brazil: Imago Editora.
(1974). *Bion's Brazilian Lectures*, 2. Brazil: Imago Editora.
(1975). *A Memoir of the Future. Book One: The Dream*. Brazil: Imago Editora.
(1976). Evidence. *Bull. Brit. Psycho-Anal. Soc.* No. 8, 1976.
(1977). *A Memoir of the Future. Book Two: The Past Presented*. Brazil: Imago Editora.
(1977). *Two Papers: The Grid and Caesura*. Brazil: Imago Editora.
(1977). Emotional turbulence. In P. Hartocollis (ed.), *Borderline Personality Disorders*. New York: Int. Univ. Press.
(1977). On a quotation from Freud: The Caesura. In *Borderline Personality Disorders*.
(1978). *Four Discussions with W. R. Bion*. Perthshire: Clunie Press.
(1979). *A Memoir of the Future. Book Three: The Dawn of Oblivion*. Perthshire: Clunie Press.
(1979). Making the best of a bad job. *Bull. Brit. Psycho-Anal. Soc.* No. 2, 1979.
(1980). *Bion in New York and São Paulo*. Perthshire: Clunie Press.
(1982). *The Long Week-End 1879–1919: Part of a Life*. Abingdon: Fleetwood Press.
(1985). All my Sins Remembered (Another Part of a life); The Other Side of Genius (Family Letters) Abingdon: Fleetwood Press.
(1988). Clinical Seminar of Four Papers. Abingdon: Fleetwood Press.

For Product Safety Concerns and Information please contact our EU representative GPSR@taylorandfrancis.com
Taylor & Francis Verlag GmbH, Kaufingerstraße 24, 80331 München, Germany

www.ingramcontent.com/pod-product-compliance
Ingram Content Group UK Ltd.
Pitfield, Milton Keynes, MK11 3LW, UK
UKHW022208190926
475702UK00003B/264
* 9 7 8 0 3 6 7 0 9 9 4 7 3 *